# SAN DIEGO PADRES:

## THE FIRST HALF CENTURY

EDITED BY TOM LARWIN & BILL NOWLIN

ASSOCIATE EDITORS: CARL RIECHERS & LEN LEVIN

FOREWORD BY RANDY JONES | AFTERWORD BY MAJOR GARRETT

Saociety for American Baseball Research, Inc.
Phoenix, AZ

San Diego Padres: The First Half Century

Edited by Tom Larwin and Bill Nowlin
Associate editors: Carl Riechers and Len Levin
Foreword by Randy Jones

Afterword by Major Garrett

Book design: Rachael Sullivan
Society for American Baseball Research
Cronkite School at ASU
555 N. Central Ave. #416
Phoenix, AZ 85004
Phone: (602) 496-1460
Web: www.sabr.org
Facebook: Society for American Baseball Research
Twitter: @SABR

Cover photography: San Diego Padres (Gwynn: Andy Hayt; Hoffman: Scott Wachter; Winfield: Media Relations); Andy Strasberg (Chicken); 1969 manager and coaches image (San Diego History Center); ticket stubs, and San Diego Bay image from Padres 2004 Christmas card (Tom Larwin).

# CONTENTS

## THE PLAYERS

## MANAGERS, EXECUTIVES, MEDIA

## SPRING TRAINING, STADIA, AND THE CHICKEN

## NOTABLE PADRES GAMES

# FACTS, FIGURES, TRIVIA

# AFTERWORD

# FOREWORD

I had missed the first four years of the San Diego Padres major-league existence, joining the club in June 1973. I ended the season 7-6 with a 3.16 ERA. I found out later that I had set a Padres record: the highest winning percentage for a left-handed pitcher in Padres history. That's when I realized I was at the start of Padres history. Now, 45 years later, I find myself blessed to still be part of the Padres organization. Whether it be talking to the young players on the team or visiting with long-time Padres fans, we share our passion for America's pastime.

In *San Diego Padres: The First Half Century*, SABR has captured some of the great players to wear a Padres uniform and also takes the true baseball fan through some of the more memorable dates in their history. Not just dates that we always read about but the ones that truly tell the story of the franchise.

I had the pleasure of knowing every player and manager/exec mentioned in the book and enjoyed reading and reminiscing with the author on their impact to Padres baseball. I remember in 1973, Nate Colbert taking a rookie left-handed pitcher under his wing and teaching him how to be a big-league ballplayer. I always appreciated what he did for me. In the '70s, Elten Schiller coming up with the Junior Padres Program where kids could get a ticket to nine games for just $1.00. Thought that was one of the greatest marketing ideas I had ever seen in baseball. Talking with Jake Peavy in the spring of 2007, telling him if he could perfect an offspeed pitch he could win a Cy Young Award. SABR has done a great job on the research on all these players.

The events talked about in the first 50 years give a different perspective to Padres baseball lore. There were way too many losing seasons but sometimes this makes the winning seasons even more special memories. I remember 1978 when we finally went over .500, 84-78, and how excited we all were with our achievements. It would be six more seasons before the Padres would win their first championship and trip to a World Series. I personally had retired from the game in 1983 and remember being a little envious of the '84 team but got a chance to be involved. Miller Beer invited myself and Detroit's Norm Cash to do the Lite Beer commercial for the World Series. It wasn't exactly how I'd seen myself in the fall classic but was proud to be a small part.

If you're a longtime Padres fan or baseball fan, you'll enjoy the wonderful stories put together by SABR on the first 50 years of the Padres franchise. I'm proud to be in the Padres Hall of Fame and have my number, 35, retired but more proud of the friends I've made and people I've met with my association with the Padres. Reading these stories has certainly brought many of those memories and I can't thank SABR enough for writing them.

ENJOY.

Randy Jones
San Diego Padres
RandyJonesbbq.com

# INTRODUCTION: A SNAPHOT OF THE PADRES' FIRST HALF CENTURY

## BY BOB CHANDLER

Big-time sports in San Diego really got going in 1961 when Don Coryell came to San Diego State College as head football coach (the school is now called San Diego State University, SDSU). About the same time the American Football League's Los Angeles Chargers moved to San Diego for the 1961 season. Then, in November 1965, voters in the city of San Diego passed a $27 million bond measure for a new stadium to be built in Mission Valley. The new stadium would have 50,000 seats and be multi-purpose, which meant it could be used for football as well as professional baseball.

In late 1965 construction was underway for another sports venue, a state-of-the-art arena, called the San Diego International Sports Arena. It opened in 1966 with the Western Hockey League San Diego Gulls as a tenant. The next year, 1967, the expansion San Diego Rockets of the National Basketball Association began play in the Sports Arena.

Another notable local sports event was in pro golf, when in 1968 Andy Williams lent his name to the San Diego Open, making it one of the major tournaments on the West Coast.

Finally, to cap off the decade, major-league baseball came to San Diego – the city was awarded a major-league baseball franchise on May 27, 1968. When that happened, it was like placing the cherry on the icing on the cake.

### 1969: Season 1

Those of us in the local media did not know for sure that San Diego was going to get a franchise until that May 27 date.

At the time, San Diego was part of the Los Angeles Dodgers' market, with the team having a strong following in the region. However, there were other Dodgers-San Diego connections, in particular one major one that involved Dodgers owner Walter O'Malley. He wanted to make room for his son, Peter, to move into the Dodgers' front office. So O'Malley helped his general manager, Buzzie Bavasi, get in on the ownership of the new franchise in San Diego. Bavasi became the Padres' first president and general manager and Bavasi's son, also named Peter, was placed in charge of the Padres' farm system.

Bavasi had teamed up with C. Arnholt Smith, who was the owner of the Pacific Coast League Padres in 1968, and had the majority financial interest in the major-league Padres. While Smith left the baseball operations to Bavasi, he did make an imprint on the club's appearance. You see, Smith had a passion for the color brown. He always wore a brown suit with a brown tie and a brown shirt. Everything the team produced was dominated by the color brown, including the uniforms.

The foundation of the first Padres team was the expansion draft held in October 1968. Of course, O'Malley knew that Bavasi had knowledge of the Dodgers' farm system. But as a patron of Bavasi's move to San Diego, O'Malley influenced the Padres to select former American League MVP, 28-year-old Zoilo Versalles, whose best years were already behind him, and 29-year-old Al "The Bull" Ferrara, who had two mildly productive years for the Dodgers, and a 21-year-old minor leaguer, Jim Williams.

The other expansion team, the Montreal Expos, had a totally different philosophy on how to go about the draft. The Padres went after young players who were available and built the team that way. Montreal went the opposite direction, going after veteran players with the idea that they could later trade those veteran players to contending teams and get some good youngsters back. Which approach worked best? At the end of the 1969 season, ironically, both teams had identical records, 52-110.

The Padres' first manager was Preston Gomez. He had been the Dodgers' third-base coach and Bavasi knew him real well. The thinking was that Preston, a Latino (from Cuba), would help draw fans from Mexico. That didn't really work out too well in that regard with the team drawing only 512,970 in its first year.

## 1970-1979: Seasons 2-11

For the new Padres the 1969 season was not too successful either, with attendance or with performance. The 1970 through 1973 seasons, were more of the same and did not offer much promise: The Padres finished in last place each year and averaged 60.5 wins and 99 losses. Home attendance averaged only 614,323.

There were several bright spots: Nate Colbert slugging five home runs and batting in 13 runs in an August 1972 doubleheader in Atlanta, and near-no-hitters pitched by Clay Kirby in 1970 and Steve Arlin in 1972.

The Padres had played only 11 games in 1972 when they fired Preston Gomez and named Don Zimmer manager. Bavasi figured that Zimmer would add a little pizzazz and give the team a lift. Zimmer managed the team for another lackluster year in 1973 … lackluster except for some turmoil in midyear caused by rumors of the team moving from San Diego.

On May 27, 1973, it was announced that the Padres had a purchase offer from a wealthy Washington, D.C., grocery magnate, Joseph Danzansky. Ironically, it was exactly five years to the day since the Padres were awarded the franchise, on May 27, 1968. It was near-certain that the team would move to Washington at the end of the season … or maybe even during the season.

The club, including nonplaying personnel, was in limbo for the next seven months. In the meantime, the City of San Diego was not sitting idly by. John Witt, the city's attorney, brought suit against the team for payment due on the remaining years of a 20-year lease for the use of San Diego Stadium. The judge hearing the case ruled that while the city couldn't stop the team from moving, it did have grounds for damages for the 15 years remaining on the stadium lease. Did that ever shake up the hierarchy in major-league baseball!

By late 1973 some of the Padres' front office had already left for new jobs while some were preparing to move to Washington. There was even a thought that the team might be operated by the National League for the 1974 season. Several groups came forward with interest to buy the team.

Then, in January 1974, Ray Kroc, the owner of McDonald's, expressed interest in ownership. Kroc and Arnholt Smith quickly agreed on a purchase price of $12 million and the deal was consummated by the end of the month.

Despite the turmoil surrounding the team, in late 1973 Peter Bavasi, now running the Padres, managed to trade for some legitimate major leaguers. The biggest name was Willie McCovey, the National League's MVP in 1969. The Padres also picked up veterans Bobby Tolan, Glenn Beckert, and Matty Alou.

For the first time in their short history, the Padres had gone after some big names and built their team in a different way. So they remained in San Diego and had some new recognizable names on the team, especially McCovey. Another important addition was new owner Kroc, whom the fans seemed to adore. Added to the mix were two key players who got their start in 1973, rookies Dave Winfield and Randy Jones.

Another offseason transaction was the hiring of a new manager, John McNamara.

For 1974's Opening Day, the Padres were in Los Angeles, and they were blown out in three straight games by the Dodgers, being outscored, 25-2. They come home to play against the Houston Astros in the team's home opener on April 9.

During this, his first home game, owner Kroc thought it a good idea to thank the fans. In the bottom of the seventh inning he approached the public-address booth and requested time. But it so happened that minutes earlier the Padres had blown a potential rally with a mental mistake. Kroc came on over the loudspeaker system saying that he had never seen such stupid ballplaying in his life!

That's how the Ray Kroc era began in San Diego. The fans seemed to love his outgoing, frank personality and it helped contribute to a significant increase in attendance. Even though the 1974 team lost 102 games, it drew over a million fans for the first time.

The Padres improved in 1975 and Randy Jones won 20 games and led the National League in earned-run average.

The next change in managers occurred in 1977 when Kroc fired McNamara in late May. Bob Skinner, a coach, managed the team for one game and then Alvin Dark was announced as the new manager. (That one game left Skinner with the best won-lost record of any Padres manager in its 50-year history, one win and no defeats.)

Dark managed the team the rest of 1977; however, while he survived the offseason, he did not survive spring training, being fired late in spring training. A rebellion of the players against Dark and his rules and restrictions, and his attitude, prompted Kroc to make a change despite the bad timing.

Pitching coach Roger Craig replaced Dark. After nine losing seasons Craig led the team to its first winning record, 84-78, with the highlight being pitcher Gaylord Perry getting his 3,000th career strikeout in the season's last game, and winning the National League Cy Young Award at the age of 40.

## 1980-1989: Seasons 12-21

Trader Jack McKeon replaced Bob Fontaine as general manager in 1980 and began building "his" team immediately. His first move, in December 1980, was to trade for a catcher, and the Padres traded Rollie Fingers and Gene Tenace to the St Louis Cardinals for Terry Kennedy.

Kennedy was McKeon's first building block. The Cardinals traded Kennedy because manager Whitey Herzog had a veteran catcher, Darrell Porter. Herzog also had the worst pitching staff in baseball in 1980, so as part of this deal, he made McKeon take a bunch of lousy pitchers, just to get rid of them and their salaries. But it was worth it to McKeon to take these pitchers so he could get Kennedy. Kennedy at age 25 was the foundation for what was to come later.

The December 1980 Rule 5 draft brought in another key player for the club's eventual 1984 season, Alan Wiggins. He was one of the fastest runners ever and a terrific outfielder.

The June 1981 amateur draft provided two more significant additions: Kevin McReynolds in the first round (at number 6) and Tony Gwynn in the third round.

In December 1981, McKeon traded Ozzie Smith to his "buddy" Herzog for the Cardinals' switch-hitting shortstop, Garry Templeton. Smith had already demonstrated that he was one of the best fielding shortstops ever but the Padres did not think he was ever going to hit.

The next big step was when McKeon brought in Dick Williams in 1982 as manager. Williams inherited a team that had been just awful in 1981. Without the addition of anybody of significance, Williams taught them to play tough, fundamental baseball and they ended the 1982 season with a .500 record.

The next key addition took place in December 1982 when the Padres signed 34-year-old free agent Steve Garvey.

A year later, in December 1983, McKeon brought in Carmelo Martinez as part of a three-team transaction that included the Chicago Cubs and Montreal Expos. Martinez was primarily a first baseman but McKeon wanted to use him in the outfield. His acquisition allowed the team to make a bold move, transferring Wiggins from the outfield to second base. The three-team trade also included another important cog in the team's eventual 1984 season, left-handed reliever Craig Lefferts.

In early 1984 the final pieces to the puzzle fell into place. First, the Padres signed free-agent relief pitcher Goose Gossage in January. The final piece came at the close of spring training through a trade with George Steinbrenner and the New York Yankees for Graig Nettles.

The 1984 team was set and the Opening Day lineup on April 3 at home against the Pittsburgh Pirates was:

Alan Wiggins 2B

Tony Gwynn RF

Graig Nettles 3B

Steve Garvey 1B

Terry Kennedy C

Carmelo Martinez LF

Kevin McReynolds CF

Garry Templeton SS

Eric Show P

The four main starting pitchers in 1984 were Show, Tim Lollar, Mark Thurmond, and Ed Whitson. However, the best starters might have been Andy Hawkins and Dave Dravecky, who shared both bullpen and starting duties.

McKeon's theory was to have a better-than-average player at every position and hope that enough of them have a good year. The team was built around a good mix of veterans and young players but a key part of it was eventual Hall of Famer Dick Williams, who was a great leader.

The Padres won the League Championship Series against the Cubs three games to two after losing the first two games in Chicago. In dramatic fashion the Padres won three in a row with Garvey winning Series MVP honors after a ninth-inning walk-off home run in Game Four. Then, in Game Five the Padres beat eventual NL Cy Young Award winner Rick Sutcliffe to capture the Series.

Up next were the Detroit Tigers, who had won 104 games in the regular season and won three straight against the Kansas City Royals in the American League Championship Series. The Padres lost the Series four games to one, with their lone win coming in Game Two in San Diego. Kurt Bevacqua, in the lineup as the designated hitter, had a three-run home run that provided the winning margin for the Padres.

Preparing for the 1985 season Trader Jack pulled off a December 1984 trade to help the Padres pitching, acquiring the Chicago White Sox' LaMarr Hoyt. Hoyt was the American League's Cy Young Award recipient in 1983 and was expected to fill a void in the Padres starting pitching staff.

The 1985 season started off well. Hoyt won 11 straight starts at one stage and was selected to start the All-Star Game for the National League. Overall, seven Padres were selected for the 1985 NL All-Star team, with four voted in as starters: Garvey, Gwynn, Kennedy, and Nettles. Gossage and Templeton were the other two selected, and Dick Williams was the manager.

During the spring the team's sparkplug, Alan Wiggins, was off to a poor start, hitting .054 in late April with no stolen bases. Then, for a game on April 25 in Los Angeles, he was initially listed on the pregame lineup card as a starter but just before the game began he was scratched from the lineup. Tim Flannery came in to play second base. It turns out that Wiggins had some serious drug issues. The result was that he never played another game for the Padres and was traded in late June to Baltimore.

The team reached its peak on July 4, being in first place by 4½ games. By the end of July the Padres were five games behind, and they never recovered. The team barely finished above .500. With Wiggins' departure they had lost a key cog in their offense. In 1984 Wiggins stole 70 bases and when he was on first base and Tony Gwynn followed him in the order, Gwynn had a .428 batting average.

McKeon rebuilt the team, which finished 1989 with an 89-73 record and made a run at the pennant, going 42-21 their last 63 games. Jack Clark had been acquired by trade in the offseason and was set for first base. Roberto Alomar, in his second season, was fixed at second base, Templeton remained at shortstop and Tim Flannery and Luis Salazar shared third base. The outfield was set with Carmelo Martinez in left, Gwynn in center, and John Kruk in right. Benito Santiago was behind the plate.

The final series of the season had drama with a tight race for the batting championship between the Giants' Will Clark and Tony Gwynn. Gwynn was chasing Clark going into the series, .332 to .333. In the first game, Gwynn was 1-for-5 while Clark went 2-for-4, and increased his lead. Over the next two games, though, Gwynn took the crown with a 6-for-8 performance while Clark went 2-for-8: Gwynn finished .336 to Clark's .333.

### 1990-1999: Seasons 32-41

McKeon thought he could win the pennant by adding slugger Joe Carter to the outfield. In December 1989 the Padres traded catcher Sandy Alomar Jr., to Cleveland and threw in a guy named Carlos Baerga. So the Padres gave up a lot and those two players did great for the Indians for many years. That Padres team just laid an egg in 1990 for some reason. It just didn't click.

A new ownership team came in 1990 led by Tom Werner, referred to as the "gang of 10." The Padres relieved McKeon. Joe McIlvaine became general manager, and Greg Riddoch took over as manager in midseason. The season resulted in a losing record, 75-87.

After the season McIlvaine traded Joe Carter and Roberto Alomar to the Toronto Blue Jays. In return the Padres received Fred McGriff, a first baseman, and Tony Fernandez, a shortstop. McIlvaine said he would rather have a great shortstop, Fernandez, than a great second basemen, Alomar. Well, Alomar was just coming into his own. Next to Gwynn, Alomar was the most talented player the Padres would ever have. Fernandez at one time was a great shortstop, but when the Padres got him he was on the downside of his career. McGriff was a home-run hitter and on the rising side of his career.

The Padres had moderately successful seasons in 1991 and 1992, with records of 84-78 and 82-80, respectively. The 1992 season highlight might have been the breakout performance of 23-year-old Gary Sheffield, who won the batting championship with a .330 average.

The new owners were not impressed and after a poor start in 1993 the Padres went on what was labeled as a "fire sale." Randy Smith was the new general manager and was under orders to trade the guys who had some value, namely McGriff and Sheffield. Two trades resulted, involving six players, one of whom acquired was Trevor Hoffman.

The 1994 season was cut short by a player strike in August. Beginning with a 5-for-5 game on April 23, Tony Gwynn was dancing around a batting average of .400. His last game before the strike was on August 11 and he finished with a .394 average. He had been locked in all season and had the perfect personality to deal with the media pressure that already had started to build

THE FIRST HALF CENTURY 15

toward a .400 batting average. As for the team, it was out of the pennant race by mid-May.

Perhaps the team's best day in 1994 was in December when general manager Randy Smith made a trade with Houston for several players, most importantly acquiring two who would contribute immensely: third baseman Ken Caminiti and outfielder Steve Finley. The sale of the club was finalized that same month and the "John Moores/Larry Lucchino era" started just days before the trade was made. A very good first step toward building a winning team.

Caminiti and Finley played for the Padres the next four years, providing superb offense and defense. Caminiti won the MVP award in 1996 by a unanimous vote, and Finley accumulated Gold Glove Awards.

Bruce Bochy was brought in to manage the 1995 team. The strike extended into the season resulting in a reduced schedule of 144 games. The Padres finished with a record of 70-74. In November Kevin Towers was promoted to general manager.

The 1996 team started winning from the start and was in first place most of the season. In September the Padres and Dodgers alternated at one-two in the league's Western Division. With three games left to play, the Padres were two games behind the Dodgers with a three-game series in Los Angeles awaiting. The Padres won the first two games and the teams were tied going into the last game of the season. Both teams would make the playoffs; the winner would be division champion and the losing team in as a wild card.

The game was tied, 0-0, through 10 innings. In the top of the 11th inning Chris Gwynn, Tony's brother, came to bat as a pinch-hitter with two men on base and hit a clutch two-run double. Trevor Hoffman came in for the save and the Padres won the division with a 2-0 victory.

This was the Padres' second-ever venture into postseason play and it ended quickly: They were swept by the St. Louis Cardinals in three games in the Division Series.

The 1997 team finished fourth and was never really in the race. However, general manager Towers had pulled off a December trade that brought pitcher Kevin Brown from the Florida Marlins. The Padres gave up a good young player, first baseman Derrek Lee. Brown at the time was one of the best starting pitchers in baseball, and was a leader in the clubhouse and on the field. Pitcher Andy Ashby had his best year and Trevor Hoffman was incredible, with 53 saves out of 54 opportunities. Hoffman and Brown finished two-three in the Cy Young Award voting at year's end. On the offense side, outfielder Greg Vaughn had quite a season. He finished the year with 50 home runs, hitting

his 50th in his last at-bat of the season. Vaughn had 119 runs batted in and finished fourth in the MVP voting.

In 1998 the Padres were in first place from mid-June on and finished 9½ games in front of second-place San Francisco. The team remained hot, winning the Division Series against the Houston Astros, three games to one, and the League Championship Series against the Atlanta Braves, four games to two.

So the Padres were going to their second World Series and would play the American League champion New York Yankees. The first two games were in Yankee Stadium.

Kevin Brown started Game One and entered the seventh inning with a 5-2 lead on the strength of back-to-back home runs by Tony Gwynn and Greg Vaughn. However, with one out and after giving up a hit and walk, Brown was pulled by manager Bochy. What followed was a three-run home run by the Yankees' Chuck Knoblauch, and a subsequent grand slam by Tino Martinez.

The Padres never recovered from that seven-run inning and lost the next three games, and the Series.

While they got close, they did not win, yet San Diego fans appreciated what the team had done all season. In November 1998, San Diego residents, feeling good about their Padres, passed a ballot proposition that resulted in the building of Petco Park. While he was not an elected official, one could credit Kevin Brown with helping to pass the measure.

The 1999 season got off to a bad start in the offseason when Brown, Caminiti, and Finley all left via free agency. The Padres ended the season in fourth place and started rebuilding. The season's highlight occurred on August 6 in Montreal when future Hall of Famer Tony Gwynn collected his 3,000th hit.

### 2000-2009: Seasons 32-41

A string of five sub-.500 seasons followed the 1998 success. Sluggers Phil Nevin and Ryan Klesko arrived by trades, Nevin in March 1999 and Klesko in December 1999. Other key players who joined the team during this period included second baseman Mark Loretta, a free-agent signing in December 2002, and outfielder Brian Giles, by trade in August 2003. The Padres' farm system also was productive, with players like Jake Peavy, coming up in 2002, and Khalil Greene, in 2003.

One of the more notable games took place on October 7, 2001, the last game of the season for the Padres, a home loss to the Colorado Rockies. The game was notable for two events: In the first inning Rickey Henderson hit a double for his 3,000th career hit; and in the ninth inning Tony Gwynn came to bat for the last time in his career. The script called for a hit but it was not to be, as Gwynn grounded out to the shortstop.

After 35 years in the team's Mission Valley stadium the Petco Park era began in April 2004. The Padres had a good season in 2004, winning 87 games but missed the playoffs. Total attendance was 3,016,752, which bested their highest prior year at by almost 500,000.

In 2005 the league's West Division underperformed and the Padres went 82-80 yet won the division by five games. They played the St. Louis Cardinals in the best-of-five Division Series. The team was seemingly void of superstar performances. Brian Giles led the team in RBIs with 83 and Klesko led with 18 home runs. Peavy led the team in wins with 13. This was the Padres' fourth venture into the postseason in its history but they did not get far, being swept by the Cardinals in three games.

In January 2006 Kevin Towers made one of his best trades, picking up first baseman Adrian Gonzalez and pitcher Chris Young from the Texas Rangers. In February Towers signed free-agent catcher Mike Piazza.

For the second year in a row the Padres made the playoffs, finishing first in the West Division, this time tied with the Los Angeles Dodgers. (The Padres were awarded first place because they won the season's series against the Dodgers.) Woody Williams led the team's pitchers with 12 wins and the three other starters each had 11 wins. The bullpen was led by Hoffman with 46 saves. The offense was led by Adrian Gonzalez with 24 home runs and a .304 batting average. The Padres again played the Cardinals in the Division Series, and again lost, three games to one.

In 2007 Bud Black took over the manager reins from Bruce Bochy. It was an interesting season in that the two teams with the best records in the National League had 90 wins, the Diamondbacks and the Rockies. Next best were the 89 wins by the Padres and the Philadelphia Phillies. Unfortunately for the Padres, they were in the same division as the Diamondbacks and Rockies, and missed the playoffs.

The next 11 seasons, 2008-2018, involved a series of rebuilding efforts. The rebuilding went for naught since in only one year, 2010, did the Padres finish over .500.

In the meantime, in December 2008 owner John Moores announced that he wanted to sell the team. Within a few months a group headed by Jeff Moorad, a former player agent, came in as a minority owner and functioned as the club's chief executive officer until March 2012. During his tenure Moorad changed general managers, firing Towers in October 2009 and bringing in Jed Hoyer. Hoyer left in October 2011 to join the Chicago Cubs organization and was replaced by Josh Byrnes.

On the business side of things, Moorad's proposed financial plan for buying the club did not pan out and the team was again up for sale.

Within a few months, in August 2012, local San Diego businessman Ron Fowler came forward representing a group and the sale was approved for $800 million … a far cry from the $12 million Ray Kroc paid for the team in 1974.

### 2010-2018: Seasons 42-50

With new owner Fowler on board, the Padres finished the 2012 and 2013 seasons with identical records, 76-86. In midseason 2014 Fowler fired GM Josh Byrnes and hired A.J. Preller to replace him.

With blessings from the ownership team, beginning in late 2014 Preller went all out for a big season in 2015. He acquired some big names, along with big salaries. Trades brought in outfielder Matt Kemp, closer Craig Kimbrel, outfielder Wil Myers, catcher Derek Norris, and outfielder Justin Upton. Veteran pitcher James Shields was signed as a free agent. Added to this new mix were returning players for whom the Padres had high hopes: infielder Jedd Gyorko, first baseman Yonder Alonso, and pitchers Andrew Cashner, Ian Kennedy, and Tyson Ross.

The 2015 team was loaded with big names, and the fans were excited about the team's prospects. The acquisition of the new players created a lot of interest and most people thought it was going to be a better team than the 2014 club, which won only 77 games. … It had to be!

The team's high point that 2015 season was a 10-5 record on April 21. On June 14 the team floated under .500, and on June 15, with the team at 32-33, manager Black was replaced by coach Dave Roberts for one game, and then Pat Murphy for the remainder of the season. The change in managers did not prove to be of any help; the Padres finished the season with a won-lost record of 74-88, worse than in 2014.

In retrospect, Black with his experience may have been the best person to handle the team with all of the veteran players. Even so, when you analyze them, the 2015 team really was not a very sound team. (Also, they did not have above-average defenders up the middle.)

By the end of July 2016 all of these players were moved except for Wil Myers. Alonso, Gyorko, Kemp, Kimbrel, and Shields were traded, and Kennedy and Upton were lost via free agency. Opening Day 2017 found Myers as the lone survivor.

Management's focus had changed from "do it quickly," relying on established veteran players, to an approach of rebuilding from within. This new approach started with the November

2015 trade of Kimbrel to the Boston Red Sox for four top tier minor-league prospects. The Fowler-Preller team also invested heavily in players from the Dominican Republic. By 2018 the Padres were rated as having one of the best farm systems in baseball, if not the best.

The model being followed by the Padres was one the Astros and Cubs used: Build a foundation within the organization with young, very talented players, and then go after one or two veteran players to provide clubhouse leadership, as Graig Nettles and Goose Gossage did for the 1984 team and Kevin Brown for the 1998 Padres. But you have to remember that the Astros and Cubs had some very poor years before they turned it around and became World Series champions.

### 2019 and Beyond: Seasons 51+

The Padres after their first half-century are still looking for their first World Series title. They have managed to reach the playoffs five times in 50 seasons, twice competing in the World Series.

In 2015 the Padres decided to try a new approach and spent about $80 million investing in young foreign talent. They also traded some key players for talented youngsters in other organizations. The club said its long-range plan was to create a minor-league system in which waves of youngsters challenge to make the major-league roster each year and keep San Diego a constant contender.

Only time will tell if this approach will work but there are some promising early indications. The 2018 rankings of the 100 top prospects in major-league baseball included 10 Padres farmhands, among them the number-two prospect, shortstop Fernando Tatis Jr. A couple of the long-term prospects made the roster in 2018 and several more were expected in 2019 with the idea that the Padres would start to legitimately contend in 2020.

Naturally, many San Diego fans are impatient and want a contender right now. Who can blame them after the team had failed to post a winning record since a 90-72 mark in 2010? Others enjoy watching the team build and following the progress of highly-rated young players.

Whatever your preference the process should be fascinating to watch … especially if it works!

# THE PLAYERS

# ANDY ASHBY

## BY STEVE FERENCHICK

There are many types of baseball lifers. Some play, then manage, like Joe Torre. Some play, then move to the front office, like Billy Beane. Some never play but still make a career of the sport, like Roland Hemond or Vin Scully. But perhaps most baseball lifers play, achieving some success but little fame, and then, after their skills decline, stick around in whatever role presents itself – spring training instructor, TV analyst … team owner? Few baseball lifers can add "team owner" to that list, but Andy Ashby can.

Andrew Jason Ashby was born on July 11, 1967, to Glendon and Rose Ashby in Kansas City, Missouri, and attended Park Hill High School, where he moved away from other sports and focused on baseball in his teens to be able to go as far in the sport as he could. He acknowledged the role his father played in his young life, saying, "My father was always there. Growing up I remember playing catch with my dad. The biggest thing for me was once I went to the big leagues, being able to bring my father into the clubhouse, seeing the expression on his face, knowing his son had achieved his goal and dream of being a major-league baseball player."[1]

After graduating from high school, Ashby enrolled in Crowder College, in Neosho, Missouri. He played baseball for the Roughriders for one season and then, on May 4, 1986, signed with the Phillies as an amateur free agent. He began his professional career that summer at age 18 for the Bend Phillies and steadily climbed through the minors, playing in Utica, Spartanburg, Batavia, Clearwater, and Reading between 1987 and 1990, and finally for the Scranton/Wilkes-Barre Red Barons in 1991 before getting called up to the Phillies to start on June 10, 1991, in Cincinnati.

Ashby's major-league debut saw him retiring the first seven batters he faced, including future Hall of Famer Barry Larkin, but the Reds' bats got to him the second time through the lineup. Five days later, on June 5, Ashby got some payback, pitching an "immaculate inning" by striking out all three Reds batters he faced in the fourth on nine pitches – just the second rookie and 33rd player overall to do so. Still, Ashby was 0-2 with an 8.00 ERA and was sent back to Triple A. He was recalled and pitched six more games at season's end with more success.

Ashby started the 1992 season in the Phillies rotation and won his first start but then broke his right thumb and missed two months of action.[2] He rehabbed in Triple A, was recalled in August, and pitched shakily. The Phillies left him unprotected in the 1992 expansion draft, so instead of playing for the 1993 NL champion Phillies team that Harry Kalas described as the "wacky, wonderful bunch of throwbacks,"[3] Ashby was selected 25th by the Colorado Rockies and started the 1993 season in the starting rotation in the thin air of Mile High Stadium in Denver.

Although Ashby served up just five home runs in 54 innings with the 1993 Rockies, his ERA at Mile High Stadium matched the park's name, and he was sent to Triple-A Colorado Springs. Then on July 27 he was the "player to be named later" in a trade with the last-place Padres. It was good fortune for Ashby, though, as Jack Murphy Stadium had a reputation as being a pitcher's park, and San Diego was where Ashby was able to get his career on track. He immediately moved into the starting rotation and while he went only 3-6 with a 5.48 ERA in San Diego, it was an improvement from his Colorado performance.

The 1994 through 1997 seasons for the Padres saw Ashby mature to become a legitimate major-league pitcher, starting all four years and posting solid ERAs. The Padres struggled for three of the four years but in 1996, when Ashby was the team's Opening Day pitcher and led the starting rotation in ERA, the Padres pulled off a surprising division win, and Ashby started NLDS Game Three against the St. Louis Cardinals. Although he left the game in the sixth tied 4-4, the bullpen couldn't hold and the Cardinals completed a sweep of the Padres. In 1997 the Padres dropped back to fourth place but Ashby continued to pitch well. In 1998 he reflected on his early career:

"[B]y the time Colorado sent me down in 1993, I felt, what in the world is going on? It seemed I was always pitching out of some jam, always one or two balls behind in the count, always just trying to keep the game close – and by the fifth inning I'd be out of there anyway. It was never the same thing. Early in my career I was wild. Sometimes I'd pitch too defensively. … I would just throw – not pitch with a purpose. Just throw. I think it was a maturity thing. I remember being up with Philadelphia and talking on the bench the whole game, until Dale Murphy finally turned to me and said, 'Ash. Watch the game, watch the game.

That's how you learn.' He was right. I had to start listening to the guys I should've been listening to."[4]

While 1998 was the year of the home run, it was also Ashby's most successful year, marking the first of his two All-Star Game appearances, his only World Series appearance, and career highs in wins (17), starts (33), innings pitched (226⅔), and complete games (5). Ashby's record was 11-5 with a 2.54 ERA at midseason; in the All-Star Game, in Denver, he pitched the fifth inning, giving up a home run to Alex Rodriguez but retiring future Hall of Famers Ivan Rodriguez and Cal Ripken. The Padres led the NL West nearly wire-to-wire, peaking with a 16-game lead and ultimately winning 98 games.

In the 1998 NLDS, the Padres faced the 102-win Astros and Ashby started Game Two but left the game down 3-0 after four innings. The Padres tied the game to get Ashby off the hook but eventually lost, 5-4. However, San Diego won the series, three games to one. In the NLCS, the Braves were favored but the Padres jumped out to a three-games-to-none lead. Ashby started Game One and pitched brilliantly, going seven innings and surrendering just one run on five hits and a walk. But when Trevor Hoffman blew just his second save of the year, Ashby was denied his first postseason win, although the Padres did go on to win the game. In Game Five, in San Diego, with the Padres leading three games to one, Ashby pitched nearly as well, scattering nine hits over six innings and giving up two runs. He was again in line for the win, but this time starter Kevin Brown came in to relieve and blew the lead, again costing Ashby credit for a victory. The Padres went on to win Game Six to advance to the World Series, against the Yankees. After the excitement of the NLCS win, the World Series was a dénouement. Ashby started Game Two but the Yankee bats were too much, scoring seven runs, three unearned, before Ashby departed for a reliever. The Yankees ended up sweeping the Padres.

The year 1999 began for the Padres with country music superstar Garth Brooks signing a minor-league contract and then, wearing number 77, going 1-for-22 for the Padres in exhibition games before switching back to guitar. From a baseball perspective, the year was much more successful for Ashby than for Brooks (including pitching again on Opening Day) but was a step down from 1998, as he ended up with a 14-10 record and a 3.80 ERA. His performance led to another All-Star Game appearance (where he pitched to just one batter) and to the role of ace of the San Diego staff. However, after failing to re-sign many of the key components of their 1998 pennant-winning squad, the Padres regressed, ending up at 74-88 and in fourth place.

In the 1998-99 offseason, facing the final year of Ashby's contract and a fading team that would drop to last place in 2000, the Padres traded him to the Phillies for three young pitchers.

The Phillies had what they felt was a strong staff in 2000, led by Ashby and Curt Schilling, but both Ashby and the team struggled, and on July 12, the Phillies traded Ashby to Atlanta. The Braves were in first place at that point and, having lost John Smoltz for the season to injury, looked to Ashby to start. The move paid dividends, as Ashby threw a complete-game win in his first appearance and ended the season with an 8-6 record and 4.13 ERA with the Braves, compared with a 4-7 record and 5.68 ERA with the Phillies. Ashby also pitched well for the Braves in the 2000 NLDS, his last postseason appearance, albeit in a mop-up relief role as the Cardinals dominated the Braves.

Ashby signed a three-year free-agent contract with the Dodgers after the 2000 season, but suffered an elbow injury in his second start of 2001, ending his season on April 12 with a 2-0 record. He returned to full strength in 2002, starting 30 games and compiling a near-league-average ERA of 3.91 and a 9-13 record. Plagued by injuries in 2003, starting with back stiffness in spring training, Ashby started just 12 games, finally shutting it down after September 1 with elbow tendinitis, at which point he underwent Tommy John surgery and was expected to miss all of 2004.[5] At age 36, it looked as though it might be the end of his career.

However, the Padres signed Ashby to a minor-league contract for the 2004 season, and by May he had begun to throw off a mound. By September he was back to throwing 90 mph and was activated on September 8, throwing a 1-2-3 inning. He pitched again on September 14, retiring three of the four Dodgers hitters he faced, ending with a swinging strikeout of Cesar Izturis in what would turn out to be Ashby's final major-league appearance.

After the season Ashby underwent another elbow surgery and signed another minor-league deal with the Padres. Returning in August, he made rehab starts for Lake Elsinore and Portland, but despite allowing just earned one run in six innings, he was not recalled to the Padres. Ashby made another valiant effort to return to the Padres in spring training of 2006 at age 38, but after he surrendered 22 hits over 11 innings, it was apparent that a return wasn't in the cards, and the team released him, putting an end to a 20-year professional career, 14 of which were in the majors.

Ashby remained busy, even without baseball. He and his wife, Tracy Tigue, a native of Pittston, Pennsylvania, whom he had met while playing for Scranton/Wilkes-Barre, married in 1993 and raised four daughters, -- Eastin, Madison, Taryn, and Ashton. The athletic talent was clearly passed on to that generation, with all four playing NCAA sports. The Ashbys maintained homes in both Pittston and San Diego. In 2014, Ashby described his life and his role as a father: "The majority of the time I'm just being Dad. I do some charity work. I hunt a lot. I fish. When I'm home, I'm running with my kids, watching them do sports. I'm just kind of being Dad, making up for the time that I missed when I was playing. Thank God for my wife. Tracy was really good about flying the girls into a city. We weren't apart a lot. When school started it was tougher, but if the girls got to a week and half where they hadn't seen Dad, that was a lot. She'd fly them in to be with Dad, then the team would go on to another city and she'd take them back to San Diego."[6]

Although Andy Ashby is not related to former catcher Alan Ashby,[7] his nephew, Aaron Ashby, was drafted in the fourth round of the 2018 amateur draft by the Milwaukee Brewers after having followed his uncle both to Park Hill High and Crowder College.[8]

Ashby returned to baseball in 2013-14 as an analyst during Padres games for Fox Sports San Diego.[9] In 2016 he was a spring-training instructor for the Padres, saying at the time, "I would love to be in the big leagues, of course, but I'd just like to be in the game – coaching or scouting or bullpen coach, something like that. This gives me the opportunity to come here and get a little taste of it."[10]

Later that year, he did get back into the professional baseball, but in a different role – Ashby bought a share of the Scranton/Wilkes-Barre RailRiders (Triple-A affiliate of the New York Yankees), near his Pittston home. Ashby had played two Triple-A seasons in the same ballpark where he was now an owner. At the official announcement, Ashby said, "I talked to my wife and she was like, 'Ownership? Are you ready for that?' And I was like, 'I don't know, but how do you know until you try it.' It's an honor for me to be a part of this. Being here 25 years ago, it's changed a lot, but for the better. I enjoyed it, the people were great."[11]

Andy Ashby has three baseball homes – Missouri (where he started playing), northeast Pennsylvania (where he played two years, met his wife, raised his daughters, and lives most of the year), and San Diego (where he blossomed as a player and was regularly welcomed back by fans). He has come full circle, from playing a season with the Roughriders to owning a piece of the RailRiders; it's clear that Andy Ashby's baseball ride continues.

## SOURCES

In addition to the sources cited in the Notes, statistics and game details were retrieved from baseball-reference.com.

# NOTES

1    "A Major League Dad," *Wilkes-Barre* (Pennsylvania) *Times Leader*, June 13, 2014, timesleader.com/archive/396243/news-news-1464912-a-major-league-dad, accessed November 29, 2018.

2    Dan Hafner, "National League Roundup: Williams Makes a Smart Move for the Phillies," *Los Angeles Times*, April 27, 1992, articles.latimes.com/1992-04-27/sports/sp-697_1_smart-move, accessed November 29, 2018.

3    Tyler Kepner, "On Baseball: Darren Daulton Was the Heartbeat of a Rowdy Phillies Bunch," *New York Times*, August 7, 2017, nytimes.com/2017/08/07/sports/baseball/darren-daulton-phillies-heartbeat.html, accessed November 29, 2018.

4    Johnette Howard, "Better Late Than Never: After Years of Frustrating Under-achievement, Padres Righthander Andy Ashby Has Joined the Ranks of the National League's Pitching Elite," *Sports Illustrated*, June 22, 1998, si.com/vault/1998/06/22/245178/better-late-than-never-after-years-of-frustrating-under-achievement-padres-righthander-andy-ashby-has-joined-the-ranks-of-the-national-leagues-pitching-elite, accessed November 29, 2018.

5    Rotoworld.com, rotoworld.com/recent/mlb/1659/andy-ashby, accessed November 29, 2018.

6    "A Major League Dad."

7    Tim Kurkjian, "Baseball," *Sports Illustrated*, July 11, 1994, si.com/vault/1994/07/11/106786713/baseball, accessed November 29, 2018.

8    Sam McDowell, "MLB Draft: Two Former Kansas City High School Pitchers Selected," *Kansas City Star*, June 5, 2018, kansascity.com/sports/high-school/article212585904.html, accessed November 29, 2018.

9    "A Major League Dad."

10   Bryce Miller, "Andy Ashby Ditches Makeup, Joins Padres at Spring Training," *San Diego Union Tribune*, March 1, 2016, sandiegouniontribune.com/sports/padres/sdut-andy-ashby-ditches-makeup-joins-padres-at-spring-2016mar01-story.html, accessed November 29, 2018.

11   D.J. Eberle, "Andy Ashby Part of Trio Joining Railriders' Ownership Group," *Wilkes-Barre* (Pennsylvania) *Times Leader*, October 19, 2016, timesleader.com/sports/railriders/598585/andy-ashby-part-of-trio-joining-railriders-ownership-group, accessed November 29, 2018.

# HEATH BELL

## BY GEOFF YOUNG

"I want to give it my all and teach my kids you can get knocked down and people can say you're no good, you're old, blah blah, but if you have passion, you can work really hard and you can go and give it your all, and if it doesn't work out, at least you can hold your head high."[1]

Former All-Star Heath Bell uttered these words in March 2015 as he made one final attempt to extend his career with the Washington Nationals. He'd shed 30 pounds after a poor showing for the Tampa Bay Rays in 2014, but the Nationals ultimately decided the 37-year-old from Oceanside, California, didn't fit in their plans and released him just before Opening Day.

Bell retired knowing he gave it his all and was able to hold his head high, teaching his four children an important lesson in the process. And although in a perfect world he would have left the game on a higher note, he could at least point back to past successes in a league and a sport where failure is far more common.

Born on September 29, 1977, to Jimmie and Edwina Bell, Heath Justin Bell grew up in Tustin, in Southern California, about 50 miles northwest of his birthplace.[2] At Tustin High School, which also produced former big leaguers Mark Grace and Shawn Green, Bell lettered in football, basketball, and baseball.[3] It was there that he developed habits that would last a lifetime.

Bell credited his father, a former Marine and auto mechanic whose busy schedule wasn't always conducive to raising a family but who found ways to make it work, for setting a good example. Despite Jimmie's long hours, he always made time for Heath: "My father worked his butt off. But if I wanted to go play catch, he could be half-asleep on the couch and he'd go play catch."[4]

Following his father's lead, Bell decided to be present for his own children despite whatever else might be going on in his life. For example, while with the Padres, he biked to school with them. As he told the *San Diego Union-Tribune* in 2011,

"I saw how my dad was, and I thought he was absolutely the coolest father."[5]

Jimmie's work ethic also passed from father to son, serving Heath well as he defied coach after coach who told him he probably wouldn't reach the next level. Undrafted out of high school, Bell attended nearby Santa Ana College (known briefly as Rancho Santiago College during his time there), which also produced entertainers Steve Martin and Diane Keaton.[6]

Bell went 8-0 with a 2.17 ERA and nine saves for the Dons as a freshman en route to being named the Orange Empire Conference Co-Pitcher of the Year in 1997.[7] He added 12 saves as a sophomore. Although those two seasons would eventually lead to his 2010 induction into the Santa Ana College Hall of Fame, his junior-college success guaranteed nothing in terms of a professional career.[8]

Again defying his doubters, Bell was selected by the Tampa Bay Devil Rays in the 69th round of the 1997 draft. The 1,583rd of 1,607 players taken that year, he did not sign, later recalling that when the Devil Rays made an offer, "I actually forgot I got drafted."[9] Instead he signed with the New York Mets as a free agent the following summer, starting his career at Kingsport of the Appalachian League, where he posted a 2.54 ERA and led his team with eight saves.

Bell was promoted to Capital City of the South Atlantic League in 1999 and enjoyed another strong campaign, again leading his team in saves, this time with 25. A year later and a level higher, it was more of the same: 23 saves for St. Lucie of the Florida State League. By this point Bell had played three professional seasons, finishing with an ERA under 3.00 and leading his team in saves each year.

But baseball wouldn't prove to be so easy in 2001. Bell struggled, posting a 6.02 ERA and earning only four saves with Binghamton of the Eastern League.

Meanwhile, Bell's life changed in other ways. He married his wife, Nicole, and adopted her young daughter, Jasmyne. Heath and Nicole had three children of their own: Jordyn, born with Down syndrome ("our blessing in disguise"[10]), Reece, and Rhett.

Back on the field, Bell responded with a stellar return to Binghamton, notching a 1.18 ERA and six saves before a midseason promotion to Triple-A Norfolk. He enjoyed less success at the higher level and again posted pedestrian numbers in a 2003 encore but now found himself just one step away from the big leagues.

From 2004 to 2006, Bell rode the proverbial shuttle between New York and Norfolk, often needed for stretches but never quite able to stick. And while his Triple-A performances dazzled, his stints with the Mets – with irregular roles and usage – didn't go so well. In 81 appearances with the Mets, he posted a 4.92 ERA and zero saves.

By the end of his tenure in New York he was already 28 years old, an age when most players have either established themselves or started preparing for their next career. As Bell later noted, even his family was ready for him to move on: "At that time, my wife was telling me to quit."[11] But, as usual, he persevered despite the odds against him.

Bell might not have endeared himself to Mets management by riding Rollerblades to spring training in an attempt to get into better shape. As Mets pitching coach Rick Peterson told the *New York Times* in 2005, "How many times do you hear about someone falling off? You can't motorcycle or sky-drive or go cliff-jumping in Mexico, and you shouldn't do this, either."[12] (Years later Bell recalled Peterson's displeasure and conceded that his training methods weren't necessarily the best.)[13]

Bell received a new lease on life when the Mets traded him and fellow reliever Royce Ring to the San Diego Padres for reliever Jon Adkins and outfielder Ben Johnson. Returning to the West Coast, Bell immediately thrived as Trevor Hoffman's set-up man in 2007, posting a 2.02 ERA in 81 appearances and fanning 102 batters.

Bell also became a legend in the Padres clubhouse, known as much for his zany antics (he was fond of flying remote-control helicopters in the clubhouse) as for his prowess on the mound. As then-teammate Jake Peavy said, "He is in his own world. And it is going to get worse because Heath is really good."[14]

Bell slipped a bit the following year in the same role, but when Hoffman departed for Milwaukee via free agency after the season, Bell filled the Hall of Fame closer's shoes with aplomb, leading the National League with 42 saves and being named to the All-Star team. Perhaps not coincidentally, he'd lost 30 pounds before the season. This time, instead of using Rollerblades to get himself into shape, he used a Nintendo game called Wii Fit that his children had been playing.

Bell cleared the 40-save mark again in 2010 and 2011, making the All-Star team each time. At the 2010 midsummer classic, in Anaheim, Bell brought his father – then fighting lung cancer – to sit with him during media appearances and share the experience. It was the least he could for someone who had always made time for him: "He says he's a proud father. I'm a proud son."[15]

In his third and final All-Star Game appearance, Bell sprinted in from the bullpen as usual before sliding into the pitcher's mound and retiring the only batter he faced. When asked about the slide, Bell said, "I wanted the fans to have fun with this.

The fans are really what matters. They're the ones that show up. They're the ones who pay our salary."[16]

After the season Bell became a free agent and signed a three-year contract with the Florida Marlins.[17] He got off to a rough start with his new team, blowing three of five save opportunities in April 2012, and never recovered. He lost his job as closer after the All-Star break[18] and found himself publicly locking horns with manager Ozzie Guillen.[19] During his struggles Nicole reminded him how much he had already overcome in life and that he would get through this difficult time as well.[20]

The Marlins traded Bell to Arizona in October 2012 and he again stumbled with his new team, allowing two home runs in his Diamondbacks debut before posting a 2.22 ERA over his next 25 appearances, notching 11 saves along the way. He held onto the closer role for another month before blowing his fifth save on July 10 and losing his ninth-inning job. Bell finished the season on a fairly strong note, albeit in a lesser role.

In December 2013 Bell found himself on the move once more, this time to Tampa Bay, the team that had originally drafted him. Bell's Rays career lasted 13 games; he was released on May 10, 2014, a week after allowing three runs in what proved to be his final big-league inning.

The Orioles signed Bell on May 18 but released him less than a month later after just 10 appearances at Triple-A Norfolk. He then spent 11 days in the Yankees organization, again at Triple-A, before being released on June 24 and sitting out the rest of the season. The Washington Nationals signed Bell in December 2014 but released him at the end of 2015 spring training. Even during his brief time with the Nationals, Bell had become known for his free-spirited nature, from making his own smoothies because "I don't like eating my vegetables" to wearing Star Wars sneakers around camp.[21]

By this time Bell had spent 11 seasons in the major leagues and made three All-Star teams. He'd led the National League with 42 saves in 2009 and finished with 168 in a career that included 590 appearances (all in relief) and a 3.49 ERA – not bad for a guy who repeatedly wasn't supposed to reach the next level but did it anyway.

Although it seems this could be where the story ends, it isn't. In 2016 and 2017 Bell pitched for the independent league Kansas Stars, playing alongside several other former major leaguers. As he told the Wichita Eagle, "I'm just here having a good time. I came here last year and had a great time talking with fans. This year I'm a little more comfortable. I want to be a personable player, not a big leaguer, I guess you could say."[22]

In 2018 Bell played with more former big leaguers for the Louisville Stars in a week-long tournament called the Bluegrass World Series.[23] As he told San Diego radio station Mighty 1090, his arm felt good: "I don't pitch as much, but last year I was still throwing 92-94, so I can crank it up for a little bit here and there."[24]

These days, Bell saves most of his fastballs for his older son: "He's 14 now, so for the last three years I've been throwing batting practice three times a week to his whole team."[25] When he isn't coaching his kids or playing in the occasional game himself, Bell is co-owner of 7 Cold Brew, a San Diego company that delivers specialty coffee to local offices, restaurants, and bars.

## SOURCES

In addition to the sources cited in the Notes, the author also relied on Baseball-Reference.com.

## NOTES

1    Anthony Rieber, "Heath Bell? Name Rings a Bell," *Newsday*, March 14, 2015, newsday.com/sports/baseball/mets/heath-bell-name-rings-a-bell-1.9988298.

2    HeathBell21.com. web.archive.org/web/20120328125620/http://www.heathbell21.com/?page_id=2.

3    Bob Keisser, "Which Tustin Baseball Players Made It in the Pros?" *Orange County Register* Anaheim, California), February 19, 2015, ocregister.com/2015/02/19/which-tustin-baseball-players-made-it-in-the-pros/.

4    "For Bell, Every Day Is Father's Day," *San Diego Union-Tribune*, June 18, 2011, sandiegouniontribune.com/sports/padres/sdut-heath-bell-its-father-son-2011jun18-htmlstory.html.

5    Ibid.

6    "Famous Santa Ana College Alumni," Ranker.com, ranker.com/list/famous-santa-ana-college-alumni-and-students/reference.

7    "Fullerton, Cypress Split Post-Season Softball Honors," *Los Angeles Times*, May 8, 1997, articles.latimes.com/1997-05-08/sports/sp-56861_1_orange-empire-conference.

8    sacdons.com/hof/members/members/bell.

9    David Brown, "Answer Man: Padres' Heath Bell Talks Toys, Conspiracies and Pez," Yahoo.com, March 25, 2010, sports.yahoo.com/blogs/mlb-david-brown/answer-man-padres-heath-bell-talks-toys-conspiracies--mlb.html.

10   Seth Livingstone, "Padres Reliever Shares First All-Star Game with Family," *USA Today*, July 13, 2009, https://usatoday30.usatoday.com/sports/baseball/allstar/2009-07-13-bell-day-with_N.htm

11   Scott Allen, "Heath Bell, Who Once Compared Himself to Han Solo, Wears Star Wars Sneakers at Nationals Spring Training," *Washington Post*, March 5, 2015, washingtonpost.com/news/dc-sports-bog/wp/2015/03/05/heath-bell-who-once-compared-himself-to-han-solo-wears-star-wars-sneakers-at-nationals-spring-training/.

12    Lee Jenkins, "By Skate or Scooter, Mets' Bell Has Arrived," *New York Times*, February 21, 2005, nytimes.com/2005/02/21/sports/baseball/by-skate-or-scooter-mets-bell-has-arrived.html.

13    James Wagner, "Heath Bell Dropped 40 Pounds This Offseason, Hopes to Compete for Bullpen Spot," *Washington Post*, February 18, 2015, washingtonpost.com/news/nationals-journal/wp/2015/02/18/heath-bell-dropped-40-pounds-this-offseason-hopes-to-compete-for-bullpen-spot/.

14    Tim Kurkjian, "Fun-Loving Bell Finally Has His Dream Job," ESPN.com, April 17, 2009, espn.com/mlb/columns/story?columnist=kurkjian_tim&id=4073444.

15    Bill Center, "This All-Star Game Special for Padres' Bell, Ill Father," *San Diego Union-Tribune*, July 12, 2010, sandiegouniontribune.com/sdut-all-star-game-special-padres-bell-ill-father-2010jul12-htmlstory.html.

16    Kevin Baxter and Bill Shaikin, "Heath Bell Doesn't Let Opportunity Slide By at All-Star Game," *Los Angeles Times*, July 12, 2011, articles.latimes.com/2011/jul/12/sports/la-sp-0713-all-star-notes-20110713.

17    Bill Center, "Bell, Marlins Agree on 3-Year Contract," *San Diego Union-Tribune*, December 1, 2011, sandiegouniontribune.com/sports/padres/sdut-bell-believes-his-future-will-be-decided-next-10-d-2011dec01-story.html.

18    Joe Frisaro, "Marlins Likely Headed to Closer by Committee," MLB.com, July 10, 2012, joefrisaro.mlblogs.com/marlins-likely-headed-to-closer-by-commit-tee-e80d1cd85f3b.

19    "Heath Bell-Ozzie Guillen Rift Widens as Teammates Support Manager," *The Sporting News*, September 26, 2012, sportingnews.com/mlb/news/4167961-heath-bell-ozzie-guillen-fight-rift-radio-fire-trade-miami-marlins.

20    Clark Spencer, "Bell's Wife Soothes His Soul with Facebook Note," *Miami Herald*, April 17, 2012, miamiherald.typepad.com/fish_bytes/2012/04/bells-wife-soothes-his-soul-with-facebook-note.html.

21    Allen, "Heath Bell, Who Once Compared Himself to Han Solo, Wears Star Wars Sneakers at Nationals Spring Training."

22    Jeffrey Lutz, "Kansas Stars' Heath Bell Has Major Fun Interacting with Fans," *Wichita Eagle*, August 5, 2017, kansas.com/sports/other-sports/nbc-baseball/article165680952.html.

23    bluegrassworldseries.com/roster/

24    Heath Bell, interview with Ben and Woods, May 22, 2018, mighty1090.com/episode/heath-bell-i-really-just-miss-the-guys-we-didnt-always-talk-baseball-we-would-just-talk-about-life/

25    Ibid.

# ANDY BENES

## BY ALAN COHEN

*"I was a biology and chemistry major at Evansville. I thought I'd go to medical school. Then, in the second or third game in my junior year, I struck out 21 batters (in a game). My velocity had gone up eight miles per hour in one season. It (the hype) was all thrust upon me at once."*

– Andy Benes speaking in 2009 about his path to becoming the number-one overall draft pick in 1988.[1]

*"As great as an athlete he was, he is even a more out-standing individual. He had such great values and such faith and a belief in family and shows by the example he sets. That, to me, is the first thing I think of when I think of Andy Benes – the person that he is."*

– Paul Gries, Evansville Central High School baseball coach (1981-2001), in 2010.[2]

This is the story of a pretty good pitcher who became an even better man.

Andrew Charles Benes was born in Evansville, Indiana, on August 20, 1967. He was the first son born to Charles and Karen Benes. Andy's sister Amy had come along the prior year. His brother Alan Benes, with whom he played on the St. Louis Cardinals, followed on January 21, 1972. A third brother, Adam, came along on March 12, 1973. Adam signed with the St. Louis Cardinals in 1995 and made it as far as Double A in six seasons.

Andy's father, a biochemist, worked in the pharmaceutical industry and his mother was a homemaker. Evansville is about 170 miles from St. Louis and Andy grew up a Cardinals fan. He first gained attention in Little League. As a 12-year-old he was named the MVP in a local tournament.[3] He spent his elementary-school years at Evansville Lutheran School, then starred in football, basketball, and baseball at Evansville Central High School. In his senior year, he passed for more than 1,400 yards on the gridiron and led the city in scoring in basketball with 19.7 points per game.[4] In baseball, he split his time between shortstop, where he was an all-city selection, and the mound, where he was 7-0 with a 0.84 ERA in his senior year.

Benes attended the University of Evansville as a pre-med student and was recruited to play varsity football and baseball. In the fall of his sophomore year, he quarterbacked the football team, and played some at tight end. By the time the baseball season rolled around, he was still recovering from the football season and did not have a good season.

Benes married Jennifer Byers, whom he had started dating in high school, on March 21. 1987. Their first child, Andrew Charles Benes II, was born on November 4, 1988. Drew, as he was known, pitched at Arkansas State University and signed with the St. Louis Cardinals after being selected in the 35th round of the 2010 amateur draft. He played three seasons in the Cardinals organization and then a year of independent ball in 2013. In 2017 he joined the Pittsburgh organization as a minor-league pitching coast and spent 2017 and 2018 with Bradenton in the Florida State League. He and his wife have three children.

Andy and Jennifer's daughter, Brynn Nicole, was born on November 1, 1993. She became a nurse. She and he husband have one child and when Andy was interviewed for this story, he was babysitting for his nine-month-old grandchild. Two other children, Bailey and Shane, followed during the next two years. In 2018 Bailey was pursuing a career as a speech pathologist and Shane was playing ball in college, hoping to play professionally. The family was not yet complete. In 2009 Andy and Jennifer adopted a 3-year-old boy from Siberia and named him Brock. They adopted a girl in January 2011 and named her Bliss. In 2010 Benes said, "Jennifer and I feel like we're blessed with so much. The Bible talks about taking care of the less fortunate. We know we can't give a home to everybody, but we can start with one or two."[5]

In his junior year at Evansville, Andy did not play football and decided to concentrate on baseball. The results were spectacular. In what was to be his final collegiate season, he was 15-3 before the NCAA tournament. He struck out 180 batters in 137 innings and his season was highlighted by a 21-strikeout performance against UNC-Wilmington.

On the eve of the 1988 draft, Benes pitched Evansville to a 1-0 win over Arizona State in the NCAA West Regional, scattering eight hits and striking out nine batters. The performance prompted ASU coach Jim Brock to say, "In all my years of college coaching, he's the best I've seen. He could be in the majors by the end of the summer."[6] The game was his 13th complete game and eighth shutout of the season.

The San Diego Padres chose Benes as the first overall pick in the draft in 1988. After the draft, Benes had a decision to make. Would he sign with the Padres or participate in the Olympic Games? Benes agreed to terms with the Padres, which included a bonus of $230,000. By not actually signing at the time, he kept his amateur status and remained eligible to participate in the 1988 Olympic Games.[7]

He was grateful to those at Evansville who helped him grow as a player, especially coach Jim Brownlee. He donated a portion of his signing bonus to the university and in 1997 established the Andy Benes Fund to help the university's athletic program.[8]

Before the Olympics Team USA played a seven-game exhibition series against Cuba. Although the USA lost four of the games, Benes performed well. In the seventh game, he pitched a complete game, allowed seven hits, and struck out seven batters in a 5-2 win.[9]

Amateur competition continued for Benes in September at the World Baseball Championships, where the United States lost to Cuba in the final round.

In the preliminary round of the 1988 Olympics, Benes pitched 6⅔ innings in a 12-2 win over Australia, allowing three hits and one earned run. In the medal round, he was put in the bullpen. He was a spectator as Jim Abbott won the game that clinched the Gold Medal for the United States, defeating Japan 5-3.

In 1989, after spring training with the Padres, Benes was assigned to Wichita of the Double-A Texas League. His first few games with Wichita were the stuff of dreams. His record through April 29 was 4-0 with 55 strikeouts in 41 innings. His two-hit shutout of Midland on April 29 lowered his ERA to 0.41.[10] He was promoted to Triple-A Las Vegas after going 8-4 with five complete games, three shutouts, and a 2.16 ERA in 16 starts. After five starts at Las Vegas, the 21-year-old was called up to the Padres.

In his Padres debut, at home against the Atlanta Braves on August 11, 1989, Benes pitched the first six innings, striking out seven. A four-run Braves fifth inning, highlighted by a three-run homer by Dale Murphy, was his undoing. Atlanta won the game, 6-5.

After losing his first two big-league starts, Benes rebounded to win his next six decisions, and finished the season with a 6-3 record and a 3.51 ERA. His first win came on August 23 at Philadelphia, when he pitched seven innings, allowing two earned runs in a 7-3 win.

The Padres' record at that point was 63-64. Including the win on August 23, the they won 27 of their last 36 games and finished second in the AL West, three games behind San Francisco. During those early games with San Diego, Benes displayed a potent bat. On September 3, in a 9-5 win over the Phillies, his two-run homer off Dennis Cook in the bottom of the second inning put San Diego ahead 3-0. He batted .250 (6-for-24) in 10 games.

In 1990 Benes spent the entire season with the Padres, going 10-11 with a 3.60 ERA. He had his first complete-game victory on May 14 at home against the Phillies. In a 5-1 win, he allowed two hits and struck out five. In 1991 Benes improved his record to 15-11 and finished sixth in the Cy Young Award balloting. His ERA, the lowest of his career, was 3.03. He logged a career-high 231⅓ innings in 1992 and finished with a 13-14 record.

On May 17, 1993, Benes pitched his fourth career shutout, a 4-0 three-hitter over the Colorado Rockies at San Diego. At the All-Star break, Benes had a 9-6 record and was named to his only All-Star team. In his last outing before the All-Star Game, on July 7, he pitched the first eight innings as the Padres limited the Mets to one hit in a win at Shea Stadium. He pitched the third and fourth innings of the All-Star Game on July 13 at Baltimore. After yielding a leadoff game-tying homer to Roberto Alomar in the third inning, he pitched scoreless ball, leaving the game with the score tied 2-2 in the middle of the fifth inning of a game the American League went on to win, 9-3. Benes pitched his second shutout of the 1993 season against the Cubs at Wrigley Field on July 27. He had a 13-7 record with a 2.62 ERA on August 6 but tailed off in the remaining weeks of the season. He lost eight of his last 10 decisions to finish at 15-15 with an ERA of 3.78.

In 1994 Benes's 6-14 record was not indicative of his performance during the season. In 10 of his 14 losses, the Padres scored two runs or less, and he was totally ineffective in only two games, a 15-1 loss on April 9 and a 14-0 loss on July 8. He had one good stretch from May 31 through July 3, going 4-0 with an ERA of 2.52 in seven starts. He topped off this stretch with a 7-0, one-hit shutout of the Mets at San Diego on July 3, striking out 13. He provided all the offense he would need with a three-run double. The no-hitter was broken up by the Mets' Rico Brogna, who hit an eighth-inning double. On the eve of the game, Padres GM Randy Smith had been quoted in *Baseball America* as saying that Benes, the Padres ace, despite his recent successes was only the third best starting pitcher on the squad. The remark annoyed the outspoken Benes, who said that "the comment really angered me. It really took the fun out of this (one-hitter). I felt that I had something to prove."[11]

Benes led the league in strikeouts with 189 in the strike-shortened 1994 season. But when he signed for the 1995 season after an angry arbitration, his days as a Padre were numbered. Matters were compounded when he started the year going 4-7 with a 4.17 ERA.

With free agency looming at the end of the 1995 season, the Padres, at the July 31 trading deadline, traded Benes to the Seattle Mariners for Marc Newfield and Ron Villone. Greg Keagle later went from the Padres to the Mariners to complete the deal. Benes left the Padres with a 69-75 record over six years. His ERA was 3.57. On 15 occasions, he struck out 10 or more batters in a single game.

The Mariners needed additional pitching as they sought to reach the postseason for the first time. In the final two months of the season, Benes was 7-2 with Seattle, although his ERA with them was 5.86. The ERA was of little consequence as the Mariners scored 10 or more runs in three of his wins. They finished first in the AL West, and in the Division Series against the Yankees, Benes started Game Two and pitched four shutout innings before yielding a game-tying run with two out in the fifth inning when Bernie Williams doubled in Wade Boggs. After the Mariners regained the lead in the top of the sixth inning, Benes surrendered back-to-back homers to Ruben Sierra and Don Mattingly and was removed from the game. The contest ended at 1:12 A.M. when the Yankees won in the bottom of the 15th inning on a Jim Leyritz homer to take a 2-0 series lead.

The series headed back to Seattle. The Mariners evened the series at two games apiece and Benes started the decisive fifth game. Benes and David Cone of the Yankees traded zeros in the early innings until Joey Cora homered for the Mariners in the third inning, then Paul O'Neill put the Yankees ahead with a two-run homer off Benes in the top of the fourth. In the top of the sixth, Benes walked the bases full and yielded a two-run double to Mattingly. It was the last hit of Mattingly's career. When Benes left the game with two out in the seventh inning, the Mariners trailed 4-2. Benes was a spectator when the Mariners won the game in the bottom of the 11th inning and advanced to the ALCS.

Benes made only one appearance as the Mariners lost the best-of-seven ALCS to the Indians. He started the fourth game and was knocked out in the third inning after allowing six runs. The Indians' attack was highlight by a pair of two-run homers by future Hall of Famers. Eddie Murray's blast in the first inning made the score 3-0 and Jim Thome's homer in the third inning put the Mariners behind 6-0. Cleveland won, 7-0, to even up the series at two games apiece and won the next two games to eliminate the Mariners.

Benes opted for free agency after the season and joined the St. Louis Cardinals in 1996. He was with them for two years. In 1996 he finished third in the Cy Young Award balloting when he recorded 18 wins against 10 losses, after starting the season 1-7. The Cardinals finished first in the NL Central and went on to sweep the Padres in the best-of-five Division Series. Benes started the second game and pitched into the eighth inning, The Cardinals went into the inning leading 4-3, but Benes allowed a single to Scott Livingstone and a walk to Rickey Henderson. Rick Honeycutt replaced Benes and allowed one of the inherited runners to score, tying the game. The Cardinals won the game, 5-4, and advanced to the NLCS when they won Game Three, 7-5.

The NLCS between the Cardinals and Atlanta was not decided until the seventh game. Benes started Game One and left the game for a pinch-hitter with the score tied 2-2 in the top of the seventh inning. The Braves won the game 4-2 with two runs in the eighth inning. Benes next appeared in Game Four. The Cardinals trailed 1-0 going into the Braves' sixth inning, when Mark Lemke led off with a homer and Chipper Jones doubled, knocking Benes out of the game. But the Cardinals were able to come from behind and win the game 4-3 and take a three-games-to-one series lead.

The Cardinals' bats then went cold. In Game Five, the Braves took no prisoners in a 14-0 rout. Andy's younger brother, Alan, started Game Six for the Cardinals and was tagged with the loss as the Braves won 3-1 to even the series. Game Seven was pretty much a repeat of Game Five. Donovan Osborne started for St. Louis and didn't make it out of the first inning, allowing six runs, topped off by a Tom Glavine triple. After the triple, Andy Benes stopped the bleeding by getting Marquis Grissom on a comebacker. Benes pitched scoreless ball in the second and third innings but yielded a two-run single to Fred McGriff and a two-run homer to Javy Lopez in the fourth inning. By the time Benes left the game for a pinch-hitter in the top of the sixth inning, the Cardinals trailed 10-0. The rest was academic, and the Braves advanced to the World Series with a 15-0 win.

In 1997 Benes went 10-7 for the Cardinals with a 3.10 ERA. After the  season, he was once again a free agent and signed a five-year, $32 million contract with the Cardinals. However, the contract was voided due to its being filed approximately two hours past the deadline. He wanted to stay with the Cardinals but, under the rules in place at the time, he could not re-sign with them until May 1, 1998. He would have missed spring training and the first month of the season.[12] He elected to seek other offers and signed a three-year contract, valued at $18 million, with the Arizona Diamondbacks.

Benes was the Opening Day pitcher for the Diamondbacks in their first-ever game, at Phoenix, on March 31, 1998. He left the game trailing 4-1 with one on and one out in the seventh inning. By the time Benes next took to the mound, the Diamondbacks were winless in five games. On April 5, against San Francisco, he pitched the first seven innings, scattering six hits. When he was removed for a pinch-hitter in the bottom of the seventh, Arizona led, 3-2. There was no further scoring and the Diamondbacks had their first franchise win. For the season, Benes was 14-13, leading the staff in wins. He also led the staff in innings pitched, equaling the 231⅓ innings he had pitched in 1992.

The highlight of Benes' first season with the Diamondbacks came on September 13. Arizona was playing the Reds at Cincinnati. Jay Bell's two-run homer in the fourth inning gave Benes all the support he would need. He took a no-hitter into the ninth inning. By then, the Diamondbacks had a 4-0 lead. With one out, Benes walked Reggie Sanders, and Sean Casey lined a single to right field, breaking up the no-hitter and putting runners on first and second. After Benes walked Barry Larkin to load the bases, Gregg Olson came in and induced Dmitri Young to hit a game-ending double-play groundball.

The following season, Benes was 13-12 as the Diamondbacks, in only their second season, won the NL West. He did not pitch in the postseason. He was left out of the rotation as Arizona was eliminated in four games by the Mets in the best-of-five Division Series. A provision in his contract with the Diamondbacks allowed him to leave the team after two years, and he returned to the Cardinals in 2000, signing a three-year deal worth $18 million.

In 2000 with the Cardinals, Benes was 12-9 with a 4.88 ERA for the NL Central champions and pitched in the postseason for the third time. Although he did not appear in the three-game Division Series sweep over Atlanta, he got his only career postseason win in the NLCS when he was the winning pitcher in Game Three against the Mets. He pitched eight innings and scattered six hits as the Cardinals defeated the Mets, 8-2. A career .143 hitter, who had three hits in his first nine postseason at-bats, Benes singled in the fourth inning and scored his team's fifth run. It was the only game they won in the series as the Mets advanced to the World Series, winning the best-of-seven NLCS in five games.

*"It's become increasingly difficult for me to pitch with what I've had to deal with. It's not a secret that my leg has made it pretty difficult for me the last year or so. It's a matter of me being unable to get people out any longer."*

– Andy Benes, April 17, 2002.[13]

After the 2000 season, Benes had surgery to address cartilage problems in his right knee and he didn't fully recover. The knee problems seriously plagued him in 2001. His record slipped to

7-7 and his ERA was a career-worst 7.38. He pitched only 107⅓ innings and at age 33 his career seemed just about over. After a good spring, he started the 2002 season in a dismal fashion. In each of three starts through April 15, he failed to go more than four innings. He was 0-2 with a 10.80 ERA when, on April 16, he decided to accept placement on the disabled list, effectively retiring. The Cardinals essentially told Benes to go home. His arthritic knee was examined by Dr. George Paletta, and Benes' status remained uncertain. He decided to press on and began working out in mid-May. He continued his workouts at the Cardinals' Jupiter, Florida, spring-training facility. He took a rehab assignment at Memphis in the Triple-A Pacific Coast league, making his first appearance on June 18. He had four rehab stints at Memphis, the last, on July 4, being a matchup against his brother Alan, who was rehabbing with Des Moines in the Cubs organization. Andy's win that night took his record with Memphis to 1-1 with an ERA of 3.12 in 17⅓ innings. He had one last rehab appearance on July 8. Since Memphis was on a break for the league's All-Star game, Benes' last tuneup was with Potomac in the Class-A Carolina League.

> *"It's a compliment to Andy to have done well enough to get this opportunity. But the real compliment he needs is to do something with it."*

– Tony La Russa, July 12, 2002.[14]

Benes joined the Cardinals after the All-Star break. The team was in San Diego. He was tuning up when his attention became diverted. At home plate, a presentation was going on. Shortly before the Padres traded Benes to Seattle in 1995, he had agreed to support a program, started by Padres owner John Moores, directed at at-risk middle-school youth in San Diego. It was a seven-year program and if a youth completed it, the Padres would fund his or her college education. On that July day in 2002, the first graduates of the program were announced.

When Benes took the mound on July 16 at Los Angeles, the Cardinals were a changed team very much in need of his services. With an injury to Rick Ankiel, the June 22 death of Darryl Kile, and little reliability from other starters, the Cardinals had recalled Benes, who was the best available arm in their system. In his first appearance, in Los Angeles, he went the first four innings in a game the Cardinals went on to win, 9-2. Four days later, they acquired 39-year-old Chuck Finley from the Indians for career minor leaguer Luis Garcia and a player to be named later (Coco Crisp). It was a major turning point for Benes and the Cardinals. Finley taught Benes the splitter, making him a far more effective pitcher. From his return on July 16 through September 1, Benes was 4-2 with a 1.98 ERA in 10 appearances.

The Cardinals headed into September with a 76-59 record and a four-game lead in the NL Central.

On September 6, 2002, the Cardinals were matched up against the Cubs as they raced to return to postseason play. The Cubs started Alan Benes. The brothers squared off for the second time in little over two months and older brother Andy came out on top. The brothers each pitched two shutout innings at the game's onset, but the Cardinals knocked Alan from the box in the third inning. A single by Andy scored Tino Martinez with the sixth run of the inning and knocked Alan out of the game. Andy pitched shutout ball for eight innings before Alex Gonzalez hit a two-run homer in the ninth inning. The Cardinals won the game, 11-2. It was the last of Benes's 21 complete games in his 14-year career and his last major-league win. Although he didn't have any other decisions in September, the Cardinals won each of Benes' four remaining starts. He finished the season with 17 consecutive shutout innings to bring his ERA for the season down to 2.78 to go with a 5-4 record. On September 29 he made his last appearance of the regular season. The Cardinals faced the Brewers at home. Benes came out of the game at the end of the fifth inning. The game was scoreless. On his last pitch, he had struck out Ryan Christenson for his 2,000th career strikeout.

On September 20 the Cardinals had clinched the NL Central with nine games remaining to be played and won the division by 13 games. Benes had the opportunity to pitch in the postseason again. He started Game Three in the Division Series against the Arizona Diamondbacks and pitched into the fifth inning. Experiencing control problems, he left the game with the Cardinals leading 4-3. The Cardinals won the game, 6-3, to sweep the Diamondbacks in three games and advance to the NLCS.

Benes started Game Four of the NLCS against the Giants. Through five innings, he kept the Giants off the board and allowed only two hits. The Cardinals led 2-0. In the bottom of the sixth inning, after striking out Rich Aurilia, he walked Jeff Kent and Barry Bonds, prompting manager Tony La Russa to bring in reliever Rick White. The Giants tied the game on a J.T. Snow double and went on to win the game, 4-3. One day later, the Giants eliminated the Cardinals four games to one. Benes elected to walk away from the game at the end of the season. He had no regrets.

For his career, he went 155-139, winning 10 or more games in 10 of his 14 seasons. His ERA was 3.97, and he had nine shutouts in his 387 starts.

His family stayed in the St. Louis area and he became a familiar face on television starting in 2003 when he began hosting a program geared at young fans. *Cardinals Crew* featured Benes and Cardinals mascot Fred Bird the Red Bird. He stayed with the program for 14 years before leaving the show to spend more time coaching youth baseball in the St. Louis area.

In 2009 he was inducted into the Indiana High School Baseball Coaches' Hall of Fame.

Benes, who had been outspoken during his early years in the big leagues, had matured over the years, especially after he threw his last competitive pitch in 2002. It was a much more mature Andy Benes who spoke on the occasion of this number being retired by the University of Evansville in 2010. (He had been inducted into the university Hall of Fame in 1994.) Speaking with the *Evansville Courier and Press*, he said, "You get pulled in a lot of different directions all because I was able to throw a baseball for a while, but now I try to make sure I don't go and do things if it's going to take away from what (my kids) have going on."[15]

In 2016 Benes received the Southern Indiana Athletic Conference Lifetime Achievement Award.

On March 31, 2018, as the Diamondbacks commemorated their 20th anniversary, Benes threw out the ceremonial first pitch. The reenactment of the first Opening Day also included Diamondbacks catcher Jorge Fabregas and the first leadoff batter, Mike Lansing of the Colorado Rockies.

Perhaps the essence of Andy Benes, as he continued to help children through his baseball camps and clinics, is in a comment he made in April 2017. "We (can) forget about the stats. We (should) think about the journey (through life) and the people we met along the way. That's truly what's important."[16]

## SOURCES

In addition to the sources shown in the Notes, the author used Baseball-Reference.com, the Andy Benes file at the National Baseball Hall of Fame and Museum, and the following:

Porter, David L. *The Padres Encyclopedia* (Champaign, Illinois: Sports Publishing, 2002), 221-223.

Author interview with Andy Benes, September 6, 2018.

## NOTES

1    Lee Jenkins, "What It Means to Be the 1," *Sports Illustrated*, June 15, 2009: 56-61.

2    Gordon Engelhardt, "Benes Humbled by SIAC Award – Former Card Pitcher Recalls Evansville Days," *Evansville Courier and Press*, July 31, 2016: 1C.

3    "Rural Freshman West Team Captures Tournament Title," *Evansville Courier and Press*, August 10, 1980: 4C.

4    Tom Collins, "Central's Benes to Sign with UE," *Evansville Courier*, April 25, 1985: 20.

5    Engelhardt, "Benes Walking into Hall Tonight," *Evansville Courier and Press*," January 23, 2009: 1C.

6    Bill Plaschke, "First Choice Benes a Real Fireball," *The Sporting News*, June 13, 1988: 28.

7    Plaschke, "Padres Sign Benes for Record Bonus," *The Sporting News*, July 4, 1988: 17.

8    Dave Johnson, "Benes Keeps Helping Out Aces," *Evansville Courier and Press*, March 2, 2004: 1C.

9    Associated Press, "Benes Hurls United States Past Cuba, 5-2," *Baton Rouge Advocate*, August 15, 1988: 3C.

10   "Around the Minors: Padres," *The Sporting News*, May 15, 1989: 40.

11   Jennifer Frey, "Benes Pitches a 1-Hitter as He Proves His Point," *New York Times*, July 4, 1994: 33.

12   Cole Claybourn, "Benes' Heart Still Beats for Cardinals," *Evansville Courier and Press*, August 24, 2014: 1C.

13   Joe Strauss, "Benes Elects to Retire, Citing Knee," *St. Louis Post-Dispatch*, April 18, 2002: D1.

14   Associated Press, "Cardinals Poised to Activate Benes," *Daily Journal* (Flat River, Missouri), July 13, 2002: 5.

15   Drew Bruno, "UE Retires Benes' Jersey Number," *Evansville Courier and Press*, April 18, 2010: 1C.

16   Chag Lindskog, "High School Baseball: Ball Field Dedicated to Longtime Coach Gries," *Evansville Courier and Press*, April 20, 2017: 1C.

# KEN CAMINITI

## BY PAUL E. DOUTRICH

The life of Ken Caminiti parallels the path of a classic Greek tragedy. He was an athlete blessed with extraordinary physical abilities who diligently worked to develop those gifts and dedicated himself to achieving excellence. A tough, tireless leader on the field, he climbed to the highest levels of the baseball world. Then, at the brink of greatness, he was seized by internal demons that drained his talent and forever scarred his success. In the end, rather than being considered one of the best of his era, he is most often remembered as a sad victim of baseball's steroid subculture.

Kenneth Gene Caminiti was born on April 21, 1963, in Hanford, California, a bustling community in Central California's San Joaquin Valley. He was the youngest of three children. From the time he could hold a ball, Kenny played whatever sport was in season. Through those early years his biggest fan and regular chauffeur was his mother, Yvonne. In high school he excelled at baseball and football, playing in California's prep all-star football game as a senior. Though he loved football, his future was in baseball. Kenny shined as a high-school shortstop. His father, Lee, was an engineer who worked on defense projects at Lockheed Martin in Sunnyvale, California. Yvonne was a homemaker taking care of three children – Glenn, Ken, and Carrie. She later worked at Lockheed Martin herself as the admininstrative assistant to the head of one of the programs at Lockheed.[1]

Lee Caminiti, who had played semipro baseball, taught his son about the game, including how to switch-hit. The lessons led to a scholarship at nearby San Jose State University following a freshman year at San Jose City College. At San Jose State he earned Sporting News All-American status and a spot on the 25-man US Olympic squad, but was among the final four players cut from the 21-man squad that went to the Olympics.[2] Impressed by his achievements and talent, the Houston Astros selected him in the third round of the June 1984 amateur draft.

Caminiti's professional baseball career began in 1985 with the Osceola Astros in the Class-A Florida State League. A 6-foot switch-hitter with a powerful physique, above-average speed, and a cannon arm, he was an acquisition whom the Astros organization immediately worked to develop. In 1985, Kissimmee, Florida, in Osceola County, was a good place to become a professional ballplayer. Like Caminiti, the area was new to professional baseball. During the previous winter the Class-A Astros relocated from Daytona Beach to Kissimmee. With the move came a new ballpark that would serve as the Astros' spring-training facility and, from April until early September, the home of the Osceola Astros. Only a handful of Caminiti's new teammates had played for Daytona Beach the season before but most had played somewhere in the minor leagues. Caminiti, or "Cami" as his teammates soon called him, was one of only two on the roster with no previous professional experience.

The season opened on a rainy mid-April night against the new Daytona Beach Admirals. Batting seventh, Caminiti started at third base, contributed one hit and an RBI, scored two runs and made a key play in the 9-8 win. By the end of the week, he had been moved up to third in the batting order. He stayed at the heart of the lineup throughout the rest of the season.

The next couple of weeks went well for the Astros and their rookie third baseman. By early May, the team was in first place in the league's Central Division. Caminiti was a key part of that success. He was leading the team in RBIs and runs scored. He had also begun to establish a reputation as a clutch player. In a game against the Tampa Tarpons, he knocked in the winning run on a ninth-inning single.[3] Over the next few months he repeated the achievement nine more times, more than anyone else in the Florida State League. When asked about his transition to professional baseball, Caminiti reported: "I feel very little pressure. … I think my biggest challenge is learning how to hit with a wooden bat again."[4]

Through the summer Caminiti established himself as one of the better players in the league. In July he was one of seven Astros selected for the league all-star game. At the time he led the league in RBIs and was third in runs scored.[5] His defensive skills had also begun to earn some accolades. He ended the season with the highest batting average, .284; most RBIs, 73; and most hits of any Osceola player who had spent at least half of the season in Kissimmee. He also banged out a team-record 26 doubles.[6] It was clear that the young third baseman had adjusted well to wooden bats and Class-A pitching.

Along with a dozen Osceola teammates, Caminiti began the 1986 season on the Double-A Columbus (Georgia) Astros in the Southern League. It was the next step up the Houston minor-league ladder. The team started slowly, finishing the first half in last place. Caminiti, on the other hand, picked up where he had left off the previous season. Batting in the middle of the Columbus order, he continued to be among his team's leading RBI producers. During the second half, the team reversed its fortunes. Climbing into first place, the Astros defeated the first-half champion Jacksonville Expos in a playoff. They then beat the Huntsville Stars to claim the league championship.[7] Ending the season with a .300 batting average, Caminiti was again among his team's leaders in several hitting categories.

The 1987 season began with Caminiti back in Columbus. While his team struggled a bit early, Cami did not. His batting average remained above .300 through the first three months of the season and he was among the league leaders in both RBIs and home runs. In July, along with Astros pitcher Rob Mallicot, Cami was selected to the league's all-star team. The all-star game turned out to be the last time that Caminiti wore a Columbus uniform. On July 16 he was called up to Houston.

Caminiti's major-league debut was spectacular. On the first play of a game against the Phillies, he made a diving catch and bullet throw to get speedy Juan Samuel. Over the next couple of innings, he made several more outstanding plays in the field. After the game Philadelphia manager Lee Elia lamented, "(Caminiti) just defensed the heck out of us."[8] As notable as his play in the field had been, it was his times at the plate that really impressed. Leading off the fifth, his second plate appearance, he drilled a triple off the right-center-field wall. Two innings later he crushed his first major-league home run. In the ninth, with the score tied, 1-1, he worked a one-out walk. Two hitters later center fielder Gerald Young banged out a single that brought Cami home with the winning run. After the game Caminiti, who two days earlier thought he was being called up to the Triple-A Tucson Toros, commented, "This might be the highest high I've had. I knew it could happen. I just didn't know it would be this fast."[9] Manager Elia put it more succinctly: "That is a heck of a way to break into the majors."[10]

The week that followed was almost as good. The day after his debut, Caminiti added two singles to his hit collection. He got his first double, another single, a run scored, and an RBI a day later. Throughout his first week, the hits and runs kept coming. He ended his first week as a major leaguer with a .500 batting average and two home runs, and was named the National League's Player of the Week. It was an auspicious start.

Through much of the rest of the season, Caminiti remained the Astros' starting third baseman. At the plate his average slid to .246 but in the field he continued to impress. Meanwhile, Houston remained in the National League West pennant race before slumping badly in September. Reflecting the disappointment that others in the organization felt, manager Hal Lanier commented, "Nobody's happy with the way we played last year, especially in the latter stages of the season."[11] At the same time, he acknowledged that "The acquisition of Caminiti and Young did good things for our ballclub."[12]

Caminiti came to spring training in 1988 with a new wife (he married his high-school sweetheart, Nancy Smith, during the offseason), a new contract, and great hopes of becoming the Astros' starting third baseman. "Lots of people I've talked to seem to think I have the job wrapped up. That's just not true I am going to go into spring training with the attitude I had when I got here," he said.[13] One of those who did not think Caminiti had the job wrapped up was Hal Lanier. The Astros manager considered the position open, saying, "It's not going to be given to Ken just because he ended up the year there."[14] Lanier had no concerns about Caminiti in the field but was not as confident about him at the plate, especially from the right side.

Spring training did not go as Caminiti had expected. Early on it became clear that Lanier had already penciled in veteran Denny Walling as the team's starting third baseman. Consequently, Caminiti was competing with Chuck Jackson, the player he had replaced the previous July, for the backup role. Jackson got off to a quick start. Caminiti did not. His ability to hit from the right side became a particular concern. Midway through camp, a $500 fine for being late to two practices further stymied the young third baseman's chances. By the last week of spring training, Caminiti's playing time had dwindled significantly. His spring play ended well, a home run from both sides of the plate in a game against the Phillies, but a day later, as the team prepared to head home to Houston, Caminiti was sent to Tucson.

The reassignment rankled Caminiti. He complained, "I think if they wanted me to play there (third base) they would have let me have more at-bats and worked with me more. … This is probably my biggest downer. It hurts."[15] A week later he was at third base in the Toros' Opening Day lineup. Batting in the middle of the Tucson order, Caminiti was expected to add some power.[16] He did not disappoint. Through the first month of the season he drove in runs on an almost daily basis. He also began to re-establish a reputation as a clutch player. It was a role he enjoyed: "I live for the tough ones."[17] Then, in early May, trying to protect a teammate in an on-the-field fracas, he tore a ligament in his right thumb. The injury kept him on the bench for a week and when he returned he struggled a bit. During the next month his batting average dropped almost 30 points and his run production slowed. Emerging from the slump in mid-June,

Caminiti started pounding the ball again, renewing speculation that he was soon destined for another call-up to the Astros.

Meanwhile in Houston, the Astros were again having problems at third base. Suffering from chronic back spasms, Denny Walling, the regular third baseman, was not hitting as the team had hoped. On June 20 he went on the disabled list, where he remained until early August. His backup, Chuck Jackson, was also having problems at the plate. The day before Walling went on the disabled list, Jackson was shipped back to Tucson. To plug the hole, the Astros traded with Cincinnati for veteran Buddy Bell. A month later, first baseman Glenn Davis pulled a hamstring and was expected to be out of action for a month. With Davis unavailable, Bell was moved to first and Caminiti was recalled.

Caminiti's second trip to Houston lasted only three weeks. By the time Walling was ready to return, Caminiti was hitting an anemic .176 and had driven in only three runs. On August 18 he was sent back to Tucson, where he stayed until the September call-ups. He ended the season with the Astros batting just .181 with one home run and only seven RBIs. The end of Caminiti's season reflected the fate of the Astros. Another dismal September dropped them out of the pennant race and into fifth place in the National League West.

The day after the 1988 regular season ended the Astros fired manager Lanier. A month later they hired Art Howe. It was a change that suited Caminiti well. The new manager soon announced that "Ken Caminiti is my third baseman."[18] Throughout the spring, trade rumors swirled around Caminiti, but he made it clear that "the bottom line is I don't want to be traded. That's all there is to it. I want to play in Houston."[19] He also made it clear that he liked playing for Howe: "It's great playing for Art. He's fun, he's stern, and he definitely knows the game. The atmosphere has really changed."[20]

Howe's confidence in Caminiti paid quick dividends. Beginning in an Opening Day win over Atlanta, the Astros third baseman established himself as an integral part of his team, contributing with both his bat and his glove. In an early April game against Cincinnati, he drove in the run that gave the Astros the winning margin and killed a threat with a sparkling play at third. Two days later he scored the winning run in a 15-inning victory over the Dodgers. The next day he hit his first home run of the season to beat the Dodgers again. Another home run in late May beat the Cardinals. Through the first two months of the season, Caminiti continued to contribute clutch hits and was part of numerous rallies that helped keep the Astros near the top of the National League West. By June, few still questioned Caminiti's place on the team. When asked what he attributed his success to, he responded, "The difference this year is I'm more relaxed. Before,

I was tense, wondering if I'd be in the lineup or not. If I got in, I knew I had to produce."[21] The season ended badly for the Astros. After battling the Giants through mid-August, the team, for the third year in a row, foundered in September, finishing third, six games behind the division-winning Giants. Though he was disappointed, Caminiti was satisfied with his play. Throughout the season he had been a solid part of the Astros lineup. Playing for the second worst hitting team in the National League, he finished with a respectable .255 batting average, comfortably above the .239 team average. He led the team in doubles, was third with 10 home runs and second with 72 RBIs. In the field he established himself as one of the outstanding third basemen in the league. By the end of season, he looked forward to being the Astros' third baseman for years to come.

For the next five seasons Caminiti remained a Houston fixture at third base, where his acrobatic stops and rifle arm regularly dazzled patrons. He also became part a young team core. Craig Biggio was another of those central players between 1990 and 1994. Caminiti and Biggio had come up from Tucson together and shared similar struggles during their initial season. The two became lifelong friends. In 1991 outfielder Steve Finley was acquired by the Astros as part of a trade with Baltimore. The same year Jeff Bagwell was brought up from the Eastern League. These four – Caminiti, Biggio, Finley, and Bagwell – became the nucleus of the team through the 1994 season. During the four seasons from 1991 through 1994 Caminiti hit between .253 (in 1991) and .294 (in 1992) while averaging 14 home runs and 73 RBIs. In 1994 he was selected to his first All-Star team. But only in the strike-shortened 1994 season was Houston a legitimate pennant contender.

Off the field Caminiti's gregarious personality and Hollywood-handsome good looks made him a fan favorite. He was a regular at celebrity golf tournaments and offseason banquets.[22] He was also a favorite among his teammates. He trained hard to develop his playing abilities, and frequently played through pain for his team. An unobtrusive enforcer, he was always ready, when appropriate, to defend teammates as well as quietly, but forcefully, rebuke players who were shirking their team responsibilities. His teammates thought enough of him that they elected him to be their representative during 1994 players union confrontation with ownership. His growing salary, steadily rising from $129,000 in 1989 to $4.6 million in 1995, further reflected his value to the team.[23]

The tensions between the players union and the owners continued throughout the winter of 1994-1995. Among the chief issues of debate was a salary cap. Anticipating the cap, Houston prepared to reduce its total salary costs by trading away several of its high-priced players. Caminiti was at the top of that list.

On December 28, 1994, along with five of his teammates, he was traded to San Diego for six Padres players. The 12-player exchange was the fourth largest in the modern era. Caminiti was not happy about the deal. In addition to leaving his home, his teammates and friends, as well as the city he had come to love, he was going to a team with the worst record in the major leagues in 1994.

In most ways, San Diego turned out to be much better than Caminiti had anticipated. While with the Padres he won three consecutive Gold Glove Awards and a Silver Slugger Award, was unanimously voted the National League's 1996 Most Valuable Player, and helped transform his new team into the 1998 National League pennant winner. But it was also in San Diego that Caminiti set the stage for his own demise.

At the time San Diego acquired Caminiti, the team's new ownership had just embarked on a rebuilding process. Their new third baseman figured prominently in those efforts. The owners were gambling that Caminiti was on the verge of stardom, and, as an eight-year veteran, could provide leadership. Their gamble paid off. In his first year in San Diego, he produced career highs in batting average, home runs, RBIs, and doubles, and helped the Padres climb out of the National League West cellar. His new manager, Bruce Bochy, later described him as "the guts of the team. … He played with maniacal zeal that left those in his wake astounded."[24] He brought a new level of toughness, intensity, and commitment to the team. Along with Tony Gwynn and Steve Finley, Caminiti and the Padres began a journey that carried them to the World Series three years later.

As well as he played in 1995, Caminiti did even better the following year. Again he produced career highs in every significant offensive category. That year also saw Caminiti's "tough guy" image grow to near-legendary proportions. Early in the season in a game against the Astros, Caminiti dived for a short flare into left field. Landing hard on his left elbow and shoulder, he tore his rotator cuff. "For the next six or seven days I couldn't lift my arm," he said. "I played for a month and a half in pure pain."[25] Through it all, his batting average remained comfortably above .300. Refusing to have season-ending surgery, Caminiti played almost the entire schedule with a severely torn rotator cuff.

Another chapter was added to the Caminiti legend in August. The Padres played a three-game series with the Mets in Monterey, Mexico. Midway through the series, Caminiti and several other players were stricken with food poisoning. Dehydrated, unable to retain food or liquids, and obviously weakened, Caminiti spent the morning of the final game on the clubhouse floor being treated intravenously. However, just minutes before game time, when he saw that he was not in the starting lineup, he confronted his manager and pleaded to start. Reluctantly manager Bochy penciled him in at third base. In his first trip to the plate Caminiti smashed a home run over the right-center-field fence. The next time up he duplicated the feat. After hobbling around the bases for a second time, he was given the rest of the day off. He spent the following two hours getting more IV treatments. In describing the sequence of events, a usually subdued Tony Gwynn marveled, "You had to see it to believe it. What we saw was not normal. It was a superhuman effort."[26] Other teammates confirmed Gwynn's assessment.

What Gwynn and most others did not know was that Caminiti's success that day and throughout much of 1996 had been significantly aided by steroids. Aware that other players had gotten through injuries using steroids and that steroids could be bought over the counter just a short drive south of San Diego in Tijuana, Mexico, Caminiti began experimenting. The immediate results were stunning. During the second half of the 1996 season he hit more home runs than he had previously hit in any full season. He finished with a batting average 24 points higher than ever before and drove in 36 more runs than ever before. His success immediately thrust him into the upper echelon of the baseball world, but it also began a tragic journey for Caminiti.

The 1997 season started slowly for the Padres' new star. Still recuperating from shoulder surgery, in typical Caminiti fashion he was in the Opening Day lineup three months earlier than his doctor had advised. To compensate for the physical limitations and pain, he again resorted to steroids. "The thing is," he said, "I didn't do it to make me a better player. I did it because my body broke down."[27] This time he was more methodical about his usage. He found a physician who prescribed a "cycle" of injections. Though not producing as he had during his MVP season, Caminiti remained one of the league's premier players, elected by the fans as the National League's All-Star starting third baseman.

The following season, 1998, Caminiti's production fell again as did his playing time. Over the winter, with the help of steroids, he had built himself up as never before. "I showed up at spring training as big as an ox."[28] Along the way, some of the hazards of steroid use began to plague Caminiti. Frequent hamstring and quadriceps strains, various ruptured tendons and ligaments, and torn muscles limited his time on the field for the rest of his baseball career. He was still an asset to the team, and helped the Padres make it to the 1998 World Series, but he was no longer the reliable force he had been since arriving in San Diego.

Caminiti became a free agent after the 1998 season. In what was described as a cost-cutting effort, the Padres chose not to negotiate a new contract with him. Instead, when the Astros offered him a two-year contract for $9.5 million, he agreed to return to Houston. He had reportedly been offered significantly more money by Detroit but instead, professing, "I think happiness is being with my family, my kids and my wife," who had remained in Texas while he was playing for San Diego, he chose to return to the Astros.[29]

Back in Houston Caminiti, despite being surrounded by family, fell into old habits and fed new addictions. He had gone through alcohol rehabilitation during the 1994-95 offseason but had resumed his drinking habits long before returning to the Astros. Beginning in 1997 he also began carrying a "goody bag" packed with assorted pain-relief medications. In the Astros dugout their new third baseman's pregame "meal" included a mixture of pills and powders that became known as a "Caminiti Cocktail."[30] More dangerously, he expanded his use of steroids. No longer relying on a physician for treatments, he developed his own steroid cycles. At some point he also began using cocaine after games to ease the depression and tensions associated with extensive use of steroids. Disregarding the apprehensions of his coaches and teammates, most notably his friend Craig Biggio, he became less concerned about concealing his medication routine. Despite it all, he performed well during his first season back in Houston. Playing fewer than half the games due to injuries, he pushed his batting average back up to .286 and drove in 56 runs.

Caminiti struggled through two more seasons. The first 10 weeks of 2000 went well. He kept his batting average near .300 and by mid-June had hit 15 home runs. Then on June 16 he went on the disabled list with tendon damage in his right wrist. He finished the season still on the disabled list. After the second and final year of his Astros contract, he again became a free agent. In December 2000, the Texas Rangers signed him with hopes that he would provide veteran leadership and help the team escape the American League West cellar. Caminiti hoped that a fresh start in the American League would revive his career. Neither prospect was realized. Batting only .232, he went on the disabled list with a pulled hamstring in mid-June. On July 2, at his request, he was released. Three days later he was signed by Atlanta. His time with the Braves was no better than his time with the Rangers. In November he again became a free agent but this time there were no takers.

As difficult as his life in baseball had become, his life away from baseball was even more problematic. A *Sports Illustrated* interview in June 2002 added to Caminiti's grief. Speaking to writer Tom Verducci for what became a pivotal investigative report, Caminiti admitted that he had begun using steroids during his MVP year in 1996. He further estimated that approximately 50 percent of major leaguers were taking steroids. Coupled with earlier statements by Jose Canseco, the report, "Thoroughly Juiced: Confessions of a Former MVP," elicited reactions from every corner of the baseball world. Eventually the responses included a congressional investigation that opened a new era of drug testing in professional baseball. For Caminiti the report, while applauded by some, brought scorn from many others. Mets sluggers Mike Piazza and Mo Vaughn, among numerous other players, questioned Caminiti's motives.[31] Phillies catcher Mike Lieberthal questioned his intelligence.[32] *Chicago Tribune* columnist Steve Rosenbloom mockingly proposed, "Guess we have proof that 'roids help your muscles, not your neurotransmitters."[33] To an ESPN radio audience just a few days after the article's release, Caminiti retracted parts of what he had said: "I never knew the interview was going to go like that. It just got real ugly."[34] However, Verducci's reporting was too convincing and the effect of the article was too powerful for retractions.

Caminiti's life continued to unravel after the *Sports Illustrated* article. To many in baseball he became a pariah. In December he and Nancy divorced. Efforts by family and friends to help had temporary success at best as he continued to swirl down ever more deeply into his addictions. Arrested in March 2001 for drug possession, he was sentenced to three years' probation which included regular drug tests. Two years later, while still on probation, he tested positive for cocaine and was ordered into a Texas criminal drug-treatment program. In September 2004, after yet again violating probation, he was sentenced to 180 days in jail. Given credit for time already served, he was released from jail on October 5.

Ken Caminiti died five days later. After being released from jail in Houston, he traveled to New York City. On October 10, at a friend's seedy Bronx apartment, he took one last hit, a speed ball of cocaine and heroin. He immediately suffered cardiac arrest, fell to the floor and died before medical attention could reach him. And so ended the spectacular but tragic life of Ken Caminiti.

In San Diego Caminiti is remembered as the greatest third baseman in Padres history. His friends and family remember him for his generosity, loyalty and dedication; but many others remember him for the role he played in exposing the insidious steroid subculture that had infiltrated professional baseball.

## SOURCES

In addition to the sources cited in the Notes, the author also consulted Baseball-Reference.com and Retrosheet.org.

## NOTES

1    Email from Ken's sister Carrie Van Solinge on January 17, 2019.

2    San Jose Sports Authority, at SJSA.org/2017-inductees.

3    "Caminiti Sparks Osceola to 8-4 Victory," Or*lando Sentinel*, May 4, 1985: 24.

4    Frank Carroll, "Ken Caminiti's Bat Propels Astros," *Orlando Sentinel* April 28, 1985: 268.

5    Tim Hipps, "7 Astros Dot FLS East Roster," *Orlando Sentinel*, July 7, 1985: 358.

6    Frank Carroll, "Astros Return to Play 3 Games with Islanders," *Orlando Sentinel*, June 15, 1986: 257.

7    "Columbus Astros Fly to League Title," *Orlando Sentinel*, September 14, 1986: 279.

8    Sam Carchidi, "Phils fall to Astros in Ninth, 2-1," *Philadelphia Inquirer*, July 17: 1987, 30.

9    "Young, Caminiti Lead Houston Past Phillies," *Arizona Daily Star* (Tucson), July 17, 1987: 31.

10   Sam Carchidi.

11   "Intending to Contend," *Del Rio* (Texas) *News Herald*, February 21, 1988: 39.

12   Reggie Roberts "Astros Have High Hopes for Andujar," *Austin American-Statesman*, January 20, 1988: 39.

13   Ibid.

14   Michael A. Lutz, "Astros Looking to Regain Magic, Consistency of '86," *Del Rio News Herald*, February 21, 1988: 11.

15   "Sambito Cut, Caminiti Sent Down," *Galveston Daily News*, April 1, 1988: 17.

16   Ron Somers, "Toros Begin Their Season Tomorrow Against Calgary," *Arizona Daily Star*, April 7, 1988: 41.

17   Ron Somers, "Toros' Sambito earns 1st win," *Arizona Daily Star*, June 1, 1988: 47.

18   Larry McCarthy, "Howe's Pitching Pains Likely to Go Away Soon," *Orlando Sentinel*, February 26, 1989: C-10.

19   Bill Haisten, "It's Final: Caminiti's a Lock at 3rd; Boggs Trade 'Dead,' *Galveston Daily News*, March 24, 1989: 15.

20   Mike Forman, "Astros Banking on Caminiti," *Victoria* (Texas) *Advocate*, March 25, 1989: 11.

21   "Caminiti Lifts Astros Over Reds," *Austin-American Statesman*, April 12, 1989: 53.

22   In 1994 Caminiti did have a brief disagreement with Astros fans. He criticized them because they "come to see a Houston game but cheer for Atlanta." The hard feelings were quickly rectified. "Home-team Blues," *Victoria Advocate*, June 12, 1994: 21.

23   baseball-reference.com/players/c/caminke01.shtml.

24   Scott Miller, The Cautionary Tale of Ken Caminiti: The Steroid Era's First Truth-Teller," bleacherreport.com/articles/2224511-the-cautionary-tale-of-ken-caminiti-the-steroid-eras-first-truth-teller.

25   Tom Verducci, "Totally Juiced: Confessions of a Former MVP," *Sports Illustrated*, June 2, 2002: 39.

26      Murray Chass, "Caminiti Becomes a Legend in His Time," *New York Times*, March 9, 1997: S2.

27      Verducci: 39.

28      Verducci: 40.

29      "Caminiti Rejoins Astros," *Galveston Daily News*, November 16, 1998: 15.

30      Scott Miller.

31      Jim Salisbury, "Steroid Use Exaggerated, Big Leaguers Say," *Philadelphia Inquirer*, May 30, 2002: E1, E4.

32      Salisbury: E-4.

33      Steve Rosenbloom, "Baseball's Power Aid," *Chicago Tribune*, June 2, 2002: Section 3, 10.

34      "Caminiti Tempers Steroid-Use Claims," *Chicago Tribune*, May 31, 2002: 45.

# NATE COLBERT

## BY GREGORY H. WOLF

Nate Colbert wasn't supposed to play on August 1, 1972. The San Diego slugger had injured his knee in a collision at home plate the night before and was listed as doubtful against the Atlanta Braves. Looking forward to hitting in Atlanta Stadium, known as the Launching Pad, Colbert decided to tough out the pain. He responded by belting a record-tying five home runs and driving in a record-setting 13 runs in a doubleheader. Colbert, an often-overlooked power hitter, averaged 30 home runs and

85 RBIs over a five-year stretch (1969-1973), becoming the expansion Padres' first bona-fide star. Chronic back problems prematurely ended Colbert's budding career after just 1,004 games and he retired after the 1976 season.

Born on April 9, 1946, in St. Louis, Nathan Colbert Jr. grew up in a predominantly African-American community on the city's north side. His father, Nate Sr., was a former semipro Negro League catcher and occasional pitcher who instilled in Junior, his two brothers, and his three sisters an uncompromising work ethic and passion for sports. "I just loved baseball," said Nate, whose fondest childhood memories included playing ball with his father and regularly seeing the Cardinals play.[1] Young Nate enjoyed going to Sportsman's Park, just about 10 minutes from his home, and marveled at his favorite players, among them Jackie Robinson, who once signed his glove, and Stan Musial. Nate was in the stands when Stan the Man belted five home runs in a doubleheader on May 2, 1954, a feat the youngster would duplicate some 18 years later.

Nate played baseball whenever he could, on nearby sandlots, and in the afternoons after attending Cole School. Nate Sr., who worked in a local mill, also coached baseball in a boys' club and taught his son the fundamentals. "I was a little bigger than a lot of the kids," Colbert told Wayne McBrayer of Padres360, "so baseball, it became easy to me."[2] At Charles H. Sumner High School, Nate dabbled in some football, but a knee injury convinced him to stay on the diamond. Tall and lithe, Nate seemingly glided in the outfield and on the basepaths and attracted major-league scouts who followed his progress in prep, summer, and local semipro leagues. According to Bruce Markusen, the New York Yankees were in hot pursuit and promised to double offers from any team;[3] however, Colbert could only think of Cardinal red. Tracked by George Hasser, an area bird-dog scout for the Cardinals, Colbert was invited by Redbirds scouting director George Silvey to Busch Stadium (the official name of Sportsman's Park since 1953) to hit a few balls for skipper Johnny Keane, who was impressed with the skinny kid's power.[4] Upon graduation in 1964, one year before the inauguration of the amateur draft, Colbert signed with the hometown team on scout Joe Monahan's recommendation for a reported $20,000 bonus.

Colbert's professional baseball career commenced just months later. The Cardinals assigned him to the Sarasota Rookie League, where the right-handed hitter split his time at first and in the outfield. His stint in the Redbirds organization was short. A fractured left hand in July ended his 1965 season with Cedar Rapids in the Class-A Midwest League.[5] Colbert got some additional experience in the Florida Instructional League, but just weeks after that season concluded, he was selected by the Houston Astros in the Rule 5 Draft on November 29.

To call Colbert's tenure with the Astros a disappointment is an understatement. Under Rule 5 stipulations, the Astros were required to keep him on their roster the entire season or risk losing him if they optioned him to the minors. The 20-year-old Colbert had just 504 minor-league at-bats and was completely unprepared to hit major-league pitching. After participating in the Astros spring training at Cocoa Beach, Florida, Colbert bided his time on skipper Grady Hatton's bench. He made just 19 appearances (12 as a pinch-runner and 7 as a pinch-hitter) and did not play in the field, not even an inning. He went hitless, though he scored three times. "It was just a year lost as far as playing is concerned," said Colbert bluntly.[6] The highlight of Colbert's season took place on July 27 when he married Carol Ann Allensworth, whom he had met while completing three weeks' training in the Army National Guard in Oklahoma City.

Colbert worked the rust off his atrophied skills in another stint in the Florida Instructional League, then faced major leaguers in the Venezuelan League with Caracas. More than anything, the 6-foot-2, 200-pound Colbert needed at-bats, and was consequently assigned following another spring training with the Astros to the Amarillo Sonics in the Double-A Texas League. Colbert showcased his power and speed, pacing the circuit in home runs (28) and stolen bases (26). He was the league's MVP, a unanimous All-Star, and was named to the Double-A Topps-National Association All-Star team. The young slugger was fully aware that he was still learning how to hit. "When I started, I didn't know much, and swung hard. Now I don't swing as hard, but hit the ball just as far," he said in 1967. "I use my wrists and reflexes more now to give me power."[7]

Assigned to the Triple-A Oklahoma City 89ers to start the 1968 season, Colbert was moved to center field to take advantage of his speed. A two-week call-up in July to the Astros proved disastrous (3-for-22). His first major-league hit was a single off fireballer Jim Maloney of the Cincinnati Reds. He was returned to the PCL, but broke his hand and played in just 92 games. He was healed enough for another two-week look-see with the Astros in September. The results weren't much better than his first stint (5-for-31) and he was still homerless in the majors.

"You can destroy a man's confidence," said Colbert, recalling his struggles with the Astros. "[Manager] Harry Walker almost destroyed mine."[8] Walker was determined to mold Colbert into his own image, a spray hitter to all fields, and constantly tinkered with his swing. A natural pull hitter, Colbert was told to wait longer for the ball, and his timing suffered, as did his power. "I got so confused, I began to doubt myself. I thought I'd never find myself again. I was terrified. Here I was 22 years old and I was being told I couldn't hit big-league ball."[9]

Colbert's stock had dropped so dramatically that the Astros made him available in the expansion draft. The San Diego Padres selected him with their 18th pick on October 14, 1968. "I had no way of checking to see if I had been drafted," explained Colbert about the days before access to around-the-clock sports news via Internet and social media. "So, I stayed up and I kept calling the newspaper. I was in Oklahoma City. And they said, 'Well, we've got nothing yet.' And I was like, 'Oh, come on.' So, the next morning, [GM] Eddie Leishman from the Padres called me to welcome me. ... And I just let out a yell because I wanted to go to the San Diego Padres."[10] Leishman, who had been GM of the PCL San Diego Padres in 1968, was well acquainted with Colbert ("Nate used to hurt us.") and was convinced that he would blossom into a star if he had a chance to play.[11]

After playing with Estrellas in the Dominican Winter League, Colbert reported to the Padres camp in Yuma, Arizona, relishing the opportunity to reset his career. "[T]he first spring training was really a unique experience, because I was with 30 or more players, most of whom I did not know," recalled Colbert.[12] The spring facilities at Keegan Field on 24th Street in Yuma were primitive. A former youth baseball field in shabby condition, the entire infield and outfield needed to be leveled and the mound elevated to major-league standards. It also lacked basic amenities, such as bleachers, dugouts, showers, locker rooms, a press box, a PA system, and concession stands.[13] "We showered in a city gym, in a recreation center," recalled Colbert.[14] The 23-year-old slugger probably wondered what he had gotten himself into, but noted that "we survived." Padres players dressed and showered at the Kennedy Swimming Pool, while visiting players traveled across town to do the same in Municipal Stadium, the former spring home of the Baltimore Orioles, which was in even worse shape than Keegan.

Skipper Preston Gomez took a decidedly hands-off approach to Colbert's swing and gave the youngster the freedom to rediscover his stroke. "Colbert has a quick bat," said Gomez, "probably the quickest on the club."[15] Nonetheless, Colbert began the season as the backup first baseman to the Jolly Green Giant, 6-foot-7 Bill Davis. About two weeks into the season, Colbert took over for the slumping Davis and held down the first-base bag for the next five seasons. His breakout game had an air of revenge. On April 24 in the Astrodome, Colbert blasted his first career home run, a game-winning three-run shot in the eighth off Jack Billingham. The next day he whacked his first home run in San Diego Stadium, a solo shot off Reds fireballer Jim Maloney, and he clouted his third home run in as many days when he connected off the Reds' Jim Merritt for a three-run dinger which also proved to be the game winner, in the eighth. Those contests inaugurated an eight-game stretch in which Colbert went 11-for-30, hit five home runs, and drove in 12 runs, becoming the Padres' first star and fan favorite. Colbert was having the time of his life playing for the Padres in what he called "big, but beautiful" San Diego Stadium. "I kept saying, 'It's the big leagues. It's the big leagues.' You know, I know we don't have a lot fans or a lot of money, but this is major league baseball. This is my goal."[16]

He was also reaching some home-run milestones. In the first game of a twin bill on May 25, in front of 13,115 hometown fans, almost twice the Padres' major-league-low 6,333 average, Colbert took the Chicago Cubs Don Nottebart deep for his first of six career grand slams. Six days later, against the Expos in Montreal, he belted two home runs in a game for the first of 14 times in his career and seemed destined for a berth on the All-Star squad. On June 11 he was batting .299 with 12 home runs and slugging .588 (fourth best in the NL), then reported to Oklahoma City for three weeks of service in the National Guard. A weekend pass enabled to him join the Padres for a four-game series in Houston, but Colbert didn't rejoin the team permanently until June 30 and subsequently struggled mightily. In his next 25 games he batted just .180 with a sole home run in 100 at-bats. "My timing was off and I started to pull everything," said Colbert.[17] He rediscovered his stroke, slugging .516 from August 1 through the rest of the season to lead the offensively challenged team with 24 home runs, 9 triples, and 66 RBIs. The Padres finished with the worst record in baseball (52-110) and

ranked last in majors in runs scored (averaging just 2.89 per game), batting average (.225), and on-base percentage (.285).

After another year of winter ball, earning all-league honors with Caguas in Puerto Rico, Colbert arrived at the Padres' brand-new training facility in Yuma with heightened expectations. His spring-training performance foreshadowed his season: He knocked in 21 runs in 60 at-bats and hit a 500-foot home run that Oakland A's coach Bobby Hofman called the longest he had ever seen.[18] On Opening Day, the 24-year-old walloped a monstrous three-run blast off Phil Niekro in the Padres' 8-3 victory against the Atlanta Braves. "If I stay healthy, I have a chance to hit 30," said Colbert, who doubted he could reach the 35 mark his skipper Gomez predicted.[19] The round-trippers kept coming. He whacked four in 17 at-bats in a three-day, four-game stretch on the road on May 6-8, including two in one game against the Phillies in the City of Brotherly Love. "[Colbert can] hit a ball as far as anyone," gushed Gomez, who compared his slugger to the hardest hitters in the game, such as Willie McCovey and Willie Stargell. "The ball just jumps off his bat."[20] Colbert blasted his former team on May 15, reaching two more milestones, by cranking his first extra-inning and first-walk-off home run, a two-run blast in the 10th to give the Padres a 10-8 victory.

Despite Colbert's success (he was tied with Hank Aaron, Dick Allen, and Tony Perez for the major-league lead with 16 home runs after hitting two against the San Francisco Giants in the first game of a twin bill on May 26), Colbert's name barely registered on the national radar. He was even left off the All-Star ballot (fans were given the right to vote in 1970 for the first time since the Cincinnati Reds ballot-box-stuffing scandal in 1957). "I could be leading the league in home runs and runs batted in and hitting .300 and people wouldn't know who I am,"

Colbert complained.[21] A 21-game homerless streak to begin June dropped him well off the NL lead, and his name further receded from national attention. After spending the All-Star break at home in San Diego, Colbert equaled his home-run output from the first half by belting 19 as the Padres kept losing, finishing with the league's worst record (63-99). In a strange statistical anomaly, the Padres ranked third in the league in home runs (172), easily led the majors with 104 on the road, yet ranked 11th of 12 NL teams in scoring. Colbert (38-86-.259 and .509 slugging) formed with his roommate Cito Gaston (29-93-.318, .543) and Ollie Brown (23-89-.292 .489) one of the most potent trios in baseball. A free swinger, Colbert finished in the NL's top nine in strikeouts in all six of his full seasons in the majors, including third in 1970 with 150 punchouts. On August 12, he became part of strikeout history when the St. Louis Cardinals Bob Gibson fanned him for the hurler's 200th K of the season to become the first major-league pitcher to reach the 200-strikeout mark in eight seasons.

Considered among the toughest parks for home-run hitters, San Diego Stadium had a deep 420-foot center field, with 375-foot power alleys, all of which were made even more imposing by a 17-foot outfield wall. "Whitey Wietelmann, one of our coaches, drew an imaginary line on his scorebook on what the dimensions were in most of the other ballparks," recalled Colbert. "And then he took where I hit every ball and he said every year routinely, I would hit 15 to 20 balls that would be off the walls, on the warning track in deep center, that would have been home runs in another ballpark."[22]

Colbert achieved success despite cognitive degeneration of his vertebrae which caused chronic lower back pain throughout his baseball career. "I have trouble getting loose," he explained, adding that he acclimated himself to the discomfort. "I feel tight a lot at the start of games and I try to compensate and wind up swinging at bad pitches. I'll have this problem all my life."[23]

Colbert's ailing back limited his participation in spring training in 1971 and raised concerns about the long-term effectiveness of the 25-year-old. Nonetheless big Nate was ready when the season commenced and he slammed two home runs against the San Francisco Giants in his second game of the season. Four days later he victimized Don Sutton of the Los Angeles Dodgers for two home runs in his first two at-bats en route to six RBIs in the Padres' 9-7 victory on April 11, leading sportswriter Ross Newhan of the *Los Angeles Times* to declare him "baseball's best young slugger."[24] Shrugging off those lofty pronouncements, Colbert developed a reputation as an emotionally charged team player who vented his frustrations after his strikeouts, but also at Padres fans, whom he once described as "impatient" and chided them for the "empty seats" in San Diego Stadium.[25] The

club finished last in the majors in attendance in 1971 for the second time in three years, averaging 6,883 per game. "I just want the team to be recognized," Colbert said. "If the team gets recognition, I will, too. Recognition is tough when you play for a last-place team."[26] The club extended its cellar-dwelling streak in the NL West to three years; however, Colbert earned a berth on the All-Star team (selected by skipper Sparky Anderson of the Reds) and struck out against the Baltimore Orioles' Mike Cuellar in his only plate appearance. Suffering through severe bouts of back pain, Colbert saw his power numbers drop, though he still led the team in home runs (27), RBIs (84), and slugging (.462), while batting .264 for the lowest-scoring team in baseball (3.02 runs per game).

Colbert enjoyed a magical 1972 season even while the Padres finished in the NL West cellar yet again with the league's lowest-scoring offense (3.19 runs per game). He arrived at spring training at a chiseled 215 pounds, having dropped about 25 pounds by "taking shots," reported sportswriter Phil Collier.[27] Eleven games into the season, delayed by 13 days because of the first players strike in major-league history, Don Zimmer replaced Gomez as skipper. Soon thereafter Colbert commenced one of his patented tears by hitting a home run and driving in a pair of runs on May 5 against the Mets, who had tried to pry the slugger away from the lowly Padres in the offseason. Eight days later, Colbert concluded a seven-game stretch on the road with five home runs and 12 RBIs and was leading the majors with nine round-trippers. He began one of the worst slumps of his career the next day, managing just 14 hits in his next 107 at-bats as his averaged plummeted to .194. A surge in July (8 home runs and 19 RBIs in 20 games) catapulted Colbert back among the league leaders in those categories and garnered him another berth on the NL All-Star squad. In the bottom of the 10th, Colbert, pinch-hitting for pitcher Tug McGraw, drew a walk off Dave McNally. Two batters later he scored the dramatic winning run in his home-away-from home, Atlanta Stadium, on Joe Morgan's single. After gaining some national recognition with that game-deciding tally, Colbert continued his July hot streak by homering in his first game after the All-Star Game, and then adding two more and knocking in all three Padres runs in a loss to the Astros at the Astrodome, setting up his fateful afternoon against the Braves in Atlanta on August 1.

Ever since Colbert was a minor leaguer with Amarillo, in 1967, he had a routine when he stepped into the batter's box. "As I walk up to the plate," he said, "I automatically touch my helmet. It gets me thinking about what I want to hit. Then I draw a Roman numeral seven in the dirt, backwards, with the end of the bat. I don't know why I do it. It just do it. It clears my mind."[28] Leading the majors with 25 round-trippers, Colbert wielded his 35-inch, 36-ounce bat to go 4-for-5, belting two homers and driving in five runs in the Padres' 9-0 laugher in the first game. Colbert recalled that he had felt exceptionally tired when the club arrived in Atlanta from Houston late the night before. "I didn't sleep well," he said. "I knew there was no way I could play both games. My back hurt, I felt down."[29] After his performance in the first game, there was no question he'd back in the field in the nightcap. He torched three different Braves hurlers to cap the best game of his life, clubbing three home runs for the first and only time and knocking in a career-high eight runs in the Padres' 11-7 victory for the twin-bill sweep. Colbert's five home runs tied Musial's record for the most in a doubleheader and his 13 RBIs set a new record, breaking the mark of 11, held jointly by Earl Averill (1930), Jim Tabor (1939), and Boog Powell (1966). Colbert's 22 total bases broke Musial's record of 21. Given the Padres' lack of home-run threats (Leron Lee was the only other player to have double-digit round-trippers that season with 12), it's a wonder that opposing pitchers even threw to Colbert. He finished the season by tying his own club record with 38 home runs (finishing in second place in the majors, two behind Johnny Bench). Colbert's 111 runs batted in set an intriguing major-league record, which still stood as of 2018, and might be among the baseball records least likely to be broken. His RBI total accounted for 22.75 percent of all the Padres' runs, breaking the mark set by the Boston Braves' Wally Berger (130 RBIs, 22.61 percent) in 1930.[30]

No one could have imagined that Colbert would go from one of the game's most feared sluggers in 1972 to out of baseball four years later at the age of 30. The initial signs of Colbert's alarming decline came in the first three months of the 1973 season, when he managed just seven home runs through June. A hot streak to start July (18 hits in 36 at-bats in nine games) helped salvage his season and earned him another berth on the All-Star squad. (He fouled out in his only appearance.) Once again the biggest offensive threat on the NL's worst team and the lowest-scoring (3.38 runs per game) club in the majors, Colbert posted career bests in batting average (.270) and on-base-percentage (.343), though he slipped to 22 home runs and 80 runs batted in.

In his final three campaigns (1974-1976), Colbert batted an anemic .186 with a .346 slugging percentage and hit only 24 home runs. After three consecutive All-Star Game appearances at first base, Colbert was moved by the Padres to left field in 1974 to accommodate the acquisition of Willie McCovey. Colbert never acclimated himself to the new position, struggled at the plate, drew the ire of the fans, and was ultimately benched by skipper John McNamara. In the offseason he was traded to the Detroit Tigers. A short, disastrous stint in the Motor City was followed by a similar one with the Montreal Expos, who released him on June 2, 1976. Signed by the Oakland A's, Colbert attempted to revive his career in the minors with the

Tucson Toros of the Pacific Coast League. He was called up by the A's in September and went hitless in two games. Granted free agency on November 1, 1976, Colbert was not selected in the inaugural free-agent re-entry draft, effectively ending his career. He participated in the Toronto Blue Jays spring training in 1977, but was jettisoned well before camp ended.

The Padres' first star and multiple All-Star, Colbert finished his career with 173 home runs, 520 RBIs, and a .243 batting average. As of 2018, he still held the Padres' career record for home runs (163) and ranked among the club's top 10 in numerous offensive categories.

Like many ballplayers, Colbert's transition into life after baseball was initially rocky. After holding down a few odd jobs and divorcing in 1979, Colbert married Kathrien (Kasey) Louis Barlow and became an ordained minister. He also gradually found his way back to the Padres, serving as an instructor during spring training and later as hitting coach for several seasons with the Riverside Red Wave in the Class-A California League. In October 1990, the day Colbert lost his job with the Padres, he was also indicted on 12 felony counts of fraudulent loan applications.[31] He eventually pleaded guilty to one count and served a six-month sentence in Lompoc, a medium-security penitentiary in California.[32] After his incarceration, Nate rededicated his life to his ministry and operated various baseball schools and camps in which youngsters learned about the sports and Christian values. He managed in two short-season independent leagues (Western Baseball League and Big South League) in 1995 and 1996, though he preferred to spend his time working with disadvantaged youths and combining his two passions, baseball and ministry. In 1999 Colbert, 1976 Cy Young Award winner Randy Jones, and former Padres owner Ray Kroc were the inaugural inductees into the Padres Hall of Fame, founded in 1999 on the team's 30th anniversary. Colbert continued his ministry work into the new millennium. As of 2018, he lived in the San Diego area and occasionally made appearances with the Padres.

"I never had a bad day in baseball," said the soft-spoken Colbert decades after retiring. "It was, I woke up, I wanted to go to the ballpark. I liked playing every day. I didn't need an offday. I played with a bad back, broken toe, fractured wrist, and concussion. I played. I just played, because I figured I'm going to hurt anyway, so I might as well play."[33]

## SOURCES

In addition to the sources noted in this biography, the author also accessed Colbert's player file and player questionnaire from the National Baseball Hall of Fame, the *Encyclopedia of Minor League Baseball*, Retrosheet.org, Baseball-Reference.com, the SABR Minor Leagues Database, accessed online at Baseball-Reference.com, and *The Sporting News* archive via Paper of Record.

## NOTES

1   "The Padres First Star -- #17 –Nate Colbert," *Padres360*, August 21, 2014. padres360.com/2014/08/21/the-padres-first-star-17-nate-colbert/.

2   Ibid.

3   Bruce Markusen, "#Card Corner: 1969 Topps Nate Colbert," baseballhall.org. baseballhall.org/discover-more/stories/card-corner/nate-colbert.

4   Arnold Hano, "Nate Colbert Is Definitely Accident Prone," *Sport Magazine*, May 1973: 50. Neal Russo, "Colbert's Brother Says Father Inspired Nate," *St. Louis Post-Dispatch*, February 8, 1971: 29.

5   Jim Sims, "Shaking Foes Hear the High Sonic Boom – It's in Colbert's Bat," *The Sporting News*, June 3, 1967: 39.

6   John Wilson, "Astros See Bright Future for Bench Kid, Colbert," *The Sporting News*, November 26, 1966: 37.

7   Sims.

8   Hano.

9   Hano.

10   Padres360.

11   Paul Cour, 'Big Colbert Booster: G.M. Leishman," *The Sporting News*, June 27, 1970: 11.

12   Padres360.

13   Sarah Wisdom, "San Diego Padres in Yuma – Spring Training 1969," Yuma County District Library, February 8, 2016. yumalibrary.org/san-diego-padres-in-yuma-spring-training-1969/.

14   Padres360.

15   Paul Cour, "Colbert New Power Man for Padres," *The Sporting News*, May 17, 1969: 18.

16   Padres360.

17   Paul Cour, "Army Chilled Nate's Bat," *The Sporting News*, October 18, 1969: 35.

18   Paul Cour, "Corkins Winning Battle With Batters and Ulcers," *The Sporting News*, April 18, 1970: 28.

19   Paul Cour, "New Padres 'Snake' Brings Foes to Knees," *The Sporting News*, April 25, 1970: 20.

20   Paul Cour, "Colbert's Cannon Shots Jolt Padre Foes," *The Sporting News*, May 9, 1970: 10.

21   Paul Cour, "Herby Proves Answer to Padre Prayers," *The Sporting News*, June 20, 1970: 21.

22   Padres360.

23   Allen Lewis, "Colbert Slams 2 Homers as Padres Best Phils, 8-2," *Philadelphia Inquirer*, May 8, 1970: 25.

24   Ross Newhan, "Nate Colbert: Name to Remember," *Los Angeles Times*, April 12, 1971: 1.

25   Paul Cour, "Barton Relaxes, Starts Belting the Ball," *The Sporting News*, May 22, 1971: 16.

26   Newhan.

27   Phil Collier, "Fewer Pounds Lift Colbert's Stock as Pounder," *The Sporting News*, May 27, 1972: 23.

28   Hano.

29   Ibid.

30   Bob Carroll, "Nate Colbert's Unknown RBI Record," *National Pastime* (2014 reissue), 1982. SABR.

31   Michael Granberry, "Ex-Padre Slugger Nate Colbert Indicted," *Los Angeles Times*, October 24, 1990: B2.

32   Alan Abrahamson, "Colbert Pleads Guilty," *Los Angeles Times*, March 31, 1991: C9.

33   Padres360.

# DAVE DRAVECKY

## BY WAYNE STRUMPFER

Doctors told Dave Dravecky that outside of a miracle, he would never pitch again. This followed a 1988 diagnosis of cancer in his pitching arm. Yet less than a year later he stood on the pitching mound at Candlestick Park in front of over 34,000 adoring fans, and retired 21 of the first 23 Cincinnati Reds batters he faced. A week later, however, Dravecky would throw his last pitch in a tragic turn of events. Despite the subsequent amputation of his arm, Dave Dravecky's story is one of happiness and hope.

David Francis Dravecky was born in Youngstown, Ohio, on February 14, 1956, the oldest of five boys born to Frank and Donna Dravecky. Frank was a machinist and Donna was a homemaker. Dave and his brothers played sports growing up and at Boardman High School, but they didn't play a lot of baseball because of the cold weather. As a teenager, Dave spent his summers across the state line in Pennsylvania playing with a Babe Ruth or Class-B team. He played outfield and first base before starting to pitch on his high-school team. As a left-handed starter, he finished his senior year with a 3-2 record.

Out of high school, Dravecky was passed up in the major-league draft and didn't receive any scholarships, so he enrolled locally at Youngstown State College. As a junior he helped lead the baseball team to its first NCAA Division II tournament appearance, with a record of 7-1 and an 0.88 ERA. In the tournament, Youngstown lost to Wright State, 26-1. Dravecky started the game and pitched 2⅓ innings. He recalled, "As each run passed home plate, Wright State players calculated my ERA and yelled it at me."[1] Up to that game, the lefty was receiving attention as the ace of the Youngstown pitching staff and a possible first- through 10th-round selection in the coming draft. In his four collegiate seasons, he struck out 252 hitters and was later elected to the Youngstown State Hall of Fame. However, the Wright State game brought a humility that would stay with him throughout his career. He realized that he was putting too much

pressure on himself to be drafted and decided to just have fun his senior year.

Dravecky happened to pitch a game during his senior year in front of scouts from the Los Angeles Dodgers and Pittsburgh Pirates – it was a two-hitter with 14 strikeouts. He had a good predraft tryout with the Pirates and was told by farm director Murray Cook to "go home and sit by the phone (on draft day) and see if it rings. If it's somebody from the major leagues, congratulations; if not, go get a real job." Dravecky was in fact drafted by the Pirates in the 21st round.

A few days later, Dravecky drove to Pittsburgh office and signed a contract to play for $500 a month. Not knowing he could ask for a bonus or additional money, he thought $500 to play baseball was a dream come true. At the Pirates' request, he picked up another newly drafted player, John Stuper, on his way to Charleston, South Carolina, the Pirates' rookie-league team. (Stuper went on to play four seasons with the Cardinals and Reds and later became the baseball coach at Yale University.)

After the season, on October 7, Dravecky married his high-school sweetheart, Jan Roh. An accountant, she was the family's breadwinner while Dave played minor-league baseball. They had two children, Tiffany and Jonathon.

Dravecky played several years in the Pirates' farm system. He grew up a Pirates fan and was thrilled to play for the organization. He played two years in Double-A in Buffalo (Eastern League). In March 1981, he worked out with the Pirates in spring training and pitched some batting practice. Pirates manager Chuck Tanner told Dravecky he liked what he saw in his bullpen sessions. But one day, Murray Cook came into the clubhouse and told Dravecky he had been traded to the San Diego Padres. Later in his big-league career, when the Padres played the Pirates, Tanner told Dravecky that he had been very upset about the

deal. Dravecky was traded for infielder Bobby Mitchell, who never played in the majors.

The Padres assigned Dravecky to their Double-A team in Amarillo. He described the 1981 season as his "sweetest year in baseball." He and his wife embraced the Christian faith that year and Dave learned the art of pitching and how to throw the cutter (taught by manager Eddie Watt). Watt and his wife would have potluck dinners and invite the team, which included Mark Thurmond, Andy Hawkins, and future Hall of Famer Tony Gwynn. Dravecky was the Padres' Minor League Pitcher of the Year in 1981, going 15-5 with a 2.67 ERA. He said his best memories of baseball were from that summer in Amarillo.

Dravecky was invited to the Padres' spring training in 1982 but was sent back to the minor leagues quickly and started the season with Triple-A Hawaii. In June he and Jan had their first baby and four days later, Dravecky was called up to the major leagues, replacing Danny Boone, who had been traded. He made his major-league debut on June 15 against the Los Angeles Dodgers, pitching one inning and allowing two hits but no runs.

Dravecky struggled early in the majors, but bullpen coach Clyde McCullough worked with him for several weeks. One day, McCullough taught him to just simply "feel it" and repeat the feeling.[2] The key for Dravecky was to slow down and keep his hand on top of the baseball so he threw the ball and did not push it. After that, pitching became enjoyable. Catcher Terry Kennedy came up to the lefty a few weeks later and told him he had become a different pitcher since spring training. Dravecky learned how to throw four different types of the fastball effectively. He later developed a "slurve" by just taking a little bit off his cutter. He said, "Moving the ball around and throwing strikes is what kept me in the majors."

In his first major-league start, against the Cincinnati Reds on August 8, Dravecky pitched six innings, giving up four hits and no earned runs as the Padres won, 3-1. He won three games in a row as a starter. The Padres manager was Dick Williams, someone Dravecky says he had tremendous respect for even though Williams could be very intimidating. According to Dravecky, off the field Williams and his wife were wonderful to spend time with.

In 1983 Dravecky was the National League's first six-game winner and first 10-game winner. He was a quick worker on the mound – his nine complete games in 1983 had an average length of 2 hours and 20 minutes. He said he didn't need time, "pitching was all instinct and feel" for him. That season, he made manager Williams, well known for hating bases on balls, happy by throwing 31⅓ consecutive innings without issuing a walk. He was selected for the All-Star Game at Comiskey Park in Chicago. When he walked into the clubhouse, he felt he didn't belong, but showed that he did by pitching two shutout innings. Jim Rice had the only hit off him – the only time Dravecky ever threw a changeup and only because the catcher called for one not knowing that Dravecky didn't have a changeup.

Later in the season Dravecky suffered from soreness in his left shoulder – the first time he struggled with pain – and sat out the rest of the season after late August. In the offseason, he worked out with Padres trainer Dick Dent along with major leaguers Alan Trammell, Paul Molitor, Terry Kennedy, Tim Lollar, and Rich "Goose" Gossage. "Sergeant Dent" met the players three days a week for a hard workout and lifting weights. This helped Dravecky develop strength in his shoulder.

Dravecky started 1984 in the bullpen and was successful with a 4-3 record, 8 saves, and a 2.80 ERA. When Andy Hawkins struggled, Dravecky returned to the starting rotation. The rest of the season, Dick Williams used him as a swingman, starting 11 games and relieving in 39. By the end of the season, Dravecky felt his arm was "a noodle" after throwing 156⅔ innings in 50 games. The 1984 Padres were a great team and a great mix of players, according to Dravecky. "We had so many characters on that team including Eric Show who was a professional guitarist." The team didn't really need a leader with so many veterans like Gossage, Steve Garvey, and Graig Nettles. Gossage told the team, "I don't want to hear any 'I or me' when you're talking to the press. This is about us as a team."[3] The strategy paid off as the Padres won the National League West. In the playoffs, the Padres dropped the first two games of the best-of-five series to the Chicago Cubs (including a 13-0 drubbing in Game One). Coming home to play the final three games, the Padres just started winning. Near the end of Game Five, when the Padres were beating Cubs ace Rick Sutcliffe, trainer Dick Dent was running up and down the dugout with smelling salts because everyone was hyperventilating about going to the World Series.

In the World Series, the Detroit Tigers, who had dominated the American League all season, beat the Padres in five games. That was when his impressive success in the postseason began. He pitched a total of 10⅔ innings, allowing only five hits and no runs and striking out 10. After Game Five and the Tigers' Series win, Dravecky had his scariest experience in baseball. Once the Padres boarded the team bus, ramped-up Tigers fans surrounded it and tried to tip the bus over. Twenty mounted police officers had to escort the bus from the ballpark to the freeway on the way to the airport.

In 1985 and 1986, Dravecky became a regular starter for the Padres, winning 13 games with a 2.93 ERA in 31 starts in 1985 and winning nine games with a 3.07 ERA in 26 starts in '86. Dick Williams left the club after 1985 and the Padres won

only 74 games in 1986, finishing fourth in the National League Western Division.

In 1987 Larry Bowa became the manager and the season did not start well. The team played poorly and Dravecky did not pitch well. By early July he was 3-7 in 30 games as a spot starter with a 3.76 ERA. On July 5 Dravecky was traded along with Craig Lefferts and Kevin Mitchell to the San Francisco Giants for Chris Brown, Mark Davis, Mark Grant, and Keith Comstock. He remembered being shocked about the trade. Mitchell didn't want to get into the cab to go the airport. Dravecky told his teammate, "Buddy, we've got to go, you don't have a choice here. We have to give it a shot." They all felt their team didn't want them anymore and were worried about what kind of reception they would receive with the new team. Once they arrived at Chicago's Wrigley Field, where the Giants were playing, manager Roger Craig set the three men down and told them, "You guys are the final pieces, we are taking this to the promised land."[4] The whole team shook the new players' hands and made them feel welcome.

Dravecky enjoyed pitching for Craig and being reunited with pitching coach Norm Sherry, and his season completely turned around. He was named the Giants' Pitcher of the Month in August and the National League Player of the Week in early September. Dravecky loved pitching at windy Candlestick Park and he started 18 games for his new team, going 7-5 with a 3.20 ERA. "Every hitter hated the 'Stick,'" Dravecky said. "Even Tony Gwynn, who never complained, hated to hit there." Roger Craig told the pitchers to use the elements to their advantage and Dravecky did, often pounding the inside of the plate. That Giants team, with the addition of the three Padres and later Rick Reuschel and Don Robinson, won the National League West.

In the postseason, the Giants faced the St. Louis Cardinals. After the Giants dropped Game One, Dravecky faced John Tudor (who was 10-2 in 16 starts that year) in Game Two in St. Louis. Dravecky pitched a two-hit shutout as San Francisco won, 5-0. Four games later, with the Giants up three games to two, Dravecky again went against Tudor in Game Six. In a classic pitchers' duel, Dravecky struck out eight and gave up one run in six innings only to lose to the Cardinals, 1-0. The next day St. Louis won again to go to the World Series.

In 1988 Dravecky started on Opening Day and the Giants beat the Dodgers and Fernando Valenzuela, 5-1, at Dodger Stadium. Steve Sax hit a leadoff home run against Dravecky but the left-hander shut Los Angeles down after that, giving up only two more hits. But 1988 turned out to be a lost season for Dravecky; he described it as, "really, really hard" – he pitched in only seven games and struggled with injuries throughout. In September he received a shocking diagnosis of cancer. He had a lump on his arm that he thought was scar tissue from throwing so much that had calcified. Dave and his wife waited in the doctor's office with the door slightly opened and they saw the doctors take the MRI film and place it under lights. That was when they heard the word "cancer" uttered. Dave and Jan just stared at each other in disbelief and then prayed quickly. The doctor told Dravecky that "outside of a miracle, you'll never pitch again." Dave called that day a "huge wake-up call" about life.

Dravecky knew the odds of a comeback were slim to none, but he was not ready to retire from baseball, so he was going to try. The cancer was treated by freezing part of the arm bone and taking out half of Dravecky's deltoid muscle – losing 95 percent of the use of it. Dr. Gordon Campbell, a doctor at the Palo Alto Clinic, where Dravecky completed his recovery program, said, "I thought Dave would be lucky just to throw a ball to his kids, I certainly didn't think he'd ever have the ability to pitch again."[5] Yet, during the 1989 season, Dravecky worked on strengthening his arm after the surgery and eventually was able to pitch in the minor leagues, making rehab starts in San Jose (Class A) and Phoenix (Triple A) for the Giants. In three starts in the minors, he posted a 3-0 record with a 1.80 ERA in 25 innings. By August 10 he was ready to start his first major-league game in over a year and since his cancer diagnosis.

It was a sunny, breezy afternoon game at Candlestick Park against the Cincinnati Reds. When Dravecky came out to warm up in the bullpen with catcher Terry Kennedy, they met up with a large crowd of media reporters and cameramen. Dave couldn't figure out what was going on; he was just warming up. Then he noticed that the fans by the bullpen began to clap and within seconds the whole stadium – the 34,810 fans attending the game – began giving him a standing ovation. Dravecky was so moved he pulled at his jersey near his heart and started pounding it quickly. Kennedy looked at him and did the same.

For Dravecky, once he was on the bullpen mound, "it was unbelievable and overwhelming." He started warming up and felt great so he threw only about 15 pitches and was ready to go. He wanted to keep things normal in the dugout before the game until it was time to walk out on the field. As he neared the pitching mound, he heard the fans again give him another standing ovation. He stood on the mound before the first pitch and remembered the words of his doctor from less than a year earlier: "Outside of a miracle, you will never pitch again." Dave thanked God for another opportunity with the game he loved so much, wound up, and threw the first pitch.

Dravecky felt it was "like a movie" as he pitched so well that day, throwing a shutout over the first seven innings – retiring 21 of the first 23 batters he faced. He had given up only a double and a walk as he headed to the eighth inning with a 4-0 lead. Manager Roger Craig later said, "I didn't really manage that game, I just sat there in awe."[6] But in the eighth inning, the fairy tale almost came to a crashing end as light-hitting infielder Luis Quinones belted a three-run homer. According to Dravecky, Terry Kennedy told him later, "Quinones was not in the script." Dravecky was able to get the third out in the eighth inning without any further damage and Steve Bedrosian pitched a one-two-three ninth for the save as the crowd stood and cheered after every out.

Five days later, in a start in Montreal, facing Tim Raines in the sixth inning, Dravecky broke his arm while pitching. The bone that had been frozen during the cancer treatment was just too weak. The snap of the break in the domed stadium sounded like a firecracker and Dravecky fell to the ground writhing in pain. Yet even after the break, he did not give up on pitching again. However, the end did come soon after during an on-field celebration after the Giants beat the Cubs in the NLCS. While Dravecky was celebrating with his teammates, he was accidentally pushed from behind and broke his arm again. Shortly after the new break, his cancer returned. On November 13, 1989, Dravecky retired from baseball.

In late 1990, Dravecky had a staph infection in his arm for 10 months. The recommendation at first was to amputate his left arm. However, nearing the time of surgery, doctors were willing to try to save the arm if the biopsy came back negative for cancer. In June 1991 Dave made the decision, telling the doctors he "didn't want the arm anymore" even though the biopsy came back negative for cancer. After the amputation, the doctors found cancer wrapped around the arm's ulna nerve.[7]

Twenty-seven years later, Dravecky said he felt the amputation saved his life. He said he calls himself the "One-armed Bandit" and travels the country as a motivational and inspirational speaker. He and his wife live in a small town in Central California. They have four grandchildren. Despite or maybe because of his cancer and amputation, Dave said, he enjoys life each day. Along with the speaking engagements, he worked part-time with the Giants as a community ambassador. Dave and Jan set up Endurance, a ministry that helps cancer patients deal with physical inflictions and depression.

## SOURCES

In addition to the sources cited in the Notes, the author consulted Baseball-Reference.com, Baseball-Almanac.com, and Retrosheet.org.

Two autobiographies by Dave Dravecky were useful:

Dravecky, Dave, with Tim Stafford. *Comeback* (Grand Rapids, Michigan: Zondervan 1992).

Dravecky, Dave, with Mike Yorkey. *Called Up: Stories of Life and Faith from the Great Game of Baseball* (Grand Rapids, Michigan: Zondervan 2004).

These articles were particularly helpful:

Curiel, Jonathan. "Ex-Giants Pitcher to Have Arm Amputated," *San Francisco Chronicle*, June 13, 1991.

Collier, Phil. "'82 Padres Capable of .500 Season," *The Sporting News*, April 10, 1982.

_____. "Padres Making Pluses Pay Off," *The Sporting News*, June 21, 1982

_____. "Dravecky Thrives on Inside Pitches," *The Sporting News*, May 30, 1983.

_____. "Dravecky Shoulders His Share of the Load," *The Sporting News*, July 16, 1984,

## NOTES

[1]    All quotations from Dave Dravecky and all specific facts regarding his childhood, college, and minor-league experiences are from an interview conducted by the author on July 16, 2018.

[2]    Dravecky interview.

[3]    Dravecky interview.

[4]    Dravecky interview.

[5]    "Dravecky to Make Big-League Return," SF Gate, August 9, 1989. sfgate.com/entertainment/article/Dravecky-to-make-big-league-return-Aug-9-1989-5660588.php.

[6]    Joe Lemire, "Dave Dravecky," *Sports Illustrated*, July 13, 2009.

[7]    Dravecky interview.

# STEVE FINLEY

## BY BILL PARKER

Statistically, a 13th-round draft pick is highly unlikely to see the majors at all; even fewer go on to make two All-Star Game appearances or win five Gold Gloves and a World Series championship. Very few four-year college outfielders who debut in the majors at age 24 go on to have 19-year careers in which they accumulate over 2,500 hits. And almost no speed-and-defense center fielders wind up with over 300 career home runs. But Steve Finley managed all of those things en route to one of the more improbable careers of the late twentieth and early twenty-first centuries.

Steven Allen Finley was born on March 12, 1965, in Union City, Tennessee. His parents, Fran and Howard, worked in education, and found jobs in the Paducah School District in Paducah, Kentucky, where Steve would grow up and become a baseball standout at Paducah Tilghman High. The only major-league baseball game Finley attended as a child – and, as of late 2017, one of only two he has ever attended as a fan – was Game Seven of the 1982 World Series at Busch Stadium, where, as a Tilghman High senior, he'd have seen Joaquin Andujar, Lonnie and Ozzie Smith, and Keith Hernandez lead the hometown Cardinals to a game and Series victory over Robin Yount and Paul Molitor's Brewers.[1]

Finley attended Southern Illinois University in Carbondale, Illinois (an hour's drive north of Paducah), impressed by coach Richard "Itch" (sometimes "Itchy") Jones and the promise of a

chance to compete for the starting job in center field from the outset. He won the center-field job in his freshman year, and with his excellence in hitting, speed, and defense, became perhaps the best all-around player the school has ever seen.

The Atlanta Braves drafted Finley in the 11th round in 1986, after his junior year, but Finley elected not to sign. Although having two parents in education was certainly a factor, it was breaking his leg in a summer league after his freshman year at

SIU that really made the decision for him; in 1989, his mother told Ken Rosenthal: "He learned from that experience that nothing is a sure thing, that in a moment your life can change." Finley returned for his senior year and completed a degree in physiology, after which – true to that goal of keeping his future options open – he was accepted into chiropractic school.[2]

Also in 1986, Finley was also selected to play for the American collegiate national team. It was a year that lacked the glamour of the Olympic teams of 1984 (which famously featured Will Clark, Barry Larkin, and Mark McGwire, among others) or 1988 (Jim Abbott, Ben McDonald, and Robin Ventura), but nonetheless gave Finley the opportunity to represent his country in the Netherlands in the Amateur World Series (whose name was changed to the Baseball World Cup the following year), along with future major leaguers including Scott Servais, Mike Remlinger, and Dave Hollins, and coached by legendary Fresno State coach Bob Bennett. Team USA finished 7-4 in the tournament and in fourth place, behind Cuba, South Korea, and Chinese Taipei.[3]

Finley had a successful senior year at SIU, wrapping up his career as the Salukis' all-time leader in numerous offensive categories.[4] Yet, he saw his draft stock *slip* from the year before – perhaps, as Rosenthal suggested in his 1989 profile, because teams questioned his commitment to the game after he chose not to sign a year earlier. Whatever the reason, the Baltimore Orioles selected him in the 13th round of the 1987 June draft – 325th overall, 57 spots later than the Braves had picked him in '86.

This time, of course, Finley did sign. He reported to short-season Newark (New York-Penn League), where he was nearly two years older than the average player, and excelled both there and in Class-A Hagerstown for the remainder of 1987, batting .303/.357/.429, with 24 extra-base hits in 315 plate appearances, and 33 steals in 40 tries.

Finley opened 1988 back in Hagerstown for his age-23 season, but as seasoned as he already was, spent just eight games there before getting a promotion to Double-A Charlotte, then played just 10 games there before he was promoted yet again, this time to the Triple-A Rochester Red Wings. At Rochester, managed by future Orioles skipper Johnny Oates, Finley batted .314/.352/.419 in 120 games, contending for a batting title and being named International League Rookie of the Year while leading the Red Wings to the West Division title.[5]

Finley's performance and meteoric rise through the minors had more than sufficed to put him on the Orioles' radar for 1989. The 1988 Orioles were one of the worst teams of the era, opening their season by losing a league-record 21 straight on the way to a 54-107 finish, and as such were in need of a youth movement heading into 1989. Manager Frank Robinson (who had taken

over for Cal Ripken Sr. just six games into that season-opening losing streak) had nearly an entire roster full of tough decisions to make, but one of the toughest was center field, where Finley was expected to compete with another young outfielder, Brady Anderson, who had been acquired from Boston, for the starting job.

The Finley-Anderson matchup was an interesting one, especially so because they were such remarkably similar players (but also because Finley and Anderson would become brothers-in-law[6]). Anderson is about 14 months older than Finley. Both hit and threw left-handed, and both were considered speed-and-defense outfielders with limited power potential, whose strengths as big leaguers (if any developed) would be getting on base and stealing bases. (And the similarities didn't end in 1989, either; both would blossom as excellent leadoff hitters in 1991-92 and develop surprising power later in their careers.) Perhaps *because* they had such similar skill sets, Robinson expected the winner to emerge in spring training, while the loser – likely Finley, if only due to their relative ages – returned to Rochester for additional seasoning. They were joined in the competition by Mike Devereaux, a soon-to-be-26 outfielder acquired by the Orioles in mid-March from the Los Angeles Dodgers.[7]

Ultimately, though, each impressed in spring training, and Robinson kept all three. Anderson opened the season as the Orioles' starting center fielder, and Finley started in right; in his major-league debut on Opening Day, April 3, Finley batted third, and flied out to right against Roger Clemens in his first at-bat, then injured himself fielding a Wade Boggs single in the fourth and was replaced by Joe Orsulak.

Finley went on the disabled list and didn't play again for nearly three weeks. He got the start in right on his return on April 22, getting his first career hit, a bloop single off the Twins' Freddie Toliver, in the third inning. He started in exactly half of the Orioles' 84 games between April 22 and July 28, but on that date, a game the Orioles would win in 13 innings, Finley came out with an injury in the 11th and wasn't able to return to the majors until September 2. He finished the year a disappointing .249/.298/.318 in 81 games. Meanwhile, led by Cal Ripken Jr., Mickey Tettleton, and Randy Milligan, and with strong showings by Orsulak and Devereaux, the Orioles rebounded all the way to 87-75 and second in the American League East, earning Robinson both the BBWAA and *The Sporting News'* Manager of the Year Awards.[8]

The 1990 season opened with Finley again penciled in as the Orioles' starting right fielder, and while he moved around the outfield quite a bit, he stayed healthy, and got 513 plate appearances in 142 games, hitting a similarly uninspiring .256/.304/.328, with 22 steals in 31 attempts. The Orioles were unable to repeat their stunning success of 1989, however, falling to 76-85 and fifth place.

The Orioles and general manager Roland Hemond believed that the team's chief problem was a lack of power; although Finley, Devereaux, Orsulak, and Anderson in the outfield and the Ripken brothers up the middle gave them one of the strongest defenses in baseball, and while the Orioles' 129 home runs were slightly above the league average, they were led by Tettleton's seemingly flukish 26 (he'd go on to be a power hitter for many more years, but he was 28 years old and his previous high had been 11), and only he and Ripken Jr. (21) topped 15. The thought was that the Orioles needed a big "run producer" in the middle of the lineup if they were going to be competitive again.

On January 10, 1991, Hemond got his guy: the Astros' Glenn Davis, a star first baseman who had averaged nearly 30 home runs and 90 RBIs a year since 1986. In return, the Orioles sent the Astros 24-year-old starter Pete Harnisch, 24-year-old middle reliever Curt Schilling, and the 25-year-old Finley. Finley and Harnisch nonetheless joined their now-former Orioles teammates on a cruise later that month: "I've got the ticket in my hand," Finley told a reporter. "I'd like to see them take it away from me now."[9]

The Sporting News, in a capsule with no byline, immediately lauded the Orioles and panned the trade for the Astros. It began: "The Houston Astros, as we have previously known them, cease to exist." The paragraphs analyzing the Astros' side of the trade were titled "HONEY, I SHRUNK THE ASTROS" and accused the team of "shed[ding] every big salary on the roster in an effort to make the team attractive to buyers. The question is: Who will buy a ticket to watch this dreadful team? ... [T]he Astros do not possess anyone resembling a major league first baseman. ... At least Harnisch, a starter of some potential, and Schilling, a middle reliever, will help fill out a pitching staff reduced to rubble by free agency. Finley, a part-time starter in the Baltimore outfield, is a speedy singles hitter who should benefit from playing in the Astrodome. But who is going to drive in runs?" The capsule concluded: "Orioles fans should rejoice; Astros fans should revolt. ... The Astros didn't receive enough for a player of Davis' magnitude and will be hard-pressed to win 60 games this season."[10]

The writer's immediate projection for the Astros wasn't off by much; the '91 squad went 65-97. But the trade, of course, was almost immediately recognized as a win for the Astros, and perhaps the worst in Baltimore franchise history. Davis suffered a freak injury in spring training in 1991, was never effective again, and was out of baseball by early 1993. (The Orioles had compounded their error by signing Davis to an extension that at the time was the richest contract in club history.)

Meanwhile, Harnisch immediately became the Astros' staff ace, posting a 2.70 ERA in 216⅔ innings and earning an All-Star nod; Schilling continued to show some promise in 75⅔ innings of middle relief (though the Astros traded him to the Phillies at the opening of the following season for slightly younger reliever Jason Grimsley); and Finley blossomed into precisely the hitter the Orioles might have hoped he would become. In 159 games, Finley hit .285/.331/.406 (a well-above-average 113 OPS+), hit 10 triples along with 8 homers, and stole 34 bases (though he was caught 18 times as well). Finley's 5.2 wins above replacement (WAR), per baseball-reference.com, led the team, just ahead of Rookie of the Year Jeff Bagwell, who'd decisively answered The Sporting News' concern over first base.

Finley was even better in 1992; he hit .292/.355/.407, a 121 OPS+, and stole 44 bases in 53 tries. He again led the Astros in WAR at nearly 6, which, along with improvements from Bagwell, catcher-turned-second-baseman Craig Biggio, and third baseman Ken Caminiti, saw the Astros climb all the way back to 81-81. Finley, Bagwell, and Biggio each played in all 162 games, the first time three teammates had accomplished that feat together since the 1974 Phillies (Larry Bowa, Dave Cash, and Mike Schmidt).[11] If there was a downside to Finley's brilliant season, it was that he still wasn't as valuable (5.7 WAR to 6.6) as rookie Kenny Lofton, whom the Astros had traded to Cleveland the previous December because he was stuck behind Finley. (So when Schilling was dealt in April of '92, that made *two* young Hall of Fame-worthy talents the Astros had given up in four months, with very little to show for them.)

The Astros and new owner Drayton McLane avoided arbitration by signing Finley to a three-year, $10.4 million contract entering the 1993 season. Probably not coincidentally, Finley donated $250,000 that winter toward establishing a charitable youth fund to keep Houston-area children in school and off drugs, and an additional $20,000 worth of Astros tickets as incentives for the children in that program. But while the Astros would improve by four wins in 1993, they didn't have Finley to thank for much of it, as he struggled to a .245/.301/.340 first-half line, and while he improved somewhat by batting .284 over the second half, he finished with just an 88 OPS+, missing 20 games along the way, mostly due to an injury in late April.

There were numerous rumors about the cash-strapped Astros trading Finley over the winter (along with Biggio, which is unthinkable in retrospect), but when Opening Day 1994 rolled around, Finley was still on the team, batting second and playing center field. He would rebound somewhat, missing another 20 games due to a mid-June injury and batting .276/.329/.424 in 94 games in the strike-shortened season – roughly league average – and setting a career high with 11 home runs.

The Astros took another huge step forward in '94, thanks largely to Bagwell's MVP-winning career year, and were on about a 93-win pace when that year's players' strike hit. But lower-than-expected attendance hit McLane's pocketbook hard even before the strike eliminated nearly 50 games worth of revenue, and so on December 28, 1994, with the strike still unresolved, the Astros traded Finley to the Padres, in a remarkable 12-player deal, the highlights of which were Finley and Caminiti, two of the Astros' higher-paid players, on Houston's side and talented younger outfielder Derek Bell on San Diego's.

The move seemed to revitalize Finley, who played all but five of the Padres' 144 games in 1995 and batted a career-high .297, posted a 110 OPS+, scored over 100 runs for the first time in his career, hit double digits in home runs with 10 for only the second time, stole 36 bases at a 75 percent success rate, and won his first Gold Glove.

Finley never stole that many bases again, but also never hit as *few* as 10 homers again until he was 41 years old, as he went through one of the more startling transformations in baseball history between the 1995 and '96 seasons. Batting in the number-two slot as usual (he'd slide down to third in the order in July, behind Tony Gwynn), Finley hit .318/.371/.598 in May after a bad April, and established a new career high with his 12th and 13th home runs on June 27, his 79th game. Finley credited Padres hitting coach Merv Rettenmund for his transformation.[12]

Finley finished the year batting .298/.354/.531, with 30 home runs, 126 runs scored, and 95 RBIs. Finley and NL MVP Caminiti presented a formidable 3-4 combo that combined for 70 home runs, and along with Gwynn led the Padres to a 91-71 record and first place in the NL West, the team's first postseason since its 1984 World Series appearance. Finley went just 1-for-12 in the three-game Division Series sweep at the hands of the Cardinals.

The 1997 season was a letdown for the Padres, who fell back to fourth place, as all of those pieces save Gwynn (who, at 37, batted .372 in 149 games) took a step back. Finley nonetheless nearly matched his shocking 1996 home-run production, with 28, scored over 100 runs again, and stole 15 bases in 18 tries. Finley was named to his first All-Star team, replacing Barry Bonds in the field in the sixth inning and striking out against Randy Myers in his only at-bat.

Then 33, Finley may have seemed to be tailing off in 1998, at about the age that players with his skillset often do – while he played all but three of the Padres' games and hit 40 doubles, he batted just .249 and dropped back down to 14 home runs, and, with a 90 OPS+, provided below-average offense for the first time in five years. The Padres had perhaps the best year in their history, however – driven by Vaughn's 50 home runs and a stellar season by mercenary starter Kevin Brown – winning 98 games and their second NL West title in three years. After another poor NLDS, Finley was instrumental in the Padres' NLCS victory over the Braves, batting .333 and drawing six walks in the six games, scoring three runs and driving in two. The Padres were then swept out of the World Series by the historically great, 114-win Yankees, Finley going 1-for-12 with a double.

After the season, Finley was a free agent, and although he expressed his preference to stay in San Diego, the expansion Arizona Diamondbacks, coming off a 97-loss inaugural season, were eager to bring in a winner, and went about it in a way that is almost never successful – luring in a slew of mid-30s free agents. They inked the 34-year-old Finley to a four-year, $21.5 million contract on December 18, 1998, a little less than three weeks after landing their real prize, a four-year, $52 million deal for Randy Johnson (35), and 10 days before they traded for Luis Gonzalez (31), Finley's former Houston teammate. They joined inaugural-season Diamondbacks Jay Bell (33), Matt Williams (33), and Andy Benes (31) to form the core of a team that certainly looked better than the 1998 squad, but whose age left a lot of reason to be skeptical.

Instead, all of those players met or exceeded their perfect-world projections, as the Diamondbacks won a shocking 100 games and the NL West in just their second season. Finley rebounded to set a new high with 34 home runs (including three in one game on September 8 against the Brewers), and scored 100 runs while driving in 103 (yet didn't lead the team in any of those categories). He won his second Gold Glove in center, and hit a brilliant .385/.500/.462 in the Division Series, though the Mets beat the D-Backs in four games.

It was around this time that baseball media and fans began seriously discussing the use of performance-enhancing drugs in baseball, and Finley (again like Brady Anderson) inevitably came up in those discussions. To be sure, with his late-career power surge, his unusual aging curve and spending several years as a teammate of admitted PED user Ken Caminiti, Finley's career had several markers that people inclined to have such suspicions might find suspicious. At the same time, though, Finley's power surges (like his brother-in-law's in 1996) all came outside his contract years; indeed, 1998, his one big contract year, was one of the worst years of his career; he fell to 14 home runs after seasons of 30 and 28. So if he was using a substance and that substance gave him his sudden power, one questions his motive for apparently stopping that usage during the year in which he stood to make the most money. Also, Finley never displayed a noticeable change to his figure; pictures of him from 1990 look startlingly similar to ones from 2006. For his part, Finley has always strongly denied any such charges, and credited his transformation to coaching from Rettenmund and Gwynn that transformed his swing from a flat, slashing type of swing to one with a more upward arc, much as hitters two decades later began to discuss creating "launch angle."[13]

The year 2000 saw the Diamondbacks slip by 15 games and into third place in the West, but Finley set a second straight career high in home runs with 35 (hitting his age in homers for the second straight year), putting up a .280/.361/.544 line and making his second career All-Star team, where he replaced Gary Sheffield in left in the seventh inning and got an RBI single off Mariano Rivera in the ninth in an unsuccessful NL comeback effort. That season also saw the Diamondbacks swing a five-player deadline deal with the Phillies that brought back Finley's former underappreciated Orioles and Astros teammate turned superstar starter, Curt Schilling, which would set the stage for the most memorable year in franchise history.

But the 2001 Diamondbacks were a pitching-first team; only three regulars provided above-average offense by OPS+ (led by Gonzalez and his 57 home runs), and Finley was not one of the three, slipping back to 14 home runs and a .430 slugging percentage, for a 91 OPS+ in 140 games. But Johnson and Schilling finished first and second in the Cy Young Award voting, the team won 92 games and the West, and Finley dazzled throughout the postseason; in the NLDS against the Cardinals, he hit .421 with a double, and knocked in the only run with a single in Game One, permitting Schilling to outduel Matt Morris, 1-0, as the Diamondbacks went on to win in five games. In the NLCS, Finley again provided the offense behind a sterling pitching performance by Schilling, driving in three of the team's five runs in a 5-1 win in Game Three, and then helped spark a big rally in their 11-4 Game Four win, as the Diamondbacks again won in five games. Finley then drove in two key runs in the Diamondbacks' thrilling seven-game win over the Yankees in the World Series; Johnson and Schilling were named co-MVPs, but Finley may have been the series' *offensive* MVP, batting .368/.478/.526 with a home run and five runs scored, and making an excellent running catch in Game Seven. In just their fourth year in existence, the Diamondbacks became the fastest expansion team to reach (and, of course, the fastest to win) the World Series. Finley has identified the world championship, as one might expect, as one of the major highlights of his career.[14]

One might reasonably have assumed again that despite his great postseason performance, Finley had entered a steep decline, having just finished his age-36 season with poor overall numbers. Instead, he again rebounded, playing 150 games for the 2002 Diamondbacks (who would win 98 games but be swept by the Cardinals in the NLDS, in which Finley was a nonfactor), hitting 25 home runs and putting up a 117 OPS+; in 2003 he

added a virtually identical year to his 2002, except that with 10 triples (up from 2002's four), he became the 17th player ever to reach double digits in his age-38 season or later, and the second ever (and first since 1922) to lead his league in that category.

The Diamondbacks were a team in decline, though, and when Schilling left Arizona for Boston via trade in November of 2003, it was clear that 2004 would be a tough season in Phoenix. When at the end of July Finley was as productive as ever (turning several of those triples into home runs, with 23 already), but the Diamondbacks were a staggering 33-72, they dealt Finley to the Dodgers. In LA, Finley continued hitting, and continued hitting home runs, adding another 13 to set another career high at 36 for the season, though none (in 2004, or his entire career) would be as important as his very last. On October 2, heading into the second-to-last game of the season, the Dodgers were 92-68 and at home to face the 90-70 Giants, a situation in which a win would clinch the NL West title. Brett Tomko had stymied the Dodgers for seven innings, then he and two relievers shut them down in the eighth, after which the Giants held onto a 3-0 lead. In the bottom of the ninth, though, a series of singles, walks, and a key error brought the game into a tie, and Finley came up against a fellow lefty, Wayne Franklin, with the bases loaded and one out. In almost exactly the moment every kid playing baseball in his or her backyard dreams of, Finley took an 0-and-1 pitch out to deep right-center – a walk-off, pennant-clinching grand slam. Finley has, unsurprisingly, named this as the top individual moment of his career.[15] The Dodgers fell to St. Louis in the NLDS – the fourth time in Finley's career that he had faced the Cardinals in that round of the postseason, and his team's third loss – as Finley went 2-for-16.

Finley signed as a free agent with the Angels for the 2005 season, and served as the primary center fielder for a team that made it to the American League Championship Series, in his age-40 season. It was the worst of his career offensively, at just a 71 OPS+, but he played 112 games and continued to start for the Angels through the postseason.

Finley was traded to the Giants for his age-41 season, and had something of a comeback, though his overall offense was still well below average, at an 83 OPS+. He did hit 12 triples (in a year in which Lofton and Finley's Giants teammate Omar Vizquel joined him in that exclusive club of players who'd hit 10 triples or more at age 38 or later), making him only the second player in his 40s to reach double digits, along with Honus Wagner. His 300th home run came on June 14, leading off the game against Claudio Vargas back at his old home park in Arizona.

Finally, just before spring training and two weeks before his 42nd birthday, Finley signed with the Colorado Rockies, making him and reliever Matt Herges (who also signed with the Rockies that season) the first two, and (through 2018) the only players to have played for all five teams in the National League West. But while the Rockies would ultimately advance to the World Series, Finley simply didn't have it anymore, drawing his release on June 13 after hitting just .181/.245/.245 in 43 games. He retired with a batting line of .271/.332/.442 and a 104 OPS+. With 44.3 WAR per baseball-reference, Finley sits (as of 2018) just outside the all-time top 400, in the same neighborhood as such very-good-but-not-quite-Hall-worthy outfielders as Rocky Colavito, George Foster, and Al Oliver. With 304 home runs and 320 stolen bases, Finley remains one of just eight players all time with more than 300 in both categories (joined by two of his former teammates, Reggie Sanders and Barry Bonds). Finley appeared on the Hall of Fame ballot in 2013, but got just four votes and fell off the ballot.

Finley returned to San Diego after his retirement, and has had various roles with the team's broadcasting crews and the team itself; as of at least 2017, he was the Padres' player development special assistant.[16] Finley is also a registered broker/dealer with Morgan Stanley Smith Barney LLC, focusing on helping professional athletes manage their money with Morgan Stanley's Global Sports and Entertainment Group.[17] He has also made an (unsuccessful) foray into the restaurant world.[18] After divorcing his first wife, Amy Jantzen Finley, to whom he was married from 1992 until 2008, Finley married Meaghan Hunt in June 2012.[19] Finley has five children, one of whom, Austin Finley, became a professional surfer.[20]

## SOURCES

In addition to the sources cited in the Notes, the author also consulted baseball-reference.com.

## NOTES

1    Steven Kutz, "Former All-Star Steve Finley on Helping Today's Players Be Smart with Money," MarketWatch.com, November 5, 2017. marketwatch.com/story/steve-finley-who-played-for-both-the-dodgers-and-astros-shares-what-its-like-to-play-in-a-world-series-2017-10-27.

2    Ken Rosenthal, "The Meteoric Rise of Oriole Steve Finley," *Baltimore Evening Sun*, May 3, 1989. articles.latimes.com/1989-05-03/sports/sp-2565_1_charlie-finley-oriole-steve-finley-orioles-manager-frank-robinson.

3    usabaseball.com/team-usa/collegiate-national-team/history.

4    siusalukis.com/hof.aspx?hof=67; Southern Illinois Salukis 2017 baseball media guide, available at siusalukis.com/documents/2017/2/15//2017_BSB_Media_Guide_spreads_small.pdf?id=6133.

5    "Around The Minors," *The Sporting News*, September 5, 1988: 39.

6    The relationship is mentioned on both players' Baseball-Reference pages and in numerous other online sources, but it isn't clear where in their families the connection was formed.

7    "A.L. East," *The Sporting News*, March 27, 1989: 31.

8    *The Sporting News*, November 13, 1989: 57.

9    "David Trade Opens Door for Tolentino," *The Sporting News*, January 28, 1991: 38.

10   "Two Minor Leaguers to Vie for Davis' Role," *The Sporting News*, January 21, 1991: 39.

11   Neil Hohlfeld, "Houston Astros," *The Sporting News*, October 26, 1992: 19.

12   *The Sporting News*, July 8, 1996: 25.

13   Finley discussed this approach – without any mention of steroids – in a segment that aired on Fox Sports' San Diego station in August 2018, available at foxsports.com/san-diego/video/1299911235524.

14   Steven Kutz.

15   Ibid. A video of the walk-off grand slam, called by Vin Scully, is available at youtube.com/watch?v=d5NdnmQ_XSA.

16   audioboom.com/posts/6148920-tincaps-interview-steve-finley-padres-player-development-special-assistant.

17   linkedin.com/in/steve-finley-68189730/; fa.morganstanley.com/rsf/mediahandler/media/9974/Steve%20Finley,%20Athletes%20Quarterly%20article.pdf

18   Tanya Mannes, "Ex-Padre Finley Strikes Out as Restaurateur," *San Diego Union Tribune*, February 21, 2010. sandiegouniontribune.com/sdut-ex-padre-finley-strikes-out-as-restaurateur-2010feb21-story.html.

19   insideweddings.com/weddings/meaghan-hunt-and-steve-finley/434/.

20   Steven Kutz; worldsurfleague.com/athletes/12791/austin-finley.

# TIM FLANNERY

## BY BOB WEBSTER

For 11 years Tim Flannery was an infielder for the San Diego Padres. During his childhood, he sang and played guitar with other family members. He took his guitar with him on the road while playing for the Padres and after retiring from his playing days, decided to take his musical career seriously. While coaching in the minor and major leagues and working radio and television for the next 25 years, Flannery and his band as of 2018 recorded 12 CDs, with another in the works.

Timothy Earl Flannery was born on September 29, 1957, in Tulsa, Oklahoma, to Ragon and Joyce Flannery.[1] His maternal grandfather was a coal miner in Illinois, while his father's side of the family originally came from Ireland in the mid-1700s and settled in the Appalachians and around the coal mines in the mountains of Kentucky.

Flannery's father left Kentucky to become a minister in Oklahoma and later moved to Southern California. They were living in Redondo Beach when Ragon Flannery gave his children a choice on their next move. Tim, who already liked baseball, wanted the family to move to Anaheim so he could see more Angels games. He won. Baseball was already in Flannery's blood as his mother's brother, Hal Smith, was a major leaguer who hit a three-run go-ahead homer in the eighth inning of Game Seven of the 1960 World Series, before Bill Mazeroski's famous homer in the ninth.[2]

Flannery played baseball at Anaheim High School, where he earned all-league honors and was elected homecoming king as a senior.[3]

Flannery met his future wife, Donna, while they attended rival high schools in Anaheim. After high school, Donna attended UCLA in Los Angeles while Tim attended Chapman University in Orange, California. The two dated on and off for seven years in high school and college and while Flannery was playing minor-league baseball. The two were engaged in 1980 and married in 1981. They had three children, a son, Danny, and daughters Virginia and Kelly.[4]

Flannery played for three years at Chapman. The second baseman had a career batting average of .399 while leading the Panthers to second-place finishes in the NCAA Division II Regionals in 1976 and 1978. He set single-season school records for batting (.435 in 1978) and hits (90 in 1976) and was named Most Inspirational Player all three years at Chapman.[5]

While at Chapman, Flannery was drafted by San Diego in the sixth round of the June 1978 amateur draft. After signing with the Padres he hit .350 for the Reno Silver Sox of the California League. The next season with the Amarillo Gold Sox of the Double-A Texas League, he batted .345. After only 960 plate appearances in the minors, Flannery was a September 1979 call-up, making his major-league debut on September 3 at the age of 21 against the San Francisco Giants. He was 1-for-3 as San Diego's leadoff hitter and delivered an RBI single off the Giants' Ed Whitson for his first big-league hit. He played in 21 more games during the remainder of the season.

Flannery started the 1980 season with the Hawaii Islanders of the Triple-A Pacific Coast League, where he kept hitting, batting .346 in 47 games before returning to the Padres and batting .240 in 95 games as a 22-year-old. Flannery split time between Hawaii and San Diego in 1981 before remaining in the majors for the remainder of his 11-year career. He hit his first career home run off the Cubs' Chuck Rainey at Wrigley Field on April 26, 1983.[6]

Batting .273 in 86 games for the Padres in their 1984 pennant-winning season, Flannery reached base in all four of his postseason plate appearances. In Game One of the National League Championship Series, Flannery was hit by a Rick Sutcliffe pitch while pinch-hitting for pitcher Eric Show. He hit a leadoff single in the fifth inning of Game Four and scored the tying run of the Padres' 7-5 victory over the Cubs. In Game Five, Flannery hit a groundball through the legs of Cubs first-baseman Leon Durham, igniting a four-run seventh-inning rally that clinched the Padres' first pennant. In the World Series, he collected an eighth inning pinch-hit single off Detroit's Jack Morris in Game Four in his only plate appearance.[7]

In the 1985 and 1986 seasons, Flannery appeared to be the Padres' regular second baseman, hitting .281 and .280 respectively while making only 16 errors in 229 games.

Flannery played his last game on his 32nd birthday, September 29, 1989. The sellout crowd greeted him with a long standing ovation, so long that the umpire had to stop play.[8]

Flannery was an all-time fan favorite in San Diego because of his hustle and all-out play. As of 2019 only Tony Gwynn, Garry Templeton, and Dave Winfield have played more games for the Padres than Flannery's 972.[9]

After his playing days were over, Flannery took a couple of years off before beginning his coaching and managerial career. In 1993 he managed the Spokane Indians of the short-season Single-A Northwest League to a 35-41 record, good for third place. Moving up to high Class-A Rancho Cucamonga, Flannery led the Quakes to the California League championship in 1994. The next year he guided the Triple-A Las Vegas Stars to a 61-83 record before going up to the Padres. Flannery was manager Bruce Bochy's third-base coach from 1996 to 2002.

Bochy's first year of managing the Padres was 1995 while Flannery was managing at Las Vegas. In 1996 Flannery replaced Graig Nettles as the Padres' third-base coach and held that position for Bochy through the 2002 season. From 2004 to 2006, Flannery was a TV and radio broadcaster on the Padres pre- and postgame shows and a color commentator during select broadcasts.[10]

Bochy continued to manage the Padres through the 2006 season before moving on to San Francisco to become their manager. (He left the Padres because they declined to give him a contract extension.)

Soon after Bochy became manager of the Giants, he asked Flannery if he would like to be his third-base coach once again. As told to ESPN's Tim Keown in 2013, Flannery said, "One day at the beginning of '07, I'm walking the dog with my wife. I'd been doing radio for four years, and at this point she thinks we're doing radio forever. I was doing 100 games a year and I loved it; it was performing without a net. So we're walking the dog and my phone rings. It's Boch. He asks me, 'You got one more ride in you?' Then he sends me the video of *Lonesome Dove,* where the two guys are sitting around kicking the pigs around the farm. I'm sitting there watching it, and Donna says, 'You're going again, aren't you?' I looked at her like this (winces and nods) and say, 'Yeah, honey, I guess I am.'"[11]

Flannery spent the next eight years in the third-base coach's box for Bochy. He became well known for his animated way of waving the runners home. He ran down the line on some plays because his mentors – Jimmy Davenport, Joey Amalfitano, and Jimy Williams – taught him the importance of buying an extra second or two to decide whether to send a runner home. Flannery wore spikes, expecting a workout every game.[12]

Flannery was not only the third-base coach, but he also counseled players. "Flan took me in as a 20-year-old kid. I didn't know how to work," said pitcher Jake Peavy, who played for Bochy and Flannery in San Diego and with the Giants. "I was sitting around twiddling my thumbs at my locker and he said, 'Come on, let's go bunt, let's go learn how to run the bases.' Me and him struck up a unique friendship. He taught me how to play guitar, a great release. He probably got me in some trouble, but he kept me out of more trouble the older I get. As anybody knows, Flan gave his heart and soul. Flan is all in."[13]

The Giants won the World Series with Bochy at the helm and Flannery in the third-base coach's box in 2010, 2012, and 2014. As the 2014 season progressed, Flannery told a sportswriter that "he is physically and emotionally spent, has done all he wants to do on the baseball field, wants to spend more time with his wife and family and devote his energies to raising money for all manner of causes through his music."[14]

In November 2014, Flannery called Giants GM Brian Sabean and Bochy to say he was stepping down as the third-base coach.[15] I call it the goddamned blessed road," Flannery said. "I've buried friends. I've put friends in rehab. I've watched marriages dissolve. There's a lot of collateral damage in this lifestyle I've had for 33 years. I'm going to send myself home safely."[16]

As spring training began in 2015, Flannery was surfing in Costa Rica. "It's still offseason for me," he said. "It'll be nice when they go to spring training and I go to Costa Rica to surf."[17]

Flannery did, however, return to baseball in 2015. He signed with Comcast Sportsnet Bay Area (now NBCS Bay Area) to be a part-time analyst and work some pregame and postgame shows.[18] After a guest stint with MLB Network in 2015, Flannery joined MLB as a studio analyst in August of 2015.[19]

On July 11, 2018, for the Giants-Cubs game, Flannery took on a new role with the Giants. Renel Brooks-Moon, the Giants' regular PA announcer, was fulfilling a once-in-a-lifetime opportunity to be master of ceremonies for the swearing-in of San Francisco Mayor London Breed, the first African-American woman to be elected the city's mayor. Flannery assumed the responsibility of PA announcer for the day. "I'm not going to do anything nuts," Flannery told the *San Francisco Chronicle*. "That's my one thing going into it."[20]

Bruce Bochy and Tim Flannery had a long history together, beginning when they first played together with the Padres in 1983 and were locker mates for parts of five years. They became good friends. Bochy retired from playing in 1987 and Flannery in 1989, but were back together in 1996 as manager and third-base coach of the Padres. They were different upbringings and according to their wives had nothing in common except baseball, but they had a chemistry that worked. Stories include one time the fans were on Flannery for sending a runner home who was tagged out and Bochy saw that Flannery was getting steamed. Flannery heard someone yelling, "Flannery, you stink, and your music stinks, too." Flannery turned to see who was yelling that and it was Bochy. That eased the tension a bit.[21]

After the 2014 season, when Flannery called Bochy to tell him he was retiring, Bochy said, "I'm happy for Flan. He's going to pursue his passion for music. You don't spend 32 years with somebody and not miss them. I'm going to miss his friendship, I'm going to miss the great job he did at third base. We're still going to see each other. This isn't a eulogy, this is a guy who's ready to go to the next chapter in his life."[22]

On December 21, 2015, a delivery arrived for Flannery. It was a World Series trophy from Bruce Bochy. The "Commissioner's Trophy," as it is known, represents the 2010, 2012, and 2014 championships. Flannery played with Bochy for five seasons and coached for Bochy for 16 seasons at San Diego and San Francisco, including three World Series with the Giants.[23]

For Flannery, there were two seasons: baseball season and music season. He and Tom, his younger brother by six years, shared a bedroom and would lie in their bunk beds and sing before turning in for the night. They sang in their father's church every Sunday along with their sister, Ragean. While in eighth grade, Tim, with his sister on banjo, sang Merle Haggard's "Okie from Muskogee" in their school's talent show. Tom taught music for many years in Kentucky and directed choirs in front of the pope at the Vatican; sister Ragean toured Europe as a pianist.[24]

Player Flannery always took his guitar with him on the road. After his playing days were over, he was in a Jimmy Buffett cover band and told ESPN's Keown in 2013 about a night playing at Dick's Last Resort in the Gaslamp Quarter area of San Diego. Flannery said, "We called ourselves Buff'd Out – can you believe that? Buff'd Out. How great is that? We got bar gigs in town through baseball, and we were pretty good. But it was the same thing every time, and I needed to make a change. One night in 1991, a couple of years after I retired, we were packing up the gear at Dick's and I turned to the guys in the band and said, 'Well boys, I have played 'Cheeseburger in Paradise' for the last time.'" That night, Flannery made a pledge to write and perform his own music.[25]

In 1993 Flannery began his coaching career, but kept on growing his musical career. Flannery said, "When I started writing my own music, I realized it isn't for everyone. People listen to music and try to write that song. At that point, you're not an artist, you're an act. When you're an artist, it's 'Here it is. Hope you like it. Don't care if you don't.'"[26]

Flannery has worked with Jackson Browne, Bruce Hornsby, Garth Brooks, Jimmy Buffett, Bob Weir, and many others. He has performed the National Anthem with Bob Weir and Phil

Lesh of The Grateful Dead many times, including during the 2012 and 2014 playoffs.[27]

On Opening Day 2011, the Giants played the Dodgers in Los Angeles. After the game a Giants fan, Bryan Stow, was savagely beaten by two men. Stow nearly lost his life and this event changed his and his family's lives forever. Flannery played in a benefit show for Stow in Oakland. The Grateful Dead's Bob Weir heard of Flannery's efforts and wanted to help. Weir invited Flannery into his home studio and they teamed up to play some benefit concerts together. Flannery became part of the Bay Area music scene. "I found a home," Flannery said of the Bay Area scene. "My kid said, "'You understand them. And they understand you.'"[28]

In 2014 Tim and Donna founded the Love Harder Project with the mission of "changing the world one bully at a time." The organization assists victims of violence and supports anti-bullying programs. Flannery and the Lunatic Fringe performed numerous times to help the Stow family with expenses: more than $300,000 as of 2018.

In 2017 Flannery was nominated for Humanitarian of the Year by All Sports United, a sports philanthropy organization.[29]

## SOURCES

Flannery's minor- and major-league stats, coaching, and managing assignments were retrieved from Baseball-Reference. com, unless otherwise noted.

## NOTES

1    findagrave.com/memorial/185823715/ragon-theodore-flannery.

2    Ron Kroichick, "SF Giants' Tim Flannery: Music Man," September 6, 2012; sfgate. com/sports/kroichick/article/SF-Giants-Tim-Flannery-Music-man-3845724.php.

3    upclosed.com/people/tim-flannery/.

4    Amy Gutierrez, "Giants Diamond Girls: Donna Flannery," July 30, 2012; nbc-sports.com/bayarea/giants/giants-diamond-girls-donna-flannery.

5    chapmanathletics.com/hof/bios/flannery?view=bio.

6    upclosed.com/people/tim-flannery/.

7    Ibid.

8    Ibid.

9    web.archive.org/web/20141203193624/http:/sanfrancisco.giants.mlb.com/team/ coach_staff_bio.jsp?.

10   upclosed.com/people/tim-flannery/.

11   Tim Keown, "Folk Hero," February 5, 2013; espn.com/mlb/story/_/id/8910268/ san-francisco-giants-third-base-coach-tim-flannery-uses-music-save-life-espn-magazine.

12   Ron Kroichick, "SF Giants' Tim Flannery: Music Man."

13   Fox Sports, "Tim Flannery Pursues New Life Away from the Baseball Diamond," February 10, 2015; foxsports.com/mlb/story/tim-flannery-pursues-new-life-away-from-the-baseball-diamond-021015.

14   Henry Schulman, "Giants' Tim Flannery Retires. 'I'm Going to Send Myself Home Safely,'" November 25, 2014; sfgate.com/giants/article/Giants-Tim-Flannery-retires-I-m-going-to-5917318.php#photo-7191323.

15   Ibid.

16   Ibid.

17   "Tim Flannery Pursues New Life Away from the Baseball Diamond."

18   upclosed.com/people/tim-flannery/.

19   Joe Harris, "Giants analyst Flannery joins MLB Network," August 17, 2015; https:// www.mlb.com/news/tim-flannery-new-mlb-network-studio-analyst/c-143728640

20   Gary Peterson, "Former Giants Coach Tim Flannery to Pinch Hit – in the PA Booth," July 11, 2018; mercurynews.com/2018/07/11/former-giants-coach-tim-flannery-to-pinch-hit-in-the-pa-booth/

21   https://www.youtube.com/watch?v=GXOoc7fzNFw.

22   "Tim Flannery Pursues New Life Away from the Baseball Diamond."

23   Dave Brown, "Look: Bruce Bochy Buys World Series Trophy for Giants' Tim Flannery," December 22, 2015; cbssports.com/mlb/news/look-bruce-bochy-buys-world-series-trophy-for-giants-tim-flannery/.

24   Ron Kroichick, "SF Giants' Tim Flannery: Music Man."

25   Tim Keown, "Folk Hero."

26   Ibid.

27   upclosed.com/people/tim-flannery/

28   Al Saracevic, "Ex-Giant Coach Flannery, Renaissance Man, Finds Broadcast Niche," June 28, 2015; sfchronicle.com/giants/article/Ex-Giant-coach-Flannery-renaissance-man-finds-6353737.php?t=faf6f1e715414c98e6.

29   loveharderproject.org/index.php/flans-story/.

# CITO GASTON

## BY ALFONSO L. TUSA

Clarence "Cito" Gaston was a National League outfielder from 1967 to 1978. At his best, he was an All-Star in 1970. He also made a vivid impression on the fans in Venezuela, where he won two batting titles in winter ball. However, Gaston attained much greater fame and respect as a manager. He became the first African-American skipper to lead his team to the playoffs and then to win a World Series. His Toronto Blue Jays won back-to-back championships in 1992 and 1993. "Cerebral, dignified, and tolerant" describe this imposing man's best qualities as a leader.[1]

Clarence Edwin Gaston was born in San Antonio, Texas, on March 17, 1944.[2] His parents were Sammy Gaston and Gertrude Coley.[3] Gaston spent his early years in the small city of Seguin, Texas, about 36 miles northeast of San Antonio, and at least one story states that he was born there rather than in San Antonio, his generally accepted birthplace.[4] Clarence had five sisters. Cito's friend of nearly five decades, Johnny Cardona Sr., said that Gertrude was remarried, to a man named Collins, when her son was young. Cardona recalled that Sammy moved to Oklahoma.

It's quite possible that Gaston inherited some of his ability. Negro Leagues legend Ted "Double Duty" Radcliffe, from Mobile, Alabama, which has a long record as a hotbed of black baseball talent, said in his biography:

"You know who else lived in our neighborhood? Cito Gaston's daddy. We used to call him 'Big Boy' 'cause he was a big heavyset fella – he could hit!"[5]

Radcliffe's collaborator, author Kyle McNary, states in another of his books that Gaston's father was a Negro Leaguer.[6] However, references for the "major" Negro Leagues do not show either a Gaston or a Collins who fits the bill. Whichever man it might have been, his experience may have come in a local circuit, the South Texas Negro League.

Cito was raised by a truck driver. Gertrude was a homemaker and at times a waitress. A San Antonio sports scribe wrote, "Religion was a big part of the Gaston family's life. His grandfather was a Baptist minister and the Gastons often attended church twice on Sundays."[7]

Young Clarence had ambitions of being either a truck driver, a singer, or a major-league baseball player.[8] Said another San Antonio sportswriter, "Some remember Gaston as a backyard preacher, the kid who always took the pulpit when the neighborhood children would gather to play church. Others remember him as a garbage man, who would trade his work gloves for a baseball."[9]

At some point in his teens, Gaston acquired his nickname from a neighborhood friend in San Antonio. In a May 2002 online chat with Toronto fans, he said it came when he was 14, but earlier stories suggest that it was a few years later as he began to play amateur ball. At any rate, the man responsible was Carlos Thompson, who later became a police detective in San Antonio. He thought Gaston resembled a Mexican wrestler whose stage name was Cito.[10]

Gaston grew up in both San Antonio and Corpus Christi. He attended Wheatley High School in San Antonio for a year.[11] After that he went to both Holy Cross High in San Antonio and Solomon-Coles High in Corpus Christi, and sources are split as to where he actually graduated.[12] However, it is clear that he was a three-sport star: baseball, basketball, and football. At Solomon-Coles, he was a pitcher. After graduating, "he returned to San Antonio, married and went to work on the midnight-to-dawn shift parking cars at a downtown garage."[13]

In 1961 the young man joined the Cardona Welders baseball team in San Antonio. Local businessman Johnny Cardona Sr. sponsored this amateur squad from 1954 to 1984. "There were some Anglos, a couple of black guys, and the rest were Mexican," said Cardona. Among other opponents, the Welders faced South Texas Negro League teams such as the San Antonio Black Sox, from the East Side, the city's traditionally African-American area. "When he first played for us, he was barefooted," Cardona told Richard Oliver of the *San Antonio Express-News* in 2006. "He showed up and nobody paid much attention to him. He went up there and hit the ball all the way out there in deep center field. I bought him his first pair of spikes, and the rest is history."[14]

More recently Cardona said, "The deal was, you bring your spikes and glove, we furnish the uniform and everything else. But Cito didn't have the spikes. I told him I'm gonna make an exception, I'm gonna call the sporting goods store. The owner,

Rudy, he said, 'Since when in the hell are you buying the guys spikes?' I said, 'Just this one, Rudy – don't tell anyone else!'"

Gaston worked for the San Antonio sanitation department in 1963. "I don't regret that nine months," Gaston told a sportswriter. "The work puts muscle on you."[15]

The Milwaukee Braves signed Gaston as an amateur free agent on March 22, 1964. George Vecsey of the *New York Times* told the story in 1989, as did Richard Oliver. Scouting legend Al LaMacchia, then with the Braves, stopped by Olmos Field in San Antonio to watch a Welders game. LaMacchia – later Cito's colleague for many years in Toronto – recalled, "Great build on him, wiry and strong. First thing he did was to chase a ball in deep center field, so I knew he could catch. Then he fired a strike so I knew he could throw. Then he beat out a groundball, so I knew he could run. And then he hit a home run, so I knew he had power." The stories went on to recount how LaMacchia beat out Houston scout Andy Andrews; the bottom line was that Gertrude said, "Sign the contract, Clarence."[16]

The young outfielder made his pro debut in 1964 with the Binghamton Triplets of the New York-Penn League (Class A), playing 11 games there before being sent to the Greenville Braves in the Class-A Western Carolinas League, where he batted .230 in 49 games. In 1965, with the West Palm Beach Braves of the Class-A Florida State League, Gaston suffered growing pains: .188 with 9 RBIs in 70 games. He was still bothered by a cracked shinbone that had gone undiagnosed during the 1964 season.[17]

In 1966 Gaston joined the Batavia Trojans in the Class-A New York-Pennsylvania League and enjoyed much better success, leading the league in homers (28) and RBIs (104) while batting .330. He was selected to the league's all-star team and was voted the league's player with the brightest professional future.[18] At the end of the season he played four games for the Austin Braves of the Double-A Texas League.

Back with Austin in 1967 after a stint in the Arizona Instructional League, Gaston had a good year (.305-10-70) with some standout moments. On June 12 he ended a scoreless pitching duel between Wally Wolf (El Paso) and Joe Cisterna (Austin) with a bases-loaded single in the ninth inning. On August 28 Gaston smacked a solo homer over the right-field wall to break a 2-2 tie with Amarillo. That earned him a cup of coffee with the Atlanta Braves in September. He pinch-ran for Tito Francona in his debut on September 14, flied out in his first, at-bat off Chicago's Rich Nye, two days later, and tripled off Nelson Briles on September 24 for his first big-league hit. In nine games, he went 3 for 25 (.120). The young man got a special mentor as roommate: Hank Aaron, whom he credited with teaching him "how to be a man; how to stand on my own."[19]

After that performance Gaston headed south to play with Cardenales de Lara of the Venezuelan Winter League in the 1967-68 season. Perhaps he had difficulty adjusting to the city of Barquisimeto, or was homesick, or the league was beyond his capabilities. He played in just 31 games, with a modest batting line of .254-0-3. The Cardenales released him. In the mid-1980s, Gaston returned to the Cardenales as a batting instructor. He declared to journalist Rodolfo Mauriello that Lara's management didn't give him the chance to recover back in '67-68.

Gaston started the 1968 spring with the Richmond Braves in the Triple-A International League. After 21 games (.239-2-8), he was sent down to Double-A Shreveport in the Texas League (.279-6-57 in 96 games).

That winter Cito's career took a great step forward thanks to Rodolfo Mauriello. Then general manager of another Venezuelan team, Navegantes del Magallanes, Mauriello offered Gaston a contract. Gaston replied that he'd had a hard time with Lara the previous season. Mauriello told him not to worry about that because he now had one more year of experience.

With Magallanes Gaston led the league in hitting (.383) and RBIs (64). His 11 home runs ranked second behind Brant Alyea's 17. In Venezuela many people still remember a weekend "a la Gaston." On December 8, 1968, the Navigators played the Caracas Lions. Cito won an exciting 13-inning game with a homer to the center-field bleachers. The next day, Magallanes played the La Guaira Sharks starting at 11 A.M. Again the game went to extra innings, as Gaston tied it with a bad-hop single over the head of his future teammate in San Diego, Enzo Hernández. He then won it in the 11th with a single to center.

The league's talent level was high, as evidenced by the long roll call of major leaguers who took part in those two games alone. Rollie Fingers, Mike Epstein, Bo Belinsky, Walt Hriniak, and Pat Kelly were some of the Americans, while the homegrown stars included César Tovar and Vic Davalillo.

The duo of Gaston and Kelly had special significance in Venezuela. According to a historian of Latin American baseball, "[They] became the first members of the Poder Negro – Black Power – era of the Magallanes team: African American import players who hit for power. Venezuelan sportswriters coined the term 'Poder Negro' after the incident at the Mexico City Olympics in 1968 when Tommie Smith and John Carlos raised black-gloved fists."[20] Carlos Tovar Bracho, a Venezuelan sportscaster, described Gaston and Kelly as a black version of Batman and Robin.

Gaston was taken by the San Diego Padres from Atlanta in the 1968 expansion draft, their last of 30 picks. In the spring of 1969, *Sports Illustrated* noted, "Their most exciting player may be a rookie named Clarence Gaston, a centerfielder with speed and power."[21] In his first complete major-league season, Gaston played in 129 games. However, in 391 at-bats, he hit just .230 with 2 home runs and 28 RBIs. The rookie was a very free swinger, especially for that era, striking out 117 times.

Gaston returned to Venezuela in October to play with Magallanes in the winter of 1969-70, but had to leave the team on December 20 because of a knee injury. However, he had enough at-bats (161 in 43 games) to win his second Venezuelan batting title, with an average of .360. His 8 doubles, 3 triples, and 7 home runs made him the leader in slugging at .578.

In 1970 Gaston enjoyed easily his best big-league season with the Padres. He played for the National League in the All-Star Game, going 0-for-2 with a walk. In 146 games, he hit 29 homers, drove in 93 runs, and batted .318. In addition to Hank Aaron, Gaston credited several men for his emergence. Richie Allen provided moral support, Billy Williams advised him to switch to a lighter bat, and San Diego batting coach Bob Skinner bolstered his confidence and adjusted his swing. Finally, Padres manager Preston Gómez stuck with him through nagging injuries and bad times during his rookie year.[22] Much of the success came from within, though – Cito had learned about pitchers and learned how to relax.[23]

Gaston returned to play 35 games with Magallanes in the winter of 1970-71, but did not approach his former peaks (.260-3-27). Then he did not sustain his fine form with the Padres in 1971. He played in 141 games, but slumped badly to .228 in 518 at-bats. His power numbers declined to 17 homers (including two solo shots on May 4 in a 3-2 win over Atlanta) and 61 RBIs. Another notable moment came on June 16, as he got the only hit off Bill Stoneman at Montreal's Jarry Park. Stoneman told *Baseball Digest* in 2005 that he regarded this outing as "The Game I'll Never Forget" – even over his two no-hitters.[24]

In 1970 Cito had shown at least some patience at the plate, walking a career-high 41 times to go with 142 K's. In '71, however, he drew just 24 passes and whiffed 121 times. On August 10 San Diego obtained speedy center fielder Johnny Jeter from Pittsburgh, viewing Gaston in turn as trade bait. However, the Padres wound up not dealing Gaston away that winter, which he again spent with Magallanes (.299-1-16 in 25 games).

During the spring of 1972, Jeter became the starter in center, and Gaston shifted to right. He would remain a corner outfielder for the rest of his career, seldom playing in center again. In 111 games, while his batting average picked up to .269, he dropped off further to 7 homers and 44 RBIs in 379 at-bats. One of those homers, off hard-throwing Don Gullett, provided the game's only run as San Diego beat Cincinnati on September 15.

Johnny Jeter was a bust, and the Padres traded him to the Chicago White Sox. However, the team's first-round draft pick in the 1971 secondary-phase draft, Johnny Grubb, was ready to take over center field in 1973. Gaston – who, as his 1973 baseball card noted, had "been plagued by injuries the past two seasons" – remained in right. He enjoyed a fairly decent season (.250-16-57 in 133 games).

The Padres made some more moves that winter. They picked up veteran first baseman Willie McCovey from the Giants and added Bobby Tolan from the Reds, who got most of the time in right. More than anything, though, Dave Winfield blossomed as the full-time left fielder. Gaston became the fourth outfielder (.213-6-33 in 106 games).

That November, San Diego dealt Gaston back to the Atlanta organization for reliever Danny Frisella. In 1975 he played in 64 games for the Braves (.241-6-15). Then, in the winter of 1975-76, at age 31, he reappeared in Venezuela to play with Magallanes. It was a successful winter (.296-5-31 in 60 games).

Gaston remained with Atlanta in 1976. He remained a reserve, although he felt he was still capable of making a greater contribution.[25] In 134 at-bats (69 games), he posted his best average in years (.291) to go with 4 home runs and 25 RBIs. On August 3, in a rare start at first base, he hit two homers and drove in five runs (a career high) off San Diego's Rich Folkers. It was the second time he'd connected twice in a game.

The 1976-1977 season was Gaston's last in Venezuela. With La Guaira, he appeared in 56 games (.262-4-38). He was taken as a reinforcement player by Magallanes to play in the 1977 Caribbean Series. Gaston joined a lineup that already had Dave Parker and Mitchell Page, the latest members of the Poder Negro tradition. He batted .300 with 4 RBIs in the Series (won by the Dominican team, the Licey Tigres). Gaston's career totals in Venezuela (seven seasons) were 31 homers, 207 RBIs, and a .307 batting average.

Gaston remained with the Braves in 1977 (.271-3-21 in 56 games) and most of 1978 (.229-1-9 in 60 games). On September 22, 1978, the Pittsburgh Pirates purchased his contract. With the Pirates at the tail end of that season, he was 1-for-2 in two games – which turned out to be his last in the majors. On October 11, Pittsburgh declined to offer Gaston a contract for the 1979 season.

Gaston decided to play for the Santo Domingo Azucareros in the short-lived Inter-American League, which featured many veteran big leaguers hanging on. Before the league folded in June, he played in 40 games (.324-1-14 in 148 at-bats). Then he left for the Mexican League to play for the León Bravos. There he appeared in 24 games (.337-1-8). In 1980 he returned to León and played in 48 games (.238-4-27). Gaston then retired as a player.

In 1981 Hank Aaron helped his friend find a spot with the Braves as their minor-league hitting instructor. "I had finished playing and Hank got me back in baseball," Gaston said. "He called me a couple times and asked me to come back as a coach. I said no. The third time he called, I said yes."[26]

The following year, 1982, Bobby Cox became manager of the Toronto Blue Jays after Ted Turner fired him in Atlanta, and took Gaston along as his batting coach. As the sixth-year expansion club matured into a winner, Gaston helped develop the likes of George Bell, Jesse Barfield, Lloyd Moseby, and Willie Upshaw. "He made a huge impression on journalists and baseball people as the rock of the clubhouse during two jittery pennant races in 1985 and 1987," the *New York Times's* George Vecsey wrote.[27]

Jimy Williams was fired on May 15, 1989, and Gaston stepped in as interim manager – the fourth black man to manage in the majors. The organization had actually been considering him for a greater role for some time:

"Two springs ago, in the roiling wake of The Campanis Affair, Blue Jays General Manager Pat Gillick approached [Cito Gaston] and asked if he would be interested in managing," wrote a *Los Angeles Times* sportswriter. "Not the Blue Jays quite yet, but winter ball. It would be an apprenticeship, servicing both the Jays' belief that Gaston might make a useful manager someday amid baseball's fresh demand for minority candidates. No matter, Cito Gaston wasn't hot on the idea. His father was ill, his second marriage (with two children added to his own two) was just getting its sea legs and life as a coach wasn't at all intolerable. So he said no."[28]

Gillick was hoping to hire Lou Piniella but was unable to do so. After encouragement from his players and Sparky Anderson, Gaston took the job full-time. Toronto was 12-24 when he took over but went 77-49 the rest of the way, winning the AL's Eastern Division (but then losing in the playoffs to Oakland). George Vecsey's article from the end of the season that year contained some other intriguing quotes:

"I never thought I'd be a manager. But once it happened it's pretty much what I expected. The worst part is the questions from the press. When the games start I relax." With regard to being a black manager, he commented, "I don't get too emotional about it. To me, it doesn't matter what color you are. I only think about it when you guys bring it up."[29]

The Jays finished second in the AL East behind Boston in 1990. They recaptured the division in 1991, but lost the pennant to Minnesota. The next year, though, in late August David Cone joined a strong talent base including Joe Carter and Roberto Alomar. Toronto was prepared to move to a higher level. Their field leader was feeling better too. George Vecsey noted, "Gaston showed courage by coming back from back surgery after 1991, showing more energy and less pain. He rarely complained or lost his temper, becoming ever more of a yup-and-nope guy." That same article compared him to "strong and silent" types such as Gil Hodges and movie star Gary Cooper.[30]

The Blue Jays beat Oakland in the AL playoffs in 1992 and then won their first World Series on October 24 by defeating the Atlanta Braves in six games. The winning run in Game Six, an exciting 4-3, 11-inning affair, was driven in by Dave Winfield. The veteran was then in his 19th season, 18 years after his emergence in San Diego prompted Gaston's trade.

George Vecsey observed, "Gaston has been skewered by a few critics in Toronto, which is normal in these critical times. 'I don't know, I don't feel any animosity in my heart toward the media,' Gaston said. … He admitted he had been hurt by inscrutable managers when he was a decent outfielder in the '70s, and he has tried to be open with his players. 'In this game, you meet good people and you meet bad people,' Gaston said. 'I guess I learned that everybody has feelings.'"[31]

In 1993 Gaston and the Blue Jays again won the World Series. Joe Carter's memorable home run lifted the Jays over the Philadelphia Phillies in Game Six. He became the first manager to win two consecutive Series since Sparky Anderson did it with the Cincinnati Reds in 1975-1976.

Gaston continued managing Toronto until the 1997 season was almost finished. But he never had another winning record – he came under fire for not developing good relationships with younger players like John Olerud and Shawn Green, and he lost support in the press. His none-too-subtle hints that racism was a factor did not help his cause. (He followed with a qualified apology.[32])

Gaston's total record as manager when he lost his job was 683-636. In July 1999 he became the fourth of nine men on the Blue Jays Level of Excellence, and his two World Series titles gained him entry into the Canadian Baseball Hall of Fame in 2002.

Gaston returned to the Jays as hitting coach for the 2000 and 2001 seasons. Yet while other teams had considered making him their manager, for over a decade he never landed another top job. Blue Jays President and CEO Paul Godfrey called it "the one big mystery in baseball, why this elegant, decent man had never been offered another job in baseball."[33] After the 1999 season, Gaston interviewed with the Indians and Brewers; the

Angels were also interested, but he withdrew from consideration for family reasons.[34] He came closest in November 2003, when the White Sox chose Ozzie Guillén.

In recent years, Gaston has served, along with former Blue Jays pitcher Pat Hentgen, as a club ambassador and special assistant to Godfrey. He also made occasional appearances at spring training in Dunedin, Florida, as a guest coach. As of 2018 Gaston lived in nearby Oldsmar with his third wife, Linda, whom he married in 2003.[35] Gaston thought the baseball life was why his first marriage, to Lena Green, ended in divorce.[36] That union produced two daughters, Rochelle and Shawn. In the late '80s, Gaston married a Canadian woman named Denise; that marriage lasted into the early 2000s.

Gaston was inducted into the San Antonio Sports Hall of Fame in 2006. He appeared to be peacefully retired, golfing and traveling the world. According to a Toronto sportswriter, "He eventually started to turn down clubs that wanted him to interview for vacant jobs." The suspicion lurked that he was being used as a token candidate.[37] But life changed for Gaston on June 20, 2008.

Amid a slump that saw the team win just four out of 17 games, Blue Jays general manager J.P. Ricciardi fired manager John Gibbons. "We know we've got a better team than this," Ricciardi said. "Right now, we just needed something to spark us, and I think Cito is the right guy for that." He cited Gaston's experience, respect, and credibility. Gaston observed that he didn't know the hitters as well as he did the last time Toronto called on him – but overall, he said, "I don't think the game has changed."[38] The Jays responded with a 51-37 record after Gaston's return, and late in the 2008 season Toronto gave him a two-year contract extension. In October 2009, he announced that his last season would be the upcoming one. After the 2010 season Gaston retired, left the dugout, and took a front-office consultant's post. He worked through 2015, and then retired from that position as well.

Perhaps his fondest memory? "The 1989 team was one of the most fun teams that I have ever managed," Gaston said. "I took over from Jimy and we came back to win the division. That was a team that could manufacture runs anytime we wanted to. All of the teams that I've had, you have to adapt as a manager and go from there."[39]

Perhaps the best expression of Gaston's even-keeled approach to baseball and life goes back to his earliest days as manager. As he told George Vecsey in 1989, "I don't mind if the guys laugh after we lose. They've got to get themselves ready for the next day. The same when we win. Enjoy it, but you can't take it with you. You've got to start again tomorrow."[40]

## SOURCES

In addition to the sources cited in the Notes, the author also consulted Venezuelan newspapers and magazines *El Nacional, El Universal, Meridiano,* and *Sport Gráfico,* as well as baseball-reference.com, baseballlibrary.com, and retrosheet.org.

Gutierrez, Daniel, Efraim Alvarez, and Daniel Gutierrez. *La Enciclopedia del Béisbol en Venezuela. Tomo II* (Caracas, Venezuela: Fondo Editorial Cárdenas Lares, 1997).

Additional research by Rory Costello and Maxwell Kates. Thanks to Johnny Cardona Sr. for his memories.

## NOTES

1    George Vecsey, "One Baseball Man Who Got His Chance," *New York Times,* September 24, 1989.

2    *2010 Toronto Blue Jays Media Guide.*

3    Harold Scherwitz, "S.A.'s 'Cito' Gaston Hopes to Make San Diego a Winner," *San Antonio Light,* January 17, 1971: 5-D.

4    "Braves Think They've Got Star in San Antonio's Cito Gaston," *San Antonio Light,* October 2, 1966: 62.

5    Kyle McNary, *Ted "Double Duty" Radcliffe: 36 Years of Pitching & Catching in Baseball's Negro Leagues* (Minneapolis: McNary Publishing, 1994).

6    Kyle McNary, *Black Baseball: A History of African-Americans & The National Game* (New York: Sterling Publishing Company, Inc., 2006), 68.

7    Tim Griffin, "Cito Gaston: Laid-back Perfection," *San Antonio Express-News,* March 20, 1994: 1C.

8    Walter Leavy, "Cito Gaston: On Top of the Baseball World," *Ebony,* May 1, 1994.

9    Harry Page, "From Sandlot, to SkyDome: Gaston's Family, Friends Will Watch Series Closely," *San Antonio Express-News,* October 17, 1992: 14D.

10   Various citations, including Scherwitz; Gib Twyman, "Gaston Makes Another Name for Himself: Champ," *Kansas City Star,* October 26, 1992: C2; John Matthew IV, "Fans Chat with Cito Gaston," mlb.com, May 7, 2002. See also Richard Oliver, "Long Journey Home," *San Antonio Express-News,* February 12, 2006: 1C. To confuse matters further, at least two stories suggest that the nickname arose in Venezuelan winter ball. See Page, "From Sandlot, to SkyDome"; Frank Hyland, "Next Black Manager? Cito Gaston," *Atlanta Journal-Constitution,* June 5, 1988: D-24.

11   Page, "From Sandlot, to SkyDome."

12   Harry Page, "Gaston Graduated from Coles," *San Antonio Express-News,* October 25, 1992.

13   "Braves Think They've Got Star in San Antonio's Cito Gaston."

14   Richard Oliver.

15   "Braves Think They've Got Star in San Antonio's Cito Gaston."

16   See both George Vecsey and Richard Oliver.

17   "Braves Think They've Got Star in San Antonio's Cito Gaston"; Scherwitz.

18   "Braves Think They've Got Star in San Antonio's Cito Gaston."

19   Walter Leavy.

20   Milton H. Jamail, *Venezuelan Bust, Baseball Boom: Andres Reiner and Scouting on the New Frontier* (Lincoln: University of Nebraska Press, 2008), 27.

21   William, Leggett, Mark Mulvoy, Peter Carry, and Roy Blount, "Old Saws Over a New Mays," *Sports Illustrated,* April 14, 1969.

22   Paul Cour, "Gaston Credits Tutors for His Swatting Rise," *The Sporting News,* March 27, 1971: 42.

23   "Gaston Concentrates on Pitchers' Styles," *San Antonio Light,* August 5, 1970: 50.

24   Al Doyle, "Bill Stoneman: The Game I'll Never Forget," *Baseball Digest,* June 1, 2005.

25   Wayne Minshew, "Braves' Gaston Eager to Shed Pinch-Hitter Tag," *The Sporting News,* August 28, 1976: 11.

26   Murray Chass, "Blue Jays Utilize a Strength Within," *New York Times,* June 6, 1989.

27   George Vecsey, "One Baseball Man Who Got His Chance."

28   Tim Layden, "Cito Gaston Is Getting Job Done as Toronto Manager," *Los Angeles Times,* June 18, 1989: 4.

29   George Vecsey, "One Baseball Man Who Got His Chance."

30   George Vecsey, "Cito Gaston Is a Baseball Man Who Finally Got His Chance," *New York Times,* October 26, 1992.

31   Ibid.

32   John Harper, "Jays' Gaston Stirs Racism Flap," *New York Daily News,* April 18, 1997; "Toronto's Gaston Apologizes," *New York Times,* April 18, 1997.

33   Dave Feschuk, "A Triumphant Renaissance for Cito Gaston," *Toronto Star,* September 27, 2008.

34   Teddy Greenstein, "Williams, Gaston Reportedly Discuss White Sox Vacancy," *Chicago Tribune,* October 1, 2003.

35   Dave Feschuk.

36   "Blue Jays Fire Williams, Look for a Manager," *Los Angeles Times,* May 16, 1989.

37   Allan Ryan, "Gaston Still Questions Past Rejections," *Toronto Star,* June 22, 2008.

38   Jordan Bastian, "Gibbons Out; Gaston Returns to Jays," toronto.bluejays.mlb.com, June 20, 2008.

39   Murray McCormick, "Cito Gaston Left His Mark on Baseball and Blue Jays," *Regina Leader-Post,* April 21, 2017. https://leaderpost.com/baseball/cito-gaston-left-his-mark-on-baseball-and-blue-jays

40   George Vecsey, "One Baseball Man Who Got His Chance."

# BRIAN GILES

## BY MARK HODERMARSKY

Were it not for the misfortune of attempting to break into the most talented major-league outfield of the 1990s, Brian Giles, as his post-Cleveland career confirms, might have earned a place in Heritage Park at Progressive Field as a member of the Indians Hall of Fame. In Giles' four seasons with the Tribe, 1995-1998, playing alongside stars Albert Belle, Manny Ramirez, Kenny Lofton, and David Justice limited the young slugger's plate appearances. Despite flashing admirable offensive stats and fine defensive range when inserted into the lineup, Giles was traded to the Pittsburgh Pirates after the 1998 season in exchange for reliever Ricardo Rincon in one of the worst deals in Cleveland baseball memory. Over the next 11 seasons, Giles made it impossible for Indians fans to forget the lopsided deal. For the Pirates and later the Padres, Giles proved to be one of the game's most consistent, though underappreciated, sluggers, until a chronic knee injury ended his 15-year career in 2009.

A native of El Cajon, California, in San Diego County and a 1989 graduate of Granite Hills High School, Giles was inducted into his alma mater's athletic hall of fame in 2008 for his exploits on the diamond, gridiron, and wrestling mat. He "slugged two homers in a game ... and scored four touchdowns in a game" among many other feats.[1] Granite Hills boasted one of the best high-school football backfields in the country. Running alongside Giles was Touchdown Tommy Vardell, a future star running back at Stanford, a first-round draft pick of the Cleveland Browns,

and an eight-year fullback in the NFL. Giles' former baseball coach, Gordy Thompson, remembered him as "a disciplined athlete with a good sense of humor" and a "work ethic that is second to none."[2] In 1989 Giles was voted the best San Diego County Male Athlete of the Year.

Bill and Monica Giles, Brian's parents, raised four children – Brian, Marcus (seven-year big-leaguer mostly with Atlanta), Kami, and Brandi. His parents "were also crazy for baseball.

Bill coached both boys in the Singing Hills Little League, and it was not unusual for the entire Giles clan to convene at a nearby ballfield for a little family BP. Dad would pitch, Brian and Marcus would hit, and Mom and the girls would play the field."[3] As is the case with most young ballplayers, Brian had a hero – Padres star and future Hall of Famer Dave Winfield. For Marcus, his hero was his big brother, Brian. Drafted by the Indians in the 17th round of the 1989 amateur free-agent draft, Giles batted .310 at Burlington (Rookie League) in 1989, .289 at Watertown (low Class A), and .310 at Kinston (advanced Class A) in his first three years of professional ball but displayed little power, hitting only five home runs in the low minors. Promoted to Double-A Canton-Akron in the middle of 1992, the young (21) outfielder saw his career blossom. In his first full season with the Indians' Eastern League affiliate, Giles' .327/.409/.452 (BA/OBP/SLG) and his 18 steals in 30 attempts began to turn front-office heads in downtown Cleveland. As prominent was a trait that separated Giles from most other players throughout his career – plate discipline. In that season he walked 57 times while striking out only 43 times in 496 plate appearances.

Giles' physique began to swell along with his statistics. As dedicated in the weight room as he was on the field, Giles transformed his 5-foot-11, 195-pound frame into chiseled granite, and the added muscle and strength produced better power numbers as he moved up to Triple A. In Charlotte (1994) and Buffalo (1995) Giles belted 16 and 15 homers, and his slash line improved. Called up to the Indians on September 16, 1995, for an end-of-the season look-see, Giles did not disappoint, going for 5-for-9 and smashing the first of his 287 major-league home runs.

Giles' 1996 stats at Buffalo (.314/.395./.594 with 20 home runs in 83 games) made it clear to the Tribe brass that he required no additional minor-league seasoning. Called up in July, he was in the big leagues for good. In 51 games for the Indians, he hit .355 with a .612 slugging average and five home runs. Over the next two years, 1997 and 1998, Giles shared left field with David Justice and played some in center and right and at DH.

From 1996 to 1998 Giles played in three American League Division Series, two American League Championship Series, and one World Series with the powerful Indians. In the gut-wrenching seven-game 1997 Series loss to the Florida Marlins, Giles had eight plate appearances in five games and was 2-for-4 with a double.

Desperate for pitching help, the Indians traded the 27-year-old Giles for Pirates reliever Rincon on November 18, 1998, in a deal that would catapult the burgeoning slugger into National League stardom while leaving a multitude of head-scratching Tribe fans bewildered. Rincon proved to be an ordinary bullpen lefty in four years with Cleveland, posting a 3.73 ERA and

crumbling in two ALDS opportunities, giving up five earned runs in 2⅔ innings.

In 1999 Giles instantly became the face of the lowly Pirates franchise by blasting 39 some runs and batting in 115 runs. His full tenure as a Pirate was equally productive. Indeed, David Golebiewski of Fangraphs makes "an argument that Giles was one of the top 10 most valuable properties in the game during his time in Pittsburgh [1999-2003]" through a sabermetric statistic, WPA/LI, that represents the sum of win expectancy per-play divided by leverage index. Golebiewski ranked Giles third in the majors in 1999 within this measurement.[4] To translate, only two players in all of baseball that year contributed more often to a win than Giles.

Another skill as a hitter that Golebiewski validated sabermetrically was Giles' plate discipline, pointing out his capacity to avoid striking out, to make contact, and to walk. As Golebiewski wrote, "If you want a player who knows the strike zone better than the man in blue behind him, then Brian Giles is your guy."[5]

For four straight seasons (1999-2002) Giles batted .300-plus with at least 35 home runs for Pittsburgh. But on August 26, 2003, before the nonwaiver trading deadline, Giles, who was enjoying another excellent year at the plate, was sent to his hometown but last-place San Diego Padres for left-handed pitcher Oliver Perez and outfielder Jason Bay.

In seven seasons with the Padres (2003-2009), Giles slammed 83 home runs despite playing at Petco Park, a very unfriendly hitters' ballpark. On April 8, 2004, in the first game at Petco Park, he got the ballpark's first hit. In 2007 he was teammates with younger brother Marcus Giles, who had a seven-year major-league career as a second baseman primarily with the Atlanta Braves.

Giles played in only 61 games in 2009 because of arthritis in his right knee. It became increasingly painful as the season wore on. He did not appear in a game after June 18. A free agent after the season, he made a comeback attempt the next year with the Los Angeles Dodgers but it lasted only briefly as the knee issues returned in a spring-training game. "Cutting in that game, I was starting to feel [knee pain]. It was getting to me, and it takes the fun out of [the game]. It's time and I'm content with it," he said at the time. "Physically, I'm not able to do what I like to do. I really have no regrets. I played the game hard, respected the game."[6]

A Padre teammate, outfielder Scott Hairston, described Giles as "one of the best I played with. He just grinded it out, each and every at-bat. ... Personally, I took it as a privilege to play with a guy like that for a few years. He brought a lot of laughs to the clubhouse. He had a great career." Another teammate, closer Heath Bell, remembered Giles as "a fun guy, upbeat, even when he was hurt."[7]

Giles' focused, hardscrabble, and fearless style of play directly contrasted with his clubhouse decorum. Former Padres GM Kevin Towers said, "I'd be in (former manager Bruce) Bochy's office having a serious meeting and Brian would come in fully naked, showing his batting stance. He's normal except for the tanning booths, shaving his body and walking around with no clothes."[8]

Giles was selected for the All-Star Game twice (2000, 2001) and named Player of the Week five times. He led NL left fielders in assists (13) in 2002. Several factors have hurt Giles' legacy and fair-minded consideration as a future Hall-of-Famer.

According to Ben Jedlovec, if Giles "had been given a lineup spot rather than wallowing in Triple-A for three seasons, his career totals would have been more noteworthy. Spending six years in Petco Park probably cost him a few dozen home runs as well."[9] Playing on small-market/mostly bottom-feeding teams (Pirates and Padres) didn't work in his favor either. In addition, Giles performed during an era of record-shattering (steroid-triggered) home-run achievements, diminishing the importance of the more than respectable number he clouted. Jedlovec only 12 players have hit more home runs with a better walk-to-strikeout ratio than Giles, including Barry Bonds and Albert Pujols. "The other 10 are Hall of Famers named Williams, Musial, DiMaggio, Gehrig, Ott, Morgan, Berra, Mize, Ruth, and Hornsby. While few would group Giles with 10 inner-circle Hall of Famers, it's clear that his combination of power and patience is in elite company."[10]

A couple of events brought national attention, albeit controversial, to Giles. The first was a domestic-violence suit brought by a former girlfriend in 2008.[11] The second, and more damaging to Giles' on-the-field reputation, concerned former Pirates catcher Jason Kendall who, in a 2009 personal divorce court filing, "disclosed that Brian Giles is someone that he has known since 1997 and when asked if Giles uses Adderall [a banned MLB substance], Kendall said, 'I believe so.'"[12] Giles never admitted using a banned substance and has never been tested positive.

The Indians of 1995 will be affectionately regarded for returning the American League pennant to Cleveland for the first time in 41 years. Not to be overlooked on this powerful squad, however, should be a 24-year-old rookie, whose career achievements matched many of those posted by the more familiar names of Belle, Ramirez, Lofton, and Justice. And as the 50th anniversary of the San Diego Padres nears (2019) and Brian Giles' remarkable tenure with the Friars is re-examined, the San Diego high school legend will spark even greater regard.

## NOTES

1    Leonel Sanchez, "Granite Hills Honors Alumnus Giles," *San Diego Union-Tribune*, January 24, 2008. Retrieved on November 2, 2017.

2    Ibid.

3    "Marcus Giles," jockbio.com, 2008. Retrieved November 4, 2017.

4    David Golebiewski, "Brian Giles Owns the Strike Zone," fangraphs.com, November 18, 2008. Retrieved on November 3, 2017.

5    Ibid.

6    Tom Singer and Corey Brock, "No Regrets: Giles Calls It a Career," MLB.com, March 11, 2010. Retrieved on October 24, 2017.

7    Ibid.

8    Bob Nightengale, "Welcome to the Quirky, Zany World of Brothers Giles," *USA Today*, March 17, 2007. Retrieved on October 29, 2017.

9    Ben Jedlovec, "Brian Giles, Hall of Fame Class of 2016?" *The Hardball Times*, July 22, 2014. Retrieved on November 3, 2017.

10    Jedlovec.

11    "Legal Battle Between Ex-Padres Player Brian Giles, Former Fiancé Cheri Oliver Headed Back to Court," 10news.com, June 9, 2013. Retrieved on November 6, 2017.

12    Vlad, "Jason Kendall Implicates Brian Giles, Bobby Crosby in Possible Adderall Use," bucsdugout.com, March 11, 2010. Retrieved on November 3, 2017

# TONY GWYNN

## BY DAN D'ADDONA

There has never been a sports icon linked to a city quite like Tony Gwynn is to San Diego. The eight-time batting champion went to college at San Diego State, spent his entire Hall of Fame career with the San Diego Padres then returned to his alma mater to become a collegiate baseball coach for 12 seasons. Gwynn's link to San Diego made him a larger-than-life icon, but meanwhile, his quiet personality balanced his play on the field, giving the city a home-grown legend who was engrained in the community.

Anthony Keith Gwynn was born May 9, 1960, in Los Angeles, the son of Charles and Vendella Gwynn. Charles was a warehouse manager and Vendella was a postal worker. Tony was the middle child between older brother Charles and younger brother Chris. The family moved to Long Beach when Tony was nine years old. To avoid breaking windows with baseballs, the brothers would use was a fig off one of the trees in their yard, or a homemade sockball for the ball. Growing up, the Gwynns were Dodger fans and Tony's favorite player was Willie Davis. But in the back yard, Tony and Chris would pretend to be the Cardinals and Pirates when they played "because they had all the left-handed hitters," Tony said.[1]

Tony attended Long Beach Poly High School in Long Beach, California, before attending San Diego State in 1977. He was a multi-sport star in high school and joined the Aztecs as a point guard on the basketball team, where he soon became a star.

He was an all-conference player twice in the Western Athletic Conference and is still the only WAC athlete in history to earn all-conference honors in multiple sports. He holds the school record for assists in a game (18), a season (221) and a career (590). Gwynn didn't play baseball until his sophomore year, and he had an immediate impact. He led the team in hitting twice and was a two-time All-American in his three seasons. His junior season, Gwynn batted .423 with six home runs and 29 RBIs. As a senior, Gwynn batted. 416 with 11 home runs and 62 RBIs. Gwynn learned to balance both sports, even when he had to switch gears quickly. One of Gwynn's legendary feats came during his final season at San Diego State. On Saturday, March 7, 1981, he concluded the basketball season with a 16-point, 16-assist performance at home against New Mexico. Two days later (March 9), he was on the baseball field for a doubleheader against the University of Southern California. In that twin bill, he went 3-for-7 with a double, three runs scored, five RBI, and a stolen base. He recorded game-winning RBIs in both contests.[2]

Gwynn's success in both sports attracted plenty of interest from professional scouts in Major League Baseball and the National Basketball Association. In 1981, the San Diego Padres drafted him in the third round and the San Diego Clippers of the NBA in the 10th round — both franchises looking to capitalize on having a home-grown star.

Tony Gwynn met his wife Alicia in elementary school. The two dated in high school and attended San Diego State together. Alicia was a member of the track and field team. The couple got married right after the draft, and Tony decided to sign with the Padres. He immediately reported to Walla Walla of the Northwest League. In rookie ball, he batted .331 to earn league MVP honors before being called up to Double A. He spent the final three weeks of the season at Double-A Amarillo, Texas, where he hit .462 over 23 games. He began the 1982 season with the Triple-A Hawaii Islanders of the Pacific Coast League. He was hitting .328 in 93 games there when he got the call to come play with the big boys.

Gwynn made his major-league debut on July 19, 1982, against the Philadelphia Phillies. He went 2-for-4 with one RBI, and went on to appear in 53 more games in 1982 after his July callup. He had 209 plate appearances and batted .289 on the season. Astonishingly, this rookie year would be the only year of his career that he didn't bat .300. Gwynn was also a part-time player in 1983, hitting .309 in 86 games.

But Gwynn's fortunes—and those of his team —changed when Gwynn became a full-time player. He made his first of his 15 All-Star Games in 1984 and would also go on to win the first of his eight batting titles with a .351 batting average. He also led the National League in hits with 213. He began to showcase his speed once reaching base, stealing 33 bases. But more importantly, with Gwynn leading the team's surge, the San Diego Padres made the playoffs for the first time in franchise history.

And their season wasn't yet over. The Padres faced the Chicago Cubs in the NLCS in 1984, and Gwynn continued to hit. He batted .368, scoring six runs and driving in three as the Padres erased a 2-0 deficit to win the final three games of the five-game series—yet another chapter in the Cubs' seemingly endless futile quest for a championship.

Unfortunately for the Friars, despite their thrilling victory over the Cubs, and their first World Series appearance, they had to play the American League monster Detroit Tigers. The Padres were no match for them. Detroit, which had opened the year 35-5 and cruised to the pennant easily dispatched the upstart Padres in five games. The Series featured the first of Kirk Gibson's pair of famous World Series home runs clinching the final-game win with a blast off of Hall of Fame closer Goose Gossage, who didn't want to walk Gibson. Gwynn batted .263 in the Series with five hits and one run scored.

The Padres' right fielder followed up his stellar 1984 season with another strong one in 1985. Gwynn batted .317 with 197 hits and 90 runs scored. It was just a taste of what the rest of the 1980s would look like. Gwynn batted .329 with a league-leading 211 hits and 107 runs in 1986, proving he was an all-around star by winning his first of five Gold Glove awards as the best fielder at his position. He then soared to a .370 mark to win his second batting title in 1987, also leading the league with 218 hits, scoring 119 runs and stealing a career-high 56 bases. It was the first of three consecutive batting titles. In 1988 he won with a .313 average, earning his 1,000th career hit against Nolan Ryan on April 22 in Houston, then followed with a .336 mark in 1989, also leading the NL with 203 hits.

Gwynn was rapidly becoming one of the greatest hitters in the history of baseball. While talent played a big role in his success, Gwynn put in the work to master his craft. "I am a natural hitter, but I have to work hard to keep it." He did so with countless hours in the batting cages and on the tee, sharpening his hand-eye coordination. But what set Gwynn apart was the way he studied hitting. He became one of the first players to accumulate and watch video of himself and of opposing pitchers during games. He was known to take multiple VCRs on road trips, taping the game on one and taping his at bats on the other, then studying them in his hotel room afterwards.[3]

Gwynn also perfected the art of hitting the ball the other way, shooting many of his hits between the third baseman and short-stop, something most left-handed hitters don't regularly do. "One of the reasons I get so many hits that way, is because it's hard to read the ball off my bat. My hands come through the zone first, and the barrel trails and it kind of hides the ball from the fielder until I've already hit it. They don't see the ball hit the bat. They just see the ball off the bat. By the time they react, they can't get to it."[4]

After three batting titles in a row, Gwynn almost amazingly didn't win another for four years. He still managed to average .324 with an OPS+ of 124 from 1990-93, the year he collected his 2,000th career hit at home off of Colorado's Bruce Ruffin on August 6.

Then came 1994, when amidst Gwynn's best season yet a labor strike by the Major League Players Union heartbreakingly ended the season prematurely. Gwynn had been flirting with the .400 mark for much of the season and would have been the first player since Ted Williams, before the US entered World War II, to bat .400 had he maintained his torrid pace. When the strike occurred he was hitting .394 with a league-leading 165 hits in 110 games. Gwynn of course was disappointed. "When you go through it in a strike year and they finally pulled the plug on the season," he said, "you get kicked to the curb like everyone else. I'd be lying if I didn't say I wanted to make a crack at .400."[5]

When after a rocky spring between players and owners big league baseball finally resumed in a slightly truncated 1995 season, Gwynn resumed his batting title monopoly for the next four consecutive seasons. He followed up his .394 in 1994 with similarly potent marks of .368, .353 and .372 in 1997, along with a career-high 119 RBIs and 220 hits, this last also leading the NL. In 1996, the Padres returned the playoffs, but lost the NLDS to the St. Louis Cardinals in in three games. Gwynne had a decent series—.308/.385/.692—but it wasn't the Padres' year.

That would come in 1998, even though for the first time he betrayed his age. The conventional performance measurements, .321/.364/.501 with an OPS+ of 133 were solid. But his WAR slipped to 1.5 from 4.3 the previous year. It was still   one of the most special seasons for Gwynn. He batted .321, ninth

highest in the NL, and led the Padres to the National League West division title and a spot for the franchise in the playoffs for the third time.

San Diego defeated Houston in four games in the NLDS (Gwynn sparked the Padres scoring the first run of the series after a hit) then knocked off the Atlanta Braves in six games to win the pennant and give Gwynn (who batted .200 in the Houston series and .231 against the Braves, but had two hits in the pennant-clinching game) and the Padres a second chance at a World Series title. But again, the Padres faced a juggernaut. The 1998 New York Yankees, one the greatest baseball teams ever, were in the midst of a 13-year stretch of straight playoff appearances that included four World Series Championships, and had no problem sweeping the Padres in the series. Despite winning in four games, the Yankees did have a problem getting Gwynn out. The crafty veteran batted .500 for the series with eight hits in 16 at-bats. He hit the only postseason home run of his career, drove in three runs, and scored twice. For many fans who missed Gwynn's first Fall Classic 14 years before, 1998 showcased the incredible abilities of a mostly unsung future Hall of Famer at Yankee Stadium and in front of record television audiences.

Gwynn's World Series finale was also the last real good-bye for him on the national stage. He would never play a full season again, playing 111 games in 1999, the season in which he passed the 3,000-career hit plateau. He got that seminal hit on August 6, 1999, at Montreal: a first-inning single to right-center off Dan Smith. First-base umpire Kerwin Danley had been one of Gwynn's college teammates, which added to the special moment. Only a single player achieved 3,000 or more hits in fewer at bats than Gwynn, Wade Boggs, and just one did it in fewer games, Roberto Clemente. (It should be noted that Boggs can make the same claim. Both he and Gwynn reached 3,000 in same number of games, 2,440.)

As his career wound down, Gwynn played just 36 games in 2000 and 71 the following season because of several injuries. He and fellow legend Cal Ripken Jr., who would both be retiring at the end of the season, were honored at the 2001 All-Star Game. Both had played their entire careers with one team, and both would be first-ballot Hall of Famers five years later.

The Hall of Fame was all but automatic for a 15-time All-Star, who was an NL starter in the Summer Classic a record 11 times, an eight-time batting champion—tying the NL record with Honus Wagner—and finished his career with a stunning slash line of .338/.388/.458 and an OPS+ of 132. In 2007 he was easily elected to the Hall of Fame on his first try with 97.6 percent of the vote by the BBWAA. Gwynne's was the eighth-highest voting percentage in Hall of Fame history.

The Hall of Fame was just the latest in a growing collection Gwynne was accumulating. In 1995, he was presented the Branch Rickey Award given to the top community activist in MLB as well as the inaugural Chairman's Award, given to the San Diego Padre who best exemplifies community spirit. He was inducted into the World Sports Humanitarian Hall of Fame in Boise, Idaho, in 1999.

Right after his retirement from major-league baseball, Gwynn became the head baseball coach at his alma mater, joining San Diego State in September of 2001, officially taking over the program for the 2002 season. He was named the Mountain West Conference Coach of the Year in his second season after leading the Aztecs to the league's regular-season title in 2004. In 2009, Gwynn led the Aztecs to a 43-21 record and its first trip to the NCAA regionals since 1991. In 2013, San Diego State returned to the NCAA regionals. Gwynn's coaching record was an even 363-363, and he developed future major leaguers like Stephen Strasburg and Justin Masterson.

Gwynn continued his devotion to community service in his hometown area after retirement from baseball. With his wife, Alicia, he established the Tony Gwynn Foundation to help fund many worthy organizations supporting children in need such as the Casa de Amparo, Neighborhood House, YMCA, and the Police Athletic League. For 14 years, he hosted the annual Tony Gwynn Celebrity Golf Classic to raise money for the foundation.[6]

Tony and Alicia had two children, Tony Gwynn Jr., who also played at San Diego State and then made it to the majors, and Anisha Nicole, who is a recording artist. Tony's brother Chris was also an All-American at San Diego State, playing for the 1984 U.S. Olympic team before joining his brother in the big leagues.

It was while he was coaching at San Diego State that health problems began cropping up for Gwynn, who at one point weighed more than 300 pounds. He had a tumor in his neck removed for the third time in 12 years in 2000. But the biggest issue stemmed from his career-long use of chewing tobacco. He was finally able to quit, but it was extremely difficult—and too late. The addiction took a toll on him as much as the effects. "I miss it every day," Gwynn said in 2011. "I screwed up. I made my mistakes. "I'm living with them. I was pretty messed up and I didn't even know it."[7]

After having two benign tumors removed, the third one turned out to be cancerous. "I just thought it was going to come back benign," Gwynn said. "And when it [didn't] your life kind of stops that day when he tells you that he found some cancer. I guess I wasn't surprised, but I was still stunned." Gwynn underwent radiation and chemotherapy for months for salivary gland cancer, and after years of treatment, he succumbed to the disease on June 16, 2014, at age 54.

Today an outsized statue of Gwynn, the "San Diego Legend," overlooks right field at Petco Park in the city. Gwynn's legacy was honored in two different ways at the 2016 All-Star Game, which was played there.

The first happened the day before the game when Chicago White Sox pitcher Chris Sale was selected as the American League starter. Sale talked about his own history with chewing tobacco and the impact Tony Gwynn's death had on him during a news conference: "He actually made a very big impact in my life. I chewed tobacco from 2007 until the day he passed away, I remember seeing thata nd just being so shocked. He was a larger-than-life person. He was an inspiration to the game for many, many people for a lot of different reasons. But I quit that day," Sale continued, "and I haven't touched it since. In a sense, I owe him a huge thank you for not only myself but for my family and, you know, hopefully I can maybe sway somebody in the right direction as well like he did for me."[8]

The other came just before the All-Star Game when Major League Baseball announced that the National League batting crown would be named after Gwynn. His wife Alicia and his children were on hand to accept the honor. "Tony is considered one of the greatest hitters in the history of the National League and there is no better place to honor him than in San Diego," MLB Commissioner Rob Manfred said in a news conference following the presentation.[9] The entire crowd at Petco Park erupted into "To-ny, To-ny!" chants that moved many, including members of the Gwynn family, to tears.

Few players have ever received that sort of reaction, ovation, and emotion after their death. But few players have ever engrained themselves so much into a community, a team, and a sport like Tony Gwynn.

## SOURCES

In addition to the sources cited in the Notes, the author also consulted Baseball-Reference.com, MLB.com, and the National Baseball Hall of Fame player file on Tony Gwynn.

## NOTES

1    "Tony Gwynn 19," http://www.goaztecs.com/sports/mbasebl/mtt/tony_gwynn_94674.html, accessed September 22, 2016.

2    Ibid.

3    Jill Lieber, "Gwynns Create A Terrific Team," *USA Today*, October 16, 1998,

4    Samantha Stevenson, "Tony Gwynn: A Portrait of the Scientist in the Batter's Box," *New York Times*, June 17, 1991.

5    Mark Newman and John Rawlings, "Man to Man," *The Sporting News*, July 28, 1997.

6    "Tony Gwynn 19."

7    Barry Bloom, "Gwynn taking fight with cancer a day at a time," April 4, 2011, MLB.com.

8    Associated Press, "Chris Sale Says Tony Gwynn's Death Caused Him to Quit Chewing Tobacco," Denver Post, July 11, 2016. https://www.denverpost.com/2016/07/11/sale-says-gwynns-death-caused-him-to-quit-chewing-tobacco/, accessed July 30, 2018.

9    Scott Boeck, "MLB Batting Titles Named After Tony Gwynn, Rod Carew, *USA Today*, July 12, 2016, https://www.usatoday.com/story/sports/mlb/2016/07/12/mlb-batting-titles-named-after-tony-gwynn-rod-carew/87013594/ accessed July 30, 2018.

# TREVOR HOFFMAN

## BY MAX MANNIS

From 1993 through 2010, Trevor Hoffman recorded 601 career saves. That was briefly a major-league record until Mariano Rivera surpassed him in 2011. Heading into the 2016 season, nobody else had as many as 500 – or will get there soon.

It was enough to get Hoffman into the Hall of Fame in 2018, when he received more than 79 percent of the baseball writers' votes in this third year on the ballot.

There is something to be said for such a reliable closer. Hoffman converted nearly 89 percent of his saves over the course of his 18-year career, ranking third out of the 50 closers with the most saves, behind only Rivera and Joe Nathan.

Moreover, Hoffman's life story is truly an inspiring one. Trevor William Hoffman was born on October 13, 1967 in Bellflower, California. As an infant of only six weeks, he had to have a kidney removed because of an arterial blockage. Because of this, Hoffman was unable to participate in certain sports that he was interested in as a kid, like wrestling and football. Now, Hoffman does a lot of charity work to help kids with similar kidney diseases. In 2005, these efforts were a big factor in winning the Hutch Award, presented annually to the baseball player best displaying "honor, courage and dedication to baseball both on and off the field."[1]

From the limited athletic options left available to him, Hoffman decided to try baseball. He was introduced to the game early

by his father. In addition to working at the post office, Ed Hoffman was an usher at California Angels games, and he would often bring young Trevor along to see the team play. Trevor's mother, Mikki, was a ballerina. She and Ed met in her homeland, England. Ed was originally a singer, and he continued to pursue his musical career for some years until he decided to quit traveling and stay with his family. At Anaheim Stadium, he became known as "The Singing Usher" – he performed the national anthem before games on various occasions.[2]

Trevor was the third of three children in the family, all boys. The oldest was named Greg; middle brother Glenn was an infielder in the major leagues for nine seasons (1980-87; 1989). Glenn also managed the Los Angeles Dodgers for much of 1998 and has since been a coach for that team (1999-2005) and the club for which Trevor starred, the San Diego Padres (2006-15).

In 1986, Trevor Hoffman graduated from Savanna High School in Anaheim, a 20-minute drive from Bellflower. He played shortstop, since his father had banned him from pitching for fear of injury to his arm. He was not offered a scholarship after high school, and so he went first to junior college – Cypress College, a short distance west of Anaheim. Undersized as a schoolboy, Hoffman eventually grew to 6-feet-1 and 200 pounds.

Hoffman went on to attend the University of Arizona, where he excelled as a shortstop. He played with future major leaguers J.T. Snow and Scott Erickson, along with future coach Kevin Long. Hoffman led the team with a .371 batting average in 1988, and showed off his strong throwing arm at short.

Upon his graduation from Arizona, he was drafted by the Cincinnati Reds in the 11th round (the 289th pick overall). He signed with the team for $3,000, a rather low amount, especially considering that he went on to be such a great player. Two years later, after watching him play shortstop for the Reds in the minors, team scout Jeff Barton told Hoffman that he felt that he could excel more as a pitcher than as a position player. Barton explained to Hoffman that while he was a relatively weak professional hitter, his ability to throw 95 miles per hour would guarantee him at least a part-time job as a pitcher with a major-league team. "He had the best arm I'd ever seen," Barton recalled more than 25 years later. "When you see someone with

*Left to right, Jeff Idelson, President, National Baseball Hall of Fame; Hoffman; Jane Forbes Clark, Chairman, Hall of Fame; Rob Manfred, Commissioner of Baseball.*

those kinds of tools, you don't go by them. Those are the tools that impact the game."[3]

Hoffman spent two years in the minors as a pitcher, developing his off-speed and breaking pitches. His fastball came easier to him because he had such a strong throwing arm. It was during these two years that Hoffman began to develop his changeup, his top pitch for years to come.

In August 1992, while he was pitching for Nashville (Class AAA), Hoffman first met Tracy Burke, the woman who would become his wife. She was a real estate agent who was also a cheerleader for the Buffalo Bills of the NFL. In the November after that season ended, the Florida Marlins picked up Hoffman through the expansion draft with their fourth pick (eighth overall).[4] A couple of months later, in January 1993, Hoffman proposed marriage to Tracy on the field of the Rose Bowl during Super Bowl XXVII.[5]

Hoffman finally reached his dream on April 6, 1993, when he made his major league debut with Florida. He kept the game close, striking out Eric Davis with the bases loaded to end the top of the ninth, but the Marlins could not score in their half of the inning and lost, 4-2. A big early moment in his career came eight days later at Candlestick Park in San Francisco. Pitching in the eighth inning as a setup man, Hoffman faced the very dangerous Barry Bonds. Bonds, pinch-hitting because he had a pulled hamstring, represented the tying run at the plate. Hoffman fooled Bonds and retired him on a little trickler to first base.

"I knew I needed to go right at him," Hoffman said. Marlins teammate Jeff Conine added, "The guy doesn't get intimated by anyone. . .he's going to be a great closer someday because he's got that mentality. He's not going to pick around. . .you could see what he was going to do just by his facial expression."[6]

In the middle of that season, Hoffman was traded to the Padres for slugger Gary Sheffield. This was part of San Diego's "Fire Sale" in which they traded many of their top players, such as Sheffield, for young talent. Fans disapproved of the trade, and Hoffman was booed during his first few appearances with the club. In his San Diego debut the day after he was acquired,[7] he gave up three runs in one inning; he allowed eight runs over his first three innings, covering three appearances. He also blew his first save opportunity of the season soon after, and he finished the season with only five saves and a 3.90 ERA.

In his first full season with San Diego, Hoffman began to show his true potential, recording 20 saves. He then began to prove himself as one of the top closers in the majors, recording 31 saves in 1995 and 42 in 1996. For all but one of the next 14 seasons, Hoffman recorded at least 30 saves. The exception was 2003, when he missed much of the season recovering from shoulder surgery.[8]

Hoffman lost his superior fastball after hurting his shoulder while playing football and volleyball during the 1994 strike. He needed surgery on his rotator cuff after the 1995 season.[9] Thus, he refined his changeup and used it to dominate hitters throughout his career. His changeup was his specialty pitch – he claims he started practicing with it as an eight-year old playing Wiffle ball in his backyard.[10] It became truly effective, though, after Padres teammate Donnie Elliott showed him a different grip.

After the bullpen doors opened, Hoffman was almost unstoppable. Intimidating hitters with his big windup, high kick, and long stare, he established himself as one of baseball's toughest pitchers to face, both physically and mentally. Starting on July 25, 1998, with AC/DC's "Hell's Bells" blasting through the PA system, Hoffman's entry gained an ominous extra dimension.

Hoffman had the opportunity to play in only one World Series during his career, in 1998, when his Padres played the powerhouse Yankees. The Yankees had 112 wins in the regular season that year, making them the heavy favorites. Hoffman was highly efficient that year, converting 41 straight saves over the course of 1997 to 1998.[11] Unfortunately for San Diego, the Yankees swept them easily. Hoffman's lone appearance in the series came in Game Three, during which he surrendered a go-ahead three-run home run to eventual World Series MVP Scott Brosius in the eighth inning. Despite the disappointing result, this World Series was one of Hoffman's most memorable experiences.

Since batting artist Tony Gwynn played on the Padres with him for many seasons, Hoffman was often overshadowed and considered the second-best player on the team despite how much he contributed to the team's success. When Gwynn retired following the 2001 season, Hoffman became the undisputed centerpiece of the franchise. He made the All-Star team again and broke Dennis Eckersley's record for most saves with one team.[12] *Sports Illustrated* even issued a May article titled: "The Secret of San Diego: Why Trevor Hoffman of the Padres is the best closer (ever)." Although he was not the main face of the Padres for much of his career, Hoffman still collected some prestigious awards. A seven-time All-Star, Hoffman led the National League in saves in 1998 and 2006. In addition, he captured the NL Rolaids Relief Man of the Year in both of these years, as well.

Following the 2003 season, Hoffman was a free agent for the first time. He had lengthy conversations with the Cleveland Indians, but even though Cleveland offered him more money,[13] Hoffman eventually ended up re-signing with the Padres.[14] San Diego's general manager at the time, Kevin Towers, said of the

Trevor Hoffman at the podium during his induction to the National Baseball Hall of Fame in Cooperstown, New York, on July 29, 2018.

new deal: "This is probably the most significant signing that I've had. This guy is the face of our organization. I can't put into words what he means to our community."

In 2004, Hoffman passed Jeff Reardon and Eckersley on the all-time saves list, securing the #3 spot. In May of 2005, Hoffman became just the third pitcher to record 400 saves, alongside John Franco (424) and Lee Smith (478).[15] Hoffman took home the NL Pitcher of the Month and Delivery Man of the Month awards for his performance. Partially due to Hoffman's success, the Padres went 22-6 that month, the best in franchise history. Hoffman finished that year 43 for 46 in save opportunities, the second-most saves in the National League. Unfortunately for the Padres, despite a successful 2005 season that brought them to the NLDS, they ended up being swept by the St. Louis Cardinals.

2006 was another eventful year for Hoffman. To start with, his brother Glenn joined the Padres as third-base coach. Trevor made the All-Star team, but he was the losing pitcher in the game. Perhaps rattled, two of Hoffman's five blown saves that year came in the week after his subpar performance in the All-Star Game. However, he recovered and later that year would pass Smith for the most saves in major-league history. In August of that same year, he appeared in his 776th game as a reliever for San Diego, breaking Elroy Face's record for most appearances by a reliever with one club. Face accomplished the feat with the Pittsburgh Pirates.

Hoffman helped the Padres clinch the NL West for the second straight season, recording his eighth career 40-save season along the way. However, the Padres again lost to St. Louis in the NLDS. Nonetheless, Hoffman was awarded The Sporting News NL Reliever of the Year for the third time in his career, and he finished as the runner-up for the Cy Young Award for the second time in his career (the other time was 1998).

In 2007, Hoffman continued to add to his already impressive collection of records and awards, but one blown save at the end of the year is what is sadly remembered from that year. In an April win over the Dodgers, Hoffman earned the save in his 803rd game pitched for the Padres, breaking the major-league record for games pitched for one team. The record was previously held by Walter Johnson of the Washington Senators and Face (it has also since been surpassed by Mariano Rivera). In June, Hoffman recorded his 500th career save, helping him to make the All-Star team again.[16] On September 8, Hoffman struck out the Colorado Rockies' Todd Helton for his 1,000th career strikeout, which was notable considering that Hoffman had only pitched 917 innings at the time.

Unfortunately for San Diego, Hoffman struggled toward the end of the year. One strike away from getting San Diego to the playoffs for the third straight year, Hoffman gave up a game-tying, two-out triple in the ninth inning to Tony Gwynn, Jr. of the Milwaukee Brewers – the son of his longtime teammate. The Padres went on to lose in the 11th inning, 4-3. Hoffman finished the year converting 42 of 49 save opportunities.

This left the Padres tied with Colorado for the NL wild-card spot. They played a one-game tiebreaker to decide who would get the final playoff spot. Hoffman blew his second consecutive save opportunity, an 8-6 lead in the 13th inning, ending on a controversial play at the plate. Matt Holliday tagged up for Colorado to score the winning run on a sacrifice fly, but to this day, it is extremely difficult to tell whether Holliday was out or safe. In the end, the only part that matters is that Holliday was called safe, putting a devastating end to San Diego's season. It was incredibly difficult for Hoffman to move past this huge blown save.[17]

Hoffman recorded 30 saves in 2008, his last season as a Padre. Unfortunately, despite Hoffman's continued excellence, the Padres struggled greatly that year. They won only 63 games, even though they were considered finally ready to be the clear top team in their division. Following that season, Hoffman – by then aged 41 – signed with the Milwaukee Brewers.[18] San Diego was in the process of rebuilding and saving money at the same time. However, it was still a surprising move; many had thought that Hoffman wanted to finish his career in San Diego.[19] Hoffman looked at the signing as a fresh start and a chance to prove that he belonged on a major-league team despite his age.[20]

Hoffman missed the first month of the 2009 season with a strained rib cage, which led to a brief injury-rehab assignment in the minors. He recovered well in May, as he was named NL Pitcher of the Month and MLB Delivery Man of the Month, recording 11 saves in 12 scoreless appearances. He made his seventh and last All-Star appearance that same year, filling in as a late replacement for the injured Jonathan Broxton of the Los Angeles Dodgers.

2010 was Hoffman's final year in the majors. Milwaukee re-signed him to a one-year deal with a mutual option for 2011.[21] After a rocky start, however, he lost his closer role to John Axford. He still got occasional chances to close, though – and on September 7, 2010, Hoffman recorded his 600th career save,[22] becoming the first major-leaguer to achieve this milestone.[23] He retired following that season,[24] after Milwaukee turned down his second-year option.[25] Hoffman felt that he could still pitch at the major league level, but with all the available closer spots filled, he was not interested in being a setup man. He retired with a 61-75 record, 601 saves, a 2.87 ERA, and 1,133 strikeouts.

Following his retirement, Hoffman joined the Padres' front office as a special assistant.[26] He also worked on both the pregame and postgame TV shows for Fox Sports San Diego. On August 21, 2011, his number 51 was retired by the team.[27] He was the ninth inductee into the Padres Hall of Fame.[28] He, his wife Tracy, and his sons Quinn, Wyatt, and Brody were all in attendance.

The Padres continued to value Hoffman, appointing him Upper Level Pitching Coordinator in September 2013.[29] He became a senior advisor for baseball operations in February 2015.[30]

Trevor Hoffman's career was filled with awards and recognition – and in 2018, he received the ultimate recognition when he was elected to the Hall of Fame.

"It's hard to describe the emotions that flood you right away," he said after receiving the call. "I know it's a very standard line, but so many things go through you. You think of your earl days in the game, you think of parts of your career, you understand what you put in on a daily basis. To be sitting there at this stage, seven years after you retire, it just comes full circle. It's kind of the cherry on top of a sundae."[31]

## SOURCES

In addition to the sources cited in the Notes, the author also consulted Baseball-Reference.com and a number of articles including:

"Padres announce plans to retire Hoffman's No. 51," *Sports Illustrated* (online edition), June 16, 2011, http://www.si.com, accessed January 2, 2016.

Center, Bill. "The Ace of Saves: Padres' Hoffman Becomes No.1 Closer of All Time," *San Diego Union-Tribune*, September 26, 2006.

Center, Bill. "Hoffman joins alumni in Padres front office," *SignOnSanDiego.com*, January 12, 2011, http://www.sandiegouniontribune.com/news/2011/jan/12/hoffman-joins-alumni-padres-front-office/, accessed January 2, 2016.

Center, Bill. "Trevor Hoffman adds coaching duties," *UTSanDiego.com*, September 12, 2013, http://www.sandiegouniontribune.com/news/2013/sep/12/padres-mlb-trevor-hoffman-coaching/, accessed January 2, 2016.

Haudricourt, Tom. "Selig reflects on Hoffman's career," *Milwaukee Journal Sentinel,* January 12, 2011.

Lin, Dennis. "Now full-time, Hoffman tackles new job," *UTSanDiego.com*, February 15, 2014, http://www.sandiegouniontribune.com/news/2014/feb/15/trevor-hoffman-padres-upper-level-pitching-spring/, accessed January 2, 2016.

Olney, Buster. "Trevor Hoffman's dive into history," *espn.go.com*, September 8, 2010, http://espn.go.com/blog/buster-olney/insider/post?id=1227, accessed December 29, 2015.

# NOTES

1    Associated Press, "Hoffman helps kids with kidney problems," June 20, 2005.

2    Chris Foster, "His Father Was a Save Artist Too," *Los Angeles Times*, July 14, 1996.

3    C. T. Rosecrans, "Longtime Reds Scout, Cross-Checker Jeff Barton Dead at 50," *Cincinnati Enquirer*, November 13, 2015. https://www.cincinnati.com/story/sports/mlb/reds/2015/11/13/longtime-reds-scout-jeff-barton-dead-50/75701346/

4    "Marlins Surprise Hoffman," *Sarasota Herald-Tribune*, November 18, 1992: 5C.

5    Tom Cushman, "Deep in the Heart Hoffman," *San Diego Magazine*, November 11, 2006.

6    S.L. Price, "Reliever Hoffman has batters feeling the heat," *The News* (Boca Raton, Florida), April 16, 1993: 3B.

7    *Pepsi Max Field of Dreams Game Program*, Cooperstown, New York: Pepsi Corporation, 2013, Print.

8    Associated Press, "Padres' Hoffman to have Shoulder Surgery," *Miami Herald* online edition, http://www.miami.com/mld/miamiherald/sports/baseball/5259774, February 25, 2003, accessed December 29, 2015.

9    Buster Olney, "Change Artist," *ESPN the Magazine*, September 11, 2006.

10    Bill Center, "One Pitch Wound Up Changing Baseball History," *San Diego Union-Tribune,* http://www.sandiegouniontribune.com/uniontrib/20060926/news_lz1x26pitch.html, September 26, 2006, accessed February 16, 2016.

11    "Alou ends Hoffman's save streak at 41," *USA Today,* July 27, 1998, Print.

12    Bill Center, "No. 321 is Vintage Hoffman," *The San Diego Union-Tribune*, May 2, 2002, http://www.uniontrib.com/sports/padres/20020502-9999_1s2padres.html, accessed December 29, 2015.

13    Tom Krasovic, "Hoffman takes San Diego discount to remain a Padre," *SignOnSanDiego.com*, November 5, 2003, http://legacy.utsandiego.com/sports/padres/20031105-1703-trevorsigns.html , accessed December 30, 2015.

14    Chuck Crow, "All-time saves leader was almost an Indian," *The Plain Dealer,* September 12, 2010.

15    Jayson Stark, "Arizona not the apple of Vasquez's eye," *espn.go.com*, May 27, 2005, http://proxy.espn.go.com/espn/print?id=2068831&type=story, accessed December 30, 2015.

16    Associated Press, "Padres' Hoffman secures place in history with 500th save," *espn.go.com*, June 7, 2007, http://espn.go.com/mlb/recap?gameId=270606125, accessed December 30, 2015.

17    Bill Center, "No relief for Hoffman: 'It still hurts,'" *UTSanDiego.com*, January 25, 2008, http://legacy.utsandiego.com/uniontrib/20080125/news_1s25hoffman.html, accessed December 30, 2015.

18    "Sources: Hoffman, Brewers have deal," *espn.go.com*, January 8, 2009, http://espn.go.com/espn/print?id=3818472, accessed December 30, 2015.

19    Tim Sullivan, "Club and closer still need each other, but can they mend the fences?", *UTSanDiego.com,* December 11, 2008, http://www.sandiegouniontribune.com/news/2008/dec/11/1s11sullivan215146-club-closer-still-need-each-oth/, accessed February 16, 2016.

20    Jack Curry, "Hoffman Savoring Fresh Start With Brewers," *NYTimes.com,* May 28, 2009, http://www.nytimes.com/2009/05/29/sports/baseball/29hoffman.html, accessed February 16, 2016

21    Buster Olney, "Hoffman to re-sign with Brewers," *espn.go.com,* October 5, 2009, http://espn.go.com/espn/print?id=4533333, Accessed December 30, 2015.

22    Tom Haudricourt, "Hoffman hits 600 save mark as Brewers win," *Milwaukee Journal Sentinel,* September 8, 2010.

23    Adam McCalvy, "Call the Hall: Hoffman gets 600th save," *MLB.com*, September 8, 2010, http://m.mlb.com/news/article/14424616/, accessed December 29, 2015.

24    Associated Press, "Trevor Hoffman's option declined," *espn.go.com*, November 2, 2010, http://espn.go.com/espn/print?id=5757290, accessed January 2, 2016.

25    Bill Center, "Hoffman retires, will wear 'different hats' for the Padres," *SignOnSanDiego.com*, January 11, 2011, http://www.sandiegouniontribune.com/news/2011/jan/11/hoffman-retires-will-join-padres-front-office/, accessed January 2, 2016.

26    Matt Snyder, "Trevor Hoffman takes position with Padres' front office," *CBSSports.com*, September 12, 2013, http://www.cbssports.com/mlb/eye-on-baseball/23613251/trevor-hoffman-takes-position-with-padres-front-office, accessed January 2, 2016.

27    Tim Sullivan, "Grand gesture is prime Trevor Time for good reason," *SignOnSanDiego.com*, August 21, 2011, http://www.sandiegouniontribune.com/news/2011/aug/21/grand-gesture-prime-trevor-time-good-reason/, accessed January 2, 2016.

28    Dennis Lin, "Hoffman inducted into Padres Hall of Fame," *UTSanDiego.com*, August 30, 2014, http://www.sandiegouniontribune.com/news/2014/aug/30/trevor-hoffman-inducted-padres-hall-of-fame-petco/, accessed January 2, 2016.

29    "Padres appoint Trevor Hoffman as Upper Level Pitching Coordinator," MLB.com, September 12, 2013.

30    Dennis Lin, "Trevor Hoffman's new title," *San Diego Union-Tribune*, February 22, 2015.

31    A. J. Cassavel, "Hall's Bells: Cooperstown Rings for Hofmann," MLB.com, January 24, 2018. https://www.mlb.com/news/trevor-hoffman-elected-to-hall-of-fame/c-265259268.

# RANDY JONES

## BY ALAN COHEN

*"It happens every time. They cheer him even before he throws a ball. It's the way he comes across. He's a humble person, the underdog making good. People can relate to him. He's not that big in stature (6 feet, 180 pounds) and he is not overpowering on the mound. Randy's the common man's pitcher."*

– John McNamara, 1976[1]

*"If I was a pitcher, I'd be embarrassed to go out to the mound with that kind of stuff."*

– Mike Schmidt, 1976.[2]

*Not overpowering is putting it mildly. His assortment of junk was frustrating to the best of the hitters in the National League. Switch-hitting Pete Rose after, at one point, going 4-for-29 against Jones, decided to try his luck left-handed. After a frustrating effort on June 30, 1976 where Rose went 0-for-3 with a walk, Rose said "Left-handed, right-handed, cross-handed, he still gets you out."[3]*

*"I'd lose something in the fifth or sixth inning of a lot of those games," he remembers. "It was a tough year. I lost a lot of confidence by the second half of the season. People said it takes a good pitcher to lose 20 games, but I never bought that."*

– Randy Jones, reflecting on his 1974 season.[4]

Randall Leo Jones was born on January 12, 1950, in Fullerton, California. His father, Jim, was a plant superintendent for a large agricultural company. Randy graduated from Brea-Olinda High School and attended Chapman University in Orange, California. In his senior year of high school, he went 8-2 with a 0.91 ERA and 110 strikeouts. He was named to the Irvine League All-Star team, and was the starting pitcher in the Orange County Prep All-Star game. At Chapman, during this first two varsity seasons, he played for coach Paul Deese. In his freshman year, his fastball was impressive. But on a pitch to the plate that season, he stumbled off the mound and pulled some tendons. Thereafter, he got by on junk. In 1970 Chapman was rated number 1 in the NCAA's College Division. After an impressive win against USC in his sophomore year, he said, "I was confident. I challenged their hitters. I threw my fastball and slider over the plate, daring them to hit the ball. They didn't."[5] Jones went 11-4 as a sophomore with a 1.75 ERA, and was named second team All-American.

Jones married his high-school sweetheart, Marie Stassi, on October 10, 1970. They had two children, Staci, born in January 1975, and Jami.

After his sophomore and junior years, Jones played summer ball for the Glacier-Pilots of Anchorage in the Alaska Baseball League. The team, managed by Paul Deese, participated in the National Baseball Congress tournament in Wichita, Kansas, in 1970. Jones pitched a complete game in the semifinals to advance his team to the finals.[6] After the 1971 season in Alaska, the Glacier-Pilots returned to Wichita and, in the final game, Jones pitched the team to a 5-4 win over the Fairbanks Goldpanners. The game wasn't decided until the bottom of the ninth inning when Anchorage tallied the winning run off Fairbanks pitcher Dave Winfield.[7] It capped off a season during which Jones went 14-1 with three wins in the National Baseball Congress tourney.[8] Deese and Jones remained lifelong friends and eventually Deese, a successful businessman, counseled Jones on his post-baseball business ventures.

By Jones's senior year, with the zip out of his fastball, and most of the scouts looking the other way, he was effective nonetheless. Under coach Bob Pomeroy, Jones went 11-4 with a 1.42 ERA during the regular season. In the NCAA District Eight Tournament he shut out Cal State on a three-hitter, prompting opposing coach Al Matthews to say, "He wasted his fastball and made us hit his breaking pitches."[9]

Although his fastball was nonexistent by the end of his four years at Chapman, Jones emerged with a degree in business, planning to go into real estate if he couldn't continue in baseball. However, one scout did keep his eye on the young Jones. Both Marty Keough and Cliff Ditto of the Padres noticed that

he could be a success. Keough said, "He threw strikes. He got a quick breaking ball and he got people out."[10] He was drafted in the fifth round by the San Diego Padres in 1972, and signed for a bonus estimated at $3,000.

Jones began his pro career in 1972 with the Tri-City Padres in the Northwest League. It was a short stay; he pitched in only one game before being promoted to Alexandria, Louisiana, in the Texas League. He went 3-5 with a 2.91 ERA and returned to Alexandria the next season. After going 8-1 in 10 starts with the Aces to start the 1973 season, Jones was called up to the Padres in June, never to return to the minor leagues. The key to his success that season was a sinkerball he learned from Padres minor-league pitching instructor Warren Hacker.[11] Hacker "showed me how to place my fingers differently and how to apply pressure with them," Jones said.[12] The lefty went 7-6 with a 3.16 ERA in 20 games for San Diego that year.

The next year, 1974, Jones was 8-22 (with a 4.45 ERA) in 40 games, and he led the National League in losses. It was a tough season. As the losses mounted, Jones said, "With any luck, my record could be 14-9 instead of 7-16. When you get people to hit the ball on the ground and the ball consistently finds a hole, it isn't bad luck – it's no luck at all."[13] Seventeen of his losses were by two runs or less. As the season wore on and the losses mounted, he was dispatched to the bullpen in September and four of his last five appearances were in relief, including a two-inning save against the San Francisco Giants on September 24. However, in his final appearance of the season, two days later against the Los Angeles Dodgers, he faltered and was charged with four runs in 2⅔ innings as Los Angeles won, 5-2, in 10 innings. It was Jones's 22nd loss and the 100th loss for the Padres, who finished last in the NL West.

After working with pitching coach Tom Morgan, Jones altered his mechanics and found success in 1975. He said Morgan "made some fundamental changes in my delivery; now my body is doing all the work, my arm isn't getting tired. I feel like I could pitch forever. It's incredible."[14] And some days, he seemingly had to pitch forever, since the team still wasn't giving him much in the way of run support.

On May 19 Jones outdueled John Curtis of the St. Louis Cardinals, pitching a 10-inning one-hitter that ended when the Padres' Johnny Grubb hit a homer in the bottom of the 10th. The next high point of the season came on July 3 against Cincinnati. He took a perfect game into the eighth inning when Tony Perez reached second on an error by shortstop Hector Torres. Showing the wisdom of former Dodger pitcher Billy Loes, Jones said that "he lost it in the stadium lights. That was obvious to me."[15] Two batters later, Bill Plummer broke up the no-hitter and shutout with a double that scored Perez, knotting the game at 1-1. Jones was prepared to pitch into the night. "I had made up my mind that they would have to drag me out of there. If [manager John] McNamara wanted to remove me, he would have had to tie me up."[16]

Although Jones could eat up the innings, he did not eat up the clock. He dispensed with the Pirates using only 68 pitches in a May 24 shutout, and defeated the Astros 6-1 in 1:37 on August 6. He won 20 games that year, led the NL with a 2.24 ERA, and was selected for his first All-Star Game, where he picked up a save. He finished second to Tom Seaver in the Cy Young Award balloting and was named the National League Comeback Player of the Year.

Jones's success continued into 1976. For his performance in 1975, San Diego owner Ray Kroc increased his pay from $24,500 to $65,000. Jones went 16-3 in the season's first half (an All-Star break win total that no one as of 2017 has equaled). His celebrity status was such that the Padres attendance figures more than doubled when he pitched. After the great start, there was speculation that he could be the next 30-game winner, but he took everything in stride. "There's no sense thinking about number 30 until you've won 29," he said. "A good start isn't necessarily an indication of what's going to happen for the whole season. I've had success taking games one at a time and omitting everything else from my mind. Guys get in trouble when their minds get astray and they start thinking way ahead."[17]

Despite his great performance in 1975, Jones did not get national hype until the night of June 9 when the Mets were in San Diego with their Cy Young ace Seaver, and 42,972 fans came to see their hero Jones. His achievements were well known to the home folks, who turned out in droves to see Randy. The game was scoreless for four innings before the Padres scored single runs in the fifth, sixth, and eighth innings to win, 3-0. Jones's record went to 11-2, as he scattered seven hits, struck out four, walked none, and sent the folks home in 2:10.

In one stretch, from May 17 to June 22, Jones tied a 63-year-old National League record by going 68 consecutive innings without issuing a walk. During that stretch, he faced 265 batters. The record had been set by Christy Mathewson of the New York Giants in 1913. On June 22, after striking out San Francisco's Darrell Evans to tie the record, he had received a standing ovation from the crowd of 29,940. The ovation continued as Jones came to bat in the seventh inning with the score tied 2-2. He singled and, with one out, came home on Tito Fuentes' two-run homer. Jones's streak ended when he walked Giants catcher Marc Hill leading off the eighth inning. The count went to 3-and-2 and Hill fouled off two pitches before taking a sinker for ball four. "Before I let it go, I knew it was going to be a ball," Jones said. "My arm was too far behind my body. I was pushing, I was too

*Jones chats with fans outside of Petco Park.*

anxious."[18] There was no further scoring, and the 4-2 victory extended Jones's record for the season to 13-3. The win put the Padres into second place, a half-game ahead of the Dodgers, and kept San Diego within five games of the league-leading Reds.

For the second consecutive year, Jones pitched in the All-Star Game. He started, and his appearance was vintage Jones. In his three innings, seven of the outs were on groundballs. There was one foul popup and one strikeout. Jones was the winning pitcher when the NL won the game, 7-1. After the All-Star Game, his numbers trailed off a bit. He also came very close to tragedy. On the evening of August 4, the Padres returned home from Atlanta after a game in which Jones lost 1-0, putting his record at 18-6. Driving home from the airport, possibly at a speed faster than that of his fastball, Jones failed to negotiate a curve near his home and, as his wife said, "The telephone pole was sitting in the front seat."[19] A passing driver took Jones to the hospital. His only injuries were cuts to his face and neck. Lucky to be alive and with more than 30 stitches, Jones was back on the mound on August 10 at New York's Shea Stadium, losing a 5-4 decision to Jerry Koosman. In all, he was 4-8 after the accident, largely due to lack of support. In his last six losses of 1976, the Padres scored three runs or less, and they were shut out twice. Nevertheless, Jones finished the season with a 22-14 record, and a 2.74 ERA. Never known for the speed of his pitches, he struck out just 93 despite leading the league with 315⅓ innings pitched.

Jones started 40 games that season and had 25 complete games, both league highs. And he worked in a hurry. His games on average lasted little more than two hours. On August 27, when he shut out the Expos 2-0, he sent the folks home in 1:38. On

September 19, in the first game of a doubleheader at Houston, Jones completed the game (a 3-2 loss) in 1:42. His quickest outing was on July 20, when he shut out Philadelphia 3-0 in 1:31. And his sinker was working to perfection. As pitching coach Roger Craig said, "It isn't so much as how much it sinks as when it sinks. It sinks late. It looks good on top of the plate and then sinks under the bat after the batter's committed himself."[20]

In 2016, reflecting on that 1976 season and the crowds that came to cheer him on, he said, "I had never seen anything like it; I don't know that anybody in San Diego had. Our ballclubs in those days weren't very good. (They had never had a winning season before 1976.) We had talent, but we didn't have consistency. But the boys really seemed to step up on the days I pitched, and the fans really got behind me."[21]

He also commented, "Everybody is mystified that I could complete 25 games. You have to remember that I completed 25 games and I didn't average 100 pitches in those games. I'd throw 89, 88, 92 pitches in a nine-inning game. That was philosophically how I approached the game. I went out in the first inning and I wanted to throw three pitches. I definitely tried to get the third one on the first pitch."[22]

But 1976 was Jones's last year as an elite pitcher. In his last start, he felt a tear in his forearm. He had severed the nerve attached to his biceps tendon. Jones had surgery after the 1976 campaign to repair a nerve injury, but never again had a season above .500. "It was years of futility and frustration," he recalled in 1998.[23]

Jones won just six games in 1977 but they included a vintage performance against the Phillies on May 4 in San Diego, his only complete game of the season. He pitched against Jim Kaat and won 4-1 in a mind-boggling 1:29 to bring his record at the time to 2-4. Of the 27 Phillies outs, 19 came on groundballs. Not everyone was happy about the swiftness of the game. Ted Giannoulas (a/k/a The San Diego Chicken) said, "That game took money out of my pocket because as an hourly wage worker back then making $4 an hour, I could only put down an hour and a half on my time card. So I made $6 on that game, then they took out taxes. For the rest of the year, I would swear the names Randy Jones and Jim Kaat under my breath."[24] But after that single major success, Jones's ERA still stood at 4.85. His record for the season wound up at 6-12 with an ERA of 4.58.

Jones began the 1978 season slowly. After winning his first decision against Atlanta, on April 20, he was ineffective in his next two starts, finishing April at 1-2. He recorded his first shutout of the season on May 10, defeating Chicago 1-0. In a season marked by inconsistency, Jones lost four games in June but came back to win three games in July. His second shutout of the season, a 1-0 win over the Dodgers on August 1, put his record at 9-9. The Padres had a disappointing season. They fell out of contention early and, despite a winning record of 84-78, finished in fourth place, 11 games behind the division champion Dodgers. Jones bounced back from a terrible 1977 to record two shutouts and seven complete games, His season's record was 13-14 with a 2.88 ERA.

Hopes were high in the spring of 1979. Manager Roger Craig said, "He's got his confidence back. I think he'll have a big year. Randy will win three or four more games because Fred Kendall is catching him again. He trusts Kendall and that's important because he never shakes off a pitch. Randy is the only good pitcher I've ever seen who doesn't shake off his catcher's signs."[25] Pitchers are notorious for bragging about their hitting, but on May 13, 1979, Jones had a stolen base that was the first theft by a pitcher in the then 11-year history of the San Diego franchise. It came at home in the third inning against Mike Scott of the Mets. He had reached on an error by Scott and manager Craig, with Gene Richards at the plate, put on the hit-and-run play. Richards swung and missed and Jones got into second ahead of the throw from Mets catcher John Stearns.[26] It was his only career stolen base. He tired in the eighth inning and did not factor in the decision as the Padres won in extra innings. Jones's 1979 season pretty much mirrored 1978, as he went 11-12, but his ERA rose to 3.63. There were no shutouts, but he did complete six games, as the Padres dropped to 68-93 and finished in fifth place in the NL West.

In the spring of 1980, things were looking up for Jones. He was 4-2 and coming off three consecutive complete-game shutouts when he faced the Pirates on May 21 in the first game of a doubleheader. He took a 3-0 lead into the bottom of the fourth inning but then the troubles started again. During the inning he felt a pain in the right side of his ribcage. "I tried to compensate by throwing with my arm instead of my body, and strained the nerve in the arm again," Jones said. "My fingers went numb. Damn, it was frustrating."[27] He remained in the game until the bottom of the sixth inning, and was not involved in the decision. Pitching in pain for the balance of the season, Jones won only one of his last 12 decisions and had a 5.32 ERA during that stretch. For the season, he was 5-13 with a 3.91 ERA.

After the 1980 season, Jones was dealt to the New York Mets for a pair of prospects, Jose Moreno and John Pacella. He won eight games over two seasons with the Mets before retiring. The 1981 season was a disaster. He lost his first five decisions, but it was a team effort: Of the 36 runs he allowed in his first eight starts, only 20 were earned. The Mets were challenged when it came to fielding groundballs. Jones's only win came on May 31 against the Cubs. He allowed one run in 6⅓ innings of his 6-1 victory. For the strike-shortened season, Jones was 1-8 with a 4.85 ERA.

Jones's first appearance of 1982 indicated that things would be different from 1981. During the offseason, he had done a great deal of running and he came to spring training in great shape. New Mets manager George Bamberger gave Jones the ball on Opening Day and he beat the Phillies and Steve Carlton, 7-2 at Veterans Stadium. Jones pitched the first six innings, scattering four hits and allowing only one run. The over-anxious Phillies were swinging at bad pitches and three of the outs were on easy comebackers. After the win, he said, "I had good concentration and, believe it or not, I warmed up on the mound (in chilly 41-degree weather). My sinker began to come around in the second inning and I got a lot of important outs with it. I had excellent concentration. My mental approach today was perfect."[28] One week later, at Shea Stadium, Jones triumphed again over the Phillies, 5-2, in the Mets' home opener.

Things were looking up for Jones and for the Mets, who were coming off five straight losing seasons. The signs outside had said, "The Magic is Back" since 1980. But was it? Jones got off to a great start, winning six of his first eight decisions. On May 10 he hurled his first complete game since 1979, beating the Padres 3-2 and reducing his ERA to 2.60. On May 18, against Cincinnati at Shea Stadium, he got his fifth win though he was charged with four runs in seven-plus innings. After his sixth win, a four-hit shutout at Houston on May 23, the Mets were in second place with a 23-18 record, 1½ games behind the National League East-leading Cardinals.

But Jones was only 2-2 at home, and Shea Stadium had been a nemesis to him over the years. It all began in 1973 when, in his major-league debut on June 16, he entered the game in relief and yielded his first major-league hit, a home run by an aging Willie Mays, and continued through his time with the Mets. In 1982 he won at home only once after May 23, and his record sank from 6-2 on May 23 to 7-10 at the end of the season. His ERA rose from a low of 2.60 on May 10 to a disturbingly high 4.60 at the end of the season. On the road in 1982 he was 4-2 with a 2.37 ERA, but he was 3-8 at home with a 7.47 ERA. As Jones's fortunes got worse, so did those of the Mets. After the good start, they finished the season in sixth place in the NL East with a 65-97 record. The Mets had several young guns coming up through the minors and Jones, hoping to catch on with another club, was released, on his own request, after the season.[29] He was philosophical when he said, "A manager can't use a pitcher who can't win at home and I understood when Bamberger took me out of the rotation."[30]

When 1983 rolled around, Jones went to spring training with the Pirates as a nonroster invitee. He was released on March 27.

For his career, Jones was 100-123 with an ERA of 3.42. He had 73 complete games, of which 19 were shutouts.

After his playing days were over, Jones returned to San Diego, where he became a fixture. His residence in Poway is about 25 miles north of San Diego. He tended to the string of car washes he had opened during his days with the Padres. His other business pursuits revolved around food; he started in his sister's catering business, became a food broker, and eventually opened his own barbecue stand at the ballpark. He also did pregame and postgame shows.[31] In his time as a food broker for AGS Foods, he traveled to military food services operations, mixing business with pleasure. In addition to making sales calls, he conducted baseball clinics for children of military personnel.[32]

Jones's number was 35 retired by the Padres in 1997, and two years later he was a member of the first group inducted into the Padres Hall of Fame. He remained, as of the end of the 2016 season, the Padres' leader in starts, complete games, shutouts, and innings pitched.

Jones also worked with young pitchers. He had put an ad in the local newspaper offering to give pitching lessons to youngsters, and had 35 students. In 1990, a 12-year-old saw the ad and his folks gave Jones a call. "I remember vividly the four, five years we spent in the backyard with Randy," said 2002 Cy Young Award winner Barry Zito. "When I did something incorrectly, he'd spit tobacco juice on my shoes, Nike high tops we could barely afford, he's spitting tobacco juice on them." In his teaching, it was Jones's goal that his best students "that showed a burning desire" would be shown his Cy Young trophy. What Zito learned from Jones was "the mental side, never giving in."[33]

Jones also worked with the Padres Volunteer Team, which was launched in February 2015 to help nonprofits, including the USO, for which in September 2015 the group put together 300 "we care" packages for US military families.[34]

He threw out the ceremonial first pitch at the 2016 All-Star Game in San Diego. In November 2016, years of tobacco use caught up with Jones and he was diagnosed with throat cancer. He started treatments at Sharp Hospital the following month, and completed his treatment on February 1, 2017. To thunderous applause, he threw out the first pitch on Opening Day 2017 in San Diego. When he was tested on May 1, he was hoping to be given a clean bill of health.[35] The following day, the call came from his doctor: he was cancer-free. "To say I'm cancer-free today will give somebody else a little hope," he commented. "If they have any hopes, don't doubt it. You've got to put the work in, but the process works."[36]

## SOURCES

In addition to the sources cited in the Notes, the author used Baseball-Reference.com, the Randy Jones player file at the National Baseball Hall of Fame Library, and the following:

Broderick, Pat. "Former Padre Still Pitching ... Food This Time," *San Diego Business Journal*, September 22, 1997: 8.

Denman, Elliott. "Jones Returns to Top of Heap," *Asbury Park* (New Jersey) *Press*, May 23, 1982: B3.

Shaw, Bud. "You've Got to Believe in Jones Now," *Philadelphia Daily News*, April 9, 1982: 93.

## NOTES

1    Ron Fimrite, "Uncommon Success for a Common Man," *Sports Illustrated*, July 12, 1976.

2    Dave Distell, "Fans Flocking to See Randy Jones," *Los Angeles Times*, June 24, 1976.

3    Ibid.

4    Al Doyle, "Former Cy Young Award Winner, Randy Jones," *Baseball Digest*, August 2001: 64.

5    Al Carr, "Randy Jones – The 'Vow Boy' of Chapman's Baseball Varsity," *Los Angeles Times*, May 7, 1970: III-14.

6    Merrill Cox, "Anchorage, Peck Here, Peck There, Colorado Tumbles," *Wichita* (Kansas) *Eagle*, August 30, 1970: 6F.

7    Bob Stewart, "Pilots Win Alaskan '71 Rush for NBC Gold," *Wichita* (Kansas) *Eagle*, September 1, 1971: 17.

8    Andy Williams, "City Pays Tribute to National Champions," *Anchorage Daily News*, October 11, 1971: 9.

9    "CHCS Down to Last Strike," *Hayward* (California) *Daily Review*, May 26, 1972: 27.

10    Dave Anderson, "Randy Jones Wins Without Fastball," *New York Times*, June 10, 1976: 49.

11    Jack Murphy, "The Best of Seasons for Randy and Marie," *San Diego Union*, July 6, 1975: H-1.

12    "Randy Jones Wins Without Fastball."

13    Phil Collier, "Pittsburgh Surges by Pirates, 7-3," *San Diego Union*, August 10, 1974: C-1.

14    Murphy, "The Best of Seasons for Randy and Marie."

15    Ibid.

16    Ibid.

17    Distell.

18    Phil Collier, "Jones Notches 13th, Ties N.L.'s No-Walk Record," *San Diego Union*, June 23, 1976: C-1.

19    Jack Murphy, "Randy in Stitches; the Padres Aren't Laughing," *San Diego Union*, August 6, 1976: C-1.

20    Jack Flowers, "Randy Jones: Shades of Denny McClain, Dizzy Dean," *Pensacola* (Florida) *News Journal*, June 24, 1976: 1-C.

21    Jeff Sanders, "'Crafty Left-Hander Had It All Working – Randy Jones Wins 1976 National League Cy Young Award," *San Diego Union-Tribune*, March 13, 2016: S-7.

22    Kirk Kenney, "Rush Hour (and a Half) – Forty Years Ago Today Padres Beat Phillies in a Mere 89 Minutes – Unthinkable Today," *San Diego Union-Tribune*, May 4, 2017: S-1.

23    Paul Gutierrez, "Catching Up With Randy Jones," *Sports Illustrated*, August 3, 1998.

24    Kenney.

25    Murphy, "Glory Was Sweet; Randy Craves Encore," *San Diego Union*, March 11, 1979: H-1

26    United Press International, "Jones's Stolen Base First by Padre Pitcher," *Lexington* (Kentucky) *Herald*, May 14, 1979: B-4.

27    Dick Young, "Ready to Play Some Hardball," *New York Daily News*, February 6, 1981.

28    Hal Bodley, "Phillies Can't Keep Up With Mets' Jones," *Wilmington* (Delaware) *Morning News*, April 9, 1982: C-1.

29    Russ Franke, "Jones Makes a Pitch for More Major Fun," *Pittsburgh Press*, February 23, 1983: D2.

30    Charley Feeney, "When Randy Jones Was a Met, Shea Was Just No Place Like Home," *Pittsburgh Post-Gazette*, February 21, 1982: 10.

31    Gutierrez.

32    Doyle.

33    "Former Cy Young Pitcher Helped Develop Zito Into Award Winner," *Hamilton* (Ontario) *Spectator*, November 8, 2002: E05.

34    Stephanie R. Glidden. "Volunteers Pitch in to Help Get Care Packages to Our Military," *San Diego Business Journal*, September 28, 2015: 41.

35    Dennis Lin, "Randy Jones Visits Padres Camp; Hopes to Be Declared Cancer-Free," *San Diego Union-Tribune*, March 23, 2017.

36    Jeff Sanders, "Padres Report – An Emotional Jones Says Cancer Is Gone," *San Diego Union-Tribune*, May 3, 2017: S-5.

# TERRY KENNEDY

## BY DAVID E. SKELTON

"As the son of former major league player, manager and [front-office executive Bob Kennedy]…Terry grew up among baseball… and had the privilege of learning about hitting from the likes of Stan Musial and Ted Williams."[1] This privileged education undoubtedly contributed to Terry Kennedy's selection as the youngest player on the 1976 College All-America baseball team. He topped that honor a year later by being named collegiate Player of the Year. In a 14-year major-league career, he earned a Silver Slugger Award, four All-Star berths and two seasons

of Most Valuable Player consideration. A fierce competitor, self-described as "high-strung,"[2] his leadership skills led two clubs to World Series play and enabled a minor-league managerial career, which extended into the twenty-first century and included Manager of the Year honors.

Born on June 4, 1956, Terrence Edward Kennedy, the youngest of five children born to Bob and Claire Kennedy, followed his father and brother (Robert, Jr.) into baseball's professional ranks. Characterizing himself as merely a fair prep player, he experienced a seven-inch growth spurt between his junior and senior years, eventually filling out a strapping, 6-foot-3, 220-pound frame. Riding a partial athletic scholarship garnered by his father's close relationship with Florida State's coach, Woody Woodward, Terry blossomed as a Seminole. "Woody was the right guy for me at that time. He let me play a lot my freshman year." En route to Tallahassee before his first semester at FSU, Terry's mother, Claire, made a slight detour into Pensacola and proudly pointed out the former location of the airfield where Terry's father had taught Ted Williams to fly fighter jets, before the Korean War.[3]

Selected to consecutive College All-American teams, Terry earned a 1982 induction into FSU's Sports Hall of Fame, but he attracted professional scouts long before then: "[B]ats left-handed with power to all fields, and a throwing arm equal to that of Jim Sundberg…the best throwing catcher in the major leagues."[4] He entered the 1977 amateur draft and found baseball bloodlines that matched his own, including members of the Francona, Kuenn, Bando, and Blyleven families. The Seminole catcher attracted vast interest, including both sides of Chicago (the interest on the north side coming from none other than Cubs vice president Bob Kennedy). "I asked my father if he would take me in the draft and he told me he would if I was still there. I told him I would go back for my senior year if he did. I saw how hard it was for my brother when he was playing under my dad in the Cardinals system, players always wondering if it was just a favor to his kid. My dad told me he would trade me after he signed me, and I said, 'Sure you will!'" But Terry was already off the board when the Cubs made their choice, having been selected with the sixth overall pick by the very organization where his brother had toiled – the St. Louis Cardinals (it was a curious choice for a team seemingly secure behind the plate with perennial All-Star Ted Simmons). Aggressively pursued by scout Chase Riddle – who soon after began a long tenure as head baseball coach of Troy University – Kennedy reportedly signed a $100,000 bonus (he states it was only half that amount), of which $5,000 was promptly donated to FSU for stadium improvements.

Terry made an immediate impression in July, going 4-for-6 in a doubleheader debut in Johnson City (Appalachian [rookie] League). A .590 clip in 39 at-bats resulted in a speedy promotion to St. Petersburg, Florida (Class A). His rapid ascent further accelerated when he led the Cardinals entry to a 31-17 record and the Florida Instructional League championship. It was during this winter campaign that Kennedy began experimenting with switch-hitting, an on-again, off-again endeavor he abandoned in the 1980s.

His offensive onslaught continued in the Texas League the following spring, resulting in still another debut on June 30, 1978, with the Springfield Redbirds in the American Association (Class AAA). Again he was impressive with two hits, including a solo home run. An ensuing 13-for-30, 15-RBI surge resulted in a combined batting line of .309-20-100, which earned Terry a September call-up. Making his major-league debut in the eighth inning of a September 4 blowout loss to the Philadelphia Phillies (and pinch-hitting for Simmons), he grounded to second base and then moved behind the plate in the final frame. Nine additional appearances followed, all in a starting role. He captured his first base hit on September 15 before a Wrigley Field crowd that included his father; it was a run-scoring single to left field off Cubs right-hander Mike Krukow. In each of Terry's starting assignments, Simmons played left field, generating speculation over the next two years that this move would become permanent when Hall of Famer Lou Brock retired.

Even if discussions of this move were serious – they were dismissed by manager Ken Boyer and balked at by Simmons – it was not going to occur anytime soon. Entering the 1979 campaign 100 hits shy of 3,000, Brock was not ready to relinquish his left-field post, thereby leaving Simmons behind the plate (in fact, by the time the Cardinals sought to fill the vacant left-field post in the spring of 1981, both Simmons and Kennedy were wearing other uniforms). Seeking full-time play for Kennedy, the Cardinals returned their young backstop to Springfield. Upset over the demotion – he'd hit at a .300 pace in the Grapefruit League and seemingly had little more to learn at the lower level – Terry ultimately accepted the change with a little help from his consoling, encouraging father.

If Terry's 1978 work in Florida represented "Exhibit A" in a case for his readiness, his early 1979 performance was "Exhibit B." On April 21, he drove in five runs with a homer and double in a 6-0 win over Iowa. A three-run homer against Denver on May 6 gave him 24 RBIs in 19 games. He rang up another five-RBI performance on May 19, in a 12-3 lashing of Wichita. "[Terry] is the finest ballplayer I've seen in my three years in the league," noted Indianapolis manager Roy Majtyka. "He is the most complete player."[5] Although his numbers and accolades made a strong argument for promotion, another development made it happen.

On June 24, 1979, Simmons broke his wrist and was sidelined for a month. Promptly recalled from Springfield, Kennedy received playing time in 23 of the next 28 Cardinal games (including 18 starting assignments). Hitless in his first seven at-bats, he went on a .364 tear (16-for-44) that included his first major-league home run, struck in grand style. On July 1, in the eighth inning of a tie game against the Philadelphia Phillies, Terry came to the plate with the bases loaded against reliever Tug McGraw and promptly put the game out of reach. Dismayed by yet another trip to the minors after Simmons recovered, Kennedy was back in St. Louis by September and produced a .400 clip in his final 20 at-bats.

His performance at the major-league level, albeit part time, drew considerable attention; no less than eight clubs were rumored to have approached the Cardinals that winter about a trade (including Bob Kennedy's Cubs). His perceived value was evidenced by the quality of trade bait dangled before St. Louis, including Atlanta Braves slugger Gary Matthews and Baltimore Orioles lefty Scott McGregor, a starter on a team that won a World Series berth in 1979. But spring arrived without any trades completed; Terry had to resign himself to a full campaign behind Simmons.

On June 20, 1980, Kennedy single-handedly dismantled the Cincinnati Reds by driving in six runs (two three-run homers, one off Hall of Famer Tom Seaver) in a 7-5 win. That game was one of the few season highlights for both player and team. The two home runs represented half of Terry's season output in a mere 64 starting assignments, nearly half of them in left field – small yield for a youngster who, according to a Houston Astros scout, "may be the 'best catcher of the decade' before he's finished."[6] The Cardinals posted their third-worst record in a quarter century as they combed through four managers (a modern record, matched by three teams). From December 8-12 they undertook a complete housecleaning, engaging in three trades that affected 22 players – including Kennedy, who shipped out to the San Diego Padres.

There were reports that Padres general manager Jack McKeon, busy with his own house-cleaning efforts, had been given his choice between Kennedy and Simmons (who was traded to Milwaukee on December 12). "I can't say enough about the new young catcher," McKeon chirped. "He'll give us stability behind the plate."[7] Weighing in on the same subject, manager Frank Howard inveighed that Terry will "be worth his weight in gold."[8] Provided an opportunity as a regular starter, Kennedy responded with his first All Star campaign. A 13-game hitting streak (a .346 pace in 52 at-bats) was interrupted days later by the 1981 strike, but Kennedy returned just as strong after the two-month delay. Another surge in September – including seven consecutive base hits before his father's watchful eyes – resulted in his becoming the only major-league catcher with more than 320 at-bats to achieve a .300 average.

Impressive as this All Star season was, one component was conspicuously missing from Kennedy's arsenal: power, a sorely-needed commodity for the Padres, who were last in the majors with 32 home runs. Kennedy had hit a mere two home runs, a matter that new manager Dick Williams set out to rectify for the 1982 campaign. "Dick took a lot of pressure off me," Kennedy said. "I knew I could swing hard and not have to worry about [my batting average] ... I switched to a lighter bat, so I could pull the ball."[9] Terry's average hardly suffered as he hit 21 homers (his career high), trailing only Hall of Famer Gary Carter among the league's catchers. He fell three short of becoming the first catcher to lead either league in doubles, while tying the NL record of 40 set by Johnny Bench in 1968 (he struck two more two-baggers as a first baseman). Terry's 15 game-winning hits helped the Padres to their second non-losing campaign since the franchise's inception in 1969; his .295-21-97 batting line earned ballot consideration for Most Valuable Player (the first of two in consecutive seasons).

"[Kennedy] is capable of hitting 30 home runs this season," opined Williams before the 1983 season.[10] This lofty projection, combined with a .390 average and a league-leading 21 RBIs, earned the 27-year-old Kennedy April Player of the Month honors. But there was more hype than that. Some boldly forecast Terry as the NL's first Triple Crown winner since Joe Medwick, in 1937. Falling far short of these soaring heights, he still made his mark by becoming the first Padre in franchise history to hit a homer in four consecutive games and, for the second straight year, led the team in home runs and RBIs. He slugged a dramatic game-winning home run against the Houston Astros on September 7, to cap a come-from-behind surge against Hall of Fame pitcher Nolan Ryan, who had led 7-0. It was his first major-league homer witnessed by his father, now the vice president of baseball operations for the Astros (Bob had "resigned" from the Cubs in 1981, a claim hotly and publicly challenged by his son), and it prompted Terry to chirp, "I've never been that excited before in my life."[11] Designated the league's "next Willie McCovey,"[12] he enjoyed his second All-Star campaign while outdistancing the Pirates Tony Pena for the Silver Slugger Award for catchers.

A sputtering offense prevented the Padres from eclipsing the .500 mark in consecutive seasons. "We play like King Kong one day and Fay Wray the next," Kennedy quipped.[13] This changed in 1984 with the emergence of youngsters such as Kevin McReynolds and Tony Gwynn. The team vaulted to its first World Series, granting Terry his first taste of postseason play. In his first at-bat in the Fall Classic, his double to right field plated two runs (the only runs for the Padres in Game One). This made Terry and Bob Kennedy into the first father-son combo to drive in runs in World Series play. The Padres lost to the Detroit Tigers in five games.

Despite the success the Padres sustained under Dick Williams, the crusty manager had his detractors – one of whom was Kennedy. Terry had stoically faced a continual barrage of criticism regarding his defensive work since the manager's 1982 arrival (criticism that continued throughout his career). He remained silent when the team explored the free agent signing of Astros catcher Alan Ashby that winter – a move that would have shifted Kennedy to first base. Admittedly, Williams' critique is supported in part by the large number of errors and stolen bases allowed throughout Terry's career; on the other hand, he placed among the league leaders in base runners thrown out and fielding percentage. "My size never made it easy to be a 'smooth' defender and it was always a chore. I envied the 5'11" to 6'1" catchers." While never considered Gold Glove material, he was not a liability behind the plate, either.

The final straw came when Kennedy's pitch calling drew unfavorable commentary. Reliever Gary Lucas, Kennedy's San Diego teammate for three seasons, commented: "[T]here's too much of an accent on the negative ... [Williams and pitching coach Norm Sherry are] always second guessing the pitcher and catcher, getting on them for pitch selection or location."[14]

During the two seasons following their World Series defeat the Padres fell out of pennant contention. Terry's name continually surfaced in connection with trade rumors as the team prepared for the emergence of catching prospect Benito Santiago. Despite appeals from the Yankees, Pirates, Orioles, and his former team, the Cardinals, Kennedy continued to produce for the Padres. In 1985, a 12-game hitting streak (.440 in 50 at-bats) brought his average to a season-high .296 on June 10, earning Terry the starting assignment in the All-Star Game when voter-selected Gary Carter was forced to rest. He established a team record with five consecutive pinch-hits the following season, and only Carter exceeded his 792 games behind the plate from 1981-1986 (a strong testament to his durability). But after Santiago received the bulk of playing time following a September 1986 callup, the Padres actively began pursuing trade inquiries for their All-Star catcher.

The mound performance of the 1986 Padres was a mere shadow of that which led to post-season play two years earlier. Injury and underperformance resulted in a near league-worst 3.99 ERA, a situation San Diego sought to remedy by acquiring Baltimore Orioles right-hander Storm Davis. On October 30, 1986, in exchange for Davis, Kennedy and reliever Mark Williamson were sent east, the Orioles thus securing a replacement for the pending free-agent departure of their aging veteran backstop Rick Dempsey. Terry responded with his fourth – and final – All Star campaign in 1987 (joining former teammate Ted Simmons as the only catcher to start an All-Star Game for both leagues), while catching a single-season club record 142 games. A second-half swoon (.230) marred an otherwise productive season. But Kennedy's slow start the following season (.172-0-5 through May) contributed to a platoon situation and a mere 265 at-bats. In January, Kennedy made way for the Orioles large, off-season youth movement when he was traded to the San Francisco Giants.

Now the Giants vice president of baseball operations, Bob Kennedy likely had influence on general manager Al Rosen's decision to acquire the 33-year-old backstop. But another factor also loomed. Poised to enter the 1989 campaign with a little-tested young catcher, Kirt Manwaring, the Giants believed Terry's veteran presence would be an asset. Much as he'd thrived in the new environs in San Diego and Baltimore before, Kennedy captured most of the time behind the plate in his first season with San Francisco. Instead of being a stopgap, Kennedy earned credit for stabilizing a pitching staff that vaulted the Giants to the World Series. "He's a very intelligent catcher when it comes to communicating with the pitchers," Dave Dravecky said. "He

develops a relationship between the lines with the pitching staff, and that's so important."[15]

A free agent at the end of the season, Kennedy was re-signed by the Giants and split time in 1990 with another free agent acquisition, Gary Carter. One of his last home runs was a near bookend to his first: a grand slam against the Mets Ron Darling on May 15, 1990, which contributed to a 6-5 Giants victory. But by 1991, the Giants committed to a younger presence behind the plate and Kennedy garnered a mere 171 at-bats. He made his last plate appearance as a pinch hitter on October 6. In 1,491 major-league games and 4,979 at-bats, Terry collected 113 home runs and 628 RBIs to accompany a .264 lifetime batting average. Despite the criticism of his defense, he placed 55th all-time for putouts by a catcher through 2013.

"[I]t's like having another manager out there…[he] can size up situations early, and the pitchers seem to have more confidence,"[16] claimed manager Roger Craig, reflecting on Kennedy's leadership qualities while also, perhaps, predicting his future. In 1993, Kennedy earned the mantle by taking the helm for the St. Petersburg Cardinals in the Florida State League. He served as manager or minor-league instructor for a number of organizations over the next two decades, overseeing youngsters and former major-league stars alike (he was the last professional to manage Rickey Henderson). A fierce competitor his entire life, Kennedy was let go by the Montreal Expos following the 1994 season for, as the organization explained, "philosophical differences; he was interested in winning and we were interested in player development."[17] Four years later he was named Baseball America Manager of the Year after leading the Iowa Cubs to a Pacific Coast League best 85-59 mark. In the early 2000s, manager Don Baylor offered a position on the Cubs coaching staff, but Terry declined: "My kids were still in high school and I did not want to be away from them. I remembered the solitude of my teen years [when my father was frequently away]." He spent 2013 as a Cubs scout and, with the children grown, hopes to follow his father into the front office someday.

From his mother's detour to the retired Pensacola airfields to his father's impact on his own career, family has had strong influence on Terry's life (by sheer coincidence, the Cardinals assigned Terry number 16, the last number worn by his father during his playing career. Terry always sought to keep the number thereafter). The message in the Kennedy house was clear: Loving baseball was optional; being a good person wasn't.[18]

In college, Terry met the love of his life, Teresa Murphy. "With all the people in the world, it still amazes me that God put us together." A dancer who taught jazz, tap, and ballet, she sought to improve Terry's agility with tap. "I attempted, only one time mind you, [but] I was a terrible student and did not pursue it any further. I am sure my wife was grateful." Married in 1978, their second child, Sarah, arrived on February 22, 1984, with her father on crutches (he had arthroscopic knee surgery that off-season, though he proudly points out that he never spent a day on the disabled list in his career). Suzanna and Bart preceded and followed Sarah, respectively, and by 2014 Terry and Teresa enjoyed the company of seven grandchildren. Terry helps Teresa run The Kennedy Realty Team in the Phoenix region during the off-season.

Although the Cardinals organization almost stymied his budding career, through 2014 Terry maintained his place among Padres all-time leaders in a variety of statistical categories (including, significantly, the most games caught, despite playing just six years for the franchise). He led two teams to World Series play while garnering the respect of fans and contemporaries alike with four All-Star appearances. A torrid start to the 1982 season – arguably his finest in the major leagues – generated speculation that he might attain heights achieved by Hall of Famers Joe Medwick (as a potential NL Triple Crown winner) and Mickey Cochrane (most doubles by a catcher). Though he fell short on both accounts, there is ample record of the respect he commanded as he strode to the plate. His defensive durability places him among the all-time leaders in baseball history.

The author wishes to thank Terry Kennedy for: (1) his invaluable review and input ensuring the accuracy herein; and (2) his extraordinary kindness shown to my 11-year-old son in 2004, prompting the desire to pursue the narrative. Further thanks are extended to Michael Lynch regarding the Cardinals' 1980 record four managers and Matthew J. Perry for editorial and fact-checking assistance.

## SOURCES

In addition to the sources cited in the Notes, the author also consulted baseball-reference.com, ancestry.com, and:

azstarnet.com/sports/baseball/professional/minor/kennedy-s-late-dad-lives-on-in-his-son/article_07f85a05-adc1-5205-892d-5e9a451a3569.html

azstarnet.com/sports/baseball/professional/minor/tucson-padres-after-years-in-pro-ball-kennedy-is-at/article_9bab98b7-35d2-5532-b11d-42c6589c5c0e.html

thekennedyrealtyteam.yourkwagent.com/atj/user/AboutUs-GetAction.do

## INTERVIEWS

Kennedy, Terry, email correspondence (from which all unattributed quotes derive), December 12-13, 2013

## NOTES

1    "Kennedy Steps Up Barrage," *The Sporting News,* May 9, 1983: 18.

2    "Kennedy in Pasture And Cards Make Hay," *The Sporting News,* July 12, 1980: 32.

3    Kennedy, Williams, and Jerry Coleman were the only major-league players to serve in both Korea and World War II.

4    "No Evidence of Juiced-Up Ball," *The Sporting News,* June 18, 1977: 53.

5    "American Association," *The Sporting News,* June 23, 1979: 37.

6    "Notebook by Stan Isle," *The Sporting News,* September 13, 1980: 16.

7    "Padres Count Youthful Blessings," *The Sporting News,* January 10, 1981: 43.

8    "Kennedy Welcomes Padres Opportunity," *The Sporting News,* February 7, 1981: 43.

9    "Padres' Kennedy Showing Muscle," *The Sporting News,* October 11, 1982: 47.

10    "Kennedy Steps Up Barrage."

11    "Kennedy's Big Bat No. 1 Padre Weapon," *The Sporting News,* September 19, 1983: 23.

12    Ibid.

13    "Kennedy Steps Up Barrage."

14    "Slumping Padres An Unhappy Bunch," *The Sporting News,* May 28, 1984: 27.

15    "Lightening in a Bottle?" *The Sporting News,* May 15, 1989: 22.

16    "Gary – Terry Combo Sparkles in Twilight," *The Sporting News,* June 4, 1990: 10.

17    "N.L. – Montreal Expos," *The Sporting News,* October 3, 1994: 43.

18    Daniel Berk, "Kennedy's late dad lives on in his son," *Arizona Daily Star* (June 17, 2012). (http://azstarnet.com/sports/baseball/professional/minor/kennedy-s-late-dad-lives-on-in-his-son/article_07f85a05-adc1-5205-892d-5e9a451a3569.html ).

# CLAY KIRBY

## BY CHARLES F. FABER

In his major-league career Clay Kirby won 75 games, yet he is best remembered for one of his losses. On July 21, 1970, Kirby, on the mound for the San Diego Padres, pitched eight innings of no-hit ball against the New York Mets before manager Preston Gomez removed him for a pinch-hitter. Kirby had given up one run in the first inning on a walk, two stolen bases, and an infield out. The Padres were trailing 1-0 with two out and nobody on in the eighth inning, when Kirby was due to bat. Gomez sent Clarence "Cito" Gaston to the plate. Gaston struck out. The Mets scored two runs on three hits and a walk against a relief pitcher in the ninth inning and won the game, 3-0. Many Padres fans, irate that Gomez had deprived the youngster a chance of a no-hitter by removing him from the game, booed long and loud. The manager's decision became a matter of intense controversy. Was Kirby treated unfairly by being removed from a potential no-hitter? Was Gomez fulfilling the manager's responsibility by making the move that he thought gave his team its best shot at a victory?

Clayton Laws Kirby, Jr. was born in Washington, D.C., on June 25, 1948, the only son of Gloria Deener and Clayton L. Kirby. Clay and his sister Carolyn both grew up in suburban Arlington, Virginia. Clay started playing Little League baseball at the age of 7 and went on to play baseball, basketball, and football at Washington and Lee High School. In one high-school contest he pitched a perfect game, while striking out 19 batters. Kirby was

selected by the St. Louis Cardinals in the third round of the June 1966 amateur draft. He was signed to a contract by St. Louis scout Charles "Tim" Thompson and assigned to the Sarasota Cardinals of the rookie Gulf Coast League, and soon earned a promotion to St. Petersburg of the Florida State League, where he won his three starts, giving up only nine hits in 20 innings. He spent 1967 with Modesto of the California League. During his first two offseasons he attended Old Dominion University in Norfolk, Virginia, and Benjamin Franklin University in

Washington, respectively. He started the 1968 season between Arkansas of the Double-A Texas League and then advanced to Tulsa of the Triple-A Pacific Coast League, winning 12 games as a starting pitcher for the two teams. At the end of the 1968 season the 20-year-old right-hander was chosen by the new San Diego Padres in the expansion draft. Kirby was the sixth player taken by the Padres.

Kirby made the Padres squad in spring training and the 6-foot-3, 175-pound right-hander made his major-league debut on April 11, 1969, against the San Francisco Giants. Giving up four runs in four innings, he was the losing pitcher. His teammates dubbed the fuzzy-cheeked youngster "The Kid." In his rookie season Kirby led the National League in losses with 20, but the Padres were not discouraged. Pitching coach Roger Craig said, "The Kid has a lot of Drysdale's competitive drive. When he was 20 in his rookie year, he wasn't afraid. And when he lost 20, it didn't get him down. I told him he had to be a pretty good pitcher to lose 20 games, because it means he was getting the ball every four days."[1] Gomez said he thought Kirby and fellow rookie Al Santorini were both potential 20-game winners. "They both have great arms and all they need to become complete pitchers in the major leagues is experience," the skipper said.[2] Kirby shared his manager's confidence in his ability. One of his teammates, pitcher Steve Arlin, said of him, "Clay was cocky, brash, arrogant, and still very popular. He was a young kid who did not back down from anything or anybody. He could beat the world and he knew it."[3] But with the woeful Padres behind him he could not beat the majority of major-league clubs he faced. In five years with San Diego he had only one winning season, and won 52 games while losing 81 for a less-than-stellar .391 winning percentage.

However, Kirby did have some outstanding games. In fact, he almost pitched three no-hitters for the Padres. The season after the game in which Gomez lifted him for a pinch-hitter, Kirby pitched no-hit ball at Houston for 7⅓ innings on September 13, 1971, before Johnny Edwards broke it up with a double. Kirby lost the game 3-2, as the Padres committed two infield errors in the ninth inning, allowing the winning run to score. In his next start, at San Francisco on September 18, Kirby set down the first 21 Giants to face him and was in pursuit of a perfect game until Willie McCovey started the bottom of the eighth inning with a home run. It was the only hit Kirby gave up in the game as the Padres won, 2-1.

Kirby caught what at first appeared to be a good break when he was traded to the Cincinnati Reds after the 1973 season for outfielder Bobby Tolan and pitcher Dave Tomlin. After five years of laboring for a team that finished in last place every season, he was now with a contender. The trade caught the pitcher by surprise, coming the day after he and his wife, the former Susan Gantt, had purchased a house in San Diego County. The Kirbys had married quite young and already had a 6-year-daughter, Theresa, and a 3-year old son, Clayton. Cincinnati manager Sparky Anderson said he was pleased to acquire Kirby. "This kid is a real competitor," said Anderson, who had managed Kirby at St. Petersburg and Modesto in the Cardinals' farm system. "I'm counting on him being a regular starter for us. He wants the ball all the time. He wants to get out there and beat you. He believes he can win and never seems to lose that feeling."[4]

Some of the Reds knew that Kirby got in hot water with the Padres by questioning manager Don Zimmer when he approached the mound to remove the pitcher one day in 1973. "What do you want?" Kirby asked. "I don't want much," replied Zimmer, "I just want the ball." The pitcher mumbled something, and the irate manager angrily said, "If you don't like the way I'm running the club, then go home."[5] Anderson, like Zimmer, wanted no questions from faltering pitchers. "Once the ole boy bounces out of the dugout, don't get excited because you're gone," pitching coach Larry Shepard told Kirby. "There are no ifs, ands, or buts about it."[6] Anderson reinforced his coach's advice. "When I go to the mound," said Sparky, "nothing is said unless I say it or ask for it. That's my role on this club, and the pitchers who don't know it will soon learn it."[7]

When he joined the Reds, Kirby asked for uniform number 31. "That's the opposite of 13; Maybe it will change my luck," he said.[8] In his third start for the Reds, in Cincinnati on April 16, Kirby retired 16 of the first 17 Los Angeles Dodgers batters he faced and was working on a one-hit shutout when pitcher Andy Messersmith hit a home run in the sixth. Kirby left the game with a stiff back after seven innings, and the Reds lost the game in extra innings. He fared better in a game against Houston on May 12, when he carried a one hitter into the ninth and survived a home run to win a two-hitter. But despite having the powerful Big Red Machine behind him, Kirby never became the 20-game winner he aspired to be. In 1974 he won 12 games. In 1975 his victory total fell to 10. In 1974 he ranked fourth on the Reds in wins behind Don Gullett, Jack Billingham, and Fred Norman. The return of Gary Nolan, who had missed almost two full seasons with shoulder trouble, and the arrival of Pat Darcy in 1975 further reduced Kirby's opportunities, and he became a spot starter and an occasional reliever. In his two seasons with the Reds, Kirby won 22 games against 15 losses for a respectable .595 winning percentage. To his dismay, he did not get into a single postseason game after Cincinnati won the 1975 National League pennant. Newspapers reported that if the World Series went beyond five games, the "baby-faced" hurler would get a start against the Boston Red Sox. The Series went the full seven games, but Kirby never got his shot. After the season was over, a Cincinnati newspaper conducted a poll of fans to see which Reds players they would most like see traded away. Kirby collected the most votes.

Not that the poll had anything to do with it, but in December the Reds traded Kirby to the Montreal Expos for infielder Bob Bailey. In January 1976, Kirby was stricken with a long bout of pneumonia before he joined the Expos in Florida for spring training. He was still weak and had a sore shoulder when the season opened. He got off to a miserable start and never recovered. He won only one game for the Expos, lost eight, and posted a 5.72 earned-run average, while walking 63 batters in 78 2/3 innings. After all the major-league clubs passed on Kirby in the offseason, Montreal released him on December 2, 1976. In January 1977, the Padres decided to give their former pitcher another chance. They invited him to their spring-training camp in Yuma, Arizona. Kirby's string of bad luck continued when he incurred a knee injury in the final week of spring training. His comeback try was delayed for almost two months. The Padres sent him to their Pacific Coast League farm club in Hawaii. He won his first game for the Islanders on June 18, but never won another. His record for the season was one win, seven losses, and an earned-run average of 7.95.

After San Diego gave up on Kirby, he tried out with the Minnesota Twins during spring training in 1978. He lasted only two weeks before he was released. Kirby's career in Organized Baseball was over before his 30th birthday. His family continued to live in San Diego County until 1983, when they returned to Virginia. Kirby became a self-employed financial securities broker. For several years he was tournament chairman for the Major League Baseball Players Alumni in golfing events to benefit the American Lung Association.

Although Kirby once listed his hobby as building miniature racing cars, his main recreational activities were hunting and fishing. "I started to fish and hunt when I was 7," he said. "I was 12 when I was allowed to carry my first gun, and I got my first deer the same year."[9] Kirby acquired his love of hunting and fishing from his father, who in partnership with two friends had bought 300 acres in the Shenandoah Mountains just so they could hunt and fish on the land. The morning after Kirby lost his chance for a no-hitter when Preston Gomez removed him from the game, Clay and his father went fishing. Afterward someone asked if they talked about the game. "We talked only about fishing," Kirby replied.[10]

On July 19, 1991, Kirby underwent a coronary atherectomy to open a blockage in an artery just above his heart. After the procedure he was advised that he had suffered a silent heart attack. The Kirbys had been living with his mother in Arlington. His sister said they thought Clay was recuperating nicely, but she later learned from friends that he had been complaining about chest discomfort and numbness in his arm. He apparently died of a heart attack on October 11, 1991, at the age of 43. His wife found him about 11 o'clock in the morning in his easy chair. It appeared that he had fallen asleep while reading and suffered the fatal attack. He was survived by his wife, Susan; his mother, Gloria; his sister, Carolyn Twyman; his son, Clayton; his daughter, Theresa Schoengold; and two grandchildren, Derek and Brandon Schoengold. He was buried in the National Memorial Park in Falls Church, Virginia.

## SOURCES

In addition to the sources cited in the Notes, the author also relied on baseball-reference.com, retrosheet.org, and his book *Major League Careers Cut Short: Leading Players Gone by 30.* (Jefferson, North Carolina: McFarland, 2011).

## NOTES

1    Paul Cour, "Kirby Rewards Patient Padre Bosses," *The Sporting News*, July 3, 1971: 10.

2    Paul Cour, "Hill Stars of Tomorrow: Padres' Kirby, Santorini," *The Sporting News*, August 30, 1969: 15.

3    *San Diego Union*, October 17, 1991.

4    Cincinnati Reds News Release, "Reds Get Clay Kirby from San Diego," November 9, 1973.

5    "National League," *The Sporting News*, August 25, 1973: 31.

6    *Cincinnati Post*, May 18, 1974.

7    Ibid.

8    *Cincinnati Post*, May 18, 1974.

9    San Diego Padres Press Release, "Padre Close Up." June 19, 1971.

10    Ibid.

# RYAN KLESKO

## BY JOEL RIPPEL

Ryan Klesko caught the attention of scouts early in his high-school baseball career. Scouts clamored for the prime spots behind home plate to watch Klesko, a freshman on the Westminster (California) High School varsity.

Klesko hit 278 home runs and batted .279 in a 16-year major-league career. But the scouts weren't there to watch him hit. They were there to watch him pitch.

"I went to Ron LeFebvre's pitching school eight years," Klesko said. "At first I was going for fun. But after a certain point I was good enough that I knew I would do something in baseball after high school. I thought it would be pitching."[1]

Klesko, a hard-throwing left-hander, struck out 138 in 96⅔ innings as a sophomore and junior and compiled a 13-6 won-lost record in his first three seasons on the Westminster varsity. After his junior season (in 1988) he was a member of the US Junior Olympic Team. But an elbow injury limited him to playing first base as a high-school senior.

"I was always a pretty good hitter, too," Klesko said. "When I was a freshman and sophomore at Ron's school, I started batting against college pitchers and I did fine. I knew I could make it as a hitter, too."[2]

Klesko credited his mother, Lorene, with helping him reach the major leagues. Klesko's parents, Howard and Lorene, divorced while he was in high school. Before the divorce, Howard Klesko was frequently gone for work in Southern California oil fields, so Lorene, who worked packing aerospace parts, took on a second job cleaning houses on weekends to pay for Ryan's pitching lessons, built a pitching mound in the backyard of their home and took on the role of catcher for him (something she also did for his two sisters, who were good softball players).

"When I was a kid, my mom would watch baseball on TV and say to me, 'See those guys? You're going to be one of them someday,'" said Klesko. "I never thought it was possible, but she always believed in me."[3]

During his senior year, Klesko hit .347 with 5 home runs and 18 RBIs and earned All-Sunset League honors for the fourth consecutive season. In early May of 1989, he signed a letter of intent to play baseball for Arizona State. In early June, Klesko was selected in the fifth round of the amateur draft. Eleven days after the draft, the Braves opened a three-game series at Dodger Stadium and invited Klesko to take batting practice.

"A lot of teams came to see me when I was in high school," said Klesko. "They thought only of me as a pitcher. It had everything to do with how hard I threw. That is what they wanted. I was a good hitter in high school but they weren't focused on anything else and I played in an awful big park so it was hard to hit it out. It all worked out after hitting with the Braves at Dodger Stadium. I think they really realized then just how good I could hit and the power I had."[4]

Several days later, the Braves signed Klesko and assigned him to their farm team in the rookie Gulf Coast League. Florida was an adjustment for Klesko.

"I remember getting to Bradenton and it was hot as crap and hot and rainy at the same time," he said. "There were also these big mosquitoes. I went in and told the coach I hated it, was depressed and wanted to go home. I said how do I get out of here? He said hit. So I did, and I was gone very quickly."[5]

Klesko responded by hitting .404 with one home run and 16 RBIs in 17 games with the GCL Braves and was promoted to Sumter (South Carolina) of the Class-A South Atlantic League. In 25 games with Sumter, he hit .289 with one home run and 12 RBIs.

Klesko returned to Sumter in 1990 and hit .368 with 10 home runs and 38 RBIs in 63 games. He was named a South Atlantic League All-Star and was named the league's top prospect. At midseason he was promoted to Durham of the high Class-A Carolina League and hit .274 with 7 home runs and 47 RBIs in 77 games.

He got off to a slow start in 1991 with Greenville of the Double-A Southern League. As the youngest everyday player in the Southern League (he turned 20 in June), he hit just .190 in April. But he regrouped to hit .347 with 9 home runs and 38 RBIs in May and June. For the season, he hit .291 with 14 home runs and 67 RBIs in 126 games. He walked 75 times and had a .404 on-base percentage as he earned the league's MVP honor and

was named the number-2 prospect (behind Royce Clayton) in minor-league baseball by Howe Sportsdata.[6]

In his fourth professional season, Klesko made his Triple-A and major-league debuts. In 123 games with Richmond of the International League, he batted .251 with 17 home runs and 59 RBIs. He was called up by the Braves on September 11 and made his big-league debut the next day in Houston. Facing veteran reliever Doug Jones as a pinch-hitter in the ninth inning, he struck out in the Braves' 9-3 victory. Over the next three weeks, Klesko saw pinch-hitting duty and made one start at first base. On October 1, against San Francisco in Atlanta, he went 0-for-4 with his first major-league RBI (on an infield grounder) in the Braves' 6-5 victory in 10 innings. In 13 games, he was hitless in 14 at-bats.

Klesko opened the 1993 season in Richmond but was recalled by the Braves on April 19. Three days later, in Miami, he got his first major-league hit – a pinch-single in the ninth inning off the Marlins' Bryan Harvey. On April 27, in Atlanta, he hit his first major-league home run – a pinch-hit, two-run home run in the ninth inning off Pittsburgh's Tim Wakefield. The home run tied the game and forced extra innings before the Pirates won 6-2 in 11 innings. Klesko hit .273 in 14 games but was returned to Richmond on May 18.

Back at Richmond, Klesko batted .274 with 22 home runs and 74 RBIs in 98 games. A highlight came when he was named the most valuable player representing the International League in the Triple-A All-Star Game after going 4-for-4 with two home runs and three RBIs in the National League's 14-3 victory over the AL.[7]

On September 10 Klesko rejoined the Braves. On September 15 in Atlanta, he hit a two-run home run as a pinch-hitter to start the Braves' five-run rally in the bottom of the ninth in a 7-6 victory over Cincinnati. In his two stints with the Braves, Klesko was 6-for-17 with two home runs and five RBIs in 22 games.

Klesko made Atlanta's Opening Day roster in 1994. Other than brief minor-league rehab stints in 1995 and 2006, he spent the rest of his 19-year professional career in the major leagues. His opportunity to make the Opening Day roster involved a move from first base to the outfield. Ron Gant, a mainstay in Atlanta's outfield the previous four seasons, suffered a broken leg in a dirt-bike accident just before the start of spring training. The injury forced Gant to miss the entire season and Braves manager Bobby Cox used a platoon of Klesko and Dave Gallagher in left field. Klesko batted .278 with 17 homers in 245 at-bats and 92 games before the season ended when the players strike began on August 12. Klesko finished third (behind the Dodgers' Raul

Mondesi and Houston's John Hudek) in the National League Rookie of the Year voting.

In the abbreviated spring training of 1995, Klesko had the best batting average (.370) of Braves regulars, but he again opened the season in a platoon with Mike Kelly. In the Braves' sixth game of the season (May 2 at Florida), Klesko suffered a thumb injury and he was placed on the 15-day disabled list. He returned to the lineup on May 18.

Klesko struggled at the plate in his return (with no home runs in his first 57 at-bats of the season), but in early June he started hitting. He broke out on June 6 with his first two home runs of the season (including the first grand slam of his career) and a career-high six RBIs in Atlanta's 17-3 victory over the visiting Chicago Cubs. One other noteworthy home run came on July 24, when he homered off Pirates reliever Dan Plesac in Pittsburgh. It was the first home run of his career off a left-hander.

For the season, Klesko hit .310 with 23 home runs and 70 RBIs in 107 games and 329 at-bats. The Braves made the 1995 post-season, and in the Division Series against Colorado, he went 7-for-15 with an RBI. Klesko went hitless in the Braves' four-game sweep of Cincinnati in the Championship Series, but he took center stage in the World Series.

After the Braves defeated Cleveland in the first two games in Atlanta, Klesko hit home runs in all three games at Jacobs Field in Cleveland to become the first player to homer in three consecutive World Series road games. His home run in the sixth inning of the Braves' 5-2 victory in Game Four landed near where his mother, Lorene, was sitting in the bleachers.

"It missed her by about 10 feet," said Klesko. "She went down and got it, but she had to bribe them for it. It cost her a baseball bat, two balls autographed by our whole team and a couple of pictures. But it was worth it."[8]

For the Series, won by the Braves in six games, Klesko was 5-for-16 with three home runs and four RBIs.

Klesko got off to a good start in 1996. He hit 10 home runs – a club record for April – with 20 RBIs and a .337 batting average. In early June he had at least one RBI in seven consecutive games (June 2-9). Healthy all season, he played in 153 games and batted .282 with a career-high 34 home runs and then career-high 93 RBIs. Klesko batted just .176 with two home runs and five RBIs in 14 postseason games as the Braves reached the World Series again (losing to the Yankees).

Klesko's production declined a little in 1997 as he hit 24 home runs and had 84 RBIs in 143 games, but he finished the regular season strong. From August 28 to September 17, he hit six home runs in 13 games. One of those home runs helped Klesko reach a milestone. On September 17 he slugged his fifth career grand slam in the Braves' 10-2 victory over the New York Mets. The grand slam – the 100th home run of Klesko's career – was Atlanta's 12th of the season, which broke the major-league record of 11 (set in 1996 by Baltimore and Seattle). In the opening game of the NLDS, his solo home run in the second inning gave the Braves a 2-0 lead in their 2-1 victory over Houston. He homered in each of the first two games (against Florida) in the NLCS.

Klesko's 1998 season was interrupted when he had an appendectomy on June 29. He missed the Braves' six games before the All-Star break and their first three games after the break before returning to action on July 12. For the season, he batted .274 with 18 home runs and 70 RBIs. But after striking out 129 times in 1996 and 130 times in 1997, he struck out only 66 times.

The 1999 season, which saw Klesko split his time between first base and left field, was his last in Atlanta. In 133 games, he hit .297 with 21 home runs and 80 RBIs. In 12 playoff games, Klesko hit .219 and one home run as the Braves made their third World Series appearance in five seasons.

On December 22 the Braves traded Klesko, second baseman Bret Boone, and pitching prospect Jason Shiell to the San Diego Padres for first baseman Wally Joyner, outfielder Reggie Sanders, and second baseman Quilvio Veras.

"I was upset at first because the Braves were so good. But (Padres manager) Bruce (Bochy) brought me in and said I was going to be an everyday player," Klesko said. "I remember when (Braves general manager) John (Schuerholz) told me about the trade. He said, 'Ryan, I think you are going to be happy.' I knew then that I was going to San Diego, Anaheim, or Los Angeles. It was fun going back home and I had good seasons there. I cut down on my swing and stride and things worked out."[9]

Klesko's first season in Southern California was one of his best overall. As the Padres' first baseman, he batted .283 with 26 home runs and 92 RBIs in 145 games. He set career highs in walks (91) and stolen bases (23).

His second season with the Padres saw him record another 20-home run, 20-stolen base season – joining Dave Winfield as the only Padre (at that point) to have accomplished that more than once – and was highlighted by his only All-Star Game appearance. In 84 games before the All-Star break, he hit 17 home runs and had 75 RBIs (a team record for RBIs prior to the All-Star break). On July 10 in Seattle, he drove in the NL's only run with a sacrifice fly in the AL's 4-1 victory. In 146 games, Klesko batted .286 with 30 home runs and career highs in RBIs (113) and runs scored (105).

In 2002, Klesko's regular-season debut was delayed as he sat out the first four games (April 1-5) for his involvement in a bench-clearing brawl between the Padres and the Anaheim Angels in an exhibition game in Tempe, Arizona, on March 9. In the first inning of that game, Klesko had charged the mound after being hit in the lower back by a pitch from Aaron Sele.

After the four-game penalty, Klesko was in the lineup almost every day as he batted .300 – his highest average since he hit .310 for Atlanta in 1995 – with 29 home runs and 95 RBIs in 146 games. The season was highlighted by a career-high 16-game hitting streak (April 9-28) and reaching base safely in 56 consecutive games from April 9 to June 14 (the longest streak in the major leagues that season). After the season, he was named the Padres' MVP by the San Diego Chapter of the Baseball Writers' Association of America.

After playing in 145, 146, and 146 games, respectively, in the previous seasons, Klesko was limited to 121 games in 2003 and missed the final month of the season after shoulder surgery. For the season, he hit a then career-low .252 with 21 home runs and 67 RBIs.

His 2004 season got off to a slow start and included a stint on the 15-day disabled list (May 28-June 16) because of a right oblique strain. But he batted .310 after the All-Star break to finish with a .291 average in 127 games. He hit 32 doubles but only nine home runs to go with 66 RBIs. He reached a milestone when he hit his 250th career home run in the Padres' 14-5 victory over the Reds in Cincinnati on August 13.

The 2005 season saw Klesko lead the Padres in home runs (18) for the third time and the Padres' return to the postseason for the first time since 1998. Klesko was 2-for-10 in the Cardinals' three-game sweep of the Padres in the NLDS.

Klesko missed all but the final two weeks of the 2006 season. Bothered by soreness in his throwing shoulder in spring training, he started the season on the disabled list. After receiving two cortisone shots, he considered trying to play through the pain. But after having an MRI, Klesko underwent surgery on April 10.

"It's probably best to go ahead and do it instead of having a roller-coaster all year," said Klesko. "The MRI did not show very good news."[10]

Klesko hoped he would be able to return around the All-Star break but wasn't activated until late September after an eight-game rehab assignment with Lake Elsinore (California League). Over the final two weeks of the season with the Padres, he was 3-for-4 with two walks and two RBIs as a pinch-hitter. He was on the Padres' postseason roster and went 2-for-3 as a pinch-hitter

in their loss to the St. Louis Cardinals in the NLDS. After the season the Padres declined the option of Klesko's 2007 contract.

On December 19, 2006, Klesko agreed to a one-year, $1.75 million contract with the San Francisco Giants, where he was reunited with Bruce Bochy, who left the Padres after the 2006 season to become the Giants manager. In 116 games in 2007, he batted .260 with six home runs and 44 RBIs in 362 at-bats. After the season Klesko filed for free agency. In April of 2008, he announced his retirement. For his 16-season major-league career, he batted .279 with 278 home runs and 987 RBIs in 1,736 regular-season games. In 62 postseason games – in seven seasons – he batted .236 with 10 home runs and 22 RBIs.

Klesko was asked about spending the early portion of his big-league career being platooned by Braves manager Bobby Cox.

"Bobby and I were always good," said Klesko, "but I wanted to play every game. I think he would want any player to want to be out there every day. What it came down to is, I played for two of the best managers in the game in Bobby Cox and Bruce Bochy. I did get to hit a lot more against lefties under Bruce but the Braves gave me my chance and we won big there."[11]

After retiring, Klesko made his home near Macon, Georgia, with his wife and son. He has invested in real estate (more than 7,000 acres in several states) and he owns 17 rental homes. He has hosted an outdoor television program called *Campfire Stories* on the Pursuit channel on Direct TV.

## SOURCES

In addition to the sources cited in the Notes, the author also consulted Baseball-Reference.com, mlb.com, newspapers.com, and retrosheet.com.

# NOTES

1    Mike Eisenbath, "Minor League Report: Making His Big Pitch at the Plate," *The Sporting News*, September 2, 1991: 33.

2    Ibid.

3    Gerry Callahan, "Baseball. Sultan of Swat," *Sports Illustrated*, April 8, 1996: 66.

4    I.J. Rosenberg, "Whatever Happened to Ryan Klesko," myajc.com, August 6, 2015.

5    Ibid.

6    Jim Keller, "Top 10 for the Future," *The Sporting News*, September 2, 1991: 33.

7    The Triple-A All-Star Game featured players from each of the three Triple-A leagues (American Association, International League, and Pacific Coast League). An MVP from each league was designated after the game.

8    I.J. Rosenberg, "Klesko Will Start in Left Despite Pain in Thumb," *Atlanta Journal/Constitution*, October 28, 1995: D5.

9    I.J. Rosenberg, "Whatever Happened to Ryan Klesko," myajc.com, August 6, 2015.

10   "Around The Majors: Padres' Klesko Out Two to Four Months," *Los Angeles Times*, April 9, 2006: D10.

11   I.J. Rosenberg, "Whatever Happened to Ryan Klesko," myajc.com, August 6, 2015.

# CRAIG LEFFERTS

## BY STEVE WEST

Craig Lefferts battled all his life to make it to the major leagues. Once he did, he stayed there for a decade, and became famous for running from the bullpen to the mound, showing his lifelong enthusiasm for the game.

Craig Lindsay Lefferts was born on September 29, 1957, in Munich, West Germany.[1] His father, Ed, was stationed there as a lieutenant colonel in the US Air Force. Ed took his wife, Bobbie, and five children across the world on various assignments. Craig lived in half a dozen cities before the family settled in St. Petersburg, Florida, where he attended high school.

As a child Lefferts suffered from asthma, as did his sister, Lynn. They took medicine to control the condition. Craig's asthma improved enough under medication that he was able to play football and later baseball, dealing with the smell of the grass that exacerbated the condition. "In the grass … I couldn't breathe, and then I'd quit," he said. "I caught a lot of flak from the players. If I couldn't practice, they didn't want me to play."[2]

Lefferts played American Legion ball, but was twice cut for being too small before making the team. At Northeast High School he was cut as a sophomore, but made the team as a junior, playing outfield. He bugged coach Larry Rudisill to give him a chance to pitch. Finally he was given the opportunity against Sarasota, the previous season's state champion. He was so nervous that his father told him to quit. The reverse psychology worked;

he said, "Dad, I can't do that." His father replied, "Well, then make up your mind and just go out there and do your best." Lefferts threw a one-hitter and beat Sarasota 1-0, kick-starting his pitching career.[3]

After high school Lefferts tried to follow his father into the Air Force, but failed the physical. He had graduated at 5-feet-10 and 140 pounds, but it was his lazy right eye that caused the failure. Instead, his father reached out to his alma mater, the University of Arizona, to see if Craig could walk on to the team.

He was given the chance to walk on, but was cut, just as he had been in high school. "He was skinny, slight, and didn't throw hard," coach Jerry Kendall said. "I cut him and said, 'Get stronger and we'll take another look."[4] "It happened a lot to me when I was young," Lefferts later said. "It's been the story of my life, everybody telling me I'm not good enough, but inside I knew that if I got the opportunity I could pitch and pitch well."[5]

Trying out again in 1979, Lefferts made the team, and turned out to be one of its best pitchers. While he was a junior, his sister, Lynn, died from an asthma attack. Craig had seemed to grow out of the condition, but Lynn had suffered all her life. Scheduled to pitch the following day, he told his parents that Lynn would want him to. He threw 11 innings over two games, giving up just three hits and two runs. He thought about his sister throughout the game, and believed that was the point that drove him to focus on baseball. "We were close. We both had asthma together. We suffered together," he said. "I know what it's like not to breathe. She's free from it now. ... I felt an inner peace because she wouldn't have to suffer anymore."[6] He later became a fundraiser for asthma and cystic fibrosis research.

Lefferts was selected and pitched for the United States in the 1979 Pan American Games in Puerto Rico, but the team failed to win a medal for the first time ever. He was drafted by the Kansas City Royals in the seventh round that year, but chose to return to school. Lefferts led the team to the 1980 College World Series, where he threw a shutout against Michigan and was the winning pitcher in the title game against Hawaii. He was named to the All-Tournament team, and later to the 1980s All-Decade team. He was drafted once more, this time by the Chicago Cubs in the ninth round, and signed a contract.

Lefferts was assigned to Geneva in the short-season New York-Penn league in 1980, and pitched well, going 9-1 with a 2.78 ERA, including a four-hit shutout in July. At the end of the season he was named to the league's all-star team. He had another complete game in the first game of the playoffs, winning 2-1, but Geneva lost the series two games to one to Oneonta.

Things weren't as easy at Midland of the Double-A Texas League the following year, where Lefferts was 12-12 with a 4.14 ERA, but he was still one of the best starters on the team. He threw another four-hitter in July, shutting out Jackson as he retired the last 17 hitters.

At Triple-A Iowa in 1982, Lefferts was 8-5 with a 3.05 ERA, and continued to step up the ladder. His July gem that season was a three-hit shutout of Oklahoma City.

Despite having almost exclusively been a starter in the minor leagues, Lefferts made the Cubs bullpen out of spring training in 1983. "He was one of those guys who wasn't overpowering, but he always seemed to get you out," manager Lee Elia said.[7] He only made the team because regular long man Mike Proly opened the season on the disabled list. Switching to the bullpen didn't faze Lefferts. "It will be an adjustment, but it shouldn't be too difficult," he said.[8]

Lefferts made his major-league debut on April 7, 1983, in the team's second game of the season. Coming on in the eighth inning with the Cubs down 6-2 to the Montreal Expos, Lefferts pitched the last two innings of the game, giving up a solo home run to Jim Wohlford in the ninth. "It was my fault. It was a nothing fastball," he said.[9]

Lefferts pitched well early in the season, but put this down to the players not being familiar with him. "The hitters haven't seen me before. They're not sure what I throw," he said. "Once they get to know me, I'll have to trick 'em a little bit."[10] He got a spot start on May 25 in Houston, and scattered six hits over seven innings, but a passed ball in the second led to the game's only run. He got three more starts in June, but after giving up five runs in five innings on June 20, he was sent back to the bullpen for the rest of the season. "I know I'm not a starter on this club. My role is in the bullpen. I'll probably be there all year, which is all right with me," Lefferts said.[11] Despite one more spot start, in a doubleheader in August, his bullpen future was settled, and he did not make another start until 1992.

Having pitched well in 1983, with a 3.13 ERA in 89 innings, Lefferts was surprised to be dealt to the San Diego Padres in a three-team trade.[12] For the Cubs, the desire was to obtain Scott Sanderson at any cost, as they believed he could become their top pitcher. Padres GM Jack McKeon was looking to stockpile young talent, and Lefferts' success in the bullpen was enough for San Diego to want him included in the deal. The Padres had included Gary Lucas and his team-leading 17 saves in the trade, and expected Lefferts to take up some of that slack. "Lefferts throws strikes and we feel like he'll develop into a good one," McKeon said.[13]

While in Puerto Rico pitching winter ball for Ponce over the offseason, Lefferts learned how to throw a screwball from teammate Gil Rondon, and it gave him an extra dimension. "I think I've just about mastered it," he said. "I can throw it for strikes. I can throw a hard screwball and I can throw it as a changeup. It has helped me a lot against righthanded hitters."[14]

As others fell by the wayside through the season, Lefferts moved up in the pecking order. He ended the season with a 2.13 ERA in 105⅔ innings, and his 10 saves trailed only Rich Gossage on the team. The team had a magical season, winning its division by 12 games. One game, on August 12, has entered into baseball lore as the Battle of Atlanta. When Braves pitcher Pascual Perez hit the Padres' Alan Wiggins to lead off the game, the Padres vowed revenge. After several attempts to retaliate (and already multiple ejections), it was Lefferts in the eighth inning who managed to hit Perez. First baseman Steve Garvey said, "When Lefferts finally hit him, I ran right to the mound and kind of held my arms out to try to help my pitcher, and about 20 guys blew right on by me after Lefferts, who by that time had hit the dirt at shortstop and was running toward left field."[15] Lefferts was one of seven players ejected after a 10-minute brawl; another six players were ejected after another hit-by-pitch in the ninth.

Down two games to none in the NLCS, the Padres came back to win the last three games and beat Lefferts' former team, the Cubs. Lefferts got the win in each of the final two games. The World Series was a letdown though; the Padres lost to the Detroit Tigers in five games. Lefferts had personal success, though, throwing six shutout innings in three appearances, including three innings with five strikeouts as he earned the save in Game Two. "Any way you want to look at it, this game was won by (Andy) Hawkins and Lefferts – they stopped us cold," Tigers manager Sparky Anderson said.[16]

An incident during 1984 was later related by Padres outfielder Tony Gwynn, which showed how valuable Lefferts quickly became to the team. In explaining the difference between a winning and losing team, Gwynn said that winning teams will ignore the little things that come up during the long season, such as a fight between Lefferts and fellow pitcher Ed Whitson:

"We're coming back from the East somewhere, and the guys are playing blackjack and sucking down a few brewskis," Gwynn [said]. "Eddie is dealing, and he's kind of toasted and not really paying attention to the card game. Whit had like 19, and Lefferts had 18, but Lefferts takes the money and Whit doesn't notice.

But somebody must have told him, because Whit goes ballistic on the bus. He starts screaming and yelling. He gets up and grabs Lefferts by the top of his hair and – pow! – just slaps the crap out of him. Guys had to get up out of their seats and grab Whitson to stop him. The quote I remember that day is, "Hey, man, you're messing with our money. He's going to help us get to where we want to go."[17]

Lefferts quickly cashed in on his postseason performance, signing a two-year contract with the Padres. A desire to start was never in the cards though. "I wouldn't turn it down if the chance came to move into the starting rotation," he said. "But for the time being, it looks like my job here is to pitch middle and late relief."[18]

Things didn't go as well in 1985, with the Padres falling to a third-place tie and Lefferts' ERA jumping to 3.35. He suffered from elbow problems, which continued into the following season. But he got off to a good start in 1986. "That confidence snowballs, and it's building right now," he said.[19] He had his career batting highlight on April 25, hitting a walk-off home run off the Giants' Greg Minton in the 12th inning. (As of 2018 he remained the last pitcher to hit a walk-off homer.) By the end of the year he'd pitched in a league-leading 83 games, but wasn't feeling good. "I'm pleased with the effort, but disappointed in a lot of other ways," he said. "I know there have been a lot of times in crucial situations when I haven't been effective." He didn't use his arm as an excuse. "My arm has been pretty good all year," he said. "I've had a sore elbow that's needed ice and treatment continually, but that doesn't keep me out of pitching."[20]

After Lefferts struggled to a 4.38 ERA in the first half of 1987, the Padres traded him to the Giants.[21] The Giants still thought highly of him. "The way he gets the left-handed hitters out, he might be finishing a lot of games for us," manager Roger Craig said.[22] Lefferts later said he was pleased with the trade. "It was definitely a great break getting traded out of San Diego the way things were going there and to San Francisco, the way things have happened here."[23]

At the time of the trade the Giants were in third place, and moved up over the rest of the season to win the NL West. Lefferts pitched just two innings in the NLCS as the Giants lost the series to the Cardinals in seven games. Once again his efforts were rewarded; he signed a new two-year deal with the Giants. He started 1988 well, and wasn't worried about his lack of publicity. "I think I could be a stopper on other teams," he said. "I don't get the saves, but the guys come up to me and tell me I've done a good job. That's good enough for me."[24]

In early 1989 Lefferts had a streak in which he retired 29 consecutive batters over six games (with two double plays on inherited runners making it 31 consecutive outs). That was part of a streak of 26 innings without giving up a run, going back to the previous season. He had a 2.69 ERA and led the bullpen with 20 saves, although he shared the closer role with Steve Bedrosian after the Giants added him in June. The Giants won their division, then beat the Cubs in the NLCS, with Lefferts finally giving up a run in the only inning he pitched, having not surrendered a run in the first 12 innings of his postseason career. They went on to be swept by Oakland in the World Series, with Lefferts pitching in three games.

Others noticed big improvements by Lefferts during the season. "He's a better pitcher now than he was in 1984," Rich Gossage said. "He's more aggressive, and he's pitching with a lot more confidence. When you're young and don't have the experience, there's always doubt in your mind." Catcher Terry Kennedy noted that Lefferts had pitched with just a fastball and screwball in his early career, but had added a slider. "Lefty's slider is much better now. … He throws the screwball for strikes better than average, and his slider is above average. He's also smarter now," Kennedy said.[25] Lefferts himself was happy in his new role. "I feel like I have more of an impact on a game. It's easy to get into a rut when you're a middle reliever or a set-up guy," he said.[26]

A free agent after the 1989 season, Lefferts returned to the Padres on a three-year, $5.35 million contract. He replaced NL Cy Young Award winner Mark Davis, who had demanded too much money from the Padres after a 44-save season. Ironically Davis had gone from the Giants to the Padres in the deal that took Lefferts in the other direction. The trade for Bedrosian was the reason for Lefferts to leave San Francisco, and the closer role in San Diego was reason for him to return. "If there was no Bedrosian deal, I probably wouldn't have filed for free agency," he said. "The biggest motivation for signing with the Padres was the opportunity to be a stopper. The timing couldn't have been better for me."[27]

Lefferts faced two big questions on his return to San Diego: How could he replace Davis, and how would his arm hold up? On the first question, he wasn't worried about replacing Davis and his 44 saves. "How many people have done that?" Lefferts said. Noting that Davis was a power pitcher while he was a finesse pitcher, Lefferts said, "Both styles can be equally as effective. And I think I've proven that over the years."[28]

The arm, meanwhile, was a different question. Lefferts had pitched through tendinitis and a sore shoulder for years, and teams were surprised he had gotten the contract he did. The Giants thought his arm was "fragile," which is why they didn't bring him back. Lefferts pointed to his history in response. "Except for the end of last year and a brief period in '87, I've pitched 100 percent of the time. … I've pitched in more games (472) than any other pitcher in the last seven years. So how can anyone make that type of argument?"[29]

The Padres stumbled in 1990, though, from preseason contenders to a 75-win team. Lefferts did his part, notching 23 saves and a 2.52 ERA despite a "dead arm."[30] The team improved by nine games the next season, and Lefferts matched his save total although his ERA jumped to 3.91. In both offseasons his name came up in trade talks, but he remained with the Padres. They even put him into the rotation to start 1992, and he exceeded expectations, going 13-9 with a 3.69 ERA in 27 starts.

With his contract approaching its end, Lefferts was traded to Baltimore on August 31,[31] where he went 1-3 as the Orioles fell out of contention. The trade to the Orioles upset the Padres. On the day of the trade they were 8½ games back in their division, but still felt they were in the pennant race. The owners were looking to cut costs and ordered general manager Joe McIlvaine to make deals. The team collapsed after that, ending up 16 games behind, and many blamed the Lefferts trade. "That was one of the hardest trades, emotionally, I ever had to make," McIlvaine later said. "My gut was telling me, 'This isn't the right thing to do.' … I pleased one group (owners) and I alienated two others (players and fans)."[32]

At the end of the season the Orioles declined to offer Lefferts arbitration, making him a free agent once more. He signed a one-year, $1.1 million deal with the Texas Rangers for 1993. Lefferts was in contention for the fifth starter role, or potentially moving to the bullpen. He began as the fifth starter but was poor, pitching to a 1-5 record with an 8.12 ERA by mid-May, when he went on the disabled list with a sore neck. When he returned, he went into the bullpen for the rest of the season, but his 4.04 ERA the rest of the way dropped his combined season ERA to 6.05, by far the worst of his career. The Rangers set him free again at the end of the season, choosing a $175,000 buyout instead of a $1.3 million option.

Lefferts signed another one-year deal, this time for $400,000 with the California Angels. He didn't pitch well, running to a 4.67 ERA before the All-Star break, when the Angels released him to avoid paying appearance incentives in his contract that could have brought him $1 million. Although naturally disappointed that his career was over, he looked back with pride. "For me, I had a wonderful career. I played 12 years in the major leagues. I couldn't have done more," he said.[33]

Lefferts had married Wendy LeBar, and they had five children. He spent a few years at home with them before Wendy encouraged him to try coaching. He reached out to Billy Beane, the Oakland A's general manager. Oakland did not have a position available, but Beane put him in touch with the Toronto Blue Jays. He was a pitching coach in the Jays system from 1999 to 2002, then in the Oakland system in 2003-14. Most of his coaching was at the lower levels; he spent 2000-03 at Double A. He was also the pitching coach for the South Africa national team at the 2013 World Baseball Classic.

In 2015 Lefferts became the A's minor-league pitching rehab coordinator in Mesa, Arizona, dealing with players recovering from injury. The team sent its injured players to live in Arizona, where they could get specialist physical and mental training. Lefferts' role expanded from being a pitching coach. "I'm a rehab coach. I'm a pitching coach. I'm a mental coach. I'm a psychologist," he said. He worked with each player on the field, ensuring that they have a plan for recovery and are following it. Although he pitched through arm problems himself, he acknowledged the changes in the modern game. "I've had to learn in these last few years that effort level is really the key initial component to having a positive rehab," he said.[34]

Lefferts himself struggled with health issues in recent years. He had spinal fusion surgery in 2016 to deal with a ruptured disk in his back. He also had ongoing issues with his eyes, having two failed surgeries to correct lifelong vision problems. Those problems helped him in working with rehabbing pitchers. "I've been through. I've dealt with that most of my life," he said.[35]

All in all, Lefferts said in 2017, he was pleased with his career and life in baseball. "I have already done my career. I'm the luckiest man around and I still get to put a uniform on and do this for a living. How about that? Couldn't be better."[36]

## SOURCES

In addition to the sources in the notes, the author consulted Baseball-Reference.com and Retrosheet.org.

## NOTES

1    Before the fall of communism and the reunification of Germany, West Germany was the non-Communist area.

2    Tom Friend, "Padre Reliever Has Met Many Challenges on His Way to Becoming a Major Leaguer," *Los Angeles Times*, June 9, 1985.

3    Dennis Georgatos, "Lefferts Faces Pressure," *Trenton* (New Jersey) *Evening Times*, April 8, 1990: C10.

4    Friend.

5    Georgatos.

6    Friend.

7    Ibid.

8    Joe Goddard, "Bullpen Very Deep; Cubs Will Need It," *The Sporting News*, April 18, 1983: 14.

9    Joe Goddard, "Rookie Lefferts Becomes a Starter," *The Sporting News*, May 2, 1983: 22.

10   Ibid.

11   Joe Goddard, "Buckner, Sandberg, Durham Halt Skids," *The Sporting News*, June 13, 1983: 16.

12   The Cubs sent Lefferts, third baseman Fritzie Connally and left fielder Carmelo Martinez to the Padres. The Padres sent pitcher Gary Lucas to the Montreal Expos.

The Expos sent infielder Al Newman to the Padres, and pitcher Scott Sanderson to the Cubs.

13   Phil Collier, "Lefferts to Work in Padres' Pen," *The Sporting News*, December 26, 1983: 43.

14   Phil Collier, "Padres' Bargain: Reliever Lefferts," *The Sporting News*, June 11, 1984: 19.

15   Michael Knisley, "A Career Year," *The Sporting News*, May 23, 1994: 14.

16   "Dirty Kurt, Handy Andy Tame Tigers," *The Sporting News*, October 22, 1984: 13.

17   Michael Knisley, "It Was in the Cards," *The Sporting News*, May 23, 1994: 13.

18   Phil Collier, "Padres Still Need Lefferts in Bullpen," *The Sporting News*, March 18, 1985: 32.

19   "Padres," *The Sporting News*, June 9, 1986: 16.

20   Mark Kreidler, "So-So Results From Lefferts' Efforts," *The Sporting News*, October 13, 1986: 27.

21   The Padres sent Lefferts, pitcher Dave Dravecky, and outfielder Kevin Mitchell to the Giants for third baseman Chris Brown and pitchers Keith Comstock, Mark Davis, and Mark Grant.

22   "Giants," *The Sporting News*, July 20, 1987: 21.

23   Casey Tefertiller, "Lefferts' Career Gets New Impetus," *San Francisco Examiner*, June 5, 1988: C6.

24   Nick Peters, "He's Caught in the Middle," *The Sporting News*, May 23, 1988: 20.

25   Nick Peters, "From Set-Ups to Saves," *The Sporting News*, June 26, 1989: 16.

26   Ibid.

27   "Giants," *The Sporting News*, January 1, 1990: 52.

28   Barry Bloom, "Lefferts Operates Under Davis' Shadow," *The Sporting News*, May 7, 1990: 16.

29   Ibid.

30   Barry Bloom, "Padres Stumble Through Ungodly Year," *The Sporting News*, August 20, 1990: 10.

31   In return for Lefferts, the Padres got pitcher Erik Schullstrom and infielder Ricky Gutierrez from the Orioles.

32   Chris De Luca, "San Diego Padres," *The Sporting News*, March 15, 1993: 18.

33   Melissa Lockard, "Former Big Leaguer Craig Lefferts Helping to Get A's Players Back on the Field," *The Athletic*, October 6, 2017. theathletic.com/117735/2017/10/06/former-big-leaguer-craig-lefferts-helping-to-get-as-players-back-on-the-field.

34   Ibid.

35   Daniel Brown, "A's Coach Craig Lefferts Recalls Memorable Blast from Giants' Past," *San Jose* (California) *Mercury News*, March 14, 2017. mercurynews.com/2017/03/14/as-coach-craig-lefferts-recalls-memorable-blast-from-the-past/.

36   Lockard.

# PHIL NEVIN

## BY JOEL RIPPEL

When Phil Nevin was an infant, he had difficulty breathing. His mother thought he had pneumonia and slept in his room to monitor his breathing. One day, at the age of 2, he had to be taken to the hospital after he started turning blue.

"They ran some tests and told me, 'Your kid has asthma, didn't you know?'" Terry Nevin said. "I lost my mother of the year

recommendation right there. But as Phil got older, he decided he was going to live a normal life and the asthma has been easy to control."[1]

It subsequently was discovered that he was allergic to grass. His mother saw one consolation in that for the future ballplayer.

"I don't think he's allergic to artificial turf," said Terry Nevin.[2]

Phil Nevin persisted and became a two-sport athlete in high school and college. In 1992 he became the first player from the baseball hotbed of Orange County (suburban Los Angeles) to be the first overall selection in baseball's June amateur draft.

Nevin was born in Fullerton, California, on January 19, 1971, to Terry, a teacher, and Norm Nevin, an electrical engineer for Southern California Edison Co. At El Dorado High School in Placentia, California, he was a standout kicker on the football team – kicking a then-Orange County record 57-yard field goal in 1988 – and the baseball team (where he was a teammate of future major leaguer Bret Boone).

In June of 1989, two days after Nevin and El Dorado won the CIF-Southern Section 5A division championship – a victory over Long Beach Millikan at Dodger Stadium – Nevin was selected in the third round of the draft by the Los Angeles Dodgers.

Nevin, who had grown up a Dodgers fan, turned down a reported $150,000 offer from the Dodgers. "It really wasn't a money decision," he said. "I made a decision (earlier in the year) to play both sports, possibly have a future in both. And I can't have a future in football if I don't keep kick. It's hard to say no to my all-time dream."[3]

After turning down the Dodgers, Nevin went ahead with plans to attend nearby Cal State Fullerton, which was less than three miles from his high school.

As a punter and placekicker, Nevin had an immediate impact on the Titans' football team as a freshman. In his fourth collegiate game, on September 23, 1989, on the field where he become a major-league All-Star, Nevin kicked a 42-yard field goal (his fourth of the game) as time expired to help the Titans tie San Diego State, 41-41, at Jack Murphy Stadium. The Aztecs' quarterback was future NFL quarterback Dan McGwire, the brother of Mark McGwire. After the season, Nevin was named first-team All-Big West Conference and the best freshman kicker or punter in NCAA Division I-A by *The Sporting News*.

In his three seasons as the Titans placekicker, he made all 69 of his extra-point attempts and kicked 31 field goals.

As a freshman on the Titans baseball team, Nevin batted .358 with 14 home runs and 52 RBIs in 59 games. As a sophomore, he batted .335 in 56 games with 3 home runs and 46 RBIs.

Titans coach Augie Garrido challenged Nevin after his sophomore season.

"Phil needed to modify his behavior and react to things properly," Garrido said. "At the same time, he was trying to be coach, general manager, owner, and chief of umpires. He wanted to wear all the hats. We told him to keep it simple and just be a baseball player, and he did make the adjustments."[4]

Nevin agreed with his coach's assessment: "They sat me down and pointed me in the right direction.[5]

As a junior, Nevin hit .402 with 22 home runs and 86 RBIs and led the Titans to the championship game of the College World Series. In the Titans' 7-2 victory over Florida State in the first round, he hit a grand slam and had six RBIs.

Two days after the victory over Florida State, the Houston Astros selected Nevin as the number-one pick in the 1992 draft.

"The Houston Astros have a job to do," Astros scout Tom Mooney said. "After what happened to us last year (the Astros had failed to sign their first-round pick, John Burke, a pitcher from Florida, in 1991), we wanted to get a player who wants to play for the Houston Astros – and will sign. We do not make the decision on 'who can we sign the cheapest. (But) you know Houston is Houston. We're a small-market club. We're just trying to do the best we can."[6]

Nevin, who was the 1992 Golden Spikes Award winner (as the nation's top amateur baseball player), was named the MVP of the College World Series, even though the Titans lost to Pepperdine in the championship game.

Nevin and the Astros quickly reached an agreement on a reported $700,000 signing bonus. After signing, Nevin spent the summer playing for Team USA, which lost to Japan, in the Bronze Medal game of the 1992 Olympics in Barcelona, Spain.

Nevin began his professional career in 1993 at the Triple-A level. In 123 games with Tucson, he hit .286 with 10 home runs and 93 RBIs. He returned to Tucson in 1994 and batted .263 with 12 home runs and 79 RBIs in 118 games.

The 1995 season was an eventful one. Nevin played for four teams in four leagues. He began the season at Tucson. He was hitting .291 with 7 home runs and 41 RBIs when he was called up by the Astros on June 10. On June 11 he made his major-league debut in the Astros' 3-2 loss to the Cincinnati Reds in Houston. Nevin delivered an RBI single in his first major-league at-bat (in the first inning off C.J. Nitkowski).

After hitting .117 in 18 games with the Astros, Nevin was returned to Tucson. On August 15 Houston sent Nevin to the Detroit Tigers to complete a trade from five days earlier in which the Astros had acquired pitcher Mike Henneman.

The Tigers sent Nevin to their Toledo farm team, where he hit .304 in seven games. On September 1 the Tigers recalled Nevin and he made his AL debut that night, going 1-for-4 with an RBI in the Tigers' 14-4 loss to Cleveland in Detroit. On Sept. 3 he hit his first major-league home run, a solo shot off Albie Lopez, in the Tigers' 9-8 loss to Cleveland.

Nevin was a regular in the Tigers' lineup over the final month of the season, appearing in 29 games. He batted .219 with 2 home runs and 12 RBIs.

During spring training in 1996, the Tigers moved Nevin, who hadn't caught since Little League, to catcher and sent him to Double-A Jacksonville so he could play every day. After hitting .294 with 24 home runs and 69 RBIs in 98 games, he was recalled by the Tigers on August 3. In his 1996 debut for the Tigers that day, he went 3-for-4 with an RBI in a 6-3 victory over the Seattle Mariners.

Nevin put together a 10-game hitting streak between August 28 and September 7. On September 21, he had the first multiple-home-run game of his career when he homered twice in a 13-6 loss in Milwaukee. Overall, in 38 games with the Tigers in 1996, Nevin hit .292 with 8 home runs and 19 RBIs.

Nevin opened the 1997 season on the disabled list after suffering a torn wrist ligament early in spring training. After a three-game rehab stint at Class-A Lakeland (the only time in his career he played below Double A) and a five-game stint with Toledo, he was activated on April 16. In 93 games with the Tigers in 1997, he batted .235 with 9 home runs and 35 RBIs.

After the season the Tigers traded Nevin and Matt Walbeck to the Anaheim Angels for minor-league pitcher Nick Skuse.

In Nevin's first full season in the majors, 1998, he batted .228 with 8 home runs and 27 RBIs in 75 games.

In the final week of spring training in 1999, Nevin and a minor-leaguer were traded to the San Diego Padres for infielder Andy Sheets and a minor-leaguer. Nevin opened the regular season on the 15-day disabled list because of a strained left hamstring suffered in spring training. He was activated on April 16 and made his Padres debut the next day with a pinch-hit single in the Padres' 7-3 loss to the Dodgers in San Diego.

After becoming the Padres regular third baseman and cleanup hitter on August 1, Nevin hit .288 with 17 doubles, 12 home runs, and 47 RBIs in 59 games over the final two months of the season. On September 7 he agreed to a two-year contract extension (with an option for a third year). For the season, he posted career highs in every offensive category: 24 home runs with a team-high 85 RBIs in 128 games. After the season he was named the Padres' MVP.

The 1999 season was the first of a three-year stretch that saw Nevin average 32 home runs and 106 RBIs for the Padres.

In 2000, his first full season as a regular, Nevin increased his production as he led the Padres in batting average (.303), doubles (34), home runs (31), RBIs (107), and slugging percentage (.543) in 143 games. He hit .346 after the All-Star break despite being slowed in September by an abdominal muscle strain. He hit just .233 with one home run in 14 games in September. For the second consecutive season, he was named the team MVP.

The 2001 season saw more improvement from Nevin, who became the only major leaguer to improve his batting average, home runs and RBI total in each season since 1998. Nevin led the Padres in batting average (.306), home runs (41), and RBIs (126) and earned his first All-Star berth. His season was highlighted by consistency – he hit .310 with 21 home runs before the All-Star Break and .301 with 20 home runs after the break. Among his 41 home runs were a club record (and the most in the majors in 2001) four grand slams.

Nevin closed out the season with a flourish. On September 27, he was 3-for-5 with two home runs and a career-high 7 RBIs in the Padres' 13-9 loss to the Colorado Rockies in Denver. On

October 6, the next-to-last day of the regular season, he hit three home runs and drove in six runs in the Padres' 10-4 victory over the Rockies in San Diego. For the season, Nevin hit 8 home runs and had 29 RBIs in 71 at-bats against the Rockies. In 10 games at Coors Field, he hit five home runs and had 22 RBIs.

When Nevin was named the team MVP for the third consecutive season, he joined Tony Gwynn (1986-1988) as the only Padres to win three consecutive team MVP awards. On November 15 Nevin agreed to a four-year extension through the 2006 season – worth a reported $34 million. The deal was the richest in club history to date.

Nevin was slowed in 2002 by two trips to the disabled list. He missed 14 games in May with a strained left elbow. After returning to action on May 27, he suffered a fractured humerus in his left arm in his third game back. He was sidelined until July 12. The Padres missed his offensive production. During his two stints on the disabled list, the Padres were 16-33. For the season, he hit .285 with 12 home runs and 57 RBIs in 107 games.

The 2003 season got off to a rough start, when Nevin dislocated his left shoulder in an exhibition game on March 7. The injury was initially expected to sideline him the entire season, but after undergoing surgery, Nevin returned to action in late July. Over the final two months of the season, he hit .279 with 13 home runs and 46 RBIs in 59 games.

Nevin rebounded solidly in 2004, hitting .289 and leading the Padres with 26 home runs and 105 RBIs. The season included one stint on the 15-day disabled list (July 5-20) with a knee injury, but Nevin became the first Padre with three 100-RBI seasons.

After hitting just .167 in the first 10 games of the 2005 season, Nevin batted .302 over his next 45 games to raise his average to .276. Included in that stretch was a career-high 13-game hitting streak (April 16-29) and a 12-game streak (May 24-June 5).

In late June, Nevin's season was again interrupted by a trip to the disabled list – June 26-July 17 with a strained oblique muscle.

Two weeks after being activated, he was traded to the Texas Rangers for pitcher Chan Ho Park. The Rangers also sent $6 million to the Padres to help offset the money remaining on the $65 million, five-year contract Park signed with the Rangers before the 2002 season.

Several days before the trade, Nevin had invoked the no-trade clause in his contract after the Padres tried to send him to Baltimore in exchange for Sidney Ponson.

At the time of the trade, Nevin was among the leaders in several Padres career categories – home runs (second, 156), slugging percentage (second, .503), RBIs (third, 573), hits (fifth, 842), batting average (sixth, .288), and games played (ninth, 806).

Over the remainder of the 2005 season, he batted .182 with three home runs and eight RBIs in 29 games with the Rangers.

The 2006 season, which would turn out to be Nevin's final season as a player, saw the 35-year-old Nevin play for three teams and make the first postseason appearance of his career.

He spent the first two months of the season with the Rangers, hitting .216 with 9 home runs and 31 RBIs in 46 games. On May 31 the Rangers traded Nevin to the Chicago Cubs for outfielder Jerry Hairston.

In 67 games with the Cubs, he hit .274 with 12 home runs and 33 RBIs. On August 31, the Cubs traded Nevin to the Minnesota Twins for a player to be named (on September 5, the Cubs received minor-league pitcher Adam Harben from the Twins.

Nevin enjoyed the month in Minnesota as the Twins bid for the AL Central title and a spot in the playoffs for the fourth time in five seasons.

After going 1-for-3 in the Twins' 6-1 victory in Cleveland on September 17 – which moved them to within one game of AL Central-leading Detroit – Nevin said, "I made the comment before the game, that it would be hard not to say that these are the finest 17 days of baseball of my life. All these years, and being part of a pennant race, even if it's a small part, has been what I hoped."[7]

The Twins went 19-11 over their final 30 games to claim the AL Central crown (edging the Tigers by one game) and opened the playoffs against the AL West champion Oakland Athletics.

The series opened in Minneapolis, and Nevin went 0-for-3 as the designated hitter in Oakland's 3-2 victory over the Twins. The A's went on to sweep the series in three games.

After the 2006 season, Nevin filed for free agency before announcing his retirement. In 1,217 games over his 12-year major-league career, Nevin batted .270 with 208 home runs and 743 RBIs.

In 2007 Nevin joined the Padres' pregame radio show. He also served as an analyst on college baseball broadcasts.

In 2009 Nevin managed the Orange County Flyers in the independent Golden Baseball League. In 2010 he joined the Tigers' organization and managed Erie in the Double-A Eastern League. In 2011 he was promoted to manage the Tigers' Triple-A farm team in Toledo.

In 2014, after three seasons as the Toledo manager, Nevin became the manager of the Arizona Diamondbacks' Reno farm team in the Triple-A Pacific Coast League. In his first season as manager of the Aces, he directed the Aces to an 81-63 record and the PCL championship series against Omaha, which Omaha won, 3 games to 2.

After three seasons as the Reno manager, Nevin was reunited with former Padres manager Bruce Bochy when he joined Bochy's San Francisco Giants coaching staff as the third-base coach.

In 2018, he moved to the New York Yankees as a third-base coach under first-year manager Aaron Boone.

Nevin and his wife, Kristin, have three children (Koral, Tyler, and Kyle). Tyler was drafted as a high-school senior by the Colorado Rockies in the first round (38th player overall) of the 2015 draft. In 2018 Tyler was listed as the number-nine Rockies prospect. Kyle, a senior at Poway (California) High School in the 2018-19 school year, planned to attend Baylor on a baseball scholarship.

## SOURCES

In addition to the sources cited in the Notes, the author also consulted Baseball-Reference.com, mlb.com, newspapers.com and retrosheet.com.

Thank you to Jason Zillo, vice president for communications and media relations for the New York Yankees, for helping the author connect with Phil Nevin.

# NOTES

1     Mike DiGiovanna, "Asthma, Allergies Haven't Slowed Down Titans' Nevin," *Los Angeles Times*, June 2, 1992: C3.

2     Ibid.

3     Robyn Norwood, "Nevin Tells the Titans He Doesn't Bleed Dodger Blue*," Los Angeles Times*, August 8, 1989: III-6.

4     Mike Penner, "Astros Get a Real Deal with Nevin," *Los Angeles Times*, June 2, 1992: C1.

5     Ibid.

6     Ibid.

7     Patrick Reusse, "Newcomer Phil Nevin Is Reveling in a Pennant Race and Marveling at the Skill of His Teammates," *Minneapolis Star Tribune*, September 18, 2006: C3.

# JAKE PEAVY

## BY GERARD KWILECKI

The 2001 *Baseball America Prospect Handbook* listed Jacob Peavy as the number two prospect in the San Diego Padres organization.[1] The report, prepared by scouts, considered him "frail and wild." That is why he slipped to the 15th round of the 1999 free-agent draft. The Padres selected the 6-foot-1 right-handed pitcher out of St. Paul's Episcopal School in Mobile, Alabama. There were also concerns regarding Peavy's commitment to Auburn. He signed with San Diego and by 2001, his fastball, slider, and changeup had propelled him to number two. He

made his major-league debut a year later against the New York Yankees. This was just the start of the long up-and-down career of one Jacob Edward Peavy.

Jacob "Jake" Peavy was born on May 31, 1981, in Mobile, Alabama. His parents were Debbie and Donny Peavy. Donny was a carpenter and built cabinets in his backyard shop. Jacob had sports in his blood from an early age. His grandfather, Blanche Peavey, played fast-pitch softball, recorded Jake's pitching. They would spend hours watching his motion to make improvements. Jake's grandfather was killed in 1994 in an accident in the family shop. Jake always had his grandfather on his mind when he pitched.

Jake excelled in every sport he played. He also began a lifelong love for the outdoors. As a freshman at St. Paul's School, he began to excel as a pitcher. He sprouted into a 6-foot-1 frame and began to dominate the competition. His record in high school was 44-1, including a 13-0 state-championship senior season. He had a touch of wildness, but he easily corrected himself to get back on track. Jacob was named the Alabama High School Player of the Year in 1999. Auburn University offered him a full scholarship, which is rare in college baseball. A scout with the San Diego Padres also began to take notice.

The 1999 draft was a mix of stars in waiting and eventual busts. The first pick was Josh Hamilton, by the Tampa Bay Devil Rays.

He would go on to have a decent career with the Texas Rangers after a long bout with substance abuse. The list of first-round draftees is littered with players who did not make it to the majors. The gem of the draft was a 13th-round third baseman from Maple Woods Community College in Missouri, Albert Pujols. He eventually moved to first base, helped guide the St. Louis Cardinals to the 2006 World Series title, and in the twilight of his career was considered an almost certain Hall of Famer.

Jake Peavy made it known he planned to honor his commitment to Auburn unless he was drafted in the first four rounds. A Padres scout begged the club to draft Peavy when he noticed he was still on the board. The Padres didn't select Peavy until the 15th round, but they offered Peavy a six-figure signing bonus and he signed. Other notables from that draft were Josh Beckett, Shane Victorino, Justin Morneau, Brandon Phillips, and Barry Zito.

Peavy began his pro career with the Rookie Arizona League Padres. He went 7-1 with a 1.34 ERA, pitching in 13 games and striking out 90 in 73⅔ innings. Late in the season he was promoted to the Idaho Falls Chukars of the faster Rookie Pioneer League, where he pitched 11 scoreless innings, striking out 13 and winning two games. He was named to the Arizona League's postseason all-star team. *Baseball America* ranked him the number seven prospect in the league.[2]

Peavy continued his rise through the Padres system in 2000, pitching for the Fort Wayne Wizards in the Class-A Midwest League and posting a 13-8 record against better competition. His ERA was 2.90 with 164 strikeouts in 133⅔ innings. *Baseball America* ranked him the number seven prospect in the league and the number two prospect in the Padres organization.[3] (The publication projected him as the He was projected to be the number three starter in the projected 2004 lineup.[4] The scouting report for Peavy heralded him as the best pick from the 1999 draft.

Peavy's 2001 season started in the high Class-A California League with the Lake Elsinore Storm. He compiled a 7-5 record with a 3.08 ERA. He struck out 144 batters in 105⅓ innings and walked only 33, helping lead the Storm to a 91-49 record and the league co-championship. (All minor-league playoff championships were canceled after the September 11 terrorist attacks. By that time Peavy had been promoted to the Mobile Baybears of the Double-A Southern League.)

For Mobile, Peavy made five starts, winning two and losing one. He posted a 2.57 ERA with 44 strikeouts in 28 innings pitched. He finished the season as the number two overall prospect in the Padres organization, and the number one pitching prospect. He was scheduled to start the 2002 season in Mobile. He spent the offseason helping sell season tickets for the Baybears front office.

Peavy started the 2002 season as the number three prospect in the Padres organization, according to *Baseball America*.[5] He made 14 starts for the Baybears and had to adjust against better competition. He had a 4-5 record with a 2.80 ERA and 89 strikeouts in 80⅓ innings of work. The Padres were suffering from injuries to the pitching staff. They called up Peavy to make his major-league debut on June 22, 2002, against the New York Yankees in San Diego. As it turned out, he was in the majors to stay.

It was 75 degrees at game time, sunny, with winds out to left about 5 mph. Peavy was assigned jersey number 44. It was a Saturday afternoon game with over 60,000 fans in attendance in San Diego. His first batter was second baseman Alfonso Soriano. Soriano lined Peavy's first pitch into left field for a double. Peavy struck out the next batter, shortstop Derek Jeter, on three pitches. It was the first of Peavy's 2,207 major-league strikeouts. The next batter, first baseman Jason Giambi, doubled to center field to score Soriano. Giambi attempted to stretch his hit into a triple but was thrown out by Padres center fielder Mark Kotsay. Peavy then got Bernie Williams to ground out to end the first inning. He pitched six innings against the Yankees, giving up one run and three hits, striking out four, and walking two. The Padres hitters could do nothing against Yankees starter Ted Lilly, losing 1-0.

Peavy lost his next two starts, but on July 16, making his fourth start for the Padres, against the Colorado Rockies, he got his first major-league victory, 5-1, pitching seven innings and giving up one run on five hits. Peavy finished his rookie season with a 6-7 record in 17 starts totaling 97⅔ innings and striking out 90 batters. The Padres finished the 2002 season with a last-place finish at 66-96.

Peavy settled in as a member of the Padres rotation. In 2004 he went 15-6 and led the National League with a 2.27 ERA. In 2005 he was named to the National League pitching staff the All-Star Game in Detroit's Comerica Park. He pitched two-thirds of an inning, coming on in the bottom of the eighth inning. He faced three batters, giving up one hit and striking out one. The American League team prevailed, 7-5.

Before the 2007 season, on January 4, Peavy was involved in an embarrassing incident at the Mobile Regional Airport. He was running late for an early morning flight to the Dominican Republic. He bypassed airline security to check his baggage at the ticket counter. He was arrested for disorderly conduct. The case was dismissed after apologies were made.[6]

Peavy's best season as major leaguer was 2007. At the All-Star break he had a 9-3 record, which earned him the starting nod for the midsummer classic at AT&T Park in San Francisco. He pitched one inning, facing four batters and giving up one hit.

The Padres finished the 2007 season with an 89-74 record and in third place under manager Bud Black. Peavy had a career-best 19 wins with 6 losses, a 2.54 ERA, and 240 strikeouts in 223⅓ innings while only walking 68 batters. He led the National League in wins, ERA, strikeouts, and WHIP (walks plus hits per innings pitched). He was the unanimous winner of the Cy Young Award, the fourth Padres pitcher to win the award.

Peavy had a reversal of form in 2008, winning 10 games and losing 11, though his ERA remained good at 2.85. In 2009, he landed on the disabled list on June 16 with a tendon tear in his right ankle. He was sidelined for 2½ months. With the Padres mired in another losing season, the club chose to free up what was left of Peavy's $11 million salary, and at the July 31 trade deadline he was traded to the Chicago White Sox for four players. The Padres had a 41-62 record at the time the trade was made. He was going to a White Sox team with a 53-51 record and needing pitching for the stretch run. After a stay at Triple-A Charlotte, he made his first start for the White Sox on September 19, lasting five innings and winning 13-3. By that time the White Sox were out of playoff contention. Peavy finished the season with two more wins for a 3-0 record. (He had been 6-6 with the Padres.)

Peavy had modest success with the White Sox. He was selected to the 2012 All-Star game in Kansas City. He had a 7-5 record but did not make an appearance in the game. In July 2013 the Boston Red Sox were in the middle of their playoff run when they acquired the right-hander in a trade deadline three-team deal. Peavy was 4-1 in 10 starts as the Red Sox advanced to the World Series. He started Game Three against the Cardinals. He pitched four innings, giving up six hits and two runs, and got a no-decision. That was his only appearance as the Red Sox won the Series.

Peavy started the 2014 season with the Red Sox but was traded to the San Francisco Giants in yet another July deadline trade. He won six games for the Giants over the final two months of the season and found himself again with a team that earned a berth in the World Series. Peavy started Game Two of the 2014 World Series against the Kansas City Royals. He pitched five innings, giving up six hits and four runs, and was charged with the Giants' 7-2 defeat. Getting another start in Game Six, he did not have a great outing. He lasted only 1⅓ innings, giving up six hits and five runs in a 10-0 loss to the Royals. His teammates bailed him out, though, defeating the Royals in seven games.

Peavy finished out his contract with the Giants in 2016. That was his last season the majors. He was not tendered a contract by a team for the 2017 season. He finished his career with 152 wins and 126 losses and a 3.63 ERA He was a three-time All-Star with two World Series rings, a Gold Glove (with the White Sox in 2012), and the 2007 Cy Young Award.

Peavy pitched in the postseason four times. He appeared two times for the Padres, in the Division Series in 2005 and 2006, and lost both his starts. In 2013 with the Red Sox he lost a game in the ALCS and had no decision in his other two starts, not lasting past the sixth inning in any of his three appearances. Peavy's final trip to the postseason was in 2014 with the Giants. He made two starts in the playoffs and two starts in the World Series, losing three of his four starts, with one no-decision. His career postseason record is one win and five losses. He was not able to match his regular-season success in the postseason. However, he was part of three deadline trades and helped two of his new teams reach the postseason.

Peavy went home to Southern Falls, his 5,000-acre plantation deep in the woods of Selma, Alabama. Southern Falls is open to guests for all occasions. Southern Falls has a wide range of activities including a bowling alley, an arcade, a live music stage, and a saloon. Groups can hunt on the forests, ride the trails, or explore the falls.[7] One of his prized possessions is one of the duck boats used in the 2013 World Series parade in Boston. He liked the boat so much that he purchased it the day of the parade. He also made headlines for purchasing a cigar-store Indian while on a trip to San Francisco. He said, "I was walking to the field on the day of my start and walked past a smoke shop, a tobacco/liquor store. And I'm Indian, my heritage is American Indian. And I walked by and saw just in the glass window this fellow looking at me."[8] Peavy earned an estimated $127,155,000 in his 15-year major-league career. By all accounts, he was set for life. On the surface, Peavy was going to be able to enjoy life after baseball, with his family on his plantation, and watch his four sons grow up. Then life threw him a curveball.

Prior to opening training camp in 2016 with the Giants, he learned that his lifelong friend and trusted financial adviser had been running a "Ponzi scheme" with his money. According to court documents filed by the United States of America against Ash Narayan, the Securities and Exchange Commission laid out their case number 3:16-cv-1417-M. The SEC alleged Mr. Narayan received more than $1.5 million in over directing over $30 million in investments from Roy Oswalt, Peavy, and NFL player Mark Sanchez. The original complaint was filed with the SEC on February 8, 2017.[9] Mr. Narayan submitted an offer of settlement without admitting or denying the allegations against him. He was suspended from appearing or practicing as an attorney or accountant with the SEC. Basically he was banned from trading or investing for himself or for clients. The

SEC filed an amended action against Mr. Narayan on April 1, 2018 adding fraud to the complaint. The amended complaint alleges how Mr. Narayan defrauded the three players, siphoning funds from the investment account for his personal use. The complaint also alleges how Mr. Narayan performed trades and opened accounts in his clients names without their consent. According to the court documents, Peavy lost his investment of $15,105,000 along with $957,432 in fees.[10] As of this writing in October 2018, Mr. Narayan has not been put on trial for his alleged crimes.

Then Peavy's wife, Katie, filed for divorce. Peavy decided to put his professional career on hold to get his family house in order. He was awarded joint custody of his sons.[11]

As of 2018 Peavy lived in Mobile and was content to watch his sons grow up and play sports at St. Paul's Episcopal School, where Peavy was inducted in the school's Hall of Fame in 1999. He still tended to Southern Falls. A few years may not have been the best, but he summed it up in a song he wrote called "Keep on Smiling."[12]

## SOURCES

In addition to the sources cited in the Notes, the author also consulted Baseball-Reference.com.

## NOTES

1    Jim Callis, *Baseball America 2001 Prospect Handbook* (Durham, North Carolina: Simon and Schuster, 2001), 354.

2    Allen Simpson, *Baseball America 2000 Almanac* (Durham, North Carolina: Simon and Schuster, 1999), 298.

3    *Baseball America 2001 Almanac*, 296-97; Callis, 350-354.

4    *Baseball America* viewed him as the number three starter in the projected Padres 2004 starter rotation. Callis, 350-354.

5    Callis, 374-78.

6    Tom Krasovic, "Wiser Peavy Has Learned Major Lesson in Discretion," *San-Diego Union-Tribune,* February 17, 2007. legacy.sandiegouniontribune.com/union-trib/20070217/news_1s17sullivan.html

7    southernfalls.com/.

8    Matthew T. Hall, "Jake Peavy Bought His World Series Parade Duck Boat," *sandiegouniontribune.com,* November 3, 2013, sandiegouniontribune.com/opinion/the-conversation/sdut-jake-peavy-duck-boat-world-series-parade-reaction-2013nov03-htmlstory.html; boston.com/sports/extra-bases/2013/10/07/jake_peavy_tells_the_mostly_true_story_of_the_luck.

9    https://www.sec.gov/litigation/admin/2017/34-79991.pdf

10    https://www.sec.gov/litigation/complaints/2018/comp24030.pdf

11    Scott Miller, "I Need a Miracle Every Day," Bleacherreport.com, February 14, 2018. bleacherreport.com/articles/2756799-i-need-a-miracle-every-day-jake-peavy-picks-up-pieces-of-a-shattered-life.

12    Mark Inabinett, "7 Questions with Cy Young Award Winner Jake Peavy," al.com, March 15, 2018. al.com/sports/index.ssf/2018/03/7_questions_with_cy_young_awar.html.

# GENE RICHARDS

## BY MICHAEL SEE

On August 29, 1977, Gene Richards was nearing the end of what was one of the finest rookie seasons in baseball history. His 56 stolen bases during that season were an all-time rookie record. However, on this particular evening, he stood silent at first base at San Diego Stadium, next to a man who had been his boyhood idol, Lou Brock. He had grown up idolizing Brock and the St. Louis Cardinals, along with players like Bob Gibson and Curt Flood.

This was also a very special night in San Diego: It was the evening that Richards' childhood hero would tie and break Ty Cobb's lifetime record for stolen bases with the 892nd and 893rd stolen bases of his career. "My greatest thrill I had in baseball was being there when Lou broke that record," recalled Richards in a 2018 interview. "I didn't say much of anything to him during that game. I was like a kid just standing in awe of his hero, afraid to say a word."[1]

In a twist of fate, here were two African-American men standing side by side, both having come from historically black colleges in the South. One was a veteran who was about to have his crowning achievement, the other a young and up-and-coming speedster who had the potential to one day challenge his idol's records. In 1977 the future was bright for Eugene Richards Jr.

Eugene Richards Jr. was born to Eugene Richards Sr. and Mary Agnes Richards on September 29, 1953, in Monticello, South Carolina. The second of seven children, he had four brothers and two sisters. Gene and his family grew up in Blair, South Carolina. His mother was a homemaker and his father worked at a rock quarry.

Richards' love of baseball began when he was a boy. "Everyone in town played baseball," he said. "The high school did not have football, so baseball was it for us." Richards attended McCrorey-Liston High School in Blair, and it soon became apparent that the talented young high-school player might be destined for great things.

Richards was recruited as a pitcher on a full scholarship to South Carolina State University. "In school, hitting was always secondary to me," he said. "I just wanted to concentrate on throwing strikes. I liked it out there." While he was a very good pitcher (he went 7-2 as a junior), it was his other tools that began to get the attention of scouts like the Padres' Gus Lombardo. Richards batted .450 during his sophomore season and .414 as a junior. He had an excellent 1974 summer season in the Shenandoah Valley League, batting .366 with 32 stolen bases.

He and his talented South Carolina State teammate, Willie Aikens, had planned to return for their senior seasons in 1975, when they received word that the Bulldogs' baseball program had been terminated to expand woman's sports.[2] "There were other avenues," Richards said. "I had spoken with Clemson and Virginia Tech, if it was at all possible, if the program was still there. I wanted to go back to SC State."[3] Richards said he had scholarship offers from both schools. Because their program had been discontinued, both Richards and Aikens were made immediately eligible for the major-league baseball draft. Richards hoped to go high in the draft, and to his surprise, he was the first overall pick, selected by the San Diego Padres. His Bulldogs teammate Aikens went second, to the California Angels. It marked the first time that a player from a historically black college was the first overall pick in the draft. "I could barely tell you where San Diego was on a map when I was drafted," said Richards. "But I was just so happy for my parents, that all of their good deeds had not gone to waste. This was the first time anything like this had ever happened in our area."

Richards began his professional career with the Reno Silver Sox of the Class-A California League. If there was any doubt as to his talent, he quickly put it to rest. He batted .381 (.499 on-base percentage) with 191 hits, 148 runs scored, and a league-record 85 stolen bases, and was named the league's Most Valuable Player. The Silver Sox won the league championship. Richards was named to the Topps National Association Class-A All-Star Team[4] and won the Louisville Slugger Bat Award.[5] His .381 average was the highest in Organized Baseball in 1975.

Though his first year in professional baseball was a success, Richards was frustrated during the season that he was not being promoted to Double A. "My goal was to make it to the majors in three years," he said. "I guess that made me play with a chip on my shoulder."

Mike Port, the Padres' director of minor-league operations at the time, said of Richards: "As a hitter, he's a lot like Ralph Garr, but I think he's going to have more pop than Garr. Defensively,

he does not seem to go back on the ball as well as we would like because of his inexperience."[6] (Richards was mostly a pitcher in high school). Richards' inexperience on defense was likely the reason that Padres left him in A-ball the entire season.

That winter, Richards went to the Arizona Instructional League to continue his work in the outfield. He was third in the league with a .375 batting average and 10 stolen bases in 17 games. Padres player personnel director Bob Fontaine came away very impressed. "Gene has a lot of things going for him," said Fontaine, "His knowledge of the strike zone is one of his pluses. He chokes up on the bat. He's on top of home plate and doesn't swing at many bad pitches. He has great acceleration as a runner and we believe he'll continue to develop. Maury Wills will be in spring training with us next year and we think he can help Gene steal even more bases."[7]

Scout Al Heist had been assigned the task of polishing Richards' outfield defense. "The biggest adjustment he has to make is playing center field after playing left field in Reno," said Heist. "Gene is not as fast as Willie Davis was at 21, but I think he has more power at the same stage, which is surprising considering the way he chokes up on the bat."[8]

Richards skipped Double A; in 1976 he was advanced to the Hawaii Islanders of the Triple-A Pacific Coast League. He hit well, batting .331 with a .435 OBP, led the league in hits with 173, and had 19 stolen bases helping lead the Islanders to the Pacific Coast League title (his second championship in two seasons). He said he enjoyed playing in Hawaii, but it was difficult to endure. "It was tougher than people might think," Richards said. "Two-week road trips, flying back and forth across the water. It was very challenging."

For 1977 the Padres rewarded Richards with a major-league contract. "They wanted me to sign a split contract, and I felt like if I were going to be in major-league spring training, that I deserved a major-league contract," Richards said. "Buzzie Bavasi called me and said, 'Son, just get on a plane out here and I'll take care of everything.'" Bavasi was true to his word, and Richards made the team as the starting left fielder, accomplishing his goal of making it to the big leagues in less than three years.

Richards' career got off to a fast start. In his debut game against the defending World Series-winning Cincinnati Reds at Riverfront Stadium on April 6, 1977, he led off the game with a single off Woodie Fryman in his first major-league at-bat. He stole his first base as well.

While his first game was a success, the rest of his first month in the big leagues did not go as well. Richards struggled to a .140 average in April and was worried that the Padres might send him back to the minors. "I have always been a second-half player," he said. "I really thought I was going to get sent down." But in a game against the Philadelphia Phillies on May 4, 1977, he went 2-for-5 against Jim Kaat with his first big-league home run. "From that point on," he said, "I never looked back or worried about going to the minors anymore."

While Richard's season was back on track, the Padres were not. After they started the season 20-28, manager John McNamara was fired and replaced by Alvin Dark. It was a situation that would become very common for Richards over the course of his career.

All-Star George Hendrick became Richards' mentor during his rookie season. "I owe everything to George Hendrick," Richards said. "He taught me about the game and all the ins and outs of being a major-league baseball player." Hendrick's influence on Richard's life went beyond the baseball field: During the 1977 season he introduced Richards to Yvette Shepard. They were married in 1979.

Richards' 1977 season was one for the record books. He batted .290 for the season with a .363 OBP, 16 doubles, 11 triples, and 5 home runs. On July 26, he had six hits in an extra-inning game against the Montreal Expos. He set a modern-day major-league rookie single-season record with 56 stolen bases, breaking the record of 49 previously held by Rollie Zeider (1910) and Sonny Jackson (1966). He finished third in Rookie of the Year voting behind future Hall of Famer Andre Dawson (with whom he shares his Topps Rookie Card) and the Mets' Steve Henderson.

The 1978 season got off to a turbulent start. Rumors were swirling that the Padres were considering trading Dave Winfield to the Yankees for Graig Nettles and Ed Figuroa (a deal that did not happen.)[9] In spring training Dark added fuel to the fire by announcing that he was shifting around the entire Padres infield. Richards would be moved full time to first base. "I was not happy about that move at all," said Richards. Dark was also moving shortstop Billy Almon to second base, Derrel Thomas to third (he had not played much third base in his career), and a rookie, Ozzie Smith, as the starting shortstop.

The team did not respond well. The Padres made a boatload of errors in the spring. Some players began to complain about what they considered to be too many rules imposed by Dark and his efforts to control all facets of the team. Richards said, "His style and the way he treated players just didn't work anymore and the players rebelled."

As the protests grew, on March 21, just 17 days before the start of the regular season, General Manager Bob Fontaine and owner Ray Kroc announced the firing of Dark. He was replaced on an interim basis by pitching coach Roger Craig. Craig was Richards' third manager on the Padres and he had played only one season.

Under Craig, things became more stable for the team (and luckily for the Padres, he decided to keep Ozzie Smith at shortstop). But Craig decided to continue the shift of Richards to center field from left, a position he was not comfortable with. "When you're talking about a young player, being yo-yoed between positions each season was very difficult," said Richards. "I felt unappreciated, because the stats and what I was doing I felt solidified me as a left fielder."

Through all of this turmoil, Richards improved his batting average to a career-high .308, though his stolen bases fell to 37. He helped lead the team to an 84-78 record, the Padres' first winning season in franchise history.

1979 would be an important and challenging year in the life of Gene Richards. First, he married his wife Yvette on Oct, 20, 1979. Second, he somehow found the time to return to school to South Carolina State University and finish his college degree.

The 1979 season though proved to be an even bigger challenge under Roger Craig. Craig had curbed Richards' basestealing. "Roger really would not let me do a lot of things free anymore," Richards said. "If I wanted to steal, he had to give me the steal sign. That was an important part of my game and the team's game. I was the igniter, and we lost that." After their breakthrough 1978 season, the Padres finished 68-93 in 1979. Richards had his worst season to date, batting .279 with a career-low 24 stolen bases.

The 1980 season brought another new manager (Richards' fourth in four seasons). This time, it was Jerry Coleman, who had been brought down from the Padres broadcast booth to lead the team. Richards was very happy with the change. "Jerry was great," said Richards. "He let me play, and I had one of my best seasons." Richards had career highs in many categories, including games (158), at-bats (642), and hits (193). He batted .301 with 61 stolen bases. The Padres became the first NL team to boast three players with 50 or more stolen bases (Richards, Ozzie Smith, and Jerry Mumphrey). He was exclusively a left fielder and led the league in outfield assists with 19 and in double plays turned by an outfielder (4). He set a team record by stealing 18 bases in a row.

The team played a little better as a whole, improving by five games, but not enough for Coleman to stay in the job; he went back to the broadcast booth. Richards would not only have another new manager in 1981, but he'd have to play it without his power-hitting teammate Dave Winfield and also faced the possibility of a looming players strike.

Winfield left in free agency, signing with the New York Yankees in 1981, leaving Richards as the dean of the Padres outfield. "Everyone knew Dave was going to leave so it was really no surprise," said Richards. "The problem was that he was really our only power source." New general manager Jack McKeon tried to replace Winfield's bat by acquiring Ruppert Jones (from the Yankees), but the vast confines of San Diego Stadium proved a challenge and the leading home-run hitter for the Padres in 1981 was Joe Lefebvre with eight. For Richards personally, Winfield's departure was offset by the arrival of his son, Eugene III, on February 3, 1981, same day the he signed a three-year, $1.1 million contract extension.[10]

Former slugger Frank Howard was Richards' fifth manager. "I really wish (the Padres) had given Frank more of an opportunity because I really liked playing for him," said Richards. "He worked three times harder than any other manager I ever had."

The Padres finished in sixth place in both strike-shortened halves of the 1981 season. Richards played in all 110 games, batting .288 and leading the league in triples (12) and outfield assists (14). As the season came to a close, GM McKeon continued his purge of the roster that had started the year before, and there were rumors that the Padres were looking to trade Richards to the Yankees for Ron Davis,[11] or that he would be included in the trade that sent Ozzie Smith to the Cardinals for Garry Templeton.[12] Richards though, was still with the Padres in 1982.

Howard did not survive the 1981 season so Richards had another new manager in 1982. This time, it was former World Series champion Dick Williams. Richards was excited by this; he had always wanted to Padres to bring in someone with Williams's experience and pedigree to try to take the team to the next level. That is what eventually happened, but it would be without Richards.

On April 9, 1982, the Padres were playing the Los Angeles Dodgers at Dodger Stadium in the third game of the season. Burt Hooton was on the mound for the Dodgers and Richards led off the game with a hit. Hooton attempted a pickoff and as Richards dove back safely, he felt a sharp pain in his knee. In Richards' words "It was a pain unlike anything I had ever felt before. My knee, instead of going the right way … went the wrong way." He did not realize it at the time, but he had suffered a partially torn ACL. The team had Richards back in the lineup just four days later, when he perhaps should have been having knee surgery, "I probably should have been out for the season," said Richards, "but I played through the pain."

For the rest of April, Richards continued to play on his damaged knee (he batted .293 and got at least one hit in 13 out of the 14 games he played, including a 10-game hit streak) before the pain became too much to bear. On May 1 he went on the disabled list for the first time in his career, and had knee surgery. Asked what was the biggest regret of his career, Richards' comment

was telling: "I wish I had listened to my mother." She had implored him to take a break from baseball, to rest himself. He did not listen. He was sure he could battle through the pain and get back into the lineup. "If I could go back and do it over, this would be the one thing I would do different. … It's a mother's intuition," said Richards. "They just know."

Richards came back a little less than a month after his surgery and pushed hard. He batted .326 in June but faded to .261 and .250 in July and August, before rebounding to .313 in September/October. He batted .286 and stole 30 bases but he was caught a career-high 20 times. Said Richards, "My best tool, my speed, was gone."

While Richards worked to rehabilitate his knee over the winter, when he reported to spring training in 1983, Dick Williams had other plans for his outfield. Alan Wiggins, a part-time player in 1982, was now manning left field, along with Ruppert Jones in center and second-year man Tony Gwynn in right. Veteran outfielder Sixto Lezcano had also been brought in and needed at-bats and young Kevin McReynolds was also tearing up the minors and was on the cusp of joining the team. This left Richards to be a part-time player, and while his speed had been seriously affected by the knee injury, he still felt that he could be a productive full-time player. "I knew 1983 would be my final season with the Padres," Richards said. "You could see the changing of the guard." Things only got worse for Richards when in late July, his mother died. There was some consolation for Richards: On September 30, 1983, he and his wife welcomed their daughter, Mary Angela "Angel" Gevette Richards, into the world.[13]

Despite all of the challenges and changes during the 1983 season, Richards still played well in a part-time role, batting .275 with 14 stolen bases, but with free agency looming, the 29-year-old outfielder looked forward to a future with a new team.

During the offseason, Richards thought that many teams seemed to be interested in acquiring his services, but throughout the winter, his phone remained quiet. In fact, it was not until midway through 1984 spring training that the San Francisco Giants offered Richards a one-year contract. But the Giants already had their starting outfield in place (Chili Davis, Jack Clark, and Jeff Leonard), and also Dan Gladden and Dusty Baker, so once again he'd be a bench player.

The highlight of Richards' season occurred on April 22 against the Cincinnati Reds at Candlestick Park. Richards went 4-for-5, including his 1,000th major-league hit, in a 9-5 victory.[14] It was one of the very few bright spots of the 1984 season for Richards.

About halfway through the season, Richards realized 1984 would be his final year. "I just had to look at it realistically. Those were the cards I had been dealt," he said. "I did not want to go out like that. I was not a good pinch-hitter. I never could adapt to the routine of coming off the bench and my knee was not better. I knew my time was done." After the season he retired as a player.

Right after retirement, Richards and his wife got into the real-estate business in South Carolina, and he opened a retail location that sold aquarium fish, a lifelong love of his. But baseball was not done with Eugene Richards yet.

Another of his childhood idols, Curt Flood, was starting the Senior Professional Baseball League in Florida. Richards could not resist the opportunity and agreed to play. He was drafted by the Winter Haven Solar Sox, playing with retired major leaguers like Cecil Cooper, Al Bumbry, Bernie Carbo, Fergie Jenkins, Bill "Spaceman" Lee, and Jim Bibby. "I really wanted to have another shot at winning a championship in baseball, and this gave me another chance," said Richards.

Richards played in the league for one season, 1989, batting .326 and stealing 11 bases. The Solar Sox made the playoffs, but fell short of a championship. But it allowed Richards to finish his playing career on a much brighter note.

The following year, his old general manager from the Padres, Buzzie Bavasi offered Richards the job of Double-A hitting coach in the Anaheim Angels organization. He served in the role from 1992 to 2001, tutoring developing players like Tim Salmon, Garrett Anderson, Troy Glaus, and Chone Figgins.

In 2002, after an organizational change, Richards moved to the Los Angeles Dodgers in a similar capacity, where he served as a hitting coach for players like Matt Kemp, James Loney, David Ross, Russell Martin, and Shane Victorino.

He wrapped up his career in professional baseball in 2005 by managing the Hagerstown Suns, the New York Mets' affiliate in the Class-A South Atlantic League, where he helped mentor a young Carlos Gomez.

As of 2018, it has been 35 years since Richard's San Diego Padres' career ended. Yet, he remains among the Padres' career leaders in a number of categories, among them:

Total WAR: 5th.
Batting Average: 5th.
Games Played: 5th.
At-Bats: 4th.
Singles: 3rd.
Triples 2nd.
Walks: 9th.
Stolen Bases: 2nd.
Runs Created: 7th.

Had he not suffered his knee injury, Richards' may have even ranked higher on the lists above.

Bill Center, a longtime sportswriter for U-T San Diego, chose Richards as the greatest left fielder in team history in 2016.[15]

Since 2006, Gene and his wife, Yvette, have spent their time between Reno and Las Vegas. As of 2018 they had been married nearly 40 years. In Reno, Richards was teaching baseball to youngsters with his company, Gene's Road to the Big Leagues.

His star may have faded too quickly, but Eugene "Gene" Richards Jr. stands amongst the all-time great players in San Diego Padres History.

## SOURCES

In addition to the sources cited in the Notes, the author consulted baseball-reference.com, baseball-almanac.com, and retrosheet.org, as well as the following:

genesroad.com/.

eastvillagetimes.com/2016/09/gene-richards-definitive-padre-leadoff-hitter-prospective-hall-famer/.

fangraphs.com/tht/cooperstown-confidential-the-1978-firing-of-alvin-dark/.

## NOTES

1    Michael See phone interview with Gene Richards, August 13, 2018. All quotations attributed to Gene Richards are from this interview unless otherwise indicated.

2    Phil Collier, "Daily Bread Tops List of Grubb's Goals (Padre Pickups)," *The Sporting News*, January 25, 1975: 41.

3    *The State* Newspaper. scsu.edu/news_article.aspx?news_id=341.

4    "Topps Salutes the Minor Leagues," *The Sporting News*, December 6, 1975: 43.

5    "1975 Silver Bat Awards," *The Sporting News*, February 28, 1976: 43.

6    "Gene Richards Player of the Month," *California League Newsletter*, June 28, 1975.

7    Phil Collier, "Padres Sing Psalms Over Kid Richards," *The Sporting News*, November 15, 1975: 43.

8    Ibid.

9    Phil Collier, "Padres Lie, Writers Unfair," *The Sporting News*, February 11, 1978: 47.

10   Phil Collier, "Padres Text of Year: Optimism," *The Sporting News*, February 28, 1981: 40.

11   Bill Conlin, "N.L. Beat," *The Sporting News*, November 14, 1981: 41.

12   "Temps Trade Call Like Clockwork," *The Sporting News*, June 20, 1981: 25.

13   Phil Collier, "Brown a Hot Hitter with Garvey Out," *The Sporting News*, August 15, 1983: 18.

14   Nick Peters, "N.L. West Notes," *The Sporting News*, May 7, 1984: 24.

15   mlb.com/padres/news/bill-centers-top-5-padres-left-fielders/c-161274608.

# BENITO SANTIAGO

## BY THOMAS J. BROWN JR.

Benito Santiago was one of the best catchers in the majors in the late 1980s and early 1990s. Santiago played solid baseball and set several catching records during a 20-year career during which he played for nine teams. His legacy was tarnished as a result of his inclusion in the steroid scandal that swept through baseball shortly before his career ended.

Benito Rivera Santiago was born in Ponce, on the south coast of Puerto Rico, on March 9, 1965. His father, José, a truck driver, died when Benito was 3 months old. José had an accident with

his rig, refused to be treated, and died shortly after the accident.[1] Shortly afterward, Benito's mother abandoned him, giving him to friends living on the opposite side of the island. He grew up never knowing his mother.[2]

Santiago not only grew up poor but he also grew up on the streets in the small town where he lived. If it hadn't been for baseball, he might have become just a poor farm worker. He reflected on this in an interview in 1989 when he returned for a visit to his hometown with a reporter and said: "See those guys out there picking tomatoes and watermelons? That used to be me. That would be me today."[3]

Santiago started out as a shortstop. He had to be talked into catching for his Little League team when the regular catcher did not show up for a game.[4] He attended John F. Kennedy High School in Santa Isabel, Puerto Rico. His coach, Luis Rosa, was also the Padres' chief scout in Puerto Rico. Santiago admired Rosa tremendously and after graduating from high school he signed with the Padres as an amateur free agent.

The Padres assigned the young catcher to the Miami Marlins of the low Class-A Florida State League in the spring of 1983. He played in 122 games and began to show the hitting prowess for which he would be recognized throughout his major-league career. He had 25 doubles and 56 RBIs. Promoted in 1984 to the

Reno Padres of the faster Class-A California League, Santiago hit .279 with 16 home runs and 83 RBIs.

After spring training in 1985, the Padres assigned Santiago to the Beaumont Golden Gators of the Double-A Texas League. He continued to demonstrate his ability to be an offensive threat even as he faced stiffer competition. Playing in 101 games, Santiago had 111 hits and raised his batting average nearly 20 points to .298. In 1986, promoted to the Las Vegas Stars of the Triple-A Pacific Coast League, Santiago batted .286 with 17 home runs and 71 RBIs. Called up to the Padres after the PCL season, Santiago made his major-league debut on September 14. He started the game against Houston and got his first major-league hit, a double off Mike Scott, in his first at-bat.

It was clear to the Padres that Santiago was ready for the majors. He became the team's starting catcher in 1987 and was a unanimous selection for the National League Rookie of the Year Award. His .300 batting average with 33 doubles, 18 home runs, and 79 RBIs, earned him a Silver Slugger Award, and behind the plate he was among the league leaders in several defensive statistics (although he notably led the league in passed balls and errors).

One of the most exciting parts of Santiago's rookie season was his 34-game hitting streak. Santiago batted .346 with 5 homers and 19 RBIs during the streak, which lasted from August 25 through October 2. His streak was the 15th longest in major-league history and the longest ever for a Padre, a rookie, or a catcher. Teammate Tony Gwynn pointed out the significance of Santiago's accomplishment when he said: "Every player but the catcher gets to rest and contemplate his next at-bat."[5]

Santiago's batting average plunged to .248 in 1988, but he won his first Gold Glove Award. In 1989 he won the first of four consecutive All-Star Game selections; he was the starting catcher for the NL team. In 1990 Santiago earned his third consecutive Gold Glove Award and third Silver Slugger Award. Chosen for the National League All-Star squad, he was injured and didn't play. For the first time, he received votes for the Most Valuable Player Award. He finished 23rd in the voting.

Santiago, who was paid $750,000 in 1990, sought a four-year, $11 million contract in 1991. The Padres offered $1.65 million for one year and they went to arbitration. Santiago lost, and said he would leave the Padres after the 1992 season and enter the free-agent market.[6] Santiago didn't let his contract situation in San Diego bother him on the field; he had one of his best offensive seasons in 1991, batting .267 with 17 home runs and a career-high 87 RBIs. Santiago was the starting catcher for the NL in the 1991 All-Star Game. (He repeated in 1992.)

Santiago went to arbitration again in 1992 and won his case, being awarded a salary of $3.3 million rather than the Padres' offer of $2.50 million. After the Padres made it clear that they were not going to re-sign Santiago or any of their other high-salaried players as a cost-cutting move,[7] he said he was sad to leave the organization that gave him his start in baseball,[8] entered the free-agent market after the season, and signed with the expansion Florida Marlins for $3.4 million.

Santiago hit the first home run in the Marlins history when he knocked a pitch by Trevor Wilson out of Candlestick Park on April 12, 1993. Santiago was solid as the Marlins' first-string catcher in 1993 and '94, but the Marlins declined to sign him at the end of 1994 because they had a young catcher, Charles Johnson, ready to step into the position.

Santiago once again entered the free-agent market and signed with the Cincinnati Reds for 1995. Sharing duties behind the plate with three others, Santiago played in only 81 games and helped the Reds get to the postseason. They defeated the Dodgers in the Division Series but lost the NLCS to Atlanta.

Once more Santiago went looking for a team after the season. He signed with the Philadelphia Phillies, for whom he hit a career-high 30 home runs, including a ninth-inning grand slam on May 3 off Greg Maddux, the first slam surrendered by Maddux in his career.[9] But the Phillies released him after the season, and Santiago signed with the Toronto Blue Jays. Injuries kept his catching load in 1997 to 97 games, and in 1998, injuries suffered in an offseason car crash limited Santiago to just 15 games.[10] He did not get into a game until September 4, and the Blue Jays released him at the end of the season.

Santiago signed with the Chicago Cubs for the 1999 season. He played in 109 games with middling results the Cubs released him at the end of the season. Santiago signed again with the Cincinnati Reds. He played in 89 games, and was released after the season.

Santiago had now played for six teams in eight years. His inconsistent play as well as injuries had made him no more than a journeyman player at this point in his career. The 36-year-old catcher's next stop was San Francisco. There, some of his new teammates questioned his ability to be a team player. There were also concerns about what skills Santiago retained, considering that he played a position that was physically difficult.[11]

After starting the 2001 season sharing catching duties with Bobby Estalella, Santiago became the Giants' regular catcher by midseason and played in 133 games. All things considered, he had a respectable season offensively; he was strong behind the plate and provided needed guidance to some of the Giants' young players. Former teammate Mark Grace said of Santiago in 2001: "He's good with pitchers and young catchers and he works hard. It's not an accident he's been around so long. He's a heck of a player."[12]

Santiago also had a strong 2002 season. Playing in 126 games, he hit 16 home runs and had 74 RBIs. He seemed to thrive when Giants manager Dusty Baker had him bat behind Barry Bonds.[13] Santiago's play earned him his fifth All-Star selection. He made the final out in the controversial game, which ended in a tie when both teams ran out of pitchers.

Santiago made his second postseason appearance in 2002, and played well. The Giants defeated Atlanta in the Division Series and St. Louis in five games in the Championship Series. Santiago hit two home runs in the NLCS, had six RBIs, and was named the series' Most Valuable Player. Santiago contributed five RBIs in the World Series, which the Giants lost to the Anaheim Angels in seven games.

Santiago played in 108 games for San Francisco in 2003. The Giants let him go at the end of the season, and he signed with the Kansas City Royals for 2004. On June 18 he was batting .274 with 6 home runs and 23 RBIs (he had hit a three-run homer in the first inning), when he was hit on the left hand by a pitch from Geoff Geary of the Phillies. The hand was broken and Santiago saw no playing time for the remainder of the season. In December the Royals traded him to the Pittsburgh Pirates for Juan Carlos Oviedo.[14]

Santiago caught in six games for the Pirates in April, the last one on the 11th. At 40, he was the third of three backstops, and the club released him in May. In June he signed a minor-league contract with the New York Mets, but was released in July after playing in nine games for Triple-A Norfolk.

Santiago played in 1,978 games in his 20-year career. He had 1,830 hits and a .263 batting average. Santiago hit 217 home runs and had 920 RBIs. His career fielding percentage was .987. He led National League catchers three times in assists, once in fielding percentage and once in baserunners caught stealing.

Santiago played winter ball in his native Puerto Rico after the 2005 season. His goal was to sign another major-league contract. He felt that he still had the arm and the skills behind the plate to contribute on a contending club.[15] No club decided to sign him.

In December 2007, after his playing career was over, Santiago was one of the players alleged in the Mitchell Report to have received anabolic steroids. The report stated that syringes were found in Santiago's locker near the end of the 2003 season. Santiago denied that he used steroids, claiming that he had collected the syringes as part of an ongoing prank by teammate Barry Bonds.[16]

Despite his positive statistics, Santiago's connection to the steroids scandal hurt his prospects for election to the Hall of Fame. He got just one vote in 2011, his first year on the ballot, and failed to get any votes in successive years. Besides the steroid allegations, some voters may have been deterred by Santiago's fielding statistics. He led the National League in errors six times and in passed balls three times.[17]

Honoring his accomplishments with San Diego, the Padres named Santiago to the club's Hall of Fame in 2015. Santiago's four starts for the NL All-Star team are the second most in franchise history, behind Tony Gwynn's 12 starts. Santiago's three Gold Gloves and four Silver Sluggers also rank second in franchise history.[18]

Santiago excelled in a difficult position for 20 years. His 1,917 games caught are 11th on all-time list. While he will be most remembered for his batting, Santiago also demonstrated solid defensive skills throughout his career.

Santiago has four children, daughters Bennybeth and Aliyah and sons Benito Jr. and Benito Ivan. He has been active in Latino events in San Francisco and his home of Puerto Rico since his retirement.

## SOURCES

In addition to the sources cited in the Notes, the author also utilized the Baseball-Reference.com and Retrosheet.org websites for box scores, player, team, and season pages, pitching and batting game logs, and other material pertinent to this biography. Fan Graphs.com provided some the individual statistical information used in this biography.

## NOTES

1    Franz Lidz, "Benito Finito at 34 Games," Sports Illustrated.com, October 12, 1987.

2    Bob Nightengale, "Santiago Puts Old Problems Behind Him," *Los Angeles Times*, March 30, 1991.

3    Bill Plaschke, "Benito Santiago's Side of the Mountains: 'Come See Where I'm From,' He Says, 'and You Understand Me Better,'" *Los Angeles Times*, January 29, 1989.

4    Lidz.

5    Ibid.

6    "Santiago Benched," *Portsmouth* (Ohio) *Daily Times*, June 1, 1991.

7    Tim Kurkjian, "Penny Pinchin' Padres," Sports Illustrated.com, March 29, 1993.

8    "Santiago Apparently Through in San Diego," *Gainesville* (Florida) *Sun*, September 22, 1992.

9    "Santiago Tags Maddux," *Tuscaloosa* (Alabama) *News,* May 4, 1996.

10    "Santiago Expects to Play After Crash," *Pittsburgh Post-Gazette*, January 6, 1998.

11    Anne Peterson, "Santiago Finds Safe Home With Giants," *Los Angeles Times*, June 3, 2001.

12    Ibid.

13    Juan Rodriguez, "Veteran Santiago Invaluable to Giants," *Orlando Sentinel*, October 12, 2002.

14    Oviedo was playing at the time, as he did for most of his career, under the assumed name Leo Nunez and under a falsified age as well. Some of the story is told by Stephen Borelli, "Marlins Pitcher Who Used Fake Name Says He's Cleared to Play, *USA Today*, May 25, 2012 at http://content.usatoday.com/communities/dailypitch/post/2012/05/juan-carlos-oviedo-leo-nunez-marlins-fake-name/1#.WQ3NTMs2y1s

15    Kevin Czerwinski, "Major League Vet Gears Up for Return," Minor League Baseball.com, November 30, 2006.

16    Jim Dooley, "Benito Santiago Misses Hall of Fame by Scant 435 Vote Margin," Chicago Now.com, January 6, 2011.

17    Ibid.

18    Dennis Lin, "Santiago, Templeton Elected to Padres HOF," *San Diego Union Tribune*, July 9, 2015.

# ERIC SHOW

## BY JOHN STAHL

Channeled into baseball by an overbearing, perfectionist father, Eric Show became a decent, if controversial, pitcher for the San Diego Padres. Although generally not considered the top pitcher for the pitching-poor club, as of 2018 he held the Padres record for career wins (100). During his major-league career, he spent 10 years with the Padres and one last forgettable year with the Athletics.

Looking back at Show's baseball life, his friends saw three common threads:

He cared about many people and things, maybe too much sometimes.

He loved to learn and strived to push the limits of his knowledge.

Though he enjoyed baseball, it didn't rank higher on his list than many of his other interests, especially music.[1]

Born on May 19, 1956, in Riverside, California, Eric Vaughn Show (pronounced to rhyme with "now") was the only son of Les and Yvonne Show. He grew up with two younger sisters, Leslie and Cindi.[2] Les was a jig builder at Rohr Industries constructing airline parts. His dad grew up fatherless in Pittsburg, Pennsylvania and loved two sports, boxing and baseball. He wanted to transfer his strong love of baseball pitching to his son. He had high baseball expectations and he punished Eric, both verbally and physically, if he failed to live up to them.

In one episode, as the family left a poor pitching performance by Eric, his father reached over into the back seat of their car and began slapping him on the side of his head. As Les continued, his screaming wife tried to cover her son. His siblings looked on in horror.[3]

Soon, as a Little League pitcher, Eric began to mirror his father's behavior. He was fine when everything was going well.

If there were problems, he would seem to pout on the mound, publicly humiliating teammates and/or umpires if he thought they made a mistake.[4]

When Eric began pitching for Ramona High School in Riverside, his father's continual verbal abuse was on full view, his "guttural" yelling aimed at Eric. Sometimes Les would stick his head into the side of the dugout and berate his son for a real or imagined pitching mistake. Sitting in the stands behind the catcher, he began calling his son's pitches. When Eric's catcher figured out what Les was doing, he confronted him. Les backed off.[5]

As a child, perhaps as a reaction to his father's domineering personality, Eric found refuge in both his guitar music and his mother's strong Christian beliefs. He taught himself the guitar and with the help of his close childhood friend, Steven Tyler, he ended up able to play rock, popular and jazz music. Tyler later became a major rock star with the group Aerosmith.

Religion also became very important to Eric, particularly in dealing with his volatile father. Nearly every Sunday Yvonne took young Eric and his sisters to church. Show became a born-again Christian in his early 20s. During his time with the Padres, he regularly attended the club's Sunday chapel services. He sometimes signed his autograph with a religious citation: Acts:12, which deals with salvation coming only from belief in Jesus Christ.[6]

Several of Show's seemingly odd behaviors may have come from his religious convictions: taking homeless strangers to dinner, calling a freelance sportswriter after midnight to discuss whether God exists, and his fascination with physics as a possible way of explaining the universe. These were among his actions that subsequently drew ridicule from both his teammates and the press for being weird.

In high school Les, baseball, and music continued to dominate Eric's life. Eric started his own band, grew his hair long, and rode a motorcycle. His home life deteriorated as Yvonne divorced Les. Despite his father's erratic behavior, he continued to "idolize" him.[7]

After high school, Eric accepted a baseball scholarship to University of California-Riverside. Les followed him. Once again, he began sticking his head inside the dugout and berating Eric.[8]

A major turning point in Eric's life came in 1975. He went to Wichita, Kansas, to play in a college summer league and met Cara Mia Niederhous. Cara Mia was "cover girl' beautiful and became a stabilizing influence on him.[9] He quickly became the number-three starter on the 1977 University of California-Riverside team that won the Division II College World Series. He made a substantial contribution to the team's success as he won

the regional championship game.[10] He maintained a lifetime relationship with his school. Later, in 1986, Show was inducted into the UC Riverside Athletics Hall of Fame.[11] In 1989 he provided the funds to endow a baseball scholarship at the school.[12]

Show had the most electric stuff on the Riverside staff – a low easy 90s fastball and a wicked slider. The influence of Les, however, continued to undermine his efforts. In stressful situations, if things didn't go his way, he would still become unglued and sulk on the mound. Memories of Les continued to slow his baseball development.[13]

Based on his potential, in June of 1978, Show was drafted in the 18th round by the Padres. The team initially sent him to Walla Walla, Washington, of the low Class-A Northwest League. He pitched 60 innings and went 5-2. Another benefit from now being a professional baseball player was that his father would not be allowed to yell at him in the dugout if he made a pitching mistake. In his second season, the Padres sent Show to Reno in the high-A California League, where he pitched 169 innings and ended with a 13-9 record.

He also married Cara Mia, who would become a key figure in his life. She provided balance. She didn't grow up immersed in the baseball world; in fact, she didn't particularly like baseball. But she recognized the challenges Eric faced and tried to help him. She knew how sensitive he really was. They never had children.[14]

In 1980 Show opened the season at Double-A Amarillo and posted a 12-6 record in 166 innings. He began 1981 pitching at Triple-A Hawaii, working 85 innings and posting a 7-3 record. He was called up by the Padres when rosters expanded in September and made his major-league debut on September 2, 1981 against the Chicago White Sox. He pitched two innings in relief as the Padres won. Used primarily as a relief pitcher, Show appeared in 15 Padres games in 1981 with a 1-3 record. His father loved it. Les had raised a major-league baseball player.

Show was in the major leagues to stay. In 1982, he posted a 10-6 record in 150 innings. By 1983, he was in the starting rotation, and posted a 15-12 record pitching 200⅔ innings.

He also formed close friendships with two other Padres pitchers Dave Dravecky and Mark Thurmond. They attended team-sponsored Sunday chapel meetings at the ballpark. The three soon became inseparable and were all considered eccentrics by their teammates, who nicknamed them Manny, Moe, and Jack after the Pep Boys. All three held strong Christian beliefs.[15]

In spring training before the 1984 season, Show, probably looking for something new to read, went into a John Birch Society bookstore in Arizona. He found their anti-communist views intriguing, so he took some of their literature. With Dravecky and Thurmond, he discussed the society's ideas, which primarily addressed anti-communism. All three decided to become members. It was a big mistake. They were unaware that some critics had stigmatized the Birch Society as racist and anti-Semitic. For Show, his association with the negative aspects of the Birch Society would dog him throughout his baseball career.[16]

In June 1984, the trio distributed literature at a John Birch Society booth at the Del Mar (California) fair. Once their Birch membership was discovered, critical media articles followed, characterizing the three as anti-Semite and anti-black.[17] As the news coverage intensified, team owner Joan Kroc ordered all the players to cease political proselytizing in the clubhouse.[18]

As Show had always prided himself on not having the same biases as Les, he was stunned. In 1984 he had a Hispanic financial adviser, a Jewish lawyer/agent and black friends in both baseball and his music world. Most of his teammates, including future Hall of Famer Tony Gwynn, agreed that Eric was no bigot.[19] His lawyer subsequently theorized that "Eric joined the Birch Society because he thought it would provide answers to how the world works. He was always looking for answers."[20]

The 1984 season was a magical one for the Padres. For the first time they won the National League West Division championship. The three "pep" boys combined for 38 wins and 8 saves or 50 percent of the team's 92 wins.[21]

Despite distractions of the Birch fiasco, Show posted a 15-9 record and pitched 206⅔ innings. His baseball success inspired a song which he titled "Padres Win Again." He recorded the song with the help of his friend Mark Augustin.[22]

Show started Game One of the 1984 National League Championship Series (at Wrigley Field) and was pounded for five runs in four innings. Key hits for the Cubs included a home run by opposing pitcher Rick Sutcliffe. Show also started Game Five and again was hit hard. In the two appearances, Show pitched 5⅓ innings and was 0-1 with a 13.50 ERA. The Padres won the series over the Cubs.

In the World Series, Show started Game Four, pitched 2⅔ innings and gave up two two-run home runs to Alan Trammel. The Padres lost to the Detroit Tigers in five games. Show finished the Series with a 10.13 ERA. Based on his 1984 regular-season performance, Show's 1985 salary jumped to an estimated $537,500.

The Padres were active during the offseason, bringing in former Cy Young Award winner Lamarr Hoyt to be the ace of their pitching staff. The move would also lessen Show's workload. With Show's record standing at 9-9 in early September, the Padres flew to Cincinnati for a three-game series. It was an important series as Pete Rose needed one hit to break Ty Cobb's career hit record. In the first game of the series, Rose, the Reds' player-manager, elected to sit out the game. In the second game, Hoyt held Rose in check by throwing nothing but high inside fastballs. In game three, on September 11, it was Show's turn. Pitching to Rose, he threw a slider that didn't slide. It looked like a "grapefruit," Tom Friend of ESPN wrote. Rose hit the pitch into left field for the record hit. Immediately Show ran over to Rose to congratulate him on breaking Cobb's record.[23]

Before the game, the Reds alerted the Padres that there would be a 20-minute delay when Rose got the record-breaking hit. They were to stay on the field until the celebrations were completed. Many speeches and gifts (including a car) were to be given to Rose.[24]

Show stood on the mound for a few minutes and then felt his back beginning to tighten up. He decided to sit down on the mound to watch the celebration. Several sportswriters and some teammates questioned Show's reasons for sitting down and criticized him for trying to show up Rose. Show lost the game, 2-0, but he won three of his last four starts and finished with a career-best 3.09 ERA for 233 innings, and a record of 12-11. However, he carried the burden of being considered the pitcher who gave up Rose's record-breaking hit for the rest of his life. Reporters wanted to know how it felt to go down in history as a goat.[25]

In 2015 an extensive review undertaken to examine Cobb's hit totals determined that Rose had really broken Cobb's record in a game against the Cubs on September 8, three days before Show's game. Show's angst was totally unwarranted. He did not give up Rose's record-breaking hit. He went to his grave believing that he did.[26]

During the offseason, Show decided to confront his father. He arranged for a sit-down with Les to talk through their issues. Show began by laying out the abuse on and off the field. Les took responsibility for nothing. He blamed either his own upbringing or his son. Nothing was resolved. Show finally threw up his hands and walked out.[27]

Show had a series of nagging injuries that limited him in 1986. He pitched 233 innings in 32 appearances 1985 but dropped to 136⅓ innings in 24 appearances in 1986. In mid-August the Padres essentially shut Show down. According to Show, the key issue was that he had broken his big left toe and then consistently aggravated the injury when he tried to pitch. Rather than risk his career, the Padres let him rest.[28]

In 1987 the Padres broke up the Pep Boys in midseason. Thurmond was traded to Detroit, and Dravecky to the San Francisco

Giants. Both of Show's best friends on the Padres were gone. On July 7 Show, with a 4-9 record, started against the Cubs in Chicago. The contest was subsequently called a "brawlgame" as seven players were ejected. Show was at the center of the action as he hit Andre Dawson, the 1987 National League Most Valuable Player, in the face with a splitter/fastball.[29]

Initially stunned, the crowd of 26,000-plus crowd became an angry mob. Rick Sutcliffe charged at Show and began pummeling him. A dazed Dawson picked himself up and began looking for Show. An umpire quickly escorted Show off the field. As he left the park with a security escort, an observer said he appeared to be in shock.[30]

The Padres issued a statement for Show that said: "I sincerely regret the unintended pitch that hit Andre Dawson. I have never intentionally thrown a pitch to hit a batter in my life, and I was not even intending to brush him back. I don't believe that throwing at a hitter is a part of the game. I apologize to the Cubs, the fans of Chicago and especially to Andre Dawson. It was unfortunate, and I'm sure I'll regret it for the rest of my life. I don't know any other words to express my feelings at this time."[31]

The incident happened in the third inning and both Dawson and Sutcliffe were ejected. The Padres felt like sitting ducks for the rest of the game. In the fourth inning, Cubs pitcher Greg Maddux and manager Gene Michael were ejected after Maddux hit a Cubs batter. In the fifth Cubs pitcher Scott Sanderson threw behind Tony Gwynn four straight times and was ejected. Seven Cubs ended up being ejected during the game. The experience unnerved Show. Overall, he finished the 1987 season with an 8-16 record, making 34 starts, and pitching 206⅓ innings.

Show's 1988 season was one of his best. He established career highs in innings pitched (234⅔), victories (16), and complete games (13). The Padres rewarded his improvement with a nearly $600,000 pay raise. His salary was now an estimated $1,450,000.

A key reason for Show's better performance may have been that he started taking an amphetamine called Fastin. According to his wife, Show had been experiencing increasing back pain. Fastin took away the pain. (Show always had trouble sleeping after games.) Initially, Fastin seemed to address the problem. In a short time, however, he began to need more. Once again, he began having trouble sleeping at night.[32]

During the 1988-89 offseason, Show released a jazz record album titled *America: 4/4 To Go*. All his five-member group contributed. Show wrote and arranged the Latin-flavored numbers. "He is on his way to mastering jazz with the musical statements he makes," said Bob Cartwright, a prominent jazz guitarist.[33]

However, Show's back pain continued. Increasing his dosages of drugs made his pain tolerable. However, by doing so he had damaged his disc area, and he had to have surgery on a disc in the lower lumbar region.[34]

To make it through the 1990 season, Show decided he also needed help from a stronger medication. To pitch without pain, he took a cortisone shot. He also upped his consumption of amphetamines, trying to deal with the drug's impact by drinking a lot of beer.[35]

As his pain continued, Show needed stronger medicines. He asked for help from the only drug addict he knew, his younger sister Cindi. Cindi, who called herself the "wild child" of the Show family, became Eric's drug supplier. Sister and brother began taking drugs together, particularly crystal methamphetamine. Eric also began experiencing hallucinations and paranoia, both possible side effects of drug abuse.[36]

Show tried many things to address his addictive issues. He went to an estimated 10-plus detox faculties. He again tried to reconcile with his father. They talked again but Les had already been diagnosed as having Alzheimer's and could not answer basic questions. Show had intended to try to help Les find Christ but Les didn't have the faintest idea of who Christ was. Cara Mia said later that he had finally made peace with Les.[37]

After the 1990 season the Padres let show go in free agency. As a Padre he had won 100 games and lost 87. Show signed a two-year free-agent contract with the Oakland A's in December 1990. The A's had good success in dealing with player drug-related issues. But with Show, their efforts produced the same results: irregular behavior and a high ERA. In 23 games he was 1-2 with a 5.92 ERA. Surprisingly, the A's picked up his option for 1992.

At the beginning of 1992 the Athletics released Show. Again, the cause was his erratic behavior probably fueled by drugs.[38]

After baseball, Show's drug troubles continued to wreak havoc with his life. He went to another detox center. Once again, he began having drug-related hallucinations. On March 16, 1994, he died in a detox center in Dulzura, California. A loaded .22-caliber revolver was found under his pillow. He was 37 years old. According to a toxicology report delivered to his wife, Cara Mia, Show died of acute morphine and cocaine intoxication.[39]

At Show's funeral only one former Padre, teammate Dave Dravecky, showed up. Dravecky delivered Show's eulogy. His Hispanic financial adviser, Joe Elizondo, also spoke and characterized him as a devoted friend. And then there were the letters. They came from all over the United States thanking Show for encouraging them to go back to church.[40]

## SOURCES

In addition to the sources cited in the Notes, the author also consulted Baseball-Reference.com, Retrosheet.org, and base-ballalmanac.com

## NOTES

1   Brent Schrotentboer, "Mystery Man," *San Diego Union Tribune*, May 18, 2008: 1-8.

2   Tom Friend, "The Tortured Life of Eric Show," ESPN.com, September 7, 2010: 1-19. espn.com/espn/print?id=5543839.

3   Ibid.

4   Ibid.

5   Ibid.

6   Ira Berkow, "Eric Show's Solitary Life, and Death," *New York Times*, March 27, 1984.

7   Tom Friend, "The Tortured Life of Eric Show."

8   Ibid.

9   Ibid.

10   Ibid.

11   Brent Schrotentboer, "Mystery Man."

12   ¹¹ Ibid.

13   Tom Friend, "The Tortured Life of Eric Show"

14   Tom Friend, "Eric Show Q&A: Whether the Subject Is Politics or Pitching, the Man Is a Puzzle," *Los Angeles Times*, May 16, 1986. ESPN, p.6

15   Tom Friend, "The Tortured Life of Eric Show."

16   Ibid.

17   Ibid.

18   Schrotentboer.

19   Ibid.

20   Ira Berkow, "Eric Show's Solitary Life, and Death."

21   Tom Friend, "The Tortured Life of Eric Show."

22   Ibid.

23   Ibid.

24   Ibid.

25   Tom Friend, "For Eric Show, It's Trivial and Probably Inescapable," *Los Angeles Times*, September 12, 1985.

26   Kirk Kenney, "Did Rose Really Set Hits Record Against Padres?" *San Diego Union Tribune*, September 11, 2015: 1-4.

27   Tom Friend, The Tortured Life of Eric Show."

28   Tom Friend, "Eric Show Q&A."

29   Bill Plaschke, "Show Hits Dawson With a Pitch, Sparks Brawlgame Won by Cubs," *Los Angeles Times*, July 8, 1987: 1, 2.

30   Ibid.

31   Associated Press, "Seven Ejected in Beanball Exchange," *New York Times*, July 8, 1987: A23.

32   Tom Friend, "The Tortured Life of Eric Show."

33   Hilmer Anderson, "San Diego Padres Pitcher Eric Show Hopes the Jazz…," upi.com/Archives/1989/02/08/San-Diego-Padres-pitcher-Eric-Show-hopes-the-jazz/7311602917200/.

34   Tom Friend, "Ailing Eric Show Not Expected Back This Season," *Los Angeles Times*, August 3, 1989.

35   Schrotentboer.

36   Tom Friend, "The Tortured Life of Eric Show."

37   Ibid.

38   Ira Berkow, "Eric Show's Solitary Life, and Death."

39   Tom Friend, The Tortured Life of Eric Show."

40   Ibid.

# GARRY TEMPLETON

## BY NICK WADDELL

his summers working for his father's auto-washing company, Templeton Traveling Washrags, which had contracts to wash fleets of vehicles. "I washed every post office vehicle in Orange County," Garry recalled.[2] He was nicknamed "Jumpsteady" by his cousin, who said he jumped more than danced to the Aretha Franklin 1971 song "Rock Steady."[3]

Templeton's parents encouraged education combined with sports, and Garry followed that plan. He was named First-Team All-County by the Los Angeles Times as a senior defensive back at Santa Ana Valley High School in Santa Ana, California. His football acumen was enough to earn him a scholarship offer from the University of California at Los Angeles. The opportunity for an education was what appealed to Templeton more. Even being drafted by the St. Louis Cardinals in the first round of the 1974 free-agent draft was not enough at first to sway a switch to baseball. Garry was set on accepting his scholarship and continuing his education, until a conversation with his father. Spiavia encouraged his son to follow whatever drove him, but reminded him that not everyone has the opportunity to be drafted and play in the major leagues.[4] After careful consideration, Templeton decided to follow his baseball path.

Templeton was assigned to the Gulf Coast League Cardinals (Rookie League) to start his career. One of his teammates was future super-agent Scott Boras. Because of his speed, the parent Cardinals had the right-handed-batting Templeton become a

Garry Lewis Templeton was born on March 24, 1956, in Lockney, Texas, a small town in the state's northern Panhandle. Templeton's father, Spiavia, played in the Negro leagues, but Garry was not aware of his father's history until he was 12 or 13. Spiavia was a backup infielder who played with Satchel Paige (who once remarked that young Garry looked like a young Spiavia).[1] The Templeton family moved from Texas to southern California when Garry was a teenager. Garry spent switch-hitter. "I was a very, very, very good right-handed hitter," Templeton said.[5] On his first day of rookie ball, Templeton got five straight hits off teammate and future major leaguer Bill Caudill. The team told him to switch to the left side, and he proceeded to go hitless. "The adjustment was more mental than physical,"[6] Templeton said. The Cardinals figured he could take advantage of his speed by being closer to first base against right-handed pitchers. In 71 at-bats Templeton hit .268 and was second on the team with eight stolen bases after 18 games. Moved up to St. Petersburg (Class-A Florida State League), he hit .211 in 95 at-bats.

Templeton began the 1975 season at St. Petersburg, and after 82 games (.264) he was promoted to the Double-A Arkansas Travelers (Texas League). He had a .395 average before having knee surgery to replace damaged cartilage. The surgery was not enough to slow him down; Templeton finished the season batting .401 and led the team with 16 stolen bases.

The 1976 season began with high hopes for Templeton based on his 1975 performance. It was assumed that it was only a matter of time until the young shortstop was fielding grounders at Busch Stadium. The Cardinals traded for Don Kessinger to play shortstop until Templeton was ready, which St. Petersburg manager Jack Krol figured would be by the middle of 1976.[7] Templeton began with the Triple-A Tulsa Oilers (American Association). Through the middle of May, he batted only .247, then caught fire and after 106 games was batting .321 with 25 stolen bases, but with 34 errors at shortstop. On June 10 Templeton got the opportunity to showcase his talents for the big-league Cardinals, who came to Tulsa for an exhibition game. Templeton impressed Cardinals manager Red Schoendienst, who said, "He's a good-looking prospect. He has the tools to be a good one if he keeps on improving."[8]

George Kissell, special assistant to the general manager, said he was "amazed" with Templeton's range, adding, "He can go in the hole and then throw with accuracy to get the man out."[9] One thing holding the Cardinals back from calling Templeton up sooner was the new four-year contract the major-league players had yet to ratify. In December 1975, an independent arbitrator had essentially eliminated the reserve clause. The new four-year deal gave teams six years of control over a player. If the Cardinals had called Templeton up before the ratification, he could have become a free agent after the 1977 season. The players okayed the new contract in July and Templeton made his debut just under a month later.

Templeton was inserted into the starting lineup on August 9, the day he was called up, and he was ready for the challenge. "I think I can handle almost anything," he said.[10] He admitted he felt no pressure, but had butterflies. "I had butterflies all throughout my career. I think all good athletes have butterflies, and you use it to your advantage," he later said.[11]

The hype surrounding Templeton and his debut were justified. Templeton went 1-for-4 in his debut, with a single in his last at-bat of the night as the Cardinals lost to the visiting Houston Astros, 13-4. Through his first nine games, he managed only 8 hits in 39 at-bats, but a 2-for-4 night against Atlanta helped change the course of his season; Templeton finished the season with a .291 batting average and 11 stolen bases. He hit his first major-league home run on September 9 off Don Carrithers of the Montreal Expos. Templeton received the John B. Sheridan Award as St. Louis's rookie of the year, sharing the honor with Hector Cruz.[12]

Templeton's 1977 season was even better. Offense took center stage. Templeton hit .322, was second on the team with 28 stolen bases (behind a 38-year-old Lou Brock), was third on the team with 79 RBIs, and led the major leagues with 18 triples. His defense was less stellar, as he was third in the National League with 32 errors at shortstop. Templeton was named to the NL All-Star team as a reserve. He hit a double in his only at-bat in the game.

The next season, 1978, was similar to 1977. Templeton's .280 batting average was third on the team among regular starters, while his 34 stolen bases led the Cardinals. He again led the league in triples with 13. Despite leading the league with 40 errors, his 5.21 Range Factor (9 times putouts plus assists divided by innings played) was best for a shortstop in the National League.

Before the 1979 season, Templeton threatened to sit out season if he didn't get a raise from $100,000 to $150,000. Templeton felt the Cardinals' contract offer, which called for a 10 percent pay cut, was an insult. General manager John Claiborne defended the offer, which he said was based on the team's 69-93 record and a drop of almost 400,000 in attendance. Templeton countered with an ultimatum: "Either get me traded or get me more money."[13] In the end he signed a one-year contract and a raise to a reported $130,000. He responded by having another strong season.

Templeton became the first player to get 100 hits from each side of the plate. Again, he led the league in errors (34), but he also led the league's shortstops in Range Factor (5.45). His first-half stats were good enough to earn him another All-Star Game bid, which Templeton turned down. He is frequently said to have declared, "If I ain't startin', I ain't departin'," but in an interview with the writer, he attributed that to Cardinals broadcaster Jack Buck. He said he told Buck he wasn't going to play in the game since he had not been voted in as a starter. Buck responded, "So if you ain't startin' you ain't departin'?"

Templeton laughed, and agreed with the veteran broadcaster.[14] Later, Templeton repeated Buck's line in interviews.

Toward the end of the season, Templeton reiterated his desire for a new contract, but without the strong trade demand from before. "Hopefully, [the Cardinals] will give me a long-term contract and show me they want me around. I'm happy in St. Louis and want to play there," Templeton said, but added, "But if they play games with me … I'm going to play out my option."[15]

Templeton's 1980 started strong. He was batting a league-leading .326 when on July 23 he broke a bone in his left hand sliding into first base.[16] The injury cost him 18 games. Templeton missed another 18 games when he fractured his right index finger during infield practice a month later.[17] Templeton ended the season with a .319 batting average, which earned him his first Silver Slugger Award. According to Range Factor he was the best defensive shortstop in the National League despite leading the league with 29 errors.

Templeton's 1981 was less about his on-field performance, and more about his supposed on-field actions. The season started with a triple play on Opening Day against the Phillies. With the bases loaded, Gary Matthews lined out to Templeton, who threw to catcher Darrell Porter, who threw to Keith Hernandez at first, who threw to Tommy Herr at second.

The most infamous event of Templeton's career came on August 26, 1981. The media and Templeton have different accounts.

## Media Account

In the bottom of the first, Templeton swung at strike three, but failed to run to first after Giants catcher Milt May dropped the ball. The fans booed his lack of effort, and Templeton responded with a middle finger. When he came to play the field in the second and third innings, the fans continued to boo. Templeton responded with another obscene gesture, and was promptly ejected by home-plate umpire Bruce Froemming. Templeton grabbed his crotch, prompting manager Whitey Herzog to race out of the dugout and retrieve his shortstop. Templeton and his manager got into a shoving match in the dugout, and had to be separated by teammates.[18]

## Templeton's Account

Templeton recalled a very different story. He remembered going back to the dugout while fans were booing. Fans behind the dugout were throwing items and he responded with a middle finger while on the top step of the dugout. "The photographer was right there and happened to catch it," Templeton said of the infamous photo.[19] Templeton's ejection was due to his grabbing his crotch. "I was on the on-deck circle. I don't remember who was in front of me, but he struck out. I was turning to go to the dugout, when three guys came down behind the on-deck circle and called me names, like the n-word. So I grabbed my crotch and told them what they could do."[20] Templeton said he thought manager Whitey Herzog heard the encounter. "He was close, he had to have. Other people did."[21] Herzog pulled Templeton down into the dugout, and the fracas ensued.

Templeton was fined $5,000 by Herzog and suspended without pay for three weeks.[22] The team agreed to lift the suspension after Templeton agreed to seeing a psychiatrist. He was checked in to a hospital two days after the suspension was lifted. A psychiatric evaluation revealed a battle with depression. He was given medication, and agreed to continue to see a psychiatrist. Templeton apologized to the fans with a press conference, but the relationship between he and the Cardinals was irreparable.[23]

Templeton played in only 80 games in 1981 and batted .288. After the season, on December 10, he was traded to the San Diego Padres in a six-player deal in which future Hall of Famer Ozzie Smith went back to the Cardinals. Templeton injured his knee just before Opening Day in 1982, and his numbers dropped. Through 1981 he batted .303 as a left-hander. In 1982 he batted .245 from the left side. The knee injury made it harder to plant and turn. He thought about asking if he could bat solely from the right side, but ultimately decided against it. Throughout his career, Templeton had seven surgeries on his knee.[24]

Templeton rehabbed his knee throughout the winter, but was forced to have arthroscopic knee surgery on March 10, 1983.[25] He was cleared just before the start of the season, but went on the disabled list at the end of April, and again at the beginning of June. The second half of the season was kinder to Templeton. On July 31 the Braves and Padres faced off in San Diego. In the top of the fourth inning, Glenn Hubbard came up to bat with runners at first and second. With the runners going, Hubbard hit a blooper into left field. Templeton raced over to make the catch. He quickly flipped the ball to Tim Flannery at second, who threw to Kurt Bevacqua at first to complete a triple play. Templeton was confident in the triple play even before it happened. "The most difficult part was getting to the ball. When I saw the runners going, I knew we had a triple play," he said.[26] Templeton finished the season batting .263, but his average from the left side, .257, was still below his career average.

Templeton again spent the offseason rehabilitating his knee. The Padres went into the 1984 season with high hopes after the acquisition of relief pitcher Rich "Goose" Gossage; however, those hopes hinged on the team staying healthy, including Templeton. Templeton responded by playing in the most games since 1979. His .258 batting average was good enough for a Silver Slugger Award. The Padres won the National League West championship and faced the Chicago in the National League Championship

Series. The Cubs won the first two games in Chicago. The Padres, aided by Templeton's two RBIs, won Game Three. The Padres won all three games in San Diego, which set up a World Series matchup with the Detroit Tigers. The Tigers and Padres split the first two games in San Diego, but the Padres dropped the next three games in Detroit, losing the series. Templeton finished the postseason with a .324 batting average. This was his only postseason action.

Templeton felt his knee did not fully respond to surgery until 1985.[27] The rehabilitation paid off; he batted .282 and was named to the NL All-Star Team for the third and final time, as Ozzie Smith's backup. Templeton singled in a pinch-hit appearance in the top of the fourth inning, but was replaced by Ryne Sandberg in the bottom of the fourth. Templeton's season came to a premature close when he chipped his shin with a foul ball, which caused him to miss the final five games of the season. The Padres overall finished a disappointing third. "I felt the 1985 team was better [than the 1984 team]," he said.[28]

The 1986 and 1987 seasons were tough ones for both the Padres and Templeton. While the team struggled to fourth- and sixth-place finishes under Steve Boros and Larry Bowa, Templeton's knee problems caused a drop in his offensive production. He used the time, though, to mentor the team's younger players, like Bip Roberts. Roberts told a Los Angeles Times reporter, "It's the sign of a special person. The first time I met him, that stuck out. He said, 'Come over and hit (at his private batting cage). Bring the family.'... Tempy's special. He's a special person."[29] Teammate Jerry Royster was not surprised. "He's a very likeable person. There's not one guy who doesn't like him," Royster said.[30]

The Padres went into spring training 1987 with high hopes under new manager Larry Bowa. Even Templeton agreed. "Best group of young kids we've ever had here, Jack," Templeton told general manager Jack McKeon.[31] Templeton was even named the second captain in Padres history, after Dave Winfield, by Bowa (manager Dick Williams never named a captain). Templeton pledged to "do my best to be the best captain the Padres have ever had."[32] Bowa commented on Templeton's managerial-like style of being a teammate: "When a guy like Tempy goes up to a player and says something, it means more. To me, that has more impact than a coach saying something."[33]

Spring training in 1988 brought trade rumors. The Padres signed Dickie Thon and traded for Mike Brumley, which led to speculation that the team would deal Templeton.[34] One possibility was the Philadelphia Phillies, but such a trade never materialized.[35] The team and Templeton both started the season slowly. Bowa was fired in late May. At that time, Templeton was hitting just .184. GM McKeon came down to manage the Padres for the rest

of the season, and the team responded by going 67-48 the rest of the way. Templeton hit .273 in that time, but overall batted .249. After the season he signed a one-year deal to return to the Padres.

The firing of Larry Bowa led Templeton to be more relaxed in the clubhouse and on the field in 1989. He felt for the first time that the title of captain meant something. Templeton was also more comfortable with Jack McKeon, who as general manager had traded for him eight years earlier. He felt McKeon drove the team to do their best. "Too many times in this game, we are told what we cannot do. Jack told us what we could do. And kept telling us," he said.[36] The Padres responded to having McKeon for a full season by finishing second in the National League West, three games behind eventual pennant winner San Francisco. Templeton himself had a rebound year, hitting .255. He belted six home runs, the most since his 1985 All-Star year. His defense was also improved. He was second in the National League in Range Factor Per Game, behind Barry Larkin.

In 1990 Templeton played his last full season with the Padres. He continued to mentor the younger Padres, like Bip Roberts and Joey Cora. "I want these guys to become a success," he said.[37] Templeton knew someone would eventually take his job, but he showed the same confidence he always had. "I'm going to keep helping Bip out all I can, but I'm not going to hand him my job.... He'll get some time in there this year ... but I'm still going to play my 130, 135 games."[38] He did even better, playing in 144 games, and tied his career high with nine home runs.

Expectations were again high for the 1990 squad, based on 1989's finish, but expectation had waned by the All-Star break. Manager McKeon resigned, to focus more on the front office. He named first-base coach Greg Riddoch manager. The team failed to improve, and finished fourth in the division. Templeton had a theory why. "[Riddoch] didn't like veteran players. He wanted everyone to listen to him and him only."[39] McKeon was fired in late September, and replaced with former New York Mets vice president of baseball operations Joe McIlvaine. McIlvaine revamped the team, and found Templeton's replacement when he traded outfielder Joe Carter and infielder Roberto Alomar to the Toronto Blue Jays for first baseman Fred McGriff and shortstop Tony Fernandez.

Templeton was used mostly as a pinch-hitter and late-inning defensive replacement before he was traded to the Mets for Tim Teufel on May 31, 1991. Templeton had almost been dealt to the Texas Rangers after the Fernandez acquisition, but he and the Rangers could not come to terms on a contract.[40] Templeton found his new team to be much different than St Louis or San Diego. "I was having fun, and I played a lot," he said.[41] Templeton played positions other than his customary shortstop:

25 games at first base, 2 in right field, and 15 at third base. He credited that time with the Mets as the spark for coaching.[42] After the season the Mets declined to offer him arbitration, but Templeton had already begun to consider alternatives. Despite having opportunities to continue playing, he was discouraged about the condition of his knee, and did not want to have more surgery. "The Mets drained my knee. ... It had blood and they wanted me to have surgery. I didn't want surgery. ... I had other opportunities but I was discouraged. ... I could have played another few years."[43]

Templeton spent 1992 and 1993 enjoying time with his wife and children and playing golf. At a banquet in 1993 the Padres asked him about coaching, but at the time he declined. Padres minor-league director Ed Lynch called Templeton a few weeks later to invite him to San Diego for a conversation. As Templeton recalled, Lynch refused to let him leave until he signed a contract to be a roving minor-league infield and baserunning instructor.[44] Templeton worked with such future major leaguers as Derrek Lee and Homer Bush, and showed them "the little things to be good."

The Anaheim Angels approached Templeton about managing in their farm system. In 1997 he accepted the manager position with the 1998 Cedar Rapids Kernels of the Class-A Midwest League. Templeton cited former manager Dick Williams as an inspiration. Williams had Templeton sit beside him on off-days.[45] Templeton was optimistic about his first team. "This is a well-rounded ballclub. We've got lots of strengths. We've got some good pitching, good defense, and I think we've got a good offense club."[46]

Templeton approached managing by teaching fundamentals. "What happens is a lot of great athletes run into the problem of trying to teach what they did instead of just teaching the fundamentals of what they did. That's the easier way to teach anybody because everybody can't do the same thing."[47] Templeton's Kernels finished 1998 at 71-69, nine victories more than in 1997. For 1999 Templeton was promoted to manager of the Erie Seawolves of the Double-A Eastern League. He guided Erie to an 81-61 record, and again the Angels gave him a promotion, this time to Triple-A Edmonton.

The Edmonton team was coming off of a 65-74 record, and looked to Templeton to turn it around. Templeton eyed Edmonton as a short layover to eventually coaching in the major leagues. "After this year, hopefully, I'll have a chance to go on to the major-league level as a coach or manager," he said. "If it doesn't happen, I can wait one more year but then I'll probably go home and be with the wife and kids and play golf because I miss playing golf in the summer."[48] The Trappers began the season at 2-7, tied for their worst start ever. Templeton knew his

team would struggle, especially after six players were called up to the Angels. After a 17-3 loss to the Las Vegas Stars, Templeton quipped, "If I had a team that was supposed to win, I think I'd be looking for that bridge over there to jump into some ice water. ... The thing that's killing us is we're getting young men who are not ready for Triple A."[49]

Templeton later spoke about how difficult it was never having a full team. "Sometimes we'd have 17 or 19 players," he said. The Angels did not want to pull from their Double-A team, so the team called up players from Edmonton, and replaced them with Class-A or Rookie ball players. Templeton jokingly told his bullpen to keep their spikes on the bench "in case you have to pinch-hit or run down balls in the outfield."[50] The Trappers finished 63-78.

After the season Anaheim and Minnesota swapped Triple-A affiliates. The Twins took Edmonton, while Anaheim took over the Salt Lake Stingers (formerly the Buzz). Templeton moved with the team and guided it to a 79-64 record. The Stingers lost their playoff opportunity over the last week of the season, and finished four games behind the Iowa Cubs. After the season, Templeton's contract was not renewed. He finished his four-year Angels minor-league managerial career with a 294-272 record.

Templeton sat out the 2002 season for personal reasons, including the death of his mother. He returned to managing when the Gary Southshore RailCats of the independent Northern League called. This time the job was different. Templeton was the on-field manager, but he was also in charge of putting the team together. "I thought about it and wondered what I could do, putting my own team together and coming up with a winner," he said.[51] Templeton was fired after going 67-119 in two seasons with the RailCats. He later recalled the challenges of managing in independent ball, namely having to find players who fit the team based on need, but also based on years of experience, since the independent leagues had rules limiting the number of players based on years. "As the years went by, I enjoyed having control of the roster," Templeton said.[52]

Templeton quickly signed up for the upstart Golden Baseball League. He spent six seasons managing in the league, including one season after the league merged with teams from the Northern and United Leagues to form the North American League. His 2010 Chico (California) Outlaws won the league championship.

Templeton stopped managing after a 2013 stint with the Newark Bears. "The independent leagues were hiring younger guys, and I was tired of traveling," he said.[53] Templeton looked back on his managerial career and recalled his simple approach: "I never gave kids more than they could handle. Keep things simple, believe in yourself. I didn't try to overhaul the kids. ... When you struggle, everybody's giving you all this advice. I would fix what's wrong, not the entire stance."[54] Templeton summed it up: "Baseball is baseball. You see ball, you hit ball. You see ball, you catch ball. Baseball has been around forever."

Garry Templeton is father to two sons and two daughters, as well as nine grandchildren and six great-grandchildren. One son, Garry Templeton Jr., played in the minor leagues and as of 2019 was a scout for the Arizona Diamondbacks. Garry's wife of 40 years, Glenda, died in March 2018.

## SOURCES

In addition to the sources cited in the Notes, the author also consulted Baseball-Reference.com and the following:

Armour, Mark, and Dan Levitt. "A History of the MLBPA's Collective Bargaining Agreement: Part 1," FanGraphs, November 7, 2016 (fangraphs.com/tht/a-history-of-the-mlbpa-collective-bargaining-agreement-part-1/).

Fagan, Ryan. "Baseball Strikes and Lockouts: A History of MLB Work Stoppages," *The Sporting News*, February 5, 2018. (sportingnews.com/us/mlb/news/mlb-free-agents-labor-dispute-history-1994-1981-strike-1990-lockout-marvin-miller-mlbpa/lhl6crvxn0ya1xrc5n9m915xf).

## NOTES

1   Author interview with Garry Templeton, December 22, 2018.

2   Ibid.

3   Tom Friend, "Tempy," *Los Angeles Times*, April 1, 1986.

4   Templeton interview.

5   Ibid.

6   Ibid.

7   Neal Russo, "Putting Redbirds Together," *St. Louis Post-Dispatch*, April 4, 1976.

8   "Templeton Gets a Preview But Cards Take the Feature," *St. Louis Post-Dispatch*, June 11, 1976.

9   Ibid.

10   Dick Kaegel, "Templeton to Make His Debut," *St. Louis Post-Dispatch*, August 9, 1976.

11   Templeton interview.

12   "Cruz, Templeton Will Share Rookie Award From Writers," *St. Louis Post-Dispatch*, January 9, 1977: 7D.

13   United Press International, "St. Louis Shortstop Sings the Blues," *Detroit Free Press*, March 28, 1979.

14   Templeton interview.

15   "Templeton's Goal: Recognition," *St. Louis Post-Dispatch*, September 26, 1979.

16   Cal Fuseman, "Garry's Injury Tempers Cards' Joy," *St. Louis Post-Dispatch*, July 24, 1980.

17   Associated Press, "Broken Finger Sidelines Templeton," *Decatur* (Illinois) *Herald and Review*, August 25, 1980.

18   Dan O'Neill, "Aug 21, 1981: Garry Templeton's Ladies Day Eruption," *St Louis Post-Dispatch*, August 26, 2016. stltoday.com/news/archives/aug-garry-templeton-s-ladies-day-eruption/article_e2ebeb70-ce60-592f-a506-99c938347842.html.

19   Templeton interview.

20   Ibid.

21   Ibid.

22   Dan Kimball, "I Say Trade Templeton," *Mattoon* (Illinois) *Journal Gazette*, August 27, 1981.

23   Tom Uhlenbock, "Templeton Apologizes for Actions," *Carlisle* (Pennsylvania) *Sentinel*, September 15, 1981.

24   Norm Cowley, "Star Teacher," *Edmonton Journal*, April 29, 2000.

25   Steve Dolan, "Templeton Must Have Operation," *Los Angeles Times*, March 9, 1983.

26   Chris Cobbs, "A Triple Play Helps Padres," *Los Angeles Times*, August 1, 1983.

27   Templeton interview.

28   Ibid.

29   Tom Friend. "Tempy," *Los Angeles Times*, April 1, 1986.

30   Ibid.

31   Tom Friend, "Templeton Setting Good Example," *Los Angeles Times*, February 28, 1987.

32   Tom Friend, "Templeton Named Captain, Only the Second in Team History," *Los Angeles Times*, March 1, 1986.

33   Ibid.

34   Peter Pascarelli, "Parrish Should Consider the Silent Treatment for Now," *Columbus* (Indiana) *Republic*, February 28, 1988.

35   Peter Pascarelli, "Merging Hope with Realism, Bystrom Works on Comeback," *Philadelphia Inquirer*, March 10, 1988.

36   Bill Plaschke, "Master Salesman," *Los Angeles Times*, February 26, 1989.

37   Bob Nightengale. "Templeton Feels Secure at Short in Padres' Plan," *Los Angeles Times*, March 30, 1990.

38   Ibid.

39   Templeton interview.

40   Scott Miller, "Templeton Traded to Mets," *Los Angeles Times*, June 1, 1991.

41   Templeton interview.

42   Ibid.

43   Ibid.

44   Ibid.

45   Norm Cowley, "Star Teacher," *Edmonton Journal*, April 29, 2000.

46   Jon Klinkowitz, "Kernels' '98 Crop Features (Nearly) All New Faces," *Iowa City* (Iowa) *Press Citizen*, April 11, 1998.

47   Norm Cowley, "Star Teacher," *Edmonton Journal*, April 29, 2000.

48   Ibid.

49   Norm Cowley, "Revolving Door Frustrates Trap," *Edmonton Journal*, May 26, 2000.

50   Templeton interview.

51   Mike Clark, "RailCats Land a Big Name," *Munster* (Indiana) *Times*, January 10, 2003.

52   Templeton interview.

53   Ibid.

54   Ibid.

# WILL VENABLE

## BY JAY HURD

On August 29, 2008, 25-year-old Will Venable, made his major-league debut with the San Diego Padres. Although the Padres lost to the Colorado Rockies that day, 9-4, outfielder Venable, brought up from Triple-A Portland, tripled to right center in the second inning, in his first at-bat, and then scored on Aaron Cook's wild pitch. Venable, the son of former major leaguer Max Venable, who was his son's hitting coach at Portland, did not see a quick transition to full-time major leaguer, but became, through athletic ability, persistent effort, and numerous minor-league stints, an everyday player with the Padres by 2011.

William Dion Venable was born on October 29, 1982, at Marin General Hospital in Greenbrae, California, 15 miles north of San Francisco. Both his parents were athletes. His father, William McKinley "Max" Venable, was born in Phoenix on June 6, 1957. He excelled in multiple sports at Cordova High School in Rancho Cordova, California. His mother, Mary "Molly" (Cross) Venable, was born in San Francisco on October 16, 1958. She played basketball at Dominican University in San Rafael. She and Max married in May 1982 in Marin, California.

Max graduated from high school in 1975 and passed up football scholarship offers to sign with the Los Angeles Dodgers, after having been selected in the 1976 amateur draft. In 1978 the San Francisco Giants acquired him from the Dodgers organization

via the Rule 5 draft. He played in the National League for nine years, with the Giants, Montreal Expos, and Cincinnati Reds, and in the American League for three years, with the Los Angeles Angels. After his playing career, he became a coach in the Korean Baseball Organization (KBO) and in Japan's Nippon Professional Baseball. Will had spent part of his childhood in Japan, "where his dad was a 'gaijin' (foreign player) in the Japanese league. He experienced Japan's baseball culture while playing for a local Little League team, enduring marathon practices in the summer months."[1] Will's time in Japan, and awareness of cultural differences influenced his senior thesis at Princeton University where he earned a B.A. degree in anthropology. His thesis, *The Game and Community: An Anthropological Look at Baseball in America and Japan,* compared American and Japanese culture by presenting histories of baseball's evolution in each country."[2]

Max went on to coach in the US minor leagues, including time with Max in the Pacific Coast League and the California League. Max and Molly had a second son, Winston James Venable, born on March 31, 1987. Winston became a professional football player with the Chicago Bears of the NFL and the Montreal Alouettes of the Canadian Football League.

Will excelled in three sports at San Rafael High School. He lettered four times in basketball, three times in baseball, and once in track and field. His name regularly appeared in newspapers as a stellar athlete, with particular attention to basketball. His notoriety included mentions in the Prep Athlete of the Week section of the *San Francisco Examiner.*[3] At the age of 16, Will said, "I think I'm naturally better at basketball. I don't work as hard at baseball as I do at basketball."[4] His senior year, he opted to run track – he "was tired of baseball. … [B]asketball was my passion."[5] After graduating from high school in 2001, Will enrolled at Princeton University. He admitted that, while he would continue academic pursuits, he had chosen Princeton for basketball, not academics.[6] "The program had a great tradition of going to the NCAA tournament, and I wanted to be a part of that," he said.[7]

At Princeton, Will felt the challenges posed by dual commitments – basketball and academics. "The academics were a little overwhelming for me my first year," he said later. "My parents hadn't wanted want [*sic*] me to be out of my league academically, and I was. You go to discussion groups and hear some of the kids talk – really smart kids – and it's intimidating."[8] This stress was real but he said he was "better for it."[9]

Basketball occupied Will's time and energy his freshman year. He was not a starter, but played in 27 games, scored 150 points and achieved a .480 two-point field goal percentage. The following three seasons, he was a starter, and was in the top 10 in the Ivy League in two-point field goal percentages each season.[10]

During his sophomore year, Venable spoke with Princeton baseball coach Scott Bradley, a former major leaguer, and joined the baseball team. His skills impressed Bradley and other Tigers players. One player told Coach Bradley that things were not fair: While he worked very hard to be good hitter, Venable "shows

up and he's a better hitter than I will ever be in my entire life." Bradley responded simply, "Will Venable will play in the major leagues."[11] From a .244 batting average in his first season, the left-handed throwing and batting Venable steadily progressed to .344 his junior year and .385 his senior year, and finished as the starting center fielder. His baseball achievements mirrored his basketball successes. In addition to All-Ivy League selections in basketball and baseball, Venable twice received the B.F. Bunn Trophy, awarded to the varsity basketball player who "through sportsmanship, play and influence has contributed most to the sport."[12] He also earned the Roper Trophy, awarded to a senior of "high scholastic rank and outstanding qualities of sportsmanship and general proficiency in athletics."[13]

Venable was the second Princeton student to be named first-team All-Ivy in both basketball and baseball. The first was Chris Young, Class of 2002, who was a teammate of Venable's with the Padres. Venable recalled his time at Princeton as a "tough four years that taught me a lot about myself and other people," adding, "I was challenged academically and athletically at all times."[14] There was "a lot of work, but both Coach Bradley and Coaches Thompson and Scott [in basketball] allowed me to do what I needed in preparation for either season; and academically, "the teachers were also understanding while holding me to the same academic standards of all the other students."[15]

By 2004, Venable was attracting interest from major-league teams. That year, the Baltimore Orioles selected him in the 15th round of the amateur draft, but he chose to remain at Princeton. In June 2005, the San Diego Padres selected him in the seventh round; ESPN's Peter Gammons identified him as "my favorite sleeper" of that draft.[16]

Venable's mother, Molly, greatly influenced his decision not to pursue a career in the NBA, via time in European professional basketball. "She told me to think about trying baseball again because she saw the opportunities that it gave my dad," Venable said. "I went to Princeton with the intentions of trying both. I didn't play my freshman year because I couldn't handle it. She just continually reminded me to keep it in mind, and it ended up working out."[17] He signed with the Padres as an outfielder. His first assignment, in June of 2005, was with the Rookie League Arizona Padres. After a month he was assigned to the Eugene (Oregon) Emeralds of the short-season Class-A Northwest League. In 2006 he was advanced to the Fort Wayne Wizards of the Class-A Midwest League.

In Fort Wayne, with the coaching of his father, Max, he impressed the Padres with a .314 batting average and 11 home runs in 124 games. After the season he joined the West Oahu Canefires of Hawaii Winter Baseball and batted .330. In 2007 Venable was promoted to the San Antonio Missions of the Double-A Texas

League, and batted .278 in 134 games, then joined the Peoria Saguaros of the Arizona Fall League. Moved up to Triple-A Portland, he batted .292 with 14 home runs in 120 games before making his major-league debut on August 29. Although he would need more time in the minor leagues, in just over three years, the basketball player turned baseball player had reached the major leagues.

Venable played the remainder of the 2008 season with the Padres, and in November, at the Padres' suggestion, headed to the Dominican Winter League to play with the Gigantes del Cibao. He did not hit well – 18 strikeouts to 15 hits, and a .200 batting average – he admitted his poor hitting "was no one's fault but my own."[18] He noted only one regret about his time in the Dominican – that he did not travel there while he was studying anthropology at Princeton. He noted, "I wished I was exposed to [the Dominican Republic] before I wrote my thesis. I would have gotten an A. I found an infinite amount of materials to write about. And the love I had for the game."[19]

The 26-year-old Venable returned to Portland from April to June 2009, and in 53 games batted .260 with 12 home runs. Called up to San Diego in early June, he played in 95 games, starting in 71. Playing mostly right field, he batted .256 with 12 home runs.

Veable was a regular in the Padres lineup from the start of the 2010 season to August of 2015, with short stints at Lake Elsinore and San Antonio in 2010 for rehabilitation of a lower back strain, which troubled him for much of that year.[20] In 2011, batting .224 at the end of May, he was sent to Triple-A Tucson. Manager Bud Black said it was "better for Venable to on his hitting in the minors rather than in big league games. ..."[21] Will was there to work "on his stance and feeling comfortable at the plate."[22] He did have trouble hitting left-handed pitching, and would specifically address this concern in 2012 and 2013, his best years in the major leagues.

In 2011 Venable batted .246 in 121 games with 9 home runs. He fared somewhat better in the 2012 season, batting .264 in 148 games with 9 home runs. Before the 2012 season, Venable had worked with Padres hitting coach Phil Plantier and said he felt more confident at the plate that season. Of his work with Plantier, Venable commented, "My dad's never forced ideas on me. And usually when we've talked hitting, it's been from a distance. But when I told him about what Phil had been doing, he liked the adjustments. My dad is another positive reinforcement."[23]

In San Diego's home opener, on April 9, 2013, Venable matched his single-game career high of four RBIs by hitting a home run and a bases-loaded triple.[24]

More stellar offense and defense would come that season. In June, against San Francisco, he "made an incredible catch to save San Diego. ...Venable's diving grab on the center field warning track with his back to home plate ended the 12th and stole a game-winning hit from Juan Perez."[25] On August 18 against the New York Mets, Venable singled to extend his 15-game hitting streak and hit a game-winning home run in the bottom of the ninth. He spent a good deal of the season in center field, filling in for Cameron Maybin, who had been plagued with injuries. For the season Venable "set career highs in nearly every offensive category" He batted .268 with 22 home runs, 53 RBIs, and 22 stolen bases.[26] In a September game against the Phillies, Venable hit his ninth leadoff home run, his 22nd of the season, off Roy Halladay.[27] This was a Padres record. Venable was named the National League Player of the Week for August 18, the only time he received this recognition. He was named the Padres nominee for the annual Hank Aaron Award;[28] and he was unanimously voted the Padres' Most Valuable Player by the San Diego chapter of the BBWAA.[29] In December Venable and his fiancée Kathryn were married in Anguilla.

Venable's overall production dropped in 2014. He played in 146 games, and finished the season with a .224 batting average and 8 home runs. In the field he had a perfect season, 1.000, with no errors in the outfield – he played right, center, and left fields.

The 2015 season brought changes in Venable's career and life. The first major event was the birth of a daughter, McKinley, to him and Kathryn on August 6. He was on the paternity leave list from August 7[30] to August 9.[31] Two weeks later, the Padres traded Venable to the Texas Rangers for catcher-outfielder Marcus Greens and right-handed pitcher Jon Edwards. Rangers general manager Jon Daniels, said Venable was "a smart player, tremendous reputation on and off the field. He can run, has some power, can play all 3 [outfield] positions. ... We're a little thin in the outfield and he gives us protection in all three spots."[32] The "thin in the outfield" referred to the injured Josh Hamilton; Daniels felt the Rangers needed depth. A great deal was happening in Venable's professional and personal lives. "Knowing I had to say goodbye to people and a place I love is not an easy thing to do," Venable said before the Rangers opened their series against the Padres at Petco Park on Monday. "Especially, when it's instant. I had to get my stuff and get out of the clubhouse in about an hour or two. It was emotional, but it's something that happens to everybody."[33] Fans felt some of those same emotions: "Venable certainly won the heart of Padres fans, who starved for players who stay longer than two or three years."[34]

Venable played in 37 regular-season games for the Rangers. He hit .182 with 3 home runs. The Rangers (West Division champions) faced the Toronto Blue Jays (East Division champions) in the first round of the ALDS. The Blue Jays won the best-of-five series, three games to two. Venable appeared in four games, as a left fielder, pinch-runner, designated hitter, and pinch-hitter. He had two at-bats, and one hit. Released by the Rangers, In February of 2016, he signed a minor-league deal with the Cleveland Indians with a nonroster invitation to spring training.[35]

When Venable realized at the end of spring training that the Indians would not put him on the major-league roster, he asked for his release; and one day later, he signed a minor-league deal with the Philadelphia Phillies with an invitation to major-league camp. Phillies manager Pete Mackanin said, "We're anxious to see what he looks like. I've seen him in the past. ... I know he's a good outfielder, he's got power, and he can run. We'll just give him three to four games to see what he looks like."[36]

Venable played in 41 games for the Triple-A Lehigh Valley Iron-Pigs and batted .205. The Phillies had seen enough. Three days after his release from the Phillies organization, the Los Angeles Dodgers signed him to a deal that would keep him on the club at least until Yasiel Puig returned from the disabled list later in June.[37] The Dodgers assigned Venable to the Oklahoma City Dodgers on June 24. He had played in 12 games and had one hit in 18 at-bats. He played his final game in the major leagues on July 6, 2106, perhaps ironically, versus the Baltimore Orioles (the first team to show real interest in him, having drafted him in 2004). He completed the 2016 season with Triple-A Oklahoma City. There he played in 46 games, hit .276 with 4 home runs.

In November Venable elected free-agency status, but no major-league playing opportunity came his way. On September 6, 2017, he officially retired as a player and joined the Chicago Cubs as a special assistant to the club's president of baseball operations, Theo Epstein, and general manager Jed Hoyer. His responsibilities, according to the Cubs, involved "several aspects of the Cubs' baseball operations department, including work with Minor League affiliates, amateur player evaluation for the MLB Draft and assistance with the Major League club."[38] Just over two months later, on November 17, 2017, Venable was named the Cubs' first-base coach. Hoyer said, "You want the experience of older coaches (such as) Chili (Davis) and (Brian Butterfield), as well as Joe (Maddon). But having a couple of guys who are not far removed (from their playing days is) a nice balance when a player has a conversation he might not feel an older guy can necessarily relate to."[39] His responsibilities also included coaching the Cubs outfielders.

Venable's philosophical summation of playing professional baseball could be applied to his approach to life: "All of us players, I think we have an idea of the player we want to be, and getting there is, a lot of times, difficult. And it's more than having a good month, or a good couple of at-bats against lefties. I know the ways that I've improved. I know the adjustments that I'm making, the improvements that I'm making. It's not something that happened."[40]

Education also remained a priority in Venable's life: He enrolled at the University of North Carolina's Kenan-Flager Business School in Chapel Hill, North Carolina.

## SOURCES

In addition to the sources cited in the Notes, the author also consulted Baseball Reference.com, Retrosheet.org, mlb/cubs, mlb.com/padres, and espn.com/mlb/.

## NOTES

1    Brett Tomlinson, "Fast Pitch, Fast Mind," *Princeton Alumni Weekly,* paw.princeton.edu/article/fast-pitch-fast-mind.

2    "Chris Young '02, Will Venable '05, Ross Ohlendorf, '05, & David Hale '11," *Princeton Varsity Club,* princetonvarsityclub.org/2013/12/chris-young-02-will-venable-05-ross-ohlendorf-05-and-david-hale-11/

3    "Prep Athletes of the Week," *San Francisco Examiner,* January 30, 1999.

4    Ibid.

5    Tim Kurkjian, "Going from Princeton to the Big Leagues," ESPN, April 16, 2010. espn.com/mlb/columns/story?columnist=kurkjian_tim&id=5094390.

6    "Celebrating Black History Month Profiles from Ivy League's Black History," "Will Venable." Ivy@50. ivy50.com/blackhistory/story.aspx?sid=12/18/2006.

7    Ibid.

8    Chris Jenkins, "Venable Has Been a Remarkably Quick Study," *San Diego Union-Tribune,* August 10, 2009.

9    Ibid.

10   sports-reference.com/cbb/players/will-venable-1.html.

11   Kurkjian.

12   *"Cubs Roster & Staff,"* Official Site of the Chicago Cubs,  m.mlb.com/chc/roster/coach/461416/will-venable.

13   "William Winston Roper Trophy," Princeton Varsity Club, princetonvarsityclub.org/award/william-winston-roper-trophy/.

14   "Celebrating Black History Month Profiles from Ivy League's Black History." "Will Venable."

15   Ibid.

16   Celebrating Black History Month Profiles from Ivy League's Black History."

17   Henry Schulman, "Max Venable's Son Shows Skills with Padres," *SFGate,* September 14, 2008. sfgate.com/sports/article/Max-Venable-s-son-shows-skills-with-Padres-3269307.php.

18   Jenkins.

19   Ibid.

20   "Will Venable 38 – MLB.com."mlb.mlb.com/documents/0/4/6/41912046/venablebio_w8p6y7gw.pdf.

21   "Padres Send Venable to Triple-A," *Akron Beacon Journal,* May 24, 2011.

22   Sarah Trotto, "Venable Hits Two Home Runs for Tucson," *Arizona Daily Star* (Tucson), May 28, 2011.

23   Bill Center, "Venable Looking to Improve With Help from Plantier," *San Diego Tribune*, February 29, 2012.

24   Bernie Wilson, "Venable's Bat Powers Pads Past Dodgers in Home Opener," *Santa Maria* (California) *Times*, April 10, 2013.

25   Jamie McCauley, "Padres Break Through for 2 in 13th, Beat Giants," *Santa Maria Times,* June 18, 2013.

26   "Will Venable Named Padres Nominee for 2013 Hank Aaron Award," MLB.com, October 7, 2013. mlb.com/padres/news/will-venable-named-padres-nominee-for-2013-hank-aaron-award/c-62629386.

27   Dave Zeitlin, "Ruiz Leads Phils to 10-5 Win Over Padres," *Lompoc* (California) *Record.* September 13, 2013.

28   The Hank Aaron Award, given since 1999 to the most outstanding offensive performer in each league, went to first baseman Paul Goldschmidt of the Arizona Diamondbacks in 2013.

29   "Will Venable 38 – MLB.com."

30   "Thursday's Sports Transactions, National League," *Tulare* (California) *Advance Register,* August 7, 2015.

31   "Transactions Baseball, National League," *Desert Sun* (Palm Springs, California), August 9, 2015.

32   Stefan Stevenson, "With Hamilton Still Out, Rangers Acquire Will Venable from Padres," *Fort Worth Star Telegram*, August 18, 2015. star-telegram.com/sports/mlb/texas-rangers/article31476940.html.

33   Stefan Stevenson, "Longtime Padre Venable Adjusting to New Life with Rangers," *Fort Worth Star Telegram*. star-telegram.com/sports/mlb/texas-rangers/article33303756.html.

34   Nick Lee, "Padres Birthday Spotlight: Will Venable," *East Village Times*. October 2018. eastvillagetimes.com/2018/10/padres-birthday-spotlight-will-venable/.

35   Matt Lyons, "Cleveland Indians Sign Will Venable to Minor-League Deal," *Let's Go Tribe*.letsgotribe.com/2016/2/26/11119966/cleveland-indians-free-agents-will-venable-signing.

36   "Venable Signs with Phillies, a Day After Indians Release Him," *USA Today*. usatoday.com/story/sports/mlb/2016/03/28/venable-signs-with-phillies-a-day-after-indians-release-him/82358566/.

37   Ken Gurnick, "Dodgers Add Vet Venable to Bench, Option Barnes," Official Site of the Philadelphia Phillies, June 14, 2016. mlb.com/phillies/news/dodgers-sign-veteran-outfielder-will-venable/c-184020880.

38   Jack Baer, "Ex-Big Leaguer Venable Joins Cubs' Front Office," The Official Site of the Chicago Cubs, September 6, 2017. mlb.com/cubs/news/cubs-hire-will-venable-as-special-assistant/c-252798732.

39   Mark Gonzales, "Cubs Counting on New Coach Will Venable Being Able to Relate to Players" *Chicago Tribune*, March 9. 2018. chicagotribune.com/sports/baseball/cubs/ct-spt-cubs-will-venable-experience-20180309-story.html.

40   Howard Megdal, "The Reinvention of Will Venable," *Sports on Earth*. sportsonearth.com/article/60291588/the-new-and-improved-will-venable-explains-his-secrets.

# DAVE WINFIELD

## BY DOUG SKIPPER

It is fitting that Dave Winfield's bust at Cooperstown wears a San Diego Padres cap. Winfield was the franchise's first superstar and represented the team in the first Major League Baseball All-Star game to be hosted the by city. Long after eight magnificent and contentious seasons in San Diego, his

charity work continued to impact "America's Finest City," even as he sustained his assault on pitchers in other venues. After he concluded one of the baseball's most glorious and eventful careers, the team retired the number 31 he sported on his navy blue and sand brown uniform on his sleek, powerful frame and he was named to the club's Hall of Fame.

Imposing, confident, complex, charismatic, and controversial, Winfield ranks as the greatest multi-sport athlete to emerge from the State of Minnesota. Drafted by five different teams in five leagues in three major sports, Winfield chose baseball and compiled a first-ballot Hall of Fame career.

At 6-foot-6 and 220 pounds, the powerfully-built right-hander wielded a menacing black bat. His long, sweeping swing started with a distinctive hitch. Then, with sudden ferocity, he uncoiled and laced line drives to all parts of the park; sometimes clearing fences and walls, more often slamming into them. He ran the bases aggressively and with purpose. He was a good base stealer, but a great base runner. He played defense with equal enthusiasm. Athletic and graceful, he gobbled up ground with long strides, sported a steady glove and boasted one of the most lethal throwing arms in the history of the game. Though blessed with tremendous physical ability, it was Winfield's preparation and determination, along with his ability to make adjustments at the plate and in the field that made him a player greater than his tremendous physical talent.

Winfield grew up in St. Paul and excelled in baseball and basketball at St. Paul Central High School and then at the University of Minnesota. "Winnie" averaged 10.3 points and 6.7 rebounds in 40 Gopher basketball games and posted a 19-4 record for the baseball squad. While at Minnesota, Winfield was a First Team All-America in 1973 and a two-time All-Big Ten selection in 1971 and 1973. He was 9-1 in his senior season with a 2.74 earned run average and 109 strikeouts in 82 innings of work. He batted .385 with 33 runs batted in in 130 at bats that season.

Winfield jumped straight from college to the major leagues, and compiled 3,110 hits, 465 home runs and a .283 batting average in 22 seasons with the San Diego Padres, New York Yankees, California Angels, Toronto Blue Jays, Minnesota Twins and Cleveland Indians. He played in 2,973 games, batted 11,003 times, collected 1093 extra base hits, stole 223 bases, made 5,012 putouts and 168 assists, and appeared in 12 All-Star games and two World Series. He was just the fifth player in the history of baseball to compile 3,000 hits and 450 home runs.

But there is so much more to the man than the numbers.

There is Winfield's charity. He was the first active athlete to establish a charitable foundation. For 22 years, The David M. Winfield Foundation provided health care, holiday meals, game tickets, educational scholarships, and hope to underprivileged families. Under Winfield's leadership, the foundation developed "Turn It On," an international community action campaign to prevent substance abuse. For his charitable work, Winfield has earned the YMCA Brian Piccolo Award for Humanitarian Service, baseball's first-ever Branch Rickey Community Service Award, the American League's Joe Cronin Award, the Josh Gibson Leadership Award, and Major League Baseball's Roberto Clemente Award. He was also awarded an honorary Doctorate of Laws from Syracuse University[1] and recognition by Derek Jeter's Turn2 Foundation. Jeter is one of a number of players who credit Winfield's philanthropic efforts for the inspiration for their own charitable organizations.[2]

There is Winfield's business acumen. In addition to serving as president of the Winfield Foundation for years, the big slugger from St. Paul – who once played for Padres owner and McDonald's founder Ray Kroc – possessed a string of Burger Kings, art galleries, a lighting design and contracting company, and a diverse and powerful stock portfolio. He has served on the board of directors for President Bill Clinton's National Service Program, the Morehouse School of Medicine and the Century Council and on the advisory boards for the Peace Corps and MLB's Baseball Players Trust.[3] Since December 2013, he has served as the special assistant to the executive director of the Major League Baseball Players Association (MLBPA), Tony Clark.

There is Winfield's literacy and culture. He is a prolific reader of fiction and non-fiction, collaborated on his best-selling 1988 autobiography, and outlined his plan of action to revitalize baseball in 2007 in *Dropping the Ball*. He penned *Turn It Around, There's No Place Here for Drugs*, authored *The Complete Baseball Player,* and collaborated on Frank White's *They Played for the Love of the Game: Untold Stories of Black Baseball in Minnesota*. A music lover, he served as host and narrator for the Baseball Music Project, a series of concerts that featured songs about the national pastime.[4]

There is Winfield's race relations leadership. As an African American youngster in St. Paul, and later as a major-league baseball player, Winfield encountered racism and battled it with dignity and determination. Granted a public forum by virtue of his occupation, Winfield has spoken and written about race relations, providing a powerful voice in the community. He helped develop the idea of the honoring former Negro League's stars at MLB's 2008 draft.[5]

Winfield's guidance is not restricted to race relations. A highly respected motivational speaker with a smooth, silky voice, Winfield has addressed clubs, schools, and business about sports, education, health, fitness, teamwork, substance abuse prevention, and youth issues.

There is also Winfield's ego. "Much of America's current self-esteem crisis could be overcome just with Winfield's excess," *Sports Illustrated* observed in 1992. "Nobody knows better than Winfield that he is handsome, buffed, richly appointed with all the options, well read, well-spoken and well paid."[6]

And then there is Winfield's pride. After eight successful seasons in San Diego, Winfield signed a contract with New York Yankees owner George Steinbrenner that made him the most highly paid player in baseball. But Steinbrenner quickly developed buyer's remorse, the two squabbled, "The Boss" publicly declared that Winfield was not worth the money, disparaged him, and tried to trade him. "Steinbrenner, who did so much to make Winfield's life miserable in the eight-plus years he played for the Yankees, never appreciated the type of player he had," the *New York Times* observed. "All he did was look at Winfield's hitting statistics. When they lacked lusty numbers, he criticized Winfield. Unlike players and managers from other teams, Steinbrenner never understood the contributions Winfield made with his outfield defense and his base running."[7]

Eventually Steinbrenner even went so far as to pay a known gambler to discredit his star slugger. "Winfield would become the target of owner Steinbrenner's downright vicious crusade to force him out," the *New York Times* observed later. "No doubt he is having the last laugh, but there are times when Winfield sounds like someone who succeeded in spite of his father, and sometimes feels the hurt an abused child must feel all his life." [8] Stung by Steinbrenner's criticism that he was great in the regular season and awful in his first postseason, Winfield cast off the "Mr. May" label with a strong 1992 World Series performance. He earned the Babe Ruth Award as the player with the best performance in the Fall Classic, and placed his decade of discontent with the Yankees behind him. After Winfield revived his career in California, won a World Series in Toronto, collected his 3,000th career hit in Minnesota, and closed out his playing days in Cleveland, he and the Boss made a form of peace. [9]

In recent years, Winfield also made peace in his complicated personal life. Devoted to the mother who raised him, he reconnected with his father after her 1988 death. That same year he married, and formed a relationship with a child from a previous relationship. Later, he fathered two more children with his wife Tonya. As a special assistant to the executive director of the Major League Baseball Players Association., he travels the world as an ambassador for baseball, delivers motivational speeches, continues his charitable work, and spends time with his family. [10]

David Mark Winfield was born in St. Paul on October 3, 1951 – the day that Bobby Thomson hit "The Shot Heard Round the World," the pennant-winning home run for the New York Giants. David was the second son for Frank Charles Winfield, a World War II veteran and a Pullman porter on the Great Northern Railroad's flagship train, the *Empire Builder*, and Arline Vivian (Allison) Winfield, a St. Paul native. Frank, who lived in Duluth before he entered military service, met Arline through her brother. The couple divorced by the time David turned 3, and Frank eventually moved to Seattle, remarried and became a skycap for Western Airlines. Though they saw one another on occasion, David and his father remained estranged for much of their lives. [11]

Arline, who never remarried, raised David and his older brother Stephen in their home in a row house on Carroll Avenue, west of the state capital and just south of the swath that Interstate 94 now cuts through St. Paul. Arline earned a modest living at her job in the St. Paul School District's audio-visual department, and raised her sons with the assistance of her mother, Jessie Hunt Allison, who lived a block away, and an extended family of aunts, uncles and cousins. Arline stressed the value of education to her sons, showed them educational films she borrowed from the school district, and taught them a new word every night. The family lived in a primarily African American neighborhood and worshipped at the African Methodist Episcopal St. James Church on Central Avenue, a couple blocks north of their home. [12] "More than anything Ma and I *did*, I learned from the example she set, learned the value of education, family, work and a positive attitude," [13]

As youngsters, Dave and Steve played baseball and hockey in St. Paul, and followed the Minnesota Twins when they moved to the Upper Midwest in 1961. Bill Petersen, a former University of Minnesota catcher, coached the pair at the Oxford Playgrounds, and the Winfield boys later led his Attucks-Brooks Post 606 baseball team to two American Legion state championships. [14]

The brothers also excelled at St. Paul Central High School, at the corner of Marshall and Lexington. Steve lettered in baseball three times, captained the team his senior season, 1968, and was named to the school's Athletic Hall of Fame in September 2007. Younger brother Dave earned All-St. Paul and All-Minnesota honors in both baseball and basketball for the Minutemen, and was named to the Central's Athletic Hall of Fame in 1995.

At the end of his senior year, Dave stood 6-foot-6 when on June 5, 1969, the Baltimore Orioles selected the younger Winfield in the 40th round of baseball's amateur draft. He passed up that opportunity, and accepted a baseball scholarship from the University of Minnesota, where older brother Steve was already enrolled.

The scholarship covered only tuition, and as a freshman, Winfield commuted 12 miles by public bus each day to attend class, to play forward for the freshman basketball team and pitch for the freshman baseball squad. He went 4-0 for the Gopher frosh in the spring of 1970, then 8-0 in the Metropolitan (St. Paul) Collegiate League that summer, before he and a friend were caught snatching a pair of snow blowers from a local business. Winfield pled guilty to a charge of felony theft and was sentenced to three years in the St. Cloud Penitentiary, a sentence that was suspended, and years later, based on his public service and good works, expunged. [15]

Winfield made a repentant return to campus and embraced his second chance. He and Steve led a team dubbed "The Soulful Strutters" to the campus intramural basketball championship, and were invited to scrimmage regularly against the Gopher junior varsity. [16] After he posted an 8-3 record and a Big Ten-best 1.48 earned run average for Dick Siebert's Minnesota varsity baseball team, Winfield pitched and played outfield for the Fairbanks Goldpanners of the Alaska Summer League, coached by college baseball legend Jim Dietz. [17]

Back on campus for his third year in the fall of 1971, Winfield worked out with the junior varsity basketball team, where he caught the eye of Gopher assistant coach Jimmy Williams. Williams invited him to try out for new head coach Bill Musselman, and Winfield earned a spot on a veteran squad that included Jim Brewer, Ron Behagen, Clyde Turner, Keith Young, Bob

Murphy, Bob Nix, and Corky Taylor. The veterans were slow to accept Winfield, but he won them over with his hard work, hustle and powerful elbows.[18] "He was the best rebounder I ever saw," Musselman, who would go on to coach in the American and National Basketball Associations, later said.[19]

"Making the team, I give up my half baseball scholarship for a full basketball scholarship," Winfield's autobiography stated. "Anyway, for the first time I can go to classes, go to practices, live away from home, and not have to worry whether I'll be able to afford my meals, my books, or transportation."[20]

If life was more settled off the court, it was frantic on the hard-wood, where Musselman coached his players to be aggressive and physical, a style Winfield embraced. "From Musselman I learned to get on that man, to get inside his jersey, his shorts, his jock. I learned first and foremost to *be* there. To get up in his face when he tried to dribble, and to stay there when he tried to shoot." [21]

On January 25, 1972, "Musselman's Musclemen" became too aggressive. Trailing late in a Big 10 showdown with Ohio State before a frenzied Williams Arena crowd, Taylor committed a hard foul on Ohio State center Luke Witte. The Gophers had been unhappy with the way Witte was throwing elbows during the game. When Taylor helped Witte up off the floor, he kneed him in the groin. Behagen who had fouled out earlier, jumped in off the bench, and stomped on Witte's head and neck. Quickly, the floor was a sea of players, fans, coaches and officials. Winfield, who had been sitting on the sidelines, entered the fray, running across the floor to throw punches ''like I was spring-loaded.'' Winfield later told *Sports Illustrated,* ''Hey, I'm not denying I was involved. There was a fight with my team. I was swinging.''[22] Though he was later blistered by media members, he escaped the punishment assessed Behagen and Taylor, season-ending suspensions.  Instead, he stepped into Behagen's spot in the starting lineup. As one of the Gophers "Iron Five," Winfield led Minnesota to its first conference championship in 35 years and an appearance in the NCAA Tournament.

The baseball season went less well. In an early season game against Michigan, Winfield damaged tendons around his right elbow and missed the remainder of the season. Despite the injury, Dietz asked him back for the summer, and Winfield hit .315 with 15 home runs for the Goldpanners as an outfielder, and struck out 36 batters as a relief pitcher. He was named team MVP after he led Fairbanks to the ASL title.[23]

Winfield returned to campus and guided Minnesota's basketball team to a second-place Big Ten finish and a berth in the National Invitational Tournament in New York. When the Gophers were knocked out, he joined Siebert's baseball team in Texas, where

he lost his season debut. After that, Winfield was magnificent. He won 13 straight, posted a 2.74 ERA, and hit .385 with 33 runs batted in to earn first-team All-America honors. Appointed team captain, Winfield led Minnesota to the Big 10 title and to the College World Series in Omaha. Along the way, he pitched a nine-inning 1-0 shutout with 14 strikeouts against Oklahoma. On the tournament's final day, the Gophers lost to Arizona State, then met Southern Cal. Thorough eight innings, Winfield limited a Trojan team that included Roy Smalley and Fred Lynn to just one hit, and struck out 15. Leading 7-0, but after nearly 140 pitches, Winfield ran out of gas and surrendered a pair of runs in the ninth. With one out, he left the mound and moved to left field. USC rallied and won 8-7. Despite a third-place finish for the Gophers, Winfield was named CWS MVP.

After the season, four different teams in four different leagues in three different sports drafted Winfield. San Diego made him the fourth pick of the major-league baseball draft on June 5. The Atlanta Hawks picked him in the fifth round of the National Basketball Association draft, the Utah Stars drafted him in the fourth round of the American Basketball Association draft, and – even though he never played high school or college football - the Minnesota Vikings selected Winfield in the 17th round of the National Football League draft. Winfield, Texas Christian's Mickey McCarty, and Colorado's Dave Logan are the only players ever drafted by professional baseball, football, and basketball teams.

Winfield signed with San Diego for $15,000 and jumped straight to the major leagues at the age of 21. He commenced his assault on big-league pitchers with a single and a stolen base in four at-bats against the Houston Astros on June 19, 1973, then collected hits in each of his next five games. Used most often in left field and against lefthanders by manager Don Zimmer, the St. Paul slugger collected 39 hits, with four doubles, a triple, and three home runs, batted .277 and drove in 12 runs in his 56-game rookie campaign. He also began to buy blocks of tickets to Padres games for families who otherwise could not afford to attend.[24]

Over the next three seasons, the youngster continued to provide tickets to poor families and power and speed to the Padre lineup. Between 1974 and 1976, he slugged 64 doubles, 10 triples, and 38 homers, despite playing his home games in cavernous Jack Murphy Stadium. He also stole 64 bases, with a career-high 26 in the bicentennial year. John McNamara, who replaced Zimmer at the start of the 1974 season, used Winfield in left and center, but most often penciled in the youngster into right field. Winfield remembered, "After the All Star Break, McNamara said to me, 'Kid, I'm going to give you a chance to play every day. Play well and the job is yours.'"[25] He did, and for his efforts, the young slugger, who created a scholarship fund for minority student athletes from St. Paul that still exists, saw his pay rise to around $40,000 in 1975 to $57,000 in 1976.[26]

Winfield was unhappy with the contract the Padres offered in 1977, and elected to play out his option at a 10 percent pay cut.[27] The contract squabble pitted him against Padres General Manager Buzzie Bavasi, and when it looked like Winfield might be dealt, signs appeared in the ballpark that urged, "Keep Dave, Trade Buzzie."[28] In early July, with the two sides $100,000 apart, Winfield's friend and representative, Al Frohman, came up with an ingenious solution. Under Frohman's plan, The David M. Winfield Foundation for Underprivileged Youth, an official 501 (c)(3) organization, was established. The team paid the Foundation the $100,000 difference between what Winfield wanted and the Padres were willing to pay, the Foundation handed it right back to the club in exchange for 100,000 game tickets at a dollar apiece, and the Foundation distributed the tickets to underprivileged families.[29] Everybody won. Winfield got the four-year, $1.4 million contract he wanted, the Padres sold an extra 100,000 tickets, thousands of kids got to sit in the Dave Winfield Pavilion at San Diego's Jack Murphy Stadium - and Frohman picked up a sizeable commission.[30]

Winfield signed the contract in early July, in the midst of his breakout season. Just 25, he batted .275 with 25 home runs and 92 runs batted in, clubbed 29 doubles, seven triples, and was named to the National League All Star team. Winfield made the first of his 12 consecutive appearances in the Mid-Summer Classic, smacked a double and drove in the winning runs with a single off Sparky Lyle in the NL's 7-5 victory.

The Dave Winfield Foundation drew support from a number of corporations, formed a relationship with the Scripps Foundation to provide free medical checkups to needy families, and delivered an anti-drug message and provided holiday dinners and scholarships to those who otherwise could not get them.[31]

In 1978, he was named the first team captain in Padres history, was the NL Player of the Month for June, hit .300 for the first time, slugged 24 homers, 30 doubles, and five triples, drove in 97 runs and scored 104, and stole 21 bases. When San Diego hosted the All-Star Game, the Winfield Foundation bought its usual allotment of pavilion tickets. On local radio, the slugger from St. Paul, scheduled to play in his second All-Star Game, urged "all the kids of San Diego" to attend. When they responded by showing up in droves, major-league baseball opened practice sessions for the first time, starting a tradition that continues to the present day.[32] It was a highlight in a special season for San Diego. Under new manager Roger Craig, with a roster that included Winfield, Rollie Fingers, Gaylord Perry, and rookie shortstop Ozzie Smith, the Padres posted a winning record for the first time, though they finished fourth in the NL's Western Division.

A year later, San Diego slid back to 25 games under .500, though Winfield enjoyed what may have been his finest season. The 27-year old batted .308 again, with 34 home runs, 27 doubles, 10 triples, and 15 stolen bases. Winfield drove in a career-best and NL high 118 runs, scored 97, won his first Gold Glove, and finished third in the league's Most Valuable Player Award voting behind Keith Hernandez and Willie Stargell. He drew a career-high 85 walks, and led the league in intentional passes with 25. "I became a lot more patient," Winfield said later. "I learned the strike zone a lot better and I realized that sometimes it's better to take a walk than to make an out on a bad pitch."[33]

Winfield grew less patient with the Padres, and there were suggestions that he was not a team player. "If the Padres go places, I will be a main reason," he said. "But it they falter, I'll still shine."[34] With his contract set to expire at the end of the 1980 season and no extension in sight, Winfield played in all 162 games for Jerry Coleman, his sixth manager in eight years, and won another Gold Glove, but slipped to 20 home runs, 87 RBIs, 23 steals, and a .276 batting average. When the season ended, so did his tenure as a Padre. Not everyone was sad to see him go. ''Dave Winfield thinks he is holier than thou,'' Smith said later. ''He always acted as if it were his God-given right to tell other people how to do things.''[35]

On December 15, 1980, New York Yankees owner George Steinbrenner signed Winfield to a 10-year, $23.3 million contract. Slugger Dave Winfield was leaving San Diego to play at Yankee Stadium and to become baseball's highest paid player.

It seemed like a match made in heaven; it would begin a decade of pure hell between the two men. From the start, there were problems. Steinbrenner, who took great pride in his negotiation skills, didn't understand or didn't fully read the cost of living escalator clause that Frohman, a man *Sports Illustrated's* Rick Reilly described as "a rumpled and retired New York caterer, a two-pack-a-day, fast-talking, 5 ft., 4 in., 220-pound chunk of walking cholesterol – with no experience as a sports agent," had negotiated for Winfield.[36] That clause made the contract worth seven million dollars more than the $16 million that Steinbrenner thought it was worth, and when alerted by a media member, the Boss was livid.[37] It was made worse when Frohman, who collected a 15%, $3.5 million commission on the deal, reportedly told the *New York Daily News*, ''If he ever touches a hair of my boy's head . . . I'll blow the lid. I've got stuff on George that if it ever came out, he would be in big trouble. It's very easy to be friends with George if you have blackmail on him."[38]

After heated exchanges, Winfield and Steinbrenner reached a compromise - an addendum to the contract that adjusted the cost of living increase, reportedly for $3 to $4 million less over the life of the contract. Winfield also reached an agreement with the Padres, mediated by Baseball Commissioner Bowie Kuhn, which called for the Dave Winfield Foundation to meet a $35,000 contractual obligation to continue to buy tickets for underprivileged children to attend Padres home games. Winfield had already arranged for $3 million ($300,000 per year for 10 years) of his salary to be donated to the Foundation, which funded the Dave Winfield nutrition center at Hackensack University Medical Center and collaborated with Merck Pharmaceuticals to create a bilingual substance abuse prevention program called "Turn it Around."[39]

In his first season in pinstripes, Winfield hit .294 with 13 homers and 68 RBIs in 105 games in the strike-shortened 1981 season. He batted .350 with two doubles and a triple to lead the first-half champion Yankees over the second-half champion Milwaukee Brewers in the AL Divisional playoffs. The Bronx Bombers went on to beat Oakland in the AL Championship Series, but with Reggie Jackson and Graig Nettles injured, and Winfield collecting only one hit in 22 at bats, dropped a 4-2 decision to the Los Angeles Dodgers in the World Series, a loss that stuck firmly in Steinbrenner's craw. After his lone hit, a single, Winfield, perhaps in jest, asked for the ball, which made the Boss even madder.[40]

The Yankees never returned to the postseason with Winfield in the lineup, though he was one of the top players in baseball over the next seven years. He was selected to play in the All-Star Game each year, won five Gold Gloves, and drove in 744 runs. In 1982, the 30-year-old slugger clubbed 37 home runs and drove in 106 runs, batted .280, and slugged a career best .560 for musical chairs managers Bob Lemon, Dick Howser, and Clyde King. A year later, Winfield batted .283 with 32 homers and 116 RBIs for Billy Martin, but the most notable day of his season came on August 4, 1983. Warming up in the outfield before the bottom of the fifth inning, Winfield hit and killed a seagull with a throw at Toronto's Exhibition Stadium. When he tipped his cap in a mock salute to the bird, the hometown crowd reacted by hurling obscenities and objects at him. When the game ended, Winfield was escorted to the Ontario Provincial Police station, booked on charges of cruelty to animals and forced to post a $500 bond before he was released, Martin joked, "It's the first time he's hit the cutoff man."[41] After the charges were dropped the next day, Winfield remarked to the media. "I am truly sorry that a fowl of Canada is no longer with us."[42] Although Winfield attempted to placate them,[43] Blue Jays fans booed Winfield every time he appeared in Toronto until he joined the Jays in 1992.[44]

In 1984, Winfield and Yankee teammate Don Mattingly waged a dramatic and wrenching race for the AL batting title. Winfield homered 19 times, drove in 100 runs, and batted .340, but Mattingly collected four hits – and a standing ovation each time he batted - against Detroit on the season's final day to finish at .343. The two walked off the field together with clasped hands after the finale, but Winfield was clearly hurt that many of his teammates – and the Yankee ownership – had openly rooted for Mattingly, who was white, over Winfield, a black man. "Most of their teammates were clearly pulling for Mattingly, raising questions about the possibility of race as a factor," the *New York Times* later observed.[45] "I've experienced racism in my life," Winfield told sportscaster and writer Art Rust, Jr. "It was all around me when I was on the Yankees and competing with Don Mattingly for the batting title. Here we both were, two guys on the same team, fighting one another for the same thing against a background of manipulative media and the perceptions of hundreds of thousands of fans that were created by that media. There was a vast difference in the amount of encouragement each of us got from the press and the public."[46] Winfield cleaned out his locker and left without speaking to the media after the final game, and some suggested he was resentful of Mattingly. ''There was nothing between Donnie and I," Winfield later said. "We lived different lives. He was a young player who had a lot of support. I just know what I experienced the entire year. It was much different than my teammate did at the same time."[47]

Already strained by the Boss's buyer's remorse and his attempt to deal his big slugger to Texas in 1984, the relationship between Steinbrenner and Winfield worsened in 1985, though New York's best all-around player drove in 114 runs, batted .275, scored 105 times and clubbed 26 home runs for Yogi Berra and Martin. Late in the season, with the Yankees out of the postseason for a fourth straight year, the Boss said bitterly, "I got rid of Mr. October (Reggie Jackson) and got Mr. May (Winfield)."[48] Winfield later told the *New York Times*, "It was irreverent, it was off-color, it was improper, it doesn't fit. I always rejected it. It doesn't apply. It was an inappropriate remark at the time. I didn't appreciate it then." [49]

Nor did he appreciate Steinbrenner's attempts – public or private – to ruin his reputation, even as he smacked 76 homers and drove in 308 runs between 1986 and 1988 for Lou Piniella and again under Martin. In 1986, Steinbrenner ordered Piniella to platoon Winfield; when he refused, the owner was livid.[50] In 1987, the Boss began to withhold payments he owed to his star slugger to be donated to the Winfield Foundation, despite three court orders to make the payments. Winfield and his new agent, Jeffrey Klein, endured lengthy, heated meetings with Steinbrenner's acerbic attorney, Roy Cohn, often on game days.[51] When Winfield sued, the Boss countersued to have Winfield removed from leadership from the foundation, suggesting that Winfield was running the foundation for personal gain and that his star slugger could not be trusted. A report in *Newsday* suggested that the foundation spent $6 for every $1 it gave away; Steinbrenner's lawyers provided the numbers. ''There is no way to fathom what was being done to me," Winfield told Reilly. ''It was immoral, improper and reprehensible. It was a battle for everything, your performance, your credibility. Do you know what it's like to have people fooling with your career?" [52]

Steinbrenner continued to make his managers bench or move Winfield down in the batting order, tried to trade him to the Detroit Tigers for Kirk Gibson in 1987, and stepped up the efforts just before Winfield's 1988 autobiography, *Winfield, A Player's Life*, was published.[53] But with 10 seasons in the majors and five for the same team, Winfield could not be traded without his consent. At times, Winfield was able to joke about the situation. "These days baseball is different. You come to spring training; you get your legs ready, your arms loose, your agents ready, your lawyer lined up."[54] After setting an AL record with 29 RBIs in April 1988, he quipped, "We go on to May, and you know about me and May."[55] Whatever levity he might have felt faded away in the Fall of 1988. His mother Arline died of breast cancer in October; he suffered a herniated disk and endured offseason back surgery. He was forced to miss the entire 1989 season, which ended his string of 12 straight All Star Game appearances. And when it looked like things between he and Steinbrenner could not get worse, they did.

Back in 1981, Frohman had introduced Winfield to Howard "Howie" Spira, a gambler with alleged mafia connections, and arranged for Winfield to make a $15,000 payment owed to Frohman instead to Spira. Five years later, Spira approached Winfield and asked for money in exchange for information that "would ruin Steinbrenner." After Winfield refused, Spira visited Steinbrenner, who was desperate for any information that would make his highly paid player look bad, and the Boss made a secret, illicit deal with the mercenary gambler. Eventually, Spira publicly accused Winfield of betting on baseball, and in the shadow of the Pete Rose investigation, the commissioner's office launched another inquisition. The investigation uncovered no evidence that Winfield had bet on baseball, but revealed that Steinbrenner had paid Spira $40,000 for his dubious information. The investigation also discovered that Steinbrenner had suggested turning over "potentially damaging" information about the Winfield Foundation to the Internal Revenue Service.[56] On June 30, 1990, Baseball Commissioner Fay Vincent ordered Steinbrenner to resign as the club's general partner and banned him from day-to-day operation of the team for life, a sanction that was lifted two and a half years later.[57] Spira was later found guilty of trying to extort an additional $70,000 from Steinbrenner, and sentenced to 30 months in prison for his role in the sordid affair.[58]

In the shadow of the inquiry, Winfield began the 1990 season in pinstripes. Angry that the Yankees left him off the All-Star ballot, he batted just .213 over 20 games with a pair of home runs and 19 runs batted in before the club traded him to the California Angels on May 11, 1990 for pitcher Mike Witt. Winfield argued that his contract did not allow him to be traded without his consent, but accepted a negotiated deal on May 16.[59] "It's been an ordeal to a large degree," Winfield said. "Maybe things didn't work out (in New York), but I know they are going to work out in California."[60]

Although he had moved to the opposite side of the country, Winfield continued to stick in Steinbrenner's craw. On July 6, Baseball Commissioner Fay Vincent ordered the Yankees to pay the Angels $200,000 - in addition to a $25,000 fine - for tampering with Winfield after he was traded to California.[61]

For the Angels, Winfield was brilliant. He batted .275 with 19 home runs and 72 runs batted in 112 games to earn The Sporting News AL Comeback Player of the Year honors. A year later, Winfield smacked 28 more home runs, 27 doubles, and drove in 86 runs for the Angels. He homered three times on April 13 at Minnesota and on June 24, he went 5-for-5 and hit for the cycle for the first time in his career, the oldest major-league player ever to do so, at 39. On August 14, 1991, Winfield became the 23rd player to hit 400 career home runs when he connected at his hometown ballpark, the Metrodome in Minneapolis. "Three-ninety-nine sounds like something you'd purchase at a discount store. Four hundred sounds so much better."[62] At the end of the year, he again became a free agent.

On December 19, 1991, Winfield embarked on the most successful year of his career when he signed a one-year contract with Toronto. For the 1992 AL East champs, Winfield batted .290, smacked 33 doubles and 26 homers, scored 92 runs, and drove in 108, the first 40-year old ever to drive in 100. His numbers as a designated hitter and right fielder were impressive, but it was his hard work and hustle that made him a fan favorite and earned him absolution for the seagull incident. Winfield, the Blue Jays' cleanup hitter, implored fans to be supportive of the team, and the phrase "Winfield Wants Noise" quickly appeared on t-shirts, signs and the Sky Dome scoreboard. "He is asked about his longevity," *Sports Illustrated* reported, "and he says, 'For the last few years people have seen me and acted surprised that I'm still playing. Still playing? I'm kicking butt.'" [63]

Winfield smacked a pair homers and a double in Toronto's four-games-two victory over Oakland in the AL Championship Series, then drove in three runs against Atlanta in the World Series. Two came home when he smashed a double down the third-base line in the 11th inning of the Game Six to give Toronto a 4-3 lead. When the game and the Series ended on Otis Nixon's unsuccessful bunt in the bottom half of the inning, Winfield went from "Mr. May" to "Mr. Jay." He was presented the Babe Ruth Award as the player with the best performance in the World Series. After the season, he also received the Branch Rickey Award, presented for exceptional community service.

''I've been thinking about this," Winfield told *Sports Illustrated*. ''If my career had ended (before Toronto), I would not have been really happy with what baseball dealt me. I would have had no fulfillment, no sense of equity, no fairness. I feel a whole lot better now about the way things have turned out."[64]

With a World Series win under his belt, Winfield set out to accomplish another calling, playing for his hometown team. On December 17, 1992, the St. Paul native signed a free agent contract with the Minnesota Twins. In 143 games, most as Minnesota's designated hitter, he batted .271 with 21 home runs and drove in 76. On September 16, 1993, he collected his 3,000th hit, a ninth-inning single off Oakland reliever Dennis Eckersley that plated Kirby Puckett.

In 1994, at age 42, he hit 10 more home runs, but the Twins fell out of contention, and on July 31, Minnesota dealt him for to Cleveland for a player to be named later. Two weeks later, on August 12, before Winfield ever appeared as an Indian, major-league baseball players went on strike, and after a short impasse, owners cancelled the rest of the season. Winfield became a free agent in October, and Cleveland never sent a player to the Twins in the deal, but when executives of the two teams went to a dinner after the season, the Indians reportedly picked up the tab to settle the score.[65] After the season, Winfield received the

Roberto Clemente Award, which annually recognizes the player who best exemplifies sportsmanship, community involvement and contribution to his team."[66]

On April 5, 1995, as baseball resumed, Winfield signed on with Cleveland. At 43, major-league baseball's oldest active player spent part of the season on the disabled list with a rotator cuff injury, appeared in 46 games, hit the 464th and 465th home runs of his career and batted .191 for the Indians, who won their first pennant in 41 years. On September 28, he rifled a pinch-hit single to center field at the Metrodome. Two days later, he collected the 3,110th and final hit of his career, at Jacobs Field, and on October 1, 1995 at Cleveland, he made his final appearance in the major leagues, a pinch-hit ground out. Cleveland won the AL title, but Winfield did not appear in the postseason. After the Indians lost a heart-wrenching World Series, the St. Paul slugger retired.

Winfield served as a Fox television baseball broadcaster, starting in 1996, hosted a Los Angeles morning drive time radio show, *On the Ball*, served as a spokesperson for the United Negro College Fund, the Drug Enforcement Administration, the Minnesota Board of Education, and the Discovery Channel. He also appeared in the film *The Last Home Run*, hosted the syndicate television show "*Greatest Sports Legends*," and appeared on *Married with Children*, the *Drew Carey Show*, and *Arli$$*.

In 1999, *The Sporting News* ranked Winfield 94th on its list of Baseball's Greatest Players, and he was nominated for MLB's All-Century Team. In 2000, he was inducted into the San Diego Padres Hall of Fame and his number 31 was retired. Winfield had one year earlier been named to the Breitbard Hall of Fame, honoring San Diego's greatest athletes, and enshrined in the San Diego Hall of Champions

Early in 2001, Winfield and Puckett each were elected to Baseball's Hall of Fame in their first year of eligibility. Steinbrenner issued a statement that said he was delighted by Winfield's election and that he was ''probably one of the greatest athletes I have ever known."[67]

Steinbrenner and Winfield had started to patch up their complicated relationship a few years earlier. ''All of that never should have happened," the Boss said in early 1998. "Dave Winfield was one of the greatest athletes I've ever known. What part of it is me, I'll take the blame."[68] Just before the HOF election, the *New York Times* reported that, "Steinbrenner also acknowledged the problems the two men encountered, though he didn't say he instigated them, and said that 'today we are good friends.'"[69]

Winfield didn't go that far, but said more than once that Steinbrenner had ''apologized for what he's said and what he's done."[70] The reconciliation survived yet another dust up when

Steinbrenner publicly stated that Winfield's HOF bust should wear a Yankees cap, and the Boss reportedly was irked when Winfield chose to be the first player represented with a San Diego Padres cap.[71]

On August 5, 2001, Winfield and Puckett became the seventh pair of teammates to be inducted into the Hall in the same year. Puckett recalled the time during his rookie year when Winfield had invited him to dinner, and imparted lessons about baseball and life. "From that point on, Dave Winfield was a friend of mine," Puckett said. ''He's a great friend of mine. Any time I can spend in his company is special, not just when we're going into the Hall of Fame."[72]

In his induction speech, Winfield was conciliatory towards Steinbrenner.[73] The two had talked earlier, and "There were a lot of things we got out in the open," Winfield said. "He said things that made me believe he regretted what had happened."[74]

Things between the two had improved enough that on August 18, 2001, the St. Paul slugger was honored with Dave Winfield Day at Yankee Stadium. "Here's a day we thought we might not see, but it's here and it's beautiful," Winfield said.[75] The Yankees unveiled his old number 31 (though they didn't retire it), painted along the first- and third-base stands, and he was presented with keys for a sports car by his old teammate, Don Mattingly. Although Steinbrenner didn't attend, he did call Winfield, who thanked the Boss for inviting him back. "I'm not the one that's been behind trying to make a Dave Winfield Day at Yankee Stadium," Winfield told the *New York Times*. "It's been his doing. Things are certainly good now."[76]

The relationship continued to thaw. In 2008, Winfield played in the final Old Timer's Day Game at Yankee Stadium in August, and took part in the Final Game Ceremony at the Stadium in September. Earlier that summer, Winfield told *Newsday* that Steinbrenner "definitely has to be considered" for the Hall of Fame. "I might not have thought this years ago," Winfield said, "but he's had a lot to do with resurrecting the Yankees franchise and their brand and they've done really, really well during his tenure."[77] However, the Boss was not elected before he died in 2010.

Meanwhile, Winfield, who had joined the front office of the San Diego Padres as an executive vice president and senior advisor in 2001, appeared as an analyst on ESPN's *Baseball Tonight* from 2009 to 2012, and become the assistant to the Executive director of the MLBPA in 2013, continued to collect honors and accomplishments.

In 2004, ESPN named him the third best all-around athlete in the history of sport, behind only Jim Brown and Jim Thorpe.[78] He was one of the inaugural class of five players named to the College Baseball Hall of Fame in 2006, and inducted on July 4, 2007. One year later, he was selected to the California Athletic Hall of Fame. In 2010, Winfield was named the All-Time Left Fielder the National Sports Review Poll, and named as one of 28 member of the NCAA Men's College World Series Legends Team.[79]

On July 14, 2014, Winfield was one of four St. Paul natives to throw out the first pitch for the 2014 Home Run Derby, along with Joe Mauer, Paul Molitor, and Jack Morris.

He journeyed to Cuba in March 2016 as a representative of Major League Baseball when President Barack Obama visited the island nation, participated in a press conference in Havana with Joe Torre, Derek Jeter, and Luis Tiant and attended an exhibition baseball game between the Tampa Bay Rays and the Cuba National Team.[80]

In July, the 2016 Major League Baseball All-Star Game at Petco Park was dedicated to Winfield, who had represented the Padres at the San Diego's first All-Star Game at Jack Murphy Stadium in 1977.

Away from baseball, as he did with his dealings with Steinbrenner, Winfield set some of the relationships in his equally complicated personal life in order.

In 1988, he married Tonya Turner in New Orleans, seven years after they had met. Arline, battling cancer, sat in the front row. Shortly before she died in October, Winfield established contact with his daughter Lauren Shanel Winfield, who he fathered with Sandra Renfro, a Houston flight attendant in 1982.[81] Renfro, who never lived with Winfield, filed a common-law marriage suit against the ballplayer in 1985, after he had supported her for several years. Renfro won a $1.6 million judgement against Winfield in 1989.[82] It was overturned in 1991, and the two reached a legal agreement in 1995 that decreed that no marriage ever existed between them. Winfield agreed to continue $3,500 monthly child support payments,[83] and continued to be involved in Shanel's life. Winfield also reconnected with his father. Frank attended Arline's funeral, and with the encouragement of Tonya's mother, the two began to communicate more frequently.[84]

Dave and Tonya welcomed twins Arielle and David Jr in 1995. Both enrolled at the University of Pennsylvania in 2013, where Arielle played women's volleyball and David Jr played men's basketball.

Winfield followed his children's athletic careers, and remembered his own. ''I miss going first to third in somebody's face," he told the *New York Times* just before he was inducted into the Baseball Hall of Fame in 2001. "I miss throwing someone out from the outfield. Going from first to third, scoring from first on a double, for a big guy, those are things I really enjoyed. You can hit a ground ball right at an outfielder and if you're busting your backside from home plate, you have a chance for a double. Those are things I enjoyed. Playing defense is something you have to work on and something you have to love. When I first started, I wasn't a good defensive outfielder. I focused on it, enjoyed it, worked on things like charging the baseball. Little things that you do consistently become big things. Defense was a big part of my game."[85]

## SOURCES

In addition to the sources cited in the Notes, the author also consulted:

### Books

James, Bill. *The Bill James Historical Baseball Abstract,* (New York: Villard, 1985).

Madden, Bill and Kerin McCue. *Steinbrenner: The Last Lion of Baseball,* (New York: Harper, 2010).

White, Frank and Dave Winfield. *They Played for the Love of the Game: Untold Stories of Black Baseball in Minnesota,* (St. Paul: Minnesota Historical Society Press, 2016).

Winfield, David with Michael Levin. *Dropping the Ball, Baseball's Troubles and How We Can and Must Solve Them* (New York: Scribner, 1987).

### Websites

www.aparchive.com, web.baseballhalloffame.org, www.baseball-almanac.com, www.baseball-reference.com, www.central.spps.org, www.davewinfield.com, www.davewinfieldhof.com, www.gophersports.com, www.mlb.com, www.retrosheet.org, www.spn.com, www.si.com/vault, www.sabr.org,www.sicnn.com, www.thebaseballpage.com, and www.upi.com/archives.

## NOTES

1  http://davewinfieldhof.com

2  Ryan Mink, "Turn2 Foundation Celebrates 10th Anniversary; Jeter's Youth Outreach Organization Helps Kids," mlb.com, June 29, 2008.

3  http://davewinfieldhof.com

4  Ibid.

5  Tim Kurkjian, "Negro League Players Will Be Recognized at Draft," ESPN.com, June 4, 2008. A group that included Winfield, then Commissioner Bud Selig and MLB executive Vice President for Baseball Operations Jimmie Solomon provided the idea and the inspiration for the June 5, 2008 special draft of former Negro League players. Each of the 30 major league teams drafted one surviving Negro League player, representing all of those who were excluded from the major leagues.

6  Rick Reilly, "I Feel a Whole Lot Better Now; Dave Winfield's 20-Year Baseball Career, Often Touched by Trouble and Trauma, Has Taken A Happy Turn in Toronto," *Sports Illustrated,* June 29, 1992. Reilly's incisive interview with Winfield at a time he was a member of the Toronto Blue Jays provides a rich look into Winfield's personality, his background and his motivations.

7  Murray Chass, "Some Slights Endure for Winfield," *New York Times,* January 18, 2001: D4.

8  Harvey Araton, "Sports of the Times; One Went; One Stayed; Both Yearn," *New York Times,* September 22, 1993: B13.

9  "Winfield Honored by Yankees," New York Times, August 19, 2001: D4.

10  http://davewinfieldhof.com

11  Dave Winfield with Tom Parker, *"Winfield; A Player's Life* (New York: W.W. Norton and Company, 1988, 39-40.

12  Winfield with Parker, 40-41 and Gene Schoor, *Dave Winfield, The 23 Million Dollar Man* (New York: Stein and Day, 1982), 9-16 both provide details about Winfield's formative years, his mother Arline, and his close relationship with his brother Steve.

13  Winfield with Parker, 43.

14  Ibid., 35-39.

15  Ibid,. 62-66.

16  Ibid., 73-75.

17  Ibid., 68-72.

18  Ibid., 77.

19  Ibid., 77.

20  Ibid., 78.

21  Ibid., 76.

22  Winfield described the incident to Reilly in the 1992 profile for *Sports Illustrated.*

23  Winfield with Parker, 83-86.

24  http://davewinfieldhof.com

25  Winfield with Parker, 111.

26  Schoor, 61.

27  According to Baseball-Reference.com, *The Sporting News* Salary Survey, published April 23, 1977, listed Winfield's salary at $90,000.

28  Winfield with Parker, 128-131

29  Ibid., 130-131

30  Reilly. Years later, according to http://davewinfieldhof.com Winfield learned that Toronto Blue Jays teammate David Wells had been one of the "Winfield Kids" who sat in the Winfield Pavilion.

31  Winfield's exceptional philanthropy is well known. Schoor, 57-58, 89-91, 160, and 161 provides details, as does the http://davewinfieldhof.com/winfield-foundation/ website.

32  http://davewinfieldhof.com

33  Phil Collier, "Hot-Hitting Winfield Shuns HR Swing," The Sporting News, May 5, 1979: 27.

34  Schoor.

35  Reilly.

36  Ibid.

37  The media member was the New York Times writer Murray Chass.

38  Reilly.

39  http://davewinfieldhof.com

40  Thomas Boswell, "Winfield's Single Merely a Souvenir," Washington Post, October 26, 1981.

41  Bill Pennington, Billy Martin: Baseball's Flawed Genius (Wilmington, Massachusetts: Mariner Books, 2016), 393.

42  UPI writer David Tucker reported Winfield's comment in "New York Yankees' slugger Dave Winfield Was Arrested Thursday" https://www.upi.com/Archives/1983/08/05/New-York-Yankees-slugger-Dave-Winfield-was-arrested-Thursday/8533428904000/. The story ran in a number of newspapers.

43  Winfield with Parker, 201-203. Winfield told Parker that he donated two pieces of art to Easter Seals charity auctions he attended in Toronto the next two off seasons, worth $70,000. Despite the charity, he was heckled by arm-flapping fans on each return to Toronto prior to 1993.

44  Herschel Nissenson, "Winfield Arrested for Killing Seagull," Daily News, August 5, 1983: 25. See also Jane Gross, "Winfield Charges Will be Dropped," New York Times, August 5, 1983: 29. Pennington, 393, provided comments from Martin. Is this the New York Daily News?

45  Murray Chass, "Some Slights Endure for Winfield," New York Times, January 18, 2001: D4.

46  Art Rust, Jr. Get That Nigger off the Field, The Oral History of the Negro Leagues (Los Angeles: Shadow Lawn Press, 1992), 190.

47  Chass, "Some Slights Endure for Winfield."

48  Murray Chass, "Murray Chass on Baseball; Familiar Problem for Piniella, New York Times, December 15, 1985: S7, and "Murray Chass, "On Baseball: Sorry, Harvey," www.murraychass.com, 14.

49  Chass, "Some Slights Endure for Winfield."

50  Bill Madden and Moss Klein, Damned Yankees: Chaos, Confusion, and Craziness in the Steinbrenner Era, Chicago, Triumph Books, 2012 (reprint). Steinbrenner denied he ordered Piniella to platoon Winfield, but that he might do so. Ross Newhan, "Baseball: Drug Death's Don't Change the Real Issue," Los Angeles Times, July 13, 1986.

51  Reilly.

52  Reilly.

53  E.M. Swift, "Yanked About by the Boss; Bringing Their Feud to a Head, George Steinbrenner Sought to Discredit, to Humiliate and Unload Dave Winfield," Sports Illustrated, April 11, 1988, and Michael Martinez, "Baseball; Dark Cloud Obscures Winfield," New York Times, May 1, 1988: S1.

54  Murray Chass, "Winfield is Hoping Yanks Will Focus on Play, Not Feuds," New York Times, February 27, 1983: S3.

55  Michael Martinez, "Baseball; Winfield Ties R.B.I. Mark as Yankees Roll," New York Times, May 1, 1988: S2. Winfield broke the AL record and tied the major-league record held by Ron Cey of the Dodgers and Dale Murphy of the Braves. Martinez wrote that Winfield reportedly be a part of a three-way trade between the Yankees, Toronto, and Houston later that week.

56  David E. Pitt, "Baseball; Steinbrenner Had Ex-I.R.S. Man Check Winfield," Publication, August 26, 1990: 2.

57  Kevin McCoy and Richard T. Pienciak, "Gone! The Boss Gets the Thumb: Loses Control of Yankees, New York Daily News, July 31, 1990: 1, 4-5. Vincent lifted the ban on March 1, 1993. "A History of Steinbrenner's Career with the Yankees," Newsday, July 13, 2010.

58  Bill Brubaker, "Steinbrenner, Winfield and Friend A Tangled Web," Washington Post, March 30, 1990: S1; David E. Pitt, "Baseball; Steinbrenner Had Ex-I.R.S. Man Check Winfield."

59  Robert McG. Thomas, Jr. "Winfield Approves Trade to the Angels," New York Times, May 17, 1990: B13.

60  Helene Elliott, "Winfield Reaches Settlement, Ready to Join the Angels: Baseball: He Gets Contract Extension for One Year, Plus Two Option Years. Package is Worth as Much as $9.1 Million," Los Angeles Times, May 17, 1990.

61  "Yanks Must Pay $225,000 for Winfield Tampering," New York Times, July 6, 1990: A17. The Times reported that "Winfield challenged the trade and threatened to take the case to arbitration. Steinbrenner met with Winfield on May 14 and said the outfielder would still have a place on the Yankees if he won in arbitration. Winfield then agreed to go to the Angels and accepted a three-year, $9 million contract extension." Baseball Commissioner Fay Vincent explained: "'Mr. Steinbrenner's statement that Mr. Winfield would be welcomed back to the Yankees if he won the arbitration and should play on a full time basis was clearly improper," Vincent said in a statement yesterday. "It follows therefore, that Mr. Steinbrenner's improper statements harmed the Angels' bargaining position.'"

62  Robyn Norwood, "No Place Like This for Winfield's 400th: Angels; He Becomes 23rd Player to Reach Home Run Milestone, Doing It in the Area Where He Grew Up," Los Angeles Times, August 15, 1991.

63  Reilly.

64  Ibid.

65  The Associated Press story that appeared in the New York Times on September 1, 1994, under the headline: "Baseball; It's a Deal: Indians Grab Winfield" said that the Indians had obtained Winfield for a player to be named later. According to Tom Keegan, "Owners Try on Global Thinking Cap, Baltimore Sun, September 11, 1994, that if the season did not resume, Indians General Manager John Hart had agreed to pay the Twins $100 and take Minnesota's Andy MacPhail out to dinner. MacPhail had already left the Twins to join the Chicago Cubs at that point. Several sources claim that Indians team personnel treated Twins team personnel to dinner after the season to settle the score.

66  https://www.mlb.com/search?page=1&q=roberto%20clemente%20award&type=all

67  Chass, "Some Slights Endure for Winfield."

68  Murray Chass, "Baseball; Mr. Break-It and Mr. Fix-It," New York Times, January 4, 1998: 1.

69  Chass, "Some Slights Endure for Winfield."

70  Tyler Kepner, "Winfield Recalls Reconciliation with Steinbrenner," New York Times, July 13, 2010.

71  Murray Chass, "Winfield Chooses Padres Over Yanks," New York Times, April 14, 2001: D1 and Harvey Araton, "Sports of the Times: Winfield and Steinbrenner and Reconciling the Past," New York Times, July 18, 2008: S1.

72    Puckett's comments were included in an Associated Press story that appeared in several newspapers, including the *Arizona Daily Sun*, which titled it "Hall Open Doors to Puckett, Winfield," on January 16, 2001.

73    Jason Stark, "Détente? Winfield Gives Thanks to the Boss," ESPN.com, Monday, August 6, 2001.

74    Araton, "Sports of the Times: Winfield and Steinbrenner and Reconciling the Past."

75    "Winfield Honored by Yankees," *New York Times*, August 19, 2001.

76    Ibid.

77    Jim Baumbach, "Even Winfield Believes in Boss," *Newsday*, July 26, 2008.

78    Jeff Merron, "The Best All-Around Athletes," ESPN.com, April 26, 2004.

79    https://amp.ncaa.com/amp/news/baseball/article/2010-05-06/ncaa-and-cws-inc-announce-college-world-series-legends-team.

80    "MLB goes to Cuba," *Newsday*, March 22, 2016; "Why Derek Jeter Agreed to Accept Spotlight of Cuba Trip," *New York Post*, March 22, 2016; Rays Beat Cuban National Team 4-1 in Havana," *Orlando Sentinel*, March 22, 2016.

81    Reilly.

82    "Winfield Loses Palimony Suit," *Los Angeles Times*, March 22, 1990.

83    "Winfield Ends 10-Year Legal Battle," UPI Archives, November 7, 1995.

84    Reilly.

85    Murray Chass, "Some Slights Endure for Winfield."

# MANAGERS, EXECUTIVES, MEDIA

# BUD BLACK

## BY NICK WADDELL

Bud Black spent 15 years as a major-league pitcher and followed that up with a long career as a manager. In 2018 he was in his 11th year as a big-league skipper.

Harry "Bud" Ralston Black was born on June 30, 1957, in San Mateo, California. He graduated from Mark Morris High School in Longview, Washington. His father, Harry Sr., was a center for the Los Angeles Monarchs of the Pacific Coast Hockey League (1945-48) and led the team in scoring in 1946.

Black pitched for Lower Columbia College (Washington) in 1976 and 1977. He was drafted twice in 1977, when the major leagues conducted two drafts a year. First, he was drafted in January by the San Francisco Giants in the third round. Then, in the June draft, the New York Mets selected him in the second round. Black declined to sign each time, deciding instead to attend San Diego State University from 1978-1979, majoring in finance. Black led the Aztecs in innings pitched and strikeouts in 1978 and 1979. Seattle drafted the left-hander in the 17th round in 1979 and Black signed with the Mariners.

Black spent the rest of 1979 in Class A, making 19 appearances with San Jose (California League) and Bellingham (Northwest League). He returned to San Jose in 1980, appearing mostly out of the bullpen. His 5-3 record and 3.45 ERA earned him a promotion to Double A to start 1981. His 2-6 record with Lynn (Eastern League) did not tell the entire story. Black led the team

with a 3.74 strikeout-to-walk ratio and was third on the team in strikeouts despite making only 11 starts. He made four appearances for Triple-A Spokane before getting a September call-up with the Mariners for two games. He made his major-league debut on September 5, 1981, coming out of the bullpen against the Boston Red Sox. In the bottom of the fifth, in the midst of a six-run Red Sox rally, manager Rene Lachemann used him as a situational lefty to face one batter, Rick Miller. Black threw a wild pitch, then surrendered a single, and was replaced. He appeared in just one other game, the next day. He came on with two outs in the bottom of the sixth, and walked the batter he faced, but then picked him off first. He worked the seventh, giving up a leadoff double and walking two while getting two outs and then handing the ball over to Shane Rawley, who closed out the inning.

Seattle traded the young left-hander to Kansas City in March 1982 to complete an October 1981 deal that sent infielder Manny Castillo to the Mariners.

Black made the Royals to start 1982. Over the first month and a half, he pitched in six games, going 0-1 with a 7.98 ERA. Opponents batted .339 against him. He was sent down to Omaha, where he excelled, going 3-1 with a 2.48 ERA in four starts. Black was recalled in June 12 when David Frost was placed on the disabled list.[1] He pitched in 16 games, making 13 starts, for the rest of the season. Black finished the season 4-6 with a 4.58 ERA.

Black started 1983 with Triple-A Omaha but was recalled in May to assume a spot in the starting rotation, taking over for Vida Blue, who was sent to the pen.[2] He pitched his first career complete game as a Royal after 27 starts. The game was a 6-2 win over the Milwaukee Brewers on August 4, 1983. Black posted a solid 10-7 season for the second-place Royals. Perhaps the most memorable game of the season for Black was the "pine tar" game on July 24. George Brett hit a two-run home run in the top of the ninth to give the Royals a one-run lead. Yankees manager Billy Martin claimed that the pine tar on Brett's bat was more than the league-allowed 18 inches. The umpires agreed, calling Brett out and giving the Yankees the victory. The Royals protested the call. American League President Lee MacPhail reversed the decision of the umpires, and the game was resumed on August 18. Both the Royals and Black benefited from this reversal. Had the called stood, Black would have been the losing pitcher. Instead, Black had a no-decision.[3]

The 1984 season was Black's best as a major leaguer. He led the Royals in wins (17), starts (35), complete games (8), strikeouts (140), and ERA as a starter (3.12). He also had the distinction of giving up Reggie Jackson's 500th career home run on September 17. Black and the Royals won that game 10-1 over the California Angels.

Black made his postseason debut on October 2 in the American League Championship Series against the favored Detroit Tigers. Black had made three starts against the Tigers during the regular season, suffering one loss and two no-decisions. His ERA approached 6.00 and the Tigers hit .319 against him. This scene repeated in Game One of the ALCS. Black lasted only five innings, giving up four earned runs, as the Tigers beat the Royals 8-1.

The 1985 season was a different story. Black had a season almost statistically opposite from 1984. He led the team in losses (15), starter ERA (4.33), runs allowed (111), and earned runs (99). The Royals made the ALCS again, this time against the Toronto Blue Jays. Black started Game Two and pitched seven strong innings. Usually reliable closer Dan Quisenberry could not hold onto the lead, and the Royals fell behind in the series two games to none. Black made two more appearances in the ALCS, both relief appearances. His 3⅓-inning relief appearance in Game Six helped the Royals force a Game Seven, and they won the American League pennant. Black made two appearances in the World Series against the St. Louis Cardinals, including a five-inning loss in Game Four. The Royals won the Series in seven games, giving Black his only World Series ring. Black did not make the postseason again in his career.

The 1986 season marked a transition to the bullpen for Black. He made four starts at the beginning of the season but was moved to the bullpen in early May. Black seemed to thrive in his role. Opponents hit .198, while he carried a 2.34 ERA. The Royals finished second though, preventing a potential repeat in the postseason.

The 1987 season was the opposite of 1986; Black started in the bullpen but returned to the starting rotation in early May. His stats as a reliever again were solid (1.90 ERA, .198 batting average against) His stats as a starter were good for a back-of-the-rotation pitcher (4.01 ERA, .279 batting average against).

Black bounced back to the bullpen to start 1988 but was traded to Cleveland in early June for infielder Pat Tabler. He pitched mainly out of the bullpen for the Indians to start, but did transition back into the starting rotation late in the season.

Black was solid in the 1989 and 1990 seasons with a bottom-dwelling Indians team. He was 23-21 over that time with a 3.44 ERA. The Toronto Blue Jays needed some pitching to help them get into the playoffs, and made a mid-September trade for Black. He appeared in three games, including two starts. His last outing was one of his best for the season, eight innings of three-hit ball against Baltimore. Ultimately, though, the Blue Jays finished in second behind the Boston Red Sox.

After the 1990 season, Black signed a four-year, $10 million contract with the San Francisco Giants. Up to that point, Black was 85-83 over nine seasons, and had won only 42 games the previous five seasons combined. An anonymous National League

*Manager Black in a dugout discussion with Padres catcher Nick Hundley.*

general manager panned the signing, saying, "Maybe Bud Black will win some games for the Giants, but it looks like one of the worst signings ever."[4]

Black's first two seasons with San Francisco were mediocre. He went 22-28 but pitched almost 400 innings. The 1993 season started well, but he could not shake the injury bug. Black went on the disabled list three times during the season for elbow trouble and he did not pitch after August 3. In late September he underwent surgery to repair a tendon in his left elbow.[5] Then before the 1994 season, he had arthroscopic knee surgery.[6]

Black did not pitch until June 1994 and made 10 appearances before the season was cut short by the players strike. During the offseason, he signed a minor-league contract to go back to the Indians in 1995 but made only 11 appearances with the Indians before being released on July 14.

The Indians named Black a special assistant for baseball operations to general manager John Hart for the 1996 and 1997 seasons, before naming him the pitching coach at Triple-A Buffalo for the 1998 season. Black returned to his special assistant role for the 1999 season.

The Los Angeles Angels named Black their pitching coach in 2000, and he helmed the mound staff that helped lead the Angels to the 2002 World Series championship. His teams finished in the top five in ERA five of his seasons. He coached Bartolo Colon during Colon's 2005 Cy Young season. This success led to Black's being considered for many managerial openings. In 2002 he was a candidate for the Cleveland Indians managerial position, but later declined to continue further with the process.[7] In 2005 he declined to be interviewed for the Los Angeles Dodgers' managerial position, citing family reasons.[8] In 2006 Black was a candidate for the San Francisco Giants opening, as was then-Padres manager Bruce Bochy.[9] When the Giants signed Bochy, the Padres turned to Black. Black was named manager of the Padres on November 6, 2006.

The 2007 season was an odd one for the rookie manager. On September 23 he had a role in one of the stranger incidents in baseball. Outfielder Milton Bradley was involved in an altercation with first-base umpire Mike Winters, accusing Winters of saying that Bradley threw his bat at an umpire.[10] In an attempt to subdue Bradley, Black pulled him away. Bradley's knee buckled. That knee ultimately cost Bradley the rest of the 2007 season and may have cost the Padres a shot at the playoffs. They were 2½ games behind the first-place Arizona Diamondbacks, and had a half-game lead over the Philadelphia Phillies. The Padres and Rockies played in game 163 to decide which would be the wild-card team. The Rockies came into the game having gone 13-1 in their last 14 games. The Padres took the lead in the top of the 13th on a two-run home run by Scott Hairston, but usually steady closer Trevor Hoffman gave up three runs in the bottom half of the inning, sending the Rockies into the playoffs (and eventually the World Series). Matt Holliday scored the winning run on a sacrifice fly by Jamey Carroll, sliding head-first into home. Replays were inconclusive as to whether Holliday had actually touched home or not.

Black narrowly missed taking the Padres to the playoffs in 2010. Going into the final weekend, the Padres were three games behind the Giants for the NL West title. The Padres won the first two, but dropped the last game, giving the Giants the division. Despite not making the playoffs, Black was named 2010 National League Manager of the Year, going 90-72. This was Black's last winning season as a manager. His 2011 Padres team went 71-91, while his 2012 and 2013 teams went 76-86, and the 2014 team was 77-85. During the offseason before the 2015 season, the Padres made bold moves, including acquiring closer Craig Kimbrel, outfielders Matt Kemp and Wil Myers, and catcher Derek Norris. The Padres were 32-33 to start the season before Black was fired.

Black was not out of work for long. He was a candidate for the Washington Nationals' open managerial position and was the leading choice by all accounts.[11] Black had accepted the position, but contract negotiations broke down.[12] The Nationals eventually hired Dusty Baker, while Black returned to the Angels as a special assistant to the general manager.

Black became a leading candidate for the Colorado Rockies managerial job when Walt Weiss stepped away after the 2016 season. On November 7, 2016, the Rockies made the hiring of Black official.[13]

The Rockies got off to a hot start and were leading the West at the end of April. The Rockies, Diamondbacks, and Dodgers fought for first throughout the first half of the season, until the Dodgers pulled away from the rest of the division en route to an eventual National League pennant. Black did lead the team to an 87-75 record, and a berth in the wild-card round against the Diamondbacks. The Rockies fell behind 6-0 in that game but fought back. "Right away, all hell broke loose and from there on it was a heavyweight fight," Black said after the game. "We got close a couple times, they stretched the lead, we came back. It was a crazy game."[14] Their efforts fell short, as they lost 11-8.

In 1992, Black was inducted into San Diego State Athletics Hall of Fame.[15] He and his wife, Nanette, donated money to fund an alumni room at San Diego State's Tony Gwynn Stadium.[16]

## SOURCES

In addition to the sources cited in the Notes, the author also used the following:

Baseball Reference (baseball-reference.com),

*2016 Los Angeles Angels Media Guide.*

*2015 San Diego Padres Media Guide.*

## NOTES

1    "Royals' Frost on Disabled List," *Los Angeles Times,* June 13, 1982: 3-5

2    "Royals' Blue Sent to Bullpen," *Atlanta Constitution,* May 24, 1983: 5-D

3    "Brett Not Only One Affected," *Los Angeles Times,* July 30, 1983: 3-2

4    Jerome Holtzman, "Black Deal Throws Free-Agent Curve," *Chicago Tribune,* November 15, 1990: 4-13

5    "Around the Majors," *New York Times,* September 26, 1993: 56

6    "Spring Training," *Washington Post,* February 20, 1994.

7    "Plus: Baseball," *New York Times,* October 17, 2002: D7

8    "Roundup," *New York Times,* November 24, 2005: D2

9    "Baseball," *New York Times,* October 24, 2006: D6

10    Michael S. Schmidt, "Baseball Suspends Umpire in Dispute," *New York Times,* September 27, 2007: D2

11    Chelsea Janes, "Bud Black, Washington Nationals' Choice to Be Manager, Known for his Communication," *Washington Post*, October 29, 2015.

12    James Wagner, "In End, Washington Nationals' Bet on Bud Black Goes Bust and They Land Instead on Dusty Baker," *Washington Post*, November 3, 2015.

13    Nick Kosmider, "Bud Black Reaches Agreement With Colorado Rockies to Become New Manager," *Denver Post,* November 7, 2016

14    Associated Press, "Rockies Fall Short in Wild-Card Loss to Diamondbacks," October 5, 2017.

15    Scott Miller, "Bud Black Among Inductees Into Athletics Hall of Fame," *Los Angeles Times,* November 12, 1992: C7

16    San Diego State University Baseball Media Guide, 2016.

# BRUCE BOCHY

## BY THOMAS J. BROWN JR.

Bruce Bochy's baseball career is filled with notable achievements. From being the first European-born manager to reach the World Series when he was with the San Diego Padres to becoming the first manager to call on his son to pitch in a game when he was with the San Francisco Giants, Bochy's long career has been remarkable and very successful.

Bochy was born on April 16, 1955, in Landes de Bussac, France, where there was a US airbase. His father, Sergeant Major Gus Bochy, was stationed there at the time. Gus Bochy's father was a West Virginian who worked in the coal mines and died in one. Gus realized that his best opportunity to avoid that fate was to join the military. Bochy's mother, Melrose, grew up on a North

Carolina tobacco farm. She met Bochy's father when he was stationed at Fort Bragg, North Carolina.

Bruce was the third of Gus and Melrose's four children. Joe, the oldest son, spent several years as a catcher and later a pitcher in the Twins organization. As of 2018 he was a scout for the Padres. Bochy's sister, Terry, is retired from the US Customs Service, and was caring for their mother, who had Alzheimer's disease. Bochy's youngest brother, Mark, was a chemical engineer living in Mobile, Alabama, in 2018.

Young Bruce "was not one to sit idle at home," Terry said. "He was always out organizing games, whether it was kickball, dodgeball, football, baseball, basketball, horseshoes, [or] darts. He could make a game out of anything, and he would lose track of time."[1]

Bochy developed a love of baseball early. His father was a rabid Cincinnati Reds fan. Bochy remembered that his father always tuned in the games no matter where they lived. When the family was stationed in Panama, Gus Bochy coached the base's baseball team. Those games "were a big deal," Bochy recalled.[2]

Bochy lived in numerous places as he grew up. Besides France, his family spent time living in the Panama Canal Zone, South Carolina, and Northern Virginia. When his father retired, the family moved to Melbourne, Florida. Bochy attended Melbourne High School.

Although Bochy played in high school, he did not begin to excel in baseball until he reached Brevard Community College in Cocoa Beach, Florida. He led the school to a state championship. Jack Kenworthy, his coach, said Bochy was a leader on that team. "I [remember] that players on my team, before they would do anything, would look and see what Boch was doing," Kenworthy said. "It was nothing he did outwardly. It was just the presence of leadership."[3] By the end of his sophomore year, Bochy had begun dating his future wife, Kim Seib.

Bochy was drafted by the Chicago White Sox in the eighth round of the January 1975 draft. He turned down the opportunity to go professional and instead signed a letter of intent to play for Eddie Stanky, the former major-league infielder and manager, who was coaching at South Alabama at the time. But when the Houston Astros drafted him in the first round of the June 1975 draft, he decided to turn professional.

The Astros sent Bochy to the Covington Astros (Appalachian League). He played 37 games during their short season. He had 34 RBIs and a .338 batting average.

In 1976 Bochy split his time between the Class-A Dubuque, Iowa, Packers (Midwest League) and the Double-A Columbus, Georgia, Astros (Southern League). He saw his offensive statistics drop against the higher level of competition. Bochy finished the season with a .234 batting average and 24 RBIs in 99 games. He played the entire 1977 season with the Class-A Cocoa Astros (Florida State League). He had 109 hits in 128 games that year as he played just up the road from his hometown.

Bochy returned to Columbus in 1978 and played in 79 games. Late in the season, the Astros called him up as a backup for Alan Ashby. Bochy made his major-league debut on July 19, 1978, against the New York Mets. He was the starting catcher and collected his first major-league hit in his first at-bat, a single to right field off the Mets' Craig Swan in the third inning. He hit another single in the Astros 2-1 loss to the Mets. Bochy and Kim Seib were married in 1978.

Bochy remained the Astros backup catcher in 1979 and 1980. He played in 78 games over those two seasons, batting .212.

The Astros made the playoffs in 1980 and Bochy played in the fourth game of the National League Championship Series, replacing Luis Pujols in the eighth inning. The game, against the Philadelphia Phillies, was tied in the 10th. Pete Rose headed for home on Greg Luzinski's double and Bochy was waiting there for the throw to tag him out. Rose crashed into Bochy and knocked the ball out of his glove. Bochy fell to the ground and was dazed with the "baseball he'd dropped resting alongside him like a period on 97 years of Phillies frustration."[4]

The Astros traded Bochy to the Mets on February 11, 1981 for minor leaguers Stan Hough and Randy Rogers.

When Bochy first made it to the majors, he had earned a reputation for having a large head. After he was called up to the Mets, he arrived but his batting helmets did not. At the time, he had custom helmets because his extra-large head size, 8, was so unusual. "When I got called up, the first question wasn't, 'How are you?' but, 'Did you bring your helmets?'"[5]

Bochy spent the 1981 season with the Triple-A Tidewater Tides (International League). He also started the 1982 season with the Tides and was called up in August. Bochy played in 17 games in the final two months of the season and batted .306.

The Mets released Bochy in January 1983. A month later he signed with the Padres. Bochy started the 1983 season with the Triple-A Las Vegas Stars (Pacific Coast League). He was batting .303 with 11 home runs and 33 RBIs when the Padres called him up to back up Terry Kennedy.

Bochy started 56 games from 1983 to 1985. He accepted his role as reserve, saying, "It might have been harder if I was just getting started but now I know my role and I can handle it. It takes a certain type of ballplayer to be able to come off the bench and do a job."[6] He made his second postseason appearance when he pinch-hit in the final game of the 1984 World Series and had a single in the Padres' losing effort against the Detroit Tigers.

The Padres traded Kennedy to the Baltimore Orioles at the end of the 1986 season since they were planning to use rookie Benito Santiago as their catcher in 1987. Bochy remained with the Padres, serving as Santiago's backup. He accepted his role, noting that "[s]ometimes I think you've got to work harder than the regulars as a backup. You never know when you're going to be called on. And you can't afford to have a bad game because you don't want to hurt the club when you're out there."[7]

Bochy started 18 games in 1987 and made it into another 20 games but was hitting just .160 when the season ended. He made his last major-league appearance as a player on October 4, 1987, when he grounded out in a 5-3 Padres loss to the Dodgers.

The Padres dropped Bochy from their roster on November 9, 1987. He signed a minor-league contract with the team and was sent to Las Vegas for the 1988 season as a player and coach. He played in 53 games while mentoring Sandy Alomar Jr.

Jack McKeon, the Padres general manager, gave Bochy his first managerial job when he hired him to run the Spokane, Washington, Indians (Low-A Northwest League) in 1989. Bochy started the season as a coach with the Riverside, California, Red Wave (Class-A California League) before getting the call to manage his own team. "He was the perfect guy to have on your ballclub. Great personality, a clubhouse leader even though he wasn't playing," said McKeon when asked why he hired Bochy.[8] Spokane finished the season with a 41-34 record.

Bochy became Riverside's manager in 1990. The team struggled to a 64-78 record. It was one of his most challenging seasons as a manager. "The year I managed there, we weren't very good," he recalled. "Of all my years, that was probably one of the toughest. We didn't play very well."[9]

But Bochy's struggles with Riverside helped him to become a better manager. "I think it helped me develop more patience. I realized, 'Hey, these guys are trying,'" he said. "It doesn't mean that you ever stop trying to win and trying to hit the right buttons, but you've got to understand that you're going to go through some (tough) times. For me to spend a whole season dealing with that, that helped make me a better manager."[10]

When the Riverside club moved to Adelanto, California, in 1991 and became known as the High Desert Mavericks, Bochy remained as their manager. The team improved to 73-63 and won the California League title.

Bochy moved up to the Double-A Wichita, Kansas, Wranglers (Texas League) in 1992. The team finished with a 70-66 record and had the second-highest batting average in the league. The Wranglers were five games out of first place with 14 games left but won 11 straight to clinch the division and went on to win the Texas League championship. Yet Bochy recognized that his role as a minor-league manager was not about winning games, saying: "It's all about development. Winning's not my job."[11]

The Padres made Bochy their third-base coach in 1993. Jim Riggleman was the manager. When Riggleman became the Cubs manager after the 1994 season, Bochy replaced him. General manager Randy Smith, explaining why he chose Bochy, said: "To me, the two most important factors were continuity, stability, and with the strength of this organization being pitching, someone who can handle a pitching staff. In my mind he's the best managerial prospect in the game."[12]

Bochy became the youngest manager in baseball and the first former Padres player to manage the team. The Padres gave him a one-year contract but Bochy was satisfied since he was finally getting the opportunity to use what he had learned in the Padres organization. "I have confidence in my ability, and Randy and I and the coaching staff, we're going to ... turn this thing around," he said.[13]

The Padres went 70-74 in Bochy's first year at the helm, winning 23 more games than they had in 1994. They improved to 91-71 in 1996 and made the playoffs for the second time in their history.

Although the Padres were swept by the St. Louis Cardinals in the Division Series, Bochy was chosen as the National League manager of the year.

The Padres fell to 76-86 in 1997 but the organization maintained confidence in Bochy. Their confidence was vindicated when he led the team to a 98-64 record, the best in Padres history. San Diego returned to the World Series for the second time in their 30-year history. *The Sporting News* named him the Manager of the Year for the second time in three years.

While Bochy was getting more and more recognition for his work, his brother Joe noted that Bochy was always focused on his team and players rather than himself, saying "[My brother will] never be comfortable going on the Leno show. His ego doesn't require notoriety. His confidence and fortitude are such that he doesn't need the spotlight."[14]

Hall of Famer Tony Gwynn described Bochy's influence that season: "He's not the type to rant and rave or kick over a [food] spread after a game, but the fire comes out. This is a veteran team that generally doesn't have to be reminded about what's at stake or what we should be thinking about, but Boch has a very good sense of timing as to when to call a meeting and when not, when to snap and when not."[15]

The Padres were swept by the Yankees in the World Series. During the offseason, they cut their payroll and the team had five losing seasons. Bochy managed the team through those difficulties and eventually the Padres returned to their winning ways of the 1990s.

In 2004 Bochy led the Padres to an 87-75 record. The team did not make the playoffs that year but they did in 2005. The team had an 82-80 record, winning the NL West. Once again, they were swept by the Cardinals in the Division Series.

Bochy led the Padres to the division crown for a second time in 2006. It was the first time San Diego played in the postseason in consecutive seasons. Once again the Padres lost to the Cardinals, three games to one.

At the time Bochy was under contract through the 2007 season. When he asked for a contract extension, San Diego CEO Sandy Alderson refused. Alderson believed that Bochy was too loyal to veteran players and wasn't willing to listen to management. He also felt that Bochy had been outmanaged by the Cardinals' Tony La Russa in the playoffs. Alderson told him he was free to look for other managing positions.[16]

The San Francisco Giants interviewed Bochy within days of his release from the Padres and hired him a few days later. They gave him a three-year contract. The Giants were hoping to rebuild from several lackluster seasons and wanted Bochy to help them do it. "I look forward to this challenge," Bochy said. He said he agreed to sign with the Giants because he wanted to "be with an organization that would be a cultural fit for me, where I would be comfortable and where there was potential to build real chemistry between myself and the front office. It would be a place where I would have a chance to make an impact and a contribution."[17]

The Giants lost at least 90 games during Bochy's first two seasons as manager. But the team turned things around in 2009. They finished with an 88-74 record. Bochy was in the final year of his contract and knew that he needed to win in order to stay on. The Giants did not make the playoffs that season but definitely seem poised for better days ahead.

The Giants rewarded Bochy with a two-year contract extension shortly after the season, their first winning season in four years. Bochy said later that 2009 was important because the time had come for the Giants to "win games. [I]f you're making a transformation (to youth), that's a little bit different. But we're trying to raise the bar and win games."[18] The team won and the Giants decided that Bochy would stay as manager.

Bochy's Giants won 92 games in 2010. They clinched the NL Western Division crown on the final day of the season, beating the Padres. After winning the game, 3-0, Bochy said of his team: "It's a group that coalesced into a team that wants to get there."[19]

The Giants marched through the postseason. First they beat the Atlanta Braves in the Division Series, three games to one. Then they beat the Phillies, four games to two, for the NL pennant. Bochy described his triumphant team as a "bunch of misfits."[20] The Giants reached the pinnacle when they beat the Texas Rangers in five games in the World Series. It was the franchise's first Series championship since 1954, when the team was still in New York.

After the World Series, Bochy deflected questions about his genius as a manager, saying: "It's not me, believe me. It's these guys. I can't say enough about how they accepted some roles. I'm not sure they were happy with me. But they stayed ready and they had one thing on their mind and that was to do this."[21]

The Giants continued to win under Bochy's leadership in 2011. They finished 86-76 but lost momentum when Buster Posey, the 2010 NL Rookie of the Year, was injured. Bochy described the loss as like "taking Johnny Bench out of the Big Red Machine."[22] The club was confident enough in Bochy's leadership that they extended his contract at the end of the season.

Bochy showed why they should maintain confidence in him when the Giants won the NL Western Division in 2012, for the second time in three years. After losing the first two games of the Division Series to the Cincinnati Reds, they won three straight games to move to the NLCS. The St. Louis Cardinals took a three-games-to-one lead in the NLCS but the Giants won the final three games to return to the World Series for the second time in three years.

The 2012 World Series was not much of a contest. The Giants swept the Tigers. As Bochy held the championship trophy over his head, he said: "It's unbelievable what happened here the last two to three weeks. I'm amazed. I couldn't be prouder of these guys."[23]

When the Giants held a victory rally several days later, Bochy told the cheering crowd, "In 2010, we characterized the club as misfits that came together and got it done. [T]he tagline of the 2012 Giants was, 'Never say die.'"[24] He wanted the crowd to remember that the Giants came back twice in the postseason to bring the trophy back to San Francisco.

Bochy's success brought him another contract extension. This time the Giants extended his contract through the 2016 season. General manager Brian Sabean, who was also rewarded with a new contract said of Bochy: "Bruce is a tough SOB, even if he doesn't come off that way. If you work with him every day, you see how he empowers the players."[25] For his part, Bochy said, "I'm very happy to continue this journey. It's been an amazing ride these past few years."

Bochy reached a managing milestone when he got his 1,500th win on July 23, 2013. The Giants beat the Cincinnati Reds 5-3 in front of a home crowd. Bochy became the 21st manager to win that many games. After the game, Bochy was modest about his accomplishment: "I'll be honest. I don't know what that number means except the fact I'm fortunate I've been doing this as long as I have. I'm very, very thankful to reach this number. To be mentioned with some of these managers is humbling."[26] Although Bochy reached a personal milestone in 2013, it was a disappointing year for the Giants. They finished the year with a 76-94 record, falling into a third-place tie with the Padres.

The Giants rebounded in 2014 to finish the season with an 88-74 record. They entered the postseason as the second wild-card team. After beating the Pittsburgh Pirates 8-0 in the one-game play-in, the Giants swept the Washington Nationals in the Division Series and beat the Cardinals in five games in the NLCS. It was their third trip to the World Series in five years. Bochy once again remained modest as he credited the Giants organization for the team's success. "We've kept our core players. The thing I love about what's happening in San Francisco is the continuity that we have, so that allows you to hopefully compete and contend every year."[27]

Bochy's Giants faced the Kansas City Royals. The Royals were hoping to win their first World Series since 1985. Although the Series went to seven games, Bochy's Giants prevailed and won their third World Series title in five years. He became the 10th manager to win three World Series.

As in past years, Bochy deflected praise from himself and gave it to his players. During the celebration in the Giants locker room, Bochy told reporters: "This group of warriors, they continue to amaze me. To see guys getting their first taste of this, that makes it even more special. I tell ya, these guys were relentless. You're so blessed to get one title, and now to have three. I'm just amazed at what they did."[28]

The Giants rewarded Bochy again by extending his contract through the 2019 season. When Chris Heston threw a no-hitter against the Mets on June 9, 2015, he became the first Giants rookie to accomplish that feat in more than 100 years. The win was Bochy's 700th as Giants manager. With the 951 games he won in San Diego, he joined an elite group of managers who won more 700 or more games with two different teams. The others were Sparky Anderson, Tony La Russa, and Jim Leyland.[29]

The Giants finished 84-78 in 2015 and did not make the playoffs but they returned to the postseason in 2016 when they finished with an 87-75 record. After beating the Mets in the wild-card play-in, they fell to the eventual World Series-winning Chicago Cubs in the Division Series.

Bochy achieved another milestone that season when he won his 800th game for the Giants. The win came on June 26, 2016, when the Giants beat the Phillies, 8-7. Bochy noted his achievement in his usual unassertive manner: "As far as the number, I know how lucky I am. I don't think John McGraw has anything to worry about."[30] He was referring to McGraw's 2,583 wins, the record for Giants managers.

Bochy also made news that season when he became the first manager since 1976 to deliberately choose to forfeit the designated hitter. The last time that his happened was when pitcher Ken Brett of the White Sox, a good hitter, batted twice in 1976, on May 27 and September 23. Bochy's star pitcher Madison Bumgarner batted against the Oakland A's at a game in Oakland on June 30, 2016. He hit a double in the third to spark the 12-6 Giants win. Bochy expressed satisfaction with his decision when he told reporters, "He smoked that ball, and he did it when he got that double. He gives you good at-bats, which he did there."[31]

The Giants struggled in 2017, winning just 64 games and finishing with the worst record in the National League. It was just the fourth losing season since Bochy took the helm of the team in 2007. Even as the Giants were struggling, Bochy continued to reach more milestones. On April 10 he won his 841st game as

Giants manager, surpassing Dusty Baker to become the team's second-winningest manager.

Bochy also won his 900th game for the Giants that season when they beat the Arizona Diamondbacks, 9-2, on September 25, 2017. The win was bittersweet for him since it came at the end of a difficult season. Half in jest, he said, "There's the old joke they may retire me for health reasons – because they're sick and tired of me, which I get.[32]

As of 2018 Bochy and his wife, Kim, lived in Poway, California, near San Diego. They have two sons, Greg and Brett. Greg spent four years playing in the Padres' minor-league system. Brett was drafted by the Giants in 2010. He was called up to the Giants in 2014. On September 13, 2014, Bochy made the call to the bullpen and handed the ball to Brett with instructions to get the last out of the inning. At the time the Dodgers had the bases loaded. Bochy was the first father to hand the ball to his son in a major-league game.[33] (Brett walked the first batter he faced, forcing in a run; the run gave the Dodgers a 15-0 lead in a game they won, 17-0.)

When Brett was asked about his father's decision, he said: "He has a habit of doing that to me. It was awesome getting out there and it was special that he was there for it." Bochy saluted his son later, saying, "Here's your son, and you're bringing him into the big leagues. It's a moment that [makes you] nervous, but at the same time, you're very proud. I was real glad to see him out there."[34]

Bochy has experienced several health issues since 2015. He underwent an angioplasty before spring training and was ready for the season. He missed part of the 2017 season when he had a minor heart ablation on April 18, and had another ablation surgery after the season. Afterward he said "I don't want anyone to think this has an effect on my work, or ability to work."[35]

Through the 2017 season, Bochy had 1,853 regular-season wins and 42 playoff victories. Only four other managers have more playoff wins. Three of them (Joe Torre, Bobby Cox, and Tony La Russa) are in the Hall of Fame.

When Bochy was asked about his Hall of Fame chances, he said, "I don't ever think about it. It's too humbling to think about. When you think of the Hall of Fame, you think of Willie Mays and great players like that. You don't look at yourself like that. I feel fortunate that I've been doing what I love for as long as I've been doing it."[36] With at least two more years on his present contract, Bochy should continue to reach more milestones in his unassuming manner before he considers walking away from the game he loves.

## SOURCES

In addition to the sources cited in the Notes, the author also used the Baseball-Reference.com, Baseball-Almanac.com, and Retrosheet.org websites for box-score, player, team, and season pages, pitching and batting game logs, and other pertinent material.

## NOTES

1    Henry Schulman, "Meet Bruce Bochy – New Head Man," SFGate.com, March 11, 2007.

2    Ibid.

3    Demian Bulwa, "S.F. Giants' Bruce Bochy Has Humble Approach," SFGate.com, October 15, 2010.

4    Frank Fitzpatrick, "Giants' Manager Part of Phillies Lore," *Philadelphia Inquirer*, October 14, 2010.

5    Lawrie Mifflin, "Bruce Bochy's Big Problem," *New York Times*, September 2, 1982.

6    Dave Distel, "Backing Up Kennedy Is a Role Bochy Accepts," *Los Angeles Times*, March 21, 1985.

7    Ibid.

8    John Shea, "Bochy Carving Out Quite a Career," SF Gate.com, September 29, 2014.

9    "Managing Red Wave Was a Challenge, Learning Experience," *Riverside Press-Enterprise*, April 13, 2013.

10    Ibid.

11    Kirk Seminoff, "Once, Twice, Three Times a Champion," *Wichita Eagle*, November 7, 2010.

12    "Bochy Named Padre Manager After Riggleman Jumps to Cubs," *Seattle Times*, October 22, 1994.

13    Ibid.

14    Ross Newhan, "Still Waters," *Los Angeles Times*, June 16, 1998.

15    Ibid.

16    Tom Krasovic, "Bochy an NL West Title Mainstay for Padres," *San Diego Union-Tribune*, May 30, 2014.

17    "Bochy Looks Forward to Challenge of Managing Giants," ESPN.com, October 26, 2006.

18    John Shea, "Bochy Has a Sense of Security in 2010," SF Gate.com, March 5, 2010.

19    "Jonathan Sanchez Eliminates Padres to Give Giants NL West Title," ESPN.com, October 4, 2010.

20    Jayson Stark, "Giant Cast of 'Misfits' Marches On," ESPN.com, October 24, 2010.

21    Susan Slusser, "SF Giants Are Champs, Dashing Bochy's Butterflies," SF Gate.com, November 2, 2010.

22    Henry Schulman, "Giants' Chances Ended with Buster Posey's Injury," SF Gate.com, September 29, 2011.

23    Henry Schulman, "SF Giants Win World Series," SF Gate.com, December 27, 2010.

24    "Giants Celebrate with Victory Parade," ESPN.com, October 31, 2012.

25    Ron Kroichick, "Giants Reward Sabean and Bochy with Contract Extensions." SF Gate.com, March 28, 2013.

26    Alex Pavlovic, "Bochy Reaches Next Level as Giants Get Unique Win," *San Jose Mercury News*, July 24, 2013.

27    Anne Killion, "With 3 Titles, Close Enough to a Dynasty," SF Gate.com, November 1, 2014.

28    Bruce Jenkins, "Savor It, The Giants Are World Champions Again," SF Gate.com, October 30, 2014.

29    Andrew Baggarly, "Chris Heston on His No-Hitter: 'I Still Can't Believe It Happened,'" *San Jose Mercury-News*, June 10, 2015.

30    Chris Haft, "Giants Walk Off for NL-Best 49th Victory," MLB.com, June 26, 2016.

31    Susan Slusser, "Madison Bumgarner Is a Hit in All Ways in Giants' Win Over A's," SF Gate.com, June 30, 2016.

32    Alex Pavlovic, "Bochy on Future: This Is 'Certainly Not the Way I Want to Go Out,'" NBC Sports.com, September 28, 2017.

33    Ryan Hood, "Bochy Gives Son MLB Debut in Tough Spot," MLB.com, September 13, 2014.

34    Ibid.

35    Andrew Baggarly, "Giants Manager Bruce Bochy Resting After Heart Procedure," *San Jose Mercury-News*, October 13, 2017.

36    John Shea, "Bochy Carving Out Quite a Career," SF Gate.com, September 29, 2014.

# BOB CHANDLER:

## A FAMILIAR VOICE THROUGHOUT THE SAN DIEGO PADRES' FIRST HALF-CENTURY

### BY TOM LARWIN

Over the team's 50-year history the San Diego Padres have played a total of 7,976 regular-season games plus another 34 postseason games. That totals 8,010 games in which the result meant something. Bob Chandler has been at the microphone broadcasting either for radio or television for about 5,100 of those games. This figure does not include an estimated 700 games in which he worked on behalf of the Padres in public relations, or worked as a pre-game/post-game host for one of the local radio or television stations. All told, Chandler has worked in some capacity for about 72 percent of the total number of Padres games played over the team's first half-century.

While Chandler has reported on more Padres losses than wins, he was in the broadcasting booth for the team's two World Series' appearances, in 1984 and 1998. Plus, he was fortunate to have seen every one of Tony Gwynn's major-league regular season and playoff games. Those games alone total 2,467.

His long-time broadcast partner and baseball Hall of Famer, Jerry Coleman, had this to say about Chandler: "The story of the San Diego Padres started in 1969, and Bob Chandler was there. In fact, he is the one person in San Diego most qualified to bring the entire Padres story to the surface."[1]

Perhaps not too well known outside of San Diego, Chandler's name, face, and soothing voice, are well-recognized around San Diego.

He is a 1961 graduate of San Diego State College (now called San Diego State University, SDSU) and began working in the San Diego television-radio market immediately. Chandler was first hired by San Diego's Channel 8 (KFMB) as a newsreel cameraman/writer. It was his first real paying job at $105 a week. For a time he also served as the weekend sportscaster and for that he received another $10-$15 per show. The gig, though, was relatively short-lived as the station found it cheaper to have the weatherman also do the sports.

Also in 1961, broadcaster Al Couppee was hired by Channel 10 (KOGO) to be the first announcer for the San Diego Chargers football team. Two years later Chandler was hired to be Couppee's assistant. He got into filming an outdoor sportsman show, writing scripts for Couppee and handling the weekend sports' updates.

In 1968 another opportunity developed and Chandler was hired as Sports Director for Channel 39 (KCST), a new UHF (ultra-high frequency) television station. The station was able to obtain the contract to televise Chargers football preseason games and a few regular season games. Also, the station picked up SDSU's intercollegiate athletic program which included football, basketball, baseball, rugby, and track and field. While the SDSU program presented a varied load, Chandler also covered professional golf tournaments, in addition to games of the San Diego Rockets (National Basketball Association), San Diego Gulls (Western Hockey League), and San Diego Padres (Pacific Coast League, PCL).[2] As a young sportscaster Chandler had all he could handle doing the play-by-play for these various sports in the continually expanding San Diego market.

By virtue of his work covering the PCL Padres in the 1960s Chandler had developed an association with Eddie Leishman, the PCL Padres' general manager.[3] So Chandler spent a lot of time with Leishman in the spring of 1968 and they were paying close attention to National League deliberations regarding the expansion of major-league baseball. Both had expected news soon but neither were sure that San Diego would be one of the teams selected.

As told by Chandler, the "big day" was May 27, 1968. He was preparing his evening sportscast when he heard bells go off, literally. Channel 39's offices had two wire machines, one for United Press International (UPI) and one for the Associated Press (AP). When a bulletin would come over the wire bells

would go off. He recalls hearing the bells, "I remember it well. I ran over to the machines to see what was coming in, and there it was. 'The National League had voted to expand to the cities of Montreal and San Diego.'"

During the team's first three years, 1969-1971, Chandler was not part of the regular broadcasting team. However, in 1970 Channel 39 made a two-year deal to televise 18 games a year, nine games from Los Angeles, and nine from San Francisco. The limited number was a result of economics since in those days it was very expensive to rent the telephone company's long lines to televise the games. On the radio side for those three years, the first announcing team for the Padres was comprised of Jerry Gross, Frank Sims, and baseball Hall of Famer Duke Snider.

In the fall of 1971 the Padres contacted Chandler and was told that Padres President Buzzie Bavasi wanted to interview him. Chandler had first met Bavasi in 1968 as the new National League San Diego Padres organization was beginning to take shape. Bavasi got to know Chandler better, as well, via the televised game broadcasts handled by Chandler.

At this same time, former New York Yankee player Jerry Coleman was being courted by the Padres for play-by-play duties. After his playing career ended Coleman handled play-by-play announcing for the Yankees, and later covered sports for the three major television networks.

It was on November 8, 1971, when the Padres announced in a joint press release the hiring of Chandler and Coleman.[4] In the release Bavasi noted "that the new Padre announcers bring both experience and skill to their assignment." He also said that "I believe they will compliment [sic] each other nicely. Jerry has both a sports and technical background, having played major league baseball and having served as a major league announcer. And Bob, who has lived and worked in the San Diego area for many years, fully appreciates the need for us to develop greater interest in the Padres through our radio and television broadcasts."

Looking back years later, Chandler mused about the hiring process orchestrated by Bavasi: "I got to know Buzzie Bavasi very well. He was a legendary general manager in baseball, and he loved to tell stories. So he hires me to join Jerry Coleman as the broadcast team and I remember going to meet him and we talked for about 40 minutes and he finally says, '...okay, Bob, you're hired. We're going to hire you as one of the announcers. Come back next Wednesday and we'll work out the deal.'"

Chandler remembered going into that meeting the next Wednesday with a bunch of things nervously going around in his mind. He characterized the meeting with Bavasi as rather typical and informal, talking about baseball. Then, all of a sudden, Bavasi stood up and said, "Great. We have a deal." And Chandler recalled his surprise: "I said 'Buzzie...' I went, 'what did I agree to?' And Bavasi, the major deal-maker, listed all these things—the salary and all that stuff—I mean, I was so over-matched! Buzzie and I had a great relationship for a long time…I used to accuse him of being the reason players got agents!"

So, Chandler and Coleman partnered as a broadcasting team for that 1972 season and it initiated a partnership that would continue together through the following 31 years. Chandler recalled that "One of the first things Jerry told me when we started together was, 'Bob, it's a long season and a small booth. We really need to get along.' And, we did!"

Most of the time Coleman would handle the play-by-play, typically doing seven innings while Chandler would do two. Chandler provided the "color" with statistics, anecdotes, and historical commentary. Chandler would also conduct the pre-game and a post-game interviews.

A number of announcers, other than Jerry Coleman, also partnered with Chandler over the years. Notable ones included: Dave Campbell, Mark Grant, Rick Monday, Rick Sutcliffe and, of course, Ted Leitner. Leitner, who joined the broadcast team in 1980 and continues into 2019, used to refer to Bob as the "B-C-P-C-" (Bob Chandler, Personal Computer) because of his ability to remember facts, figures, and stories and tell them on the air." [5]

Beset by a Padres team that achieved a record of .500 or better 16 times in 50 years Chandler agreed that it is easier to announce for a winning team. However, he also said that he was always excited to be a major league baseball announcer and truly enjoyed the gig. He noted that many of the players and coaches became friends of his off-the-field. To this day, regular golfing buddies include: Roger Craig, Bobby Klaus, Bob Skinner, and Alan Trammell.

Still, Chandler admitted "It's much harder to do broadcasts when the team is not winning. You know that your listeners aren't hanging on every pitch and so you have to try to make it entertaining, telling stories and so forth. In the beginning I didn't

have a lot of stories." He made up for any lack of stories with a stupendous memory and soothing voice tone that made for interesting commentary and relatable stories during the game. Many of these stories can be read in the 2006 book Chandler authored with local baseball historian Bill Swank titled *Bob Chandler's Tales from the San Diego Padres*.

Chandler retired from the booth and full-time announcing after the 2003 season. By that time he worked for five different San Diego television stations, delivering regular evening sportscasts, interviews, and play-by-play broadcasts. On the radio-side he was a regular voice for the Padres for nearly two-thirds of the Padres' first 50 years.

While no longer actively involved in broadcasting Chandler is routinely invited to offer commentary on Padres baseball, past as well as present. Ask him a question about the Padres, for instance, about a former player? Or, about a particular game? Or, about McNamara's Band? Or, about Tony Gwynn's batting average with Alan Wiggins on first base during the 1984 season? Or, about Ray Kroc's rants at the home opener in April 1974? Or, about the number of pitches from one of Randy Jones' quickest games pitched in 1976?

Or…well, you get the idea!

## NOTES

1    Bob Chandler with Bill Swank, *Bob Chandler's Tales from the San Diego Padres* (Champaign, Illinois: Sports Publishing L.L.C., 2006), "Foreword."

2    The PCL Padres played in San Diego from 1936 through 1968 and were the predecessor to the major-league Padres.

3    Leishman was with the PCL Padres from 1960 through 1968, and then served as Vice President-General Manager with the major-league Padres until his passing in 1972.

4    Press Release, *San Diego Padres*, November 8, 1971.

5    Chandler, "Foreword."

# JERRY COLEMAN

## BY C. PAUL ROGERS III

Jerry Coleman was a true American war hero who played a little baseball for the New York Yankees during the times the Marines did not demand his services. He was the only major-league ballplayer to see combat in both World War II and the Korean Conflict.[1] And he saw more than just a little combat as a fighter pilot in both wars, flying 57 missions in a dive bomber in World War II and 63 missions in a fighter plane in Korea. For his service he was awarded two Distinguished Flying Crosses in addition to 13 Air Medals and three Navy Citations.[2]

Altogether Coleman spent nearly five years in the Marines and sandwiched in a nine-year big-league career with the Yankees that was plagued by injuries around his service in Korea. When healthy he was a fine ballplayer, graceful and acrobatic at second

base and a dangerous slash hitter.[3] He was the Associated Press American League Rookie of the Year in 1949 but his best year was 1950, when he hit .287 and was named the MVP of the World Series.[4] After retiring from his playing career at the age of 33, Coleman went on to become a Hall of Fame broadcaster, first for the Yankees and then for more than 40 years for the San Diego Padres.

Gerald Francis Coleman was born on September 14, 1924, in San Jose, California, the second of two children of the former Pearl Beaudoin and Gerald Griffin Coleman. His sister, Rose-marie, was born two years earlier. Although the children were born in San Jose, the family lived in San Francisco. Their father was a backup catcher in the Pacific Coast League for a couple of years and continued to play semipro baseball while working as a bank teller.[5]

But as Coleman related in his memoirs, his and his sister's childhoods were anything but idyllic. Their father had a drinking problem and was verbally and physically abusive. Their mother left him when Jerry was about 8 years old, taking the children with her. Shortly thereafter, Jerry's father shot his estranged wife three or four times as she came out of a dance. Pearl was seriously injured and was in the hospital for about nine months as her children went to live with relatives and her husband left town. Her husband was apparently never prosecuted, although the shooting made front-page news.[6]

Jerry and his sister were reunited with their mother when she finally got out of the hospital. Pearl had permanent injuries; her left elbow would not bend and for the rest of her life she had to wear a brace on her left leg to be able to walk. She was unable to work and with two children was forced to go on welfare. Meanwhile, Jerry's father moved back to San Francisco after a couple of years. Pearl had divorced him in the interval, but he had gotten a steady job with the post office and so she actually remarried him so that he would provide for the family. Fortunately for Jerry and his sister, their father worked the 4 P.M.-to-midnight shift so they seldom saw him.[7]

As Jerry grew up he began to play a lot of sandlot baseball in Golden Gate Park. He was also a good basketball player and his athletic prowess got him admitted to the prestigious Lowell High School in San Francisco.[8] There he played basketball and baseball and as a senior made All-City in the former sport, setting a city single-game scoring record with 23 points against Commerce High on March 8, 1942.[9] While in high school he began to play for the Keneally Yankees, the premier semipro baseball team in the Bay Area.[10] There his teammates included future New York Yankees teammates Bobby Brown and Charlie Silvera as well as future major leaguers Bill Wight and Dino Restelli.[11]

During Coleman's senior year in high school, the Brooklyn Dodgers offered him a $2,500 bonus to sign after a tryout camp, but Jerry's mother wanted him to go to college, so he accepted a combined basketball/baseball scholarship to USC.[12]

December 7, 1941, right in the middle of Coleman's senior year, changed all that. In March he heard a presentation at his high school about the Navy's V-5 flight-training program from two naval aviators and immediately decided that he wanted to become a Navy fighter pilot. Although he graduated from high school in June 1942, he would not turn 18 until that September. Joe Devine, a Yankees scout who had followed him during his high-school years and who had recruited him to play for the Keneally Yankees, offered him $2,800 to sign with the Yankees organization and Coleman accepted since he was not yet old enough to enlist.

The Yankees assigned him to Wellsville, New York, of the Class D PONY (Pennsylvania, Ontario, New York) League, where two of his teammates were CharlieSilvera and Bob Cherry, both of whom had also been teammates in the San Francisco sandlots. Hampered initially by a cut finger from an uncovered fan, Coleman struck out his first six times at bat. Eventually he found his swing and batted .304 for the season in 83 games and 289 at-bats while shifting between shortstop and third base. A Wellsville groundskeeper worked with him before games to develop a hit-and-run stroke that he used his entire career. Although Coleman didn't know who he was, he turned out to be Chief Bender, one of the greatest pitchers of the early twentieth century.[13]

When the season ended Coleman returned to San Francisco and was accepted into the Navy's V-5 flight training program. He was first assigned to train at Adams State College in Alamosa, Colorado, where he first soloed. He subsequently trained at St. Mary's University in California; Olathe, Kansas; and Corpus Christi, Texas, where he decided to become a Marine pilot. Coleman was commissioned as a second lieutenant in the Marine Corps on April 1, 1944.[14] From there he was assigned to Jacksonville, Florida, where he learned to fly the SBD, also known as the Dauntless dive bomber. He wanted to fly dive bombers because they had the potential to sink aircraft carriers.[15]

After short stints in Cherry Point, North Carolina, and the Miramar Naval Air Station in California, Coleman was sent to Guadalcanal in a troopship on which he joined a squadron known as the Torrid Turtles.[16] Guadalcanal was by then a staging area and Coleman flew raids from Green Island to the Solomon Islands. Later he transferred to the Philippines, where he flew raids to Luzon and other Japanese-held strongholds. While there he was able to play a little baseball and basketball during down times.

Coleman was sent back to San Francisco in July 1945 after flying 57 combat missions, because he was qualified to fly off aircraft carriers. After a leave, he was to be assigned to an aircraft carrier to prepare for the invasion of the Japanese mainland. But the Japanese surrendered in August, so Coleman was reassigned to Cherry Point, North Carolina, before his discharge in January 1946.[17]

After missing three seasons because of his war duty, Coleman, still only 21 years old, returned to professional baseball for the 1946 season. The Yankees promoted him to the Binghamton Triplets in the Eastern League where he played under the legendary Lefty Gomez. There he batted a solid .275 in 134 games and 487 at-bats, earning a brief late-season call-up to the Kansas City Blues in the American Association. Shortly after the season, Coleman married Louise Leighton, who had also graduated from Lowell High in San Francisco. The couple had two children, Diane and Jerry Jr., before divorcing in 1980.[18]

Coleman stuck with Kansas City in 1947 and batted .278 in over 500 plate appearances while playing shortstop and third base under manager Billy Meyer.[19] That performance earned him an invitation to the Yankees' 1948 spring training, where he was the last man cut by New York manager Bucky Harris.[20] The Yankees sent him to the Newark Bears of the International League to learn how to play second base as a potential replacement for George "Snuffy" Stirnweiss on the parent club.[21] He ended up playing a lot of shortstop and third base as well and saw his average slip to .251 in 562 plate appearances.

Even so, the Yankees called Coleman up for the last couple of weeks of the season, although he did not appear in a game. The time he spent on the bench proved beneficial, however, because he quickly figured out that as a 160-pound right-handed hitter, he was not going to be able to hit home runs in Yankee Stadium. Bill Skiff, his manager with Newark, had urged him to learn to bunt and to exercise better bat control. And with the Yankees Coleman noticed that his old semipro teammate Bobby Brown choked up on the bat and had much better bat control than he did, so he decided to follow suit.[22]

Coleman had forced himself to learn to smoke when he was overseas but Skiff told him that with his slight build, smoking was sapping his strength. Coleman related in his memoir that he quit immediately and never smoked another cigarette.[23]

He made the Yankees out of spring training in 1949 as a 24-year-old rookie, set to back up Stirnweiss at second base. When Stirnweiss got spiked on Opening Day, Coleman found himself starting at second and leading off the second day of the season in Yankee Stadium against the Washington Senators. The first ball hit to him went right between his legs for an error, but, after a popup, he started a double play when Buddy Lewis  hit a one-hopper to him. [24] Coleman grounded out to shortstop Sam Dente to first baseman Eddie Robinson in his first at-bat, leading off the bottom of the first against Paul Calvert, and went 0-for-4 on the day on four groundouts as the Yankees won 3-0. He got his first big-league hit leading off the next day, singling to left field off Forrest Thompson in another Yankees win.

With his first hit out of the way, Coleman went off on a hot streak and on April 26, his seventh game, had a 4-for-4 day against the Philadelphia Athletics, including his first major-league home run, off Alex Kellner, a two-run shot to left in the eighth inning that won the game for the Yankees, 5-4.[25] That game increased his batting average to .417. Yankees coach Frankie Crosetti worked with Coleman on the hit-and-run, bunting, and bat control and he hovered around .300 for much of the season, although he was out at one stretch because of a sinus condition.[26] Coleman finished his rookie season with a .275 batting average in 128 games and 523 plate appearances. He led American League second basemen in fielding percentage and teamed with shortstop Phil Rizzuto to quickly become the top keystone combo in the league.

The 1949 pennant race went down to the final game of the season with the Yankees and Red Sox tied for the league lead and playing at Yankee Stadium. The Yankees led 1-0 heading into the bottom of the eighth when Tommy Henrich's leadoff home run off Mel Parnell made it 2-0. The Yankees then loaded the bases against Tex Hughson with two out, which brought Coleman to the plate. He fought off a high inside fastball and

hit it on the trademark just beyond the reach of second baseman Bobby Doerr and hard-charging right fielder Al Zarilla inside the line for a bases-clearing double to make the score 5-0. The drama wasn't over, however, as the Red Sox rallied for three runs before Vic Raschi was able to retire the side and secure the pennant.[27]

The Yankees went on to defeat the Brooklyn Dodgers in the World Series in five games, with Coleman playing all five and batting .250 with three doubles and four runs batted in. After the season he was named the American League Rookie of the Year by the Associated Press.

For many years Coleman was apologetic about his dying swan double[28] against the Red Sox until he ran into former Yankees manager Joe McCarthy at a banquet. "You swung at it, didn't you?" McCarthy said, meaning that he put the ball in play and didn't strike out.[29] Many years later, Coleman visited Ted Williams in the hospital in San Diego. Williams was recovering from a serious stroke and had trouble speaking. But the first thing he said when he saw Coleman enter his hospital room was, "That f-----g hit you got," a very clear reference to Coleman's bloop double some 40 years before.[30]

Coleman had his career year in the 1950 season that followed. He got off to another blazing start and was still batting above .290 when he was named to the American League All-Star team for the midsummer classic. For the season he played in all but one game and batted .287 with a career-high 69 RBIs. The Yankees won their second straight pennant and then swept the Philadelphia Phillies, known as the Whiz Kids because of their youth, in four straight low-scoring games in the World Series. Coleman continued his timely postseason hitting, driving in Bobby Brown with a fourth-inning fly ball for the only run of a Game One 1-0 Yankees victory. Coleman had three hits in Game Three, including a walk-off single to left-center off Russ Meyer that fell between Richie Ashburn and Jack Mayo and scored Gene Woodling with the winning run in a 3-2 win. For his efforts, Coleman was named  the MVP of the Series. The Yankees scored only 11 runs in the Series, but Coleman knocked in three of them, including two game-winners.

With the Korean Conflictgoing full tilt, Coleman knew that he was subject to recall by the Marines. After World War II, officers were not discharged but simply put on reserve or inactive status, meaning that they could be recalled to active duty. And Coleman realized that it was much more efficient for the military to recall trained fighter pilots than to train new ones.[31]

Uncle Sam did not call Coleman that winter and he was able to play the entire 1951 season, batting .249 in 121 games, as rookies Gil McDougald and Billy Martin pushed for playing time on the infield. The Yankees won their third consecutive pennant, by five games over the Cleveland Indians. During the World Series, won by the Yankees over the New York Giants in six games, Coleman shared second base with McDougald and went 2-for-8.

After the season, Coleman embarked on a two-month tour of US military bases in Europe that was organized by the commissioner's office. He was joined by Stan Musial, Jim Konstanty, Frankie Frisch, Charlie Grimm, Elmer Valo, Steve O'Neill, Dizzy Trout, and two umpires. He knew his recall by the Marines was imminent, but he did manage to play the first two weeks of the 1952 season and appear on the *Ed Sullivan Show* before reporting for duty at the Los Alamitos Naval Air Station in early May. In 11 games before his recall, he batted .405 in 47 plate appearances.[32]

Once he regained his flying skills at Los Alamitos, Coleman was transferred to the El Toro Marine Station, also in California, to learn to fly Corsair attack planes.[33] He went into action in Korea in late January 1953. Over the next four months Coleman flew 63 combat missions, had two near-death experiences, and saw Max Harper, his tentmate and close friend, shot down and killed by antiaircraft fire right in front of him.[34] The physical and emotional toll of those experiences was enough to get Coleman grounded and he finished his tour of duty performing intelligence work from the front of the DMZ.[35]

Coleman was discharged in time to return to the Yankees by mid-September of 1953 as his team was on its way to its fifth consecutive pennant and world championship.[36] Coleman made eight mostly token appearances and was not on the World Series roster.[37] He was ready for spring training in 1954 but found that the pressure and fatigue he had experienced in Korea had affected his depth perception and thus his batting eye.[38] Although still only 29 years old, Coleman struggled the entire season and batted only .217 in 107 games.

The 1955 season was even worse for Coleman, although he became the player representative for the Yankees in spring training. In the first week of the season, he was caught in a run-down between third base and home and tried to plow over Red Sox shortstop Owen Friend in front of the plate. Friend dodged and Coleman landed on his left shoulder instead, shattering it. Surgery would have meant missing the rest of the year, so Dr. Sidney Gaynor, the Yankees' orthopedist, manipulated the bones back in place and put a large plaster cast over his left shoulder and arm to immobilize it.[39]

Coleman returned to action on July 19, but in his first game back was beaned in Comiskey Park by Harry Byrd, a White Sox reliever. Fortunately, Coleman was wearing a batting helmet, still not mandatory in 1955, but he still suffered a serious concussion that landed him in the hospital for two days and

*Jerry Coleman with his wife, Maggie, standing beside the statue of him in his Marine aviator uniform at the Petco Park.*

kept him out of the lineup for over a week.[40] For the season, he appeared in only 43 games, mostly at shortstop and third base, and hit .229 in 112 plate appearances. The Yankees won the AL pennant and then lost the World Series in seven games to the Brooklyn Dodgers, their longtime rival. Coleman got into three games as a pinch-runner and defensive replacement, going 0-for-3 at the plate.

Almost immediately after the season, the Yankees embarked on a six-week tour of Hawaii, Japan, and the Philippines, playing exhibition games against local competition. When they played a game in Hiroshima, they were among the first group of Americans to visit there since World War II.

Although Coleman had the reputation of being a very smart, heady ballplayer, he occasionally supplied some comic relief. His Yankees teammate Eddie Robinson remembered the first time southpaw pitcher Bill Wight started a game for the Baltimore Orioles against the Yankees in Yankee Stadium after being out of the American League for a while. Coleman had played with Wight in the sandlots in San Francisco and before the game went around telling his teammates that Wight had a great pickoff move. He said, "You've got to be very careful. If you just take your foot off the base, he'll pick you off." Coleman then got on first base in his first at-bat and Wight promptly picked him off.[41]

Coleman was among several interchangeable infielders in 1956 for manager Casey Stengel and shared time at second base, third base, and shortstop with Billy Martin, Gil McDougald, and Andy Carey after Phil Rizzuto was released. He batted .257 in 80 games and 203 plate appearances as the Yankees won their seventh American League pennant in eight years. They went on to reclaim the world championship in seven games against the Dodgers but Coleman played in only two of those.

The following year, 1957, would be Coleman's last as a player. He appeared in 72 games, mostly in a utility role, and batted a solid .268 in 180 plate appearances. The Yankees comfortably won their eighth pennant in nine years by eight games over the Chicago White Sox. This time they faced the Milwaukee Braves in the World Series and lost in seven games as former Yankees farmhand Lew Burdette won three games and pitched two shutouts against his former organization. Coleman started all seven games at second base and batted .364 for the Series, the highest on the team. He singled against Burdette in the ninth inning of Game Seven, in what was the last at-bat of his career.

Coleman's lifetime batting average for nine big-league seasons is .263 with a .340 on-base percentage. Although he hit only 16 home runs in his career, he struck out only 218 times in 2,415 plate appearances. Casey Stengel, never one to lavish praise, said of Coleman, "Best man I ever saw on a double play. Once I seen him make a throw while standing on his head. He just goes 'Whish!' and he's got the feller at first."[42] He became so proficient at the double play that "it almost seemed the ball would ricochet in and out of his glove without actually touching it." Overall, he played second base "with grace and style."[43]

Although Coleman's playing career was over at the age of 33, his baseball journey was just beginning. Even with his great World Series in 1957, Coleman understood that he was headed for a backup role to incoming second baseman Bobby Richardson and was afraid of being traded and having to uproot his family.[44] Thus, when Yankees General Manager George Weiss offered him a job as director of player personnel, Coleman jumped at it. His responsibility was to work with the Yankees' scouts and provide players for all the Yankees farm teams except their top team in Richmond, Virginia.[45]

Coleman aspired to eventually become the general manager of a big-league team, but his travel as personnel director had him away from home the majority of the time and was difficult because of his young family.[46] In 1960 he left to go to work in promotions and marketing for the Van Heusen Shirt Company, a position he obtained at the behest of his friend Howard Cosell.[47] He had been offered a broadcasting job with CBS Television by Bill MacPhail right after he retired as a player, but he turned it down because he had just taken the front-office job with the Yankees.[48]

But in 1960 MacPhail again offered Coleman the opportunity to get into broadcasting by conducting pregame interviews on CBS's *Game of the Week* and doing occasional game broadcasts when Dizzy Dean and Pee Wee Reese, the regular broadcasters, were not available. Since the CBS games were only on the weekends, he was able to keep his position with Van Heusen. He was completely ill-prepared for the job[49] and recalled that his first pregame interview was with future Hall of Famer Red Schoendienst who saved him from disaster by talking nonstop for five minutes or so after Coleman asked, "How's it going, Red?"[50]

Coleman's inexperience also showed early on when he was interviewing Washington Senators manager Cookie Lavagetto during a pregame show. The National Anthem began and Coleman, unaided by his director, continued with the interview, thinking that perhaps the audience could not hear the anthem. Although CBS received a number of letters in protest, as Coleman recalled, "My military background saved me."[51]

He must have improved rapidly because in 1963, after his third year with CBS, Ballantine Beer, which sponsored the Yankees telecasts, invited Coleman to join the Yankees broadcast team. He accepted, resigned from Van Heusen and CBS, and joined the Yankees for spring training in March. He was the newest member of the Yankees legendary broadcast team of Red Barber, Mel Allen, and Phil Rizzuto, his old keystone partner.[52] The first season he broadcast only road games because Barber was not traveling and typically would broadcast half the home games on radio and half on television.[53] Barber took Coleman under his wing and became a mentor, for example telling him not to guess on the air but to make sure what he said was "right."[54]

Coleman broadcast the Yankees games for seven years and worked with Joe Garagiola after the team fired Barber. During that period, in 1967 he traveled to Vietnam to visit troops with Joe DiMaggio, Pete Rose, and Tony Conigliaro.[55] By 1970 his wife very much wanted to move back to the West Coast and Coleman hoped to get a job broadcasting for the expansion San Diego Padres. The team did not have an opening and so Coleman took a sports broadcasting job with KTLA-TV in Los Angeles.[56] There he alternated doing the nightly sports news with Tom Harmon, the former Heisman Trophy winner at Michigan, who was also a decorated World War II pilot.

Howard Cosell helped Coleman also get a job doing weekend sports shorts for the ABC radio network. Then, in 1972, Buzzie Bavasi, the Padres' president, offered Coleman a broadcasting job and he snapped it up.[57] It was a job he held, with the exception of one year, until he died 42 years later. In the mid-1970s he also began broadcasting CBS Radio's *Game of the Week* and did so for 22 years.

That exception was 1980, the year Coleman served as manager of the Padres. He and Bob Fontaine, the Padres general manager, had grown up together. After the Padres finished 68-93 in 1979, Fontaine persuaded Coleman to succeed Roger Craig as manager. Coleman received a three-year contract for a total of $200,000 with the understanding that he could return to the broadcast booth if the managing stint did not work out.[58] Unhappily for all concerned, it did not. The club started the season with a promising 22-19 record but then went into a nosedive. The club owner fired Bob Fontaine shortly before the All-Star break and replaced him with Jack McKeon, who had been the assistant general manager. Although the everyday lineup featured Dave Winfield and Ozzie Smith and had great team speed with three players stealing 50 or more bases, the club struggled getting on base. The Padres also had Rollie Fingers in the bullpen, but the staff was overall mediocre. The team finished last in its division with a 73-89 record, 2½ games behind the fifth-place Giants, and, during the final week of the season, Coleman was told that he would not be coming back as manager.[59]

After his season as manager, Coleman did return to the broadcast booth with the Padres. He also remarried in October 1981, marrying the former Maggie Hay. He was 57 and she was 31 and the couple had a daughter named Chelsea in 1985.[60] Coleman gravitated to broadcasting mostly on radio because he enjoyed describing the action for the fans. He juggled broadcasting the Saturday *Game of the Week* on CBS radio with Padres games until 1997, taking red-eyes and early-morning flights to get back for Sunday Padres games.[61]

Over the years Coleman became so popular that he was almost an iconic figure in San Diego. He became known as "The Colonel" on radio broadcasts and around Petco Park since he had retired from the Marines as a lieutenant colonel. Broadcasting highlights were when the Padres went to the World Series in 1984 and 1998.[62] He sometimes remarked, however, that he, because of the Padres habitually weak teams, had broadcast more losing games than anyone in history.[63]

Coleman became known for his "rich and intimate" but concise delivery[64] and developed two trademark calls with the Padres. When a Padres player made a great defensive play, Coleman would say, "Hang a star on that one, baby!" During home games, Coleman would then hang a two-foot-wide gold star out the broadcast booth on a broomstick. Radio station KFMB broadcast the Padres games and at one point gave out "Hang a star on that one" membership cards to fans. His other call "Oh, doctor!" was first used by Red Barber. Coleman related that it just came out of his mouth once early during his time with the Padres and he continued to use it when something extraordinary occurred on the field.[65]

Coleman was also known for his malapropisms on the air, which came to be called "Colemanisms." Perhaps the best known is when he described Dave Winfield going back for a long fly ball. Coleman allegedly said, "Winfield goes back. He hit his head against the wall. It's rolling back toward the infield."

On another occasion, he reputedly described a double by saying, "He slid into second with a stand-up double."

Then there was the time that he noted that "Gaylord Perry and Willie McCovey should know each other like a book. They've been ex-teammates for years."

He reportedly said, "George Hendrick simply lost that sun-blown popup."

He once introduced the starting pitcher by saying "On the mound is Randy Jones, the left-hander with the Karl Marx hairdo."[66]

Padres President Buzzie Bavasi once said, "I made some good acquisitions here ... Nate Colbert, Cito Gaston, Dave Winfield, Randy Jones, Rollie Fingers, Ozzie Smith. But the best acquisition I made for this town was Jerry Coleman."[67]

Coleman was universally respected and admired within baseball. Jeff Torborg, who worked with him for several years on CBS Radio, said, "I don't think I've ever heard anyone say anything negative about Jerry." He was also unfailingly humble and self-deprecating. Joe Garagiola remembered an occasion when Coleman was conducting a pregame interview with an infielder and asked the player how he made the double play. Afterward Garagiola told Coleman, "You asking him how to do a double play is like the pope asking somebody how to say Mass. You did it better than anybody."[68]

In 2005 Coleman was honored by the Baseball Hall of Fame in Cooperstown, receiving the Ford C. Frick Award for excellence in baseball broadcasting. That same year he was inducted into the Marine Sports Hall of Fame; along the way he was also inducted into the National Radio Hall of Fame, the San Diego Padres Hall of Fame, and the Bay Area Sports Hall of Fame. In 2012 the Padres honored Coleman by unveiling a statue outside Petco Park of him in his Marine aviator uniform.

Jerry Coleman died on January 5, 2014, from complications after a fall.[69] He was laid to rest with full military honors including a 21-gun salute and an F-18 flyover in the missing-man formation. At his death, Coleman was 89 years old and had led a remarkable life, starting with a very difficult childhood. He became a bona-fide war hero in two wars, had a baseball playing career that earned him Rookie of the Year and World Series MVP honors, and then transitioned into a Hall of Fame broadcasting career. Through it all, he remained a very humble man with a great sense of humor and an appreciation for his good fortune in surviving two wars and for his ability to play major-league baseball. Jerry Coleman was not only a San Diego treasure, but an American treasure.

# NOTES

1    Ted Williams was also a fighter pilot who famously served in both World War II and Korea but Williams saw combat only in Korea.

2    Dan Daniel, "Quiet Coleman Speaks Out With His Bat," *The Sporting News*, October 18, 1950: 3.

3    Peter Golenbock, *Dynasty – the New York Yankees 1949-1964* (New York: Prentice-Hall, Inc., 1975), 53.

4    "Gerry, Don – Top Rookies," *New York World-Telegram*, November 4, 1949. Roy Sievers of the St. Louis Browns was voted Rookie of the Year by Baseball Writers Association of America, with Coleman finishing third in that vote. The official designation of the World Series MVP was not instituted by the major leagues until 1955, but the BBWAA voted Coleman the Babe Ruth Award as its Most Valuable Player in the 1950 World Series. As a result, most authorities have recognized Coleman as the MVP of that Series.  See, e.g., George Vecsey, "Jerry Coleman, 89, Yankee Infielder, Fighter Pilot and Voice of the Padres," *New York Times*, January 6, 2014: A15.

5    Jerry Coleman with Richard Goldstein, *An American Journey – My Life On the Field, In the Air, and On the Air* (Chicago: Triumph Books, 2008), 14-15.

6    Coleman, 15-16.

7    Coleman, 17-18.

8    Graduates of Lowell include Supreme Court Justice Stephen Breyer, California Governor Pat Brown, actress Carol Channing, author J.D. Salinger, and sculptor Alexander Calder. Coleman, 20.

9    Coleman, 27.

10    According to Coleman, the team was sponsored by the Keneally Bar in San Francisco which was owned by a guy who never drank. Josh Board and Joe Hight, "The Man Who Hung the Stars," *San Diego Reader*, April 7, 2005: 30. The bar owner was Neil Keneally. The team had been called the Keneally Seals but Keneally renamed the team the Keneally Yankees in honor of New York Yankees scout Joe Devine, who later signed Coleman. Bob Stevens, "This Is Jerry Coleman," *Baseball Digest*, January 1950: 4.

11    Coleman, 27-28; Stevens: 4.

12    Coleman, 29.

13    Bender had apparently been given a job by George Weiss, general manager of the Yankees.  Although Coleman was a willing student, Bender shortly disappeared, and Coleman never saw him again. Coleman, 31-33.

14    Coleman, 37-38.

15    Todd Anton, *No Greater Love – Life Stories from the Men Who Saved Baseball* (Burlington, Massachusetts: Rounder Books, 2007), 93-94; Todd Anton and Bill Nowlin, eds., *When Baseball Went to War* (Chicago: Triumph Books, 2008), 80. Bob Cherry, who had played with Coleman in San Francisco and in Wellsville, went through pilot training with him and also chose the Marines. Coleman, 39.

16    Board and Hight: 30.

17    Coleman, 41-49; Anton, 94-96.

18    Sadly, Louise battled alcoholism much of her life and committed suicide with a drug overdose in 1982. Coleman, 149-150.

19    After the season, Coleman went to see a doctor to see what he could do about his weight loss and thus strength loss during the long season. He was a teetotaler until the doctor told him to drink two beers a day to help him maintain body fluids.

Coleman, 57. Coleman later related that he hated beer and that the last one he ever drank was after his last game in 1957. Anton, 97-98.

20    According to Coleman, it seemed as if he was always the last man cut. Board and Hight: 31.

21    Coleman, 56-57.

22    Coleman, 57-59; Stevens, 5.

23    Coleman gave Skiff a lot of credit for getting him to the big leagues and possibly saving his life by telling him to stop smoking. Coleman, 61. David Halberstam, *Summer of '49* (New York: William Morrow & Co., 1989), 39-40.

24    Coleman, 65-66. About the error, Coleman was quoted as saying, "My first big league play and I booted it like the rankest busher. I could hear the train whistle back to Newark right then." Stevens, 6. See also "Keystone Kid of the Champs – Jerry Coleman," *Sport Life*, August 1949: 53.

25    "I was walking on clouds that night." Stevens, 7.

26    Coleman, 68-71; "Keystone Kid of the Champs," 90.

27    Coleman, 87-88.

28    In 1950 Coleman was quoted as saying, "It was embarrassing to hit a ball like that. I just hit it off my hands. Disgusting little blooper. ... It was a shamefully weak hit." Stevens, 8.

29    Coleman, 92; Halberstam, 249; Dom Forker, *The Men of Autumn: An Oral History of the 1949-53 World Champion New York Yankees* (Dallas: Taylor Publishing Co., 1989), 202.

30    Interview with Bobby Brown, June 25, 2018.

31    Coleman, 98.

32    Coleman often joked that he was the first .400 hitter since Ted Williams in 1941. Coleman, 105.

33    Fellow major leaguers Ted Williams and Lloyd Merriman were also recalled to Korea to fly fighter planes and teammate Bobby Brown, by now a medical doctor, was recalled, serving in a MASH Unit and later in a military hospital in Japan.

34    On one occasion Coleman's was the last plane coming in for a landing after a successful raid. The control tower became confused, however, and gave clearance for a wounded Sabrejet from another airfield to land at the same time. The two pilots saw each other at the tip of the runway and the Sabrejet pilot gunned his engine, missing Coleman's plane by inches. The Sabrejet pilot crashed and was killed. Just two weeks later Coleman's engine conked out during takeoff when his Corsair was loaded with 3,000 pounds of bombs. As he tried to brake, he released the bombs which fortunately did not detonate. However, one of the bombs caught his tail wheel and flipped the plane upside down. Coleman ended up upside down inside the cockpit with his arms pinned to his side and his safety harness choking him. By the time the emergency crew reached him, he had passed out and was blue in the face. Coleman, 113-114. Coleman remembered thinking, "What a way to die, at least I could be right side up." Phil Rizzuto with Tom Horton, *The October 12 – Five Years of New York Yankee Glory, 1949-1953* (New York: Forge, 1994), 111.

35    Coleman, 109-117.

36    George Weiss of the Yankees knew that Coleman was near the end of his tour and tried to hasten Coleman's return from Korea so that he could join the Yankees late in the season. Coleman, 117-118; Anton, 105, 106; Nowlin & Anton, 85-86.

37    Because he appeared in a few games in both 1952 and 1953, Coleman was one of 12 players to play in the Yankees' run of five straight world championships. In the mid-'50s the Yankees had a commemorative plaque made of those five straight world championships and gave one to each of the 12 players. When interviewed

in the early '90s Coleman was told that he was the only one of the 12 not to have the plaque on display. Coleman, who lived in LaJolla, California, and had a great view of the Pacific Ocean from his house, responded, "If you can't feel good when you pick up the paper and look out over the Pacific Ocean, coming back into the house and seeing pictures of yourself in baggy pinstripes is not going to help you feel any better." Rizzuto with Horton, 111.

38    Coleman, 122-123; Jim G. Lucas, "Coleman: A Real Bomber," *New York World Telegram Saturday Magazine*, July 11, 1953; Forker, *The Men of Autumn*, 204.

39    Coleman, 123; Dan Daniel, "Coleman Injury Hits Yanks Hopes to Trade for Top-Flight Hurler," *New York World Telegram and Sun*, April 23, 1955.

40    Coleman had been hit behind the left ear in 1947 without a helmet while playing for the Kansas City Blues and reported that it affected his equilibrium for weeks, so he always wore a helmet when they became available. Coleman, 123-124.

41    Eddie Robinson and C. Paul Rogers III, *Lucky Me: My Sixty-Five Years in Baseball* (Dallas: SMU Press, 2011), 110.

42    Arthur Daley, "Sports of The Times/Return of a Hero," *New York Times*, August 24, 1953; Carlos DeVito, *Scooter: The Biography of Phil Rizzuto* (Chicago: Triumph Books, 2010), 176.

43    Coleman was also a fastidious dresser, including the way in which he wore his uniform, and that coupled with his smooth and acrobatic play at second base earned him the nickname "Fancy Dan." Golenbock, 53.

44    Several teams including the Boston Red Sox were reportedly interested in acquiring Coleman when he retired. Dan Daniel, "Class Always His Top Trait," *New York World Telegram*, January 11, 1958. Bobby Richardson later recalled that during his rookie year Coleman would show up early and work with him at second base, even though Richardson was trying to take his job. He said, "I owe a lot to Jerry Coleman." Dom Forker, *Sweet Seasons: Recollections of the 1955-1964 New York Yankees* (Dallas: Taylor Publishing Co., 1990), 3.

45    Coleman, 147.

46    Golenbock, 272-273 (describing long hours working for George Weiss).

47    Brian Jensen, *Where Have All Our Yankees Gone?* (Lanham, Maryland: Taylor Trade Publishing, 2004), 63-64.

48    Coleman had gotten to know MacPhail when he played for the Kansas City Blues and MacPhail was the traveling secretary for the team. He subsequently went into the broadcasting business. Coleman, 153.

49    Curt Smith, *The Storytellers* (New York: Macmillan, 1995), 45-47. (Coleman describing his first broadcasting experience).

50    Coleman, 153-154; Joe Vella, "Coleman Recounts Fun of Games," *Oneonta Star*, August 11, 2005.

51    Coleman, 154; Curt Smith, *Voices of Summer* (New York: Carroll & Graf, 2005); Smith, *The Storytellers*, 119.

52    According to Coleman, initially "Scooter [Rizzuto] and I were kids who had a wonderful time but [were] maybe not as professional as you'd like." Smith, *The Storytellers*, 47. See also DeVito, 225,226.

53    Coleman, 161-163.

54    Coleman, 165-166.

55    Coleman, 170-171.

56    He, through Pat Summerall, apparently turned down a job to become President of the Oakland Seals hockey team. Jensen, 65.

57    Coleman, 175.

58    Coleman, 191-192.

59    Coleman, 197-199.

60    Coleman, 203-205.

61    Coleman, 156.

62    According to Coleman, his most memorable game as a broadcaster was Game Four of the NLDS when the Padres had to defeat the Cubs to force a fifth game and Steve Garvey hit a ninth-inning two-run home run to win for the Padres 7-5. *See* Smith, *The Storytellers*, 171, for Coleman's call of Garvey's home run.

63    Jensen, 67.

64    Baseball broadcast historian Curt Smith described Coleman's play-by-play as "rich and intimate; he was the bearer of a clean meticulous story line." Curt Smith, *Voices of the* Game (South Bend: Diamond Communications, 1987), 370.

65    Coleman, 176.

66    A more complete list of "Colemanisms" is at funny2.com/coleman.htm. and Smith, *Voices of the Game,* 370-371. *See also* Smith, *The Storytellers*, 73, 101, 109, 117-118.

67    Board and Hight: 42.

68    Jay Posner, "Hang a Star on Mr. C," *San Diego Union-Tribune*, July 31, 2005.

69    Vecsey: A15.

# RAY AND JOAN KROC

## BY BOB LEMOINE

*Owner Joan Kroc in the windup of the first pitch on October 4, 1984, Game Three of the National League Championship Series, against the Chicago Cubs.*

If it were not for the San Diego Padres, this biography on the lives of Ray and Joan Kroc would never have to be written. Not that the reader would be bereft of materials on this celebrated billionaire couple. Ray and Joan Kroc were both American celebrities long before they ever became associated with baseball. Hundreds of news articles from the mid-twentieth century to the early twenty-first century tell their remarkable stories of business and philanthropy. One can read Lisa Napoli's aptly titled 2016 biography of the couple: *Ray & Joan: The Man Who Made the McDonald's Fortune and the Woman Who Gave it All Away*, which brought their stories alive to a new generation. Also in

2016 was John Lee Hancock's *The Founder*, a FilmNation Entertainment 2016 production starring Michael Keaton. The story of the Krocs continues to appear on the American landscape, and for good reason. Ray Kroc's fame came late in life when he masterfully persuaded the American public that they deserved a break today with a burger, fries, and a milkshake. The story of Ray's third wife, Joan, the philanthropist with a political slant much different than his, is also well known. The San Diego Padres are just a small part of each of their stories. However, this joint biography needs to be written because we cannot tell the story of the San Diego Padres without telling the stories of Ray and Joan, who owned the club from 1974 to 1990. There probably would not even be a San Diego Padres franchise today if it were not for Ray, who, with his Golden Arches worth $8 billion by the time of his death, needed a hobby in his golden years and turned to his childhood love of baseball.[1] It is a story of burgers, baseball, and benevolence.

The exact origins of the hamburger are obscured in mystery, but its evolution from a beef patty served on a plate to one slapped between a bun was first displayed to the public at the 1904 St. Louis World's Fair. While the White Castle restaurant chain was the first trendy place to get a burger, it wasn't until Ray Kroc revolutionized the mass production of the hamburger decades later that the concept of "fast food" began. Before long, billions were sold, and Kroc became one of *Time* magazine's top 100 Persons of the 20th Century.[2]

Raymond Albert Kroc was born on October 5, 1902, in Oak Park, Illinois, a bustling suburb of German and Czech immigrants on Chicago's West Side. Ray's parents were Louis and Rose Mary (Hrach) Kroc. Louis was from Bohemia, now part of the Czech Republic, and worked for Western Union. Rose's father was an immigrant from Austria and she was born in Illinois. Rose gave piano lessons to support the family, which included Ray's brother, Bob, and sister, Lorraine. They lived in their own home at 1007 Home Avenue, just two miles up the road from a young boy named Ernest Hemingway.[3]

Ray played baseball in the alley behind his house, where a garbage-can lid served as home plate, and players swung at a ball bandaged with black tape. "How agonizing it was though when my mother would step out onto the back porch and call, 'Raymond! It's time to come in and practice,'" Ray remembered. The other boys would mimic her as Ray scooted off to his piano lesson. Louis would take young Ray to West Side Park to see the Chicago Cubs and their famous infield of Tinker to Evers to Chance. Joe Tinker and Louis were close friends, and a teenage Ray saw Babe Ruth and the Red Sox beat the Cubs in the 1918 World Series.

Ray's ambitious nature earned him the nickname Danny Dreamer. In grammar school he started his own lemonade stand, then later worked at his uncle Earl's drugstore and soda fountain. "That was where I learned that you could influence people with a smile and enthusiasm and sell them a sundae when what they'd come for was a cup of coffee," Ray remembered. He and some high-school friends opened a short-lived sheet-music store. "I was the piano man, and I did a lot of playing and singing but not much selling."[4]

Ray dropped out of high school and sold coffee beans door-to-door. "I was confident I could make my way in the world and saw no reason to return to school," he said. He persuaded his parents to let him volunteer for the Red Cross to drive an ambulance during World War I. He lied about his age to do so. During training in Connecticut, Kroc and others partied around town at night while another boy his age spent his time drawing pictures. He was Walt Disney. Ray was ready to board a boat for France, but the Armistice was signed and the war was over. He came home and tried school again but soon dropped out again.

Ray started selling ribbon novelties. He also worked at a summer resort in Paw-Paw Lake, Michigan, playing the piano on a steamboat. He drew the attention of Ethel Janet Fleming, daughter of an engineer father and a mother who ran a hotel. A romance was started, but Louis Kroc forbade them to get married until Ray had a steady job. They married on June 2, 1922, after Ray became a salesman for the Lily-Tulip Paper Cup Company.[5] Ray sold paper cups by day and played the piano nights for radio station WGES. He also hired talent at the station, including a comedic duo named Sam and Henry, who later became the legendary Amos & Andy. Kroc found a new customer in Bill Veeck, a young vendor at Wrigley Field, where fans realized paper cups were perfect for grabbing a beer during the game.

In 1924 Ray and Ethel had their only child, Marilyn. Ethel rarely saw Ray, who worked long hours and never grew close to his daughter. But he found time to attend ballgames and cheered on his Cubs in the 1929 World Series. Ray remembered seeing famous and infamous celebrities like Al Capone, Sophie Tucker, and Tommy Dorsey. The paper-cup business was going so well that Kroc bought a new Model T Ford and took the family to Florida, seeking to cash in on the real-estate boom. Ray worked for realtor W.F. Morang & Son but soon discovered that the investment properties he was selling were a scam. Out of a job, Ray worked in a nightclub that was raided by the police for violating Prohibition laws. The family soon returned to Chicago.

Ray drove to Wrigley Field in his Model A Ford at 2 A.M. on October 1, 1932, to get a ticket to the World Series. Kroc witnessed Babe Ruth's alleged "called shot." "I saw the motion," Kroc remembered of the Bambino pointing, "but I don't think he really called it. That was all in the minds of the sportswriters."[6]

Returning to Lily-Tulip, Kroc worked his way up to Midwest sales manager by 1937. One major client brought new success to his paper-cup sales. Earl Prince ran the successful Prince Castle ice-cream parlors chain and Kroc's paper cups were perfect for his milkshakes. Kroc became mesmerized by Prince's new Multimixer, which could make six milkshakes at once. Kroc became Prince's exclusive sales agent for this shiny new object in 1939. He spent the next several years traveling the country, selling the Multimixers to Tastee-Freeze and Dairy Queen.

By 1954 business had slowed since Hamilton Beach and other competitors sold their own multimixers and downtown soda fountains began to disappear. However, a hamburger drive-in in San Bernardino, California, had purchased eight of Ray's Multimixers. Kroc went to visit this place, which was busy enough to make 48 milkshakes at a time, and talk to the owners, Maurice "Mac" and Richard "Dick" McDonald.

Mac and Dick were originally from Manchester, New Hampshire, the sons of a shoe-factory worker. They went west to California in the 1920s, looking for fortune in the movie business. They purchased a rundown movie theater in Glendora. Successful initially, they suffered during the Great Depression and in 1937 sold the theater to run a hotdog and fruit stand they called the Airdrome near an airport in Monrovia. Success led to two more stands and in 1940 they opened a drive-in restaurant in San Bernardino. Patrons came for the popular McDonald's Barbeque. In 1948 they upgraded their business model and their restaurant ran like an assembly line of burgers, fries, and milkshakes in 20 seconds.

Ray Kroc had never seen a restaurant like this before: It was clean, fast, and efficient. Customers came for the 15-cent hamburgers with warm french fries courtesy of infrared heating lamps. Kroc envisioned McDonald's restaurants all over the country, and the brothers agreed to let him franchise their design for 1.9 percent of the gross sales. Dick and Mac would keep 0.5 percent as royalties. Ray opened his first store in Des Plaines, Illinois, in 1955. By 1960, there were 200 McDonald's restaurants around the country. "Now the evolution of the hamburger has reached its zenith," wrote Lucy Key Miller in the *Chicago Tribune* in 1957, "with the adoption of assembly line methods by Ray Kroc."[7]

While discussing business over dinner at the Criterion restaurant in St. Paul, Minnesota, in 1957, Kroc heard beautiful music emanating from a Hammond organ. He was introduced to the organist, Joan Smith. "I was stunned by her blond beauty," Kroc wrote. "Yes, she was married. Since I was married, too, the spark that ignited when our eyes met had to be ignored, but I would never forget it."[8]

The two went their separate ways, but Ray's own family was coming apart.

"As long-suffering Ethel became increasingly frustrated with her husband's workaholic lifestyle, his reluctance to settle down, and his mortgaging of the family finances to underwrite his whimsical ideas, their daughter had sided with her mother, pained by her suffering," Napoli wrote. "Home had not, for a long time now, been a welcoming, nurturing place for any of the Kroc family."[9]

In 1958 Rawland F. "Rollie" Smith, Joan Smith's husband, was managing a McDonald's, which gave Ray an ample excuse to visit with Joan while "checking on business." Their shared interest in music led to duets at the piano at the Criterion. She also saw a side of Ray she never saw before: the screaming baseball fan. They both were dressed to the nines while they sloshed through the mud after a storm to watch the minor-league St. Paul Saints.[10] Ray continued to find the need to have extensive business conversations with Rollie and Joan. Rollie opened several McDonald's in South Dakota. Despite both being married, Joan accepted Ray's proposal for marriage in 1961.[11] It was complicated.

Both Ray and Joan left their spouses and secured a house in Woodland Hills, California, then established residence in Las Vegas, waiting the six weeks to be able to legally marry. But Joan backed out after five weeks and returned to Rollie. Ray still went through with his divorce from Ethel, signed over the house, and agreed to pay $30,000 a year in alimony. Ray also had to part with his most crucial asset, the Prince Castle Sales Company he had created by selling his Multimixers. His employees bought him out for $150,000. At the time of the divorce, it was reported that Ray oversaw 323 hamburger stands in 37 states as chairman of McDonald's Corporation.[12]

Ray also divorced himself from the McDonald brothers, asking to buy the company with all its trademarks and copyrights. The brothers asked for $2.7 million, which Kroc paid through a loan from Harry Sonneborn and a group of investors dubbed "the Twelve Apostles."[13]

By the time all expenses of the deal were paid off in 1972, Kroc had spent $14 million. But that was a drop in the bucket considering the profits that would soon be made. The McDonald brothers retained sole rights to the original San Bernardino store, now called The Big M. Kroc didn't like this, and soon new Golden Arches appeared across the street, and the brothers soon gave up the burger business.

In 1963 Ray met Jane Dobbins Green, John Wayne's secretary. She was born Jane Elizabeth Dobbins to David and Grace (Duncan) Dobbins in Walla Walla, Washington, in 1911. "A rarefied whiff of glamour and refinement enveloped everything about the petite, elegant beauty: her golden blond hair, her stylish dress, her resemblance to Doris Day," Napoli wrote. Jane had already had three marriages when she met Ray in California, who was taken by her "sweet disposition."[14] They were married on February 23, 1963, two weeks after meeting.

By 1966, McDonald's was grossing $200 million yearly and was now public on the New York Stock Exchange. McDonald's now boasted "Over 2 Billion Sold." Hamburger University was created in 1961 as an employee training center. Their new mascot, Ronald McDonald, was portrayed by future *Today Show* weatherman Willard Scott. Kroc bought a 210-acre ranch he called the J and R Double Arch Ranch for $600,000 and created the Ray A. Kroc Foundation, managed by his brother Bob. The foundation focused on research for diabetes and arthritis, which afflicted Ray, and multiple sclerosis, which his sister Lorraine suffered from.[15]

Joan and Rollie attended a McDonald's meeting in 1968, and Ray invited them to his suite. Ray and Joan rekindled their romance at the piano, while a frustrated Rollie stormed off. Ray and Jane had planned a cruise to celebrate their fifth wedding anniversary, but Ray lost interest. With McDonald's executives present, Ray instructed his lawyers to break the news to Jane that he wanted a divorce and the trip was off. His chauffeur whisked him away as gathered guests consoled the devastated wife. Ray met Joan again in Las Vegas to establish residency.

She was born Joan Beverly Mansfield in August of 1928,[16] in Saint Paul, Minnesota, to Charles and Gladys (Peterson) Mansfield. Charles was a railroad telegraph operator. Gladys played the violin and instilled in Joan a love for music. During the Great Depression, Charles took the family to California, where Joan's only sister, Gloria, was born. The family soon moved back to St. Paul and Charles returned to the railroad. Young Joan fell in love with animals and she treated sick pets in the neighborhood. She also loved music and would travel by streetcar to the MacPhail School of Music in Minneapolis. As a teenager, Joan played and taught the piano.[17] "Though other blondes may fade and tire, Joan will set men's hearts afire," was the caption in her high-school yearbook.[18]

After graduating, Joan worked at a hotel and bar in Whitefish, Montana, where she met Rollie, who had recently been discharged from the Navy. Rollie was fascinated with this young piano player and joined her in some songs at the piano. Six weeks later, on July 19, 1946, they were married. Their daughter Linda arrived on July 12, 1947, after the family had moved back to St. Paul. Rollie worked on the railroad while Joan taught keyboard, provided musical programming on KSTP-TV, as well as working at the Criterion restaurant.[19]

Both Ray and Joan terminated their marriages and got married on March 8, 1969. But when Ray returned to Chicago from business in 1971, he was issued a summons. Joan was filing for divorce. The court papers read, "The defendant has a violent and ungovernable temper and has in the past inflicted upon the person of the plaintiff physical harm, violence and injury." The news hit the headlines, reporting Joan's suffering "on the grounds of extreme mental cruelty."[20] The couple reconciled in early 1972, and the matter was never discussed again.

Joan celebrated Ray's 70th birthday by donating $7.5 million to various museums and hospitals. "I was finding it increasingly difficult to keep up," Ray confessed. "Some days I could hardly get around because of the way arthritis was warping my hip. Yet pain was preferable to idleness, and I kept moving despite Joni's urging that we settle down on our ranch."[21] Ray wanted to stay busy but not have as grueling a schedule, so he returned to his childhood love of baseball.

"I wanted to own the Chicago Cubs, the baseball team I had been rooting for since I was seven years old," he said. The Cubs weren't for sale. But on the plane from Chicago to Los Angeles he read stories of the impending sale of the San Diego Padres. When Joan picked him up at the airport and he said he

*Padres owner Joan Kroc being saluted at the Salvation Army's Ray and Joan Kroc Corps Community Center in San Diego.*

was considering buying the Padres, she asked, "What on earth is that? A monastery?"[22]

The San Diego Padres began as an expansion team in 1969. They were owned by Conrad Arnholt Smith, a California banker who had owned the team since 1955 when they were a minor-league club in the Pacific Coast League. Smith held a controlling interest in United States National Bank, which collapsed under a $400 million debt. Smith would later go to prison for embezzlement and commingling of funds from various businesses. It was revealed that President Richard Nixon's former law firm had made secret deals with the Nixon administration to funnel assets from Westgate-California Corporation, owned by Smith, into the United States National Bank, to keep it from collapsing. Smith had raised over $1 million for the Nixon campaign.[23]

In May of 1973, it was announced that Smith had sold the Padres to supermarket magnate Joseph Danzansky and others in Washington, D.C., for $12 million. The new owners planned to relocate the club to Washington for the 1974 season. Baseball cards depicting the Padres players playing in Washington had already been printed. But antitrust and breach-of-contract lawsuits were filed against the National League by San Diego Mayor Pete Wilson and City Attorney John Witt. The Padres still had 15 years remaining on their lease of San Diego Stadium from the city. Kroc appeared with his lawyers on January 17, 1974, asking to review the team's financial books.

It was the proverbial eleventh hour on January 23, 1974, and boxes were packed and ready to be moved to the nation's capital. Kroc arrived to buy the club. "I'm hopeful it will work out, it looks very good," he said. "Baseball is my sport. I want to have fun with an expensive hobby." The Padres organization, desperate and on the cusp of uprooting, were now in the hands of a billionaire who just wanted a hobby. "And I can afford this expensive hobby," he announced, with plans on keeping the franchise right where it was.[24] "I won't be an absentee landlord," he promised. "I'll be involved. I want our athletes to be proud men. I don't feel I ever worked a day in my life – working is doing what you hate to do. I want ballplayers who enjoy baseball."[25]

Two days after purchasing the club, Kroc negotiated a restructuring of the lease on San Diego Stadium, guaranteeing that the team would have a home through 1980. The final price to buy the club was $12 million. Buzzie Bavasi, team president, and his son, Peter Bavasi, general manager, would remain in their positions. "Now we can unpack," a relieved Buzzie said.[26] The move was approved by the National League a few days later. In early February, John McNamara was named the Padres' new manager.

The Padres were coming off a 60-102 season in 1973, their third season of 100-plus losses in the first five years of the franchise, but had already added a future Hall of Famer in Willie McCovey. The '73 Padres finished last in batting average (.244) and had the second-highest ERA (4.16) in the National League. They also ranked last in the league in attendance.

Opening Day was on April 5 at Los Angeles. Kroc went down to the Padres' dugout to inspect his new "hobby." "The important thing is," he told McNamara, "that we hold our heads up and look like pros." "I'm going to be patient," he promised, despite the fact that he had never shown patience in building a fast-food empire. He didn't have much patience earlier in the day, either, when he visited a local McDonald's. "The food was terrible," he griped. "I raised hell. It was a company store."[27] The Padres lost, 8-0, then continued to disappoint with 8-0 and 9-2 losses as they were swept in the opening series.

Their home opener was on April 9 against Houston. Kroc received a standing ovation during pregame ceremonies as fans showed appreciation for the man who kept their team in San Diego. He grabbed the mike and shouted, "With your help and God's help, we'll give 'em hell tonight." But the Padres again looked like hell, trailing 9-2 in the middle of the eighth. Kroc went into the public-address announcer's booth, grabbed the mike, and yelled, "Ladies and gentlemen, I suffer with you." Just then a naked man streaked across the field. "Get that streaker off the field and throw him in jail," Kroc bellowed. "I have good news and bad news," he continued. "The good news is that the Dodgers drew 31,000 for their opener and we've drawn 39,000 for ours. The bad news is that this is the most stupid baseball playing I've ever seen." The crowd cheered, but Kroc was denounced for the outburst by players on both teams as well as Commissioner Bowie Kuhn and Players Association chief Marvin Miller. "I've never heard anything like that in my 19 years in baseball," McCovey said. "None of us like being called stupid."[28] "I used a bad choice of words and I'm sorry," Kroc said apologetically. "I was bitterly disappointed and embarrassed before almost 40,000 people. I

should have said the team wasn't playing good ball and have urged the fans to stick with us. At McDonald's, we try to look out for the customers. It's the same with our baseball fans. I want them to get value, to have a square deal and a fair deal."[29]

Some weren't satisfied with Kroc's apology. "He knows as much about the sport as Willie McCovey knows about an Egg McMuffin," slammed sportswriter Melvin Durslag. "The world is too quick to accept apologies as instant redress for mischief and atrocity," Durslag said, ripping Kroc as another one of "the sports ignoramuses who have purchased franchises."[30]

Kroc wanted his Padres to be the class of the league, even if he felt they were years away from being competitive. "I want it to be so that kids would rather play for the Padres than any team in the majors," he said. "I'm going to buy the team a DC-9 and I would like for the team to stay in hotels that are at least a little better than the ones the other teams stay in." Kroc also spent $60,000 in 1974 to field a team in the Arizona Fall League.[31]

One of Ray Kroc's lasting legacies off the field also began in 1974 when he created the Ronald McDonald House. The facility, first begun in Philadelphia, was designed to provide housing for families with sick children who couldn't afford to stay in nearby hotels or travel great distances. Families could give a donation of $5 per day or not pay at all if they could not afford it, as no family was ever turned away.

The Padres finished 1974 with an identical 60-102 last-place record as the previous year. However, the Padres fans supported the team; attendance was 1,075,399, eighth in the league. The team batting average dipped again to a league-worst .229 and pitchers had a league-worst 4.58 ERA.

The 1975 team improved to 71-91 and leaped to fourth place. Their batting average was tied for last (.244) and the Padres hit only 78 home runs, 23 by McCovey. But the pitching (3.48 ERA) was greatly improved behind Randy Jones's 20 wins (league-best 2.24 ERA) despite no other starter winning more than eight. Attendance improved to 1.2 million fans (seventh).

Baseball entered a major turning point as pitchers Catfish Hunter and Andy Messersmith won free agency. Kroc might not have known how to grow talent from the ground up, but he knew how to open his wallet on the open market. He made bids for both, but both went elsewhere.[32] Kroc anticipated more free agents being available after the 1976 season.

While waiting for new baseball players, Kroc decided to add professional hockey to his list of hobbies. In August of 1976 he purchased the fledgling San Diego Mariners of the World Hockey Association for $450,000.[33] He felt San Diego needed all four major sports, even if he himself knew little about hockey. "They were going to leave town," he said, "and it wouldn't be good for the town to lose hockey. At first I was going to loan some money to the hockey team. But I decided I'd rather own it. If I'm going to lose the money, I'll own it and lose it rather than loan it and lose it."[34] Ray and Joan sold their Fort Lauderdale home and moved to the La Jolla section of San Diego.

On July 4, 1976, the Padres were 42-37 and in third place, but they went 31-52 from that point on, finishing 29 games back in the division at 73-89. Despite the late-season woes, this was still the most wins in franchise history. Jones (22-14) won the NL Cy Young Award. The team continued to draw well; 1.4 million came out to the park, fourth best in the league.

After the season Kroc gave $1.25 million and a six-year deal to veteran free-agent catcher-first baseman Gene Tenace. "He's Kroc's favorite player," Buzzie Bavasi explained of Oakland's popular player, "and what Kroc wants, he usually gets."[35] Kroc also wanted slugger Reggie Jackson, but a $3 million deal for five years was not enough and Jackson signed with the Yankees. Disappointed but not defeated, Kroc signed another Oakland star, bullpen ace Rollie Fingers[36] and veteran outfielder George Hendrick. On paper, the Padres appeared to be a contender.

Kroc resigned as chairman of the board of McDonald's in late September 1976 but continued as senior chairman.[37] Also in 1976, Joan first stepped into the world of philanthropy. She brought publicity to alcoholism, a disease few would ever publicly discuss at the time. She founded CORK (Kroc spelled backwards), an organization that worked with families of alcoholics. There was more than one meaning to the name: The secret everyone knew but Ray refused to admit was his alcoholism. Wanting to help families that suffer through a member's alcoholism, Joan recruited advice columnist Abigail Van Buren ("Dear Abby") to publicize the organization, and thousands of readers sent in donations. CORK had a $1 million operating budget in 1978 and provided an $800,000 grant to the Dartmouth Medical School to develop a curriculum for studying alcoholism. "Our main focus is on the family members of the country's 10 million alcoholics," Joan said. "For each alcoholic in a family, four or five family members are being severely affected. We want to show them what they can do, and how they can get help. I'm just not business-oriented," she said, distinguishing herself from Ray. "I have a good head, and I'm logical, but my real concern is for human problems."[38] Joan also funded made-for-TV movies dealing with the subject. She was part of a cultural revolution, while hiding the secrets at home of why this topic was so important to her.

The best team Ray thought money could buy had fallen apart before Memorial Day 1977. With the Padres limping along at 20-28 and already 14½ games behind the division-leading

Dodgers, McNamara was fired. "In all of baseball there's not a finer man than Mac," Kroc said. "He is a gentleman among men. Everybody thinks this is a glamorous business, but it can be very tough. I'm tough on the outside, but I'm soft on the inside. Mac is a very wholesome guy but we're in the baseball business, not the fellowship business. The players by their performances have shown us we aren't getting the leadership we need."[39] Kroc's new manager was Alvin Dark, the former Oakland manager who had been on the Cubs coaching staff. The team played better under Dark (48-65), but it was a lost season at 69-93. Fingers led the league in appearances (78) and saves (35), but the team ERA (4.43) was second worst in the NL. While Hendrick (.311/23/81) and Dave Winfield (.275/25/92) provided power in the lineup, the .249 team average was also next to last. Attendance dropped to 1.3 million.

If the Padres were a disappointment, Kroc's hockey ventures were even worse. He sold the Mariners in May to an ownership group in Florida that couldn't secure a stadium, so the team folded. Kroc lost $1.4 million on the club.

In September 1977 Kroc named himself the Padres' president after Bavasi resigned. Kroc's son-in-law Ballard Smith became executive vice president. GM Bob Fontaine would have the final say on trades. "I'm going to take over," Kroc said, "and I'm going to turn this club inside out."[40] Kroc doubled the television revenue to $200,000 and the radio revenue to $360,000.[41] To try to boost the lineup and attendance, Kroc signed outfielder Oscar Gamble to a six-year contract for $2 million.

Despite $3.3 million in ticket revenues, the Padres suffered a net operating loss of $2.1 million in 1977. "San Diego has given the ballclub marvelous support over the past four seasons," Ballard Smith said, "but Ray is just about even at this point. We went into the 1977 season with cash reserves of $1.8 million. That's gone. People have the impression Ray is making a lot of money off the Padres, but that is hardly the case. My ambition right now is to see that we break even this year."[42] Contradicting themselves, the Padres acquired 39-year-old pitcher Gaylord Perry and 37-year-old pitcher Mickey Lolich. In early February 1978, Kroc purchased for the team a 727 jet from Northwest Airlines for $4.5 million.[43] So much for breaking even.

Kroc fired manager Alvin Dark in spring training after a player revolt. "Alvin had a tendency to overmanage," Kroc said. "It was too much."[44] Pitching coach Roger Craig became the manager. The change didn't result in success and the Padres were under .500 for much of the season in 1978. "The crybaby ballplayers complained about Alvin Dark, and they get Roger Craig, who's the epitome of a great guy on and off the field. And they're playing for him like they played for Alvin," Kroc ranted. "Roger Craig can't make up for a bunch of guys who don't give a damn and don't work at it. I'm sick and tired of the way this ballclub has been playing. It's pitiful. I'm thoroughly disgusted. I don't think they've got any guts or pride. They may not give a damn, but I've got news for them – I do. I want ballplayers. I'm not going to subsidize idiots. I don't know what these guys want. You give them a private plane, a players' lounge, everything under the sun. And they still respond like juveniles." Kroc singled out Tenace. "He needs to go to an eye doctor. He can't tell a strike from a ball. He hasn't given this club one thing since we got him. Tenace is the most overrated player on this team – he's a disgrace." Kroc later retracted the comments, saying, "I was probably a little hard on Gene. He's a perfect gentleman and he has a good attitude."[45]

Kroc and San Diego hosted the 1978 All-Star Game with 51,549 on hand, the largest crowd to see a baseball game in San Diego at that point. The team went 42-33 in the second half of the season to finish fourth at 84-78, with attendance at just over 1.6 million (fifth). This was the first team to finish above .500 in the history of the franchise. Perry (21-6) won the NL Cy Young Award, but Gamble, his production dropping from 31 home runs to seven in 1978, was traded away to save money. When asked if his team played better since he bought them their own airplane, Kroc said, "They play the same whether they ride in an airplane or a mule-drawn cart. And I'm not sure some of them know the difference."[46]

In November Kroc flew to Tokyo for the opening of his 5,000th McDonald's.[47] The business of baseball was much more difficult. "When I was selling, I always believed each new year would be a high for me," he said. "I'd be a year older, I'd have more experience and be more knowledgeable. Now, why can't ballplayers be like that? Why do they suddenly want to be paid before they achieve their goals? I can't understand that. Some of the risk has got to be borne by the individual. You have to do it first. You can't get paid first."[48]

The 1979 team did not follow the previous year's success, and on August 13 were 53-66. Kroc, who publicly stated he had lost money every year since he bought the club, promised more shakeups. "Whatever we've done is not good enough. I want to do better," he said. Roger Craig was fired in the offseason. Kroc made headlines when he promised to "spend $5 million to $10 million" to "try signing Graig Nettles and Joe Morgan if they become free agents this fall. You bet your boots I'm going after 'em."[49]

For these statements, Kroc was fined $100,000 by the league for player tampering. "Baseball has brought me nothing but aggravation," Kroc complained. "It can go to hell."[50] He gave up control of day-to-day operations to Ballard Smith. "There's a lot more fun in hamburgers than baseball," Kroc said. "The

fun in it is all gone for me. Baseball isn't baseball anymore. I've been disillusioned by everyone I met."[51] Kroc contemplated selling the team. "I've never seen him so depressed," Joan said. But he changed his mind. "I can't get out of baseball," he said. "It means so much to me. I'll keep the club another five years and give it a try."[52]

Kroc brought in free-agent pitchers Rick Wise and John Curtis and traded for second baseman Dave Cash. Jack McKeon was hired as assistant general manager, and Padres broadcaster Jerry Coleman became manager. Kroc suffered a stroke just before Christmas of 1979 and had to curtail his drinking habits. Coleman's tenure lasted just a year as the Padres finished back in last place (73-89) in 1980. The season was overshadowed by the impending free agency of Winfield. The future Hall of Famer was seeking a 10-year contract for over $1 million per season. "Who's going to pay him?" Kroc asked. "I'm not going to pay him. The customers aren't going to pay him. He doesn't mean a damn thing."[53] The Yankees felt otherwise and gave all that and more to make the star outfielder the highest-paid player in the game.[54] Kroc reported he had lost $2.7 million in 1980 as rumors of a players strike circulated in early 1981. "It's ridiculous," he said. "I have a (Kroc) Foundation that gives $5 million a year to fight diseases like multiple sclerosis and arthritis. They haven't found the cures yet, but at least I can feel like that money is doing some good. I don't get that feeling in baseball anymore. I said when I got into this business that the last thing I needed was another dollar's worth of income. I've never taken a penny out of the ballclub. I decided long ago that I'd just write the Padres off (tax-wise). I don't want to sell them. I wouldn't even mind losing $50,000 to $100,000 a year with them. But $2.7 million is ridiculous." He believed his free-agent signings of Fingers, Tenace, Gamble, Wise, and Curtis were a waste of money along with the team jet, which he decided to sell.[55] Frank Howard lasted only the strike-shortened 1981 campaign as manager, as the Padres finished last in both halves.

Ballard Smith and Jack McKeon, who began earning his nickname of Trader Jack, were busy after the 1981 season. They shipped out Fingers, Tenace, and pitcher Bob Shirley in a 10-player trade with St. Louis, receiving promising young catcher Terry Kennedy. Young speedster Alan Wiggins was taken in the Rule 5 draft and young pitchers Tim Lollar and Dave Dravecky emerged. They also traded Gold Glove shortstop Ozzie Smith to St. Louis for veteran shortstop Garry Templeton. Dick Williams, who had success previously in Boston, Oakland, and Montreal, became the Padres' new manager.

Kroc celebrated an early 80th birthday at the newly renamed Jack Murphy Stadium on October 2. The team finished the 1982 season 81-81, eight games behind division winner Atlanta. The

Padres were second in stolen bases, fifth in ERA, and first in defensive efficiency. Four players had 27 or more stolen bases, and a 22-year-old rookie named Tony Gwynn was called up in July, the first of his 20 Hall of Fame seasons in San Diego.

Still lacking in star power, the Padres in late December made headlines when they signed first baseman Steve Garvey to a five-year, $6.5 million contract. "Steve, I think you can make a difference here," Kroc said to Garvey when they met at Kroc's home."[56] On his way to the podium for the press conference, Garvey stopped and greeted Ray and Joan. "We're going to have some fun. We're going to have a winner," he promised.[57]

The 1983 season was an identical 81-81 record for the Padres as Garvey was limited by a thumb injury. Meanwhile, McDonald's reported $8 billion in sales and Kroc's fortune was now estimated at $500 million. Ray was hospitalized for 10 days in September, returned home, and then was readmitted on December 5. Needing a closer but unsure if the team could afford one, Smith and McKeon visited Ray in the hospital. When McKeon said he thought Goose Gossage could help the team win the pennant, Kroc responded, "Sign him."[58] On January 6, 1984, Ray had a visitor at the hospital. It was Gossage, who had just signed with the Padres for what was reported as the largest contract ever given a pitcher: a five-year deal for $6.25 million.[59]

Ray would never return home. He died of heart failure on January 14 and was buried in El Camino Memorial Park in San Diego.[60] The Padres wore a patch on their sleeve that season with the initials "RAK" in his memory. By the time of his death, McDonald's was grossing $12 billion per year in sales through its 9,400 restaurants.[61] "Ray Kroc was many things," wrote Bud Poliquin of the *San Diego Union-Tribune*. "Philanthropist. Entrepreneur. An internationally known figure. But beyond all of that, beyond the fortune he accumulated through his development of the McDonald's restaurant chain, he was a hot-dog-eating, peanut-shelling, foot-stomping baseball fan."[62] Joan Kroc now controlled a baseball team.

Ray didn't live to see the Padres finally acquire Nettles, years after the $100,000 tampering incident. The veteran was now 39 but provided power at the plate and presence in the clubhouse, along with Garvey and Gossage. Ray also didn't live to see his dream of the Padres playing in the World Series. Everything came together for the 1984 team. Gwynn (.351) won the NL batting crown and Wiggins stole 70 bases. The team led the league in defensive efficiency. Young outfielders Carmelo Martinez and Kevin McReynolds were hyped as the new "M&M Boys," combining for 33 home runs. Lollar (11 victories), Ed Whitson (14), Mark Thurmond (14), and Eric Show (15) gave the Padres four starting pitchers with double-digit wins. Gossage was supported in the bullpen by a cast of low ERAs: Dravecky

(2.93), Craig Lefferts (2.13), Greg Booker (3.30), and Greg Harris (2.70). "When I took over, I had a five-year plan, and I thought we would win by 1985," McKeon said. "We've gotten there earlier than I expected because Ballard and Joan were able to spend the money to sign free agents like Steve Garvey and Goose Gossage."[63]

The Padres took over first place for good on June 9 and never looked back, winning the NL West by 12 games. In what would have been a bittersweet time for Ray, they played his first love, the Cubs, in the National League Championship Series. The Padres dropped the first two games in Chicago but swept the next three to get to the World Series. Whitson guided the Padres to a Game Three win, the first playoff game ever in San Diego. Game Four would go down as a classic. Leading 5-3 in the top of the eighth, Gossage couldn't hold off the Cubs, who scored two to tie. With Cubs closer Lee Smith on the mound, Gwynn singled, then Garvey hit a walk-off home run to right field to send the series to a decisive Game Five. The Cubs jumped out to a 3-0 lead, but four Padres relievers shut the door from then on. With the Padres trailing 3-2 in the bottom of the seventh, Cubs first baseman Leon Durham let a grounder go between his legs to allow the tying run to score. The Padres then tagged three straight hits off Rick Sutcliffe to score three more runs, and prevailed, 6-3.

"We dedicated this season to Ray and that's why we're in the World Series today," Joan said. "This team was committed, they were determined, they have the best fans in America, they worked harder than anybody – I could go on and on. Any team could win if they had what we've had this year."[64] The Padres lost to the heavily favored Detroit Tigers in five games in the World Series. They would not see the postseason again for 12 years.

During their championship season, two off-field incidents tested Joan's leadership abilities. In July, pitchers Show, Dravecky, and Thurmond each revealed that they belonged to the ultra-conservative John Birch Society, known for its anti-Semitic and racist views. Joan believed the clubhouse was no place to air political commentary and that it risked alienating teammates and fans. "I'm concerned about our team being a forum for political beliefs and aspirations," she said. "It has nothing to do with sport – and I don't think the boys mean it to be – but I think it should be dropped. Anybody who knows anything about politics knows that the John Birch Society is a radical – let's say ... controversial – organization. And sports isn't the place to get into controversial politics. The clubhouse is not a place for it."[65] Decades later, Dravecky said the trio had no idea about the racist overtones of the society and were drawn to its conservative small-government ideals.[66]

On July 18, 1984, gunman James Oliver Huberty entered a McDonald's in the San Diego neighborhood of San Ysidro and opened fire, killing 21 people and injuring 19 before being taken down by a SWAT team. It was the largest mass shooting in US history at the time. Joan donated $100,000 of aid for survivors and families of the victims, while McDonald's Corporate donated $1 million. "The only thing I thought about McDonald's in that regard was, 'Thank God, Ray never lived to see it,'" Joan said. "Because he wouldn't have believed that something like that could have happened at all."[67] Some were angered when Joan also contributed to Huberty's wife and children. "Surely everyone would agree that this compassion must extend to Mrs. Huberty and her two children," she said, "so that they too can begin to rebuild their shattered lives."[68]

Joan was now out of the Ray's shadow, although she had been involved in numerous charities herself over the years. She had always let Ray do the talking throughout their public appearances. "I've always been opinionated and committed to things I believe," she said, "but I didn't feel the need to espouse them to the world. Anytime you are involved with a man like Ray, who was so charismatic and strong, you can't have two people vocalizing at once. Politically, we were at separate ends of the spectrum. [He was a staunch Republican; she a registered Independent.] It wouldn't have been ladylike or proper to differ with him at public forums." Joan was now felt free to articulate her own beliefs. "Two words I wish we could remove: guilt and regret," she pronounced. "We all make mistakes and we all do things we wish we hadn't. What good do guilt and regret do? They're counterproductive. We have to move forward. (Life) is no kinder to one person than the other."[69]

In July of 1984, Joan sold 300,000 shares of McDonald's stock for well over $20 million, but she still owned over 6 million shares, or 10.5 percent of the holdings.[70] Ballard Smith had already become a member of the McDonald's board of directors, where he would remain until 1997. In December the Joan B. Kroc Foundation donated $1 million to famine relief in Africa.[71]

One of Joan's primary causes was nuclear disarmament. In April of 1985, she was in the audience to hear a speech by Rev. Theodore M. Hesburgh, the former president of the University of Notre Dame. She was impressed with his vision of a nuclear-free world and peace. She had several meetings with Hesburgh over the next few months. In December, she donated $6 million to create "a center for multidisciplinary research and teaching on the critically important questions of peace, justice, and violence in contemporary society." The Joan B. Kroc Institute for International Peace Studies at Notre Dame was created, thanks in part through her donation of $69 million.[72] "To me, the nuclear freeze issue transcends politics," she said. "We live in a world

in which nuclear weapons are casting a pall of fear and helplessness over us that may be as tragic as their detonation."[73] The institute awards academic degrees and says its alumni are "at all levels of society to build a more just and peaceful world."[74]

The remainder of Joan's years as owner of the Padres never reached the heights of 1984. In 1985 Wiggins was dealt to Baltimore after being connected to drug use, violating Joan's zero-tolerance policy. The team dropped to third (83-79) and friction emerged in the front office. McKeon and Smith offered to buy out Dick Williams's contract, unbeknownst to Kroc, who denounced the move. "That will never happen," she said. Smith and McKeon will "have to use their own money because I'm not using mine. There is something inherently indecent about buying out contracts in this kind of situation. If Dick chooses to walk away, not only will that sadden me, but he will walk away empty-handed. And I don't expect him to do that."[75]

Williams resigned during spring training, or was forced out, depending on who you believed, and Steve Boros took over as manager in 1986. The Padres again finished fourth (74-88) and star pitcher Lamarr Hoyt was also shipped out after the discovery of drugs. Kroc also forbade drinking in the clubhouse, which led to a suspension of Gossage. "She's poisoning the world with her cheeseburgers and we can't have a beer after a game," Gossage said. The two later reconciled. "I said something very disrespectful and she fired right back at me. She was as tough as she was nice ... and she was probably the nicest, kindest lady I ever knew. At the end of that meeting, we hugged."[76]

At the end of the 1986 season, Kroc put the Padres up for sale, but sought a buyer who would keep the club in San Diego. The lease on Jack Murphy Stadium, however, was extended by the city until the year 2000. Ballard Smith resigned as team president as he and Linda were filing for divorce.[77] The Padres fell to last place (65-97) under new team President Chub Feeney and manager Larry Bowa, who was fired after the club started 16-30 in 1988. McKeon managed the remainder of the season and in 1989 when the team improved (89-73). In April of 1990 Joan sold the Padres to television producer Tom Werner and nine other partners for $75 million. Werner had produced such television hits as *The Cosby Show* and *Roseanne*.[78]

In 1997 Joan anonymously donated $15 million to flood victims in North Dakota and Minnesota. A reporter nevertheless discovered she was the source of the gift, and she was dubbed the Angel of Grand Forks, but she declined to receive any public recognition. Her net worth was estimated at $2.1 billion by 1998. She donated $87 million to the Salvation Army for a 12-acre youth center in San Diego. Only at the urging of friends did she publicly reveal herself as the benefactor. She often said her giving was a continuation of Ray's generosity. "Ray was once asked why he gave so much of his wealth away," Joan said. "He said, 'I've never seen a Brinks truck following a hearse.' Have you?"[79]

"When she walked into a room, she radiated joy," said San Diego Mayor Maureen O' Connor.[80] Joan contributed to homeless shelters, AIDS and cancer research, the Special Olympics, and the Betty Ford Center. She contributed $25 million to the University of San Diego to establish the Mohandas K. Gandhi Institute for Peace and Justice.[81] Her $100 million donation expanded the Ronald McDonald House into the broader Ronald McDonald Charities, which as of 2018 included 365 Ronald McDonald Houses in 43 countries and regions and 50 mobile medical-care units, and provided assistance to 5.5 million children and families around the world.[82] She donated $1 million to the Democratic Party and $2 million for the construction of the Kroc-Copley Animal Shelter.

Lisa Napoli spends nearly eight pages documenting Joan's various financial donations, even though it is not nearly an exhaustive list.[83] Her life was one of philanthropy and when Joan died of brain cancer on October 12, 2003, at the age of 75, money continued to be distributed according to her wishes. She bequeathed $1.5 billion to the Salvation Army, $225 million to National Public Radio, and $60 million to the Ronald McDonald Charities. The University of San Diego and the University of Notre Dame, where she established peace initiatives, each received $50 million.

"Joan Kroc could have used the fortune that she and her husband amassed to insulate herself," said the *San Diego Union-Tribune*. Instead, she became very involved with a variety of good works that have benefited countless people. Those who were fortunate enough to have known her marveled at her unpretentiousness. This wonderful woman, who wasn't born to wealth, never stopped believing she should use much of her treasure to help others. The many lives she touched in so many ways will remain her enduring legacy."[84]

## SOURCES

Special thanks to Cassidy Lent, reference librarian at the A. Bartlett Giamatti Research Center at the Baseball Hall of Fame in Cooperstown, New York, for providing access to the Krocs' extensive files. Other sources include:

Associated Press. "'Fanatic' Set to Ante $10 million," January 1974 article of unknown origin in Kroc's Hall of Fame File.

Associated Press. "Padres Moving to Washington," *San Francisco Chronicle*, May 28, 1973: 47.

Baseball-reference.com.

Boas, Max, and Steve Chain. "Mr. Mac: Maestro of Munchland," *Daily News* (unknown place of origin), June 1, 1976: C9. Article is from Kroc's Hall of Fame file.

"Kroc Hospitalized After Stroke," *San Diego Union*, January 3, 1980: F1.

"Life and Times of Joan B. Kroc," *San Diego Union*, October 13, 2003: A12.

Retrosheet.org.

## NOTES

1    Nancy Ray and Dave Distel, "Ray Kroc, 81, Builder of McDonald's Chain, Dies," *Los Angeles Times*, January 15, 1984: 1.

2    content.time.com/time/magazine/article/0,9171,26473,00.html Retrieved May 5, 2018.

3    Hemingway, born in 1899, lived at 600 North Kenilworth.

4    Ray Kroc and Robert Anderson. *Grinding It Out: The Making of McDonald's* (New York: St. Martin's Griffin, 1977), 13.

5    Kroc and Anderson, 14-19.

6    Kroc and Anderson, 24-25.

7    Lucy Key Miller, "Front Views & Profiles," *Chicago Tribune*, October 29, 1957: F5.

8    Kroc and Anderson, 113.

9    Lisa Napoli, *Ray & Joan: The Man Who Made the McDonald's Fortune and the Woman Who Gave It All Away* (Boston: E.P. Dutton, 2016), 55.

10   Napoli, 64-65.

11   Napoli, 81.

12   Napoli, 88-92; "Wins Divorce, $30,000 a Year, $100,000 House," *Chicago Tribune*, April 19, 1962: F4.

13   Napoli, 94; Kenan Heise, "Ex-McDonald's Exec Harry J. Sonneborn, 77," *Chicago Tribune*, October 6, 1992.

14   Napoli, 97.

15   Napoli, 108-109.

16   According to Napoli, Joan Kroc always claimed August 27 as her official birth date even though August 26 is given on the birth certificate. Napoli, 42.

17   George Flynn, "San Ysidro Tragedy Struck at the Heart of Joan Kroc," *San Diego Union*, July 29, 1984: B1.

18   Napoli, 44.

19   Napoli, 45.

20   Napoli, 130; United Press International, "Executive Sued for Divorce," *Indianapolis Star*, November 12, 1971: 55.

21   Napoli, 175.

22    Napoli, 176.

23    Holcombe B. Noble, "C. Arnholt Smith, 97, Banker and Padres Chief Before a Fall," *New York Times*, June 11, 1996; Denny Walsh and Tom Flaherty, "Tampering with Justice in San Diego," *Life*, March 24, 1972: 30; "Arnholt Guilty of Evading Taxes," *Washington Post*, May 4, 1979.

24    Jack Murphy, "Kroc Agrees to Purchase Padres, Seeks League's OK," *San Diego Union*, January 24, 1974: 1.

25    Murphy, D4.

26    Phil Collier, "City, Kroc, OK Stadium Lease; Padres to Stay," *San Diego Union*, January 26, 1974: 1.

27    Jack Murphy, "Kroc Is Brimming with Pride and Patience," *San Diego Union*, April 6, 1974: C1.

28    Phil Collier, "Kroc Rips Club on P.A. as Astros Romp, 9-5," *San Diego Union*, April 10, 1974: C1.

29    Phil Collier, "Padre Kroc Eats Humble Pie After 'Stupid' Slur," *The Sporting News*, April 27, 1974: 25.

30    Melvin Durslag commentary of unknown origin marked May 4, 1974, from Kroc's Hall of Fame File.

31    Phil Collier, "Kroc Goal for Padres: That Old Yank Pride," *The Sporting News*, July 6, 1974: 8.

32    Jack Murphy, "He Loses Messersmith But He's Not Defeated," *San Diego Union*, April 12, 1976: C1.

33    Jack Murphy, "It's Official: WHA Okays Kroc's Mariner Purchase," *San Diego Union*, August 10, 1976: C1.

34    Charles Maher, "Ray Kroc. McDonald's Magnate Makes His Break to be Near Padres," *Los Angeles Times*, March 6, 1977.

35    Phil Collier, "Tenace Accepts Padres' Pact," *San Diego Union*, November 17, 1976: C1.

36    Jack Murphy, "Signing Fingers Brightens Kroc's Thanksgiving Day," *San Diego Union*, November 26, 1976: C1.

37    "Dow Jones Reports," *San Diego Union*, September 30, 1976: B6.

38    Judy Klemesrud, "For Alcoholics, Treatment in a Mansion ... and a Program for the Families," *New York Times*, July 10, 1978: 9.

39    Jack Murphy, "Kroc Asserts Himself, and McNamara Is Gone," *San Diego Union*, May 29, 1977: H1.

40    Jack Murphy, "Bavasi Out as Padres' President," *San Diego Union*, September 21, 1977: 1.

41    Phil Collier, "Padres Drag in More Loot from Radio and TV," *The Sporting News*, January 28, 1978.

42    Jack Murphy, "$2.1 Million Deficit for the Padres in '77," *San Diego Union*, January 23, 1978: C1.

43    "4 Padre Players Reported Signed," *San Diego Union*, February 10, 1978: C1; Jack Murphy, "Air Kroc's Inaugural Flight a Happy Event," *San Diego Union*, April 25, 1978: C1.

44    Phil Collier, "Padres Name Craig to Succeed Fired Dark," *San Diego Union*, March 22, 1978: C1.

45    "Kroc's Timing Off by a Day," article of unknown origin in Kroc's file, labeled June of 1978; Dave Distel, "'Offend the Players? They Offend the Fans,'" Globe-Democrat-Los Angeles Times News Service. Article of unknown date in Kroc's Hall of Fame file.

46    "Insiders Say," *The Sporting News*, August 26, 1978: 4.

47    Dick Young, "Ideas," article of unknown origin in Kroc's Hall of Fame file marked 11/11/78.

48    Steve Bisheff, "Baseball Too Protective of Weaker Sisters, Says Big Brother Kroc," *The Sporting News*, May 12, 1979: 9.

49    Associated Press, "Padre Shakeup in Works," article of unknown origin in Kroc's Hall of Fame File marked 8-14-79.

50    Phil Collier, "Kroc's Tampering Penalty: $100,000," *San Diego Union*, August 24, 1979: D1.

51    Murray Chass, "Kroc, Citing $100,000 Fine, Gives Up Control of Padres," *New York Times*, August 25, 1979.

52    Jack Murphy, "Kuhn Almost Drove Kroc From Baseball," *San Diego Union*, August 30, 1979: D1.

53    Phil Collier, "Kroc: Winfield Out," *San Diego Union*, August 6, 1980: C1.

54    Phil Pepe, "Winfield a Yankee for 10 Years, $13M," *New York Daily News*, December 16, 1980: 88.

55    Phil Collier, "Upset Kroc Won't Sell Padres," *Sporting News*, March 28, 1981: 28.

56    Garvey, quoted in "Triumph and Tragedy: The 1984 San Diego Padres." Major League Baseball Network. Retrieved April 29, 2018. youtube.com/watch?v=W-GVrkSmEPs.

57    Phil Collier, "Steve Garvey Is Now a Padre," *San Diego Union*, December 22, 1982: 6.

58    "Triumph and Tragedy."

59    Phil Collier, "Padres: 'Goose' Signs on for Five-Year Stint – Gossage for $6.25 Million," *San Diego Union*, January 7, 1984: C1.

60    Eric Pace, "Ray A. Kroc Dies at 81; Built McDonald's Chain," *New York Times*, January 15, 1984; Tom Blair column, *San Diego Union-Tribune*, September 29, 1983: B1.

61    Kroc and Anderson, 205.

62    Bud Poliquin, "Ray Kroc: a Fan and a Friend," *San Diego Union-Tribune*, January 16, 1984: C1.

63    Phil Collier, "Title Brings Thoughts of Kroc and Struggle," *San Diego Union-Tribune*, September 21, 1984: C10.

64    Mark Sauer and Ed Jahn, "Dreams Can Come True – Padres Win Flag for Kroc – Series Opens Tomorrow – Delicious, Delightful Delirium," *San Diego Union*, October 8, 1984: A1.

65    Nick Canepa, "Birch Comments Stir Concern – Kroc, Smith Worry About Club's Image," *San Diego Union-Tribune*, July 13, 1984: E1.

66    "Triumph and Tragedy."

67    Suzanne Choney, "Joan Kroc – A Year of Wins, Losses," *San Diego Union-Tribune*, October 19, 1984: A1; Christopher Reynolds, "McDonald's Will Establish Fund," *San Diego Union-Tribune*, July 20, 1984: A14.

68    Flynn, "San Ysidro Tragedy."

69    Choney.

70      Donald Coleman, "Largest Shareholder – Joan Kroc Sells Block of McDonald's Shares," *San Diego Union- Tribune*, October 23, 1984: A17.

71      Frank Green, "Joan Kroc Gives $1 Million in Famine Aid," *San Diego Union*, December 12, 1984: A14.

72      "History," kroc.nd.edu/about-us/history/, retrieved April 28, 2018; "Joan B. Kroc's Legacy," kroc.nd.edu/about- us/history/joan-b-krocs-legacy/, retrieved April 28, 2018.

73      Choney.

74      "About Us," kroc.nd.edu/about-us/ retrieved April 28, 2018.

75      Bob Slocum, "The Buyout Fiasco – Kroc Insists on Honoring Williams' Contract," *San Diego Union*, December 4, 1985: C1.

76      Bill Center, "Padres of Yesterday Remember Kind, Caring Lady Who Led Team," *San Diego Union*, October 13, 2003: A13.

77      Mark Kreidler, "Joan Kroc Will Keep the Padres," *San Diego Union*, May 30, 1987: A1.

78      Mark Kreidler, "Joan Kroc to Sell Padres – Talks Begin – Lakers Boss Plans to Bid for Padres," *San Diego Union*, October 18, 1989: A1; Kevin Kernan, "Werner Group Signs to Buy Padres – Kroc's Sale of Club Could be Final in 45-60 Days," *San Diego Union*, April 3, 1990: C1.

79      Tony Perry, "Joan B. Kroc, 75; Widow of McDonald's Chief, 'Radiated Joy' as Philanthropist," *Los Angeles Times*, October 13, 2003: B13.

80      Ibid.

81      "Joan Kroc: She Acted with an Enormous Heart and a Checkbook to Match," *People*, December 28, 1998.

82      "RMHC Program Facts," rmhc.org/our-impact Retrieved April 23, 2018.

83      Napoli, 276-285.

84      "Joan Kroc – Private Person Who Gave So Much to So Many," *San Diego Union-Tribune*, October 14, 2003: B6.

# JACK MCKEON

## BY THOMAS J. BROWN JR.

*Jack McKeon with his cigar (left) and Padres owner Ray Kroc (right).*

Jack McKeon never made it to the major leagues as a player but he eventually made his mark in the majors as a manager and general manager during his long career in baseball. Along the way he earned numerous accolades and will be remembered as one of the more colorful managers and general managers in baseball.

John Aloysius McKeon was born on November 23, 1930, in South Amboy, New Jersey. His parents were William and Anna McKeon. They had four children, two boys and two girls. McKeon's father owned a garage, a taxicab, and a towing business and spent most of his days working at one of his businesses. His father imparted a love of baseball on his son from an early age. "My dad started the 'McKeon Boys Club,' and we played other local teams," Jack said. "I was managing and making out schedules when I was 12. My brother (Bill Jr.) and I put up chicken wire in Dad's garage, which served as our batting cage."[1] (Bill Jr. played in the Milwaukee Braves system as a catcher.)

McKeon attended St. Mary's Catholic School in South Amboy. His passion for baseball did not wane as he grew older. He said, "[I] would catch a game in the afternoon, turn [my] uniform inside out and rush across town to catch in a city league game."[2] He graduated from high school in 1948 and his play attracted the attention of pro scouts. His father did not want him to follow in his footsteps, and insisted that Jack attend college.

His parents were devout Catholics and they imparted their faith to McKeon, who remained faithful to his Catholic upbringing throughout his life. He told an interviewer that it might have been divine intervention that finally got him into baseball. Every evening as he returned to his dorm at Holy Cross College, McKeon stopped at the shrine of the Blessed Virgin Mary. He prayed for her divine intercession, always asking her to persuade his father to let him leave school and play baseball.[3]

McKeon attended college for one semester before persuading his father to let him sign a pro baseball contract. The elder McKeon finally relented but only before getting his son to promise to get his college degree later. McKeon would eventually take offseason courses at Seton Hall University and Elon College to fulfill his promise. He earned a bachelor's degree in physical education from Elon in 1957. He missed his graduation because he was busy managing Missoula of the Pioneer League. Eventually the university mailed him his diploma.[4]

McKeon signed a contract with the Pittsburgh Pirates and played in their minor-league system from 1949 to 1954. The Pirates assigned him to Greenville (Alabama) in the Class-D Alabama State League. The right-handed McKeon caught in 116 games that season. He batted .251 and while he had 98 hits, only 14 were for extra bases.

"I got $450 to sign and I made $215 a month. That's not too much money, but I came home with $600," McKeon said in 2015. "Of course, you could stay with a family for $5 a week, and it might cost you $1.50 to eat, all day."[5] What mattered most to McKeon was that he was playing baseball. Little did he know that his career would last another 62 years.

McKeon played one game for the York (Pennsylvania) of the Class-B Interstate League at the start of the 1950 season before being sent to Gloversville-Johnstown (New York) of the Class-C Canadian-American League. He played in 72 games and his batting average slumped to .215 with the Glovers.

In 1951 McKeon served in the Air Force at Sampson Air Force Base in upstate New York. While there, he was the player-manager of the base's baseball team. He left the service and played for Hutchinson (Kansas) of the Class-C Western Association in 1952. Although he still struggled at the plate, batting .218, he played solid defense.

During spring training in 1953, Danny Murtaugh, who was managing the Pirates' Double-A New Orleans Pelicans, asked him if he ever considered being a manger. "I guess he thought I had some things going for me," McKeon said. "When I got my first big-league job, I kind of leaned on Danny for advice. He was good about it."[6]

At Class-B Burlington-Graham (North Carolina) of the Carolina League in 1953, McKeon played in all 140 games, and batted only .181, so the Pirates sent him back to Hutchinson team in 1954. He hit .207 in 46 games before returning to Burling-ton-Graham, where he continued to struggle at the plate, hitting just .133 in 17 games. His hopes of making the big leagues were starting to dim, and he returned to college, continuing his studies at Elon. McKeon said Branch Rickey, who was running the Pirates, called him in the fall of 1954 and encouraged him to continue his studies.[7]

In 1954 McKeon married Carol Isley, whom he met while playing in Burlington. As of 2018, they had been married for 64 years and lived in North Carolina.

McKeon planned to manage the Pirates' Hutchinson team in 1955 but the opportunity never materialized when the team folded before the season. Instead he started the season as a part-time player with Fayetteville (North Carolina) of the Class-B Carolina League, a Baltimore Orioles farm team. In midseason the manager was promoted and McKeon became player-manager.

He said all but two players on the team were older than he was. (McKeon was 24.) One of his pitchers showed up every four days since he had another job, and other players showed up as needed. His relief pitcher would show up by the sixth inning every night for the same reason.[8] Yet McKeon led the team to a 30-22 record during his two months at the helm. "I kept my dream of getting to the big leagues but just changed the direction," he said of his time with Fayetteville.[9] McKeon realized that "all these guys were hitting .250 or better and I was only hitting .180 so I became a good salesman. I convinced people that I could be a manager."[10]

At the time, many minor-league managers also played, and McKeon was no exception. He managed the Missoula, Montana, Timberjacks of the Class-C Pioneer League from 1956 to 1958. The team was independent in 1956 and McKeon said that when he took the job, the owner said, "We have three players. Can you find us some more?" He went on the road to scout amateur leagues in North and South Carolina to find players.

He led the team to 61-71 record and a seventh-place finish. He batted .170 that season. The following year, the team became a Washington Senators affiliate. McKeon's team finished in fourth place that season with a 62-64 record. He played in 102 games and batted .217. Years later he said, "I was the only player who hit three ways: left, right, and seldom."[11]

In 1958 McKeon enjoyed his biggest success as both a player and a manager up to then. He batted .263, hit 8 home runs, and had 51 RBIs. Manager McKeon led the team to a second-place finish with a 70-59 record.

The Senators were pleased with McKeon's efforts and moved him to Fox Cities of the Class-B Three-I League for 1959. The team, based in Appleton, Wisconsin, finished in fourth place with a 59-67 record. He returned to North Carolina for the 1960 season when the Senators made him the manager of Wilson of the Carolina League. At 29, he dropped "player" from his job description; for the first time, he was just the manager. Wilson had a 73-65 record and finished in second place. In 1961 McKeon led the team (83-56) to a first-place finish. The team was now an affiliate of the Minnesota Twins after the Senators moved in the offseason.

The Twins continued to be impressed with McKeon's leadership and promoted him to the Triple-A Vancouver Mounties (Pacific Coast League) in 1962. He led the team to a 72-79, seventh-place finish. The team moved to Dallas-Fort Worth in 1963 and became the Rangers. McKeon stayed at the helm and managed them to a 79-79 record.

When the Twins moved their Triple-A affiliate to Atlanta for the 1964 season, McKeon moved with them. The Crackers, now playing in the International League, ended up with a 55-93 record. McKeon stepped aside after the season and served as a scout in the Twins organization for the next three years.

By 1968, McKeon was restless to get back on the diamond. He joined the expansion Kansas City Royals and managed their winter instructional league team in the winter of 1968. When the season ended, he took the reins of High Point-Thomasville in the Carolina League. The team played just up the road from McKeon's home in Burlington. The team was independent but had 14 players signed by Royals on their roster. Despite a 69-71 record, the team made the playoffs in the two-division league, and won the league championship.

McKeon managed the Triple-A Omaha Royals (American Association) from 1969 to 1972. He called this "the turning point of my career." He explained: "That led to my first big-league job. And it just so happened I was in the right organization to achieve that."[12]

McKeon compiled a 298-259 during his four years in Omaha. The team finished in first place and won league titles during his first two years as manager. McKeon was chosen as the American Association manager of the year in both years. Omaha's only losing season during McKeon's tenure came in 1971, when the team finished 69-70.

At the time, McKeon was facing a decision about whether he should continue to manage at the minor-league level or look for a chance to coach with a major-league team. When he took the job in Omaha, he said, "I made up my mind that I would stay managing until age 44, and if I didn't get to the big leagues by then I would take a coaching job. And fortunately I got there at age 42."[13]

McKeon reflected on the difference between managing in the minors and the majors. In the minors, "my goal was to develop the players. When you are in the majors, your goal is to win. I learned that the more that I developed my players, the more I won. If I could make my players 10 to 15 percent better each year, then I was successful."[14] He said it was his ability to develop his players that eventually got him to the major leagues as a manager.

The Royals made McKeon their manager in 1973. He replaced Bob Lemon, whose team went 76-78 record during the previous strike-shortened season. Playing in their new ballpark, the 1973 Royals improved to 88-74 and a second-place in the American League West. It was a record number of wins for the young franchise.

One of the highlights of McKeon's inaugural season at the Royals' helm came when the team arrived in New York to play the Yankees. His hometown of South Amboy honored its native son. As McKeon recalled, "They honored me with proclamations and gifts and what have you. My mother and my wife and my kids were there. My mother leaned over and said, 'Boy, your dad would be proud of you.' With that I just figured that I had reached my goals, making the major leagues and making my parents proud."[15]

The Royals slumped in 1974 and finished fifth in the division with a 77-85 record. The team improved in 1975 and its record was 50-46 on June 23 when the Royals fired McKeon, replacing him with Whitey Herzog. The Royals said that the reason for the change was that "there was really no rapport between the team and Jack."[16]

McKeon returned to managing in the minor leagues in 1976. The Atlanta Braves hired him to manage Triple-A Richmond (International League). The team finished with a 69-71 record. Oakland owner Charlie Finley hired McKeon to manage the A's in 1977. Finley was in the process of getting rid of all his star players before they could enter the free-agent market. Even with the diminished talent, McKeon managed the team to a 26-27 record, when he was fired by Finley on June 8 and replaced with Bobby Winkles. When McKeon asked why he was fired, Finley told him that "a change had to be made." Several days earlier, McKeon said, Finley had told McKeon he was proud of the job the manager was doing.[17]

McKeon stayed with the A's as an assistant general manager. The team played well when the 1978 season began. But Winkles had become frustrated with Finley's meddling. At one point there were rumors that Finley was going to make Winkles wear earphones so he could talk to him in the dugout.[18] Winkles resigned on May 22. At the time the team had a 24-15 record and was in first place.

Finley put McKeon back in the dugout to manage the team almost a year after he was fired. Asked why he was bringing McKeon back, Finley said: "He is smarter this year."[19] The team stayed in first place through the middle of June but Finley had not learned his lesson with Winkles' resignation.

Finley continued to meddle with managerial decisions. An example: Finley insisted on starting the A's two draft picks from that season's June draft, so the team would know if they were ready for the majors.[20] Draftee Mike Morgan was given a start against Baltimore. "He pitched well for the first four innings but then he got in trouble so I decided to take him out," McKeon said. "I got a phone call in the dugout. It was Charlie. He told me to keep him in the game. When Morgan reached the seventh inning, I decided to pull him but then the phone rang again. It was Finley and he told me that I needed to keep him in the game. He said that Morgan's high-school coach was up there and had told him that Morgan had pitched 10 innings on previous occasions."[21]

McKeon stayed as the A's manager for the rest of the season. The team struggled in the final months of the season and finished 45-78 with McKeon as manager. McKeon's analysis: "You couldn't win no matter what" with Charlie Finley.[22]

McKeon joined the Montreal Expos organization for the 1979 season, managing the Triple-A Denver Bears (American Association) to a 62-73 record. McKeon saw the effect of Denver's high altitude on hitting. On July 4, "We were down 14-7 with a runner on and two outs in the bottom of the ninth. We scored nine unearned runs, with Jim Cox hitting a three-run homer to win it, 16-14."[23]

The 1980 season found McKeon in San Diego. He started the year as assistant to general manager Bob Fontaine. The team struggled in the first half of the season. Owner Ray Kroc and club President Ballard Smith fired Fontaine during the All-Star break and gave the job to McKeon.

McKeon remained the general manager of the Padres through the 1988 season. It was during those years that he earned the nickname "Trader Jack." He explained: "I'd be lying if I said I didn't like trades. If another GM asks me if I want a certain guy, I rarely say no. Maybe I don't have a need for a guy but maybe I can acquire the guy anyway, and trade him for someone that I do need."[24]

Kroc, the Padres owner, was frustrated that the team had not had a winning season since he became owner. New GM McKeon "asked Mr. Kroc if there were any players on the roster that he considered untouchable. When he said 'No,' I said, 'Good, let's shake things up.'"[25]

The first big deal of McKeon's tenure as general manager came at the end of the 1980 season. He acquired Terry Kennedy in an 11-player trade with the St. Louis Cardinals. That deal was the start of his efforts to build the Padres into the team that would win the 1984 National League pennant. Other players McKeon acquired through trades were Garry Templeton (from the Cardinals in a trade for Ozzie Smith), Graig Nettles, Carmelo Martinez, and Dave Dravecky.[26]

McKeon continually moved players during his tenure with the Padres. "If I can improve the Padres with a trade, I'll consider anything," he said. "I'm a gambler. I always have been. I'm aggressive and I'm confident. I'm not worried about making a mistake because I think I'm going to be right much more often than I'm wrong."[27]

Sometimes McKeon made trades to help out other teams. Dallas Green, the Cubs general manager in 1983, wanted Scott Sanderson from Montreal but couldn't come up with players the Expos would trade for. McKeon heard about this and told Green, "I'll get him for you." So, I called John McHale, the Expos general manager and said 'You need a good relief pitcher. I'll give you Gary Lucas.' And I swung the deal for all three clubs. [Green] got Scott Sanderson, the pitcher he wanted. [McHale's] Expos got Gary Lucas, the relief pitcher they wanted."[28]

McKeon got Carmelo Martinez and Craig Lefferts from the Cubs. "It worked. The Cubs won the National League East the next year, the Padres won the West and won the National League pennant"[29]

During his years with the Padres, McKeon never hesitated to make a trade. Many of them made headlines across the baseball world. But that was not his goal. "That's how this business works. Like [I've] said, I'm not in this business to rip people off. I'm here to smoke cigars and make a trade or two."[30]

McKeon returned to the dugout in 1988. The team started the season with a 16-30 record. On May 28 skipper Larry Bowa was fired and McKeon took over as manager. He also remained as general manager. "I like both jobs," he said. "It's Skipper Jack from 2:30 until midnight and Trader Jack the rest of the time."[31] He led the Padres to a 67-48 mark for the rest of 1988 season. As McKeon remembered it, "I had put together the team through trades and drafts. I might as well prove that we were on the right track."[32]

McKeon said it was an asset to the team for him to be both manager and general manager. "The guys don't want to be honest with themselves. When I was general manager, they would come to me and I would tell them that if you have any complaints, talk to the manager. When I became manager, guys were complaining and I called a team meeting in Atlanta. I told them, 'You guys ought to get on your hands and knees and thank the lord that you have a job. I tried to trade you but I can't find anyone to take you.' We went on to win 20 of the next 28 games as I recall."[33]

After the season, Chub Feeney, the Padres' president, told McKeon that he didn't care for the idea of one man holding both jobs. McKeon's success in the dugout led to pressure from the organization and the players for him to choose the manager position. He eventually persuaded Joan Kroc, who ran the team after her husband died, to let him keep both jobs. "I think he likes being in the dugout chewing tobacco or chomping on a cigar before a game," Cardinals manager Whitey Herzog said.[34]

McKeon stayed as the Padres manager in 1989 and the team finished 89-73. But the Padres struggled in 1990. They had a 37-43 record at the All-Star break. McKeon resigned as manager, and made first-base coach Greg Riddoch his successor. He kept the GM portfolio, but several months later he was fired by the Padres' new owner, Tom Werner.

McKeon was out of baseball for the 1991 and 1992 seasons. He returned to North Carolina to spend more time with his wife and family. McKeon returned in 1993 when the Cincinnati Reds signed him as a scout and then senior adviser for player personnel under general manager Jim Bowden. He served in that capacity until July 25, 1997.

Ray Knight, the Reds manager, was causing disruption in the dugout and disillusionment in the Reds front office. The Reds were 43-56, nine games out of the lead in the National League Central Division when Knight was fired. McKeon was asked to take over as manager. "McKeon is going to take over this ballclub on an interim basis through the end of the '97 season to help stabilize the situation," said Bowden, who believed that McKeon's more even-tempered approach would be more helpful to the team.[35] "We feel that a change might help the progression of our young guys between now and the end of the season."[36] McKeon managed the team to a 33-30 mark for the rest of the season.

McKeon stayed on as manager in 1999 and the team continued to improve. He led them to 96 victories and a tie for the National League wild-card slot. However, the Reds were defeated 5-0 by the Mets in a one-game tiebreaker at Cinergy Field. McKeon was named 1999 National League Manager of the Year.

The Reds acquired center fielder Ken Griffey Jr. in a trade with the Seattle Mariners on February 10, 2000. Griffey hit 40 home runs in 2000, but the Reds' record fell to 85-77, and they fin-

ished 10 games behind the St. Louis Cardinals. After the season, McKeon was fired. Bowden said, "Jack has been a part of the development of the good, young Reds players you see on the field today. But the organization has decided to take a different decision in its leadership from the dugout."[37]

McKeon retired from baseball and returned to his home in North Carolina. He was mostly enjoying life, spending time with his wife and grandchildren, but said that while he enjoyed working in his garden during the day, he hated "[s]itting in the same damned chair till midnight, watching games. That used to be my working day."[38] That would change. Florida Marlins owner Jeffrey Loria fired manager Jeff Torborg in May of 2003 and asked the 72-year-old McKeon to take over. He jumped at the chance.

When Torborg arrived in Florida, he called a team meeting. His impressions? "I saw these guys that weren't prepared. They didn't have a good work ethic. I told the players that I don't need this job. I am here to show you how to win. If you want to pay the price, we can play in October. But it's all up to you. How bad do you want it? If you want it, we're going to have to change a few things. Change your attitude, change your work habits, you're going to have focus a little bit better and you're going to have to leave your egos at the door. It took a few weeks but they bought into my program."[39]

The Marlins went 75-49 under McKeon's leadership. McKeon used his experience to guide his young team. He "didn't need computer readouts or piles of data to tell him how to manage. He's from the old school; he told his players to … do the best they can, relax and have fun."[40] Josh Beckett, one of the Marlins' young stars, described McKeon's approach: "He's a fun guy to play for. He expects a certain amount out of you, and if you don't give it to him, he won't even talk to you. He ignores you. That's his way of motivating you. It gets under your skin, but that's how he is."[41] McKeon worked the young players extremely hard. "I rode them," he said. He told Beckett that "I'm going to make you a 20-game winner."[42]

The result was that Marlins made the playoffs as the NL wild-card team in 2003. Before they faced the Giants, who had finished with the best record in the National League, McKeon said, "[The] pressure is on everybody else because we aren't supposed to win."[43]

The Marlins beat the Giants in the Division Series, three games to one. Then they won the pennant by beating the Chicago Cubs in seven games. In the World Series, the Marlins faced the Yankees. McKeon's young Marlins team beat the Yankees in six games to claim the club's second World Series championship. After the Series, the New Jersey native said that he had always "wanted to have my first World Series in Yankee Stadium. Win or lose, I wanted to play it in Yankee Stadium."[44]

McKeon won his second Manager of the Year award, becoming the first manager who was hired during a season to be honored with the award. At 72, he was the oldest manager to win a World Series.

The win was special for McKeon. He was general manager the last time one of his teams made the World Series. "I always was hoping that I'd get one more chance. After 1999, it kind of left a sad taste in my mouth. Then getting fired the next year. After all the years in baseball, you never were afforded the opportunity to even make the postseason, let alone get to the World Series. That's why this has been a great ride."[45]

McKeon managed the Marlins for two more seasons. The team finished 83-79 both seasons. His 2005 team looked was a contender but lost 12 of their last 17 games to finish in third place in the division.

At the end of the season McKeon announced that he would retire. "The last couple of years, I haven't had as much fun as I'd like," he said. "Since I'm the leader, I'll take full responsibility for the poor year we had."[46] McKeon stayed with the team as an adviser although he said that he was open to other offers. "Sometimes you need to step back and maybe take a breather for six or seven months and get recharged. I haven't given up the thought of managing again."[47]

McKeon held the adviser's post for five years. The Marlins struggled early in the 2011 season and Edwin Rodriguez resigned as manager on June 20, after the team had lost 10 straight games and 18 of 19. McKeon was brought back as interim manager. He said, "I love doing [the managing], and I decided to come back here and give it my best shot to get this team back to respectability. That's what I aim to do."[48]

When he was hired, McKeon became the second oldest manager in major-league history, after Connie Mack, who was 87 when he managed his last game. (Mack also owned the team he managed, the Philadelphia Athletics.) McKeon was hired to finish out the season while the club searched for someone to take over when the team moved to a new ballpark in 2012. At his introductory news conference, McKeon said "I've managed since I was 14 years old. I'll probably manage until I'm 95."[49]

Under McKeon, the Marlins were 40-50. They did not make the playoffs as many had expected at the beginning of the season but they played better under his leadership. When Dusty Baker, the Reds manager, heard about McKeon's hiring, he said: "They're looking for the same magic from Jack they had before."[50]

When he came on board, McKeon shook things up with the young Marlin players. He had been in baseball for more than 40 years and was not interested in "relating" to the players. "Someone's got to come in and show them some discipline," he said. "These guys are rushed to the big leagues. They're babied all their lives. They don't know how to play the game, because of the inexperience. It's just like having kids or grandkids. There's a certain amount of discipline that's necessary."[51]

For 2012 the Marlins had a new manager, Ozzie Guillen. McKeon stepped aside and returned to his retired life in North Carolina. "My family, I think I owe it to them to be with them a little bit," he said. "They were very gracious to let me come down this time."[52]

When he retired, McKeon had won more than 1,000 games as both a minor-league and major-league manager. His record in the minor leagues was 1151-1152 and in the major leagues it was 1050-990. As of 2018 he was the only manager in Organized Baseball to accomplish this feat.

As of 2018 McKeon still lived in Elon, North Carolina, with his wife, Carol. Their three children, Kasey, Kelly, and Kristi, have all been involved in baseball. Kasey was a former minor-league player in the Detroit Tigers system. He later became a scout with several major-league teams and as of 2018 was the director of player development for the Washington Nationals. As a scout for the Padres, Kelly signed major leaguer Greg Booker, who married his sister, Kristi. Jack's grandson Kellan scouts for the Phillies. Two other grandsons, Avery and Zach Booker, were assistant coaches for the Greensboro College baseball team.

Throughout his playing days, McKeon never lost his Roman Catholic faith. When he was playing or managing, he attended Mass daily. He credited his success to his faith in many ways. When he was fired by the Reds in 1999, he prayed to St. Therese of Lisieux. "She's the prodigy of miracles, and I needed a miracle," McKeon said. "I don't know God's plan but I don't think my career has been fulfilled. And then came the Marlins."[53]

McKeon said in an interview with the author that he would never stop loving the game. He still "like[s] how it's a kid's game. Grown men play it, but when you really look at it, for what it is, it's a bunch of fun."[54] He said he watched baseball as much as possible and "manages every game that I see."[55]

If Trader Jack has his way, he may still make it back into baseball someday. He just trusts that God will show him his plan. McKeon said it best: "Instead of taking things so seriously, worrying and fearing failure, you simply do what you can, be generous with those around you, and let God take care of everything else."[56]

## SOURCES

In addition to the sources cited in the Notes, the author also used the Baseball-Reference.com and Retrosheet.org websites for box-score, player, team, and season pages, pitching and batting game logs, and other pertinent material.

## NOTES

1  John Gearan, "Give Another Hoiah – The Tales of Trader Jack," *Holy Cross College Magazine*, Spring 2012.

2  Ibid.

3  Ibid.

4  Jack McKeon, personal interview, February 26, 2018. (McKeon interview).

5  Paul Post, "McKeon Aiming to Be MLB's Oldest Skipper," MLB.com, February 5, 2015.

6  Ibid.

7  McKeon interview.

8  Ibid.

9  Stephen Schramm, "Jack McKeon's Long Career in Baseball Began in Fayetteville," *Fayetteville* (North Carolina) *Observer*, June 11, 2016.

10  McKeon interview.

11  Sheryl Peterson, *The Story of the Florida Marlins* (Mankato, Minnesota: Creative Education, 2008), 47.

12  Rich Kaipust, "Jack McKeon Got on Track in Omaha," *Omaha World-Herald*, April 21, 2014.

13  Ibid.

14  McKeon interview.

15  "Jack McKeon Interview: Trader Jack," interview by Mitch Pittman, Elon College, 2008, video.

16  "Royals Fire McKeon, Hire Angels' Herzog," *Milwaukee Sentinel*, July 25, 1975.

17  "Winkles Takes Over as Oakland Skipper; McKeon Gets Axe," *Gadsden* (Alabama) *Times*, June 11, 1977.

18  David Schoenfield, "The Strange Saga of the 1978 Oakland A's," ESPN.com, May 6, 2014.

19  McKeon interview.

20  Ibid.

21  Ibid.

22  Ibid.

23  Irv Moss, "Colorado Classics: Jack McKeon, Former Denver Bears Manager," *Denver Post*, April 22, 2011.

24  Kirk Kenney, *100 Things Padres Fans Should Know & Do Before They Die* (Chicago: Triumph Books, 2016).

25  Bill Center, "Trader Jack Is 14th member of Padres' HOF," MLB.com, March 29, 2017.

26  Ibid.

27  Ibid.

28  Joseph Durso, "Baseball's Leading Matchmaker," *New York Times*, December 7, 1988.

29  Ibid.

30  Kenney.

31  Murray Chass, "McKeon Faces Problem: To Manage or Be General Manager," *New York Times*, August 28, 1988.

32  McKeon interview.

33  Ibid.

34  Murray Chass, "McKeon Faces Problem."

35  Murray Chass, "Reds Change Approach: Knight Out, McKeon In," *New York Times*, July 26, 1988.

36  Ibid.

37  Joe Kay, "Cincinnati Reds Fire Manager Jack McKeon," ABC News.com, October 2, 2000.

38  Roger Angell, "Gone South," *New Yorker*, November 24, 2003.

39  "Jack McKeon Interview: Trader Jack," interview by Mitch Pittman, Elon College, 2008, video.

40  Hal Bodley, "On Baseball," *USA Today*, October 26, 2003.

41  Ibid.

42  McKeon interview.

43  Hal Bodley, "On Baseball."

44  Ibid.

45  William C. Rhoden, "McKeon Takes His Act on the Road, and Wins," *New York Times*, October 19, 2003.

46  "McKeon Resigns as Florida Manager," *Seattle Times*, October 3, 2005.

47  Ibid.

48  Mike DiGiovanna, "Florida Marlins' Rehiring of 80-Year-Old Jack Mckeon as Manager Is One for the Ages," *Los Angeles Times*, June 20, 2011.

49  "Marlins Hire 80-Year-Old Jack McKeon," ESPN.com, June 21, 2011.

50  Ibid.

51  Dave Sheinin, "At 80 Years of Age, Marlins' Jack Mckeon Still Has His Fastball," *Washington Post*, July 27, 2011.

52  Al Yellon, "'Trader Jack' McKeon Says He's Retiring," SB Nation.com, September 26, 2011.

53  Richard Sandomir, "A Career Sustained by Unwavering Faith, *New York Times*, August 2, 2011.

54  Trent Beattie, "Oldest Manager to Win World Series Still Enjoys Kid's Game," *National Catholic Register*, October 1, 2012.

55  McKeon interview.

56  Beattie.

# EDUARDO ORTEGA:

## THE PADRES' SPANISH-LANGUAGE VOZ

### BY JORGE IBER

At the start of the 2018 season, Latinos comprised slightly less than one-third of major-league rosters and about one-half of those in minor-league baseball. As a result, the sport is seeking diligently to expand its base of *fanaticos* of this background. An example of such efforts was MLB's *Ponle Acento* program from 2016, which saw the placement of tildes on jerseys, so that surnames would appear correctly in Spanish. Other efforts include broadcasting games in that language. As of 2018, 22 of the 30 major-league teams offered such broadcasts. Prior to the efforts of pioneers such as Buck Canel, Felo Ramírez, and the arrival of the Dodgers in Los Angeles (with the labors of René Cardenas and Jaime Jarrín), the "Spanish-speaking fans in the United States had no avenues for listening to any games in their native tongue."[1] Things have changed dramatically as the major leagues moved into markets with large Latino constituencies, and other markets witnessed the rise of the Spanish-speaking demographic.[2] One of the longest running of the *voces* servicing these constituents is that of Eduardo Ortega. His story provides not just a sense of the international appeal of baseball, but also the power of sport to unite individuals of differing backgrounds.

Ortega's path to the booth began in the late 1960s. He was born on June 5, 1963, and raised in the *Colonia Juárez* neighborhood of Tijuana. Like many other Mexican youths, he loved to play baseball, but said, "I was so bad. They sent me to right field, but I was always benched."[3] Ultimately, he would scamper up a tree and "broadcast" the action before him, imitating the stylings of Mario Thomas Zapiáin (known as "Don Mario"), the first Spanish-language voice of the Padres (starting when the team became a major-league franchise in 1969), and his sidekick, Gustavo López Moreno. He quickly earned a local reputation for his aptitude in describing athletic contests.

Ortega's capabilities also came to the attention of one of his teachers, Juan Manuel Martínez- Pérez, who provided encouragement and even helped him get his first job: serving as master of ceremonies at local graduations (Eduardo was 12 at the time). In turn, this led to a plethora of narrating opportunities: boxing matches, bullfights, beer commercials, and serving as a disc jockey at a local radio station. He even attained another pinnacle of Mexican broadcasting: working as an announcer for *lucha libre* contests alongside Juan Manuel Martínez. Still, his dreams of broadcasting baseball were at the forefront of his mind. Ultimately, Ortega moved on to broadcast both winter (with the Tijuana *Potros*) and summer league contests (with the Torreón *Algodoneros*) in México.[4]

While his dulcet tones graced the airwaves throughout his teen years and early 20s, there was one person, his biggest fan, who could not hear any of it: his beloved mother, Amparo Díaz. Eduardo's parents divorced when he was 3, and his mother, who had been deaf since she was 14, had to work diligently to support her family. The many jobs Eduardo held in his early career helped, and his mother grew to love baseball because of her son's passion for the sport. In an interview with Curt Smith for the book *A Talk in the Park*, Ortega recalled how his mother reacted to his first appearance on the radio. "Your brothers tell me there was a beautiful voice on the radio. … Remember, while you may not be before me, I will always listen with my heart."[5] Amparo Díaz died during the offseason of 2011. "It gets me sentimental … because I took inspiration from her. … I wanted to make her proud," Ortega said.[6]

The voice of Don Mario was not the only connection between Eduardo and the Padres. One of the most important memories of his youth took place in the mid-1970s when Ortega got the opportunity to attend a home game courtesy of another San Diego legend. He recalled the importance of the Dave Winfield Pavilion and how he appreciated all that the player did to assist disadvantaged youths on both sides of the border. When, in 1995, the broadcaster (then working the World Series for the CBS Americas Radio Network) had an opportunity to visit with the Hall of Famer, he thanked Winfield for using his wealth and the sport of baseball to reach out to the needy above and below the international divide. "I just wanted to tell you, on behalf of my family, thank you very much. You motivated me to pursue a life in baseball."[7] A friendship developed between the two, and when Winfield was inducted into the Hall of Fame in 2001, he asked Ortega to be in attendance at Cooperstown.

After several years of success in Mexico, Ortega, through the efforts of Gustavo López Moreno, was offered his dream job in 1986: sitting in the booth next to the legendary Spanish-language voice of the Padres franchise. Fulfilling a childhood flight of the imagination, Ortega shared the microphone next to his idol for the final 11 years of Don Mario's career, through 1997. Don Mario died in 2009.

Curt Smith, a noted historian of baseball broadcasting, argues that "Hispanic broadcasters call baseball in a lively way," which he refers to as a "*mi casa es su casa*" style that involves great storytelling and a great deal of emotion.[8] This is certainly true for Eduardo Ortega's broadcasts. One of the stories Ortega related to Smith of such differences occurred during a spring-training game with the Brewers in Chandler, Arizona. The attendance at the contest was minuscule, and Ortega began to count up the balls and strikes in "our festive Latin style." Not surprisingly, not everyone appreciated his narrative methodology. Several retirees seated in the stands in front of Ortega stared intently and asked, "Who the heck are you and what are you doing here?" "By game's end, no one was sitting directly in front of us, moving to different sections to get away. I haven't taken it personally," Ortega recalled.[9]

Over the past 30-plus years, Eduardo Ortega has become the *voz* of the Padres for the local Latino community, as well as for fans in Mexico. Not only does he work for the franchise, he also, since 1993, has broadcast games in Spanish for *ESPN Deportes* radio and other entities. Among these have been World Series, All-Star Games, and World Baseball Classic contests. He is also active as a volunteer on both sides of international divide: raising funds for scholarships, leading toy drives, and being a presence in the wider communities and classrooms. His professionalism also led to his nomination for the most important recognition in baseball broadcasting, the Ford C. Frick Award. Although he did not receive this honor in 2013, no less of a legend than the late Dick Enberg (himself a Frick winner in 2015) proclaimed, "Oh, he's going to be in the Hall of Fame one day. He's that good."[10]

Even more significant than his accomplishments with the Padres are Ortega's efforts to connect the Latino community with the broader society of the United States; and baseball is a perfect mechanism with which to accomplish this. He is a consummate professional, and always argues that the presence of the Spanish-surnamed in our nation is a promising development. Not only are there more Latinos than ever on the field, but also by introducing these players to a national audience, broadcasters such as Ortega help to unite our nation's different groups through our mutual love for the sport. Here, he follows in the grand tradition of his other idols: Canel, Ramírez, and Jarrín.

*Tito Avila (left) inducts Eduardo Ortega into the Hispanic Heritage Baseball Museum Hall of Fame, June 28, 2015.*

Eduardo Ortega is a shining example of the power of baseball to unite individuals of various backgrounds through a passion for the "national pastime."

# NOTES

1    Samuel O. Regalado, "'Dodgers *Beisbol* is on the Air: The Development and Impact of the Dodgers Spanish-Language Broadcasts,1958-1994," *California History*, Vol 74, No. 3 (Fall 1995): 280-289. Quote on pages 283-284.

2    For a discussion on this trend, see Jorge Encinas, "How Latino Players Are Helping Major League Baseball Learn Spanish," NPR.org, March 26, 2017, npr. org/sections/codeswitch/2017/03/26/519676864/how-major-league-baseball-came-to-officially-speak-spanish; Jerry Milani, "On the Airwaves and Online, Spanish Language Baseball Business Grows," *Portada*, March 27, 2018, portada-online. com/2018/03/27/on-the-airwaves-and-online-spanish-language-baseball-business-grows/; and Mike Elk and Karina Moreno, "Baseball, Latino America's Pastime, Faces New Challenges in Age of Trump," *The Guardian*, March 29, 2018, theguardian.com/sport/2018/mar/29/baseball-latino-trump-mlb.

3    Bryce Miller, "Padres' Eduardo Ortega Is a Spanish-Language Star," *San Diego Union Tribune*, March 27, 2016, sandiegouniontribune.com/sports/padres/sdut-eduardo-ortega-baseballs-boy-in-a-tree-2016mar27-story.html

4    Author interview with Eduardo Ortega, April 26, 2018.

5    Curt Smith, *A Talk in the Park: Nine Decades of Baseball Tales from the Broadcast Booth* (Washington: Potomac Books, 2011), 230-231.

6    Miller. See also Matt Calkins, "The Padres' Hall of Fame Nominee You Might Not Know," *San Diego Union Tribune*, October 11, 2013, sandiegouniontribune. com/sports/padres/sdut-padres-eduardo-ortega-calkins-2013oct11-story.html.

7    *A Talk in the Park*, 226.

8    Author interview with Curt Smith on March 16, 2018.

9    *A Talk in the Park*, 227.

10   Miller. See also Alexandra Mendoza, "Eduardo Ortega: 30 Anos Como La Voz de los Padres," *San Diego Union Tribune*, April 9, 2016, sandiegouniontribune.com/ hoy-san-diego/sdhoy-eduardo-ortega-30-anos-como-voz-de-los-padres-2016apr09-story.html.

# ELTEN SCHILLER

## BY TOM LARWIN

*Schiller on the field at Omaha Municipal Stadium
(later renamed Johnny Rosenblatt Stadium). (July 1961)*

"Combining a career since 1947 in professional baseball with an interest in stamps since age ten has brought a lifetime of enjoyment. To be able to combine these two childhood interests into business and pleasure in adulthood has been my good fortune."[1] Those were Elten Schiller's words penned in a 1982 book he authored about "baseball … stamps … autographs."

By the time he retired from the San Diego Padres in 1988, Schiller's professional career as a baseball executive spanned 42 years, 26 of them with the Dodgers organization and his last 16 with the Padres.

Along the way Schiller built a reputation as a shrewd baseball business executive. He was often referred to as an "innovator," and sometimes with additional adjectives, such as "prolific innovator" or "productive innovator." Other descriptions included being an "operational genius," being an "astute baseball man," and the best man if you wanted to learn "the business of baseball." There was more to Schiller than the business side: He was also described as being a "modest man," a "caring executive," and someone who "lives, breathes, and sells baseball."

In terms of miles, Schiller's path to San Diego, was a long one. It started in Germany, where he was born. His parents, Wilhelm Schittek and Freda Bertsch Schwittay, were also born in Germany. They married on September 30, 1922. When Elten Frederick Schittek was born in Buer (Gelsenkirchen) on October 17, 1923, the family lived in a small village outside of the city of Essen in northwestern Germany.[2] He was the second child for the Schitteks, with Helene having been born in 1921. In addition, Elten had an older half-brother, Erich Bertsch, living with the family. (He was born in 1915.)

Soon after Elten's birth the Schittek family readied for a move across the Atlantic to the United States. Elten's father, Wilhelm, had gone alone to the U.S. and stayed with an uncle living in the Willow Grove mining community, just outside of Neffs, Ohio, a small village along the Ohio-West Virginia border near Wheeling, West Virginia. He found Willow Grove to his liking,

*Schiller with wife Valorie in front of the Los Angeles Dodgers' private team plane in Albuquerque, New Mexico. (June 1966)*

got himself a job at the nearby Willow Grove coal mine and that's where the family decided to settle. On November 1, 1924, mother Freda and the three children arrived on the S.S. Veenden at Ellis Island and were soon on their way to Willow Grove.

Over the next 16 years the Schittek family gradually expanded with three sisters joining Elten, Helene, and Erich: Gertrude (born in 1926), Irene (1930), and Darlene (1940).

In April 1939 Elten's father, Wilhelm, became a naturalized US citizen and at the same time the family changed their last name from Schittek to Schiller. Soon after, in March 1940, disaster struck the family, as Elten's father was one of 72 men killed in the Willow Grove coal-mine explosion, one of the deadliest mine accidents in US history.

Elten lived in Willow Grove through his teen years, graduating from Bellaire (Ohio) High School in June 1941.

After graduation Schiller decided to join his sister Helene in Canton, Ohio, where he found work as a machinery operator. While there was not much that was notable about his job, he did have an experience that remained with him for the rest of his life: An industrial accident caused the loss of the first two digits of his left ring finger.

The accident didn't prevent Schiller from joining the US Navy in February 1943. In 1944 Yeoman Second Class Schiller was assigned to Bougainville in the Solomon Islands. However, before he could make the transfer, the ship Schiller was assigned to was sunk in combat off Bougainville. Instead, according to Elten's daughter, Linda, his shorthand and typing skills learned in high school resulted in his being assigned to the Navy's legal department in Guadalcanal and he never saw war action.[3]

The war over, Schiller in late 1945 was stationed in Corpus Christi, Texas. There he met a 27-year-old WAVE,[4] Valorie Anne Gorz. Shortly after being mustered out of the Navy Elten and

Valorie were married in her hometown of St. Paul, Minnesota, on February 23, 1946.

The Schillers proceeded to establish roots in St. Paul and Elten was employed with the Veterans Administration helping vets get work, and also looking for a job for himself. One notice got his attention, a part-time position with the St. Paul Saints of the Triple-A American Association that was part of the Dodgers organization. This one notice he kept for himself, a decision that launched his career in professional baseball.[5]

Schiller remained with the Saints for 13 years, from his entry position in 1947 through 1960. He worked his way up to being the assistant to the president/general manager, Mel Jones.

During this period in St. Paul, Valorie and Elten had three children, Linda Susan (born in 1950), Jeffrey Alan (1954), and Carol Lynn (1955).

In November 1960 it was confirmed that the American League's Washington Senators would be moving to Minneapolis-St. Paul. The team would be known as the Minnesota Twins and begin play in the 1961 season.

Major-league baseball's decision to expand to the Twin Cities prompted the Dodgers to move their Triple-A franchise from St. Paul to Omaha, Nebraska. The Dodgers offered Jones and Schiller the opportunity to move with the team. Schiller accepted it. Jones declined, and the Dodgers made Schiller the new president and general manager.

Omaha had been a St. Louis Cardinals farm team since 1947. In early 1960 the Cardinals pulled up stakes and Omaha was left without a team in Organized Baseball for the year. Schiller was coming into a dormant baseball community and had only three months to launch and promote the new team, the Omaha Dodgers. A March article in *The Sporting News* noted Schiller's challenge and reported that he "plunged into the assignment with enthusiasm" and 12-hour and longer workdays were common.[6]

The 1961 season was not a very good one. Omaha finished with a record of 62-87 and in last place, 23½ games out of first.

Yet, in December 1961 Schiller was surprised to learn that he was selected to receive an award from *The Sporting News* as Minor League Executive of the Year (for the higher classifications). Along with Roger Maris, Warren Spahn, and Ralph Houk, Schiller's face was one of eight on the front page of the paper's January 3, 1962, issue.[7] The award touted Schiller's ability to "rebuild interest" in Omaha after the city lost its team the year before, and doing so with "no chance to do early spade work."[8]

The award was an early sign of what would become a trademark of Schiller: his ability to promote fan interest.

The 1962 season turned out to be a better one with the team finishing in second place at 79-68. Given the positive team performance and the Dodgers' apparent interest in being in Omaha it seemed that the Omaha Dodgers would be around for more seasons to come. However, the American Association disbanded after the 1962 season and for 1963 four of its six teams were folded into the two remaining Triple-A leagues, the Pacific Coast League and the International League. Since the Dodgers already had a PCL team in Spokane, Omaha again ended up without a team in Organized Baseball.

Schiller fared better. In November 1962 Dodgers' executive vice president Buzzie Bavasi confirmed that the Albuquerque Dukes of the Double-A Texas League would become a Dodgers farm team, and that Schiller would be the general manager.[9] It was to be a second baseball move for the Schiller family after less than two years in Omaha. The 1963 season was the Dukes' second in the Texas League. Schiller quickly got a season-ticket sales drive underway.

An April 1963 article in the *Albuquerque Journal* spotlighted Schiller's promotional ability. It said, "Schiller is a shrewd one when it comes to tickling the fancy of the fan." The article listed nine promotions, one of which was "Pony nights … the most popular thing to hit Albuquerque since the first wagon train."[10]

The 1963 Dukes finished 67-73, in fifth place, 12 games out of first. In 1964 they improved to 75-65 and they finished in third place.

In November 1964 Peter Bavasi joined Schiller's management team. Bavasi was barely out of college and hoping to get an apprentice job in baseball when his father, Buzzie, now the Dodgers' general manager, called him and asked, "How fast can you get to Albuquerque? If you want to learn the business of baseball, the best man in all of baseball to teach you is Elten Schiller. He'll be your boss at Albuquerque. Just keep your eyes and ears open and your mouth shut, and you might learn something."[11]

"From the first day, I started my real education," Bavasi said recently. "They didn't teach you how to sell scoreboard ads in college, nor how to stretch the mustard at the concessions stands (cut it with white vinegar), or how to talk the city public-works department out of gallons of green and yellow pavement striping paint so we could paint the old ballpark. … He was the best professor I'd ever had."[12]

As January 1965 arrived, Schiller was busy introducing some new promotions. First, he decided to change the team's nickname from Dukes to Dodgers. He said it would better relate its affiliation to the parent club and provide Albuquerque more

publicity: "People don't know if the Albuquerque Dukes are a band or a lumber company or what we are."[13]

The other idea was the formation of an Albuquerque Dodgers Booster Club, called the Dukes. The Boosters, comprising 60 members who were prominent businessmen, had a preseason ticket drive with a goal of selling $60,000 worth. As an incentive, Schiller arranged for the group to be flown to a game at Dodger Stadium by the Dodgers' team plane.[14]

During his time in Albuquerque, Schiller also tinkered with other ideas like speeding of play. He was an advocate of using a clock as early as 1962; he felt clocks would speed up the tempo of the game by putting players into a "speed-up" frame of mind.[15] Slow play was being noted as one of the causes for poor baseball attendance in both the major and minor leagues. Schiller was still advocating a speedier game in 1966 when he offered several more ideas, among them reducing the number of balls for a walk to three and the number of strikes for a strikeout to two, and allowing the pitcher to wave a batter to first for an intentional walk instead of making the pitches.[16] Not all of Schiller's ideas caught on but by 2017 clocks had been introduced in major-league games, and the intentional-walk rule no longer requires pitches.

After four years in Albuquerque, the family moved again when Schiller became general manager of the Triple-A Spokane Indians (PCL). Schiller stayed in Spokane for five seasons, 1967-1971, and the team had a successful run with three first-place finishes.

In September 1971 the Dodgers decided to move the Spokane club to Albuquerque.[17] Schiller agreed to move back to Albuquerque to take over the management of the Albuquerque team, which would move up from Double A to Triple A and once again be called the Dukes.

While getting resettled in Albuquerque, Schiller was offered a job with the San Diego Padres by his former boss, Buzzie Bavasi.

*Los Angeles Dodgers' farm director, Fresco Thompson (left) with Schiller in Albuquerque. (1966)*

Bavasi had left the Dodgers in 1968 to join the new National League franchise in San Diego as both a part-owner and top executive with the team. In its first three years the Padres had won only 36 percent of its games, averaging 59 wins and 103 losses. Attendance averaged slightly over 7,000, and had fallen in season three (1971) by 15 percent.

By 1971 Peter Bavasi had joined his father and was the Padres' head of minor-league operations. In a 2018 email he wrote that the team was in real bad financial, artistic, and management shape and the prospects weren't very bright for recovery anytime soon. "Buzzie was very fond of Elten, and he knew how talented Elten was in every business-side operational area," Peter wrote.[18]

Within three weeks after the close of the season Buzzie had hired Schiller as the Padres' director of business operations, with jurisdiction including ticket sales and distribution, day-of-game operations, and promotions.[19]

Schiller and his family had just moved from Spokane back to their former home in Albuquerque in September –a Schiller family baseball move number four – and now, at the end of 1971, would be on the move again. The move to San Diego would be the family's fifth baseball move in a decade.

One idea Schiller implemented immediately after joining the Padres was to create a Padres Action Team, patterned after his Albuquerque booster club, the Dukes. In the San Diego version it was more a community-based group made up of Padres fans from all walks of life who volunteered to help "sell the Padres" – and, oh, by the way, sell season-ticket plans, too.

In the spring of 1973 the Padres' majority owner, C. Arnholt Smith, initiated efforts to sell the team. In May Joseph Danzansky, who owned several grocery stores in the Washington, D.C., area, agreed to purchase the Padres for $12 million. It was also understood that Danzansky would move the team from San Diego to Washington for the 1974 season. The sale and relocation of the Padres was approved by the other 11 National League owners in December 1973. Things had progressed so far that Danzansky was touting Frank Robinson to manage of the team, and the team was scheduled to open the season at RFK Stadium against the Philadelphia Phillies on April 4, 1974.[20]

Jeff Schiller indicated that the family was ready for baseball move number six, from San Diego to Washington, and that his father's office files were packed and Allied Van Lines had been scheduled for pickup.[21] However, the City of San Diego threatened an $84 million lawsuit against Smith for breaking the lease on San Diego Stadium. In response, Smith canceled the deal and began seeking another suitor. By the end of January 1974, a sales agreement was finalized with Ray Kroc, head of the McDonald's empire, and the team would stay in San Diego.

And the Schiller family would remain in San Diego.

In coming to San Diego, Schiller's challenge with the Padres was daunting. When he came aboard in late 1971, his main task was to build fan interest in an expansion team that was off to a poor start during its first three years. San Diego was one of major-league baseball's smallest population markets. Average game attendance those three years, at about 7,000, was less than half of major-league average game attendance.

By the end of the 1976 season average game attendance had increased to about 18,000, a 180 percent increase over 1971. That five-year attendance growth, coming despite the obstacles faced with continued sub-.500 seasons, represented a significant and positive turnaround in fan interest. Factors included adding some new exciting players, like future Hall of Famers Willie McCovey and Dave Winfield and pitcher Randy Jones. Also, Kroc's arrival on the scene in early 1974 with Schiller in charge of business operations was seemingly paying off.

Buzzie Bavasi resigned as Padres' president in September 1977 and within three days owner Ray Kroc announced a new management team that included the promotion of Schiller to vice president and business manager.[22]

As 1978 rolled around Schiller was optimistic more gains were ahead. "The interest in the team is very encouraging," he said. "… Once we become a contender we'll have no problem drawing two million fans a season."[23]

The 1978 All-Star Game was scheduled for San Diego. Schiller came up with an idea that would invite more San Diego fans to experience the thrills associated with the event. On his initiative, for the first time the All-Stars Monday batting-practice sessions would be opened to the public.[24] Fan interest was beyond expectations: 15,000 were expected but the team stopped counting when the turnstiles reached 30,000.[25] Since then the Monday All-Star batting practice sessions have become a popular and integral part of the two-day event.

In 1982 Schiller was promoted to the Padres' senior vice president/business operations, which remained his title until he retired in 1988.

A colleague who got to know Elten well was Andy Strasberg, a former Padres executive who worked under Schiller's direction for 13 years. Strasberg felt that Schiller instilled a professional culture to the office along with a deep understanding of the business of baseball resulting from his extensive minor-league experience. "He was especially great at giving responsibility and authority to his employees," Strasberg said.[26]

Strasberg cited examples of practices begun by Schiller, among them computerized ticketing systems: One reduced "deadwood" ticket printing that saved the team money by reducing the number of tickets printed to be consistent with expected game attendance. In another, called Teleseat, the Padres partnered with local businesses to let fans purchase game tickets with identical seat selection as available at the ballpark ticket windows.[27]

There was another important side to Schiller's interest in baseball, and it related to postage stamps and autographs.

From childhood on, Schiller had an interest in stamp collecting. This hobby, together with his career in baseball, spurred him to develop a specialty collection of stamps and envelope covers with baseball-themed art. In 1978 he expanded his collecting focus to include autographs from Hall of Famers and record-breaking stars. His focus was on two baseball-related stamps in particular, one issued on June 12, 1939, to commemorate the dedication of the National Baseball Hall of Fame in Cooperstown, New York, and one issued on September 24, 1969, to commemorate the 100th anniversary of professional baseball in the United States.

As he continued to develop his hobby, Schiller found that there were more than 1,000 baseball-motif covers and cachets. His collection was considered to be the largest in the world of stamped baseball covers. Discovering that no record was kept of what had been produced, Schiller wrote a book on the subject, *Baseball ... Stamps ... Autographs*, published in 1982.

The book focused on a specialty, a hobby. The publisher, George Hentzell, characterized the book in his foreword as follows: "There are books that are published for profit, and there are those which are published because their contents insist on being preserved for prosperity. This is one of the latter."[28]

When Schiller retired from the Padres in 1988, his baseball friends and colleagues saluted him with a couple of retirement parties, one of which was a surprise put on by Padres management and office personnel at Jack Murphy Stadium. While the party was a surprise, perhaps an even bigger one turned out to be a gift – a trip to Germany courtesy of the Action Team and Padres' President Ballard Smith. The trip allowed Elten and Valorie to visit northwestern Germany, where he had been born 65 years before but to which he had never been back.

In August 1997, at age 80, Valorie died away in San Diego. The Schillers had been married 51 years.

Even during retirement, baseball was never too far from Schiller's mind as evidenced in 2005-2006 when he was given a part-time assignment by his former assistant, Peter Bavasi. Peter and brother Bob owned a summer college-league team, the Yuba-Sutter Gold Sox, and Schiller was brought in as a senior adviser.[29]

Schiller died in his San Diego home on March 10, 2012, at the age of 88. The cause of death was cardiac arrhythmia. The ashes of both Elten and Valorie, both Navy veterans, were scattered at sea by the Navy. Surviving the Schillers were their three children, Linda Barclay of Nipomo, California, Jeffrey Schiller of San Diego, and Carol Lewis of Austin, Texas; and two grandsons.

Words of friends and baseball colleagues describe Schiller in various ways. "Elten Schiller was an innovator in the business of baseball and was sensitive to the common fan concerns and desires," his obituary in the *San Diego Union-Tribune* wrote of him. "He loved baseball and it was his life's passion. He was often quoted as saying, 'I had the best job in the world for over 40 years.'"[30]

Peter Bavasi well-summarized Elten Schiller as a baseball man:

He taught me everything I know about the business side of the baseball business. Elten was among baseball's most prolific innovators. He was such a modest man that you might not know it was Elten who invented bat day (via his broken bat day concept), pioneered computerized ticketing, created a series of All-Star Game promotions, launched the idea of sponsored giveaways, and organized the early mathematical principles of schedule-making.[31]

## SOURCES

In addition to the sources cited in the Notes, the author consulted Baseball-Reference.com, and Retrosheet.org.

## NOTES

1      Elten F. Schiller, "Introduction," *Baseball ... Stamps ... Autographs* (San Diego: Hentzell Publications, 1982), vii.

2      Schiller's birth name was Eitel. He never possessed a birth certificate; however, the name listed on the ship's manifest for his voyage to the U.S. in 1924 lists his name as Eitel, and an affidavit from April 15, 1942, confirmed his name as Eitel Frederick, as obtained from a "German Family Book." The 1940 US Census has his name listed as Alton.

3      Caroline Dipping, "Elten Schiller, Longtime Padres Senior VP, Was an Innovator," *San Diego Union-Tribune*, April 9, 2012.

4      This is an acronym for Women Accepted for Volunteer Emergency Service, which was the women's branch of the United States Naval Reserve.

5      Author interview of Jeff Schiller, January 9, 2018.

6      Bob Williams, "A.A. Return Welcomed by Omaha Fans," *The Sporting News*, March 8, 1961: 18.

7      "No.1 Men of the Year," *The Sporting News*, January 3, 1962: 1.

8    C.C. Johnson Spink, "Yanks Cop Trio of 'Bible' Prizes," *The Sporting News*, January 3, 1962: 14.

9    Carlos Salazar, "Albuquerque New Farm Club in Dodgers' Westward Move," *The Sporting News*, November 24, 1962: 9.

10   LeRoy Bearman, "Dukes Fans Will Get Specials as Well as Baseball This Year," *Albuquerque Journal*, April 21, 1963: 35.

11   Peter Bavasi, email to author, January 22, 2018.

12   Peter Bavasi, email to author, February 3, 2018.

13   LeRoy Bearman, "Albuquerque Who? Dodgers! No, No, the Baseball Team!" *Albuquerque Journal*, January 17, 1965: 34.

14   "60 City Businessmen Planning Ticket Drive," *Albuquerque Journal*, January 16, 1965: 20.

15   "Texas League May Be First to Use 20-Second Time Clock," *Albuquerque Journal*, November 30, 1962: 45.

16   LeRoy Bearman, "Baseball Anthem Would Change if Schiller Has His Way," *Albuquerque Journal*, July 1, 1966: 49.

17   "Albuquerque Is Chosen as New Coast Farm Team," *Berkshire Eagle* (Pittsfield, Massachusetts), October 13, 1971.

18   Peter Bavasi email, February 3, 2018.

19   Paul Cour, "Padres' Front Office Gets New Look," *The Sporting News*, November 13, 1971: 49.

20   Jake Russell, "San Diego Padres Were Once So Close to Moving to D.C. They Had Uniforms and Everything," DC Sports Blog, *Washington Post*, June 16, 2016. washingtonpost.com/news/dc-sports-bog/wp/2016/06/16/the-time-the-san-diego-padres-were-this-close-to-moving-to-d-c/?noredirect=on&utm_term=.472e8dcfa119

21   Jeff Schiller interview.

22   Phil Collier, " 'I'll Be the Judge,' Declares Padre Boss Kroc," *The Sporting News*, October 15, 1977: 19.

23   Phil Collier, "It's Third Base or Else for Ivie, Kroc Asserts," *The Sporting News*, December 31, 1977: 57.

24   "Baseball Executive Information Sheet," 1978 All-Star Game.

25   Dipping, *San Diego Union-Tribune*, April 9, 2012.

26   Author interview of Andy Strasberg, January 24, 2018.

27   Ibid.

28   Schiller, "Publisher's Forward [*sic*]," *Baseball ... Stamps ... Autographs*, v.

29   Peter Bavasi, email, February 3, 2018.

30   "Schiller, Elten F.," *San Diego Union-Tribune*, March 15, 2012.

31   Peter Bavasi, email, January 29, 2018.

# KEVIN TOWERS: TOP FRIAR

## BY MARK SOUDER

Tony Gwynn is clearly Mr. Padre. Perhaps Kevin Towers should be called Top Friar.

Towers bled brown and orange. He was drafted by the San Diego Padres as a pitcher, pitched in their minor-league system for eight years, became a scout and minor-league pitching coach for the club, was promoted to director of scouting, and spent 14 years as general manager of the Padres.

During his time as GM, the Padres won the National League West four times and made their only World Series appearance. To put that into perspective, from 1969 until the 1996 season, when Towers took over, the Padres won the division once. Since 2009, when Towers left, the team (as of 2018) has not yet again appeared in the playoffs. The team's success on the field during that period was vital to San Diego voters' approval of the funds necessary to build Petco Park, which was constructed during Towers' time as GM. Many people contributed to the Padres periods of success, but Towers' record deserves Top Friar billing.

Kevin Towers began his life in professional baseball as a San Diego Padres minor-league pitcher, after being selected as the Padres' top pick in the secondary phase of the June draft.

Post-draft, Towers reported to the Walla Walla Padres, a short-season, Northwest League team for which he went 1-4 with a 4.74 ERA. He performed well enough that he was promoted to Double-A Beaumont in 1984, where he was selected to the

Kevin Towers in a parade in downtown San Diego along with his wife, Kelley.

Texas League Western Division All-Star team.[1] Having been a minor-league all-star pitcher obviously established some extra credibility as a future scout and during his time as a general manager. In 1985 he returned to Beaumont but blew out his arm. An article in the *Reno Gazette-Journal* in 1985 reported that Towers had "the same type of surgery performed on Tommy John."[2] In other words, Towers had the surgery back when Tommy John was still known as a baseball player, not a medical term.

Towers and his reconstructed arm made the Reno Padres of the California League in the spring of 1987, but he had been recast as a reliever. He had some success. In July of 1987, two years after his injury, the Reno newspaper noted: "Reno extended its winning streak to 15 games, Padres' reliever Kevin Towers extended his consecutive scoreless innings streak to 30. 'When you get in a streak like this and you're winning games, the breaks always seem to go your way,' said Towers, 3-6, who pitched the final three innings for the victory. 'When you're losing, everything seems to go against you.'"[3] In late August, after his success in Reno, Towers was promoted to the Padres' Triple-A team in Las Vegas with the intention of becoming the team's closer but he did not pitch. In 1988 he began the season as a relief pitcher for Las Vegas but on June 20, he started his first game.[4] Towers finished the year with 15 relief appearances and 12 starts. Further arm injuries effectively ended his pitching career, although he pitched 1⅔ innings in relief in one game in 1989, back in the A-level Northwest League, where he had begun.

As a player, Towers never made it to the major leagues but his steady path through the minors to Triple A, his injury and Tommy John surgery, and his transition from a starter to reliever and eventually a closer, helped him make him a better scout and at least gave him an understanding of, if not empathy for, players he was signing, promoting, or trading, and/or going through medical challenges. He had been there and done that.

Towers' time as a minor-league baseball player ended at age 27, but his career in baseball was still in its early stages. Instead of fading into baseball oblivion, spending his life talking about what might have been, Towers became an area scout for the Padres and spent summers as pitching coach for their Class-A short-season team. In 1991 the Pittsburgh Pirates hired him as a regional and national cross-checker for two years. Then, in August 1993, at the age of 32, Towers was named the director of scouting for the Padres. By 1995, he was general manager.[5]

When Towers died of anaplastic thyroid cancer in January of 2018, praise flowed from those in major-league baseball throughout the nation. Even allowing for tribute inflation, the comments were impressive. And instructive about the type of man Towers was. Those who did not know him began to grasp how he could have moved up the system so rapidly. The common element was that Towers was a gregarious people-lover, who actually cared about others.

Two examples came from the 2018 Chicago Cubs brain trust, Theo Epstein and Jed Hoyer. Epstein was a 21-year-old intern under Towers and viewed him as a mentor. Epstein described himself as just out of college, "a nobody, a faceless kid trying to be invisible and not get in the way. But there was never such a thing as a nobody to Kevin Towers – he just wasn't wired that way." Epstein was a powerless kid when he met Towers. Hoyer

was not. He replaced Towers as GM, after the Padres got rid of Towers. Yet his description sounds the same: "I took over for him and he always treated me so well. We would meet for beers or talk on the phone and it was always KT wanting to help me do a better job." [6]

Another key element of Towers' personality was his detailed memory related to baseball players. He considered himself a scout first and foremost. He liked to analyze players, draft players, and trade players. It was behind his famous nickname, "The Gunslinger." At least that was what Jeff Moorad, the man who fired him from the Padres, called Towers. Moorad was attempting to purchase the Padres on the cheap. He claimed to want to hire a GM with a more "strategic vision." Towers did not particularly take offense at the label, changing his canceled Padres email account to one with "gunslinger" in it. Towers said that when he thought of a gunslinger, "I think of a guy that shoots first, or throws the first punch, he wins the battle."[7]

It should be noted, however, that Towers did not seem to lack strategic vision. When the Padres played some games in Mexico, he showed San Diego a partial potential path to escaping San Diego's geographically constrained market within the United States. He did churn his rosters, in part because San Diego was a small-budget market, but also because of other financial pressures that forced short-term strategies. A piece here, a piece there. He may have been a gunslinger, as Moorad charged, but his lack of vision was likely (to keep the analogy) more a shortage of bullets than lack of a strategy.

Whatever other reasons demanded such an approach, the fact is also that Towers certainly loved to trade. He loved to talk. He loved the process. Towers said in 2011: "Part of making trades is about developing relationships, and you can't do that through texting."[8] Towers sought face time, phone conversations, and/or chatting at a bar.

Towers' friendships were widespread and deep. He traded players frequently with Randy Smith, the Tigers GM, who happened to be the man Towers had replaced at San Diego. He remained friends with Jed Hoyer, who had replaced him as the Padres GM. Towers was friends with Brian Cashman, who had been GM for the New York Yankees when they defeated the Padres in the 1998 World Series, and who later hired Towers as a scout for the Yankees between his GM jobs at San Diego and Arizona. He followed a "build bridges, don't burn them" strategy. Kevin Towers made friends of many, which also proved to be useful for his career. He justified it by saying that it made him a better GM, which it likely did, but he also clearly enjoyed playing the role of a talkative riverboat gambler.

Four admittedly imperfect ways to measure the impact of a general manager are 1) drafts, 2) player development, 3) trades, and 4) the team's record (how the pieces come together).

Towers' record in trades was pretty much reflected his own definition of a gunslinger: Fire first, fire often, and keep firing. He made some bad trades, many trades that added nothing to either team, and enough good ones at the right time to win four division titles. He didn't get a lot of cash to work with, so trading was a critical part to winning those titles.

San Diego drafts were not a major part of the team's success during the Towers era. Their boom/bust records (division championships but also seasons trailing by 20 to 36 games) at least sometimes led to top draft choices. In 1999 San Diego had six first-round draft choices, choosing three high schoolers and three college players. Vince Faison, the top Padres' choice at number 20, did make Triple A for 10 games in 2004 before falling back. That was the high point of the group. But the 15th-round choice, number 472, in 1999 proved to be an essential Padres piece: Jake Peavy.

Khalil Greene, the 2002 Padres' top pick, was a rookie All-Star in 2004. He was the best number-one pick the team had in the Towers era. Some draft choices were eventually traded, like 2001 fourth-round choice Josh Barfield, who had one good year, then was traded for Kevin Kouzmanoff, a useful puzzle piece. Kouzmanoff played with San Diego from 2007 to 2009, hitting 59 home runs, driving in 246 runs, and setting a National League single-season fielding percentage record for third basemen.

In other words, Towers' 25 first-round choices were largely a bust, and even among the later choices, there were no other Peavys and Greenes, nor even many tradeable Barfields. The combination of touted draft choices who did not pan out combined with lower choices in the division-winning years contributed over time to the Padres going from a top-10 farm team to one of the lower-ranking systems over Towers' career. And, as always, money was also a factor. Potential financial bargains often influenced draft decisions, as was taking college players, whose peak potential was more visible and likely lower, but who had less risk and potentially could help the major-league team faster. The Padres could not compete for top free agents (e.g., Kevin Brown to the Dodgers), or even retain their top stars, which forced trades (e.g., Greg Vaughn to Cincinnati). At times San Diego came under intense criticism for not using revenue-sharing to boost its spending (one of the reasons Moorad did not receive Major League Baseball's approval to take control of the Padres was a fear that he would pocket it to pay off his debt).

It was Towers' constant hunting for a trade that was fundamental to his reputation. From 1995 through 2007, in only one year, according to Baseball-Reference, did San Diego not make a "significant trade." Many of the trades were similar to the March 22, 1996, trade with the Detroit Tigers: San Diego sent Raul Casanova, Melvin Nieves, and Richie Lewis to the Tigers for Todd Steverson, Sean Bergman, and Cade Gaspar. It was a trade in which both teams hoped to find something but not a major piece. But clearly the Padres from 1995 to 1997 were preparing to make a major push. That year they won the West after finishing an average of 17 games out of first since 1984. Those teams became the core of the 1998 team, the only Padres team to go to the World Series.

In 1995 Towers acquired first baseman Wally Joyner in a trade with the Kansas City Royals. Free agent Fernando Valenzuela, thought to be finished and not highly sought after, gave the Padres two decent years. Overlooked Bob Tewksbury went 10-10 in 1996, a typical supplemental piece signed by GM Towers. Yet another "former great," Rickey Henderson, was signed, and he "contributed 37 stolen bases, a .410 on-base percentage, and a positive, fun-loving influence in the clubhouse," according to Bill Swank and Bob Chandler.[9]

The Milwaukee Brewers couldn't sign slugger Greg Vaughn, but the Padres ownership freed up funds to sign him for two years during their push for Petco funding. He did not contribute much in the last half of 1996 or in 1997, but in 1998 he jumped to 50 home runs, trailing Mark McGwire and Sammy Sosa in their epic steroids-aided home-run derby slug-off. Towers also traded for key pieces Sterling Hitchcock and Quilvio Veras. Hitchcock had a 1.23 ERA in the 1998 postseason, and was MVP in the Championship Series with the Braves. Veras offered valuable speed to the lineup. In the winter of 1997, Towers traded Derrek Lee and two others to get pitching ace Kevin Brown. During his one World Series year with the Padres, Brown went 18-7 with a 2.38 ERA and 257 strikeouts.

Many of the key anchors of the 1996 and 1998 teams were added by previous GM Randy Smith. Hall of Fame relief pitcher Trevor Hoffman had been picked up in the Gary Sheffield trade. Pitcher Andy Ashby came in another trade by Smith. The big trade was with the Houston Astros on December 28, 1994. GM Smith's father, Tal Smith, was president of the Houston Astros. When the new ownership of the Padres gave Randy Smith the green light to add payroll, the teams completed a 12-player trade. The key Padres pieces were Ken Caminiti and Steve Finley.[10]

Randy Smith played a foundational role in constructing the greatest teams in San Diego history (i.e., best won-loss records, only National League championship, World Series appearance) with Towers adding the pieces necessary to push the team to the top. Ultimately it is the team's won-lost records that the reputations of not only the GMs but the team managers and team presidents are established. Towers is unusual in this way: He won in 1996 and 1998 with teams that had foundations built by GM Randy Smith, but the Padres again won the West in 2005 and 2006 with teams built by GM Towers. For the purely Towers' division titles, the pitching ace had been drafted by Towers (Peavy), and before the 2006 season began, he stole star first baseman Adrian Gonzalez and number-two starter Chris Young from the Texas Rangers in one of the more lopsided trades in modern baseball history.

Towers didn't just win with a small-market team: He was a San Diego guy. However, his career did not end in San Diego. He had brief advisory stints with the New York Yankees and the Cincinnati Reds, but also was back in a general manager's seat in Arizona as GM of the Diamondbacks from 2011 until he was fired in 2014. In 2011, when Towers took over, Arizona went from last place in 2010 to winning the West in 2011, going from 65 to 94 wins. The next three years, Arizona slipped backward. In 2014 they hit bottom, finishing with the worst record in either league. Towers was then fired. Among other things, he had made a series of trades that looked bad at the time but also left some assets for the Diamondbacks. His biggest contribution was to sign Paul Goldschmidt, then fewer than 200 games into his career, to a five year-contract extension in 2013.

Regardless of how one tries to explain it away, a GM does not walk in and single-handedly add nearly 30 wins. It helps to have added rookie star Goldschmidt and for Justin Upton to have a bounce-back season. Still, in the case of Towers, as GM, he won the NL West with two small-market teams. And, to note it again, no one before or since (as of 2018) has begun to match his record of success in San Diego. And he hit Padres peaks twice.

As remarkable as the Kevin Towers/San Diego story of success is, there are two very significant other baseball issues that undoubtedly greatly affected the Padres' on-field success. They are important to note because they are problems endemic to many, if not most, baseball teams.

One relates to the ownership investing in a team in order to promote public financing for construction of a new ballpark (in this case, Petco Park). The other second is steroids, an issue about which Towers broke baseball's code of silence. Neither issue was the direct responsibility of Towers, but they do, in fact, partly explain his success in San Diego whether it is comfortable to say so or not.

The ballpark issue can be more easily explained, since San Diego lost its longtime football team, the San Diego Chargers, over basically the same issue. San Diego cannot offer the same revenues to owners as teams in cities like Los Angeles and San Francisco, or in other markets with big geographic regional followings. San Diego is hemmed in, with Los Angeles to its north and sand between it and Phoenix. Like it or not, public financing of ballparks in such situations is essential or teams move away. Only pressure from the league offices can hold a team in place (e.g., the Oakland A's). The ownership of the Padres built the greatest Padres teams (1996 and 1998) leading up to the public referendum to fund Petco Park, held in November of 1998. The Padres went to the World Series in 1998, the referendum passed the next month, and then the team dumped salary and players.

This is not an opinion, but an uncomfortable fact. In 1998 the Padres went 98-64. The next year they finished 26 games out of first, the next 21, the next 13, the next 32 games behind, and in 2003 they finished 36½ games behind. Petco Park opened in April of 2004. Teams in most new ballparks (for example, Atlanta in 2018) suddenly improve dramatically. Generally, it is not just because the locker rooms are new and the stadium is attractive. The Padres cut the division leader's lead by 30½ games in 2004, and finished first in 2005 and 2006. They did not have that success in subsequent years. That success helped launch Petco, just as the success in 1998 boosted the referendum that provided the funding to build it.

The second problem – drug abuse designed to improve performance – is even more tragic. It physically damaged young people all the way down to high school as they tried to emulate their heroes and to improve their odds of success through cheating.

Ken Caminiti, once a Most Valuable Player in the NL, confessed to his drug abuse, including steroids. The Mitchell Report, by former Senator George Mitchell, provided significant evidence that ace pitcher Kevin Brown used steroids. Wally Joyner admitted using them three times in 1998. There has long been wide speculation about other Padres. To be fair, the Padres' World Series year of 1998 happened during the McGwire-Sosa home-run derby that captured America. Sluggers in both leagues, and probably key pitchers, were also juiced, so the Padres were hardly unique. While the number of players using illegal substances was possibly exaggerated by those who want to excuse themselves, including by Caminiti, they were undoubtedly a significant number. In other words, it is impossible to prove that San Diego or some teams gained an advantage with any certainty because so many stars were abusing.

Trailblazing writer Tom Verducci, along with Joe Torre, wrote an article in *Sports Illustrated* headlined "The Man Who Warned Baseball About Steriods" that focused on the 1998 season. They wrote that at the winter meeting of the Executive Board of the Major League Baseball Players Association that followed that season (1999), the player representative of the Texas Rangers, pitcher Rick Helling, stood up and told his fellow union leaders that steroid use had grown rampant and was corrupting the game. Helling said: "It's so prevalent that guys who aren't doing it are feeling the pressure to do it because they're falling behind. It's not a level playing field."[11]

The arguments about drug abuse in baseball and pressures for drug testing went back even further. In May 1985 the *Austin American-Statesman* interviewed Texas League players and staff members from the Beaumont Golden Gators, Arkansas Travelers, and San Antonio Dodgers, all of whom supported mandatory drug testing ("although they might not like it," the newspaper noted). A young Beaumont pitcher named Kevin Towers was quoted: "In the minor leagues it'll be a big scare. They'll be worried that it'll cost them their minor-league career if they get caught."[12] In other words, these issues were not suddenly new to Towers in the late 1990s.

A special report on steroids by *Sports Illustrated* in 2002 focused on Caminiti, while he was still alive and could talk about his abuse. In that story, Kevin Towers acknowledged that the Padres organization had a problem, though he focused on the minor-league players: "The word's out in our organization, but the trend we're seeing is that most of the players who tested positive were in A ball. That tells me the problem is spreading fast. I think it's prevalent in college and high school – even before we get them."[13]

Buster Olney wrote a story in *ESPN The Magazine* titled "Towers on Caminiti: 'I feel somewhat guilty'" that came out about a month before the famous congressional hearing in 2005 that featured Canseco, McGwire, Sosa, and Palmeiro. Towers told ESPN: "I feel somewhat guilty, because I felt like I knew. I still don't know for sure, but Cammy came out and said he used steroids, and I suspected. Selfishly, the guy was putting up numbers, and I didn't do anything about it. That's just the truth." Olney commented that Towers wasn't finished purging his soul. "We're in a competitive business, and these guys were putting up big numbers and helping your ballclub win games. You tended to turn your head on things." Olney then let loose with his opinion: "Finally comes a voice lending credence to everything our eyes have told us through the many years since baseball players started showing up with Popeye arms and medicine ball-sized heads. Finally comes the admission of a man with a guilty conscience whose instincts screamed that what he was seeing was wrong."[14]

Like many baseball fans, I agreed with Buster Olney and most of the other baseball beat writers of the period. Where had the management been? After a disastrously long baseball strike, the home-run derby approach by the major leagues had drawn back even larger crowds and enthusiasm for baseball. The owners, not just the players, had benefited. Unlike most baseball fans, I was privileged to ask and complain about it at the hearing because I was a senior congressman on the committee holding the investigation. Kevin Towers, the GM of the Padres at the time, was the only MLB executive to acknowledge that they were a significant part of the problem.

The *San Diego Union-Tribune* reported on Towers' bravery the next day: "Padres general manager Kevin Towers looked out of place alongside Selig, union leader Donald Fehr and others representing baseball's leadership. Towers was there because he spoke openly and honestly over his concerns about Ken Caminiti's health. Towers' honesty was not lost on Rep. Mark Souder (R-Ind.) who noted: 'Can we trust baseball? It seemed like they gave us the 'Hear no evil, see no evil, do no evil' speech. You heard Kevin Towers, after he realized Caminiti was taking steroids. Why didn't anyone else?'"[15]

Kevin Towers was not a perfect man. No one is. But from the beginning to the end of his life, as he proved in so many different roles and in the future leaders he helped develop, Kevin Towers loved the game of baseball, every part of it. And he wanted to preserve it for future generations as well.

# NOTES

1    "All-Star Rosters," *Jackson* (Mississippi) *Clarion-Ledger*, July 10, 1984: 34.

2    Guy Clifton, "Cal League Notes," *Reno Gazette-Journal*, July 28, 1985: 26.

3    Jeff Jardine, "Towers Silences Stockton, 7-2, in 11 Innings," *Reno Gazette-Journal*, July 22, 1987: 17.

4    "Las Vegas Hands Dukes 5-2 Loss," *Sante Fe New Mexican*, June 21, 1988: 12.

5    Steve Gilbert, "Former D-Backs, Padres GM Towers Dies," mlb.com, January 30, 2018.

6    Jay Paris, Associated Press, "Kevin Towers Remembered for His Love of Baseball and People," February 25, 2018.

7    Dennis Lin and Tom Krasovic, "Kevin Towers, Who Guided the San Diego Padres to the World Series, Dies at 56," *San Diego Union-Tribune*, January 30, 2018.

8    "Former D-Backs, Padres GM Towers Dies."

9    Bob Chandler and Bill Swank, *Bob Chandler's Tales from the San Diego Padres* (Champaign, Illinois: Sports Publishing, 2006), 118.

10    Nelson Papucci, *San Diego Padres: 1969-2002* (San Diego: Big League Press, 2002), 152.

11    content.time.com/time/arts/article/0,8599,1881350,00.html.

12    Mark Wangrin, "Testing Bothers Some Players," *Austin American-Statesman*; May 19, 1985: 192.

13    Tom Verducci, "Special Report: Steroids in Baseball: Confessions of an MVP," *Sports Illustrated*, June 3, 2002: 44.

14    Buster Olney, "Towers on Caminiti: 'I Feel Somewhat Guilty,'" *ESPN the Magazine*, February 27, 2005.

15    sandiegouniontribune.com/sdut-baseballs-closet-turn-heroes-into-tragedy-2005mar20-story.html.

# DICK WILLIAMS

## BY ERIC ARON

Dick Williams was regarded as one of baseball's premier managers and turnaround artists. He was only the second skipper to win pennants for three different teams – Boston, Oakland, and San Diego.[1] As a rookie manager in 1967, Williams led the Red Sox from ninth place the year before to the World Series. Both personally and tactically, he took a no-nonsense, aggressive approach, which electrified several teams that he managed. His

A's won back-to-back World Series, and he pushed the Padres to their first-ever postseason.

As a manager Williams compiled a record of 1,571 wins and 1,451 losses in 21 seasons, 20th on the career victory list as of 2014. Williams also enjoyed a fine playing career. As a versatile utilityman, he played with five teams in 13 seasons. After an appearance in the 1953 World Series with the Brooklyn Dodgers, Williams had three separate stints with the Baltimore Orioles, playing for manager and key mentor Paul Richards.

Richard Hirschfeld Williams was born on May 7, 1929, in St. Louis. He and his brother, Ellery, were raised in their grandfather's house during the Great Depression. Dick's father, Harvey, quit high school to join the Navy, and afterward found jobs delivering fish, cleaning brewery vats, and collecting insurance debts. Dick had fond memories of attending Browns and Cardinals games at Sportsman's Park.

"I belonged to the Knothole Gang in St. Louis, and the seats were in left field. So (Browns left fielder) Chet Laabs and (Cardinals left fielder) Joe Medwick were my favorites," he said.[2]

When the elder Williams found regular employment, the family moved to Pasadena, California. Dick graduated from Pasadena High School and Pasadena Junior College, lettering in seven sports and even winning a city title in handball. Baseball, however, was his first love; he was 6 feet tall, weighed 190 pounds, and threw and batted right-handed.

In 1945, while playing a junior college football game, Williams suffered a leg injury. His father ran on to the field to check on him, only to suffer a fatal heart attack. Williams blamed himself for his father's death and never forgot how he felt that day. Harvey Williams left a lifelong impression on his son. A stern man, he accepted nothing but excellence from his boys, at times even physically abusing them. Consequently, Williams never accepted losing and constantly had to prove to himself that he was not a failure. Despite it all, he loved his father.

While playing for Pasadena Junior College, Williams was spotted by Brooklyn Dodgers scout Tom Downey and signed his first professional contract in 1947. After graduation he reported to Santa Barbara in the Class-C California league. In 79 games he hit .246 with 4 home runs and 50 RBIs, playing the outfield and third base.

The next season Williams was invited to spring training with the Dodgers. Through repetition and systemization, the Dodgers drilled young players in basics like bunting, hitting the cutoff man, and breaking up double plays. As a manager, Williams himself stressed those details. He began the 1948 season in Santa Barbara (California League), earning a promotion to Double-A Fort Worth (Texas League) after batting .335 with 16 home runs and 90 RBIs. He played mainly the outfield, with a few games at third while playing for Fort Worth.

Williams played in Fort Worth again in 1949, under the tutelage of another influential manager, Bobby Bragan, and was a Texas league all-star, thanks to 23 home runs, 114 RBIs, and a .310 batting average. Although Bragan bore a losing record in the major leagues, Williams credited him for all of his own victories. Bragan taught Williams about discipline, winning at all costs, and not being afraid to demonstrate how much you hate losing.

Williams said, "Players give you 100 percent not because they want something, but because they hate something. Me I gave a hundred percent because I hate losing … for the ones who treated losing and failure lightly, I figured I'd better get something ever better to hate. Me."[3]

Despite his progress, Williams had a hard time getting promoted in the Dodgers' deep organization. In 1950 he was back In Fort Worth, and in 144 games he hit .300 with 11 home runs and 72 RBIs. After the season, he played winter ball in Havana, and faced a young pitcher named Fidel Castro in batting practice. That winter he was drafted into the US Army, but with two weeks left in basic training, he reinjured his knee during a camp baseball game and got a medical discharge. Missing all of 1951

spring training, Williams expected to play at Triple-A St. Paul, but baseball, trying to maintain competitive balance, required that minor leaguers returning from the service had to go through waivers. Both the Pirates and the Cardinals claimed Williams, so the Dodgers had to put him on the Brooklyn roster to keep him in the organization. As a returning serviceman, he was the 26th man on the 25-man roster and, not surprisingly, was first relegated to the bench. But he worked hard to earn playing time, and his opportunity finally came.

Williams made his major-league debut in the first game of a doubleheader against Pittsburgh at Ebbets Field on June 10, 1951. Pinch-hitting for Gene Hermanski, he grounded out to the pitcher. He started the second game in left field, batting leadoff, and went 4-for-5 with three singles and a triple. With an outfield of Carl Furillo, Duke Snider, and Andy Pafko, however, there simply wasn't a lot of playing time for Dick. He played in only 23 games in 1951, hitting .200 with one homer and five RBIs.

In 1952 Williams was on the verge of succeeding Pafko as left fielder but was injured again.[4] On August 25 in St. Louis, he suffered a shoulder separation while diving for a ball. Unable to play the rest of the season, he sat on the bench during the 1952 World Series against the Yankees.

In 1953 Williams played for Brooklyn and Triple-A Montreal. The Dodgers won the pennant again. Williams batted three times as a pinch-hitter in the World Series, getting a hit and a walk as the Dodgers fell in six games.

In 1954 Williams again spent time with the Dodgers but also played for Triple-A St. Paul. He spent the entire 1955 season back in Fort Worth, where he hit .317 and, in a season-ending doubleheader on September 5, he won the first game with an inside-the-park grand slam, and played all nine positions in the second game, pitching a scoreless eighth inning.[5]

On June 25, 1956, while playing for Triple-A Montreal, Williams was sent on waivers to the Baltimore Orioles. He became the team's starting center fielder, batting .286 with 11 home runs. In 1957 Williams was a true utility guy for the first time, playing all three outfield positions by first base and third base for the Orioles before being traded to the Cleveland Indians for outfielder Jim Busby in June. He continued to play multiple positions for the Indians, as he did the rest of his career.

Just before the 1958 season, Williams was traded back to the Orioles, with outfielder Gene Woodling and pitcher Bud Daley, for outfielder Larry Doby and pitcher Don Ferrarese. He went on to play 128 games, all over the diamond, hitting .276. After the season, Williams was traded to the Kansas City Athletics for shortstop Chico Carrasquel. Playing multiple positions, A's he batted .266 with 16 home runs and 75 RBIs.

Once again, the Orioles felt compelled to call for Williams's services. Early in the 1961 season, he was on his way back to Baltimore, traded with pitcher Dick Hall for catcher Chuck Essegian and pitcher Jerry Walker. He did poorly this time, batting.206 in 103 games. Back the next season, he raised his average to .247 in 178 at-bats.

On October 12, 1962, Williams was sold to the Houston Colt .45s, then in December he was traded to the Boston Red Sox in exchange for outfielder Carroll Hardy. Williams spent the last two years of his big-league playing career in Boston, as a utility player. The Red Sox teams of 1963 and 1964 hardly reminded him of the "Boys of Summer." He even claimed that Boston management did not expect the players to win. Moreover, he observed that players were treated differently depending on team status, aggravating natural resentments between highly competitive athletes.

"The place was a country club," Williams said. "Players showed up when they felt like it and took extra work only when it didn't interfere with a card game."[6]

During the winter of 1964, Williams was named manager of Boston's Triple-A affiliate in Toronto. He led the Maple Leafs to records of 81-64 in 1965 and 82-65 in 1966, winning Governors' Cup championships in both seasons. While in Toronto he managed players who would later come with him to Boston, including Billy Rohr, Mike Andrews, Joe Foy, Russ Gibson, and Reggie Smith. Foy was the batting champion and MVP of the International League in 1965. Smith led the International League in hitting the following season, batting.320.

After the 1966 season, Red Sox general manager Dick O'Connell promoted Williams to replace Boston manager Billy Herman. At 37, he was the youngest manager in the American League.

Williams inherited a club that had grown complacent. In 1965 the team finished ninth in the 10-team American League with a dreadful mark of 62-100. In 1966 the Red Sox finished ninth again, 26 games behind the Orioles, although they played well in the second half. The 1967 Red Sox were considered a young team with talent, but no one could have predicted that they would win the pennant. Signing a one-year contract, Williams felt that he had a lot to prove. Remembering his own years with the Red Sox, he understood the country-club atmosphere and had a wealth of ideas about turning it around.

At spring training in Winter Haven, Florida, Williams made it perfectly clear that there would be only one person in charge – him – and that he would bring many changes to management's processes and rules. He began by stripping Carl Yastrzemski of his captaincy. All unmarried players were required to lodge at the team hotel. If players were late, they were fined. Williams stressed fundamentals, pitching, and defense. He was one of the first managers to use videotape to improve the adjustments.

Williams required his pitchers to play volleyball in the outfield to develop footwork skills while pushing their competitive instincts. Winning teams had to do only half of their post-workout sprints. When the great Ted Williams, incensed over the "boot camp" approach, walked out of spring training, the manager did not seem to mind.

In Las Vegas, Jimmy "The Greek" Snyder rated the Red Sox a 100-to-1 shot at winning the pennant. Williams promised that "we will win more games than we lose."[7] Opening Day at Fenway Park drew only 8,324 fans. The Red Sox were among the youngest teams in the league. Led by Yastrzemski, Jim Lonborg, Rico Petrocelli, Tony Conigliaro, and George Scott, these still-young veterans were surrounded by ex-Maple Leafs Foy, Smith, Gibson, and Rohr.

Williams was not afraid to exert his authority. If someone played poorly, he was benched and even embarrassed in front of his teammates. Williams chastised first baseman George Scott for being overweight, and described discussions with Scott as "talking to cement."[8] So many players were in the skipper's doghouse that it became a gag. One player said, "Listen, this thing is so full we're lucky we can field a team."[9]

On July 24 the team had rattled off a 10-game winning streak, including six on the road. Returning to Boston, the Red Sox were greeted wildly by thousands of fans. "I will never forget that night we landed at Logan Airport with that wild reception," Williams said later. "… I felt the franchise was practically reborn."[10]

Despite the odds, the Red Sox kept on winning, even overcoming Tony Conigliaro's beaning on August 18 that which sidelined the slugger for the remainder of the season. All season, it was a tight race. On October 1, the last day of the regular season, the Red Sox won the pennant by beating the Minnesota Twins. In the World Series, the Red Sox lost to the Cardinals in seven games. After the amazing season, Lonborg won the Cy Young Award, Yastrzemski, who won the Triple Crown, was voted MVP, and Williams won *The Sporting News'* Manager of the Year Award.

For re-establishing the team as a winner, Williams received a three-year contract extension. In 1968 Boston's pitching staff was decimated by injuries to Lonborg and Jose Santiago, and Conigliaro missed the entire season. The team finished in fourth place at 86-76, 17 games behind pennant winner and World Series champion Detroit.

In 1969 the Red Sox improved their victory total by one. Williams, however, was fired with nine games remaining in the season. His dismissal was attributed primarily to his acrimonious relationship with owner Tom Yawkey. Williams believed Yawkey was undermining his authority; pampering players after Williams had disciplined them. Media reports also claimed that Yawkey considered Williams disrespectful and unrealistic. In a game on August 1, Williams benched Yaztrzemski and fined him $500 for not hustling. Williams did not give special advantages to his star players. Rather, he was tougher on them *because* they were stars.

Williams spent the 1970 season with the Montreal Expos as Gene Mauch's third-base coach. That winter, he accepted an offer from Oakland owner Charlie Finley to manage the A's, becoming the 10th manager of the Athletics in Finley's short regime. John McNamara had been fired after leading the A's to a second-place record of 89-73. Finley charged that McNamara seemed unable to prevent bickering among his players. Backup catcher Dave Duncan remarked, "There's only one manager who manages this club – Charlie Finley … and we'll never win so long as he manages it."[11]

Right from the beginning, Williams knew he had talent on his team. There were outfielders Reggie Jackson and Joe Rudi, third baseman Sal Bando, shortstop Bert Campaneris, and pitchers Vida Blue, Blue Moon Odom, Catfish Hunter, and Rollie Fingers. Williams said, "This club is head and shoulders above the Boston club I had in '67."[12]

Oakland finished the 1971 season 16 games ahead of the Kansas City Royals, winning 101 games. Williams once again won the Manager of the Year award. Hunter went 21-11, and Blue finished a remarkable 24-8, winning both the Cy Young and MVP awards. But the A's didn't make the World Series: They were swept in three games by Baltimore in the American League Championship Series.

The 1972 A's were famous for their facial hair. It began when Reggie Jackson arrived at spring training sporting a mustache. When others decided to follow Jackson's lead, Finley seized another marketing opportunity, offering to pay anyone a $300 bonus if he would grow a mustache by Father's Day. The Mustache Gang was born. By now, Williams had changed as both a manager and a person, growing a mustache himself. Sal Bando said, "I think a lot of things are mislabeled on Dick, I mean, he was a strong disciplinarian, in terms of fundamental baseball and what he expected. … [But] as far as being a disciplinarian in terms of your curfew, your dress, your hair, Dick was very flexible there."[13]

The A's finished the season 93-62, winning the West by 5½ games over the Chicago White Sox. They won the League Championship Series by defeating Detroit three games to two.

In the World Series, the Oakland A's were matched up against the Big Red Machine, Sparky Anderson's Cincinnati Reds. With the hippie-like A's and the cleancut, conservative Reds, the Series was dubbed "the Bikers against the Boy Scouts."[14] Sparky and Williams had been friends since they were teammates in the Dodgers organization. The A's led the Series two games to one when in Game Four, Williams' aggressive managerial moves paid off. With Oakland trailing 2-1 in the bottom of the ninth, Williams used two pinch-runners and three pinch-hitters for a 3-2-comeback victory. The A's lost Games Five and Six, but rallied in Game Seven to win the Series.

In 1973 Oakland had three 20-game winners, Ken Holtzman, Vida Blue, and Catfish Hunter. The team won the American League West with a 94-68 record, and then defeated Baltimore in the ALCS, three games to two. The World Series against the New York Mets, however, marked the beginning of the end of Williams's tenure in Oakland. In Game Two, with the score tied, 6-6, in the 12th inning, Oakland second baseman Mike Andrews made two costly errors that gave the Mets four runs. After the 10-7 loss, Andrews blamed himself for his mistakes. Remembering his own experience with the death of his father, Williams consoled Mike. Mental errors upset Williams, not physical ones.

After the game Finley told Williams that Andrews should be placed on the disabled list with a shoulder injury. In reality, Finley was trying to add Manny Trillo to the postseason roster. Andrews was coerced into signing a medical statement indicating that he was injured, and did not accompany the team to New York.

Before Game Three Finley announced that Andrews was officially unable to play. Sal Bando, the team captain, retaliated by asking all of his teammates to wear Andrews' number 17 on armbands to show their support. Finally, Commissioner Bowie Kuhn intervened, arguing that a player could be replaced on a postseason roster only after suffering a new injury. Kuhn added, "The handling of this matter by the Oakland club has had the unfortunate effect of embarrassing a player who has given many years of able service to professional baseball."[15]

In Game Four, Williams sent Andrews up as a pinch-hitter to a standing ovation from the 54,817 fans at Shea Stadium. For Williams, the Andrews incident was the last straw; he told his team in the locker room that he would resign immediately after the Series. After the A's defeated the Mets in Game Seven, 5-2, Finley announced that he would "not stand in [Williams's] way" should he decide not to return as manager.[16] (Finley later said he meant not standing in the way of NON-baseball-related activities.)

It was no secret that Williams wanted to fill the managerial vacancy for the New York Yankees, and it was no secret that they wanted him. Before baseball's winter meetings, Yankees general manager Gabe Paul asked Finley for permission to talk to Williams. Since Williams had one year remaining on his Oakland contract, Finley demanded player compensation. Eventually American League President Joe Cronin intervened, determining that Finley was acting within his rights in retaining his manager. The Yankees hired Bill Virdon as their manager.

Williams left baseball to work for John D. MacArthur, one of the richest men in America, but realized that he missed baseball. California Angels general manager Harry Dalton persuaded Finley to allow him to hire Williams as manager. Williams replaced Bobby Winkles and interim manager Whitey Herzog on July 1, 1974. He took the job despite having been warned by former Tigers manager Mayo Smith against accepting it, saying, "I've scouted them and I know: They've got no talent in the major leagues and nothing in the minor leagues. Nothing … But enough about me. Good luck."[17]

Nine of the Angels' first 13 seasons had resulted in losing records, and 1974 was no exception. Behind Nolan Ryan, Frank Tanana, and an aging Frank Robinson, Williams led the Angels to a 36-48 record the remainder of the season. The team finished last in the American League West at 68-94, 22 games behind the eventual three-peat world champion A's. The Angels fared no better in 1975, again finishing in last place at 72-89. The entire infield consisted of rookie or sophomore players: first baseman Bruce Bochte, second baseman Jerry Remy, shortstop Orlando Ramirez, and third baseman Dave Chalk.

Williams's frustration was epitomized by a 1976 incident. While talking to sportswriters in Chicago on June 30, he accidentally penciled Nolan Ryan in as the game's starting pitcher. Although it was not Ryan's turn in the rotation, league rules stipulated that the starting pitcher must face at least one batter. After Ryan retired Chicago's leadoff hitter, Chet Lemon, Williams yanked him. Unable to cope with the Angels' losing attitude, Williams was fired on July 24.

After three disappointing seasons in California, Williams got an offer to return to Montreal to manage the Expos. The 1977 Expos had nowhere to go but up. The previous season they had lost 107 games. Williams knew that a promising farm system generated the opportunity to build a winner. Montreal's young outfield consisted of future Hall of Famer Andre Dawson, Warren Cromartie, and Ellis Valentine. Larry Parrish was at third base and Tony Perez at first. Chris Speier was shortstop. And then there was a catcher nicknamed "The Kid": future Hall of Famer Gary Carter.

The team finished in fifth place in 1977 at 75-87. In 1978 the Expos were one game better at 76-86, rising to fourth place in the National League East. In his autobiography Williams recalled, "As we entered the 1979 season, [we] helped put together a team that would make people actually come to the park to watch baseball."[18]

The biggest pitching star in Montreal was Steve Rogers, who pitched his entire 13-year major-league career for the Expos. Montreal also had Ross Grimsley, who had won 20 games in 1978, and added Bill Lee, who had broken in under Williams with the 1969 Red Sox. The team was in the divisional race until the final weekend of both 1979 and 1980. In 1979 the Expos finished at 95-65, two games behind Pittsburgh, and in 1980, they went 90-72, just one game behind Philadelphia. Attendance soared, and pennant fever arrived in Montreal.

The strike-shortened season of 1981 was split into two halves. In the first half, the Expos finished 30-25 for third place behind Philadelphia. In the second half, the team was 14-12 when Williams was fired on September 8. Team president John McHale cited "lack of communication with players and poor clubhouse skills."[19] The team went on to win the "half-pennant," making the playoffs for the only time in franchise history, but after defeating the Phillies in the division series, the Expos lost to the Dodgers in the NLCS.

Williams's next stop was San Diego. In their first 13 seasons, the Padres had finished over .500 only once, in 1978. In 1981, the team finished 26 games out of first place. Credit for building the Padres into a pennant contender belonged to Jack McKeon, general manager since 1980. In 1982 McKeon gave Williams a three-year contract as manager, asking him to turn a franchise into a winner. Williams said in his autobiography, "At all my managerial stops I'd molded winners out of players already present. Doing it the San Diego way was perhaps a more difficult feat, considering that there was a chance that guys wouldn't just hate me, but hate each other."[20]

McKeon drafted outfielders Kevin McReynolds and Tony Gwynn in 1981. He traded shortstop Ozzie Smith to the Cardinals for Gary Templeton in 1982. He also signed Dodgers first baseman Steve Garvey as a free agent in 1983. Additional trades netted Carmelo Martinez and Craig Nettles. McKeon also signed closer Goose Gossage.

Under Williams, the Padres finished 81-81 in 1982 and 1983. They started the 1984 season poorly, losing seven consecutive games in May. They moved into first place on June 9, however, and never looked back. The Padres clinched the National League West on September 20.

On August 12, 1984, the Padres were involved in one of the ugliest scenes in major-league history. A brushback game in Atlanta resulted in two bench-clearing brawls, 16 ejections, and five fan arrests. On the very first pitch of the game Atlanta starter Pascual Perez plunked Padres second baseman Alan Wiggins in the ribs. For the rest of the game, the Padres tried to retaliate. By the time Perez was struck in the eighth inning, Williams had long been ejected from the game. For his role in the brawl, Williams was suspended for 10 games and fined $10,000, while Braves manager Joe Torre was suspended for three games.

The 1984 National League Championship Series against the Chicago Cubs provided the Padres with one of the greatest comebacks in playoff history. In Game One of a best-of-five series, the Cubs blanked the Padres, 13-0. After losing Game Two, 4-2, the Padres faced elimination. Only the 1982 Milwaukee Brewers had rebounded from a two-game deficit to win a best-of-five series. In a scene similar to the '67 welcoming at Logan Airport in Boston, the Padres were greeted by thousands of fans upon arriving in San Diego.

The Padres won Game Three, 7-1. In Game Four, Steve Garvey hit a walkoff home run in the ninth to win, 7-5. Game Five completed the comeback as the Padres, after trailing 3-0, won 6-3. Meeting Williams's old foe Sparky Anderson again in the World Series, the Padres were clearly overmatched by a Detroit team that had won 104 games during the regular season, and fell in five games. Still, Williams finished third in voting for National League Manager of the Year.

In 1985 Williams led the Padres to an 83-79 record, 12 games behind the division champion Dodgers. However, constant struggles with management forced him to resign on the first day of spring training in 1986. He wasn't out of work very long. A few weeks into the season, Williams accepted an offer to manage the Seattle Mariners. Knowing that it was likely his last chance at managing, he wanted to prove that he could still turn a bad team around. He signed a three-year deal to pilot a club for whom 76 wins marked a record high. He took over a 9-20 team (led by manager Chuck Cottier and Marty Martinez) and finished the 1986 season in last place at 67-95.

In 1987 Williams led Seattle to a then record finish of 78-84, seven games behind West Division champion Minnesota. However, he resented management for preventing him from replacing Billy Connors with a pitching coach who he felt would not coddle players or offer preferential treatment. Moreover, he lambasted pitcher Mark Langston for asking to be removed early from games rather than "tough it out." Clearly, Williams's hard-nosed management style had lost its effect. With the Mariners in sixth place at 23-33 on June 6, 1988, Seattle owner George Argyros fired him. Williams never managed again in the major leagues.

Williams became a skipper in the short-lived Senior Professional Baseball Association in Florida. Beginning play in November 1989, the eight-team league was made up of former players 35 and older. Williams managed the West Palm Tropics, who featured former A's Rollie Fingers and Dave Kingman.

In retrospect, a league consisting of aging stars seemed rather silly. As Williams remarked, "With pitchers who could barely throw and runners who could barely run [practice] games took nearly six hours."[21] Williams enjoyed the spirit of the game, however, as his Tropics led the league with a 52-20 record. They came within one game of winning the championship, losing 12-4 to the St. Petersburg Pelicans. The league folded after its second season.

Williams worked as a scout for the New York Yankees until 2002. He also broadcast games for the University of Nevada-Las Vegas and the Las Vegas 51s of the Pacific Coast League. On November 9, 2009, Williams was inducted into the Red Sox Hall of Fame for managing the Impossible Dream team of '67.

Williams got the call from the National Baseball Hall of Fame just a year earlier. On July 27, 2008, after being voted in by the Veterans Committee, Williams was enshrined in Cooperstown along with Rich Gossage.

Williams, who had been married to his wife, Norma, since 1954 and lived in Henderson, Nevada, died on July 7, 2011, of a ruptured aortic aneurysm. He was 82. Besides his wife he was survived by three children, Kathi, Marc, and Rick, and five grandchildren.

Rick Williams was a Red Sox batboy for his father in 1967, and later pitched college ball under coach Eddie Stanky at the University of South Alabama. He was drafted by the Montreal Expos out of school. In 1977, he went 3-1 with a 2.90 ERA for the GLC Expos, and 1-0 in four innings for the Jamestown Expos. In 1978, he reached Triple-A, pitching for the Denver Bears, but an arm injury derailed his career. He was the first pitching coach of the Florida Marlins and Tampa Bay Devil Rays. He was an assistant to the Tampa Bays general manager and scouted for the Yankees. As of 2014, he worked for the Atlanta Braves as a special assistant to the general manager for pitching development.

# SOURCES

Chandler, Bob, with Bill Swank, *Bob Chandler's Tales From the San Diego Padres* (Champaign, Illinois: Sports Publishing LLC, 2006).

Crehan, Herb, *Red Sox Heroes of Yesteryear* (Cambridge, Massachusetts: Rounder Books, 2005).

Reynolds, Bill, *Lost Summer: The '67 Red Sox and the Impossible Dream* (New York: Warner Books, 1992).

Arbel, Allen, "Dick Williams Can Remember Baseball's 'Angry Days,' " *Baseball Digest*, July 1980.

baseball-almanac.com

baseballlibrary.com

baseball-reference.com

# NOTES

1  The first was Bill McKechnie, who won pennants with the Pirates, Cardinals, and Reds.

2  Phone interview with Dick Williams by Jeff Angus, January 2006.

3  Dick Williams and Bill Plaschke, No More Mr. Nice Guy (New York: Harcourt Brace Jovanovich, 1990), 78.

4  Williams, 62.

5  The Sporting News, September 14, 1955: 42.

6  Williams, 71-72.

7  "Dick Williams; Sox Skipper for Impossible Dream Season" (obituary), Boston Globe, April 8, 2011.

8  Williams, 93.

9  Bill McSweeny, The Impossible Dream: The Story of the Miracle Boston Red Sox (New York: Coward McCann, 1968), 186.

10  Glenn Stout and Richard Johnson, Red Sox Century (Boston: Houghton Mifflin, 2004), 323.

11  Bruce Markusen, A Baseball Dynasty: Charlie Finley's Swingin' A's (Haworth, New Jersey: St. Johann Press, 2002), 1.

12  Markusen, 6.

13  Markusen, 117.

14  Markusen, 171.

15  Markusen, 248.

16  Markusen, 263.

17  Markusen, 183.

18  Williams, 206.

19  Williams, 225.

20  Williams, 233.

21  Williams, 316.

# SPRING TRAINING, STADIA, AND THE CHICKEN

# SPRING TRAINING IN YUMA, 1969–1993

## BY JIM PATRICK

On July 2, 1968, San Diego Padres vice president/general manager Eddie Leishman announced that the new National League franchise had chosen Yuma, Arizona, as its spring-training base.

This was cause for celebration in Yuma, since the community had been trying to attract another major-league club ever since the Baltimore Orioles reluctantly trained at Yuma's Municipal Stadium in 1954.[1] Yuma's city officials and baseball boosters were thrilled that the town had been given a second chance to host a big-league club, but they also realized that much work needed to be done in a short time to get Yuma ready for major-league baseball – particularly since Municipal Stadium was no longer a viable location for big leaguers; after neighboring 1st Avenue had been widened in 1965, the right-field fence at the ballpark was only 280 feet from home plate. As this article will illustrate, Keegan Field, the Padres' temporary facility in 1969, was certainly no field of dreams, but thanks to hard-working volunteers, generous local businesses, and enthusiastic community support, Yuma and the Padres successfully completed the first year of their mutually beneficial 25-year spring-training partnership.

Why Yuma? The city began officially courting major-league teams in 1950 when the Chamber of Commerce established a baseball committee. News stories in that decade occasionally mentioned teams that were "considering Yuma" for spring training, including not only the St. Louis Browns [Baltimore Orioles], but also the Pirates, Giants, and Dodgers. While none of the latter three clubs conducted serious negotiations with Yuma, a

Padre coach Wally Moon (in jacket, far right) leads Padres in exercise drill at Padres' spring training camp in Yuma, Ariz.

[1969 Inaugural Yearbook]

positive result of the city's outreach efforts was the friendship established between Dodgers general manager Buzzie Bavasi and newspaper publisher Don Soldwedel, a member of Yuma's baseball committee. Bavasi resigned as Dodgers GM in June 1968 to become president and part-owner of the new San Diego ballclub. In a 1984 article Soldwedel recalled, "[I]n 1968, before the Padre franchise came about, Buzzie called and told me that he was going to be involved in a new franchise. He said if it was granted, Yuma would get a team. About a month later he called back and said the franchise had been okayed."[2] Yuma's selection may not have been quite as automatic as Soldwedel remembered. John "Doc" Mattei, the Padres team trainer and traveling secretary, described being sent by Bavasi to scout several potential spring-training sites. According to Mattei, Apache Junction, Arizona, was eliminated from consideration when he walked into the clubhouse and found it "crawling with rattlesnakes."[3] Mattei also recalled visiting Borrego Springs, California, but he sensed that "Yuma was much more gung-ho," adding, "I said to Buzzie, 'The people really want us there.'"[4]

Much of Yuma's "gung-ho" attitude could be attributed to the Caballeros de Yuma, a civic group formed in 1962 as the official greeting organization for the city. The Caballeros signed on as the sponsoring organization for the 1969 Padres spring-training season, a role that they maintained for all 25 years of the Padres' tenure in Yuma. During the first year, an ad hoc group called the Community Baseball Boosters complemented the efforts of the Caballeros by holding a fundraising barbecue, a dance, and a golf tournament. They also sold thousands of "Be a CBB" bumper stickers for a dollar each.[5]

In 1968 Keegan Field was an unadorned youth-baseball facility located near Kennedy Park and Kennedy Swimming Pool. The field's dimensions were adequate for professional baseball, but nearly everything else needed by the Padres at Keegan would have to be cobbled together – largely by volunteer labor using donated materials. Bleachers, fences, dugouts, locker rooms, showers, batting cages, sliding pits, concession stands, a press

box, and a PA system were all absent. The field needed to be leveled and the pitching mound had to be raised to professional standards. Doc Mattei described the impressive community effort: "The Marines built the lockers. The electric company took light poles and made a batting cage. Tanner Construction leveled the field. We raised $3,000 from a raffle, $3,000 from a barbecue, another $3,000 selling bumper stickers."[6] Some of the bleachers were purchased at "going out of business" prices from a Las Vegas racetrack.[7]

The Padres held their first workout in Yuma on Saturday, February 22, 1969. The high temperature that day was a brisk 52 degrees, making the temporary outdoor shower facilities less than comfortable. The Padres used the locker rooms at Kennedy Swimming Pool while training at Keegan Field, but the additional outdoor showers were also needed. Another amusing Doc Mattei story concerns the need for a telephone at the training facility so that the players could call their wives and girlfriends. "If we put in a free one," Mattei reasoned, "the bills will be outrageous. So I had a pay phone installed. Put a roll of dimes on top of it. Worked very smoothly."[8]

The Padres played 14 games at Keegan Field in 1969. The total attendance was 14,987, a per-game average of 1,070. In the opening game, on March 7, the recently unretired Johnny Podres led the Padres to a win over the California Angels before 2,500 fans. An even larger crowd of 2,604 saw Juan Marichal and the San Francisco Giants defeat the Padres on March 21. Only 530 fans attended the midweek 1:00 P.M. Padres-Seattle Pilots game on March 27, but since former Yankees pitcher Jim Bouton happened to be a member of the Pilots squad, the game and its host city garnered an unflattering description in one of the best-selling sports books ever published. In *Ball Four*, his classic tell-all baseball diary, Bouton did not remember his Keegan Field experience fondly. He described the teams playing in front of "about twelve people ... at a place that doesn't even have a visiting clubhouse, so that we had to dress on the back of an equipment truck."[9]

When Yuma officials signed their initial five-year spring-training contract with the Padres, they agreed to have a multi-field baseball facility ready for the opening of spring training in 1970. To finance the construction of Desert Sun Stadium, which was built at an approximate cost of $400,000, the city passed a 2 percent hospitality tax and sold $100,000 worth of recreation bonds that had been obtained with voter approval seven years earlier. Desert Sun Stadium, which was three miles south of Keegan Field and just up the road from the Yuma Greyhound Park, consisted of a primary grandstand field adjoined by three practice fields. The complex's 12,000-square-foot clubhouse seemed especially luxurious after the swimming-pool locker rooms and double-wide trailer offices at Keegan Field. The original configuration at Desert Sun had a seating capacity of 4,000, but by the end of the Padres' tenure in 1993, seating capacity had been expanded to 7,894. Several other improvements were made over the years, including a lighting system provided by the Padres in 1983, a weight room donated by Japan's Yakult Swallows in 1984, and added bleachers and box seats obtained with funds from benefit games.[10] When Desert Sun Stadium opened in February 1970, general manager Eddie Leishman claimed, "This complex will be head and shoulders above the other spring-training areas."[11] Visiting players also took notice. In 1976 Cubs first baseman Andre Thornton expressed frustration with his team's venue, old Scottsdale Stadium with its single field: "Look at that facility in Yuma. ... Here's a club that's been in existence less than 10 years. The Cubs have been around for 100. Chicago ought to have the best, but I don't find it to be true."[12]

Before the start of the 1984 regular season, owner Ray Kroc died at the age of 81. The Yuma City Council voted to name the complex the Ray Kroc Baseball Complex in his honor, while keeping the name Desert Sun Stadium for the primary field at the complex. Kroc's wife, Joan, attended the dedication ceremony held before the Padres-Angels game on March 11, 1984.

Moving to the Desert Sun training facility in 1970 was a major upgrade for the Padres, the visiting teams, and the fans, but attendance didn't increase substantially in the early years of the new complex. In 1973, for example, the home games drew a total of 13,735 fans for an average of 1,145 per game.[13] The March 24, 1974, game versus the world champion Oakland A's set an attendance record of 3,257.[14] By 1983 attendance had risen sharply to a spring-season total of 47,676, with a per-game average of 3,667.[15] In 1989 eight of the Yuma games were sell-outs for a total attendance of 69,541 and an average of 5,795.[16] These numbers were not sustained the following year due to the 32-day lockout imposed by the owners at the beginning of the 1990 exhibition season. The labor impasse caused scheduling havoc and economic hardship for all of baseball's spring-training sites. A handful of hastily rescheduled games were played before Opening Day, but attendance was predictably poor.

Yuma's year-round residents and seasonal "snowbirds" supported the Padres throughout their 25 years, but it was the influx of fans from San Diego, including one organization known as the Hot Stove League of San Diego, that accounted for the full occupancy of Yuma's hotels and motels, particularly for weekend series. In February 1987 Sylvester Stallone and the producers of *Rambo III* discovered a lodging scarcity in Yuma when the crew wanted to stay for several days while filming battle scenes in the nearby desert. (Stallone's company did return the following January, well before the Padres and their fans were due to hit town.)[17]

The Padres' lodging accommodations varied throughout the Yuma years, presumably because traveling secretary Doc Mattei would negotiate with local hotels for optimal prices and availability. The team stayed at resorts including the Flamingo, the Stardust, the Park Inn International, and the Ramada Inn. Players in camp from Padres minor-league affiliates, including the Hawaii Islanders and the Las Vegas Stars, were more likely to stay at the Motel 6. Future Padres general manager Kevin Towers recalled his experience: "Yuma, 1983. Our lodging was a Motel 6. Had a black-and-white TV. Towels were so small they wouldn't fit around your waist. Air conditioning was a westerly breeze through the window."[18] Things weren't necessarily better with the big-league accommodations, at least according to 1988-1995 team President Dick Freeman: "Most of us stayed at the Stardust. The name was the only thing impressive about that place. The mattresses had lumps."[19]

Padres players and team officials frequently commented about Yuma's nightlife and entertainment scene – or lack thereof. As he neared the end of his eighth and final Yuma spring-training camp in 1980, Dave Winfield complained to the *Los Angeles Times,* "There's nothing to do here. Nothing."[20] Another future Hall of Famer, Ozzie Smith, expressed a more positive view: "I was there to play baseball, so I really didn't care that there wasn't much else to do."[21] Outspoken reliever Goose Gossage explained in his autobiography the difference between Yuma (home of Marine Corps Air Station Yuma) and Fort Lauderdale, Florida, where his previous team, the Yankees, trained: "Down in Florida, you get to see a bunch of beautiful young girls in bikinis. Out here we get to see jarheads."[22] According to catcher Terry Kennedy, "Yuma was the best. We played baseball all day and cooked out every night. That was it. When we left there, we were ready for the season." Infielder Tim Flannery, another key member of the 1980s Padres teams, would find rental housing in Yuma each spring so he could be joined by his family. Flannery recalled fondly, "We would barbecue every night out there with the family. My son, he learned to walk here; he learned to swim here."[23] Dick Williams, who managed Kennedy and

Flannery, expressed a contrarian view in his autobiography: "Perhaps because their spring training facility in Yuma, Arizona, is too relaxed and too close to San Diego ... this organization traditionally has the slowest starts in baseball."[24] Greg Riddoch, manager in 1990-1992, noted the friendliness of Yuma's winter visitors: "I'd go out jogging in the morning and there would be all those RVs out there. ... Someone would always have a pancake for me. Then I would jog on back to the ballpark and get ready for the game."[25] It might seem impossible to find common ground in such mixed reviews of Yuma, but reliever Randy Myers' existential description of the town comes close: "It's not where you'd probably like to be, but it's a nice place when you're there."[26]

Yuma's relatively short distance from San Diego (170 miles, approximate three-hour driving time) was a major factor in its choice as the Padres' spring-training site. As GM Leishman explained, "This proximity makes it easy for many San Diego fans to attend the exhibition games."[27] He also noted that the team's training location enabled many of the players' wives and children to attend weekend games in Yuma. Visiting teams didn't benefit from this proximity, however, and complaints about long bus rides to and from the Phoenix and Tucson camps were common. The scenic drives through the desert could also be tiresome for the Padres, but a bigger challenge for the team was gaining access to ballfields when on extended spring road trips. In 1986, for example, the team played 12 games during a 10-day stay in the Phoenix area. Manager Steve Boros explained, "We just don't have access to the fields and the time. But we've got to play somebody, and they don't want to come to Yuma all the time."[28] Greg Riddoch, manager of the 1992 squad, shared similar frustrations: "We can't work on fundamentals. We don't have our own facility. ... We have to find a field each day that the guys who aren't playing in the game can work on."[29] When the California Angels moved their training site from Palm Springs, California, to Tempe, Arizona, after the 1992 season, Yuma's

isolated location became even more of a logistical issue for the Padres and the other Cactus League clubs.

There were no rainouts during the first 22 years of Padres spring-training games. This remarkable streak is understandable given the city's average annual rainfall of 3.36 inches, but rainouts did occur in both 1991 and 1992.[30] High winds in Yuma are not uncommon, and on March 13, 1971, a Padres-Indians game had to be canceled due to a sandstorm. Manager Preston Gomez said, "It would have been risky to try and play – someone could have gotten hurt."[31] And when acclaimed rookie pitcher Jim Abbott of the Angels made his professional debut on March 3, 1989, in a B-squad game at Desert Sun Stadium, his biggest challenge was not the Padres hitters, but the wind gusts approaching 30 miles per hour.[32] It's rare to hear anyone complain about a *lack* of humidity, but in 1987 manager Larry Bowa did just that in commenting about the weather in Yuma that spring: "The facilities are nice and the people are great, but the weather was terrible. ... It was windy every day. ... It's hard for a pitcher to throw breaking balls here. There is no humidity in addition to the wind. I prefer training in Florida."[33]

Of course, Yuma is known for the extreme heat of its summers, but the town is also renowned for its typically mild winter weather. On March 19, 1978, however, an 81-year-old San Diego woman was overcome by the 84-degree sunshine during the Padres-Indians game. After she was revived by paramedics and asked how she felt, Frances Price replied, "I think I'm okay. The only thing that bothers me is that the Padres are playing such lousy baseball."[34] Unknown to Mrs. Price, manager Alvin Dark would be fired just two days later – a rare spring training firing – and new manager Roger Craig would lead the team to its first-ever winning season in 1978.

Throughout their Yuma stay, the Padres had signed and renewed a series of five-year contracts with the city, but the final contract was only for two years (1992 and 1993). Consequently, it was not a surprise when the team announced in July 1992 that the San Diego organization had signed a 20-year contract to train in Peoria, Arizona, beginning in 1994.[35] A local headline best expressed the feelings in Yuma regarding the upcoming 1993 lame duck training camp: "Celebration, Sadness in Store for Padres' Swan Song."[36]

At the conclusion of their 1993 spring training season – their final one in Yuma – a couple of San Diego icons weighed in on the impact of the long Padres-Yuma relationship. After the team's March 31 finale, against the Chicago Cubs, Tony Gwynn said, "I've been here for 12 years, and I've really enjoyed it. ... I'm going to miss Yuma. I'm going to miss the short drives over. I'm going to miss the way the people treated us here with a lot of respect."[37] And broadcaster Jerry Coleman, never one for understatement, proclaimed, "We owned this town. Nobody has been treated better than we were treated here. I don't believe that, in the history of baseball, has a city embraced a ballclub the way Yuma embraced the Padres."[38]

The goodwill and good memories shared between the Padres and Yuma was evident in the annual series of split-squad games staged in Yuma between 1998 and 2007. The Arizona Diamondbacks, who joined the National League in 1998, were the "visiting team" for most of these well-attended exhibitions. After complaining that the Diamondbacks had brought only one of their frontline players, Tony Womack, to play on March 24, 2002, a Caballeros de Yuma member commented, "We're really happy with the Padres. They bring big players to this game every year – it's their game, they're the home team. They get great support from Yuma."[39]

After the Padres' departure following the 1993 exhibition season, professional baseball maintained a bumpy existence in Yuma through 2011. After conducting spring training in Yuma from 1974 to 1999, the Yakult Swallows decided in 2000 to resume training in their home country with the other Japanese teams. In 1995 Yuma attracted an independent minor-league team called the Desert Dawgs who played a grand total of 10 games before their league folded. From 2000 to 2002 the Yuma Bullfrogs struggled to draw fans to summer baseball games in Yuma. Similarly, the 2005-2011 Yuma Scorpions experienced many roster and management changes, along with one constant: poor attendance.

In 2015 the city made the difficult decision to convert the primary field at the Ray Kroc Baseball Complex to a soccer field. The grandstand field had rarely been occupied after 2011, and a professional soccer team agreed to pay for the conversion. The pro soccer enterprise was not a success. Finally, in September 2017 Yuma residents witnessed the opening of the Pacific Avenue Athletic Complex, a six-field facility designed solely for ... softball.

The Cactus League of today is dramatically different from that of 50 years ago when Yuma hosted the Padres' inaugural spring-training camp at Keegan Field. The team has spent the past 25 years sharing the massive Peoria Sports Complex with the Seattle Mariners. The Peoria facility consists of 13 full-size baseball fields spread over 145 acres. The main stadium has a seating capacity of 12,518.[40] In 2018 average attendance for the Padres home exhibition games was 5,887, up slightly from 2017's average of 5,617.[41] And the reduction in travel has been an even more dramatic change for the 15 Cactus League clubs that now train in Arizona. The teams all train in the Phoenix metropolitan area – 10 complexes total, five with dual occupancy. Yuma would never have a place in today's centralized, corporate-style Cactus League, but at the outset, the community's exceptional hospitality and eagerness to be a baseball town made Yuma an ideal match for the young San Diego Padres franchise.

# NOTES

1    After St. Louis Browns owner Bill Veeck contracted the team to train in Yuma in 1954, he sold the club to a group from Baltimore who did not hide their preference for having their newly-christened Orioles train in Florida.

2    Tom Jolliff, "The Padres Bring Fun, Folks and Fame to Yuma in Spring," *Yuma Daily Sun* [Destination Yuma supplement], November 11, 1984: 7C.

3    Dave Distel, "Padres Traveling Secretary Handles Road Trips, Players' Barbs," *Los Angeles Times*, September 7, 1979: 48-49.

4    Barry Lorge, "Major Leagues," *San Diego Union-Tribune*, March 6, 1991: D-1.

5    "Yuma Field Funds Grow," *Arizona Republic*, November 9, 1968: 11.

6    Lorge.

7    Tom Cushman, "The Doc Who Delivered Newborn Padres to Yuma Has Snapshots to Share," *San Diego Union-Tribune*, February 28, 1993: C-1.

8    Ibid.

9    Jim Bouton, *Ball Four: The Final Pitch* (New York: Rosetta Books, electronic edition, 2012).

10   Tokyo's Yakult Swallows, who were also sponsored by the Caballeros de Yuma, conducted spring training in Yuma from 1978 to 1999. Their annual departure from Yuma usually overlapped with the arrival of the Padres, allowing for annual benefit exhibition games between the two teams.

11   Joe Heath, "Plush Clubhouse, 4 Diamonds Awaiting Padres at Yuma Base," *The Sporting News*, February 28, 1970: 7.

12   Richard Dozer, "Training Facilities Hurt Us: Thornton," *Chicago Tribune*, March 28, 1976: 79.

13   "Cubs Drop San Diego in Exhibition Finale," *Yuma Daily Sun*, April 5, 1973: 11.

14   "Record Crowd," *Yuma Daily Sun*, March 25, 1974: 1.

15    Jim Frederikson, "Caballeros Sighs Its Relief," *Yuma Daily Sun*, March 31, 1983: 17.

16    "Padres," *The Sporting News*, April 10, 1989: 44.

17    Mark Kreidler, "Yuma Their Town, and Padres Run Rambo Out of It," *San Diego Union-Tribune*, February 28, 1987: C-6.

18    Tom Cushman, "Padres Spring Training Has Come a Long Way Since Yuma," *San Diego Union-Tribune*, March 7, 2004: C-4.

19    Ibid.

20    Chris Cobbs, "Padres Find It Easy to Stay Out of Trouble in Yuma," *Los Angeles Times*, March 28, 1980: 28, 30.

21    Ozzie Smith and Rob Rains, *Wizard* (Chicago: Contemporary Books, 1988), 17.

22    Richard "Goose" Gossage and Russ Pate, *The Goose Is Loose* (New York: Ballantine, 2000), 192-193.

23    Bob Romantic, "A Spring Tradition," *Yuma Daily Sun*, March 28, 1993: 15, 19.

24    Dick Williams and Bill Plaschke, *No More Mr. Nice Guy: A Life of Hardball* (New York: Harcourt, 1990), 250.

25    Mark Saxon, "Riddoch Chronicles Return to Padres," *Yuma Sun*, March 26, 2007: C1, C2.

26    Bill Center, "Gwynn Stays the Extra Day for Yuma and Alma Mater," *San Diego Union-Tribune*, March 29, 1999: D-13.

27    Jackson Borjes, "Padres' Manager Says Club Happy over Yuma," *Arizona Republic*, January 19, 1971: 8.

28    Stan Isle, "Caught on the Fly," *The Sporting News*, April 14, 1986: 30.

29    Murray Chass, "Baseball Notebook," *New York Times*, March 22, 1992: A-5.

30    John Cardinale, "Padres-Angels Rained Out; Doubleheader Scheduled Today," *Yuma Daily Sun*, March 8, 1992: 19.

31    Wire Services, "Storm Cancels 2 Games," *Arizona Republic* (Phoenix), March 14, 1971: 2-D.

32    Michael McQuain, KYMA-TV sports report, March 3, 1989. youtube.com/watch?v=UPT3oz9g5jg&list=PL4B281AD49EFF0F01&index=28&t=0s.

33    Stan Isle, "Caught on the Fly," *The Sporting News*, April 20, 1987: 32.

34    " 'Winter' Sun Is Too Much for Ball Fan," *Yuma Daily Sun*, March 20, 1978: 1.

35    M.E. Saavedra, "Peoria Moves Into the Big Leagues," *Arizona Republic*, July 23, 1992: 15, 20.

36    Bob Romantic, "Celebration, Sadness in Store for Padres' Swan Song," *Yuma Daily Sun*, February 21, 1993: 17, 20.

37    Eric Beato, "Gwynn Signs Off After Long Stay in Yuma," *Yuma Daily Sun*, April 1, 1993: 15-16.

38    Nick Canepa. "Yuma Will Keep Rolling 'Cause City's on Wheels," *San Diego Union-Tribune*, April 1, 1993: D-1.

39    Jon Greenberg, "Padres Still Reign in Yuma," *Yuma Sun*, March 25, 2002: C1, C5.

40    "About Peoria Sports Complex." peoriasportscomplex.com/spring-training/find-info/about-sports-complex, accessed December 21, 2018.

41    Brandon McClung, "Spring Training Attendance Up for Grapefruit, Cactus League Games," *Street & Smith's Sports Business Daily*, March 29, 2018. sportsbusinessdaily.com/Daily/Issues/2018/03/29/MLB-Season-Preview/ST-attendance.aspx. Accessed December 21, 2018.

# SAN DIEGO STADIUM /
# JACK MURPHY STADIUM
# / QUALCOMM STADIUM

## BY CURT SMITH

"People don't know how good the Pacific Coast League is," a onetime miner named H.V. "Hardrock Bill" Lane said in 1935. "There's Oakland, or San Francisco."[1] A year later he moved the then-Double-A Hollywood Stars to San Diego, renamed them Padres for a nearby mission, opened single-tier 9,100-seat Lane

Field, and began to fill a baseball chapel. Early priests included Bobby Doerr, Vince DiMaggio – and native Ted Williams, already worshiped at nearby Herbert Hoover High School. In 1938, The Kid, 18, leapt to Triple-A Minneapolis, batting .366. Later the Pads boasted Minnie Minoso, Al Rosen, and Luke Easter, who hit the center-field scoreboard, more than 500 feet from the plate. By 1949, San Diego drew a record 493,780, fully 222,844 more than the American League St. Louis Browns. Without wishing to be sacrilegious, when the term *higher power* was bandied about, it was often unclear who was meant.

In 1957 C. Arnholt Smith bought the franchise for nearly $350,000. Shiver me timbers: Termites were eating wooden Lane Field. Smith soon built 8,200-seat Westgate Park, whose gate opened to minor-league profit but without, as San Diego wanted, a major-league team. Place that against the backdrop of baseball's top late-'50s tale. In late 1957, the Dodgers of Brooklyn since 1890 suddenly and stunningly decamped for Los Angeles, "mak[ing] the greatest impact on Southern California's millions since the 1933 earthquake left them shimmying and shaking,"

Frank Finch wrote.[2] Signs scripted "Ball Game Today: Win Dodgers." Storefront windows sold team jackets and $300 suits. A welcoming parade jammed 300,000 downtown. Team owner Walter O'Malley then told a civic luncheon, "I hope the next time you will be asked to stand up will be for Duke Snider's first home run in Los Angeles."[3]

Brooklyn had drawn 1,028,258 in 1957. The 1958 Dodgers lured 1,845,556 to the Los Angeles Memorial Coliseum, two years later adding a sublime 2,253,887. Then more than now, the City of the Angels intimidated San Diego, its 1960 US Census populace more than four times larger. As counter, many increasingly hyped a new park to give LA's neighbor to the south its own big-league leg-up, most effectively *San Diego Union* sports editor and columnist Jack Murphy, brother Bob Murphy a New York Mets announcer. In 1965 its City Council OK'd a multisport "facility" with a baseball bent. A referendum backed the $27.5 million site in Mission Valley, the San Diego River coursing through the plot. Engineers diverted it, then moved 2.5 million cubic yards of dirt. San Diego Stadium flaunted 1,715 huge pieces of precast concrete in 2,345 shapes, some weighing 39 tons.

Its address hinted absolution: 9449 Friars Road.

At the time, the Southland was mostly small town and suburban, middle-class, and white: *Grapes of Wrath* émigrés from the Dust Bowl and beyond. It mimed the late-'60s national pastime, drawing largely from the ordered and traditional. "Partly because it was small," read *The Ballparks*, built decidedly more for baseball than football, "and partly because of its rather odd shape," the stadium resembled "a box with only three sides."[4] Five tiers circled home plate to the left- and right-field corner, moored by each bullpen. Four levels half-enclosed the park from left to center field. In right field, a bleacher section fronted a large scoreboard on pillars, hillside seen beyond. You entered below ground level, passed through tunnel-type gates, and walked through one of six concrete coil-shaped towers to each level and any of then-47,634 multicolor seats: 6,394 lower box,

8,183 reserved, 1,918 press-level box, 11,224 upper box, and 19,915 general admission.[5]

The stadium opened August 20, 1967, evincing professional football's recent merger: Detroit Lions 38, hometown Chargers, 17. A February 1968 open house hailed a different sport: 15,000 – ogled Santa Ana Bermuda grass, a 17-foot concrete outfield wall, and uniform lengths – each foul line, 330 feet; alleys, 375, and center field, 420. On April 5, the Giants and Indians played a Cactus League exhibition game in the then-Triple-A PCL Padres' home. In May San Diego and Montreal both received a National League expansion team, that year's Friars leading the minors in attendance. How would the big-league team do? "I said, 'We'll walk, then we'll run,'" Emil J. "Buzzie" Bavasi, Dodgers general manager turned new Pads president, recalled a decade later.[6] It was assumed they would draw. On November 2, 1967, financier C. Arnholt Smith, later named the team's first owner, wrote a letter to O'Malley, head of the NL expansion committee, enclosing a brochure touting San Diego's "population, the means, and the desire to support major league baseball," in what had become America's "15th-largest city,"[7] its population nearly doubling since 1960.

From the start, the Friars tried to flee the Dodgers' shadow by bettering the Dodgers' way –pitching, defense, and speed; accent the fundamentals; never beat yourself. Their front office bulged with ex-Los Angeles personnel – Bavasi, as head; son Peter Bavasi, farm-system director; coach Preston Gomez, manager. Missing was Dodgers cash, Smith emptying his vault on the NL $10 million expansion franchise fee. By the mid-1970s, after a change in ownership, McNamara's Band, named for skipper John McNamara, would rove through the stands playing songs like "Happy Days Are Here Again" and "California, Here I Come."[8] In the late 1960s and early '70s, the group might have played a dirge: "Brother, Can You Spare a Dime?" The question was rhetorical.

"In the [October 14, 1968] expansion draft we went for young players, figuring to build the future around them," Peter Bavasi said, noting Smith's inability to afford older – thus, marquee –players.[9] Some drafted later shaped a fine career. At the time, most brooked near-invisibility. Expansion roster pitchers were Steve Arlin, Mike Corkins, Tom Dukes, Dave Giusti, Rick James, Fred Katawczik, Dick Kelley, Clay Kirby, Al McBean, Billy McCool, Frank Reberger, Dave Roberts, Al Santorini, and Dick Selma. Other players included Jose Arcia, Ollie Brown (first choice), Nate Colbert, Jerry DaVanon, Al Ferrara, Clarence "Cito" Gaston, Tony Gonzalez, Fred Kendall, Jerry Morales, Ivan Murrell, Roberto Pena, Rafael Robles, Ron Slocum, Larry Stahl, Zoilo Versalles, and Jim Williams.[10] Given most of their youthful anonymity, the Pads wisely promoted rival personnel.

It didn't help enough. Neither did geography that let radio's magical Vin Scully gild baseball for much of Southern California. The Voice of the Dodgers was sportscasting's Roy Hobbs, "the best there ever was,"[11] beamed over their powerful 50,000-watt KFI far-flung network toward, among other places, San Diego. The Padres were the sole NL team near enough to Los Angeles to be daily reminded of Scully's art. In 1969-71, Frank Sims, Jerry Gross, and Duke Snider did Pads WOGO wireless and Channel 10 TV. To visit, you drove between two steep Mission Valley ridges, near Tijuana, golf courses, and endless miles of beach, desert, and mountain range, to about eight miles from the Pacific, near Interstates 15 and 8. Inside the Padres' abbey, checkerboard-cut grass replaced dirt on each side of both lines. Corner pens bisected them – the only park in which a foul could be caught out of sight of umpires and players. The setting was lovely – save empty seats.

The Padres opened at home on April 8, 1969, edging Houston, 2-1, before just 23,370, their lineup Robles, shortstop; Pena, second base; Gonzalez, center field; Brown, right field; Bill Davis, first base; Stahl, left field; Ed Spiezio, third base; Chris Cannizzaro, catcher; and Selma, starting and winning pitcher. First batter/hit: Houston's Jesus Alou. Homer and RBI: Spiezio.[12] "The first game in the National League was like the last game of the World Series for us," said Kendall, the Pads starting 3-0.[13] They should have quit while ahead. On one hand, Joe Niekro hurled their first complete-game shutout, 5-0 – against LA. The other: Kirby lost 20 games on a 52-110 team that drew 512,970 – *eight* empty seats for each seat filled. Next year the Friars won 11 more as Colbert hit 38 homers and 30th and last expansion pick Gaston added 29. Neither kept San Diego from being no-hit by the Bucs' Dock Ellis or struck out 19 times by New York's Tom Seaver. Attendance rose to 643,679 – again 12th in a 12-team league.

The 1971 Padres were the sole NL club *not* to draw a million. For the first time players from Selma to Niekro were dealt for prospects, "build[ing] our farm system through trades," said Peter Bavasi. "It was a holding action" – a price paid for hope tomorrow.[14] San Diego was last in the West its first six years, four times losing 100 or more games. Amid carnage, consolation rarely made a call. In 1970 San Diego had somehow won the season series, 10 games to 8, from the league titlist Big Red Machine. 1971: Roberts vaunted a 2.10 ERA. 1972: In an August 1 doubleheader at Atlanta, Colbert hit five home runs, had an otherworldly 13 RBIs, scored seven runs, and totaled 22 bases – "the whole team, and even Nate," said Kendall, "in a daze just watching him do it"[15] – tying a twin-bill record for homers and breaking it for ribbies and total bases. Colbert became the first Friar with 100 RBIs, gloom lifting. Inevitably, it returned.

In 1972 Gomez was fired after 11 games, replaced by an infielder of the 1955 titlist Brooklyn Dodgers and 40-120 1962 Mets. Don Zimmer's team was more Metsian than champion, a 611,826 gate in 1973 not enough to help C. Arnholt Smith thrive or locally sell. As the NL tried to move it, San Diego Mayor Pete Wilson and city attorney John Witt went to court. Said Bavasi Jr.: "If the city had turned its back on the ... Padres, the club might very well have been moved."[16] Instead, to make it saleable Smith threw the dice, getting big-time veterans Matty Alou, Glenn Beckert, Willie McCovey, Bobby Tolan, and Dave Tomlin. The public cheered. Green eyeshades recoiled at *déjà vu*: empty coffers. "We were out of options, and our bank account showed a balance of two thousand dollars," said Bavasi Sr.[17] Later Smith went to prison for $8.4 million in embezzlement and tax fraud. By January 1974, businessman Joseph Danzansky, tentatively buying the team, pledged it to Washington, D.C. The Pads seemed as good as gone – files packed, new uniforms sewn – until a reprieve as good as gold.

For eight years McDonald's Corporation founder and chairman Ray Kroc had tried to buy his hometown Cubs. Thwarted, he read of the D.C. sale's snag. An official called Bavasi for a meeting. Midway through lunch, "Mr. Kroc shook hands with Mr. Smith, and the rest is history," said Buzzie, Ray's effect as rapid as the quickest fast food. Entering Bavasi's offices for the first time, Kroc bayed another first: "Give everyone in this room a raise."[18] On Opening Night, Friars, losing, 9-5, he grabbed the public-address mike to snarl, "This is the most stupid ballplaying I've ever seen."[19] A day later Ray apologized, most not grasping why. "The reaction," said a baseball original, 1972-79 and 1981-2012 Pads Voice Jerry Coleman, "was finally a guy who wants to *win*."[20] The '74ers set every then-franchise attendance peak, including season 1,075,399. Next year Randy Jones became the franchise's first 20-game victor with a league-best 2.24 ERA and closed a 6-3 All-Star Game. San Diego won a franchise-high 71 games to finish higher than it had ever placed, fourth in its division.

By now, the Padres promoted like McDonald's – "more than any other baseball club," Bavasi Sr. said, about 80 percent of playing dates.[21] Shakespeare wrote, "Fair and foul." The Pads' fairest blessing became baseball's foulest bird. In 1974 a journalism student at San Diego State heard that KGB FM Radio needed someone to wear a chicken costume. Needing the $2 a day, Ted Giannoulas shortly gave candy Easter eggs to children at the San Diego Zoo. Job over, he executed a neat one-two. He got the team and station OK to wear his henhouse outfit to a game. Soon other clubs were hiring him: "No grand plan," he said. "It was the laughter from the grandstand that carried me onto the field." When KGB later fired him, Ted won a patent suit, forced to change costume, but rehatching his career as the Chicken before a sellout: He recalled watching TV as a kid with Mom – "Laurel and Hardy, the Marx Brothers, what I learned … was a simple value: no laughs, no life" – the San Diego Chicken helping to define the Pads.[22] Especially for the huge local military battalion, another draw became the afore noted McNamara's Band led by "The Tuba Man" – US Marine Jim Eakle – eagerly sought between innings, his cult tying the sign man, the flute lady, the drum man, and the tambourine lady.[23] "For the first time," said Coleman, "you could see young adults bringing their dates."[24]

In 1976, the public saw Jones lead the National League in innings (315⅓), complete games (25), and victories (22). The Padres lefty tied Christy Mathewson's 1913 NL mark of 68 straight innings without a walk – broken by Greg Maddux in 2001 – threw three scoreless innings to start and win the All-Star Game, and took the Cy Young Award. Gaylord Perry's 21-6 in 1978 encored the honor – the first to win each league's. The 84-78 Pads topped .500 for the only time in their first 10 years, drew a team-high 1,670,107, and hosted the midsummer classic: NL, 7-3. Other league highs included Rollie Fingers' 35 and 37 saves in 1977-78, respectively – and Dave Winfield's total bases (333) and RBIs (118) in 1979. On January 6, 1981, the San Diego City Council voted 6 to 2 to rename San Diego-Jack

Murphy Stadium – said Kroc, "He beat the drum to get us big-league ball" – for the late *San Diego Union* sports editor, who died September 24. 1980. Today mascots thrive for one team after another – Mr. Met, the Philly Phanatic. Blessedly, another 1960s through '80s trend, the truly multipurpose stadium, had a briefer life than the Chicken – or Padres' longtime official mascot, the post-1968 Swinging Friar.

In 1908, vaudevillian Jack Norworth wrote what still is baseball's full-throated anthem: "Take Me Out to the Ball Game." Its first two steel and concrete ballparks, Shibe Park and Forbes Field in Philadelphia and Pittsburgh, respectively, opened a year later. By 1923, 14 other parks, most fitting on an urban parcel, rose from the grid of city streets. Like other bad ideas from the 1960s, a different generation of stadia reversed what had worked. Planners sought "super blocks" to flank freeways, abut parking, and spur ease, vainly trying to help baseball's and football's oil and water coexist. Each pre-cookie-cutter had a different personality: League Park, Comiskey Park, Briggs (later Tiger) Stadium. By contrast, multipurpose stadiums seemed dismally alike, conformity choking their vast foul turf, bad sightlines, and seating a seeming time zone from the field. Cookie-cutters were dull, duller, dullest. Happily, most today are dead, deader, deadest. How could baseball so lose its way?

Computers and steel design helped concrete better cantilever and build multiple tiers. Loge seats multiplied, hanging beneath a deck. The effect was to recess stands farther from the field. Some baseball parks were fatally compromised even before they opened by attempting the impossible – accommodate the mutually destructive DNA of baseball (triangular) and football (rectangular). As noted, San Diego's park was built primarily for baseball: small, intimate, and odd. The Giants' Candlestick Park and Angels' Anaheim Stadium were built solely for baseball; the A's Oakland-Alameda County Coliseum, mostly football. *After* opening, each was among parks refitted and rearranged. "The Murph" was sadly "Chargerized" in the 1980s. Three decks rose to enclose left-center field to right-center field. Capacity soared far beyond what its 1960s founders planned. San Diego built an 8½-foot inner fence, alleys dipping to 370 feet, center field to 405, and each line 327 feet from home plate. A 329-foot pole split it from the outer wall, "making it possible," read *The Ballpark Book*, "for a line drive to cross the fence in fair territory and hook in front of the pole into foul."[25] The Pads moved the plate five feet toward the backstop, added a black hitting backdrop, and put ivy on the wall. Nothing restored rapport.

For that, the early 1980s Padres again had only to look at a team smashing almost each attendance record, having been first to note the Spanish-speaking market and to broadcast bilingually. By 1980, Hispanics totaled 25 percent of Dodgers attendance.

In April 1981 a 20-year-old Mexican rookie made the club. On Opening Day, Fernando Valenzuela blanked Houston. Soon Southern California seemed to signify his name. In time, San Diego seemed bent on making up for *lost* time outside America's 50 states. Domestically, its target was the Angelenos. In the 1982-83 offseason, the Dodgers lost Ron Cey to the Cubs and Steve Garvey to San Diego. As a Padre, the latter dislocated a thumb next year in a home-plate collision to end his National League consecutive-games streak at 1,207. LA clinched that September 30 as Dodger Stadium's Diamond Vision scoreboard showed that San Diego downed Atlanta. Given their Death Valley of the past decade, the Pads were about to discover how the other half lived.

Prior to 1984, the Friars had never even placed *third*. Casey Stengel might have said of that year's Padres what he had of the '69 New York Metropolitans, taking everything after seven years of nothingness: "The team has come along *slow* but *fast*."[26] San Diego won the West by 12 games over Atlanta and Houston and 13 over the Dodgers, luring a record 1,983,404. Garvey and Graig Nettles keyed first and third bases, respectively. Goose Gossage ruled the bullpen, saving a 3-1 All-Star Game victory. Bottle-shaped Tony Gwynn climbed his first step toward hitting's Mount Rushmore by forging 213 hits into a first batting title at .351 – his greatness such that those totals later became too easy to dismiss. Tart and bright, manager Dick Williams became the only skipper other than Bob Skinner (records, 337-311 and 1-0, respectively) to reach .500 among the Padres' first 11 managers.[27] In 1984 America outside of San Diego County seemed to hope that the Friars would fall on their postseason face against the Cubs, unfeeling how the League Championship Series could become the Pads' recompense for 1969-83. "It's like we're in 'The National League playoffs starring the Chicago Cubs. Also with the San Diego Padres,'" said Gwynn afterward. "Nobody gave us a chance but the [Padres fans]. They believed in us, and we started to believe in us."[28]

San Diego lost Game One, 13-0, at Wrigley Field, largely on five Chicago homers, including winning pitcher Rick Sutcliffe's. Next afternoon Steve Trout bested Mark Thurmond, 4-2. Behind, two sets to zero, the Padres hosted the rest of the then-best-of-five, trailing the third game, 1-0, in the home half of the fifth inning, five frames from extinction. Cubs starter Dennis Eckersley then yielded three singles and Garry Templeton's double: 3-1, San Diego. Kevin McReynolds' sixth-inning bomb sealed a 7-1 final. Starter Ed Whitson recorded the Friars' first postseason *W*. Gossage, who played from 1972-94, relieved, hailing "the loudest crowd I've ever heard."[29] The next day an unpredictable fourth match had an unanswerable conclusion. San Diego tied at three in the fifth inning, fronted, 5-3, two innings later, and was tied as Garvey batted in a one-out ninth. "Hit high to

The San Diego Padres
Cordially invite you to attend the

## Final Weekend at the Q
## VIP Reception

Saturday, September 27
5:00 - 7:00 p.m.
Reception tent on the Plaza Concourse
Inside Gate A

Please respond to Lauren Heiser
by September 24, at 619-881-6643
or
lheiser@padres.com

A game ticket is required
for admittance to the stadium.
Enter through Gate A.

Invitation is non-transferable.

right-center field! Way back! Going! Going! It is gone! The Pads win it!" Coleman cried. "In a game that absolutely defies description, Steve Garvey, in the ninth inning, hit one over the 370 mark, and the Padres beat the Cubs, 7-5. "Oh, doctor, you can hang a star on that baby!"[30]

The final had a shape few soon forgot. Chicago led, 3-0, behind Sutcliffe, a sublime Cy Young 16-1 in only 20 games. In the sixth inning, its lead had shrunk to 3-2. Then, in lucky *7*, the Pads' Carmelo Martinez walked to lead off, Templeton bunting him to second base. Tim Flannery's grounder passed under first

baseman Leon Durham's glove for an error, scoring Martinez with a 3-all run. After Alan Wiggins singled, he and Flannery scored on Gwynn's double: 5-3. Series MVP Garvey slapped a run-scoring single before Gossage mopped up the Cubs, 6-3, who outscored San Diego, 26-22, but made three muffs, one lethal, to the Friars' one. "As for Cubs fans everywhere," read *Sports Illustrated,* twitting the home-run call of "[their famed Voice Harry] Caray, 'They might be … they could be … they're not [world champions for the first time since 1908]!' Holy cow!"[31] The Murph's largest crowd – 58,359 for Game Five vs. September 1973's 1,413 smallest – agreed. Chicago's rendezvous with destiny would have to outlast the last 15 years of the twentieth century and first 16 years of the twenty-first.

In the fall classic, Detroit took a 3-2 opener. Kurt Bevacqua's three-run dinger evened things, 5-3. The Tigers then swept at home, 5-2, 4-2, and 8-4, battering the Padres for a 4.71 Series ERA. NBC-TV's 14-camera coverage etched Detroit's Alan Trammell's long-ball solo; mate Kirk Gibson's aria, going deep; and Dick Williams's dirge, telling reliever Andy Hawkins, "We've got a long way to go." A Padres fan hoped that at least *making* the Series would prophesy H.G. Wells' *The Shape of Things to Come.*[32] Their *park's* shape continued to change. Before 1984, The Murph was open beyond the right- and center-field bleachers, a view of the Mission Valley enhancing the game's lulls and other rhythms. To please the Chargers, that winter, bleachers swelled to fully enclose the field, making capacity 59,022. The 1985 Padres tested it, drawing 2 million at home for the first time – 2,210,352. On September 11, it played a foil for another team. "It's into left-center! There it is!" Reds Voice Ken Wilson said. "Rose has eclipsed [Ty] Cobb! ... [Pitcher] Eric Show becomes a spectator as this city mobs its native son! The moment we've all waited for – hit number 4,192 that makes Pete Rose the all-time baseball hit leader!" Added *Time* magazine: "By the number and beyond he is what he does. Rose is baseball."[33] Its opinion, like most of America's, would change.

Fall 1985 brought the Pads, quoting Warren Harding's 1920 campaign for president, "Back to Normalcy" – on October 2, the Dodgers clinched the West, their third time since 1981. 1986: Gwynn led the league with 211 hits. Montreal's Tim Raines led with a .334 average. 1987: The batting title reverted more or less to Tony's permanent possession (.370). Rookie of the Year Benito Santiago debuted with a franchise-record 34-game hitting streak. 1988: Gwynn encored as titlist (.313) as San Diego placed third. On August 30 LA's Orel Hershiser yielded a run, then threw the first of 59 straight scoreless innings to break Don Drysdale's 1968 big-league mark of 58. On September 28 he threw his last 10 innings. "There's a drive to right field!" bayed Coleman. "He's going to put it away! Oh, doctor! History was born right here!" At Jack Murphy, now-Dodgers Voice Big D joked that at least Hershiser had kept it in the family. Meanwhile, in the Pads' *famille,* Mark Davis next year became the team's third Cy Younger, Gwynn three-peated a batting crown, and in the saddest "shape of things," as Wells had said, San Diego reclaimed last.

Churchill said: "We shape our buildings and afterwards our buildings shape us."[34] Barely a quarter-century old, The Murph, starting to prematurely age, now began to show why a great baseball franchise needed a baseball-only site. Earlier, it had been sustained by a past to hail –Jack Murphy as the first big-league park to laud a Negro League player – and present to eye. "The Claw" referenced a man sitting in the first outfield row of seats with a rod and a claw on its end. Upon a homer, he lowered the claw and it collapsed on the ball. At worst, a right-field mural showed a crowd support profanity – actress Roseanne Arnold (nee Barr)'s 1990 National Anthem. At best, the park housed quality – Gwynn's six hits in a game and NL-best-since-1930 .394 in 1993 and 1994, respectively, and a war hero and former big-league infielder who fused Mrs. Malaprop and Dizzy Dean.

"On the mound is Randy Jones, the left-hander with the Karl Marx hairdo," said Jerry Coleman, who once fretted about such "Colemanisms" but ultimately "figure they add to my sex appeal." Jesus Alou was "in the on-deck circus." Winfield was "going back ... back ... he hits his head against the wall. It's rolling toward second base!" A man "slides into second with a stand-up double."[35] NBC's Bob Costas defined the most memorable personality, with Gwynn, in Pads history. "He'd have been inimitable in any event. These magnificent departures from norm made him unforgettable."[36] Sit back and "put a star on that baby"[37] – Jerry's signature, akin to Mel Allen's "How about that!" or Caray's "Holy Cow!" Most announcers blur. Coleman's identity entered San Diego's bloodstream.

Baseball's sterling linguist knew the way from San Jose, born September 14, 1924. After high school, he delayed entering baseball to serve in World War II as a Marine Corps fighter pilot, flying 57 missions. Returning home, Coleman moved from Yankees' Class-D Wellsville to the Bronx in 1949 to next year's Babe Ruth Award as the World Series' most valuable player. Leaving baseball, the lieutenant colonel then flew 63 missions in the Korean War before rejoining the Yanks. "Bob Feller and Ted Williams were right," Coleman said. "What you do for America counts most" – in his case, 13 Air Medals, three Navy citations, and two Distinguished Flying Crosses.[38]

Retiring as a player in 1957, Coleman became the Yankees' personnel director. His CBS-TV pre-*Game of the Week* began in 1960. Instantly it almost closed. Jerry was interviewing Cookie Lavagetto when the "Star-Spangled Banner" started. "Better keep talking," the apprentice thought, and did through the Anthem. Letters swamped CBS. "Believe me," he later said, "when the Anthem starts I stop, whether I'm taping, talking, or eating a banana."[39] Jerry covered 1963-69 Yankees radio/TV, at first so insecure that "you need someone to pat you on the back." Instead, a sadist mailed a record to him titled "Famous Jungle Sounds." In film's *Mary Poppins* a character moans, "Things began to happen to me." Working, Jerry's never stopped. Once, interviewing Baltimore pitcher Dave McNally's wife, Coleman said, "I guess you ladies wear the pants when your husbands are gone." She smiled, saying, "And we take them off when they come home." Another warm day Jerry stripped to shorts in Kansas City. A woman complained. "So I had to put my pants back on," he said. "Not that I took them off that often, anyway."[40]

Jerry next aired the 1970-71 Angels, then moved down the coast, where he aired the Padres for nearly four decades. In 1980 he briefly left to manage them to a 73-89 *finis*. Some blamed a "generation gap" between Jerry and especially some of his younger players. Coleman, showing class redolent of his generation, blamed no one, returning a year later to radio, "where I'm probably more comfortable. Most players think I was born at 45," he said.[41] That puzzled most listeners, for whom Jerry eternally and endearingly seemed 12.

In 1979 Winfield had nearly made a leaping catch. "If he had made that play," said Coleman, "they'd be throwing babies from the upper deck."[42] At the end of the Pads' 1984 World Series, hoods rushed the field upon his postgame show. "At Tiger Stadium, it's only 30 feet from the field to the booth," Jerry stated a quarter-century later, having dodged trash and almost sent the Detroit club his dry-cleaning bill.[43] In 1993 he did CBS Radio's LCS, saying on-air, "It was a fantastic game last night. I'm still trying to figure out who did what, and why?"[44] In 1999 Gwynn got hit number 3,000. "Right-center field! Base hit!" one Mr. Padre spoke as the other swung. "Oh-ho, doctor, you can hang a star on that baby! A star for the ages for Tony Gwynn!"[45] In 2002 Jerry became baseball's oldest full-time Voice. The 2004 Pads gave him an open-ended pact at 80. Several years later he voluntarily curbed his work.

In 2005 Coleman got the Hall of Fame's Ford C. Frick Award for broadcast excellence. A San Diegan recalled, "Here's [Johnny Grubb] under the warning track." A hitter lined "up the alley. ... Oh, it's foul." On one hand, Jerry denied saying, "'Rich Folkers is throwing up in the bullpen.' I said, 'He's throwing them up.'" On the other, he *did* say, "This is the only afternoon day game in the National League"; "They throw Winfield out at second, and he's safe"; [George] Hendrick simply lost that sun-blown popup"; and "Next up is Barry Carry Garry Templeton."[46] In 2012 the Pads dedicated a statue of its most beloved Padre in his most beloved garb – Coleman, in military dress. Upon his 2014 death, people bought bouquets and other floral arrangements to lay at the statue. "Sometimes big trees grow out of acorns. I think I heard that from a squirrel," Jerry would say. Sometimes legends grow out of little boys from California, who dream of playing ball.[47]

Another World War II hero, George H.W. Bush, loved baseball as much as any president, having followed, played, and coached the game in every permutation. In 1992 his popularity temporarily at sea, he was heartily booed by the crowd at The Murph on throwing out the first ball at the All-Star Game.[48] The AL battered NL pitchers as Bill Clinton would Bush in that fall's election, 13-6. A Padre won the batting title, as had become customary. It wasn't Gwynn, hitting .317, as had become the rule. Gary Sheffield wed a .330 average, another league-high 323 total bases, and 33 home runs. Mate Fred McGriff led with 35 homers. In 1991 Joe Carter had been dealt to Toronto. In 1993 McGriff and Sheffield were traded, the Friars again placing last, like the bad old days. Worse, the 1994 season ended with a players lockout that began August 12, lasted 234 days, canceled a World Series for the first time since 1904, ended in April 1995, and capsized statistics. Gwynn ended 1994 with a franchise-record *.394* average. "Who knows," said Coleman, "if he'd have hit .400 with seven weeks more to hit?"[49]

In retrospect, the lockout's end began a crucial part of Jack Murphy's story, scripted largely by a man who loved Pittsburgh's lyric Forbes Field as a boy "and saw the damage"[50] when the Pirates left in 1970 for multisport Three Rivers Stadium. By the 1980s, Baltimore Orioles VP/general counsel Larry Lucchino had become owner Edward Bennett Williams's choice to chart aging Memorial Stadium's successor. First, the club vetoed a baseball/football plant to replace it. The O's then hired a new architectural design firm Helmuth, Obata, and Kassabaum (HOK Sport), whose first plan mimicked bland new Comiskey Park. Lucchino and Williams banned that, too, razing an 85-acre plot parallel to old trolley tracks, near historic Camden Railroad Station of the old Baltimore & Ohio, a pop fly from Inner Harbor. Bricks and mortar followed, the product Oriole Park at Camden Yards, opening in 1992 – a new park that became an outlier, not built at the vortex of interstates, but actually *in* the city; better, becoming *part* of it.[51] Before his 1988 death of cancer, Williams made Lucchino O's president.

Lucchino recalled A. Bartlett Giamatti asking, "Why can't we have modern amenities *and* idiosyncrasy? Give me sharper quirks and odder angles,"[52] the past Yale University and future commissioner evoking his first game, at 10, dad taking him to Fenway Park. Oakland seats half-circled each foul line. Camden's nuzzled them. New Comiskey's no-man's land separated seats from an inner fence. Camden's wall and bleachers fused, "fielders grabbing a homer from the stands," Lucchino said. Fences at most parks then curved. The Yard's – few called it "Oriole Park" – leapt angularly and irregularly, tying features of Ebbets Field, Wrigley Field, Shibe Park, and old Comiskey Park. The 46,500-seat arc drew a then-O's record 3,567,819 in 1992 – to the *New York Times*, "the best plan for a major

league baseball park in more than a generation." In December 1988, Giamatti said, having seen a model: "When this park is complete, every team will want one. Baseball can be like life – the keys to the future often lie in the past."[53] Camden Yards keyed 21 sites, including San Diego, in the next 21 years. In 1994 expansion made the NL West briefly a four-team division. That year Lucchino left the Orioles' 41,000 paid and waiting season-ticket list to become San Diego president, CEO, and minority owner.

The 1994 Pads and Astros made the majors' largest deal, involving 12 players, since 1957. Such peddling was one way to retain marquee. Another presented itself when "the [1996] Republican [National] Convention kicked us out of our stadium," said Larry. "So we went to Monterrey [Mexico, vs. the Mets] because we were trying to become a regional team," Estadio Monterrey hosting the bigs' first game outside the United States or Canada. Fernando Valenzuela won the inaugural, 15-10, San Diego alive with Spanish-speaking people. "We're the only team next to the border," said Lucchino, starting Spanish oral and written ads, "and we'd ignored them for years."[54] The Pads revived their swinging Friars mascot. San Diego bought a 24-by-33-foot JumboTron, closed the top outfield deck, cut capacity to 48,639, but built field-level seats behind the plate, and put an 86-foot-long by 9½-foot-high board atop the right-field fence, making lefties clear a 17½-foot barrier. Cordiality would market, if The Murph were made over. A P.A. mike rotated Top 40 and organ music. A gourmet might inhale barbecue at the Randy Jones BBQ Grill, where ironically the "Super Big Slugger Dog" became a menu favorite of the ex-pitcher's clientele.[55]

Above all, the Padres aimed to make good by playing well, nothing marketing like success. The 1996 Friars won a final-day West title. In 1995 Ken Caminiti had become the first to homer from each side of the plate thrice in four games. Now the NL Most Valuable Player set a new team high in homers (40), RBIs (130), and slugging (.621). Steve Finley had 348 total bases. John Flaherty hit in 27 straight games. In October, Golconda crashed in the best-of-five Division Series, born a year earlier – a Cardinals sweep.[56] In 1997, The Murph became Qualcomm Stadium, after rights sponsor Qualcomm Corp. The general stadium site was named "Jack Murphy Field." More rousing: reliever Trevor Hoffman's wonderwork (37 saves), Gwynn's Honus Wagner-tying NL eighth batting title (.372 average, in addition to 119 RBIs!), and travel to Hawaii's Aloha Stadium during Qualcomm's construction. "We couldn't play in San Diego," said Pads co-owner John Moores, "so we moved a [three-game] series." Old habits lingered. St. Louis won twice.[57]

How to top the topper? The '98ers topped 1984's as the best Padres team, their regular-season path to a pennant starring a potpourri of precedent – Hoffman's 53 saves, Greg Vaughn's 50 homers, Bruce Bochy as manager of the year, and 98-64 record – each a franchise high. San Diego's second Division Series went better, the highest-scoring NL team, Houston, batting .182. Game One: Vaughn homered and Kevin Brown fanned a Division Series record 16, beating Randy Johnson, 2-1. Two: After Pad Jim Leyritz's ninth-inning blast tied the score, the Astros untied it, 5-4. Three: The first baseman again homered, Friars, 2-1, set and lead. Four: Padres winning, 6-1, Leyritz ended his season in a series with a third dinger in a week after joining San Diego from Boston with eight. Ahead: The LCS vs. Atlanta, the "Team of the Decade," having won 106 games in the regular season and swept its DS from the Cubs.

A different Braves team unaccountably lost the first two sets at home – 3-2 in 10 innings as Caminiti homered and Donnie Wall saved, and 3-0 as Brown blanked Atlanta on three hits. In Game Three at Qualcomm Stadium the Braves thrice loaded the bases – twice with less than two out – and failed to score, losing, 4-1, to Sterling Hitchcock. Atlanta's three future Hall of Fame starters now had an opening no-decision (John Smoltz) and two losses (Game Two-Three's Tom Glavine and Greg Maddux). Rallying, the Braves countered, 8-3 and 7-6, the latter pivoted by Michael Tucker's three-run bolt off Brown briefly converting Pad congregants to church mice. Go figure: In five of six games the LCS road team won, including the clincher: San Diego, 5-0, in Georgia, Hitchcock beating Glavine, his series ERA 0.90.[58]

The Padres' World Series rival had a different blood type. The Yankees had ended the regular season with an American League record 114-48, swept Texas in the DS, and beaten Cleveland in the LCS. If they could sweep the fall classic, they would record an overall 1998 won-lost 125-50 – the majors' most single-season victories and among best percentage of all time.

In 1937 Lou Gehrig had hit a long home run off Dizzy Dean at the All-Star Game in Washington. Irked, Ol' Diz threw a fastball to the next batter, Earl Averill, whose drive smashed off Dean's left toe. Diz was removed and examined by a doctor. "Your big toe is fractured," the doctor said. "Fractured, hell," Diz stormed, "the damn thing's broken!"[59] In the 1998 Series opener, a like incident occurred. In the second inning, New York's Chili Davis lashed a line drive off Kevin Brown's left shin. Gamely, Brown kept pitching as the Padres built a 5-2 lead on two homers by Vaughn and one by Gwynn. Brown exited in the seventh inning, still ahead, before the bullpen crumbled, Chuck Knoblauch's three-run home run preceding Tino Martinez's grand-slam – Yanks win, 9-6. "If he's not hurt," Jerry Coleman said, "he stays in. Probably the whole game and Series are different."[60]

In Game Two, the pinstripes sprayed 16 hits off four Padres pitchers down the peewee lines and to the gaping alleys of the historic Bronx arcade, romping, 9-3. Game Three returned to Qualcomm, where a year earlier more than 10,000 seats were placed behind the outfield for the Super Bowl to make football capacity 67,054 – and palm trees put between the stands and fence to suggest the breezy and informal merely affirmed the antiseptic and artificial. The Friars led, 3-2, in the eighth inning, before 64,667, Hoffman then yielding a three-run homer to Scott Brosius, the third baseman's second in as many innings: 5-4 final. A day later Andy Pettitte and two relievers threw a 3-0 shutout before 65,427. Overall the Dismal Swamp/Sweep embodied the team gulf, the Bombers outscoring San Diego, 26-13. Once again Hitchcock's ERA was sterling: 1.50.

On cue, the '99ers then evoked the title of Bel Kaufman's 1964 best-selling novel, *Up the Down Staircase*,[61] so characteristic of their lineage. *Down:* The Pads finished two games from the cellar. *Up:* "The season brought back baseball in San Diego," said Coleman.[62] Several lights offset the dark. Hoffman pitched in the July 13, 1999, All-Star Game at Fenway Park. Gwynn, on the disabled list but naturally named to the National League team, flew in from San Diego, saying, "I finally got to see it! Fenway!"[63] Was the batting Matisse 39, or 9? Before the game a native San Diegan, 80, frail, and The Greatest Hitter Who Ever Lived, rode a golf cart from center field to the pitcher's mound, the ovation so huge that American League starting pitcher Pedro Martinez said, "I thought the stadium was going down."[64]

All-Stars rushed to greet Ted Williams as Fenway shook. Baseball's Grand Old Man asked Mark McGwire, "Do you ever smell the wood burn?" of bat hitting ball. Rafael Palmeiro refused to leave. "The game can wait. That's the chance of a lifetime."[65] The Expos' Larry Walker noted tears in Ted's eyes – and his. Saint Francis Xavier said, "Give me a child until he's seven, and you may have him afterward." Even now, The Kid made children of us all. Seldom did baseball play memory's soundtrack more exquisitely than the evening No. *9* tossed out the first ball in the Fens. Ironically, it occurred at the same time another great hitter readied to retire – and the team in Ted's place of birth signaled that it might leave its park.

The prior November a $476 million taxpayer-funded referendum had passed to build a new San Diego ballpark. On August 6, 1999, the man who most helped pass it batted in Montreal. At Qualcomm, thousands chanted his name, watched the game free on a giant-screen TV, and celebrated hit 3,000. A week later nearly 61,000 jammed the yard on Gwynn's return. His reply –a pair of two-run homers. Life begins at 40, which Tony turned in 2000, retiring a year later. He holds a virtual patent on San Diego's big-league batting history: most games (2,440), at-bats (9,288), runs (1,383), hits (3,141), batting average (.338), doubles (543), triples (85), total bases (4,259), RBIs (1,138), extra-base hits (763), and stolen bases (319), among others. Gwynn trails in only home runs (135) to Nate Colbert's 163 and three others. No. *19* was retired by the Pads, like Steve Garvey's *6*, Dave Winfield's *31*, Randy Jones' *35*, Jackie Robinson's *42* (by baseball), and Trevor Hoffman's *51*.

In 2001 Tony and Rickey Henderson, 42, became the first mates in their 40s in the same outfield since Detroit's Doc Cramer and Chuck Hostetler in 1945. Henderson set baseball's all-time walk record (2,063). In October, he got his 3,000th hit in Gwynn's final game. Pro: Winfield entered Cooperstown that year, having played 1973-80 in San Diego, for which he twice batted .308, hit up to 34 home runs, and thrice had more than 90 RBIs – the first Hall of Famer to have a Padres emblem on his cap, followed by Gwynn in 2007 and Hoffman in 2018. Con: A swarm of bees on the right-field auxiliary scoreboard halted a 2001 Pads-Dodgers game. They didn't stay long enough: LA, 5-4. Unless you were there, most of the public in time forgot the incident – but not the splendor of Gwynn's life on and off the field, ended in 2014 of cancer. Remembered, too, was the taxpayer referendum to build downtown Petco Park – business, groups like the nonpartisan City Club of San Diego, and the taxpayer, above all.

Named for local pet supplies retailer Petco, which paid for naming rights until 2026, Petco was built in the downtown area of San Diego with a capacity of 40,219. It was designed by HOK Sport to anchor a Ballpark District of offices, homes, and retail shops – "vital," said Lucchino, his oceanside La Jolla home between LA and San Diego, "to making a seedy area a year-round jewel."[66] Jacaranda trees, palm courts, and water malls conjured an early-Spanish mission. Nearly 4,000 could stand or sit on an incline beyond center field. Bookending them: "two-tiered left- and right-field bleachers, like the grandstand individual sections, each facing the mound," said the 2010-16 TV Voice of the Padres, legendary Dick Enberg.[67] The beautiful and historic brick and timber Western Metal Supply Co. building, once an abandoned warehouse, abutted left field, a corner painted yellow – Petco's new foul line! "This is how we sited the ballpark," HOK architect Joseph Spear said.[68] "We worked from the corner of that building. We worked backwards. The tip of home plate created that 'X' [magical] dimension, and the field and grandstand went around that."

An environmental dustup postponed the Padres' debut at Petco Park. Thankfully, justice delayed there did not become justice denied. The club played its last game at The Murph on September 28, 2003: Colorado, 10-8. San Diego drew a season 2,030,084 to watch its third last-place club of the new century. The Chargers played there through 2017, vainly seeking a new local home, then egressed to LA, leaving the Friars as the sole big-league club not sharing its city with another pro team in football, hockey, or hoops. It housed two World Series (1984 and 1998), two All-Star Games (1978 and 1992), and three Super Bowls (1988, 1998, and 2003) – given "retro" baseball parks, almost sure to remain the only place to host a Series and Super Bowl in the same year (1998.)

The San Diego University Aztecs and several college bowls still call the former Murph home. In 2017 the San Diego County Credit Union bought Qualcomm's naming rights through 2018 and almost farcically redubbed it SDCCU Stadium. The original San Diego Stadium closed for baseball with 11 seat prices for sites from standing room to field-level infield box. At one end, the 1969-2003 Padres only nine times placed even higher than fourth. At another, when San Diego hit it big the Pads almost ran the table, taking the division thrice and NL pennant twice.

On March 11, 2004, the first baseball game at Petco Park involved a four-team NCAA invitational tournament hosted by the Aztecs, coached by Gwynn, beating Houston. The first big-league match was April 8, the Padres edging San Francisco, 4-3, in 10 innings. Lucchino had left two years earlier to become Red Sox president, the '04 Olde Towne Team winning its first world title since 1918. Meantime, his West Coast bequest became widely hailed and often filled – a first-year franchise high 3,016,752, next-season 2,869,787, and yearly near or more than 2 million since.

Like Camden Yards, Petco Park was asymmetrical – the left-field line and straightaway left field originally 336 and 357 feet, respectively, and left-center field a potent 402 feet from home plate. Center field stood 396 feet away, right-center field a fearsome 411, straightaway right field 382 feet, and the right-field line 322 – more of a pitchers' park than first thought, the ball not carrying. Thus, some lengths were cut – left-center field to 390 feet, right-center field to 391, and straightaway right to 349 – offense rising, without harming the ballyard's look.

By any length, Camden West is a grand venue by which to watch on television, gentle camera angles welcoming. In person, it seems an especially fine fit for the pastime after The Murph's bastardization to help football thrive. Yet for more than a third of a century San Diego-Jack Murphy Stadium kept baseball in San Diego alive, even well, prefacing Petco Park. We can all say *Amen* to that.

## SOURCES

Unless otherwise indicated, baseball statistics are derived from baseball-reference.com and retrosheet.org.

Grateful appreciation is made to reprint all play-by-play and color radio text courtesy of John Miley's The Miley Collection. In addition to the sources cited in the Notes, most especially the Society for American Baseball Research, the author also consulted Baseball-Reference.com and Retrosheet.org websites for box scores, player, season, and team pages, batting and pitching logs, and other material relevant to this history. FanGraphs.com provided statistical information. In addition to the sources cited in the Notes, the author also consulted:

## Books

Angell, Roger and Walter Iooss Jr. *Baseball* (New York: Harry N. Abrams, 1986).

Coffin, Tristram Potter. *The Old Ball Game: Baseball in Folklore and Fiction* (New York: Herder and Herder, 1971).

Cohen, Richard M., David S. Neft, and Roland T. Johnson. *The World Series* (New York: Dial Press, 1976).

Halberstam, David. *The Teammates* (New York: Hyperion, 2004).

Koppett, Leonard. *Koppett's Concise History of Major League Baseball* (Philadelphia: Temple University, 2015).

Lowry, Philip L. *Green Cathedrals: The Ultimate Celebration of Major and Negro League Ballparks* (New York: Walker and Company, 2006).

Patterson, Ted. *The Golden Voices of Baseball* (Champaign, Illinois: Sports Publishing, 2002).

Seymour, Harold, and Dorothy Seymour Mills. *Baseball: The People's Game* (New York: Oxford University Press, 1990).

Smith, Curt. *Storied Stadiums: Baseball's History of Its Ballparks* (New York: Carroll & Graf, 2001).

___. *Voices of Summer: Ranking Baseball's 101 All-Time Best Announcers* (New York: Carroll & Graf, 2005).

Williams, Ted, with David Pietrusza. *Ted Williams: My Life in Words and Pictures*. (Toronto: Sports Media Publishing, 2002).

## Newspapers

*The Sporting News* was a primary source of information about San Diego Stadium, especially its embryonic and youthful years. The *San Diego Union-Tribune* was another principal source of information. Other contemporary sources include Associated Press, *Baseball Digest*, *Houston Chronicle*, *Los Angeles Times*, *St. Petersburg Times,* Sunbelt Publications, *New York Times*, and United Press.

## Interviews

Emil J. "Buzzie" Bavasi, with author, November 1978.

Jerry Coleman, with author, May 2003 and April 2010.

Bob Costas, with author, July 1993 and April 1997.

Dick Enberg, with author, October 2014.

Larry Lucchino, with author, August 2011 and July 2012.

## Appreciation

To the late Jerry Coleman and Dick Enberg, Padres broadcasters and recipients of the Ford C. Frick Award for broadcast excellence from the National Baseball Hall of Fame and Museum – the Everest of their field, as each freely said. As a writer and member of the Frick committee, I knew both well. Both loved baseball deeply – and cared for the Padres intensely. Each loved America, and leaves a lesson for how life should be lived. To each this essay is dedicated.

# NOTES

1    Bill Swank, *Echoes from Lane Field: A History of the San Diego Padres, 1936-1957* (Paducah, Kentucky: Turner, 1997).

2    Frank Finch, *The Los Angeles Dodgers: The First Twenty Years* (Virginia Beach, Virginia: Jordan & Co., 1977), 10.

3    "Dodgers Welcomed by Los Angeles," *Washington Post and Times-Herald*, October 29, 1957: A18. SKM_284e18082714590.pdf.

4    Bill Shannon and George Kalinsky, *The Ballparks* (New York: Hawthorn, 1975), 216.

5    Ibid.

6    Emil J. "Buzzie" Bavasi interview with author, November 1978.

7    "This Day in Walter O'Malley History." November 2, 1967, letter from C. Arnholt Smith to Walter O'Malley. walteromalley.com/en/biography/this day.

8    Henry Berry, *A Baseball Century: The First 100 Years of the National League* (New York: Rutledge, 1976), 132.

9    Ibid, 133.

10   *The Sporting News Official Major League Baseball Fact Book 2001 Edition* (St. Louis: The Sporting News, 2001), 467.

11   In the film *The Natural*, a line spoken by star Robert Redford as Roy Hobbs, based on Bernard Malamud's 1952 novel. Produced, TriStar Pictures, 1984.

12   *Official Major League Baseball Fact Book 2001 Edition*, 467.

13   Berry, *A Baseball Century*, 133.

14   Ibid.

15   Ibid.

16    Ibid., 135.

17    Ibid., 136.

18    Ibid., 137. Both quotes courtesy Bavasi.

19    Ron Smith, *The Ballpark Book: A Journey Through the Fields of Baseball Magic* (St. Louis: The Sporting News, 2000), 78.

20    Jerry Coleman interview with author, April 2010.

21    Berry, *A Baseball Century*, 139.

22    "Ted Giannoulas – 42 Years as the San Diego Chicken," *National Herald*, August 30, 2016.  www.thenationalherald.com/134870/ted-giannoulas-42-years.

23    Berry, *A Baseball Century*, 132.

24    Ibid., 137.

25    Smith, *The Ballpark Book*, 83.

26    great-quotes.com/quotes/author/Casey/Stengel/pg/5.

27    *Official Major League Baseball Fact Book 2001 Edition,* 464.

28    Steve Wulf, "You've Got to Hand It to the Padres," *Sports Illustrated*, October 15, 1984: 43. si.com/vault/1984/10/15/627634/youve-got-to-hand-it-to-the-padres.

29    Joe Hughes and Jay Johnson, "Full House Beats Nine Cubs," *San Diego Union-Tribune,* October 5, 1984: A-1.

30    Unless otherwise indicated, this and following play-by-play courtesy of The Miley Collection.

31    Wulf.

32    H.G. Wells, *The Shape of Things to Come* (New York: Macmillan, 1933).

33    Tom Callahan, "A Rose Is a Rose Is a Rose," *Time,* August 19, 1985: 46.

34    "Churchill and the Commons Chamber," on Parliament's official website in London: parliament.uk/about/living-heritage/building/palace/architecture/palacestructure/ churchill. Quote from Churchill's speech to the House of Commons after that chamber's destruction by Nazi bombing during The Blitz.

35    baseball-almanac.com/quotes/quocole.shtml.

36    Bob Costas interview with author, July 1993.

37    Coleman, April 2010 interview, discussing his frequent use of "Hang a star on that baby!"

38    Ibid.

39    Ibid.

40    Ibid.

41    Coleman interview with author, May 2003.

42    Ibid.

43    Ibid.

44    Play-by-play courtesy of CBS Radio.

45    Play-by-play courtesy of Padres Radio.

46    azquotes.com/author/27359-JerryColeman. All Coleman quotations in this paragraph.

47    Coleman April 2010 interview.

48    Bush's booing continued despite the presence next to him on the field of native San Diegan Ted Williams.

49    Coleman April 2010 interview.

50    Larry Lucchino interview with author, July 2012.

51    Smith, *The Ballpark Book*, 148.

52    Lucchino July 2012 interview.

53    xroads.virginia.edu/~MA01/Lisle/Memory. From my story, "Comeback!" for *The American Enterprise* magazine in 1997. Giamatti's quote was taken from my interview of the then-National League president in December 1988.

54    Lucchino July 2012 interview.

55    sandiegorestaurants.com./randy-jones-all-american-sports-grill/ Randy Jones BBQ Grill.

56    *Official Major League Baseball Fact Book 2001 Edition,* 347 and 467.

57    Ibid., 348.

58    Ibid., 348-49.

59    thestacks.deadspin.com/the-genius-of-baseballs-hillbilly-philosopher-1612606054. John Schulian, "The Genius of Baseball's Hillbilly Philosopher," August 1, 2014.

60    Coleman April 2010 interview.

61    Bel Kaufman, *Up the Down Staircase* (New York: Prentice Hall, 1964).

62    Coleman May 2003 interview.

63    Dan Shaughnessy, "Ted Williams the Star as All-Stars Come to Fenway Park," *Boston Globe,* July 14, 1999.

64    Hayden Bird, "5 Times That Ted Williams' Legend Loomed Over the All-Star Game," *Boston Globe,* July 17, 2018.

65    Ibid.

66    Lucchino August 2011 interview.

67    Dick Enberg interview with author, October 2014.

68    Tim Newcomb, "Ballpark Quirks: Petco Park's Historic Western Metal Supply Co. Building," *Sports Illustrated,* July 21, 2014. si.com/mlb/2014/07/21/ballpark-quirks-san-diego-petco-park-western-metal-supply-company.

# MORE THAN A BALLPARK
# PETCO PARK, SAN DIEGO

## BY MIKE MADIGAN AND DAVE NIELSEN

### Introduction

Petco Park has been home to the San Diego Padres since 2004. It has proved to be popular with fans and is largely credited with stimulating significant development of the East Village neighborhood in which it is located, development that was necessary to generate tax revenues necessary for the City of San Diego to meet its financial obligations for the ballpark project. Its beneficial impacts on the neighborhood have exceeded expectations even of its supporters.

Achieving public support and building a facility in a decaying urban neighborhood was very challenging. It took seven years from early discussions to opening. It involved a citywide vote and prevailing in 16 lawsuits that sought to halt the entire ballpark project or otherwise affect elements of it. It required the club owner to finance and gain approval of development in the vicinity of the ballpark. Most important, it required a diverse group of individuals and entities to learn how to work together and to do so on the fly. To their credit they did that and they all deserve praise for the results.

### Background

### New Club Ownership

In 1994, John Moores, a wealthy Texas entrepreneur, philanthropist, and baseball fan, purchased the San Diego Padres for a reported $80 million. This chapter tells the story of the decision by Moores and his team to seek a new venue for the team's home games. In 1994 times were not good for either major-league baseball or for the club. A strike that began on August 12 resulted in the remainder of the 1994 season being canceled, including the playoffs and World Series. It was the first World Series cancellation in history.[1] It also deprived the Padres' Tony Gwynn of his best opportunity to be the first major-league player to bat .400 since Ted Williams in 1941. At the time, the club had a bad record, attendance was low and so was revenue. A very unpopular trade known as the "fire sale" had sent well-known, highly-paid players to the Miami Marlins for what at that time were by and large a group of unknowns, although few suspected at the time that among the "unknowns" was a future Hall of Famer, Trevor Hoffman, who became one of the most popular players in the Padres' history.

Still, Moores' timing was good in many regards. A trade orchestrated by general manager Randy Smith that would bring future All-Stars Ken Caminiti and Steve Finley needed only his approval in December 1994. Moores also inherited a strong cast of inexpensive but productive pitchers headed by Trevor Hoffman, Andy Ashby, and Joey Hamilton, plus a $21 million payroll that he would double within three years.

From 1995 to 1998, the Padres prospered under Moores. In 1996 the team won its first National League West title since 1984. In 1998, the Padres reached the World Series

When Moores purchased the club, he brought in Larry Lucchino as a partner and club president and CEO. Lucchino had served as president and CEO of the Baltimore Orioles and was credited with developing the ballpark at Camden Yards, the first of the so-called "retro" facilities with old-fashioned charm and smaller seating capacities.

Early on, the new ownership group made it clear that they wanted to pursue a new ballpark for the Padres. They had concluded that the current home of the Padres, the joint-use Jack Murphy/Qualcomm Stadium was inappropriate for baseball, citing incompatibility between the needs of football (the Chargers) and baseball (the Padres). As well, the Padres held a distinct second place to the Chargers in terms of stadium revenues. The owners declared that the community deserved a state-of-the-art ballpark. Their shared objective with the city was to make major-league baseball sustainable in San Diego.

### Community and City Involvement

### San Diego International Sports Council

Early efforts for a new ballpark occurred at the San Diego International Sports Council, which on May 10, 1996, released a report titled "Stadium and Arena Financing Options for San Diego." The study had been a "team project" conducted by a group of students at San Diego State University as part of the school's MBA curriculum. The group was led by Erik Judson, who presented the study to the Sports Council. Lucchino was impressed and ultimately hired Judson as the Padres' first special assistant. The findings of the study proved to be useful in subsequent discussions about a new ballpark for San Diego.

### Mayor's Task Force on Padres Planning

Meanwhile, San Diego Mayor Susan Golding had appointed a Task Force on Padres Planning to identify what was needed to guarantee a sustainable future for major-league baseball in San Diego. The task force was chaired by Ron Fowler, who as of 2018 was the Padres executive chairman and a co-owner of the club. The task force's final report was submitted to the City Council in September 1997 and concluded among other things that:

The Padres were an important asset to the life and economy of the San Diego/Tijuana region, and that a community partnership with the owners of the franchise was necessary to protect, preserve, and enhance that asset.

The Padres under their current ownership had set new industry standards for regional marketing and community involvement and had been exceptional corporate citizens.

Given the significant economic benefits provided by the Padres, the city should play an active, meaningful, and responsible role in assuring the existence of major-league baseball in San Diego well into the millennium.

The economics of professional sports had changed significantly. The national trend was away from multisport stadiums to separate baseball-oriented and football-oriented facilities with revenue streams dedicated to the primary sports tenant. Unless some action was taken to change the Padres' circumstances, they would fall further behind the pack.

The Padres could not generate the revenue necessary to become economically viable and remain competitive in Qualcomm Stadium. Their ballpark-related revenues were said to be below the National League and major-league average and far below average in comparison to those clubs with baseball-oriented ballparks.

Given the limited size of the San Diego market and media opportunity, the potential popularity and increased revenue streams generated by a new baseball-oriented ballpark were essential to the future economic and competitive success of the Padres and their long-term survival in San Diego.

A new baseball-oriented ballpark, properly located and designed, could be a catalyst for both revitalization and expanded economic activity in a city or an area of the city.

San Diego had an opportunity to build a ballpark that would be so unique, beautiful, and integrated into its surroundings that it could become an internationally recognized symbol of the city.

Although the Padres had made significant strides in corporate development, corporate support was still inadequate when compared to other major-league baseball franchises.

San Diego was a community rich in small and midsized businesses. Given this significant "middle market," the Padres must continue to appeal to those thriving enterprises.

While the Padres had been extraordinarily successful in the area of community outreach, the unique circumstances of the San Diego region would require the team to reach out even further into the community and create a network of mutually beneficial relationships.

In a new baseball-oriented ballpark with the type of atmosphere and amenities that enhanced the fans' experience and increased revenues in other cities such as Baltimore, Cleveland and Denver, the Padres could potentially become a stable, competitive, healthy franchise for years to come.

**City of San Diego Task Force on Ballpark Planning**

The City Council, upon officially receiving the report of the Task Force on Padres Planning, approved a proposal by Mayor Golding to establish a City of San Diego Citizens Task Force on Ballpark Planning to be chaired by Patrick Shea, a partner in the Pillsbury Madison and Sutro law firm. City Councilman Byron Wear was appointed an ex-officio member. Their charge was to look at location and financing options for a ballpark. Specifically, the task force was directed to do the following:

SITE SELECTION: To recommend a site that would maximize economic development and vitality for both the Padres and San Diego as a community and be consistent with long-range urban planning principles.

FINANCE: To recommend a viable preliminary financing plan that would identify a preferred financing structure to include public, private, corporate, and project-related financing components.

DESIGN AND CONSTRUCTION: To develop a preliminary project cost estimate for a new ballpark based on analysis of factors such as land assembly, infrastructure requirements, environmental impacts, and design and construction issues, and a construction timetable.

The work of the task force commenced in January 1997. Their final report was submitted to the mayor and City Council in January 1998.

While not official members of the task force, the Padres played an important support role. They provided information and data throughout the process. They provided material from Major League Baseball, other major-league clubs, and outside consultants and experts to assist task force members in their analysis. Padres players and employees gave public comment at various public forums and committee meetings. They also assisted in many of the task force's special events including the Design and Construction Committee's public workshop and children's competition as well as a public forum on January 7, 1998, that included ballpark presentations from other major-league communities.

In the course of its deliberations the task force considered five sites, all within the city limits:

The General Dynamics site in Kearny Mesa.

Mission Valley, near Qualcomm Stadium.

North Embarcadero (Navy property south of Broadway on San Diego Bay).

The vacant Lane Field site (home of the minor-league Padres from 1936 to 1957).

The South Embarcadero site in the Centre East area of the city.

The General Dynamics site was eliminated early in the process for lack of interest by the owner. The Lane Field site was eliminated next because it was found to be too small to accommodate

a project of this size. Subsequently, both the North Embarcadero and Mission Valley sites were eliminated—the former due to the uncertainty of its availability and the difficulty of confirming a real-time process for obtaining access to the property, and the latter mainly due to locational aspects.

That left the South Embarcadero site (a/k/a East Village or the Historic Warehouse District), and the task force recommended that the mayor and city council select it as the preferred site for a new baseball park. It was described as being immediately adjacent to the thriving Gaslamp Quarter and to have "an approximate site range" bordered on the north by K Street, the south by Commercial Street, the east by 12th Avenue, and the west by 7th or 8th Avenues.

In addition, the task force recommended that the mayor and city council:

Create a "Ballpark District" surrounding the ballpark site and establish a "Ballpark District" Board to expedite development of the ballpark and surrounding area.

Ensure that the public portion of a financing plan would be justifiable to taxpayers and fair to all parties involved. It would limit City General Fund participation to Transient Occupancy Tax revenues paid by visitors to the city with no other General Fund obligation beyond the specific revenues identified in the financing plan.

Promptly enter into negotiations with the Padres for planning, constructing, developing, and operating a new ballpark.

The new ballpark in that location would in the words of the task force become the "anchor tenant" in a revitalized section of the city. It would be surrounded and complemented by commercial and residential development, restoration of existing buildings and landmarks and a variety of parks, promenades, and other public amenities.

With regard to financing, the task force recommended that the agreement between the city and Padres should not guarantee the Padres a profit, but should afford them the opportunity to make a profit.

With regard to design, the report concluded that the ballpark should be one of the signature structures of the downtown skyline and part of an attractive, welcoming "front door" to a beautiful city with a world-class waterfront. The ballpark should express San Diego's unique character and beauty. It should be in a parklike setting with extensive landscaping and open to the sky, with ample vistas of San Diego. It should be a high quality, state of the art facility with careful attention to every aspect of design and construction. It could be the first step in dramatic neighborhood improvement.

In summary, what became commonly known as the East Village site met most of the parties' objectives. From the city's point of view it would quite likely revitalize a portion of the downtown redevelopment area that in the words of former Councilman Byron Wear was financially upside down. Moores and Lucchino had come to appreciate the potential of tax increment financing in order for the city to meet its financial obligations. And Lucchino, looking back at his experience in Baltimore, wanted to expand the scope of this effort to include a comprehensive master plan for the entire surrounding neighborhood. Finally, the city's Centre City Development Corporation (CCDC) had what a former Padres executive years later called an "army" of experts with a record of success. They understood the complexities of California redevelopment law and financing, and had experience in land assembly and negotiations with diverse landowners. They also had in-house urban planning and design expertise.

The final challenge was to select the precise location of the ballpark within the boundaries of the East Village. The site agreed to was between 7th and 10th Avenues and Imperial Avenue and J Street. While some wanted it to be farther to the east, the selected site was close enough to be more easily "fitted into the fabric of downtown." Several participants in those discussions, in particular master plan architect Boris Dramov, pushed hard for a location close enough to "spark the gap" between the ballpark and the Gaslamp Quarter, which was thriving.

The ballpark was expected to hold up to 46,000 people by means of approximately 42,000 fixed seats, standing-room locations for up to 1,500, and picnic and lawn seating areas in a "Park at the Park" for approximately 2,500. It would be an open-air, natural grass, state-of-the-art, multiple-use ballpark.

On February 23, 1998, the City Council officially received the task force report and authorized a negotiating team recommended by the city manager to negotiate with the Padres. The council directed the city manager to return in three weeks with the necessary timeline to get the matter before the public for a vote as early as November. The timeline presented included a measure on the November 3, 1998, ballot.

**The Design and Construction Teams**

Even before the task force report was released, the Padres had retained an architectural team which included:

Design architect Antoine Predock

Executive architect Joe Spear, HOK + Venue + Event

Master plan architect Boris Dramov, ROMA Design Group

In June 1998, well in advance of the November election, the Padres unveiled renderings of "A Ballpark for San Diego."

Meanwhile Ballpark Builders was formed, a joint venture composed of Clark Construction Group, Inc., Nielsen Dillingham Builders, and Barnhart PCL. The joint venture retained Hines Interests Limited Partnership to act as construction manager for development of the ballpark.

## Ballpark Design

From the beginning, the Padres and their team worked to design a ballpark that would reflect San Diego's position on the ocean and in the semi-arid Southwest. Thus, the final design, unlike other ballparks being developed at the time, would be clad in sandstone rather than brick, to reflect images of the iconic cliffs in the nearby Torrey Pines State Preserve. Other distinctive features to be included were a large waterfall at the home plate entrance as well as planters filled with a variety of plants throughout the facility.

One feature of the ballpark did, however, harken back to Lucchino's experience in Baltimore – incorporation of the historic Western Metal Supply Company building into the ballpark design, similar to the B&O Warehouse at Camden Yards. One corner of the building in San Diego became the left-field foul pole, thus setting the precise location of the field. This novel idea required approval of Major League Baseball. Ultimately the building would house the Padres' team store, a bar and grill, party suites to be rented for individual games with balconies for viewing games, and bleacher seating on top of the building.

The design included a 2.8-acre "Park at the Park" just outside the center-field fence. It was to include a grassy area, a play area for children, a miniature Wiffle Ball diamond, and a sand "beach" where children could play while parents watched the action on the field from the higher ground. The park would be available to the general public except during games. Admission during games was to be $5 per person and a video display would be installed for those sitting in view-obstructed areas.

## Memorandum of Understanding

Meanwhile the Padres, the city, the City Redevelopment Agency and CCDC had begun to work on a draft Memorandum of Understanding (MOU). The MOU covered a Ballpark District, Construction of a Baseball Park, and a Redevelopment Project. It outlined the responsibilities of each party for the project, including:

Land acquisition, construction, and installation of the ballpark,

Parking facilities and other public improvements.

Requirements for ancillary development, including hotels, retail and residential facilities, and office space,

The estimated project cost was $452.6 million, to be funded by four key elements of investment:

City of San Diego, $225.0 million.

Redevelopment Agency, $ 61.0 million.

Padres/Private Sources, $145.6 million.

Other/Port, $21.0 million.

Responsibilities for developing the project were to be spread among the various parties as follows:

The city was to be responsible for the planning and construction of infrastructure improvements in the area.

CCDC was to be responsible for the acquisition of land.

The Padres were to be responsible for building the ballpark facility.

The Padres, or developers the Padres could designate, were to be responsible to build the ancillary development.

## Proposition C

On November 3, 1998, in a citywide election, 59.64 percent of those voting approved the MOU after a very spirited campaign in which the Padres played a major role. Larry Lucchino recalled that the club treated it as a political campaign and they and their representatives "spoke everywhere." It certainly helped that the credibility of the club had improved with the division championship in 1996 and, in particular, the National League pennant in 1998, just before the voting took place.

## Early Progress

Construction of the "Ballpark Facility" officially commenced in May 2000, when the city issued a "Project Site Notice to Proceed," although demolition of existing buildings had begun on February 10, 2000. The first highly visible construction event occurred on April 1, with the "Ballpark Blast," the implosion of a former San Diego Gas and Electric building. This was a major media event and helped keep momentum going for the project. Lucchino strongly believed that momentum was important in major projects and tried to use media events related to the ballpark's progress to maintain public interest. On August 12, "Ballpark Blast II" brought down the former San Diego Refrigeration building, the last building to be cleared within the ballpark's footprint. The first concrete for the new ballpark had been poured the previous month.

In January 2001 the city manager reported that between the city, CCDC, the Padres, and private developers, $138 million had been expended toward completion of the project. The manager also reminded the City Council and public that he was to provide a maximum of $225 million to the construction of the project from the net proceeds of a financing. But the report ominously noted that legal challenges remained to be resolved before city financing could commence.

## Litigation

Initially the project proceeded smoothly. But in spite of broad public support and the popularity of the club and its leadership, there was serious and protracted opposition. Some opponents argued that the public investment was not justified given the projected economic benefit. Others argued that public funding of facilities for private use was wrong. The latter group, led by former City Councilman Bruce Henderson, initially objected to placing the matter on the ballot at all and took the matter to court. They were overruled and Proposition C was approved handily.

But approval of Proposition C was only the beginning of what proved to be a succession of court cases. The opponents filed a series of lawsuits challenging follow-up actions of the City Council to approve the project. It was a complex process. Each step implementing the MOU required a separate vote of the council and each in turn resulted in new lawsuits, ultimately amounting to 16, incorporating more than 70 separate causes of action, six of which were appealed. The city and the Padres prevailed in all of them. But it took considerable time to achieve success.

## Suspension of Construction

One of the consequences of the ongoing litigation was that the city could not sell bonds to cover its obligations under the MOU. In order to sell tax-exempt bonds, public agencies such as the city must obtain a legal opinion confirming that the process has been conducted according to all applicable laws, and that there is no outstanding litigation considered relevant to this determination. Not knowing when all this could be resolved in court, the city and the Padres were forced to suspend construction in October 2000.

By then 20.3 percent of the estimated budget had been spent on various portions of the ballpark facility, including all demolition, all foundation work, some portion of the underground utility work, partial construction of the concrete structure, and work relating to the creation of the main seating bowl.

On January 30, 2002, the San Diego Superior Court dismissed the last of the lawsuits, and two weeks later the city sold bonds to finance the project, raising $130 million. Construction resumed on February 28, 2002, after a delay of 16 months.

During that period however, some important work had proceeded, most importantly delivery of structural steel from Korea beginning on December 22, 2000. While buying the steel was expensive and at the time seemed risky, it turned out to be a wise move, as steel prices increased substantially and delivery times lengthened during the 16-month delay.

### Public Relations and Outreach

From the beginning of this project, the Padres demonstrated considerable skill in garnering and maintaining public awareness and support. During the Proposition C campaign, Lucchino and other members of his staff and consulting team were involved in literally hundreds of presentations. Lucchino successfully recruited influential fans and business leaders to lend their support and appear at public meetings and hearings.

Throughout this process, even during the suspension period, Lucchino worked constantly to maintain public support for the project, to never lose momentum and to maintain a sense that a new ballpark in East Village was a good thing and inevitable. Events and announcements large and small were staged regularly including:

6/8/98: Unveiling of the first renderings of "A Ballpark for San Diego."

2/15/99: Unveiling of a scale model of the ballpark.

8/4/99: JMI presentation of design plans for a 33-story hotel and tower to be built just west of the ballpark, connected by a sky bridge over Seventh Avenue.

2/12/2000: Symbolic right-field foul pole ceremony to mark the site with San Diego native Ted Williams.

4/1/2000: "Ballpark Blast I," implosion of the former SDG&E building.

8/12/2000: "Ballpark Blast II," implosion of last building in the ballpark footprint.

10/7/2001: Announcement of the ballpark's address: 19 Tony Gwynn Drive.

All during this time Lucchino was busy. During games he used his private box at Qualcomm Stadium to meet and greet as many people as possible. They were each hosted for an inning or two and then dispatched to some other prime location, often the press box, making room for the next group. He never missed an opportunity to garner goodwill and promote the project.

### Neighborhood Issues

Leading up to final approval by the City Council, residents of the communities near the proposed ballpark expressed serious concerns about the impact to their neighborhoods, in particular traffic, parking, noise, and light impacts in Barrio Logan, Logan Heights, Sherman Heights, Golden Hill South Park, and North Park. Lucchino dispatched his consulting team to meet with these groups to try to allay their fears and develop mitigation measures to minimize impacts should they occur. At a critical juncture, he brought in a former citizen activist from Baltimore who lived near Camden Yards and had originally opposed a ballpark in his neighborhood. He met with people in their homes, responded to their questions and offered suggestions as to how the city and the Padres could deal with their issues. His presentations and suggestions proved to be very helpful for the neighbors as well as the City Council in its deliberations.

### Traffic and Parking Impacts

Fears concerning potential traffic and parking impacts proved to be largely unfounded. The majority of games and events would not occur during rush hour. Unlike the traffic pattern at Qualcomm Stadium, there were multiple points of ingress and egress, including Interstate 5 and State Routes 163 and 94, and a grid system of surface streets. There would be three trolley stations within easy walking distance.

For event parking the Padres identified available parking spaces in the downtown area and showed them on a map that was widely distributed. They worked with the city and East Village businesses to implement street parking restrictions on event days. And for the adjoining residential neighborhoods, the city prepared a parking permit program that proved not to be needed. Thus, opposition fears that there would be too few parking spaces proved not to be true as other parking-lot owners adapted both availability and pricing to match Padres games.

### Historic Preservation

A number of buildings on the ballpark site and elsewhere in the proposed Ballpark District were considered to be of historical significance. These concerns were well articulated by, among others, the National Trust for Historic Preservation and the local Save Our Heritage Organization. The Padres, JMI, and the city worked with these organizations and were able to develop a comprehensive agreement for the preservation of historic buildings in the Ballpark District. In all, 11 buildings were preserved and seven allowed to be demolished. The most challenging historic undertaking was the relocation of the Showley Brothers Candy Factory, a building constructed of unreinforced masonry. Historic preservationists insisted that the building be moved intact the one block to its new home within the project boundaries rather than be dismantled and rebuilt. This was a very expensive proposition, but one the Padres successfully (with nervous members of the planning and construction teams holding their collective breath), managed to accomplish. It is now the headquarters of Bumble Bee Tuna.

Another structure, Rosario Hall, the oldest wooden building built in downtown, had to be relocated across the trolley tracks, which necessitated closing a trolley line and a midnight move. It, too, was successful.

### Resumption of Construction and Ballpark Completion

On February 16, 2002, then-Mayor Dick Murphy issued an official "Notice to Proceed" with construction, thus ending a 16-month suspension. Construction proceeded relatively smoothly from there and included the following milestone dates:

7/8/2002: Arrival of first shipment of "Padre Gold" sandstone.

8/22/2002: Construction one-third complete

12/18/2002: Construction 50 percent complete.

12/22/2002: Padres and Petco Animal Supplies, Inc. announced a 22-year sponsorship agreement that included naming rights.

2/14/03: "Topping Out" ceremony.

5/5/03: Installation of first "Pacific Blue" seat.

8/4/2003: 75 percent of construction complete.

9/3-4/2003: Installation of Bull's Eye Bermuda sod on playing field.

9/22/2003: Relocation of Showley Brothers Candy Factory,

9/28/2003: Last Padres game at Qualcomm Stadium – 35th and final season. Home plate transferred to Petco Park.

1/21/2004: First players workout.

2/20/2004: Substantial completion. Keys and certificate of occupancy handed to the Padres.

3/11/2004: First event: Aztec Invitational College Baseball Tournament.

4/3/2004: First exhibition game: Padres vs Mariners.

4/8/2004: Opening day: Padres 4, Giants 3.

### Conclusions

Development of the Ballpark District was the culmination of a larger effort launched by then-Mayor Pete Wilson and shopping center developer Ernest Hahn in the early 1970s.

Wilson very much wanted to redevelop the downtown and Hahn was a willing partner provided the city first commit to construction of a convention center and housing in the area. Based on his experience in Las Vegas, Hahn felt strongly that a convention center would attract out-of-town visitors and new residents and be the necessary first step in stimulating downtown redevelopment. Wilson launched the effort to develop a convention center, which culminated in its approval under Mayor Roger Hedgecock and first-phase completion under Mayor Maureen O'Connor. Hahn in turn developed Horton Plaza, a major shopping center in the geographic center of the downtown area.

While the shape of retail has changed dramatically since then and the center will soon be repurposed, the two projects provided the spark that resulted in the transformation of the areas west of the Ballpark District.

The challenge of those who planned the ballpark and ancillary development in East Village was to build on those successes and create the spark necessary to bridge the physical gap between the vibrant Gaslamp Quarter to the west and the mostly deserted and rundown East Village. By almost any measure they were successful beyond anyone's expectations. And it was accomplished with only minimal disruption, requiring relocation of only 22 people.

The ballpark, especially the Park at the Park, has created a unique personality and feel in the neighborhood. Thousands of new residents have moved into high-rise, townhouse, and loft homes. A luxury hotel is linked to the ballpark by a pedestrian bridge. A new Central Library with its distinctive design has been built immediately east of the ballpark.

Only two other features of the original Ballpark District plan remain unfinished. Due to regulatory delays and financing issues, the at-grade rail crossing at Park Boulevard was not open as of 2018 although a dramatic pedestrian bridge at that location provided some access to the nearby hotel, convention center, and waterfront. And the "D-1" parcel near the railroad tracks remained vacant. Originally planned for a hotel, its development seems dependent on future expansion of the convention center.

Since Petco Park opened in 2004, nearly all of the early hopes for the project have been fulfilled. The ballpark itself gets high marks from both locals and visitors. The decision to rely on light-rail transit, buses, and other alternative transportation systems, as well as private parking lot entrepreneurs, has justified the minimal dedicated parking lot capacity. Rock and Pop concerts (the Rolling Stones, Madonna, the Eagles, etc.) as well as corporate and civic events, have turned the ballpark into a year-round activity center and the project continues to catalyze new development in the East Village.

## SOURCES

City of San Diego, "Report of the Mayor's Task Force on Padres Planning," September 19, 1997.

City of San Diego, "The Report of the City of San Diego Task Force on Ballpark Planning," January 29, 1998.

Stanford Graduate School of Business, "PETCO Park as a Catalyst for Urban Redevelopment," February 19, 2008.

Moores, Jennifer, and Jim Forni, foreword by Tony Gwynn. *The Sweet Spot: The Story of the San Diego Padres' Petco Park* (Solana Beach, California: Canum Entertainment, 2004).

The authors wish to thank the following for assistance in preparing this article: Larry Lucchino, Eric Judson, former City Councilmember Byron Wear, Rick Vogle, and Jim Chatfield.

## NOTES

1    The first World Series was held in 1903, with the Boston Americans triumphing over the Pittsburgh Pirates. In 1904, the New York Giants declined to play the Boston team. From 1905 on, the World Series has been held on a regular basis, with the exception of 1994.

# TED GIANNOULAS

## (AKA THE SAN DIEGO CHICKEN, THE FAMOUS CHICKEN)

### BY FRED O. RODGERS

They say the best things come in small packages and this is quite true when analyzing Ted Giannoulas's career as a 5-foot-4 costumed chicken for four decades and counting. Baseball fans in San Diego consider The Chicken as their own but as time passed The Famous Chicken took his act around the world, mesmerizing fans with his sketches and antics, cavorting around ballparks, stadiums, and arenas. He has been a joy to watch by anyone, of any age. He is the very first, and the most famous, professional mascot in sports history to most observers.

Ted has entertained more than 5,000 times at sporting events in over 900 different facilities in all 50 states and 8 countries. Counting all his appearances from all events he has appeared more than 17,000 times around the world. Moreover, he has played to more than 60 million people in live audiences, which ranks up there with best entertainment ever.[1]

His parents, John, a restaurateur, and Helen, a seamstress, emigrated from Greece to Canada in the early 1950s with just $17 to their name. They settled in London, Ontario, where Ted was born on August 17, 1953, and two sisters followed. His father traveled to San Diego in 1965 and 1966 to visit Ted's godparents, who were the first to leave the harsh winters of Canada. He returned raving about the climate – very similar to that of his homeland.

The family applied for residency and their application was accepted in 1969. They left Canada in the family station wagon during the Woodstock Music Festival. Ted remembered vividly that trek while he was 16 years old. "I enjoyed all the stops along the way, and was especially fascinated by all the big-league stadiums we passed en route."[2] His dad was not a sports fan of any kind but Ted kept up on baseball by reading copies of *The Sporting News* from cover to cover.

The family settled into a neighborhood that enrolled Ted at Herbert Hoover High School, the same high school that Ted Williams attended. "It was a thrill to learn that Ted Williams walked the same halls as I did," Giannoulas said. "They also had a large picture of him at the end of one of the halls."

When Ted was at Hoover High, there was an open tryout for the school mascot and a lot of his friends wanted him to try out. "I thought I was too hip to be doing anything like that," said Ted. "They really thought I was that stupid to do anything that goofy."

Ted took journalism classes at Hoover hoping one day to be a sportswriter. He immediately began winning California state awards for high-school journalism. He was soon named editor of the school paper. "I actually declined becoming editor-in-chief because I just wanted to focus on sports," Ted said.

His favorite memories in high school included taking drama classes at which his teacher encouraged him to be expressively creative in his body language while on stage. Although he never committed himself to being in any of the school's major stage productions, his teacher strongly suggested he might have a career as an actor. Prophetic advice seen in hindsight.

A straight-A student at Hoover, Ted took his education to another level at nearby San Diego State University, majoring in journalism. He graduated with honors in 1976. For somewhat political reasons, he never worked for the student-run *Daily Aztec*. "It was clearly a case of who you knew to get any plum assignments like covering Aztec sports," he lamented. "But I have no sour grapes about it because it merely created other fateful opportunities as a result."

On the day before spring break in March 1974, the campus was deserted of students who had taken off early. "I decided to hang out for a few minutes at the small, student-run radio station, KCR," said Ted, "to shoot the breeze with anyone still left that were hanging out."

"There were four other kids casually lounging about as I joined them, settling in toward the back corner of the cramped lobby area. Within minutes, a representative from KGB radio appeared at the doorway to address us. He himself was an alum of KCR a few years back. He was in search of quick intern help on a short promotion the station was planning."

"All five of us volunteered on the spot, no questions asked – anything to get a foot in the door of an honest-to-goodness real rock 'n' roll station! He immediately cautioned that KGB was

only willing to pay two dollars an hour. No problem, we all said! Then he cautioned that this wasn't going to be a conventional assignment. Again – no problem, we all repeated. We'll clean bathrooms, empty trash or shine records!"

"When the rep mentioned next that one of us would have to wear a chicken suit at the [San Diego] Zoo as a promotional stunt, there was a brief pause in our enthusiasm … but then – no problem, we restated with all our hands raised. … Bring it on!!!!"

"The rep was taken aback, I think, by our continued spirit for the job as he still stood in the doorway. He glanced about the room quickly, looking for a polite reason for one of us to be selected before having to disappoint the other four.

"When he saw me towards the back corner, he immediately had his answer, "You … the short guy. You'll fit the chicken suit the best of all!!!"

"This hiring episode took two minutes – no audition, no job application to fill, and no interview to process. He said, 'You start tomorrow.' And it began."

After Ted's 10-day stint at the San Diego Zoo ended, he mentioned to station management that it might be a good publicity idea to send him to the Padres Opening Night. "Personally, I was just hoping to get in free anyway!" he said.

They agreed and when the press expressed how quirky it was to see a "red, ragtag chicken" at the game, KGB's brass were thrilled by the attention. "They kept me on as a result and allowed me to continue attending Padres games."

That one-week gig turned into a five-year run with the radio station. It was not unusual for The Chicken to appear at six or eight events a day. At the ballpark he would traipse up and down the aisles handing out "eggs" to the fans. Eventually he found his way onto the field, where his dancing and casting a spell on the visiting team thrilled the fans. Attendance nearly doubled his first year. At one point, The Chicken appeared at 520 consecutive Padres home games.[3] His knew that he had made it as a guy dressed in a chicken suit when he was asked to appear at the All-Star Game in San Diego in 1978.

Before The Chicken came on the scene the only music one heard at the ballpark was organ music. Ted changed all that by introducing popular prerecorded music at games.[4] "Stadium Rock" has its roots from his act in the 1970s. Ted was also the first to use a game's time-out breaks, including between innings, to perform his comedy gags on the field. The audiences were thrilled. No more boring interludes.

His escapades on the field included all baseball personnel – the players, the umpires, the grounds crew. They all became tools in his act.

"The umpires have been the most overlooked and under-appreciated part of the game," Ted said. "Yet, through the magic of humor, I engaged them in comedic bits on the field."

One night in San Diego before a game, umpires Joe West and Frank Pulli suggested to Ted a gag in which they would turn their backs standing in tandem outside the infield. Ted would then beeline his three-wheeler at them from across the diamond. Within feet of them he would yell a signal and they would split apart at the last second. As he buzzed right through them, the crowd shrieked with laughter. "Little did they know that the whole sketch was designed by the umpires themselves," smirked Ted.

Employing an eye chart for the umpires has always been one of his best pranks.

In 1977 the KGB Chicken almost caused an international incident. The San Diego Mariners hockey club scheduled an exhibition game with the champion Russian hockey team in San Diego. They were not amused about a red chicken sporting the letters KGB mocking their goalie behind the glass and hexing all their skaters and even mooning them.

But when it was time to begin the game, the Russians refused to come out of their dressing room. They sent word that they would only take the ice when "that fowl" was removed from the premises. They had had enough of that insulting Chicken, who they believed was hired for the evening to ridicule them with his "KGB" logo on his vest.

The game was delayed 20 minutes. A sudden meeting under the grandstands to straighten things out was convened among the coaches, ambassadors, executives, and interpreters. The Russians came to finally understand that it would make bigger news if The Chicken was evicted from the arena and that his KGB insignia had nothing to do with their spy agency. Grudgingly, they relented and The Chicken was allowed to stay. Flustered as they were, the Russians fell behind early in the game before coming back to win it handily.

"I had no idea at the time I was the focus of their ire!," said Ted.

As the years progressed and the KGB Chicken's popularity increased, he was often spotted at other sporting events: NHL games, NBA games, concerts, and conventions. Ted's growing career ambitions increased faster than the radio station's management policies.

As feathers were ruffled in the media regarding the spiff between Ted and KGB, the radio station abruptly fired him in May 1979.

It tried to stop him from going out on his own. But Ted decided to contest the lawsuit accusing him of appropriating the station's "intellectual property." He said, "How can you sue a guy for intellectual property wearing a chicken suit?"

"I designed my own new caricature which I still wear to this day," Ted said, "and I had my mom, a professional seamstress, sew it together. I then approached the San Diego Padres about appearing in their games for a fee. They were all for it!"

But for his return debut night, on June 29, 1979, Ted requested an attendance-based bonus if the event drew more than the Padres' average crowd of 18,000. The front office essentially laughed off such a notion and agreed to an arrangement in order to humor Ted, he thought. Ted would be paid $1.50 per person above the average crowd.

Meanwhile, through media interviews Ted heavily promoted his return night as "The Grand Hatching," and had a professionally constructed eight-foot Styrofoam egg built that he would break out of during a pregame ceremony on the field to introduce his new coat of feathers. The public was excited.

That evening, more than 41,000 fans sold out Jack Murphy Stadium to witness the spectacle. It featured a parade of the egg – with Ted inside it – atop an armored truck onto the field, led by a California Highway Patrol escort. The entire Padres team helped to lower the egg from the truck and onto the field. Then, as the soundtrack to *2001: A Space Odyssey* played, the new Famous Chicken burst out of the shell to a 10-minute standing ovation. Baseball historians have said this was one of the greatest public-relations spectacles in the game's history.

"The next day, the Padres cut me a check for more than $43,000 – more than eight times what the highest major-league player (Rod Carew) was paid per game," Ted said. "The entire amount was gobbled up by attorney fees as I defended myself from KGB's litigation. Still, the fans' turnout that night saved my bacon to continue onward in my career." He was now a free bird.

Over the next couple of decades The Famous Chicken became popular all over the world. Three US presidents – Gerald Ford,

Ronald Reagan, and George W. Bush – requested his presence at their events. He co-starred with Johnny Bench and Pete Rose on the Emmy-winning children's show *The Baseball Bunch* for five seasons. *The Sporting News* named him one of the 100 most powerful people in sports for the twentieth century. The *New York Times* has characterized him as "perhaps the most influential sports mascot in history."[5]

In 2011 Giannoulas was inducted into the Baseball Reliquary Shrine of the Eternals.[6]

His feathered chicken suit was sent for display in the National Baseball Hall of Fame in Cooperstown, New York. "I'm thrilled that my costume is now enshrined," Ted said, "The Hall of Fame is about stats, not lore. My Hall of Fame is getting thousands of people to laugh whenever I perform. Having said that, Cooperstown has a players wing and a broadcasters wing. Maybe one day they'll have a chicken wing!"

Those wings are getting tired after flying more than two million miles over four decades. Ted's appearances have dwindled from approximately 260 a year to about 40 in 2018. He has never missed a scheduled appearance and there has never been a replacement for him either.

There was the possibility of keeping his "legacy" continuing if he sold The Famous Chicken rights to a ballclub. But Ted said in 2019 that he was unsure if having someone else wear the costume was the right way to go. "I'm going to keep going until it isn't fun anymore, he said. "It's not the end, but I can see it from here."

## NOTES

1    Chris Jenkins, "The San Diego Chicken's Still Kickin'," *San Diego Union Tribune*, June 24, 2015. sandiegouniontribune.com/sports/padres/sdut-giannoulas-chicken-famous-padres-2015jun24-story.html.

2    Author interview with Ted Giannoulas on January 3, 2019. All quotations otherwise unattributed come from this interview.

3    Pete Croatto, "The San Diego Chicken Heads Into a Sunset," *New York Times*, August 27, 2016. nytimes.com/2016/08/27/sports/baseball/ted-giannoulas-san-diego-chicken.html.

4    Unknown author, "The Famous SD Chicken," 2016. famouschicken.com/biography.html.

5    Pete Croatto.

6    "Shrine of the Eternals," Baseball Reliquary. baseballreliquary.org/awards/shrine-of-the-eternals/shrine-of-the-eternals-alphabetical-list-of-electees/.

# NOTABLE PADRES GAMES

# PADRES WIN INAUGURAL MAJOR-LEAGUE GAME

## APRIL 8, 1969: SAN DIEGO PADRES 2, HOUSTON ASTROS 1, AT SAN DIEGO STADIUM

## BY GREGORY FUNK

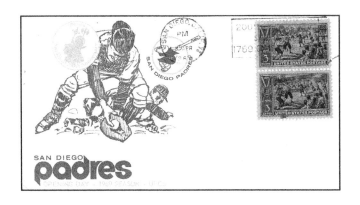

San Diegans rejoiced in May 1968 when the National League announced the awarding of expansion teams to Montreal and San Diego, beating out Buffalo, Milwaukee, and Dallas, after a 10-hour owners meeting with 18 ballots. Montreal was the first choice, and Buffalo initially had votes from eight of the 10 owners. However, the two West Coast owners, Walter O'Malley and Horace Stoneham, held out and eventually persuaded the others to go with San Diego. Less than a year later, the Padres

were playing their first game, debuting at home in recently built San Diego Stadium, hosting the Houston Astros.

E.J. "Buzzie" Bavasi left the Dodgers to partner with San Diego businessman and financier C. Arnholt Smith to secure the franchise. Smith became two-thirds owner and supplied the bulk of the capital, with Bavasi owning the other third, serving as president, and providing the experience. Smith had owned the Pacific Coast League Padres and, although at the time he was known for his banking and financial empire, he also preferred to stay out of the spotlight, and was something of a mystery man to all but his closest friends.[1] Eddie Leishman, general manager of the PCL Padres, became GM of the new team as well.

The roster was filled primarily through an expansion draft, during which each team received 30 players from the existing clubs. Winning the coin toss, the Padres selected right fielder Ollie Brown as the first choice. Montreal went after several veterans, but Bavasi's plan was to draft plenty of young talent with a sprinkling of experienced players, and therefore he expected some possible lean seasons at the start. Only six players who appeared in a game for San Diego that first season were over 30 – Tony Gonzalez, Chris Cannizzaro, Roberto Pena, Johnny Podres, Jack Baldschun, and Al McBean.

The Opening Day outfield consisted of Brown, 13th pick Larry Stahl, and nine-year veteran Gonzalez, a career .293 hitter at the time who had hit .339 just two years earlier, and was chosen a surprisingly late 19th from the Phillies. The starting infielders were Bill Davis, Pena, Rafael Robles, and Ed Spiezio. Davis was a 26-year-old, 6-foot-7 slugging first baseman, acquired from Cleveland in a trade for shortstop and 1965 MVP Zoilo Versalles, the Padres' 10th pick. Pena, drafted 24th as a shortstop, moved to second base so Robles, a rookie picked 26th, could play shortstop. Robles wound up playing only six games for the Padres in 1969 and 47 for his career. Spiezio, acquired from St. Louis along with three others for second pick Dave Giusti, started at third base. Catcher Chris Cannizzaro had still been a Pirate just two weeks before Opening Day. The starting pitcher was third pick Dick Selma.

Clarence Gaston, the name he was known by at the time and the final draftee, was due to start in center field, but came up with an infection from too many foul balls off his left foot.

The Padres were confident they had an excellent outfield of Brown, Gaston, and Gonzalez, with Al Ferrara (drafted 15th) as a fourth outfielder needing to get playing time. Bavasi said he would not trade his outfield corps for the entire Dodgers picket line of Ron Fairly, Willie Davis, Andy Kosco, Len Gabrielson, and Willie Crawford.[2]

Padres manager Preston Gomez, who had been a coach with the Dodgers, proclaimed that his team would hit better than the Dodgers.[3]

On Tuesday evening, April 8, 1969, as fans and sportswriters gathered for the first major-league game in San Diego, optimism was in the air. The club expected 35,000, but only 23,370 showed up. The original take on that was that this was a glass half-full. *San Diego Union* sports editor Jack Murphy wrote, "This was a gala occasion, and a festive crowd came to the stadium on a pleasant spring evening convinced that youth was not wasted on the young. This is the youngest, rawest team in baseball – a team with a high potential for excitement. It just might be the perfect team for San Diego."[4]

Houston manager Harry Walker called San Diego "another happy city. Another hot spot for baseball." Walker exulted that San Diego's attractive new stadium was one of the finest he'd ever seen.[5]

Former catcher Ken Retzer was in the stands, and declared that the Padres were better than the original 1961 expansion Senators, on which he played.[6]

Not everyone saw the Padres in such a positive light. Astros starting pitcher Don Wilson had said a night earlier that he would "enjoy" pitching the opener and told Dick Selma, "You know, don't you, that you are going to lose tomorrow night?"[7]

At 8:15 P.M., Selma delivered a first-pitch strike to Jesus Alou, who eventually singled, stole second, and scored on a single by Doug Rader. In the home half, Rafael Robles, the first Pade batter ever, reached base on an error by Joe Morgan, but was left stranded after stealing second.

The Padres also got a runner into scoring position in the third inning when Cannizzaro walked and was balked to second, but the game reached the fifth still 1-0. Ed Spiezio tied the game with a one-out solo home run over the 17-foot wall in left field, for the team's first homer and first run. It was also the Padres' first hit. Then in the sixth inning, Pena led off by getting hit by a pitch, and Brown doubled him home with one out. Both runs came off Wilson, who went six innings.

Houston threatened in the fourth (a single by Curt Blefary and a passed ball) and fifth (a triple by Alou), but couldn't score, and after that got a runner to second base only once. Selma, a spring-training flop, pitched a masterful 2-1 complete-game victory, allowing five hits and two walks, striking out 12.

San Diego made several outstanding defensive plays, the first of which came right after Rader's RBI single. With two on, Pena made a difficult snag of a blistering liner hit by Blefary. Brown made an exceptional catch of a second-inning foul fly by Johnny Edwards, and in the eighth, with a runner on second, Gonzalez crashed into the concrete wall in left-center to grab a 370-foot drive by Rader.

Selma, by the way, had a perfect day at the plate with two of the team's four hits and a sacrifice bunt.

The Padres' record would reach 3-0 with consecutive 2-0 wins over Houston, behind Podres, allowing two hits in seven innings, and Dick Kelley, allowing one hit in 8⅓ innings, the hit coming in the seventh. Podres had been a candidate to be the Opening Day starter[8] although he did not pitch in 1968.

Reality set in soon thereafter, to a lack of both victories and fan interest. The lower-than-expected Opening Night crowd foreshadowed five years of concern about San Diego's ability to support baseball. Attendance figures for games two and three with the Astros were both under 5,000.

San Diego fell to 3-6 before winning again, but interestingly had six winning streaks of at least three games (including one at six) among its lowly 1969 win total of 52.

As for Gomez's prediction that the Padres would outhit the Dodgers, they did out-homer them, 99-97, but hit .225 and scored the fewest runs in the league. The Dodgers outscored them 645-468, and every other team outscored the Padres by more than 100 runs.

Three of the Padres' starting nine in the opener would be gone by mid-June. Selma, Davis, and Gonzalez were traded for younger players. Davis, suffering from an Achilles tendon injury that kept him out of all of 1968, never recovered, and did not play again in the majors after leaving the Padres. His departure was hastened by the development of another young first baseman, Nate Colbert.

## SOURCES

In addition to the sources cited in the Notes, the author consulted Baseball-Reference.com, Retrosheet.org, and the following:

Kaegel, Dick. "Sweating, Waiting ... As N.L. Debated," *The Sporting News*, June 8, 1968: 5.

Lang, Jack. "Hill Gems Scarce, Expos, Padres Discover," *The Sporting News*, October 26, 1968: 11.

Cour, Paul. "Padres Hopes Hinge on Comeback Trio," *The Sporting News*, April 19, 1969: 22.

Porter, David, and Joe Naiman. *The San Diego Padres Encyclopedia* (Champaign, Illinois: Sports Publishing LLC), 2002.

## NOTES

1  Bob Ortman, "Scouts Are No. 1 on Bavasi's Lists of Musts," *The Sporting News*, June 22, 1968: 9.

2  Paul Cour, "No Poverty in Padres' Picket Line," *The Sporting News*, March 15, 1969: 9.

3  Ibid.

4  Jack Murphy, "Happy City, Beautiful Stadium Impress Diamond Veteran Walker," *San Diego Union*, April 9, 1969: C1.

5  Ibid.

6  Jerry Magee, "Pad Fans Hopeful, Optimistic, Daring," *San Diego Union*, April 9, 1969: C1.

7  Phil Collier, "Padres Sparkle in Debut, Selma Beats Astros, 2-1," *San Diego Union*, April 9, 1969: C1.

8  Paul Cour, "Podres Takes Vows With Padres," *The Sporting News*, April 5, 1969: 15.

# CLAY KIRBY'S NEAR NO-HITTER

## JULY 21, 1970: NEW YORK METS 3, SAN DIEGO PADRES 0, AT SAN DIEGO STADIUM

### BY RORY COSTELLO

Through 2017 – the franchise's 49th season – no San Diego Padres pitcher had thrown a no-hitter. No other major-league team holds that dubious distinction. Yet the Padres might have gotten one as early as their second year in the National League. On July 21, 1970, righty Clay Kirby held the New York Mets hitless for the first eight innings at San Diego Stadium. With two outs in the bottom of the eighth, however, manager Preston Gómez lifted Kirby for a pinch-hitter as the Padres trailed 1-0. San Diego failed to score, and the no-hitter was lost in the top of the ninth. Gómez's decision was controversial then, and the debate has lingered.

"It's not that I'm bitter," said Kirby in 1990, a year before his untimely death. "But ... when I try to look at the logic behind it, I don't see it. We ... needed something to drum up interest in the ballclub. A no-hitter would have given the franchise a much bigger boost than one more victory. If it had been the seventh game of the World Series, I could understand it, I guess. But we were in last place."[1]

On the night of July 21, 1970, San Diego fell behind right away, mainly because of Kirby himself. Tommie Agee walked to

open the game and stole second. With one out, Ken Singleton also walked. The Mets then worked a double steal – "I wasn't careful," said Kirby.[2] Agee scored on a fielder's choice.

The hole was shallow, but Mets pitcher Jim McAndrew allowed just three hits and no walks while striking out nine. Just two Padres reached second base. Ed Spiezio doubled to start the third inning, and Al Ferrara had a two-out two-bagger in the fourth. After that, all they could muster was a two-out single by Bob Barton in the fifth.

Meanwhile, Kirby had "a real good breaking ball and his fastball was moving," said Mets outfielder Art Shamsky. Kirby walked just three more; McAndrew came closest to getting a hit. In the eighth, he "drilled a hot grounder to first baseman Nate Colbert, who threw out [Joe] Foy at the plate."[3]

Kirby then struck out Agee "on three pitches – fast, faster, and fastest, and see you later. I figured I had a no-hitter in the bag.

"When I came in after that inning, I got a drink of water, and I saw [pitching coach] Roger Craig coming in with a long look on his face. He was really upset, because he obviously wanted me to proceed.

"I knew then that something was up. When I put my helmet on, Gómez called me back. He basically said, 'Get your butt back here.' I said, 'What?' and that was it. [Clarence] Gaston felt bad. He didn't want to go up and hit for me."[4]

Gaston – the Padres' leader in batting average in 1970 – hadn't started because of a strained leg muscle.[5] Kirby was due to bat third, after Spiezio and Barton. Gómez recalled, "If Spiezio hits a home run or if one of them gets on and I can bunt with Kirby, then he stays in. But my mind was made up to hit for him if neither one of them got on."[6] At the time, he said that if Spiezio had led off with a hit, he'd have had Barton sacrifice and then lifted Kirby. Mets broadcaster Ralph Kiner commented, "The game doesn't belong to the pitcher. The manager has no choice but to pinch-hit."[7]

Gómez had scant precedent. As of 1970, there had been just two combined no-hitters in the majors, and only one was recognized as such at the time.[8] That was the bizarre game on April 30, 1967, in which Baltimore's Steve Barber and Stu Miller held Detroit hitless yet still lost, 2-1. When Orioles manager Hank Bauer yanked Barber after 8⅔ no-hit innings, there was no dispute – Barber had walked 10 and wild-pitched in the tying run.

In just two other big-league games had a pitcher been lifted with a no-hitter in progress after seven innings.[9] The closest parallel to Gómez's situation came on May 26, 1956. Cincinnati was trailing 1-0 in the top of the eighth when – "shunning tradition and sentimentality"[10] – manager Birdie Tebbetts sent up a pinch-hitter for Johnny Klippstein, who'd walked seven. The crowd that day booed, yet the *Cincinnati Enquirer* didn't second-guess Tebbetts, writing, "There's no room for sentiment in baseball. ... It was the correct move."[11]

On May 22, 1962, Yankees manager Ralph Houk removed Whitey Ford in the bottom of the seventh with the game tied 1-1 – but there was a key difference: a strained back muscle forced Ford to leave his potential no-hitter.[12] After Kirby's game, Houk said he'd have done the same as Gómez.[13]

Gómez cited success in a similar spot when he managed the Spokane Indians in the Pacific Coast League. His account, however, does not square with the available facts. It has not been possible to determine whether such a game took place.[14]

Mets ace Tom Seaver said the New York bench "gasped in disbelief" when Gaston was announced.[15] The San Diego crowd was a modest 10,373 – but booed loudly. A couple of enraged fans went after Gómez but were restrained.[16]

Gaston struck out, and Jack Baldschun relieved Kirby. He promptly gave up the Mets' first hit, a single by Bud Harrelson. Two runs eventually scored to make it 3-0.

McAndrew then set the Padres down in order in the bottom of the ninth to complete his shutout. He retired the last 13 men to face him.

"The reporters ... wanted me to say something about Preston," Kirby recalled. "I couldn't do that. I respect him as a man and as a manager."[17]

Gómez said, "It would have been the easy way out for me to let the kid go up and hit. I hated to take him out, but we needed runs. I don't play for the fans."[18] He added that winning was also important because the Mets and Pittsburgh Pirates were battling for first place.[19]

Gómez thought the same way 20 years later. "I always felt that when you're playing this game, you play to win. I don't care if we were 160 games behind. I'd do the same thing. The commissioner (Bowie Kuhn) called me and so did several other managers, and they all said it was the only way to play the game."[20]

Cito Gaston and Roger Craig – who'd both become managers themselves by then – agreed. So did Dave Campbell, a Padres second baseman in 1970. On September 4, 1974, Campbell was with the Houston Astros – managed by Gómez. Houston's starter versus Cincinnati, Don Wilson, was in the same boat as Kirby. He had a no-hitter through eight innings but trailed 2-1 because of two walks and an error. Gómez's strategy was consistent: He pulled Wilson for a pinch-hitter. Campbell said, "I sure do" when Gómez asked if he remembered seeing it before.[21] The end result was similar. The Astros couldn't tie it, and reliever Mike Cosgrove gave up a single to open the top of the ninth.

After that game, Kirby – who'd been traded to Cincinnati after the 1973 season – walked into Gómez's office at the Astrodome and shook his hand.[22] He said, "Preston told me he'd never change his ways." Indeed, Gómez reiterated, "I play this game to win."[23]

Starting in 1975, there have been nine more combined no-hitters in the majors. Also, from 1996 through 2017, eight pitchers have been removed after going at least seven no-hit innings, and the bullpen subsequently gave up hits.[24] Managers today have another excuse to pull a starter during a no-no: pitch limits/protecting pitchers' arms. Dodgers skipper Dave Roberts did so twice in 2016; for him the decision was hard but clear.[25] Marlins manager Don Mattingly did the same in both 2016 and 2017.[26]

By contrast, when Johan Santana pitched the Mets' only no-hitter to date[27] in 2012, skipper Terry Collins agonized about leaving Santana in even after exceeding his 115-pitch limit. Many argue that the cost of ending the club's notorious 50-year no-hitter drought was high – Santana made just 10 more starts in the majors.[28]

Preston Gómez, who died in January 2009, didn't suffer such doubts. After the Kirby game, he said, "I never second-guess myself. And I can always go home after a game and sleep, figuring I did what I thought was right."[29]

Clay "The Kid" Kirby said, "I'm only 22 and I'll have a lot more chances to pitch one [a no-hitter]."[30] He never did, though he came close twice more as a Padre, in consecutive starts in September 1971. Various other San Diego pitchers have also had chances but been denied. One of them, 1976 Cy Young Award winner Randy Jones, discussed it in 2015: "I've got a feeling the no-hitter is going to come out of nowhere. We keep waiting for that night." Padres broadcaster Ted Leitner added, "There's going to be one. The question is just who and when."[31]

# NOTES

1    Bob Wolf, "Near Miss Haunts Pitcher," *Los Angeles Times*, June 9, 1990.

2    "No-Hitter Less Vital Than Win?" *Florida Today*, July 23, 1970: 7C.

3    Paul Cour, "Clay Cool in Heat of No-Hit Fuss," *The Sporting News*, August 8, 1970: 18.

4    Bob Wolf.

5    Joseph Durso, "8-Inning No-Hitter Irks Fans on Coast," *New York Times*, July 23, 1970: 34.

6    Bob Wolf.

7    Durso.

8    In September 1991, the Committee for Statistical Accuracy reclassified the game of June 23, 1917 – in which Ernie Shore retired 27 straight batters after Babe Ruth's ejection – as a combined no-hitter.

9    Two other pitchers had thrown games of seven-plus hitless innings without being relieved. They were also declassified as no-hitters in 1991 because they did not go the regulation nine. On August 27, 1937, Fred Frankhouse pitched 7⅔; on September 26, 1959, Sam Jones pitched seven. Rain ended both of those games.

10    Gregory H. Wolf, "Ray Crone," SABR BioProject.

11    "Fowler Faces Braves; Buhl Battles Redlegs," *Cincinnati Enquirer*, May 27, 1956.

12    "New York Wins on Four-Man One-Hitter," *Emporia* (Kansas) *Gazette*, May 23, 1962: 10.

13    Durso.

14    "Padres' Kirby Loses No-Hit Bid," *Tucson Daily Citizen*, July 22, 1970: 31. According to Gómez, "Phil Ortega was pitching a no-hitter for eight, I batted for him in the bottom of the eighth, the pinch-hitter, Tony Roig, doubled and we won the game 2-1." Gómez managed Spokane from 1960 through 1962. During this period, Roig played for Spokane only in 1960, and Ortega pitched just seven innings in three games for Spokane that year.

15    Durso.

16    Brian Hiro, "Forty Years After the Infamous Clay Kirby Game, the No-Hitter Drought Lives On," *San Diego Union-Tribune*, July 17, 2010.

17    Bob Wolf.

18    Durso.

19    Bob Chandler with Bill Swank, *Bob Chandler's Tales from the San Diego Padres Dugout* (New York: Sports Publishing, 2006), 49.

20    Bob Wolf.

21    Ibid.

22    Chandler, *Tales from the San Diego Padres Dugout*, 53.

23    Bob Hertzel, "'I Play to Win,'" *Cincinnati Enquirer*, September 5, 1974: 41.

24    In addition to the four cited in notes 25 and 28, they were David Cone (September 2, 1996), Damian Moss (May 3, 2002), Kevin Slowey (August 15, 2010), and Aaron Harang (April 18, 2014). Also, on April 10, 2010, CC Sabathia would have been lifted because of his pitch count even if his no-hitter hadn't been broken up after 7⅔ innings.

25    On April 8, 2016, Ross Stripling left his big-league debut after 7⅓ no-hit innings because he'd thrown exactly 100 pitches. Ken Gurnick, "Tiring Stripling Agrees With Exiting No-Hitter," MLB.com, April 9, 2016. On September 10, Roberts lifted Rich Hill after seven perfect innings. Ken Gurnick, "Health Over Accolade Fuels Decision to Pull Hill," MLB.com, September 10, 2016.

26    Mattingly pulled Adam Conley after 7⅔ on April 29, 2016, and Wei-Yin Chen after seven on April 18, 2017.

27    As of 2018.

28    Phil Taylor, "No-No Regrets: Johan Santana Would Not Alter a Thing. Terry Collins Might," *Sports Illustrated*, June 1, 2015. For a counter-argument, see Ted Berg, "Did Johan Santana's 134-Pitch No-Hitter Really Ruin His MLB Career?" *USA Today*, April 14, 2016.

29    Paul Cour, "Second-Guessers Pouring It On Poor Preston," *The Sporting News*, August 8, 1970, 18.

30    Cour, "Clay Cool in Heat of No-Hit Fuss."

31    Sam Gardner, "Somehow, Only the Padres Have No History of No-Hitters," Foxsports.com, August 24, 2015.

# PADRES' STEVE ARLIN ONE STRIKE AWAY FROM NO-HITTER

## JUNE 18, 1972: SAN DIEGO PADRES 5, PHILADELPHIA PHILLIES 1, AT SAN DIEGO STADIUM

### BY GREGORY FUNK

The Padres are well-known for not (as of 2018) having a pitcher throw a no-hitter. They have, however, been no-hit 10 times: by Dock Ellis in 1970, Milt Pappas in 1972, Phil Niekro in 1973, twice in 2001 (A.J. Burnett and Bud Smith), Jonathan Sanchez in 2009, and Tim Lincecum in consecutive years, 2013-14,

plus two combined no-no's by the Braves (1991) and Dodgers (2018; the first-ever major-league no-hitter in Mexico). There was also an 11th time, in 1995, if we count Pedro Martinez's perfect game that wasn't – nine perfect innings forced to a 10th inning by a 0-0 score, then broken up by Bip Roberts' double. This one never got on the books because of a 1991 ruling that all no-hitters would have to cover an entire game, no matter how long. Another perfect game near-miss was Pappas losing out after getting an 0-and-2 count on the 27th batter, with the next four pitches just missing the strike zone.

Padres pitchers have got close many times over the years. Probably the most famous is Clay Kirby throwing eight hitless innings, only to be pinch-hit for because the team was losing 1-0, and reliever Jack Baldschun allowing multiple hits. This occurred in 1970, only the Padres' second season.

There have been had four other occasions in which Padres pitchers carried a no-hitter into the ninth inning: Steve Arlin in 1972, Andy Ashby in 1997, Chris Young in 2006, and Aaron Harang plus four relievers in 2011. There have been five one-hitters in which the hit came in either the eighth or ninth: Kirby in 1971 (Willie McCovey's eighth-inning homer ruined an otherwise perfect game), Randy Jones in 1975 (a perfect game through seven), Greg Harris and Craig Lefferts in 1991, Andy Benes in 1994, and Chris Young and Cla Meredith in 2006. A special mention should go to Kirby; his near-perfect game was his second straight start taking a no-hitter into the eighth inning.

Through the 2018 season, there have been 300 no-hitters in baseball history, 132 since 1969. During the Padres' time, that comes to about 2.6 per season, and one every 10.4 years or so per team.

The Padres closed the 2018 season 44 games short of breaking the Mets' all-time record of 8,019 games before pitching a no-hitter. As of the start of play in 2019, they are the only active franchise without one.

Getting two strikes on the final batter with one out to go is about as close as one can get. That was Steve Arlin's fate on July 18, 1972. It also happened in 2011 when the Padres sent five pitchers to the mound on July 9, with Luke Gregerson allowing a double on a 1-and-2 pitch to Juan Uribe of the Dodgers, but the Arlin story has a more interesting ending.

Arlin, a dentist in the offseason and after his career ended, was drafted by Philadelphia in 1966, and made a deal with the Phillies that he would be permitted to complete his dental-school studies each spring before reporting to the minors. But possibly because of that, he was left open in the 1968 expansion draft, from which the Padres selected him 26th out of 30 picks.

Not many people remember that Arlin had been on a tear in midseason 1972. Beginning on June 18, four of his seven starts before his no-hit bid were gems of at least nine innings allowing just one hit or two hits. On June 23 he beat the Giants on a one-hitter and on July 6 he threw one-hit ball for 10 innings in a 14-inning 1-0 win against the Mets.

The game on July 18 was at San Diego Stadium against the Phillies before a crowd of just 4,764. Through the first four innings, Arlin allowed only a first-inning walk to Tom Hutton. San Diego scored in the first on Jerry Morales's walk and Nate Colbert's double.

The Padres loaded the bases in the second and put two on in the third, but it was still 1-0 in the fifth inning.

In the Phillies' fifth, Willie Montanez walked, but two outs later was caught stealing. The Padres scored twice in their half when Morales singled and Colbert homered.

A two-out walk to Larry Bowa in the sixth produced the only other Phillies baserunner before the ninth. The best defensive play of the game came next. Second baseman Derrel Thomas dived to his left to stab a smash by Denny Doyle and threw him out from a sitting position.

In the seventh, Arlin induced three groundballs, by Hutton, Greg Luzinski, and Montanez.

The Padres padded their lead to 5-0 with a triple by Morales, an intentional walk, Cito Gaston's double, and a groundout.

In the eighth, Arlin struck out Don Money, then retired Oscar Gamble and John Bateman on grounders to third base.

After the Padres failed to score in the eighth, Arlin faced pinch-hitter Deron Johnson to begin the ninth. Third baseman Dave Roberts made a leaping catch of Johnson's liner. Next up was Bowa, who popped out to second baseman Thomas for the second out.

Denny Doyle was all that was left between Arlin and history. Roberts had been playing the normal strategy of moving in at third base to cover a possible bunt, and as soon as there were two strikes on Doyle, Roberts moved back. But Padres manager Don Zimmer, fearing a possible two-strike bunt attempt, motioned for Roberts to stay in, so Roberts moved back in about eight feet on the grass. With the count 1-and-2, Arlin threw a slider inside, and Doyle hit a one-hop chopper that bounced over Roberts' head into left field. Roberts probably would have caught the ball with ease had he played back at normal depth.

The no-hitter gone, Arlin appeared to lose his composure and balked Doyle to second, then gave up a run-scoring single to Hutton. Fans urged Arlin just to finish the game, which he did by getting Luzinski to fly out.

Arlin originally thought he had the no-hitter. Not realizing where Roberts was positioned, and seeing the path of the poorly hit ball, Arlin said he was ready to begin celebrating.[1]

After the postgame radio show, Zimmer took the blame, approaching Arlin with a razor blade and, pointing to his throat, said, "Here. Just make it quick."[2]

But Arlin defended his manager, saying he thought both Bowa and Doyle might try to bunt in the final inning.[3]

Years later, Arlin had this to say: "I should have had my no-hitter. It's stupid how I lost my no-hitter. It was a case of over-managing. We knew he wasn't going to bunt with two strikes."[4]

Arlin's start had originally been scheduled for the following night, but was moved up a day so that he could be ready to pitch in the All-Star Game. But National League manager Danny

Murtaugh elected to leave Arlin off the nine-man staff,[5] despite his run of allowing only 33 hits in 71 innings.

The near-miss was his third two-hitter, along with the preceding two one-hitters in a 31-day span. After that, his career started to spin downward, and although the next season, 1973, featured a four-game span highlighted by three shutouts, the first hit came very early in each of those games. Steve Arlin never came close again.

## SOURCES

The box score can be found at retrosheet.org/boxesetc/1972/B07180SDN1972.htm.

The author attended the game and had a home-plate view of Doyle's single.

In addition to the sources cited in the Notes, the author consulted Baseball-Reference.com, Retrosheet.org, and the following:

Keidan, Bruce. "Doyle Ruins Arlin's No-Hitter in 9th," *Philadelphia Inquirer*, July 19, 1972: 25.

## NOTES

1    Bill Conlin, "No-No by Zimmer Costs Arlin No-Hitter," *Philadelphia Daily News*, July 19, 1972.

2    Phil Collier, "Low-Hit Gems Are Arlin's Specialty," *The Sporting News*, August 5, 1972: 17.

3    Ibid.

4    Mel Antonen, "Despite Close Calls, Padres Only Members of the No No-Hitters Club," https://www.si.com/more-sports/2012/06/13/padres-no-hitters, June 13, 2012.

5    Bruce Keidan, "When Baseball's Inept Meet, Arlin Performs Like a Master," *Philadelphia Inquirer*, July 19, 1972: 28.

# COLBERT'S RECORD-SETTING DAY LEADS PADRES TO SWEEP OVER BRAVES

## AUGUST 1, 1972: SAN DIEGO PADRES 11, ATLANTA BRAVES 7, AT ATLANTA STADIUM (SECOND GAME)

### BY CHUCK JOHNSON

On the team flight to Atlanta after the Padres' 3-2 loss at Houston on July 31, manager Don Zimmer sat down next to first baseman Nate Colbert and asked how he felt. Atlanta was the third stop on a five-city, 16-game road trip and Zimmer was concerned about his big slugger, who had recently twisted his left knee in a home-plate collision. Colbert reassured his boss that he was fine, figuring Atlanta was a good place to get healthy.

Colbert signed with his hometown St. Louis Cardinals after graduating from high school in 1964, and then spent three seasons in the Astros organization before heading to San Diego in the expansion draft.

Colbert's propensity for the long ball quickly made him the face of the franchise, giving the Padres fans something to look forward to during an otherwise dismal 110-loss first season. Colbert hit 38 homers in 1970 and his 27-homer season in 1971 was highlighted by his being named to his first All-Star team.

Colbert started off slowly in 1972, even by his standards. A career .258 hitter entering the season, Colbert was at a season-low .194 on June 15. As the San Diego summer started to warm up, so did Nate, raising his average to .233 on the eve of the All-Star Game, coincidentally played in Atlanta. Colbert scored the winning run in the National League's 4-3, 10-inning victory and then hopped a plane to join his teammates in Cincinnati.

A two-homer game against the Astros in Houston in the second game of a July 30 doubleheader gave Colbert the National League lead by one home run (25-24) over Johnny Bench, and his 68 RBIs ranked third behind the 75 posted by Bench and Willie Stargell.

The Tuesday, August 1, doubleheader in Atlanta was the first of a four-game series and despite Colbert's earlier optimism the day didn't start as planned. Plagued with chronic back issues that would ultimately end his career at the age of 30, Colbert woke up and could barely move, so he took an early cab to the ballpark for treatment. After a while, Colbert went into Zimmer's office and said he didn't think he could play; Zimmer asked him to wait until after batting practice to decide.

"I took 10 swings and hit all 10 into the seats, seven fair and three foul," Colbert recalled. "I walked past Zim and he said, "You're in.""[1]

Clay Kirby scattered seven hits in pitching a complete-game shutout in the Padres' 9-0 victory in the first game. Ron Schueler took the loss. Colbert paced the way on offense, going 4-for-5 with two homers and driving in five runs. He hit a three-run homer off Schueler in the first inning, which held up as the game-winning hit. A solo home run to lead off the seventh against Atlanta reliever Mike McQueen added the Padres' eighth run.

In the first inning of the second game, Larry Stahl drew a two-out walk and Colbert came to the plate to face right-hander Tom Kelley. Colbert hit Kelley's first pitch into the upper deck just foul down the left-field line before also drawing a walk. Cito Gaston then hit a chopper back to the mound which Kelley threw wildly past first base, allowing two unearned runs to score and giving the Padres the early lead.

After Fred Stanley grounded out leading off the second inning, Kelley walked the next two hitters and was replaced by righty Pat Jarvis, who allowed a run-scoring single to Dave Roberts and walked Stahl. This brought Colbert to the plate with the bases loaded. Colbert took the first pitch for a ball, then lined a

high slider deep into the left-field stands for a grand slam and a 7-0 Padres lead.

Colbert grounded to third in the fourth inning. Meanwhile, San Diego starter Ed Acosta had held the Braves to just one run through six innings.

Colbert came up for his fourth at-bat in the seventh against right-hander Jim Hardin. Larry Stahl grounded a one-out single to center and Colbert followed up by lining a Hardin slider just inside the foul pole in right, a two-run homer that extended San Diego's lead.

Acosta tired in the bottom of the seventh and was charged with four runs. The Braves chipped away, adding two more runs in the bottom of the eighth, cutting what had been a 9-1 deficit to 9-7 heading into the top of the ninth. Side-arming righty Cecil Upshaw was now pitching for Atlanta. Stahl once again gave Colbert a chance to hit, grounding a two-out single to right. "Upshaw always gave me problems," Colbert recalled. "For some reason, maybe to fool me because I was swinging early in the count, he threw me a fastball overhand and I hit that one out." As Colbert rounded second base he said to umpire Bruce Froemming, "I don't believe this," to which Froemming replied, "I don't, either."[2]

It was 11-7 in the Padres' favor and when Atlanta failed to score in the bottom of the ninth, that stood as the game's final score.

On May 2, 1954, 9-year-old Nate Colbert and his father were seated in the upper left-field grandstand in St. Louis to watch their beloved Cardinals take on the New York Giants in a doubleheader. The Cardinals' superstar outfielder, Stan Musial, hit five homers that day and drove in nine runs. For the day, Musial set the record for the most homers in a day with five, the most runs batted in (nine), and the most total bases (21).

The Padres completed the first four-game road sweep in franchise history in Atlanta, then continued to Los Angeles and San Francisco before returning home to face the Dodgers on August 11. Before the game the Padres honored Colbert for his accomplishment and surprised him by him by flying in Musial to take part in the ceremony.

Colbert's day included breaking Musial's RBI record with 11 (broken in 1993 by Mark Whiten) and his total-base record with 22. His five homers came off five different pitchers and he reached base eight times in 10 plate appearances.

Colbert was an All-Star again in 1973 at the age of 27 but then his back problems intensified and finally forced him out of the game after he was released in spring training in 1977 by the Toronto Blue Jays at the age of 30.

Colbert drove in 111 of the Padres' 488 runs in 1972 or 22.75 percent, a record that still stood as of 2018.[3] He is the Padres' career home-run leader with 163.

## SOURCES

In addition to the sources cited in the Notes, the author also consulted Retrosheet.org,

Baseball-Reference.com, and Padres360.com.

## NOTES

1 All quotes taken from the transcript of a phone interview between Colbert and historian Seth Swirsky unless otherwise noted. seth.com/coll_histbseballs_18.html.

2 Phil Collier, "Just Night's Work for Nate: 5 HRs, 13 RBIs," *The Sporting News*, August 19, 1972.

3 Bob Carroll, "Nate Colbert's Unknown RBI Record," *The National Pastime* (SABR, 1982).

# PADRES OVERCOME EIGHTH-INNING 8-0 DEFICIT TO WIN

## JUNE 10, 1974: SAN DIEGO PADRES 9, PITTSBURGH PIRATES 8, AT SAN DIEGO STADIUM

### BY GREGORY FUNK

The year 1974 started as a season of optimism for San Diego as the Padres were rescued from their aborted move to Washington, DC, and ultimately purchased by Ray Kroc. During the offseason, even before Kroc's name came up, the Padres, in anticipation of better times, traded for Willie McCovey, Matty Alou, Glenn Beckert, and Bobby Tolan, players past their prime, but names nonetheless, something Padres fans were not used to. However, their sixth season's beginning resembled the previous five. Starting 0-6, they were at 23-39 when the Pirates came to town on June 10.

Lowell Palmer, purchased from the Yankees 10 days earlier, was making his second San Diego start, while Jim Rooker was on the mound for the Pirates. Pittsburgh had a terrific hitting lineup that year: first in batting and top three in most offensive categories. The first seven in that day's lineup were named Clines, Hebner, Zisk, Stargell, Oliver, Sanguillen, and Stennett.

Palmer got into trouble in every inning, while Rooker breezed. In the first, Palmer got out of a bases-loaded jam, but in the second he allowed a sacrifice fly by Gene Clines after Rennie Stennett and Mario Mendoza singled. A third inning two-run homer by Manny Sanguillen made it 3-0, and Palmer managed to strand a runner at second in the fourth. In the fifth, another two-run homer, this time by Willie Stargell, and a one-out single by Sanguillen finished Palmer.

In the seventh, off Dave Tomlin, Stargell tripled home Richie Zisk, and then scored on a single by Al Oliver to make it 7-0.

Meanwhile Rooker was sailing along with a five-hit shutout through seven innings. Other than a third-inning hiccup during which Enzo Hernandez walked and reached second, but was thrown out after hesitating when Tolan lined off the right-field wall, Rooker appeared to be in total command of the game.

In the eighth, Rooker himself upped the score to 8-0 when he doubled to left and scored on Richie Hebner's single.

It looked like just another game in which the Padres were headed for their sixth consecutive last-place finish and fourth 100-loss season. One of the bright spots in this particular season was a young tuba player named Jim Eakle, a Marine who had begun showing up at games near the end of the dismal 1973 season, playing hand-clapping tunes and familiar songs on a green-painted tuba. By 1974, a Pied Piper-like following had formed, marching down the stadium aisles generating enthusiasm throughout, playing flutes, drums, and other assorted instruments. Calling themselves McNamara's Band, after newly hired manager John McNamara, they marched around virtually every game.

But on this particular day, with many of the 7,309 spectators already on their way home by the middle of the eighth inning, even the Tuba Man wasn't getting much response during this one-sided affair.

Bobby Tolan led off the bottom of the eighth, and, before the inning started, was engaged in some sort of squabble with home-plate umpire Andy Olsen. Tolan, standing in the batter's box, but facing away from the mound, with his bat in only one hand, arms dropped at their sides, continued to bark at Olsen. The umpire, appearing to have heard enough, signaled to Rooker to begin pitching. Rooker wound up and only after the pitch was on its way did Tolan turn around and drop a perfect drag bunt past the mound toward second base for an infield hit. Whether or not this was any kind of catalyst could be open for debate, but it's a matter of record that the next five batters all reached base.

Dave Winfield doubled to center, scoring Tolan, Nate Colbert walked, and even though it was still only 8-1, manager Danny Murtaugh replaced Rooker with Bruce Kison. Cito Gaston greeted Kison with a three-run home run to make it 8-4. Fred Kendall walked, and Dave Roberts reached base on an error by Stennett. But a strikeout and two flyballs ended the eighth.

Vicente Romo pitched a perfect ninth for the Padres.

Ramon Hernandez, who had come in to get all three outs in the previous inning, retired Tolan to start the ninth. But Winfield shot a home run over the center-field fence to make it 8-5. At that point, Murtaugh elected to go to his ace reliever, Dave Giusti, who, after throwing a strike, issued consecutive walks on eight straight balls to Colbert and Gaston. Murtaugh quickly yanked Giusti, and brought in a young rookie pitcher named Kent Tekulve. Called up from Triple-A Charleston in May, Tekulve was making his eighth appearance for the Pirates. Kendall singled to right, loading the bases. Roberts then grounded the ball back to Tekulve who threw home for the second out.

Tekulve got two strikes on pinch-hitter Derrell Thomas, who then lined a base hit into left-center to make it 8-6. Bob Barton, also pinch-hitting, and also with two strikes, hit a routine grounder into the 5.5 hole[1] that barely eluded shortstop Mendoza. Two runs came in and the game was tied.

Horace Clarke was next. Tekulve again got two strikes on the batter, but Clarke hit a soft liner over second base, scoring Thomas, for the unexpected victory.

An hour before the game, Pirates general manager Joe L. Brown had said, "This club is built on two things – our hitting and our bullpen."[2]

After the game, an enraged Rooker said, "The job isn't being done by the bullpen and that's the truth. No matter how well I pitch, they figure out a way to put men on and to let them in." It was the fourth time in 10 starts that Rooker reached at least the seventh inning with a lead that the bullpen failed to protect. He was also upset after being pulled with a seven-run lead.[3]

For Padres fans, though, it wasn't the usual victory celebration. Many walked away stunned at what they had just witnessed: the greatest Padres comeback ever, accomplished in the last two innings. No San Diego team (as of 2018) has ever been behind by more runs at any stage in a game and won.[4]

## SOURCES

In addition to the sources cited in the Notes, the author consulted Baseball-Reference.com and Retrosheet.org, and relied on his personal memory of the game, which he attended. The following two articles were also helpful:

Collier, Phil. "Padres' Five-Run Ninth Startles Pittsburgh, 9-8," *San Diego Union*, June 11, 1974.

Feeney, Charles, "Padres Explode to Whip Bucs," *Pittsburgh Post-Gazette*, June 11, 1974.

## NOTES

[1]    The term "5.5 hole" is one that is very familiar to Padres fans. It was invented by Tony Gwynn to describe his favorite target: hitting a line drive between third base and shortstop.

[2]    Bob Smizik, "Bullpen Leaves Pirates for Dead," *Pittsburgh Press*, June 11, 1974.

[3]    Ibid.

[4]    On May 23, 1970, San Diego fell behind 8-0 to San Francisco, but closed the gap to 8-7 by the fourth inning, and won 17-16 in 15 innings.

# GAYLORD PERRY GETS 3,000TH CAREER STRIKEOUT AND OZZIE SMITH PERFORMS HIS FIRST PREGAME BACKFLIP

## OCTOBER 1, 1978: SAN DIEGO PADRES 4, LOS ANGELES DODGERS 3 (11 INNINGS), AT SAN DIEGO STADIUM

### BY TOM LARWIN

"The game will go down in the history of the San Diego Padres as perhaps one of the most dramatic ever played. Gaylord Perry, in the final game of the 1978 season against the Los Angeles Dodgers, accomplished a feat that only two other pitchers in the history of baseball before him were able to do."[1]

This game, played on Sunday afternoon, October 1, was the last game of the 1978 season. It was Fan Appreciation Day and a crowd of 37,185 turned out. This game marked the conclusion of the Padres' 10th major-league season. Over this 10-year span the team had lost almost 60 percent of those games – but this day's extra-inning win concluded the Padres' first winning season. With a record of 84-78 (.519) they finished in fourth place, 11 games behind the West Division leaders, the Los Angeles Dodgers.

The Padres' Gaylord Perry, at 21-6, was going up against the Dodgers' Don Sutton with a record of 15-11. Perry was on his

*Future Hall of Fame pitchers Don Sutton (left) and Gaylord Perry (right) warming up during the October 1, 1978 game.*

way to a Cy Young Award for the season and started the game with a career mark of 2,991 strikeouts. The trouble was that the fans – and the local media – thought Perry was actually at 2,990 career strikeouts.

This meant that the journey to 3,000 that was being watched over the course of the game was predicated on the wrong career strikeout number. What follows is the story of the game as viewed by fans at the game, and by the local media as reported the next day in the news.

While not part of the publicized activities, this game also featured a pregame surprise for the fans. The Padres' shortstop, Ozzie Smith, was finishing his rookie season and decided before the game to perform a backflip as he went to his position in the first inning. While fans may have noticed the flip, no one in the media apparently paid any attention.

Meanwhile, Perry started strong with seven strikeouts through the first four innings, by which time the Padres led 3-1.

With the National League Championship Series looming in three days, Dodgers manager Tommy Lasorda began resting his starting lineup in the bottom of the third inning. In the bottom half of the fifth, it was left fielder Dusty Baker's turn to take a rest when 26-year-old Joe Simpson, a Dodgers September call-up, took over with the score 3-2 in favor of the Padres.

The game progressed into the sixth inning and the San Diego Stadium scoreboard kept the crowd aware of Perry's march toward history as he rang up strikeout number 2,998. Reporter Dan Berger, in the next day's *San Diego Union*, noted that the tension started to mount when "the scoreboard flashed the word to the assembled. The word was 2,998."[2] In reality the tally was off by one, and the number flashed should have been 2,999.

There were no Dodgers strikeouts in the seventh and the game entered the eighth with the score remaining 3-2. With everyone believing Perry was still at strikeout number 2,998 after one

out, Joe Simpson came up with the bases empty. Into this at-bat Simpson had a career batting average of .194 in 62 plate appearances. With two strikes on him, he obliged Perry with a swing and miss and Perry's strikeout total now was said to stand at 2,999. In reality, it was strikeout number 3,000.

After Simpson's strikeout the Dodgers went on to tie the game, 3-3. Neither team scored in the eighth inning. The Dodgers came up in the ninth and Perry continued to put the crowd in "delightful agony" as fans were aware of a potential history-making strikeout.[3] The Dodgers did not comply as they went down without a score and without a strikeout. It appeared likely that Perry would exit the game with a presumed 2,999 strikeouts.

In the bottom of the ninth the Padres rallied and the game's end looked imminent. With one out they loaded the bases with Perry scheduled to bat. Perry had gone nine innings already and a deep fly ball or hit would win the game, so the situation called for a pinch-hitter. However, manager Roger Craig decided to stay with Perry – who had a .093 batting average for the season. After the game Craig admitted wanting to try to help Perry get strikeout number 3,000.[4] So he left Perry in the game. Craig also figured that if Perry was successful in getting the run home, he would pick up the win – number 22 for the year – which would cinch his chances of receiving the National League's Cy Young Award.

The drama ended quickly as Perry grounded into a pitcher-catcher-first double play … and the game went into extra innings.

Due up for the Dodgers in the top of 10th inning were Manny Mota pinch-hitting for reliever Rick Sutcliffe, Jerry Grote, and Simpson again. Both Mota and Grote went to two-strike counts but neither contributed to Perry's strikeout total, Mota flying out and Grote grounding out. That brought up left-fielder Joe Simpson – who was Perry's last strikeout victim, in the seventh inning.

Perry "tantalized" the crowd by getting two strikes on Simpson.[5] His next pitch was on the outside corner and Simpson looked at it while home-plate umpire Lee Weyer signaled it a strike. With that pitch Perry had ended the inning with his 10th strikeout of the game and what all understood to be career whiff number 3,000.

The scoreboard announced the historic event with the large number "3000." Anyone not aware of the milestone being achieved might have thought the Padres had won the pennant. "There was a 2½-minute standing ovation. … His teammates poured onto the field to pound his back."[6] Perry had become the third major leaguer to achieve 3,000 career strikeouts.

The game continued and the Padres did not score in their half of the 10th. The 11th inning arrived and reliever Rollie Fingers came in for the Padres. The Dodgers managed a hit and a walk but were not able to push across a run. Up came the Padres and Dave Winfield led off with a double to left field. A sacrifice moved him to third base and pinch-hitter Oscar Gamble came through with a single to end the game with Winfield scoring and the Padres winning, 4-3.

Rollie Fingers picked up his sixth win of the season to go with a league-leading 37 saves that were good enough for him to win the league's Rolaids Relief Man of the Year and *The Sporting News* Fireman of the Year Awards.

Going into 1978, the 3,000-strikeout club included only two pitchers: The first to reach that plateau was Walter Johnson in 1923. It took 51 years before a second pitcher joined the ranks with Bob Gibson getting number 3,000 in 1974. It took another 14 years before Perry achieved that number on October 1.

As for Ozzie Smith, the game articles the next day had no mention of his backflip.

Years later Smith offered background on the backflip. He said the idea for one started in spring training when he had been "goofing around … doing some flips."[7] Catcher Gene Tenace noticed him doing the flips and told Smith he would like him to do it sometime during the season when his daughters could see him perform it. The timing finally came together when Smith learned that Tenace's daughters would attend the season's last game. After being urged on by Andy Strasberg, the Padres promotion director, Smith decided to do the backflip on his way out to the field at the top of the first inning.

The backflip became so much a part of Smith's career that words on his Hall of Fame plaque note his "trademark backflip."[8]

Fast-forward 40-plus years and looking back at this game, it does not rise up to the importance that some thought it would have back on that day in October 1978. Yet at the time, it was a very entertaining game – a memorable one even – and matched

two starting pitchers who both would go on to win over 300 games, strike out more than 3,500 batters, and be inducted into the National Baseball Hall of Fame.[9] The game was memorable in another aspect: There were seven Hall of Famers active in the two dugouts, six on the Padres side and one for the Dodgers.[10]

As for the factual error on Perry's strikeouts, the record books got it right even though the team and local media were wrong. The mistaken count did not change two important aspects of the record strikeout: The batter was Joe Simpson and it occurred on October 1, 1978.

## SOURCES

In addition to the sources cited in the Notes, the author consulted Baseball-Reference.com, Retrosheet.org, and the following:

Armour, Mark. "Gaylord Perry," SABR Baseball Biography Project, sabr.org/bioproj/person/f7cb0d3e.

Faber, Charles F. "Ozzie Smith," SABR Baseball Biography Project, sabr.org/bioproj/person/a6663664.

San Diego Padres, *1978 Official Program and Souvenir Magazine*, 1978.

## NOTES

1    *San Diego Padres Report*, Vol. 1, Issue 17, November 1978: 15.

2    Dan Berger, "Perry Makes Padres Part of a Baseball Legend," *San Diego Union*, October 2, 1978: C-1.

3    Earl Gutskey, "Perry's 3,000th Strikeout Livens Up 4-3 Padre Win," *Los Angeles Times*, October 2, 1978: 179.

4    Phil Collier, "Perry Collects 3000th Whiff in 4-3 Victory," *San Diego Union*, October 2, 1978: C-1. Had Craig realized that Perry already had 3,000, he might well have brought in a reliever.

5    Gutskey.

6    Berger. Despite the timing of the ovation, everyone present had indeed witnessed a very special moment in baseball history. And it was indeed Simpson whom Perry had struck out for number 3,000.

7       Ozzie Smith with Rob Rains, *Wizard* (Chicago: Contemporary Books, 1988), 27.

8       Ibid.

9       In a curious and ironic twist in the Padres' history, what turned out to be a memory of equal – or more – importance from the game would be Ozzie Smith's first backflip and not Gaylord Perry's career number 3,000 strikeout.

10      Of the seven, only one was a Hall of Famer at the time, Padres' coach Billy Herman. Six others would go on to be inducted (in order by year of induction): Perry, Fingers, Lasorda, Sutton, Winfield, and Smith.

# TONY GWYNN'S FIRST MAJOR-LEAGUE GAME AND HIT

## JULY 19, 1982: PHILADELPHIA PHILLIES 7, SAN DIEGO PADRES 6, AT JACK MURPHY STADIUM, SAN DIEGO

## BY FRED O. RODGERS

As the sun rose over San Diego on July 19, 1982, San Diego Padres fans were excited that the Tony Gwynn era was about to begin. The sports stations were announcing all day that the Padres had brought up Gwynn, their third-round pick from 14 months earlier, from Triple-A Hawaii.

The day before, Hawaii manager Doug Rader had called Gwynn into his office after Gwynn made the last out of the game at home plate on a baserunning mistake. Gwynn figured he was in for a chewing-out. "He went through the whole thing, ripped my butt, then said, 'Anyway, you are going to join the Padres tomorrow.'"[1]

In May, Padres manager Dick Williams had asked general manager Jack McKeon to promote Gwynn to the Padres. But Gwynn was off to a slow start, hitting .239, while Alan Wiggins was hitting .319, so the Padres promoted Wiggins instead.

At the All-Star break, on July 11, the Padres were only two games behind the first-place Atlanta Braves in the National League West Division. It was their best showing at the break in their history. After the break the Padres hosted the Montreal Expos for four games. The Padres lost all four games and fell to five games out of first. The front office looked for more help.

Since early May, Gwynn had got hot and was hitting .328, so McKeon brought him up, hoping to help end the Padres' losing streak.

On the flight to San Diego, Gwynn thought about his chance to play in front of his buddies from San Diego State (he had to hand out 24 tickets), and his whole family was coming down from Long Beach, California. He had been told he would be facing star Phillies pitcher Steve Carlton.

The Padres had given him wrong information. He would be facing right-hander Mike Krukow, who was 9-6 with a 2.56 ERA,

fourth in the National League. Krukow wasn't Steve Carlton but he was still a very competitive pitcher for Gwynn's first game.

Gwynn got to the ballpark 5½ hours early. He wasn't really nervous, just eager to get his major-league career started. After getting him situated at his new locker, clubhouse man (and former coach) Whitey Wietelmann handed Gwynn his first uniform, number 19. Whitey said, "I wore this number playing for the PCL Padres so don't disgrace it!"[2]

The Padres started left-hander John Curtis, who was 6-5, against the Eastern Division's first-place Philadelphia Phillies. The Phillies had future Hall of Famers Pete Rose and Mike Schmidt in the lineup besides pitcher Steve Carlton in the dugout. Also on the field was future Hall of Fame umpire Doug Harvey at first base.

The Phillies went down one-two-three in the first as leadoff hitter Bob Dernier lined out to second baseman Tim Flannery, Pete Rose grounded back to Curtis, and Gary Matthews popped out to Flannery.

The first three Padres batters singled for a 1-0 lead. Sixto Lezcano bunted and Krukow nailed him for the first out of the inning, Flannery, taking third with one out. The scene was set for Tony Gwynn's first major-league at-bat. It was 7:21 P.M. when Gwynn got in the batter's box for the first time.

"I wasn't nervous on the on-deck circle," said the rookie. "As I walked to the plate, obviously you could hear the crowd cheering for you but when you're playing you just try to focus in on what you're trying to do."[3]

That first inning at-bat produced Gwynn's first major-league RBI when he lifted a fly ball to center field and Flannery scored. The Tony Gwynn era had begun. Now he needed his first hit.

In the top of the second inning, Mike Schmidt and Bo Diaz hit back-to-back home runs to tie the game at 2-2.

After singles by Broderick Perkins and Luis Salazar in the second, John Curtis struck out but Gene Richards singled to center field for his second hit of the game and the bases were loaded.

That was it for starter Krukow. In came reliever Sid Monge, and he walked Flannery to force in a run, making it 3-2, San Diego. Monge got the next two batters out.

Curtis never got an out in the third. Monge walked and Bob Dernier and Pete Rose singled (number 3,799 for Pete), loading the bases for Gary Matthews. He singled in Monge to tie the game, 3-3. Dick Williams brought in right-hander Floyd Chiffer, who got Schmidt on a short fly ball but gave up a single to Bo Diaz, knocking in a run. The Phillies now led, 5-3. Chiffer then got Bill Robinson on a grounder, but Matthews scored and it was 6-3.

In the bottom of the third, Gwynn batted for the second time. He hit the ball hard but right at shortstop Ivan DeJesus, just missing the "5.5 hole" that Gwynn would make famous during his career – the area between third base and shortstop.

The fourth, fifth, and sixth innings were scoreless. In the Padres' fifth inning Gwynn faced left-hander Monge for the second time, his third at-bat in the game. Lezcano was on second base with one out. During his career, striking out would become a rarity for Gwynn but Monge got him on a nasty slider.

Pete Rose led off the top of the seventh inning with his second hit of the game (number 3,800), off Eric Show, who in 1985 would give up Rose's record-setting 4,192nd hit. George Vuckovich doubled, scoring Rose for a 7-3 Phillies lead.

In the bottom of the eighth, Lezcano led off with a home run off Monge. Gwynn congratulated him after he rounded the bases. Now it was Gwynn's turn to hit against Sid Monge for the third time. Gwynn doubled to left-center field for his first major-league hit, the first of 3,141.

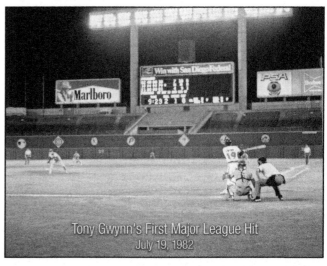

Tony Gwynn's First Major League Hit
July 19, 1982

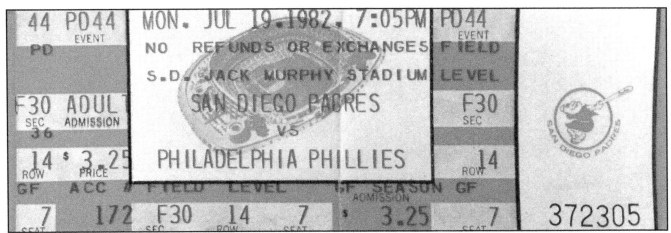

Pete Rose, playing first, backed up the play at second base. Rose noticed the ball was being retrieved and told Gwynn, "I didn't realize this was your first game. Nice going, kid."[4] That impressed Gwynn forever.

Sparky Lyle relieved Monge and gave up a run as Luis Salazar grounded out and Gwynn scored his first major-league run. Kurt Bevacqua's pinch-hit single plated another run, bringing the Padres to within a run of tying the game.

Gwynn's night wasn't over yet. After Padres reliever Luis De-leon set down the Phillies in the top of the ninth, it was time for Gwynn's last at-bat in the game. He came up against reliever Ron Reed after Templeton and Lezcano made the first two outs.

Like Gwynn, Reed had been a basketball star in college, at Notre Dame, and had played two seasons in the NBA for the Detroit Pistons. Gwynn, who set a record for assists at San Diego State, had been drafted by the San Diego Clippers in the 10th round of the NBA draft on the same day he was drafted by the Padres.

Gwynn lined a single to center field to solidify a successful major-league debut, going 2-for-4 with a double, a run scored, and a run batted in on the sacrifice fly. As Gwynn stood at first base after his ninth-inning hit, Pete Rose told him, "Don't try to catch me all in one night."[5]

Terry Kennedy grounded out to the pitcher to end the game. Tony Gwynn's first two hits were in the books. The Padres had lost their fifth straight game but through no fault of the rookie center fielder.

**Sidenote:** Gwynn went hitless in his next game and then hit in 15 straight games, the longest streak by a Padre in 1982. Gwynn hit .289 in 54 games that season. He would never again hit below .300 in his career.[6]

**Personal Note:** I was blessed to be there that night and I was able to stand behind the cutout windows behind the plate due to the friendship of major-league umpire Joe West. I took pictures of the game with a 24-picture throwaway camera. I recorded Gwynn sitting in the dugout moments before his first at-bat; the scoreboard showing the exact moment of his first plate appearance (7:21 P.M.); his first major-league hit (9:23 P.M.); and the scoreboard announcing "That was T. Gwynn's 1st major lge hit." In 2007 Gwynn took the hit picture to Cooperstown and former head archivist Pat Kelly asked me to donate it, which I did. The Hall of Fame sent me a certificate describing my donation. It truly was a moment of being in the right place at the right time

## SOURCES

In addition to the sources cited in the Notes, the author relied on Retrosheet.org.

## NOTES

1    Rich Wolfe, *Tony Gwynn: He Left His Heart in San Diego* (Phoenix: Lone Wolfe Press, 2014), 143.

2    Kirk Kenney, "Gwynn's Debut Impressive, but Padres Lose 5th Anyway," *San Diego Union-Tribune*, July 19, 2014: C-4.

3    Ibid.

4    Tony Gwynn with Jim Geschke, *Tony!* (New York: Contemporary Books, 1988), 48.

5    *Tony!*, 49.

6    Bill Center, *Padres' Essential* (Chicago: Triumph Books, 2007), 70.

# A DAY AT THE BRAWL PARK

## AUGUST 12, 1984: ATLANTA BRAVES 5, SAN DIEGO PADRES 3, AT ATLANTA-FULTON COUNTY STADIUM

### BY JEFF FINDLEY

In 11 years of major-league baseball service, Pascual Perez hit exactly 25 batters. Known as much for his lack of navigational skills and unique pickoff move, it was his elusiveness as a hitter in an August 12, 1984, game between the San Diego Padres and the Atlanta Braves that spurred one of the ugliest games in baseball history. The "Brawl Game" contest featured ejections of both managers in addition to two acting managers and 13 players before the game ended.[1]

Tension started with the first pitch of the game, as Perez drilled Alan Wiggins in the lower back. The Padres, who had a commanding 10½-game lead over the Braves in the National League West, questioned the intent of the pitch. Wiggins took his base without incident, and was retired in a double play, but Perez's pitch proved to be the catalyst for an afternoon of fisticuffs.

"I wasn't trying to hit him," Perez said. "I was trying to get inside on him, and the ball slipped. The San Diego players got mad at me, and I don't know why."[2]

Padres manager Dick Williams had his own viewpoint. "There was no question in our minds that Perez hit Wiggins on purpose," Williams said. "He hit only two batters in 135 innings this year. If that's the way Joe Torre [Atlanta's manager at the time] wants to play, that's a shame. But we didn't throw at the first guy up. We played hardball before. We're not supposed to lie down."[3]

In the bottom of the first, Atlanta put two runs on the board with a Glenn Hubbard walk, which was immediately followed by Claudell Washington depositing a home run in the right-field seats.

The Braves came to bat in the second with the same margin, and after a Rafael Ramirez single and Bruce Benedict's popout, Perez strolled to the plate. Padres pitcher Ed Whitson threw at Perez, but wise to the situation, Perez backed away from the plate and Whitson missed. The resulting wild pitch moved Ramirez to second, and home-plate umpire Steve Rippley issued a warning to both teams against attempted retaliation. Perez struck out, but the Braves pushed across another run when Jerry Royster's single plated Ramirez.

Trailing 3-0, the Padres had unfinished business beyond the scoreboard.

Both teams were scoreless in the third and the Padres were retired in order in the top of the fourth. Perez came to the plate again with one out in the bottom half of the inning. After a first-pitch ball, Whitson threw three consecutive inside pitches in an obvious attempt to hit Perez. He missed each time, walking Perez, and Rippley ejected both the pitcher and Padres manager Williams.

Greg Booker relieved Whitson, and a subsequent wild pitch moved Perez to second, where he stood just mere feet from Wiggins.

"If Wiggins wanted to settle the issue, he could've done it right there," said Braves backup infielder Bob Watson, in his final season in the majors. "It was just him and Pasqual."[4]

"I wish I would have done something," Wiggins said, "but I didn't."[5]

Royster singled to score Perez, and the Braves led 4-0 through four innings.

Perez tossed another scoreless inning in the fifth, and the Braves added to their margin in the bottom of the inning when Rufino Linares, after walking with two out, scored on Ramirez's double.

In the midst of a strong pitching performance despite the ongoing headhunting by San Diego, Perez again retired the Padres without yielding a run in the sixth. Through six innings, Perez had allowed only three hits, which earned him his third at-bat to lead off the bottom half of the frame. Padres pitcher Greg Booker promptly threw at (and missed) Perez, earning himself an ejection, along with acting manager Ozzie Virgil, who had assumed the role when Williams was tossed in the fourth.

"It would've been a lot simpler if we'd hit Perez his first time up," Padres catcher Terry Kennedy said later. "We missed him three times at bat. The whole thing got pretty ridiculous. It's bad to have kids watch something like this."[6]

The Padres finally got on the board when Graig Nettles homered to lead off the seventh inning. It was the only run Perez would allow, and after again holding San Diego scoreless in the eighth (Atlanta also failed to score in the bottom of the seventh), he made a fourth plate appearance in the home eighth.

Lefty Craig Lefferts toed the rubber and, unlike the three Padres pitchers before him, he successfully hit Perez. Chaos ensued when both benches emptied onto the field, and with Perez standing in the dugout away from the fray, the Padres' Champ Summers rushed toward him, only to be confronted by Bob Horner and pelted with various objects by Atlanta fans, several of whom entered the field to join the scuffle.

When order was restored, Lefferts and acting Padres manager Jack Krol (the third manager of record) were ejected, along with five other players.

Torre finally replaced Perez, sending Brad Komminsk in as a pinch-runner. The Braves were retired by reliever Rich Gossage, and the game advanced to the ninth, with the Atlanta still leading 5-1.

It was now the Braves' turn.

Donnie Moore, now pitching for Atlanta, promptly plunked Graig Nettles, and the benches again cleared. Moore and Torre were ejected, as well as four other players. Umpire and crew chief John McSherry, looking disheveled after trying to break up several fights, decided to send all nonparticipating players to their respective clubhouses, calling the incidents "the worst thing I have ever seen in my life," and adding, "It was pathetic. It took baseball down 50 years."[7]

The Padres pushed across two runs in the ninth off Braves reliever Gene Garber, with both Kevin McReynolds and Carmelo Martinez delivering sacrifice flies for the final tallies. Atlanta won 5-3.

By the time the final out was recorded, bullpen coach Harry Dunlop was the manager of record for the Padres.

Atlanta police confirmed that five spectators were charged with being "disorderly while intoxicated" after they joined the fray in the eighth inning. One fan had the added charges of simple battery and resisting arrest.[8]

"There was a danger of a riot once the fans got involved. This is scary," Torre said. "It was getting to where pretty shortly it would have been San Diego and us against the fans."[9]

In the aftermath. National League President Chub Feeney fined or suspended 18 players. San Diego manager Dick Williams received a 10-day suspension and a fine of $10,000 for ordering his pitchers to continually throw at Perez. Bobby Brown and Champ Summers each received three-day suspensions and $100 fines, and coaches Jack Krol and Ozzie Virgil, as well as players Ed Whitson, Greg Booker, Craig Lefferts, Kurt Bevacqua, Tim Flannery, Graig Nettles, and Rich Gossage all were fined $300.

For the Braves, manager Torre received a three-day suspension and $1,000 fine because "as a field manager you must be held responsible for precipitating the incident," Feeney said in his ruling.[10] Steve Bedrosian was fined $600 and given a three-day suspension for fighting and returning to the field after being ejected, as was Rick Mahler, although his fine was $700. Moore was fined $350 for hitting Nettles; Gerald Perry $700 for returning to the field after being ejected; and Perez, who was not ejected, was fined $300 for making threatening gestures with his bat.

On September 22, with the Padres still boasting a 9½-game lead over the Braves, Whitson and Perez again opposed each other, this time in San Diego. Perez tossed eight innings in a 5-2 Atlanta victory.

The game saw no ejections.

## SOURCES

In addition to the sources cited in the Notes, the author also consulted Baseball-Reference.com and SABR.org.

## NOTES

1    Some discrepancies exist in descriptions of this game. The author relied on the box score and play-by-play data as reported by Retrosheet at retrosheet.org/boxesetc/1984/B08120ATL1984.htm.

2    Joseph Durso, "BeanBall Brawl Stirring Baseball," *New York Times,* August 15, 1984.

3    Ibid.

4    Steve Dolan, "14 Are Ejected as Padres Lose, 5-3, in Beanball War," *Los Angeles Times,* August 13, 1984.

5    Ibid.

6    "This Day in Baseball: Braves, Padres Engage in Mega-Brawl," *Sports Illustrated,* August 12, 2015. si.com/mlb/2015/08/12/atlanta-braves-san-diego-padres-brawl-fight-1984.

7    Chris Mortensen, "McSherry Calls Brawls the Worst He Has Ever Seen; Umpire Holds Padres Responsible," *Atlanta Constitution,* August 13, 1984.

8    Jonathan Vitti, Associated Press, "Braves and Padres Playing Base 'Brawl," *Hanover* (Pennsylvania) *Evening Sun*, August 13, 1984.

9    "Brawl Mars Braves-Padres Game," *Daily Herald Suburban Chicago,* August 13, 1984.

10   Jerry Fraley, "Feeney Fines, Suspends 18 in Braves-Padres fight," *Atlanta Constitution*, August 17, 1984.

# ANOTHER CLUTCH MOMENT FOR STEVE GARVEY

## OCTOBER 6, 1984: SAN DIEGO PADRES 7, CHICAGO CUBS 5, AT JACK MURPHY STADIUM, SAN DIEGO (GAME FOUR OF THE NATIONAL LEAGUE CHAMPIONSHIP SERIES)

### BY JOEL RIPPEL

Before Game Four of the 1984 National League Championship Series, Chicago Cubs manager Jim Frey and San Diego Padres manager Dick Williams were scrutinized for their starting-pitcher choices.

A headline in one newspaper said, "Padres Go With Lollar, a Questionable Starter."[1]

The writer said, "An entire San Diego Padre season rests this evening on the left shoulder of pitcher Tim Lollar. And the shoulder has been a sore spot lately."[2]

Lollar, who was 11-13 with a 3.91 ERA in the regular season, started on September 25 but missed his final scheduled start of the regular season on September 30. He had thrown on the sidelines twice since and had thrown well enough to be deemed fit to pitch in the NLCS game on October 6.

Williams's plan was that everyone but Eric Show, who was scheduled to be the Game Five starter, and Ed Whitson, who had pitched eight innings in Game Three, would be available in relief of Lollar.

Frey was going with Scott Sanderson, who had spent 21 days on the disabled list after recurring back spasms earlier in the season, instead of going with ace Rick Sutcliffe on three days' rest. Sutcliffe, who had pitched seven innings the Cubs' 13-0 victory in Game One, had gone 16-1 in the regular season after joining the Cubs in June. Sanderson was 8-5 with a 3.14 ERA in 24 starts, but had won just two of his last 10 starts. He had pitched five shutout innings in the Cubs' regular-season finale on September 30.

"I didn't want to move (Sutcliffe) out of his normal routine," Frey explained. "I want to give him his full rest so he'll have the best chance to do his best. I want all the conditions right for him."[3]

Game Four was an important one for both franchises.

The Padres, making their inaugural playoff appearance in their 16th season of existence, had lost the first two games of the series, 13-0 and 4-2, in Chicago. After avoiding a sweep with a 7-1 victory over the Cubs in Game Three in San Diego, the Padres were trying to prevent their first foray into the postseason from being brief.

The Cubs were trying to get to the World Series for the first time since 1945. They hadn't won a World Series since 1908.

The Padres staked Lollar to a 2-0 lead with two runs – on a sacrifice fly by Tony Gwynn and an RBI double by Steve Garvey – in the bottom of the third inning.

The Cubs rallied for three runs off Lollar in the top of the fourth. Lollar walked Gary Matthews, then Jody Davis, and Leon Durham hit back-to-back home runs to give the Cubs a 3-2 lead.

Neither Lollar nor Sanderson made it out of the fifth inning. After retiring the first batter in the top of the fifth, Lollar walked the next two and was replaced by Andy Hawkins. Hawkins got a double play to end the threat.

In the bottom of the fifth, Garvey's single off Sanderson tied the score and ended Sanderson's outing.

Garvey's single off reliever Tim Stoddard in the seventh inning came after an intentional walk to Gwynn. Gwynn eventually scored on a passed ball to make it 5-3.

The Cubs got those two runs back in the eighth inning – on an RBI single by Keith Moreland and a double by Davis off Goose Gossage – to tie the score, 5-5.

The Cubs then threatened in the top of the ninth. With one out, Bobby Dernier doubled down the left-field line and stayed at second when Ryne Sandberg popped to third. Craig Lefferts intentionally walked Matthews to get to Henry Cotto, a rookie who had hit .274 in 105 games and 146 at-bats during the regular season. (Cotto had pinch-run for Moreland in the eighth inning.)

The strategy backfired when Lefferts hit Cotto with a pitch to load the bases. But Ron Cey grounded out to second baseman Alan Wiggins to end the inning.

With one out in the bottom of the ninth, Gwynn singled to center. Garvey, who was the only Padre with more than 75 RBIs during the regular season (he had 86), then hit Lee Smith's 1-and-0 fastball into the right-field stands.

"He's a great clutch hitter, what else can you do?" Jody Davis said of Garvey. "We had our best reliever and we gave him our best pitch. He just beat us tonight, and there's no second-guessing around here."[4]

Padres reserve Kurt Bevacqua, Garvey's roommate on the road, predicted Garvey's role in the playoffs.

"I don't want to say I told you so," Bevacqua said, "but I told people before the series: Watch Gary Matthews and watch Garvey.

Why? Because that's him. He's been a great clutch performer all these years and he's going to do it for a lot of years to come."[5]

The 35-year-old Garvey, in his second season with the Padres after playing on four World Series teams with the Los Angeles Dodgers, had rescued the Padres with a historic day. The home run, his fourth hit of the game, gave him a playoff-record-tying five RBIs. Each of his first three hits came with two outs.

Williams, in his 17th season as a major-league manager, said, "No question, it was the greatest playoff game I've ever been associated with, or World Series. I had (Carl) Yastrzemski when he was MVP in 1967 and I've never watched a player have a year like he had, but I don't recall him ever having a day like Steve did today. It was utterly fantastic."[6]

For Garvey, the game-winning home run was rarity after a regular season that saw him hit just 8 home runs in 161 games and 617 at-bats. Garvey, who had averaged a little over 20 home runs in his final nine seasons with the Dodgers, had hit just three home runs after the All-Star break and none in the Padres' final 43 regular-season games. The home run was his first since August 15.

The home run gave Garvey 20 RBIs in 21 games in 21 League Championship Series games.

"I've thought about why," Garvey said. "I get myself up for these moments. I look at the statistics and it gives me a lot of satisfaction."[7]

The next day, in Game Five, Garvey went 1-for-3 and drove in a run as the Padres beat the Cubs, 6-3, to earn their first World Series berth. The Padres became the first NL team to win a playoff series after trailing 2-0 in the series.

## SOURCES

In addition to the sources cited in the Notes, the author consulted Baseball-Reference.com, Newspapers.com, and Retrosheet.org.

## NOTES

1    Steve Dolan, "Padres Go With Lollar, A Questionable Starter," *Los Angeles Times*, October 6, 1984: Part III, 17.

2    Ibid.

3    Jerome Holtzman, "Eliminating DH Might Even It Up," *Chicago Tribune*, October 7, 1984: Section 3, 3.

4    Gordon Edes, "Garvey Has a Night to Remember," *Los Angeles Times*, October 7, 1984: Part III, 1.

5    Ibid.

6    Ibid.

7    Mike Littwin, "When Spotlight's on Garvey, He Always Shines," *Los Angeles Times*, October 7, 1984: Part III, 1.

# THE SAN DIEGO PADRES COME FROM BEHIND AGAIN TO CLAIM THE 1984 NLCS

## OCTOBER 7, 1984: SAN DIEGO PADRES 6, CHICAGO CUBS 3, AT JACK MURPHY STADIUM, SAN DIEGO

### BY BOB WEBSTER

The San Diego Padres advanced to the 1984 World Series by defeating the Chicago Cubs, 6-3, on October 7 at San Diego's Jack Murphy Stadium in front of a crowd of 58,359. After dropping the first two games of the best-of-five National League Championship Series in Chicago, the Padres came from behind in each of the next three games to claim the National League title. It was the first time a National League team won a postseason series after losing the first two games.

The stakes were high for both teams entering Game Five of the NLCS: The Padres had never won a postseason series in their 16-year existence and the Cubs had not appeared in postseason play since 1945. They had not won a postseason series since they took the 1908 World Series over the Detroit Tigers. This was the last year of the best-of-five NLCS format; the major leagues went to a best-of-seven format for the League Championship Series the next season.

Because the umpires went on strike after the close of the regular season, the first four games of the Series were officiated by replacement umpires. The walkout was settled in time for the regular umpiring crew of John Kibler, Paul Runge, John McSherry, and Doug Harvey to be back for Game Five.[1]

The Cubs won the first two games of the series at Chicago's Wrigley Field, 13-0 and 4-2. After Game Two the Padres' plane was delayed on the tarmac at Chicago's O'Hare Airport to allow the Cubs' plane to depart first. Then, after arriving at San Diego's Lindbergh Field, the players learned that the bus route back to Jack Murphy Stadium was being detoured.[2]

"We weren't told about why we were being delayed or detoured," Tony Gwynn recalled years later. "All we knew is that a long day was getting longer. We weren't happy."[3]

Then, as the Padres neared their Mission Valley home, the reason for the delay and detour became apparent. Friars Road was backed up by traffic. More than 15,000 fans were in the parking lot to greet the Padres. Because the team's return had been delayed, the throng had started partying without them.[4]

"It was unbelievable, great chaos," said Gwynn. "The fans were celebrating and we had lost two straight. It got to us. It got to all of us. It was crazy. We're on the verge of getting swept out of the playoffs and the fans came out to welcome us. What I saw was a lot of hope and frustration of the (16-year) losing history boiling over. I didn't know if we were going to win the series, but I knew we weren't going to lose the next day."[5]

As the series shifted to San Diego, the Padres came from behind to take Games Three and Four, the latter capped off by Steve Garvey's walk-off two-run homer to give the Padres a 7-5 victory, setting the stage for Game Five.

On the mound for the Padres was Eric Show, the Game One starter. Rick Sutcliffe, the Cubs' starter, had been picked up in a trade with the Cleveland Indians on June 13 coming with George Frazier and Ron Hassey for Joe Carter, Mel Hall, Don Schulze, and minor-leaguer Darryl Banks. Sutcliffe went 17-1 the rest of the season, including the 13-0 blowout in Game One. Including Game One of this series, Sutcliffe was 3-0 with a 0.37 ERA against the Padres this season.[6]

With two outs in the top of the first, Gary Mathews walked and stole second. Leon Durham homered to give the Cubs a 2-0 lead against Show. Cubs catcher Jody Davis led off the top of the second with a home run to give the Cubs a 3-0 lead. After Larry Bowa flied out to left, Sutcliffe singled to right, chasing Show. Reliever Andy Hawkins got Bobby Dernier to ground into a 4-6 fielder's choice, then was caught stealing to end the inning. Hawkins pitched a scoreless third inning and gave way to pinch-hitter Mario Ramirez, who fouled out to the catcher. Alan Wiggins followed with a walk, but was stranded at first to end the inning

The score remained 3-0 going into the bottom of the sixth with Sutcliffe holding the Padres to two singles. Wiggins reached on a bunt single to open the inning. Tony Gwynn followed with a single to left, Wiggins stopping at second. Steve Garvey walked and the Cubs bullpen was warming up in a hurry. Graig Nettles' fly ball to center scored Wiggins with Gwynn taking third. Terry Kennedy followed with a sacrifice fly to left, cutting the Cubs' lead to 3-2. Bobby Brown grounded out to first baseman Leon Durham to retire the side.

The Cubs went down in order in the top of the seventh. Carmelo Martinez walked to open the Padres' seventh. Garry Templeton sacrificed Martinez to second. Tim Flannery batted for Padres pitcher Craig Lefferts and his grounder went through Durham's legs, scoring Martinez and knotting the score at 3-3. Wiggins

singled to left, Flannery stopping at second. Gwynn's potential inning-ending double-play ball took a hop past Cubs second baseman Ryne Sandberg and rolled into center field for a double, scoring Flannery and Wiggins with Gwynn taking third on

the throw home. Steve Garvey drove in Gwynn with a single, chasing Sutcliffe. Cubs manager Jim Frey called on Steve Trout to relieve Sutcliffe and he retired Nettles on a grounder to first and struck out Kennedy, but the Padres now led, 6-3.

Of Flannery's groundball to Durham, the Cubs first baseman said, "It was a routine ball and it stayed low. I was anticipating a hop." The grounder to Sandberg took a hop when he thought it was going to stay low. "If either groundball is caught," Frey said, "Sutcliffe gets out of the inning."[7]

Rich "Goose" Gossage came in for the Padres in the top of the eighth. With one out, he hit Richie Hebner with a pitch. One out later Sandberg singled Hebner to third. After Sandberg stole second, Gary Matthews struck out swinging to end the inning.

Keith Moreland singled with one out in the Cubs' ninth, but Gossage got Ron Cey to pop out to first and Jody Davis to hit a force-play grounder to third, ending the game and the series.

The Cubs were ahead in every game of the Series and seemed about to put it away at any time, but the Padres and their fans were not about to give up. More than 58,000 spectators showed up for each of the San Diego games and were constantly loud nonstop. The PA system at Jack Murphy Stadium was playing "Cub-Busters," a parody on the title song from the movie *Ghostbusters,* which came out earlier that year. A popular item during the series was Cub-Busters T-shirts. During the clubhouse celebration after Game Five, many of the Padres players took off through a tunnel to the parking lot and through a chain-link fence greeted the fans.[8]

"If it wasn't for Wednesday night, when all those people were out at the stadium when we got off the bus, this might not have happened," said Tim Flannery. "On the airplane back from Chicago, we were all looking through travel magazines trying to figure out where we are going on vacation."[9]

Author Studs Terkel even found a silver lining in the loss. "I think they're more endearing in defeat than in victory," he said of Cubs fans. "I like their loser-like quality. At least this will force all the Johnny-come-suddenlys off the bandwagon. But they were a great team. Far better than the teams of the 1930s."[10]

Steve Garvey, who batted .400 with 7 RBIs, was named the series' Most Valuable Player.

The Padres went on to meet the Detroit Tigers in the 1984 World Series.

## SOURCES

In addition to the sources cited in the Notes, the author also accessed Retrosheet.org, and Baseball-Reference.com for player and game information.

## NOTES

1    Associated Press, "Umpires End Their Strike," *San Francisco Chronicle,* October 8, 1984. The article explained, "Substitute umpires had been working both the American and National League championship series since the strike began after the close of the regular season last Sunday."

2    Bill Center, "NLCS Victory Over Cubs Capped Historic 1984 Season," Friar-Wire, padres.mlblogs.com/nlcs-victory-over-cubs-capped-historic-1984-season-b2541c11a7d3. accessed November 21, 2018.

3    Ibid.

4    Ibid.

5    Ibid.

6    David Bush, "Rally Stuns Cubs, Wins NL Pennant," *San Francisco Chronicle,* October 8, 1984.

7    Bernie Lincicome, "The Fold of '84 Came in Hurry," *Chicago Tribune,* October 8, 1984.

8    Steve Wulf. "You've Got to Hand It to the Padres," *Sports Illustrated,* si.com/vault/1984/10/15/627634/youve-got-to-hand-it-to-the-padres, accessed November 21, 2018.

9    Phil Hersh, "Suddenly, a Serious Love Affair," *Chicago Tribune,* October 8, 1984.

10   Associated Press, "No Joy in Wrigleyville," *Peoria Journal Star,* October 8, 1984.

# WIN ONE FOR THE FRIARS

## OCTOBER 10, 1984: SAN DIEGO PADRES 5, DETROIT TIGERS 3 AT JACK MURPHY STADIUM, SAN DIEGO

### BY SETH MOLAND-KOVASH

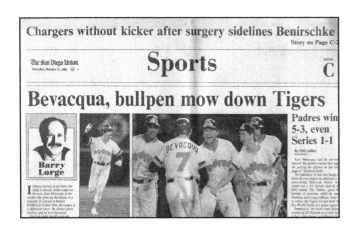

The San Diego Padres have been in existence since 1969 and as of 2018 had played nearly 8,000 games but just nine games in the World Series. Of those nine games, fans of the Padres have only one World Series game victory to celebrate. That victory came at home in Game Two of the 1984 World Series.

Managed by Dick Williams, the 1984 Padres finished with a record of 92-70, winning the National League's West Division

by 12 games over the Atlanta Braves. It was a truly dominating season, as the Padres took over the division lead for good on June 9 and were in first place for 138 days during that year. The Padres were paced by All-Star right fielder Tony Gwynn in the first full season of his Hall of Fame career and got great contributions from closer Rich "Goose" Gossage, youngsters Kevin McReynolds and Carmelo Martinez, and veterans Steve Garvey and Graig Nettles. In the National League Championship Series, the Padres edged past the East Division champion Chicago Cubs with each team winning their home games in the five-game series. The NLCS Most Valuable Player was Garvey who went 8-for-20 with 7 RBIs to lead the Padres into the World Series for the first time.

San Diego's opponent from the American League was the Detroit Tigers. Sparky Anderson's squad, which finished a baseball-best 104-58 and swept the Kansas City Royals in the American League Championship Series, came to San Diego for Game One on October 9. The Tigers won, 3-2, on a masterful

complete game by ace Jack Morris supported by a two-run home run by left fielder Larry Herndon.

As the time for Game Two approached on Wednesday, a capacity crowd of 57,911 streamed into Jack Murphy Stadium. Joining the Padres fans in attendance was former President Gerald Ford. Greeting them on the scoreboard was the face of late owner Ray Kroc with one of his favorite sayings, which the Padres faithful hoped applied to their team as well: "Dreams can come true."[1] Right-hander Ed Whitson (14-8, 3.24 ERA) took the mound for the Padres. Whitson had won the do-or-die third game of the NLCS for the Padres, holding the Cubs to one run in eight innings.

From the umpire's call of "Play Ball!" it was clear that the Tigers were not going to be so compliant with Whitson. Detroit's dangerous 1-2 punch of Lou Whitaker and Alan Trammell led off the game with back-to-back singles. Kirk Gibson followed with a run-scoring single and stole second, Lance Parrish scored Trammell on a sacrifice fly into the Padres' bullpen in left-field foul territory, and Darrell Evans brought Gibson home with another single. After a pop fly and another single to Johnny Grubb, Williams had seen enough. Whitson's first (and, as it would turn out, only) World Series start ended with two-thirds

of an inning pitched, five hits given up (all singles), and his team in an early 3-0 hole. Williams called on swingman Andy Hawkins to stop the damage and keep the Padres in the game. Hawkins had worked in relief in Game One, giving up one hit in 2⅔ innings. Hawkins induced a Chet Lemon groundball to end the half inning.

In the home half of the inning, the Padres faced the Tigers' Dan Petry. The first two men, Alan Wiggins and Gwynn, reached on a bunt single and a walk. Steve Garvey's sacrifice and Nettles' sacrifice fly scored Wiggins but that was all the Padres could manage. Hawkins threw perfect innings in the second through fifth. The Padres got a runner on in the second and third innings, but no significant threats emerged as Petry settled in as well. In the bottom half of the fourth, Padres designated hitter Kurt Bevacqua[2] led off. Bevacqua was a 37-year-old utility player who was mostly used as a corner infielder or pinch-hitter. He had played for six teams in his 14-year career[3] and was in his second stay in San Diego. "I've been so many places," he said, "I have my own ZIP code."[4] In 59 games and 95 plate appearances for the Padres in 1984, Bevacqua had hit .200/.326/.275 and had one home run. In fact, he had only 24 home runs in a major-league career that began in 1971. He would not have figured to be the best candidate for offensive heroics in the World Series. Bevacqua's true heroics would come later. In the fourth inning, however, he led off with a single, took third on Garry Templeton's one-out single, and scored on a fielder's choice groundball to shortstop by Bobby Brown, cutting the Tigers' lead to 3-2.

Hawkins' perfect fifth continued his streak of setting down the first 13 batters he faced after relieving in the first inning. He was giving the Padres time and it was time for the bats to do their job.

Garvey led off the bottom of the fifth as Petry had to face San Diego's 3-4-5 hitters. Garvey flied out to center, but Graig Nettles walked. Terry Kennedy followed with a single on a tough groundball to Tigers second baseman Whitaker. Bevacqua stepped in. He took a strike but did not take a second one. He drove Petry's second pitch, a belt-high slider, into the first row of seats in left field to drive in three runs and put the Padres up, 5-3.[5] Bevacqua knew it was gone from the moment he hit it and put both his arms up and danced around first base before continuing his trot. The Padres had their first-ever World Series lead. Anderson brought in Aurelio Lopez to relieve Petry and he ended the inning. Hawkins gave up a single to Gibson to lead off the sixth but faced the minimum again as Gibson was eliminated in a line-drive double play off the bat of Darrell Evans to end the inning and complete Hawkins' outing. He had faced 16 batters in 5⅓ innings pitched, striking out three, and giving up just one hit. It was all his manager could have asked of him.

The Tigers turned to another reliever in the sixth, bringing in Bill Scherrer to face Gwynn, Garvey, and Nettles. He gave up a single to Gwynn but picked him off and retired the other two for a quick inning. In the Tigers' half of the seventh, the Padres manager turned to lefty Craig Lefferts, who set down the Tigers in order. Scherrer and Doug Bair combined to strand one Padres baserunner in the home seventh and Lefferts came back with a clean top of the eighth as the tension built. In the Padres' half of the eighth inning they were retired 1-2-3 by Willie Hernandez, setting up a top of the ninth with the home team still clinging to the 5-3 lead bought by Bevacqua's blast.

Lefferts took the mound again for the Padres and prepared to face Detroit's 4-5-6 hitters, Lance Parrish, Darrell Evans, and Larry Herndon. The 35 pitches he had thrown to that point did not hold him back. Parrish battled Lefferts through a seven-pitch at-bat but was out on a called third strike. Evans did not leave the call in home-plate umpire Larry Barnett's hands as he struck out swinging on five pitches. Larry Herndon stepped in trying to keep the game going, pinch-hitting for Ruppert Jones. He swung at the first pitch and popped it foul behind first base. Wiggins made the long run from his position at second base and squeezed the final out, securing the first World Series game win for the San Diego Padres.

After a travel day on Thursday, October 11, the Series moved to Detroit for Games Three, Four, and Five. The Tigers won all three of their home games and the World Series was not to return to San Diego until 1998, when the Padres were swept by the New York Yankees.

## SOURCES

In addition to the sources cited in the Notes, the author also used YouTube.com, Baseball-Reference.com, and Retrosheet.org.

## NOTES

1    Bill McGraw, "Padres Storm Back, Rock Tigers," *Detroit Free Press*, October 11, 1984: D1.

2    Yes, you read that correctly. There was a DH in a World Series game in a National League ballpark. When the DH was introduced in the American League in 1973, there were no designated hitters at all in the World Series. Beginning in 1976, the DH was used in the entire Series (in both ballparks) in even-numbered years. This practice lasted through 1985, when the current format of using the DH only in American League ballparks was instituted. This rule likely allowed Bevacqua to be in the lineup and in position to play the hero.

3    One team not included in that number was the Cincinnati Reds. Bevacqua started his professional career in the Reds organization but was cut during spring training 1971 by manager (and 1984 Tigers manager) Sparky Anderson.

4    Dave Distel, "Bevacqua a Journeyman Who Enjoys His Journey," *Los Angeles Times*, October 11, 1984: III-1.

5    Chris Cobbs, "Petry Let Game 2 Slide Through His Hands," *Los Angeles Times*, October 11, 1984: III-14.

# TONY GWYNN EDGES WILL CLARK ON LAST DAY FOR BATTING CROWN

## OCTOBER 1, 1989: SAN DIEGO PADRES 3, SAN FRANCISCO GIANTS 0, AT JACK MURPHY STADIUM, SAN DIEGO

### BY RICHARD CUICCHI

San Francisco Giants first baseman Will Clark was having a career year in 1989 as he helped lead the team to a division championship. He had been a model of hitting consistency throughout the season and heading into the final series of the year, against the San Diego Padres, he had a good shot at capturing the National League batting title. However, the Padres' Tony Gwynn, who already had three batting crowns in his trophy case, would have something to say about that.

Gwynn was no stranger to batting races, although none had been as close as the one in 1989. The contact hitter had already established himself as one of the top hitters in baseball, having led the league in batting average (.351) in his first full major-league season (1984) and then in 1987 (.370) and 1988 (.313).

As for Clark, it was his first run at a batting championship. His previous high was .308 in 1987. During his first three seasons, he was considered more of a power hitter, with sixth- and third-

place finishes in home runs and a league-leading 109 RBIs in 1988. Clark was on the verge of becoming the first San Francisco Giant to win the batting championship.[1]

Clark's hitting had been unswerving throughout the entire season: .375 in April, .351 in May, .303 in June, .307 in July, .352 in August, and .316 in September/October. He hit .325 at home and .341 on the road, and batted .321 against left-handed pitchers and .340 against righties.[2]

He had suffered a bruised knee on September 21 and sat out three games to give it a rest. The Giants had already clinched the National League West Division and led the second-place Padres by four games. Clark could have easily taken off some or all of the final series. But he told Giants manager Roger Craig he didn't want to miss any more games: "If I'm going to win the title, I'm not going to win it sitting down. My job is to play."[3]

Going into the Padres-Giants series that started on September 29 in Jack Murphy Stadium, Clark led Gwynn in batting average, .3333 to .3316. The Giants won the first game, 7-2, as Clark went 2-for-4 while Gwynn collected only one hit in five at-bats. The Padres took the second game, 11-5, with Gwynn getting three hits in four at-bats. Clark managed only one hit in four at-bats, but still held a very narrow lead (.0006) over Gwynn, .3339 to .3333.

So the final game of the season, on Sunday, October 1, wouldn't have any effect on the final standings in the NL West; but what was at stake was the individual honor of a batting crown.

Kelly Downs (4-7) was the starting pitcher for the Giants. He had been on the disabled list from May 2 to August 12, but had secured a spot in the starting rotation upon his return. Greg W. Harris (7-9), who had been used exclusively in relief during September after getting seven starts in July and August, drew the starting assignment for the Padres.

In a low-scoring game, most of the drama centered on the battle for hits between Gwynn and Clark. Here are the sequential at-bat results of their pursuit.

| Player | Inning | Pitcher Faced | At-bat Result | Current Average |
|--------|--------|---------------|---------------|-----------------|
| Clark | 1st | Greg Harris | Grounded out to first base | .3333 |
| Gwynn | 1st | Kelly Downs | Lined a single to right field | .3344 |
| Gwynn | 3rd | Kelly Downs | Grounded out to first base | .3339 |
| Clark | 4th | Greg Harris | Grounded out to second base | .3328 |
| Gwynn | 5th | Jeff Brantley | Beat out a grounder to shortstop that scored Alomar | .3350 |
| Clark | 6th | Greg Harris | Looped a single to left field | .3339 |
| Clark | 8th | Mark Davis | Flied out to center field | .3333 |
| Gwynn | 8th | Craig Lefferts | Grounded a single into right field that scored Alomar | .3361 |

The Padres scored their first run in the second inning when Phil Stephenson slammed a solo home run off Downs. Combined with Gwynn's RBI hits in the fifth and eighth innings, the Padres won the game, 3-0. Clark's lone hit was one of only four the Giants mustered against Harris and reliever Mark Davis.

Gwynn's hit in the fifth inning came close to being an out. He hit a two-out chopper over the mound that shortstop Chris Speier fielded and threw to first base. Umpire Ed Montague initially raised his fist to indicate an out, but changed it in mid-signal to a safe call. Giants first-base coach Bob Lillis was ejected on the play for his animated dispute with Montague over the call.[4]

Harris got credit for the win, giving up only the four hits and three walks in seven innings, while striking out seven. Downs took the loss, yielding one run on four hits and a walk in four innings. The Giants used the last four innings to provide work for the bullpen in preparation for the playoffs. Jeff Brantley and Craig Lefferts gave up the other two Padres runs.

Gwynn said that Clark congratulated him at first base after his hit in the eighth inning. He told Clark, "It's no big deal. You're going where I want to go. I'd trade a batting title to be going to the playoffs."[5] Well aware of the batting title consequences, the hometown crowd was pulling for Gwynn each time he stepped up to the plate. On the other hand, Clark had to listen to boisterous heckling and booing from fans who obviously wanted to see him fail in each at-bat. While Gwynn acknowledged Clark's challenging situation throughout the game, Clark said, "The fans' jeering had no effect on me. Confidence is not one of my problems."[6] Gwynn said, "I ended up winning it, but that doesn't take anything away from Clark's year."[7]

After the game, a disappointed Clark said, "It's too bad my whole season had to come down to one at-bat. If I get a hit and he doesn't, I win. If I don't get a hit, he automatically wins. That's why this game is fun." In admiration of Gwynn, Clark added, "I got beat by the best, and there's no disgrace in that. The thing about Tony Gwynn is, when everything is said, he goes out on the field and gets it done. That's what separates him."[8]

Gwynn's third consecutive batting title was the first time any player had accomplished the feat since Stan Musial did it for the St. Louis Cardinals in 1950-1952. Gwynn went one better 1994 to 1997, winning four consecutive batting crowns including one with a .394 average in the strike-shortened 1994 season. Ty Cobb holds the record for most batting titles (12) in a career,[9] while Gwynn is tied with Honus Wagner for second with eight.

Clark finished the 1989 season with a slash line of .333/.407/.546. He led the league in runs scored (104) and finished second in hits (196), hit 23 home runs, and drove in 111 runs. His overall performance earned him a runner-up finish in the National League MVP Award voting behind teammate Kevin Mitchell, who led the league in home runs (47) and RBIs (125). He continued his torrid hitting during the National League Championship Series against Chicago, batting .650 (13-for-20).

There was similar drama in the American League batting race on the last day of the 1989 season. Minnesota Twins outfielder Kirby Puckett was less than a percentage point ahead of Oakland A's infielder Carney Lansford heading into Sunday's action. Puckett got two doubles in five at-bats to claim the title, ultimately beating Lansford by three points (.339 to .336).

## SOURCES

In addition to the sources cited in the Notes below, the author also consulted Baseball-Reference.com.

## NOTES

1    Willie Mays was the last Giant to win a batting championship, in 1954, when he played for the New York Giants.

2    Seymour Siwoff, Steve Hirdt, Peter Hirdt, and Tom Hirdt, *The 1990 Elias Baseball Analyst* (New York: Collier Books, 1990), 228.

3    "Bottom Line: 3 in a Row for Gwynn," *The Sporting News*, October 9, 1989: 23.

4    Ray Ratto, "Gwynn a Hit in the Finale," *San Francisco Chronicle*, October 2, 1989: D1.

5    Ratto.

6    Associated Press, "Gwynn Edges Clark for Title," *New Orleans Times-Picayune*, October 2, 1989.

7    Ratto.

8    Ratto.

9    Baseball-Reference.com shows Cobb (baseball-reference.com/players/c/cobbty01. shtml) winning 12 batting titles (1907-1915, 1917-1919), while Retrosheet.org shows Cobb winning 10 titles (retrosheet.org/boxesetc/C/Pcobbt101.htm). Two of his titles (1910 and 1914) have been the subject of dispute over the years. The MLB.com website for Cleveland Indians history (cleveland.indians.mlb.com/cle/history/story1.jsp) addresses the controversy for 1910, with two hits being mistakenly credited to Cobb. The dispute in 1914 centered on whether Cobb had the minimum number of plate appearances to qualify for the batting title (baseball-reference.com/leagues/AL/1914-standard-batting.shtml).

# A MEXICAN BASEBALL FIESTA

## AUGUST 16, 1996: SAN DIEGO PADRES 15, NEW YORK METS 10, AT ESTADIO BEISBOL DE MONTERREY, MONTERREY, MEXICO

### BY PAUL E. DOUTRICH

Monterrey, Mexico, lies 100 miles south of the Texas border. It is the third largest city in Mexico, the capital of Nuevo Leon state, and an industrial city that produces a broad array of goods. It is also a city passionate about baseball. On August 16, 1996, the San Diego Padres attempted to tap into that passion by playing the first of a three-game series against the New York Mets in Monterrey. It was the first regularly scheduled major-league game outside of the United States and Canada.

The three games in Monterrey were part of a Padres strategy to broaden their fan base and to promote baseball in Mexico. Since Larry Lucchino and John Moore acquired the team 20 months earlier, the Padres had actively pursued relations with Mexican fans. Efforts had been taken to make Jack Murphy Stadium warmer and friendlier for Latinos. Spanish-speaking ushers were hired, and some concession stands were expanded to include Mexican food and beer. On Sundays throughout the season the Padres bused in as many as 2,000 Mexicans from Tijuana. Special prices and seating sections were set aside for the Sunday visitors and the Mexican flag flew alongside the American flag inside the ballpark.[1]

The opening game began amid a festive backdrop like an Opening Day or a World Series game. Rush-hour traffic along Avenida Gonzalitos was stopped while a police motorcade escorted the two teams from their hotel to Estadio Monterrey. Inside the ballpark mariachi bands entertained 23,699 anxious fans as they shuffled into their seats. When the 7 o'clock game time arrived, players from both teams lined up along the two baselines and were individually introduced. So too were players from the local team, Los Sultanes (the Sultans), who had just won their third Mexican League championship in four years. The players then threw ceremonial baseballs that had been stitched with red and green thread, the colors of the Mexican flag, into the stands. The honor of throwing out the first pitch was given to one of Mexico's baseball heroes, Fernando Valenzuela, who was also the Padres' starting pitcher.

With the preliminaries out of the way, the two teams got down to business. Amid chants of "Tor-o, Tor-o, Tor-o," it was obvious immediately that Valenzuela was the fan favorite.[2] "The crowd didn't just root, they ranted and rode home-plate umpire Joe West with each close call against Valenzuela. … (They) gave him a standing ovation when he flied out to center. They rose in salute again in the fourth and they applauded again when Fernando struck out."[3] His supporters didn't care that he was clearly no longer the young hurler who, 15 years earlier, had been voted both the National League Rookie of the Year and the Cy Young Award winner. They didn't mind that his fastball no longer zipped past batters as it once had. Instead they idolized his unmistakable eye-rolling skyward windup. They were delighted that he still had a vicious screwball and they appreciated that he had compensated for his loss of velocity with an arsenal of off-speed pitches. They also expected that, at least on this night, he would still be as savvy as ever. Most importantly, they were proud that he was one on their own.

Despite giving up a single and a walk, Valenzuela held the Mets scoreless in the opening frame. His rookie counterpart, Robert Person, did not fare as well. He walked the Padres' leadoff hitter, Tony Gwynn, then gave up a one-out home run to center fielder Steve Finley. Two innings later Gwynn started another assault on Person. He led off with a single, went to second after a walk to first baseman Wally Joyner, and scored on a double to right by Finley. Joyner and Finley both scored on a two-out double by catcher John Flaherty. Meanwhile Valenzuela continued to outsmart Mets hitters, giving up only a third-inning double to third baseman Alvaro Espinoza and a fifth-inning single to center fielder Lance Johnson.

The end of Person's night came in the bottom of the fifth. He surrendered a three-run homer off the bat of Ken Caminiti. One out later Flaherty knocked one over the left-field fence and Person was replaced by reliever Derek Wallace. After the game the Mets' young right-hander rationalized his outing, proposing, "It was in a foreign country, on foreign ground. It's a great park, but not a major-league park. The ball flies out of it."[4] In some ways Person's laments were hollow. A little over a month earlier he had beaten the Expos "in a foreign country and on foreign ground." On the other hand, there was some credence to the observation. Though it was the largest baseball stadium in Mexico, by major-league standards it was small: 325-foot fences down both lines and 400 feet to dead center with a seating capacity of 25,644. To bring the playing field up to major-league standards, the Padres grounds crew had spent a week of 14-hour days replacing the rocky crushed-brick infield, baselines and mound with topsoil. The turf was trimmed down from 2½ inches to 1 inch and meticulously manicured. To brighten the field, 24 floodlights were added. New locker rooms were built.[5]

In the sixth Valenzuela, aided by a double play, breezed through another three-up, three-down inning. In the bottom half of the inning, already up by nine runs, the Padres piled on more when left fielder Greg Vaughan belted a grand slam, San Diego's fourth home run of the day. After another pitching change, Derek DiPoto took over for Wallace, and two more Padres runs scored, stretching the lead to 15-0. Later Mets manager Dallas Green cynically professed, "I guess we showed those Mexicans how to play baseball. Was that a fine big-league game or what?"[6]

The seventh inning began with four new Padres names on the scorecard. Gwynn, who was replaced by his brother Chris, first baseman Joyner, third baseman Caminiti, and catcher Flaherty were given the rest of the night off. Not much later Valenzuela was also replaced. He had surrendered a run on a walk sandwiched between two singles, and it was clear that Fernando had run out of gas. Dustin Hermanson was called upon to put out the fire. Though two more markers were charged against Valenzuela, he left with an apparently insurmountable 14-run lead. As he departed, fans stood and gave him a roaring sendoff. After the game Valenzuela assessed the evening affirming, "Tonight was good for baseball, good for Mexican baseball."[7]

Though they were down by a dozen runs, the Mets did not surrender without a fight. Neither team scored in the eighth, but New York mounted a comeback in the ninth. The Mets opened the inning with a single, a walk, and a double to plate a run. After two groundouts, including one that drove in another run, Andy Tomberlin, who had replaced Bernie Gilkey in left field an inning earlier, smacked a home run. With two outs and a runner on second, Sean Bergman replaced Hermanson on the mound but had no success. Five more hitters came to the plate and three more runs scored before Dario Veras, the Padres' third pitcher in the inning, finally shut down the Mets' comeback with the final score 15-10. After the game manager Green griped, "We just unload and battle and claw and scratch and never give up but it was a little too late."[8]

By most standards major-league baseball's first official venture into Latin America was a success. National League President Leonard Coleman called the game "a significant step in the international growth of baseball."[9] The publisher of the quarterly journal *Latinos in the Major Leagues* agreed, saying, "Major League Baseball should be praised for doing this."[10] Further confirming the game's success was a father who had traveled 435 miles with his son from Mexico City, and said, "This is wonderful because it opens the doors for baseball in all Latin America."[11] And at least one player, Padres pitcher Tim Worrell, also recognized the historic significance of the game. "We're the first to do it – there isn't going to be another first time."[12]

# NOTES

1    Kevin Baxter, "Padres Go for Title: 'Mexico's Team,'" *Los Angeles Times*, August 16, 1996: 49.

2    Mark Kriegel, "Mania Still Remainia," *Daily News* (New York), August 17, 1996: 36.

3    Mark Fineman, "Fernandomania Is Alive and Well and Living in Monterrey," *Los Angeles Times*, August 17, 1996: 40.

4    Thomas Hill, "Padres Plate Mets with Mex Hex," *Daily News* (New York), August 17, 1996: 37.

5    Fineman.

6    Hill.

7    Kriegel.

8    Hill.

9    Associated Press, "Beisbol Takes a Trip South of the Border," *San Bernardino County Sun*, August 17, 1996: 25.

10    Ibid.

11    Ibid.

12    Ibid.

# THE END OF LA PRIMERA SERIE: PADRES AND METS

## AUGUST 18, 1996: SAN DIEGO PADRES 8, NEW YORK METS 0, AT ESTADIO MONTERREY, MONTERREY, MEXICO

### BY PAUL E. DOUTRICH

The third and final game between the San Diego Padres and New York Mets, the first regularly scheduled major-league games played in Mexico, took place under a broiling 100-degree sun. The finale drew another 22,810 enthusiastic fans who again heartily greeted players from both teams as they took the field.[1] As in the first two games,[2] a roving mariachi band entertained before the game and between innings. However, by Sunday the impact of the adventure had begun to affect players. After two comfortable night games, the dry, desert-afternoon heat immediately took a toll. Meanwhile, several players had fallen victim to food poisoning. A few other players had also begun grumbling about the Estadio Monterrey playing field. Conditions that had been tolerable two days earlier had, by Sunday, become a point of concern.

The game began well for both pitchers. Joey Hamilton put the Mets down in order, the first two by strikeouts. In the bottom of the inning, Rickey Henderson, who was playing left field,

led off for the Padres. Henderson had not started in the first two games. When he came to the plate for the first time, he received a roaring salute. After the game he conceded that he probably had more fans in Monterrey than anywhere in the National League – including San Diego.[3] Mets hurler Paul Wilson got both Henderson and Tony Gwynn to ground out. The inning ended on a Steve Finley fly out to left.

In the second inning Hamilton chalked up his third strikeout but also gave up two-out singles to catcher Brent Mayne and second baseman Edgardo Alfonzo. Fortunately for Hamilton, Rey Ordonez, the Mets shortstop, grounded out to third before any runs could score.

The Padres' second inning opened with some fireworks. Lead-off hitter Ken Caminiti blasted Wilson's fourth pitch into the left-center-field stands for a home run. A Gold Glove winner the previous year, Caminiti was recognized as one of the best fielding third basemen in baseball. At the plate he was having a career season that would culminate in a Silver Slugger Award as well as the league's Most Valuable Player Award. Caminiti was also one of the Padres players suffering from the effects of the team's foray into Mexico. He had spent the previous night vomiting and the morning getting intravenous medication to counter food poisoning and dehydration.[4] That he was able to play was a testament to his fortitude.

Caminiti came to the plate again in the third inning, this time with Henderson on second, pitcher Hamilton on third, and two outs. As he had an inning earlier, the Padres third baseman smacked a Wilson pitch for another home run. This one went into the right-center-field stands. Amid a standing ovation from appreciative fans, Caminiti slowly loped around the bases and back into the Padres dugout.[5] His day ended two innings later when second baseman Craig Shipley moved to third and Jody Reed took Shipley's place at second base. Shipley, who hailed from New South Wales, Australia, had the distinction of being the first Australian to play major-league baseball during the modern era.

Despite a bases-loaded threat in the fourth, Hamilton continued to rack up strikeouts and keep the Mets off the scoreboard through the middle innings. When he left in the eighth he had struck out 10 Mets batters and given up only six hits. For Wilson it was a different story. In the fourth he gave up another home run, this one to Hamilton. The Padres scored again in the fifth on doubles by center fielder Steve Finley and first baseman Wally Joyner. Then, in the seventh, Wilson was finally lifted for a pinch-hitter. After the game he lamented, "Sometimes I don't have it. I can't say I'm pitching the way I was in spring training. Physically and mentally, I'm different now. … I'm just not getting the job done."[6] Mets manager Dallas Green was a bit more philosophical about his rookie pitcher's performance: "With young people they don't learn too much when you take them out of the game."[7]

The Padres scored their eighth and final run in the eighth. Meanwhile, Dario Veras picked up where Hamilton had left off. After Lance Johnson singled leading off the fifth inning, the Mets failed to put another runner on base until the ninth, when Trevor Hoffman, the Padres closer, gave up a walk and a single. The 8-0 win pushed the Padres into a tie with the Dodgers for first place in the National League West while the Mets slid nine games beneath .500.

Many involved in the three-day series considered it a grand success. Padres CEO Larry Lucchino was at the top of that list. It had been his idea and organizing that had brought major-league baseball to Monterrey. The previous winter he had learned that the Republican Party was considering holding its presidential nominating convention in San Diego and might use Jack Murphy Stadium. Already focused on developing a Latino fan base, Lucchino decided to schedule games in Mexico while the GOP was in San Diego. His goal, as stated by the Padres director for Hispanic marketing, was simple: "We want to become Mexico's team."[8]

There were several players who shared Lucchino's aspiration. The most outspoken was Carlos Baerga, a native of Puerto Rico. Baerga commented, "I was ready to come here. … Baseball needs to be Spanish. We're idols in Latin America. A lot of these kids can't come to the States to watch us play."[9] He told the Rockland Journal News: "It has been good, it has been good for baseball."[10] During their visit, Baerga, two other players, and four coaches gave instruction to 200 local children on a field across the street from the ballpark. Tony Gwynn liked the relative anonymity he experienced in Monterrey: "Once we left the hotel today, nobody said, 'Mr. Gwynn can I have your autograph?' in English or in Spanish."[11] Mets pitcher John Franco observed, "It's a lot nicer than I would have thought from what everybody said."[12]

Of course, there were a few players who had a different opinion about their experience in Monterrey. In addition to Caminiti, at least three Mets, catcher Todd Hundley, second baseman Edgardo Alfonzo, and outfielder Chris Jones, complained about stomach problems. Hundley was blunt about playing in Mexico again: "You can have this place. It ain't worth coming here."[13] Teammate Bernie Gilkey grumbled, "They better call me because I'm not coming. Dangerous man. I'm glad nobody got hurt."[14] Center fielder Lance Johnson agreed. "These are probably the hardest conditions I've played in in years. You couldn't even charge a ground ball. … One ball that went by Wally (Joyner) he didn't even see."[15] The language barrier was also a problem for some players. However, manager Green summed up the general attitude: "I don't speak Spanish, so I don't know what the hell they're calling us. But they're fine. They like their baseball and they know this game."[16]

Despite the complaints, Lucchino returned home satisfied. Attendance for the three days averaged 22,461, a bit more than either the Padres or Mets were drawing at home.[17] Assessing the three-day experiment, the Padres CEO contentedly remarked, "I feel like the Padres flag is pretty firmly planted in Monterrey soil and we'll have to come back and tend to it."[18]

# NOTES

1    Mark Fineman, "Padres Beat Mets as Monterrey Fans Toast Their Success," *Los Angeles Times*, August 19, 1996: 32.

2    The Padres won the first game of the series, 15-10, and the Mets won the second, 7-3.

3    Ibid.

4    Kit Stier, "Mets Bow in Mexico Finale, 8-0," *Rockland Journal News* (White Plains, New York), August 19, 1996: 19-20.

5    Fineman.

6    Thomas Hill, "Gives Up 3HRS as Padres Have a Fiesta," *Daily News* (New York), August 19, 1996: 43.

7    Ibid.

8    Kevin Baxter, "Padres Go for Title: 'Mexico's Team,'" *Los Angeles Times,* August 16, 1996: 49.

9    Thomas Hill, "Water's Fine, but Hundley Is Out at Plate," *Daily News* (New York), August 19, 1996: 43.

10    Stier. The other player was Mets third baseman Alvaro Espinosa. The Mets coaches were Rafael Landestoy and Frank Howard. The Padres coaches were Davey Lopes, Merv Rettenmund, and Rob Picciolo. The coaches did the instruction and the players talked to children. Baerga advised the kids to stay in school, telling them, "[I]f you stay in school and get a degree you'll always be able to get a job."

11    Thomas Hill, "Players Adjust to Whole Enchilada," *Daily News* (New York), August 17, 1996: 37.

12    Ibid.

13    Hill, "Water's Fine, but Hundley Is Out at Plate."

14    Stier.

15    Hill, "Water's Fine, but Hundley Is Out at Plate."

16    Fineman.

17    Ibid.

18    Stier. In 1999 the Padres returned to Monterrey to open their season with a game against the Colorado Rockies. They made a third trip to Monterrey in May 2018, playing a three-game series against the Los Angeles Dodgers. The Rockies won the 1999 game, 8-2. The Dodgers won the May 4, 2018, game, shutting out the Padres, 4-0, but San Diego prevailed in the next two games, beating the Dodgers 7-4 on May 5 and shutting out LA, 3-0, on May 6.

# PADRES COMPLETE SWEEP OF DODGERS FOR NL WEST TITLE

## SEPTEMBER 29, 1996: SAN DIEGO PADRES 2, LOS ANGELES DODGERS 0, AT DODGER STADIUM

## BY PAUL HOFMANN

On September 29, 1996, the last day of the regular season, the Padres and Dodgers were in a dead heat, tied for first place and scheduled to play each other at Dodger Stadium. The winner would be the National League West champion, while the loser would advance to the playoffs as the NL wild card. While both teams were guaranteed to play beyond that afternoon, there was still a division title at stake. Not since 1908 had an NL league or division title been decided in a head-to-head matchup on the last day of the season, but that's exactly what happened that Sunday afternoon.[1]

The Padres came to Los Angeles with no margin for error. Trailing the Dodgers by two games, they needed a sweep to win the division title. The stage was set for the season finale when the Padres took the first two games of the series. Ken Caminiti won the September 27 series opener with a 10th-inning double, giving the Padres a 5-2 victory and assuring San Diego of at least a tie for the wild-card berth. Tony Gwynn was the hero the next day, breaking a 2-2 tie in the eighth with a two-run single as the Padres assured themselves of a postseason spot and gave them a shot at the division title with a 4-2 win.

For the third game, the Padres passed on starting the team's number-two hurler, Joey Hamilton (15-9, 4.17), on three days' rest and instead turned to right-hander Bob Tewksbury, who hadn't started since September 17.[2] Tewksbury entered the contest with a 10-10 record and a 4.46 ERA. The Dodgers countered with right-hander Ramon Martinez (15-6, 3.44), who was 7-0 in his last nine starts. He hadn't lost since August 7. On paper the pivotal contest seemed to favor the Dodgers.

It was a perfect day for baseball in Los Angeles. Dodger Stadium basked in a sun-drenched 78 degrees against the picturesque backdrop of the San Gabriel Mountains when Martinez threw the first pitch at 1:05 P.M. The lanky, hard-throwing Martinez retired the Padres in order on 11 pitches in the top of the first. Tony Gwynn lined out to shortstop, Steve Finley followed with a groundout to first and Caminiti struck out swinging. Tewksbury matched Martinez's first-inning effort and needed only 12 pitches to set the Dodgers down 1-2-3.

Right-hander Pedro Astacio came on in relief of Martinez in the top of the second. Knowing a playoff spot was already clinched, the Dodgers opted to remove their streaking right-hander to allow him to start Game One of the NLDS against either the Braves or Cardinals. The 27-year-old Astacio was earmarked to come out of the bullpen during the NLDS and was called upon to eat as many innings as he could. The Dodgers hurler had been particularly effective in this area throughout the year and entered the game with record of 9-8 and a 3.55 ERA over an impressive 205⅓ innings pitched.

Astacio picked up where Martinez left off. From the second inning through the seventh, the right-hander yielded only a pair of hits to Wally Joyner (a one-out double in the second and a leadoff single in the seventh) and a pair of walks in the fifth. Tewksbury was equally as effective for the Padres. He scattered three hits over seven innings and only twice allowed a Dodger baserunner to advance to second base.

The first real threat of the game was mounted in the top of the eighth inning. Jody Reed, the Padres' dependable second baseman, started the inning by grounding out to short. Scott Livingstone, pinch-hitting for Tewksbury, followed with a seeing-eye roller that found the hole between short and third. Sensing that the next run might be a pennant clincher, Padres manager Bruce Bochy lifted Livingstone in favor of pinch-runner Doug Dascenzo. Tony Gwynn walked, sending Dascenzo to second and ending Astacio's afternoon. Dodgers manager Bill Russell played the percentages and called on left-hander Scott Radinsky to face the left-handed-hitting Finley. The Padres center fielder greeted Radinsky with a groundball into right field, where Raul Mondesi came up throwing and nailed Dascenzo at the plate. Radinsky intentionally walked Caminiti and escaped the inning when he struck out Greg Vaughn to keep the game scoreless.

Bochy brought in rookie right-hander Dario Veras to face the Dodgers in the bottom of the eighth inning. The 26-year-old Dominican responded with a scoreless frame in which he yielded a one-out walk to Delino DeShields, who advanced to second with a two-out stolen base.

Russell, who had replaced the legendary Tommy Lasorda after he suffered a midseason heart attack, summoned closer Todd Worrell to pitch the ninth for the Dodgers. Worrell, who recorded a career-high and league-leading 44 saves that season,

retired the Padres in order and kept the game scoreless. It was his only inning of work. Veras kept the game scoreless when he pitched around a leadoff walk to center fielder Wayne Kirby in the bottom on the ninth to send the game into extra innings.

Right-hander Chan Ho Park, the Dodgers' rookie reliever from South Korea, came on in the 10th inning and easily retired the Padres. After striking out Reed to start the inning, Park retired future Hall of Famers Rickey Henderson and Tony Gwynn on consecutive grounders to shortstop Greg Gagne. Veras, working his third inning, navigated his way around a one-out single to Tim Wallach in the bottom of the inning to send the game into the 11th.

Finley led off the top of the 11th with a groundball single up the middle. He advanced to third when Caminiti singled to right. With runners at the corners and no one out, Bochy called on Chris Gwynn, Tony's younger brother, to hit for Veras. Gwynn, who was raised in the Dodgers organization, became the man of the hour when he sent a double to deep right-center, plating Finley and Caminiti.[3] (Chris Gwynn had been cast aside by the Dodgers during the previous offseason. The at-bat was the last regular-season plate appearance of his career.) Park settled down and retired Joyner, Chris Gomez, and Brian Johnson to keep the score at 2-0.

The Padres turned to closer Trevor Hoffman, who had already saved 41 games, to nail down the team's first division title since 1984. Hoffman came through. He retired Greg Gagne on a groundball to short and pinch-hitter Dave Hansen on a fly ball to deep right-center before he ended the game with his signature changeup that caught Chad Curtis. It was Hoffman's third save of the weekend.

The victory was sweet revenge for the Padres. On September 30, 1995, they had been forced to watch as the Dodgers celebrated their Western Division title at Jack Murphy Stadium. One day short of a year to the day, at Dodger Stadium, the Padres celebrated the franchise's second division championship.[4]

Both teams advanced to the NLDS. The Dodgers faced the defending World Series champion Atlanta Braves and were swept in three straight, losing to future Hall of Famers John Smoltz, Greg Maddux, and Tom Glavine. The Padres fared no better against the Cardinals and were also swept in three straight as future Hall of Famer Dennis Eckersley saved all three games for St. Louis.

# NOTES

1    "Padres History: 1996 Season Recap," mlb.com.

2    The Padres had shortened the rotation in an effort to keep pace with the Dodgers.

3    Bob Nightengale, "Dodgers Must Gwynn, Bear It: Former Dodger Chris Gwynn Leads Padres to Division Title," *Los Angeles Times*, September 30, 1996. Retrieved from articles.latimes.com/1996-09-30/sports/sp-49102_1_chris-gwynn.

4    "Padres History: 1996 Season Recap."

# SIMPLY STERLING: ON SHORT REST, HITCHCOCK LEADS PADRES TO THE FALL CLASSIC

## OCTOBER 14, 1998: SAN DIEGO PADRES 5, ATLANTA BRAVES 0, AT TURNER FIELD
## GAME SIX OF THE NATIONAL LEAGUE CHAMPIONSHIP SERIES

### BY BRIAN WRIGHT

As the 1998 NLCS began, two statements seemed certain. Given the way they dominated the National League, the Atlanta Braves were nearly a consensus choice to capture their fifth pennant of the 1990s. If they did not, and the San Diego Padres did, Kevin Brown would be the main reason why.

Contrary to expert opinion, the Padres managed to dethrone the presumed NL kings – advancing to their first World Series since 1984. And it wasn't their ace right-hander who got them there.

In fact, Brown had his opportunity to slam the door on Atlanta two nights earlier. After San Diego had unbelievably taken a commanding three-games-to-none series lead, highlighted by a masterful three-hit Game Two shutout by Brown at Atlanta's Turner Field, the Braves pummeled Padres relievers to salvage Game Four. Then, clinging to a 4-2 lead in Game Five at Qual-

comm Stadium, manager Bruce Bochy rolled the dice. Instead of saving Brown for a potential Game Six on the road, he used him in the unconventional role of closer.

The move backfired in the eighth. Atlanta had two runners on and one out. Brown tried to throw a fastball past Michael Tucker. He didn't. Tucker launched the pitch over the right-center-field wall and turned the game (and the momentum) around.

The Braves now led 5-4. They'd go up 7-4 and hold on to win, 7-6. The once-sleeping giant had been fully awakened. San Diego still held a three-games-to-two lead heading back to Atlanta, but it certainly didn't feel that way.

The immense pressure once squarely on the heavily favored Braves to fulfill expectations and claim what seemed rightfully theirs was squarely on the trembling Padres – now trying to avoid the ignominious distinction of becoming the first team to relinquish a 3-0 series lead in a best-of-seven series.

Out of these pressure situations emerge unlikely heroes – those who avoid receding to the background and instead come to the forefront. That was the sentiment of Sterling Hitchcock, a 27-year-old unsung left-hander who began 1998 in the bullpen but was eventually shifted to the starting rotation and was the winner in Game Three.

After Brown's Game Five demise, Hitchcock went to pitching coach Dave Stewart, no stranger to postseason excellence, and expressed his desire to start Game Six, despite not being on full rest.

"In my career I haven't thrown very well on three days," Hitchcock said after the game. "But the two starts prior to this I didn't throw a lot of pitches. I knew pretty well that I could go out there and contribute for our team."[1]

Stewart relayed Hitchcock's message to Bochy.

"Hitch wanted the ball," Bochy said. "Which was the best news I heard."[2]

Hitchcock did not let his manager, or his teammates, down. He kept the Braves offense, which had scored 15 runs in the past two contests, from building on its momentum. That was immense – because his opposite number, Tom Glavine, was doing the same to San Diego bats.

Through five innings, neither starter had yielded a run. Come the sixth, the stalemate was broken – and it was the Cy Young Award winner, not the journeyman, who gave in.

Back-to-back one-out singles by Greg Vaughn and Ken Caminiti placed runners at the corners. Jim Leyritz, who haunted Atlanta with his 1996 World Series homer heroics as a Yankee, was up next. Instead of a blast, Leyritz poked a weak grounder to third base – slow enough that Vaughn was able to score and break the scoreless tie.

As it turned out, one run would be enough. But the Padres went for more. Wally Joyner followed with a bouncing single up the middle, past diving shortstop Walt Weiss, which sent Caminiti home. Another single and a walk brought up the ninth spot in the batting order with the bases loaded. Bochy didn't go to his bench.

Hitchcock was understandably far less spectacular at the plate than on the mound. Yet he made enough contact on a Glavine offering to send it into shallow left field. Danny Bautista misjudged the ball as he dove toward it. The ball ricocheted off his glove and led to three unearned runs – a boon for the Padres, a backbreaker for the Braves.

San Diego's bullpen picked up where Hitchcock left off, not allowing a hit the rest of the way. Trevor Hoffman, as he did so often during his Hall of Fame career, set the Braves down in order in the bottom of the ninth. The Padres completed the upset.

"I also knew that should we have lost today, I'd put my money on Kevin Brown any day of the week," Hitchcock said. "Fortunately, we didn't have to go to that."[3]

Coupled with his victory in Game Three, in which he allowed one run in five innings, Hitchcock's two wins and a 0.90 earned-run average made him the choice for the NL Championship Series MVP. Taking into account his success during the Division Series against the Houston Astros, the unheralded pitcher had defeated three of the era's best starters, Randy Johnson, Greg Maddux, and, finally, Glavine.

"It's incredible to think about what he accomplished, about what he helped us accomplish," Bochy said. "He stepped up every time we needed him to, and he gave us what we needed on three days' rest. It just goes to show he has the heart of a competitor."[4]

"I'm extremely happy for those guys over there in our locker room, for our organization, and for the city of San Diego," said Tony Gwynn, the only remaining player from the '84 pennant-winning club. "We all have waited a long time, and the fact that we're going to the World Series again is great. But I'm going to tell you now: We want to win."[5]

If the Padres could topple the 102-win Astros in the Division Series, then follow it up with a triumph over the Braves and their 106 victories, who would stop them now with a championship in reach?

The 114-win Yankees would.

San Diego ran straight into the Bronx Bomber buzz saw – swept in four straight. Its best chance to seize any momentum came in Game One. Homers by Tony Gwynn and Greg Vaughn put the Padres up 5-2. But there was a reason why the Yankees were so dominant in '98. Specifically, their resourcefulness.

The seventh inning proved to be San Diego's undoing. New York struck for a seven-spot, capped by Tino Martinez's grand slam down the right-field line.

The Padres never recovered. A lead in Game Three resembled a mirage. That night at Qualcomm Stadium, the Yanks did the inevitable, scoring five unanswered runs in the late innings to put the series out of reach.

Considering how many opponents shared a similar fate of being outmaneuvered by a Yankees club considered to be among the greatest in baseball history, there is no shame in how the World Series turned out for the Padres.

The 1998 season should be remembered less for the fall classic and more for how they got there – and what followed. It revived baseball in San Diego and set the stage for a new ballpark initiative that passed and, subsequently, the construction of a state-of-the-art home that proved to be a sharp contrast from the cookie-cutter multipurpose facility that was Jack Murphy-turned-Qualcomm Stadium.

"I'm sure that the team's success and the atmosphere did get people to vote for it," hitting coach Merv Rettenmund said. "You had to be a sports enthusiast afterward, if you were at the games."[6]

Game Six of the NLCS, led by Sterling Hitchcock's take-charge attitude, confirmed 1998 as the greatest season in San Diego Padres history.

## SOURCES

In addition to the references cited in the Notes, the author also consulted Baseball-Reference.com, Retrosheet.org, and Ultimatemets.com

## NOTES

1    Jason Diamos, "World Series Pits Padres vs. Yankees," *New York Times*, October 15, 1998: 1.

2    Ibid.

3    Ibid.

4    Jason Reid, "Padres Bury the Hatchet," *Los Angeles Times*, October 15, 1998: 1.

5    Ibid.

6    Tom Krasovic, "1998 Padres Take Pride in Helping Make Downtown Ballpark a Reality," *San Diego Union-Tribune*, May 10, 2018: 1.

# VAUGHN HOMERS TWICE AND GWYNN ONCE, BUT YANKEES RALLY TO TAKE GAME ONE OF THE 1998 WORLD SERIES

## OCTOBER 17, 1998: NEW YORK YANKEES 9, SAN DIEGO PADRES 6, AT YANKEE STADIUM

### BY MARK S. STERNMAN

Heavy underdogs against the Yankees, who with 114 wins set a since-broken American League record, the Padres in the 1998 World Series opener faced David Wells, who "before the Series … proclaimed … that the Yankees would beat his hometown Padres in five games."[1] After leading the 1998 AL with only 1.2 walks per nine innings, Wells surprisingly issued a base on balls to leadoff hitter Quilvio Veras. Playing hit-and-run,[2] Tony Gwynn, the marquee player in the first half century of the San Diego franchise, singled. With Padres on first and second with none out, Wells induced a double-play grounder from Greg Vaughn and fanned Ken Caminiti to escape the jam.

San Diego starter Kevin Brown retired the first four Yankees, and none of the first eight New York batters hit the ball out of the infield. Like Wells, Brown also averaged fewer than two walks per nine innings in 1998, but in the bottom of the second

with one out Chili Davis had an infield hit, and Tino Martinez walked. With two outs, Jorge Posada also walked to load the bases for Ricky Ledee, the least formidable of the Yankee starters. A 24-year-old rookie who had played in just 42 regular-season games, Ledee had gone 0-for-5 in the ALCS against Cleveland. But he pulled a double down the right-field line to put New York up 2-0. Brown fanned Chuck Knoblauch to end the frame.

The Padres quickly rallied, likewise sparked by a bottom-of-the-order hit. Ninth-place batter Chris Gomez singled over a leaping Derek Jeter. With one out, Gwynn hit sharply to Martinez, who boxed the ball and could only retire Gwynn at first. The failure to turn the double play cost New York as Vaughn took a low-and-away offering by Wells over the 385-foot sign in right center for a homer that tied the game at 2.

Both pitchers settled down after shaky starts. With two outs in the bottom of the fourth, Scott Brosius hit into the left-center gap. Steve Finley, centerfielder for the Padres, made the defensive play of the game. After briefly playing hot potato with the ball, Finley recovered to unleash a strong throw to second that beat Brosius to the bag. With Veras waiting with the ball, Brosius tried a swim move into the keystone sack but was easily tagged to end the inning.

San Diego broke through in the top of the fifth. With two outs, Veras blooped a single over Jeter. The lefty Gwynn followed by pulling a homer to deep right, and, on the next pitch, the righty Vaughn pulled a no-doubter to deep left. The back-to-back blasts put the Padres up 5-2.

After the game, reporters seemed surprised about the power displayed by the usually singles-hitting Gwynn. Tom Verducci of *Sports Illustrated* asked the future Hall of Famer about the reaction, and Gwynn said, "It's not like it's the first home run I've ever hit. I've hit a few before and I've hit a few longer than that. Give me a break."[3]

Consecutive singles by Ledee and Knoblauch put two Yankees on in the bottom of the fifth. With Joey Hamilton and Mark Langston warming up in the bullpen, Brown got grounders from Jeter and Paul O'Neill to protect the three-run San Diego lead.

In the top of the sixth with one out, Wells walked Wally Joyner. Holding Joyner, Martinez had the ideal position from which to field a line drive off Finley's bat and step on the pillow for a double play before the runner could retreat.

Hamilton and Langston both warmed up as the bottom of the sixth began, but Brown had a 1-2-3 inning that featured strikeouts of Bernie Williams and Martinez. Wells also had a 1-2-3 frame in the top of the seventh.

The bottom of the seventh began innocently enough as Brosius grounded to Veras. After the out, Fox ran a graphic showing that the Yankees had a league-leading 50 come-from-behind wins. On cue, Posada singled over Veras. At 102 pitches, Brown readied to face Ledee with Donne Wall getting ready in the pen. Manager Bruce Bochy faced his first crucial decision of the contest. Ledee had two line-drive hits off Brown, who probably had few effective pitches left.[4] Bochy stayed with Brown, who proceeded to walk Ledee on four straight pitches, none of which came close to the plate. Bochy then pulled Brown and brought in Wall.

Wall threw only four pitches. Facing Knoblauch, Wall missed with the first two before grooving one that Knoblauch hit high and barely inside the foul pole and over the left-field wall to tie the game. On the next pitch, Jeter smacked a line-drive single up the middle. Bochy, who had Langston warm up the last three innings, finally brought him in to face the heart of the New York batting order.

O'Neill flied out to leave Jeter on first with two outs and a 5-5 score. But then Langston wild-pitched Jeter to second, walked Williams intentionally, and walked Davis to load the bases with two outs for Martinez. Fox showed a graphic entitled No Mr. October. At that point, Martinez with New York had a .184 career postseason batting average with only 1 HR and 5 RBIs. Fox also showed Martinez's career stats with the bases loaded, which looked much better as Tino had a .326 batting average with six grand slams .

Perhaps less sharp than usual after having loosened for so long, Langston fell behind Martinez 2-0 and then, surprisingly, given his wildness and the location of the game, got the call on a borderline pitch to make the count 2-1. With a 2-2 count, Langston threw a similar borderline pitch, more over the plate but possibly a little low as catcher Carlos Hernandez jerked his glove up in the strike zone after receiving the ball. The argument about whether this borderline call or the one earlier in the at-bat appeared more egregious became moot when Martinez hit a grand slam on the full-count pitch that followed, making the 3-2 pitch famous and the 2-0 pitch forgotten.

"It was obvious we would have liked to have had it [called strike three]," … Bochy said. "Langston, he thought it was there."[5]

The grand slam, the 17th in World Series history and the first since Atlanta's Lonnie Smith on October 22, 1992 off Toronto's Jack Morris, gave the Yankees a 9-5 lead.

The Padres needed four runs against the formidable back end of the New York bullpen. Facing Jeff Nelson, Gwynn singled under Martinez's glove. Vaughn broke his bat and reached on a fielder's choice as Nelson got the force at second. Mariano Rivera warmed up for the Yankees. Caminiti walked to put the tying run on deck. The lefty specialist Graeme Lloyd joined Rivera in the New York bullpen. Nelson struck out Jim Leyritz before yielding to Rivera, who needed four outs for the save.

San Diego could not get the ball out of the infield against Rivera. Joyner grounded to Knoblauch, but the shaky second baseman booted the ball as Vaughn scored. Rivera then retired Finley on a grounder to Martinez.

Leading 9-6, the Yankees had a big opportunity to pad the lead after loading the bases without a hit in the bottom of the eighth, but Randy Myers struck out O'Neill and Williams to keep the score the same.

Rivera had an easy ninth. He struck out pinch-hitters Greg Myers and the future Yankee John Vander Wal before Veras fouled out to Brosius to seal the New York victory.

Fox named Knoblauch and Martinez co-players of the game, and their homers clearly proved pivotal toward the outcome. But the inability of the Padres' pitchers to retire the unheralded Ledee really proved the difference in the game and hurt San Diego throughout the championship. Ledee went 2-for-3 in Game One and in Games Two and Four as well, helping to lead the powerful Yankees to a four-game sweep of the overmatched Padres.

## NOTES

1    Jon Heyman, "New York," *The Sporting News*, October 26, 1998: 60.

2    All observations of the game come from the author's reviewing a soundless video recording of the Fox broadcast available at www.youtube.com/watch?v=JvMCT-NX1eJ0 (accessed May 9, 2018).

3    Tom Verducci, "Tony Gwynn was a joy to watch at the plate, and in life," *Sports Illustrated*, June 16, 2014.

4    "A weary Brown began sending up red flares in the fifth inning, when he told Bochy, 'You might want to have somebody ready [for relief].' Then, before the seventh, Brown told his manager to 'pay attention' to him." Tom Verducci, "Tourist Trap Awestruck--And Awful--On Their First World Series Visit To The Bronx, The Padres Had To Contend With Both The Yankees And History," *Sports Illustrated*, October 26, 1998.

5    Jack Curry, "Finally, for Martinez, His October Moment," *New York Times*, October 18, 1998.

# TONY GWYNN'S 3,000TH HIT

## AUGUST 6, 1999: SAN DIEGO PADRES 12, MONTRÉAL ROYALS 10, AT OLYMPIC STADIUM, MONTRÉAL

## BY AMY ESSINGTON

On August 6, 1999, at Stade Olympique (Olympic Stadium) in Montréal, San Diego Padre right fielder Tony Gwynn singled off Montréal Expos pitcher Dan Smith in the first inning to collect his 3,000th major-league hit.

At the start of the season, the march to 3,000 looked as though it might not happen in 1999. The 39-year-old Gwynn missed 44 games in the first half of the season with calf injuries. After a memorable All-Star Game in Boston where Gwynn assisted Ted Williams in throwing out the ceremonial first pitch, he returned to regular play. At the end of July, Gwynn was within nine hits of 3,000. On August 4, three hits against the St. Louis Cardinals, including a grand slam, brought Gwynn to 2,998. On August 5, he had one hit in four at-bats, a ninth-inning double to reach 2,999. This was the same game in which Mark McGwire hit his 500th and 501st home runs. From St. Louis, the San Diego Padres traveled to Montréal for a series against the Expos.

On Friday, August 6, 1999, at 7:00 P.M., the crowd of 13,540 at Olympic Stadium[1] watched Quilvio Veras begin the game with a single off Expos rookie pitcher Dan Smith. Gwynn, the second batter, hit a 1-and-2 pitch into center field. Those listening to the Padres broadcaster Jerry Coleman heard, "There's a drive,

right-center field, base hit. And there it is. Ohhhh, doctor! You can hang a star on that, baby. A start for the ages for Tony Gwynn. Number 3,000."[2] After arriving safely on first base, with the crowd offering a lengthy standing ovation, Gwynn hugged Padres first-base coach Davey Lopes and shook the hand of Expos first baseman Brad Fullmer. The first-base umpire, Kerwin Danley, one of Gwynn's college teammates at San Diego State University, also congratulated Tony with a handshake and hug. The full roster of Padres coaches and teammates soon joined Gwynn at first base to congratulate the newest member of the 3,000-hit club. Gwynn also received a hug from his mother, Vandella Gwynn, who was celebrating her 64th birthday; his wife, Alisha; and his daughter, Anisha. Teammate Reggie Sanders retrieved the ball, which the center fielder had thrown to second baseman Mike Mordecai. The first-base bag was also collected.[3] Of the hit, Gwynn said, "The relief that you feel is the first thing that hits you. And then I started to feel emotional and then all these guys started coming over to me. When I got back to the dugout I could not sit down."[4]

After the congratulations for the historic moment and an out by Reggie Sanders, Phil Nevin doubled to bring in both Veras and Gwynn. The rest of the Padres' at-bat included advancing

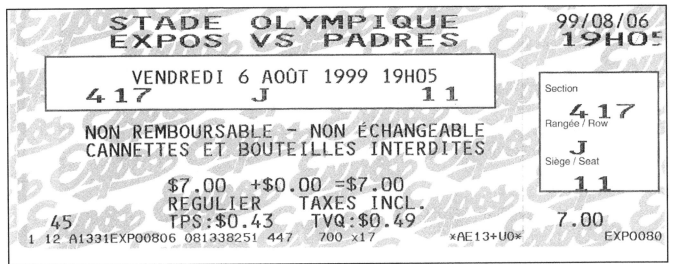

two runners on errors in the first inning and scoring two runs. Montreal manager Felipe Alou replaced Dan Smith, who lasted just two-thirds of the first inning on the mound, with J.D. Smart, who ended the inning with a strikeout of pitcher Sterling Hitchcock, the ninth batter. The Expos responded in the bottom of the first with two home runs, including one from future Hall of Famer Vladimir Guerrero. In the top of the second inning, Gwynn reached first base with a hit to center field and second base on an error by Michael Barrett, the third baseman. The first Expo to bat in the second reached base on an error by the second baseman, Quilvio Veras.

Eric Owens provided the only hit of the third inning. The fourth inning saw the leadoff batter for the Padres, Gwynn, ground out to start the fourth, and Phil Nevin hit a home run to deep left field. The leadoff batter for the Expos reached based on a Phil Nevin error and Chris Widger hit a home run that made the score Padres 7, Expos 3. Six batters registered six outs in the fifth inning. In the sixth, Gwynn saw a wild pitch, singled to right field, advanced to second base on an error by right fielder Vladimir Guerrero, and advanced to third base by a second error by Guerrero on the very next batter. The Padres also scored a run. The Expos responded in the bottom of the seventh with four runs on four hits.

In the top of the eighth, in his last at-bat of the game, Gwynn sent a line drive to right field and Ruben Rivera ran for him. In that inning, the Padres scored two runs on two hits. San Diego added two final runs on two hits and the Expos responded with three runs on two hits and an error in the ninth. Padres manager Bruce Bochy sent future Hall of Famer Trevor Hoffman to the mound to pitch to the final two batters and record the save.

The winning pitcher for the Padres, starter Sterling Hitchcock, gave up six runs in six innings. The Padres had 17 hits and scored 12 runs. The Expos fell two runs short with their nine hits. Tony Gwynn had a total of four hits to help San Diego defeat Montréal, 12-10, bringing the Padres' record to 52-57 and raised his batting average from .316 to .326. The game lasted 3 hours and 18 minutes and added Tony Gwynn to the record books. Both teams finished the season second to last in their respective divisions.

Back home in San Diego, the Padres had opened Qualcomm Stadium that day for local fans to watch the historic game. About 5,000 people, seated in the Plaza level above the third-base dugout, saw Gwynn's hit on the video board above the right-field bleachers. The celebration of the achievement included fireworks, which produced smoke which obscured the screen and they were unable to watch the victory celebration in Montréal.[5]

Three seasons after the Minnesota Twins' Paul Molitor reached 3,000 hits, Tony Gwynn had become the 22nd player to join the elite club – and did so only one day ahead of Wade Boggs of the Tampa Bay Devil Rays, who showed Gwynn's historic hit on the Jumbotron at Tropicana Field in St. Petersburg, Florida.[6]

As the 22nd player to reach the milestone, Gwynn achieved his 3,000 hits in fewer games (2,284) or at-bats (8,874) than any other hitter born after 1900. He was the 11th player to hit all 3,000 hits with one team. Gwynn reached 3,000 in 2,284 games, third fastest behind Ty Cobb and Nap Lajoie. Gwynn is the only player to reach the 3,000-hit milestone on foreign soil. Gwynn donated his helmet, spikes, pants, and bat from the game to the National Baseball Hall of Fame in Cooperstown, New York. He presented the items to Hall of Fame President Dale Petroskey and Vice President Jeff Idelson during an on-field ceremony at Qualcomm Stadium on August 13.[7]

Gwynn was the only major leaguer (as of 2018) to compile 3,000 hits, 200 intentional walks, and 300 stolen bases. August 6, the day he got number 3,000, was the sixth anniversary of Gwynn's 2,000th hit.

After the game, Gwynn said, "When you talk about 3,000 hits, you talk about passion and a love for the game. I love playing the game."[8]

## SOURCES

In addition to the sources cited in the Notes, the author consulted Baseball-Reference.com and Retrosheet.org.

# NOTES

1    The crowd included the author and two other research interns from the library at the Baseball Hall of Fame.

2    MLB video on YouTube. youtube.com/watch?v=Taw0BloL8ns.

3    MLB video on YouTube. youtube.com/watch?v=Taw0BloL8ns.

4    Campbell Clark, washingtonpost.com/wp-srv/sports/baseball/daily/aug99/07/gwynn7.htm.

5    Kirk Kenney, "Remembering Tony Gwynn's 3,000th Hit," *San Diego Union Tribune*, August 6, 2016.

6    Clark.

7    exhibits.baseballhalloffame.org/museum_bound/donation.htm.

8    Aimee Crawford, "#TBT: Tony Gwynn collects hits Nos. 2,000 and 3,000 on his mom's birthday," espn.com/blog/sweetspot/post/_/id/61353/tbt-tony-gwynn-collects-hits-no-2000-and-3000-on-his-moms-birthday, August 6, 2015.

# RICKEY HENDERSON SLIDES INTO RECORD BOOK AS CAREER RUNS SCORED LEADER

## OCTOBER 4, 2001: SAN DIEGO PADRES 6, LOS ANGELES DODGERS 3, AT QUALCOMM STADIUM

### BY MIKE HUBER

As future Hall of Famer Rickey Henderson approached Ty Cobb's career runs-scored record of 2244,[1] he said that when the moment arrived, he "promised he would slide into home plate to officially mark his reign as baseball's career runs leader."[2] In the 159th game of the 2001 season, before a home crowd of 21,606, Henderson, a 23-year veteran of the majors, kept his word.

The fourth-place San Diego Padres were playing the final game of a three-game series against the visiting Los Angeles Dodgers. The LA squad was stuck in third place, but they were seven games ahead of the Padres. San Diego had lost five of its last six games, guaranteeing that the Padres would not have a winning season. (They came into the game with a record of 77-81.) Rookie right-hander Jason Middlebrook got the nod as starting pitcher for the home team. He was making his third start and fourth appearance in the majors since joining the Padres in

mid-September. Middlebrook was opposed by Dodgers righty Luke Prokopec, who entered the contest with a record of 8-6 and an ERA of 4.86. The 166-pound Prokopec had been working out of the bullpen; his last start was on August 25 against Atlanta.

Middlebrook was a bit shaky from the get-go, walking both Tom Goodwin and Gary Sheffield in the top of the first, but he escaped without allowing any runs. Prokopec was not so fortunate. Henderson and D'Angelo Jimenez each flied out to open the bottom half of the opening frame, but Ryan Klesko stroked an 0-and-2 pitch down the right-field line for a double. Prokopec got two quick strikes on cleanup batter Phil Nevin as well, before Nevin lined an RBI single to right, giving the Padres a 1-0 lead.

Both teams were retired in order in the second, but the Dodgers scored in the top of the third. With Goodwin on first, Shawn

Green doubled to deep center, plating Goodwin. Sheffield followed with a single up the middle, and Green was waved home but was called out on a close play at the plate. That brought up Henderson's historic moment.

With one out in the bottom of the third, Henderson settled into the batter's box. After pitching ball one, Prokopec tried to get a 93-mph fastball past Henderson, but failed. Henderson swung and launched the ball off the top of the left-field fence. It was his 2,998th career hit, his eighth homer of the season, and when he crossed home plate with his 2,246th career run scored, the record was his. As he rounded the bases, "fireworks erupted from beyond the right-field stands, [and] the instrumental theme from 'The Natural' was blasted over the stadium loudspeakers."[3] And then Rickey slid into home plate.

"Sliding into home plate was a really a treat for my teammates," Henderson told reporters. "I think they were expecting me to go headfirst into home plate, but I told them I hate sliding into home plate headfirst, so I eventually went feet first." When he popped back to his feet, he was mobbed by his team.[4]

Teammate Tony Gwynn described the scene: "And he comes sliding into home plate, and the guys loved it. They were all over him. To me, that's what the game is all about."[5] Henderson could not take home plate out of the ground, so Gwynn presented the new leader with a gilded home plate that had a plaque commemorating the milestone. Henderson held that over his head instead.

Prokopec must have been a bit rattled by all of the fanfare and delay. He worked a full count to Jimenez before getting him to fly out and then walked both Klesko and Nevin. Bubba Trammell also had a full count (which took nine pitches) but grounded to short to end the mini-rally. Henderson's homer had given San Diego the lead for good.

The Padres padded the lead in the fourth on a two-out double by Damian Jackson and an RBI single by Middlebrook. Two innings later, they struck again. Mike Trombley came in to pitch for the Dodgers, replacing Prokopec. Trammell sent his first pitch through the hole in short for a single. After two fly outs, Jackson singled, and Gwynn pinch-hit for Middlebrook. The future Hall of Famer worked a full count before drawing a walk to load the bases (and Kevin Witt came on to pinch-run for Gwynn). That brought Henderson to the plate, and he drew another walk, bringing in a run. Jimenez drove a liner into right for a double, and Jackson and Witt scored. The Padres now led 6-1. Klesko walked, again loading the bases, but Trombley struck out Nevin to end the inning.

In the eighth, three singles by McKay Christensen, Goodwin, and Bruce Aven resulted in a Dodgers tally, and then in the ninth

Los Angeles threatened again. Jeremy Fikac had entered the game in the eighth as the fourth Padres hurler, and he started the ninth by retiring two of the three batters he faced, sandwiching groundouts around a single by Adrian Beltre. San Diego skipper Bruce Bochy made the call to the bullpen for Jose Nunez. Dodgers manager Jim Tracy countered by sending in Phil Hiatt to bat for Dave Hansen. Hiatt took the first pitch for a ball and then smacked a double into right field. Beltre circled the bases and scored, pulling the Dodgers within three runs. Bochy called for Trevor Hoffman to save the game. It took four pitches for Hoffman to strike out pinch-hitter Marquis Grissom to end the game. Henderson's record had come in a San Diego victory, 6-3.

Henderson, the new runs-scored king, had gone 1-for-4 with a walk and a pair of runs batted in, and after the game he admitted, "Scoring so many runs, it's not just an individual record. It's a record that you've got to have your teammates help you out."[6] He added, "When I first started in the big leagues, I felt that as the leadoff hitter my job was to get on the basepaths, create stuff and score some runs to help my teammates win some ballgames. It just so happens that over the 23 years I think I went out there and did my job as well as I could do … and all of a sudden it's a record breaker … it's just an honor."[7]

The Hall of Fame asked Henderson for his spikes to put on display in Cooperstown.[8] Henderson said he wanted the actual home plate.

In earning the victory, Middlebrook equaled the longest outing of his career – six innings. He scattered five hits and two walks, allowing only the one earned run. San Diego saves guru Hoffman picked up his 43rd save.[9] Prokopec took the loss.

In addition to owning the career runs-scored record (2,295), Rickey Henderson holds the stolen-base record (1,406), the unintentional-walks record (2,129)[10] and the leadoff home-run record (81). Coincidentally, only hours after Henderson set his record, San Francisco's Barry Bonds blasted a 454-foot home run into the upper right-center-field bleachers at Houston's Enron Field,[11] giving him 70 homers for the season and tying Mark McGwire's single-season record. But on this day, San Diego was celebrating Henderson's accomplishment.

## SOURCES

In addition to the sources mentioned in the Notes, the author consulted Baseball-Reference.com, MLB.com, and Retrosheet.org.

# NOTES

1    baseball-reference.com/players/c/cobbty01.shtml.

2    Bernie Wilson, "Henderson Slides Into Record Book," *Pittsburgh Post-Gazette*, October 5, 2001: 53.

3    Paul Gutierrez, "Record Run for Rickey," *Los Angeles Times*, October 5, 2001: 105.

4    Wilson.

5    Ibid.

6    Ibid.

7    Gutierrez.

8    Paul Gutierrez, "Henderson Breaks Cobb's Run Record," *Los Angeles Times*, October 5, 2001: 22.

9    This was Hoffman's 314th career save.

10   Bonds holds the career record for most bases on balls with 2,558, but 688 of them were intentional walks (also a record), giving him 1,870 unintentional walks.

11   Ross Newhan, "Right on the Mark," *Los Angeles Times*, October 5, 2001:105.

# RICKEY HENDERSON GETS 3,000TH HIT IN TONY GWYNN'S FINAL GAME

## OCTOBER 7, 2001: COLORADO ROCKIES 14, SAN DIEGO PADRES 5, AT QUALCOMM STADIUM

### BY FREDERICK C. BUSH

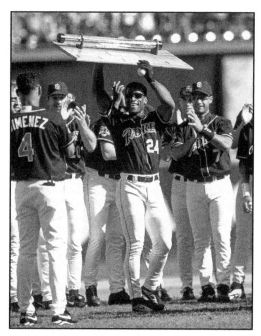

*Padres teammates on the field saluting Henderson after getting his 3,000th hit.*

Americans will always remember 2001 for the terrorist attacks that were perpetrated on US soil on September 11 of that year. Although baseball seemed trivial in the immediate aftermath of that day's events, President George W. Bush – in a decision reminiscent of President Franklin Roosevelt's "green light" letter during World War II – encouraged major-league baseball to play out the season. Thus, baseball provided a diversion for a troubled country, culminating in a World Series between the Arizona Diamondbacks and New York Yankees that was not decided until the bottom of the ninth inning of Game Seven. Along the road to that climax, one of several other memorable moments was baseball's all-time runs, steals, and walks leader, Rickey Henderson, becoming a member of the 3,000-hit club before a crowd of 60,103 at San Diego's Qualcomm Stadium on October 7, the final day of the regular season.[1]

The game itself was meaningless, as neither the San Diego Padres nor the Colorado Rockies were playoff-bound. The sellout crowd was on hand to say goodbye to Tony Gwynn, who was set to retire upon the conclusion of the season. Gwynn had become "Mr. Padre" by spending his entire 20-year career with the team, amassing 3,141 hits, a .338 batting average, and eight NL batting titles. Gwynn later said about his last game, "My whole approach was just to have fun, but everybody kept coming up to me crying, and that made it hard. I wanted to have fun. It's a celebration."[2]

Though the fans had turned out to show their affection for Gwynn, he was reduced to a pinch-hitting role because of an injured right knee and was not in the starting lineup. Gwynn was happy to share his final game with Henderson, who had respectfully offered to bench himself so that the spotlight would remain on his teammate. Gwynn would have none of that, however, recalling in 2007 that Henderson had told him, "Rickey need to let you enjoy your last day in the big leagues," to which Gwynn responded, "There are going to be 65,000 people in this ballpark tomorrow, coming to see you get your 3,000th hit, too, so I appreciate the thought, you know, but you gotta be out there tomorrow."[3]

Henderson decided to play, and he started the game in his customary leadoff spot. When he came to bat in the bottom of the first, he wasted no time in giving the fans the thrill they had hoped for, as he hit Colorado starter John Thomson's first pitch down the right-field line. Rockies first baseman Todd Helton, second baseman Terry Shumpert, and right fielder Mario Encarnacion all made a run at the fly ball, but it dropped onto the field for a double that made Henderson, who was playing in his 23rd season, the 25th major leaguer to accumulate 3,000 hits.

The game was delayed as the Padres rushed out of the dugout to congratulate Henderson, and Shumpert, who had fielded the ball on a bounce, handed it to him as a memento. A brief on-field ceremony was held in which Henderson received a plaque that commemorated his accomplishment. Dave Winfield, another member of the 3,000-hit club who was now on the Padres' board of directors, also was present and gave Henderson a hug near the foul line. Henderson was known for being ostentatious – upon breaking Lou Brock's career stolen-base record, he had held the base over his head and asserted his greatness to the crowd – but he was humble in describing his latest feat, saying, "It's a great feeling, a feeling that you can't really describe."[4] He also conceded, "I thought I would never get there because I walk so much. If you continue to play as long as I've been playing, you get the opportunity to do it."[5]

Once the action resumed, Henderson added to his career-record run total. After D'Angelo Jimenez struck out and Ryan Klesko reached first on an error, Phil Nevin smacked a liner to right field that drove in Henderson for a 1-0 Padres lead. Thomson then struck out the side by getting both Bubba Trammell and

Ben Davis on swinging strike threes; he went on to strike out 12 batters over seven innings of three-run ball to earn the win.

The Padres added to their lead in the bottom of the second when Cesar Crespo led off with a double and scored on Damian Jackson's triple to left-center field. Padres starter Brian Lawrence contributed to his own cause with a sacrifice fly that gave San Diego an early 3-0 advantage. Unfortunately for Lawrence and the hometown fans in attendance, he did not help himself on the mound. He surrendered two runs in the third on a Juan Pierre home run that also scored Ben Petrick, but it was the fourth inning that would prove his undoing.

In the fateful fourth, Juan Uribe led off with a double and the next batter, Jacob Cruz, homered to give the Rockies a 4-3 lead. Encarnacion followed with a base hit but was retired on Petrick's fielder's-choice grounder to second base. When Lawrence struck out Thomson, it looked as though he might be able to limit the damage done. But Petrick stole second base and Pierre knocked him in with a single. After Pierre stole second and Shumpert drew a walk, Padres manager Bruce Bochy lifted Lawrence in favor of Chuck McElroy.

However, on this day, McElroy was a reliever in name only. With Helton at bat, Pierre stole third and then scored on a throwing error by the second baseman, Jackson. Rockies runners continued to circle the bases as Helton doubled, Jeff Cirillo singled, and Uribe hit a two-run homer. There was no consolation in the fact that McElroy brought the inning to an end by striking out Cruz, since the Padres were now in a 10-3 hole.

Although "It ain't over 'til it's over," as Yogi Berra once said, the outcome of this game now seemed to be a foregone conclusion.[6] Shumpert added another Rockies run with a solo homer in the sixth, the Padres scored two in the eighth (one on a Jimenez round-tripper), and Uribe added a three-run circuit clout in the ninth that finished the scoring in a 14-5 Colorado victory. Uribe was the game's hero, going 3-for-5 with a double, two homers, three runs scored, and five RBIs.

The crowd still wanted to see Gwynn bat one last time, and Bochy obliged by sending him to the plate as a pinch-hitter for reliever Jeremy Fikac with one out in the bottom of the ninth. He hit Jose Jimenez's first pitch to Uribe, who easily threw him out. Gwynn described the at-bat, saying, "I just hit it a hair forward instead of letting the ball get deeper. I just got out in front of it."[7]

That Gwynn could describe in precise detail what had happened in his last plate appearance was par for the course for a player who probably remembered every single pitch he had ever seen in his career. Gwynn's memory was on display prior to the game, when a radio reporter asked him to autograph a bat Gwynn had broken in 1987. Gwynn recalled the last hit he had made with that bat: "I hit a game-winning homer. Hanging curveball from Jesse Orosco."[8]

After the game, another on-field ceremony was held, this time to honor Gwynn, who spoke to the crowd, saying, "It's been unbelievable. Never in my wildest dreams did I imagine I'd be standing here after 20 years feeling good about a decision I made a year and a half ago. But I do. I feel I've done all I can do as a baseball player."[9] The Padres announced that their new ballpark, Petco Park, which was scheduled to open in 2004, would be located at No. 19 Tony Gwynn Drive. As a parting gift, Gwynn's teammates presented him with a Harley-Davidson motorcycle that he could ride into retirement.

Tony Gwynn was elected to the National Baseball Hall of Fame in 2007, his first year of eligibility. Rickey Henderson joined him in baseball's hallowed hall two years later, also in his first year of eligibility.

# NOTES

1    Henderson's 2,295 runs scored and 1,406 stolen bases were still career records as of May 2018, but his 2,190 walks have been surpassed by Barry Bonds' 2,558.

2    Steve Springer, "Finishing Touches: Padres Combine Gwynn's Farewell with the 3,000th Hit by Henderson," *Los Angeles Times*, October 8, 2001: D13.

3    MLB Network Radio, "(2007) Hall of Famer Tony Gwynn tells his favorite Rickey Henderson story," soundcloud.com/mlbnetworkradio/2007-hall-of-famer-tony-gwynn-tells-his-favorite-rickey-henderson-story, accessed May 14, 2018.

4    "Henderson Steals Show, Hits No. 3,000 on Bloop," *Baltimore Sun*, October 8, 2001: 1D.

5    Ibid.

6    Yogi Berra, *The Yogi Book: "I Really Didn't Say Everything I Said"* (New York: Workman Publishing, 1998), 121.

7    Springer, "Finishing Touches."

8    Ibid.

9    "Padres Say Goodbye with Harley for Gwynn," *Arizona Republic* (Phoenix), October 8, 2001: C2.

# PADRES WIN ON CONTROVERSIAL CALL FOR FIRST BACK-TO-BACK DIVISION TITLES

## OCTOBER 1, 2006: SAN DIEGO PADRES 7, ARIZONA DIAMONDBACKS 6, AT CHASE FIELD, PHOENIX

### BY THOMAS J. BROWN JR.

When the San Diego Padres defeated the Arizona Diamondbacks, 3-1, on the afternoon of September 30, 2006, the victory clinched a playoff berth for the team. But on October 1, the final day of the season, they remained tied with the Los Angeles Dodgers for first place in the National League Western Division.

The Padres had won the division in 2005 and were hoping to repeat. If they did, it would be the first time they had won consecutive division titles. They had overcome a 9-15 record (.375) in April but with one game left in the season their record was 87-74. Since baseball began using a wild-card team in the postseason, only one team, the 2001 Oakland A's, had a sub-.400 record in April and later made the playoffs. The Padres and the Minnesota Twins both made the playoffs in 2006 after recording a .375 winning percentage in April.

The Padres were closing the regular season against the Diamondbacks. A crowd of 48,946 packed the Phoenix ballpark on this final day of the season. Many had come to bid farewell to

Luis Gonzalez who would not be returning next year since the team had announced that they would not exercise their option on his contract. The team painted a purple "20" in left field and showed tributes from fans on the center-field videoboard between innings.

Bruce Bochy, San Diego's manager, sent Woody Williams to the mound. After struggling in 2005, Williams had pitched well this season. He came into the game with an 11-5 record and had won his previous four starts, maintaining a 1.90 ERA during that span. The Diamondbacks started Brandon Webb. Although Webb eventually won the Cy Young Award, he had struggled in the latter part of September, losing on the 21st and going eight innings without getting a decision on the 26th.

San Diego jumped out to a 1-0 lead in the first inning. Adrian Gonzalez hit a two-out single to center field and came home when Mike Piazza doubled down the right-field line. Piazza had signed with the Padres as a free agent the previous winter and had a good season, hitting .283 as the Padres' starting catcher and cleanup hitter.

The Padres broke through for six runs in the fourth inning. Gonzalez led off with his second single of the game, went to third when Piazza hit his second double of the game, and scored on Webb's wild pitch. Webb struck out Russell Branyan and Terrmel Sledge and then things fell apart for him.

First, he gave up a single to Geoff Blum that scored Piazza. Josh Barfield singled, then Woody Williams hit an RBI single. Webb needed just one more out but it remained elusive. He walked Dave Roberts to load the bases and then walked Brian Giles to bring home the Padres' fourth run of the inning.

Gonzalez came to bat for the second time in the inning and hit a two-run double, his third hit of the game. Webb finally got out of the inning when he struck out Piazza for the third out.

The Diamondbacks slowly climbed back in the game when they scored a run in the fourth and another in the fifth. They got two more runs in the bottom of the seventh when Chad Tracy hit a two-run blast over the center-field wall. They might have been able to score more runs but Giles made a sensational catch on a fly ball by Carlos Quentin. The Padres' lead was cut to 7-4.

As they drew closer, the Diamondbacks relied on their bullpen to hold the Padres in check. Arizona manager Bob Melvin used four pitchers from the fifth inning through the eighth

The Padres almost scored another run in the top of the ninth when Adrian Gonzalez and Rob Bowen hit consecutive singles. But Jose Valverde came out of the bullpen to get the next two outs.

With a one-run lead, the Padres called on their closer, Trevor Hoffman. Hoffman had recorded 45 saves that season, the second-highest total of his career. He would finish second to Webb in the Cy Young Award voting. With Hoffman on the mound, the Padres felt reasonably confident about clinching their second consecutive division title.

Hoffman got leadoff batter Eric Byrnes to pop out to the second baseman, but then he gave up consecutive home runs to Tracy and Conor Jackson. Suddenly the score was 7-6 and the Padres' division title was not looking as secure.

Hoffman walked Quentin. When Chris Snyder hit a groundball that forced out Quentin at second, Melvin replaced Snyder with pinch-runner Chris Young and sent Alberto Callaspo to the plate to hit for Valverde.

Callaspo hit a grounder past first. Second baseman Josh Barfield fielded and threw wildly to first, forcing Gonzalez to come off the bag. Gonzalez quickly threw to Khalil Greene at second base. The throw beat Young but Greene failed to tag him. Second-base umpire Larry Poncino initially called Young safe because of the no-tag. Bochy immediately ran from the dugout and argued that the Padres' failure to get an out at first had kept the force play at second in force, and no tag was needed. Poncino changed his call after hearing Bochy's protestations. The game was over.

"It was strange," said Gonzalez, who tied a career high with four hits. "When Callaspo hit it, I saw Young jump and try and get away from the ball. I saw him fall, didn't think anything of it at the time, but when Barfield's throw was a little off line I knew I still had a shot at second."[1]

Television replay showed that Greene was off the bag, and that the original safe call might have been correct. "It's kind of the way it's gone," said Bochy. "Nothing is easy."[2] When the umpire finally called Young out, the crowd at Chase Field let out a loud chorus of boos as the teams left the field.

The save was Hoffman's 482nd. Later in the day Los Angeles beat the San Francisco Giants to remain tied with San Diego. But the Padres had won the season series against the Dodgers so they won the division title for the second season in a row, and the Dodgers were the wild-card team.

## SOURCES

In addition to the sources cited in the Notes, the author used Baseball-Reference.com and Retrosheet.org for box-score, player, team, and season information as well as pitching and batting game logs, and other pertinent material.

## NOTES

1    "Padres win second straight division title," ESPN.com, October 3, 2006.

2    Ibid.

# PADRES' HOFFMAN CLOSES OUT DODGERS FOR 500ᵀᴴ CAREER SAVE

## JUNE 6, 2007: SAN DIEGO PADRES 5, LOS ANGELES DODGERS 2, AT PETCO PARK

### BY MIKE HUBER

It took just 10 pitches. The ninth-inning play-by-play line for the Dodgers read:

0 R, 1 H, 0 E, 1 LOB.

After striking out Russell Martin with a runner on third and two outs, San Diego Padres closer extraordinaire Trevor Hoffman earned his 500th career save, preserving a 5-2 win over Los Angeles.

A Wednesday evening crowd of 31,541 came out to Petco Park to watch the first-place Padres seek their fourth consecutive win. San Diego was tied with the Arizona Diamondbacks atop the National League West, while the Los Angeles Dodgers were a half-game back. Greg Maddux started for San Diego, opposed by Randy Wolf, in his first season with LA after eight with the Philadelphia Phillies.

Maddux faced the minimum through the first four innings. He did allow a leadoff single to Jeff Kent in the second, but

Martin grounded into an inning-ending double play after Luis Gonzalez had flied out. Maddux's teammates gave him a lead in the bottom of the second. Kevin Kouzmanoff sent a line-drive single into left-center to start the inning. Hiram Bocachica doubled through the right side, sending Kouzmanoff to third. Geoff Blum followed with a double down the left-field line, knocking in both runners and giving Maddux a 2-0 advantage. Wolf retired Maddux, Marcus Giles, and Jose Cruz in order to avoid further damage.

The Padres padded their lead in the third. With two outs and Adrian Gonzalez on second (after a single) and Josh Bard on first (walk), Bocachica bashed his second double of the game. Gonzalez scored and Bard held at third base. Up next was Blum, who swung at Wolf's first offering and lined a single into center field, good for two more runs batted in. San Diego now led, 5-0.

In the top of the fifth, Maddux faltered. Kent swung at the first pitch of the inning and dribbled a weak ball down to third, reaching on an infield single. Luis Gonzalez grounded a ball up the middle for another single, advancing Kent to third. Martin then lifted a fly ball into right and Kent came home. After Andre Ethier lined out to third baseman Kouzmanoff, Tony Abreu roped a ball deep down the left-field line. Gonzalez rounded the bases and was waved home, and Abreu headed for third, but he was gunned down by left fielder Cruz before Gonzalez crossed the plate.

In the seventh, Maddux faced Kent with one out and the Dodgers slugger blasted his ninth homer of the season beyond the wall in left-center, making the score 5-2. Maddux walked the next batter, Luis Gonzalez, and Padres first-year manager Bud Black signaled for a pitching change, bringing in Heath Bell, who made two pitches to Martin, inducing the pitcher's best friend, a 6-4-3 double play, to end the inning. Scott Linebrink pitched a scoreless eighth for San Diego, and after the Padres were retired in the top of the ninth, the stage was set for history.

The 39-year-old Hoffman strode to the mound to the familiar chimes of AC/DC's "Hell's Bells." The first batter he faced, Nomar Garciaparra, greeted San Diego's right-hander with a double off the left-center-field wall. Kent sent a weak grounder to short for out number one, while Garciaparra held at second base. When Gonzalez grounded out to second, Garciaparra trotted to third. Martin moved into the batter's box and Hoffman threw four pitches, the last one getting a "Strike Three!" call from home-plate umpire Jeff Kellogg. Hoffman had earned the milestone save.

Catcher Bard raced to the mound to embrace his closer. The rest of the Padres "converged in the infield before carrying Hoffman toward the dugout."[1] A sign with "500" brightly lit on it was

raised onto a platform in beyond the center-field wall. Hoffman tipped his hat to the cheering crowd and then put on a hat with the number "500" on it.

The bottom of the Padres' lineup did the damage against the Dodgers. Kouzmanoff, Bocachica, and Blum each had two hits. Blum knocked in four runs and Bocochica batted in the fifth tally. Two future Hall of Famers pitched bookends for San Diego. Starter Maddux pitched 6⅓ innings en route to his fifth win of the season, and Hoffman earned the save, his 18th of the 2007 campaign. Wolf took the loss for the Dodgers, his record dropping to 7-4.

Hoffman had spent the last 15 seasons closing games for the Padres. In fact, the converted shortstop[2] had pitched for San Diego in all but his first 28 games. (He came into the major leagues with the Florida Marlins in 1993 and was traded to the Padres in June of that year.) This was save number 500 overall, number 498 with the Padres. Both were records. At the end of the 2006 season (September 24), Hoffman had eclipsed Lee Smith's career mark of 478, when he pitched one shutout inning against the Pittsburgh Pirates, striking out Ryan Doumit

and Jose Bautista and retiring Freddy Sanchez on a groundout to end the game and earn his 479th save. He finished the 2006 campaign with 482 saves and was voted the National League's Fireman of the Year by *The Sporting News* and the Rolaids Relief Man of the Year. Hoffman, a seven-time All-Star and two-time runner-up for the National League Cy Young Award, said, "I take a lot of pride in being a guy that could be accountable to his team as a player and also as my career progressed, just having the opportunity to be valuable in other capacities."[3] Dodgers skipper Grady Little summed up Hoffman's accomplishment best: "He's the definition of a closer. He's there for them every day and he's very consistent."[4]

New York Yankees star reliever Mariano Rivera broke Hoffman's career saves record in 2011, the season after Hoffman retired with 601 saves. Rivera finished with 652. Hoffman (1998) is tied for fifth-most saves in a season (53) with Rivera (2004) and Randy Myers (1993).

Hoffman was humble with reporters after the game, saying, "It's a special moment from an individual standpoint to be at a number that looks a bit different than some of the other guys that have accrued a lot of saves. But our focus is definitely on winning a division and moving deep into the postseason and winning a championship."[5]

In reaching this historic mark, Hoffman had blown only 58 saves. That is a conversion rate of 89.6 percent.[6]

## SOURCES

In addition to the sources mentioned in the notes, the author consulted Baseball-Reference.com, MLB.com, and Retrosheet.org.

## NOTES

1    Ben Bolch, "Dodgers Closed Out by Hoffman," *Los Angeles Times*, June 7, 2007: 39.

2    Hoffman was drafted as a shortstop in the 11th round of the 1989 draft by the Cincinnati Reds.

3    Dennis Lin, "Hoffman Keeps 'Trevor Time' Going," *San Diego Union-Tribune*, February 3, 2014. Found online at sandiegouniontribune.com/sports/the-52/sdut-52-trevor-hoffman-padres-saves-leader-mlb-2014feb03-story.html.

4    Bolch.

5    "Hoffman Gets 500th Save as Padres Win," newson6.com, June 7, 2007. Found online at newson6.com/story/7662107/hoffman-gets-500th-save-as-padres-win.

6    For his entire career, Hoffman converted 601 of 677 opportunities, for a save rate of 88.8 percent.

# GAME 163

## OCTOBER 1, 2007: COLORADO ROCKIES 9, SAN DIEGO PADRES 8, AT COORS FIELD

### BY LAUREN CRONIN

After the full 162-game schedule had been played, the Colorado Rockies and San Diego Padres were tied for second place in the National League West at 89-73. That was better than any other wild-card contender, so a 163rd-game tiebreaker was required to determine the wild-card team. On both September 29 and 30, the Padres had lost potentially clinching games in Milwaukee. The Rockies had won 13 of their last 14 games, to squeeze into the tie on the scheduled last day of the season.

The Rockies had won the season series, going 5-4 in Denver and 5-4 in San Diego. Josh Fogg took the mound for the Rockies in front of a raucous Coors Field crowd of 48,404. He quickly dispatched Brian Giles and Scott Hairston, but after getting ahead 0-and-2 to Kevin Kouzmanoff gave up a bloop single to right. Fogg then got Adrian Gonzalez swinging on a full count to end the inning.

Jake Peavy took the mound for the Padres. Peavy led the league in wins, ERA, and strikeouts that season, and won the Cy Young Award.[1] Rockies manager Clint Hurdle had told the media that his team would be aggressive against the Padres ace, and the truth of that statement showed in the bottom of the first.

Second baseman Kazuo Matsui led off by lacing a ball to right-center, sprinting around first, and taking second. Rookie shortstop Troy Tulowitzki, who would finish two points behind the Brewers' Ryan Braun in NL Rookie of the Year voting, slapped a grounder up the middle from his deep crouch. Padres shortstop Khalil Greene knocked the ball down, but Tulowitzki reached and Matsui moved to third. Matt Holliday approached the plate to deafening "M-V-P!" chants from the crowd, and worked a walk to load the bases. The Rockies then got on the board with a sacrifice fly from Todd Helton. Third baseman Garrett Atkins then dropped a single into shallow right that drove in Tulowitzki and made the score 2-0. Brad Hawpe's pop fly in foul territory and Ryan Spilborghs' fly to center ended the inning.

Rockies catcher Yorvit Torrealba's leadoff home run in the bottom of the second extended the Rockies' lead to 3-0. But Fogg ran into trouble quickly in the top of the third. Peavy smacked a single up the middle past a diving Tulowitzki, and then Fogg walked Giles and allowed a broken-bat single to Hairston to load the bases with nobody out. After Kouzmanoff flied to left, Gonzalez furthered his reputation as a Rockies killer by taking Fogg's first pitch, a sinker that didn't sink, into the stands in right field for a grand slam that gave the Padres a 4-3 lead and silenced the crowd. Greene's single, Josh Bard's double, and an intentional walk to Geoff Blum loaded the bases again. On Brady Clark's groundball to shortstop, Tulowitzki fired to Matsui at second for the out, but the throw to first skipped in front of Helton, allowing Clark to reach and Greene to score, and giving the Padres a 5-3 lead.

In the Rockies' third, Helton smashed a low pitch into the right-field seats, bringing the Rockies to within one run.[2] The game settled for a bit after that, as Peavy retired the side and both teams went down 1-2-3 in the fourth inning.

After a leadoff double by Gonzalez in the fifth, Taylor Buchholz took over for Fogg and retired the side.

In the Rockies' fifth, Tulowitzki doubled and Holliday singled him home with the tying run. This locked up the batting title for Holliday, and tied him with Ryan Howard for the NL RBI lead. A combination of Buchholz, Jeremy Affeldt, and Ryan Speier held the Padres scoreless in the top of the sixth. In the bottom of the inning, the Rockies grabbed the lead again when September call-up Seth Smith tripled to center and Matsui brought him home with a sacrifice fly.

Blum began the Padres' eighth with a single off new pitcher Brian Fuentes, the ball reaching Cory Sullivan, who had replaced Spilborghs in center. Clark hit a foul pop to the right side, where Helton, who led all NL first basemen in 2007 with a .999 fielding percentage, made an over-the-shoulder Willie Mays-style catch for the first out. Michael Barrett struck out swinging, but a wild pitch on the third strike allowed Blum to make it to second. On a 1-and-1 count, Giles hit a fly ball to left field, where a misplay by Holliday allowed Blum to score and tie the game, 6-6.

Neither team scored in the ninth, 10th, 11th, or 12th, though each had runners in scoring position in the 11th and the Padres did again in the 12th.

In the 13th inning, Rockies manager Hurdle called on Jorge Julio to pitch to the Padres. Julio walked Giles on five pitches, and San Diego had its leadoff batter on base for the third straight inning. Hairston then drove a ball to left-center. Like a ball Atkins hit in the seventh, the ball appeared to hit the top of the wall. Hairston's bounced into the stands for a two-run homer. After Chase Headley's pinch-hit single, Ramon Ortiz came on to pitch for the Rockies – their 10th pitcher of the night – and retired the next three batters.

The Rockies' predicted win percentage for the game had dropped to 8%.[3]

As the Rockies came to bat in the bottom of the 13th down by two runs, the fans at Coors Field cheered as loudly as they had all night, donning their rally caps in hopes of swaying the baseball gods. Coming off their stretch drive, the Rockies had cultivated a reputation as a team that wouldn't give up.

This time they had to overcome Trevor Hoffman, who was at the time baseball's all-time saves leader.[4] First to face him was Matsui, who after two quick balls watched a ball go by him for the first strike, then slapped two fouls down the third-base line. Finally, he smacked a ball into right-center, where it rolled to the wall before Jason Lane, who had come into the game the previous inning, could track it down and fire it to second; Matsui was already there. Tulowitzki, at this point just a home run short of the cycle, worked a full count, then lined a pitch high in the strike zone to left-center, Lane once again firing in to second, where Tulowitzki got in just before the tag, popped up and pounded his fists in elation.[5] The Rockies now had the tying run in scoring position with nobody out.

Holliday, who had misplayed the ball in the eighth that allowed the Padres to tie the game, strode to the plate. He went after Hoffman's first pitch, driving it to right field where it hit the bottom of the manual scoreboard, bounced over the head of right fielder Giles, and ricocheted back toward the infield. Tulowitzki, who held at second until the ball hit the wall, scored easily and Holliday slid headfirst into third with a triple. Padres manager Bud Black then called for Hoffman to intentionally walk Helton, leading to derisive boos from the home crowd. Black and catcher Michael Barrett went to the mound to chat with Hoffman, and Black motioned for the outfielders to come in as shallow as they dared to fend off the winning run on a sacrifice fly.

Jamey Carroll approached the plate, kicked at the dirt, and adjusted his batting gloves. He then swung his bat toward Hoffman a few times, glanced back at third for the briefest of moments, and settled the bat above his shoulder. Connecting on Hoffman's first pitch, Carroll drove the ball to right field. "I was just trying to get a ball up in the zone," he said after the game.[6] Giles reached over his head to catch it, and at that moment Holliday, who had tagged up as soon as the ball was in the air, put his head down and ran. "The ball appeared to beat Holliday to the plate," wrote the New York Times.[7] Holliday slid headfirst, and his head bounced off the ground as Barrett reached back to tag him. The ball popped loose. Dazed, and with blood dripping down his chin, Holliday lay on the ground for what seemed like an eternity until home-plate umpire Tim McClelland finally called Holliday safe, ending the game and sending the Rockies to their first playoff berth since 1995.[8]

320 SAN DIEGO PADRES

## SOURCES

In addition to the sources cited in the Notes, the author consulted
Baseball-Reference.com.

## NOTES

1      Against the Rockies, however, his record coming into the game was only middling.
       He'd gone 4-4 lifetime against them, including a 3-3 record at Coors Field.

2       It was only the second time all season that Peavy had allowed more than one
       home run in a game.

3      baseball-reference.com/boxes/COL/COL200710010.shtml.

4      Hoffman was elected to the Hall of Fame in 2018.

5      Adrian Gonzalez also finished one hit short of a cycle, lacking only a triple.

6      Associated Press, "Rockies Score Three in 13th to Beat Padres," *Baton Rouge
       Advocate,* October 2, 2007: 34.

7      Pat Borzi, "Rockies Have One Last Rally in Them, Scoring 3 Off Hoffman in
       13th," *New York Times*, October 2, 2007: D2.

8      Holliday admitted he didn't know if he'd been safe or out, blocked by Barrett's
       foot. "I don't know. He hit me pretty good. I got stepped on and banged my chin.
       I'm all right." Padres manager Bud Black allowed that Holliday was probably
       safe, "It looked to me like he did get it." Associated Press. Ortiz got the win, and
       the Padres had lost their third consecutive opportunity to clinch.

# PADRES WIN IN 18ᵀᴴ INNING ON GONZALEZ'S WALK-OFF HOME RUN

## MAY 25, 2008: SAN DIEGO PADRES 12, CINCINNATI REDS 9, AT PETCO PARK

### BY RICHARD CUICCHI

San Diego Padres fans had already witnessed three extra-inning games of 13 or more innings (including one for 22 innings) during the first seven weeks of the 2008 season, so when the game on May 25 against Cincinnati was tied after nine innings, it really wasn't a big surprise. What the 36,508 Petco Park fans didn't fully expect to play out, though, was an 18-inning affair won by the Padres on a dramatic three-run walk-off home run.

A classic matchup between two future Hall of Famers, pitcher Greg Maddux and slugger Ken Griffey Jr., might have been anticipated as the main draw for the game between the two last-place teams. But it turned out they weren't the biggest story of the marathon contest.

Instead, the two stars of the game were lesser-known Padres players, first baseman Adrian Gonzalez and pitcher Josh Banks. Gonzalez delivered the game-winning home run nearly six hours after the game started. Banks, in only his fifth major-league game, claimed his first career win when he pitched six innings in relief without yielding a run to the Reds.

Padres manager Bud Black started Maddux, who had won 14 games for the Padres the year before. The 41-year-old with 350 career wins had been struggling in May 2008, barely exceeding five innings per game, while giving up double-digit hits in two of his last four starts.

Reds skipper Dusty Baker countered with right-hander Matt Belisle, loser of his three previous starts. The Reds lineup featured 38-year-old center fielder Griffey, who was on the verge of hitting his 600th home run.

Brothers Jerry and Scott Hairston were in the starting lineups for the Reds and Padres, respectively. They were members of a three-generation family in the major leagues that included father Jerry Hairston Sr. and grandfather Sam Hairston.

Another pair of brothers were on the Padres roster: Adrian Gonzalez was the starting first baseman, while brother Edgar was a utility infielder in his rookie season.

The Padres got the scoring started with three runs in the second inning. Khalil Greene's double scored Kevin Kouzmanoff, who had led off the inning with a single. Greene advanced to third on a throwing error by shortstop Jerry Hairston, and scored on a fly ball to deep left by Michael Barrett. Paul McAnulty followed with his third homer of the season for a 3-0 lead.

The Reds scored a run in the fourth inning. Griffey, whom Maddux had struck out in the first inning, doubled and scored on Javier Valentin's two-bagger.

Kouzmanoff made the score 4-1 when he homered to lead off the bottom of the fourth.

The Reds tied the score in the fifth. Jerry Hairston singled and stole second after Griffey struck out. He scored when Brandon Phillips' fly ball to center was mishandled by Scott Hairston as a result of poor communication with left fielder McAnulty. Adam Dunn followed with a two-run home run, the 251st of his career and the second-most in Reds history by a left-handed hitter (after Ted Kluszewski).

In the bottom of the fifth inning, Tadahito Iguchi doubled to left and scored on Gonzalez's double to right.

Maddux came out of the game in the top of the sixth inning with the Padres leading 5-4. In the top of the seventh, the Reds took the lead on Phillips' two-run home run off Cla Meredith.

With David Weathers pitching for the Reds, the Padres tied the game again in the eighth on Kouzmanoff's second home run of the game. It was the first multi-homer game of his career and his fourth home run in six games.

The Reds went ahead again in the top of the ninth, off closer Trevor Hoffman. After he gave up singles to Griffey and Phillips, Ryan Freel beat out a grounder to second and Griffey scored.

Just as quickly, the Padres' Scott Hairston tied the game in the bottom of the inning, 7-7, with a leadoff home run to left field off Reds closer Francisco Cordero.

Each team scored twice in the 11th inning. Griffey led off the top of the inning with a double, his 1,117th extra-base hit, tying him with Ted Williams and Jimmie Foxx for 13th place on the career list. After Phillips singled and stole second, Reds pinch-hitter Paul Janish hit a two-run single. In the bottom of the inning, after two singles and a sacrifice, Iguchi drove in a run on a grounder and Brian Giles doubled in another one.

Josh Banks came into the game in the 13th inning for the Padres and shut out the Reds for six innings, scattering five hits and two walks. In the bottom of the 13th, with the Reds out of relief pitchers, Dusty Baker looked to starter Aaron Harang to keep the Reds at bay. He succeeded by striking out nine batters in his four-inning appearance, striking out the side twice.

Paul Bako, the Reds' last position player, pinch-hit for Harang and struck out with the bases loaded to end the top of the 17th.

With one out in the bottom of the 18th, Scott Hairston drew a walk off Edinson Volquez, another Reds starter, who had thrown a scoreless 17th inning. (Volquez had just pitched on Friday night when he struck out 12 in the Reds' victory.) Hairston stole second as Iguchi went down swinging for the second out. Giles kept the inning alive when he hit a hard grounder to first baseman Joey Votto, who fumbled it and then threw behind Volquez as he went to cover first base.

With two outs and a full count, Adrian Gonzalez ended the marathon contest with a three-run home run to dead center. The Padres were 12-9 winners. Reds catcher David Ross had called for a fastball, but Volquez shook him off. After the game Volquez offered an explanation: "I wanted a changeup. It was my best pitch today. It went right over the plate."[1]

Some sportswriters wondered why Baker didn't have Volquez pitch around Gonzalez, the team's best hitter. That would have loaded the bases for Kouzmanoff, who already had two homers in the game. Black's observation: "A lot of times it's tough to be a pitcher in a bases-loaded situation because you don't know how a pitcher might respond. Dusty knows his players better than any of us, but Volquez has a little bit of a walk (issue)."[2] Gonzalez was known to expand the strike zone, and it seemed as though the Reds were counting on that. But it didn't happen on this at-bat.

The game lasted 5 hours and 57 minutes. At the time it was the Reds' longest game ever. The Padres lost a 22-inning game to the Colorado Rockies five weeks earlier.

The Reds' 10 pitchers struck out 19 Padres, Iguchi five times and Greene four. The only unused pitcher on the roster, Johnny Cueto, would have relieved Volquez if the game had gone longer. After the game, Baker commented, "I've never used a starter (as a reliever) in a game, much less two in a game. We were so close to getting everything lined up. That game really hurt."[3] Baker was referring to the fact that his staff had blown three saves in the game while recording two in the previous 49 games.

Adrian Gonzalez, who was in his third season with the Padres, went 4-for-9 in the game and knocked in four runs. He finished the season with his best performance to that point in his career:

36 home runs, 119 RBIs (third most in the National League), and a slash line of .279/.361/.510. Gonzalez earned his first All-Star selection. He became one of the organization's best hitters during the 2000s and as of 2018 remained second to Nate Colbert in career home runs for the Padres. His Mexican heritage contributed to his immense popularity among the San Diego baseball community.

Banks finished the season with a 3-6 record and 4.75 ERA in 17 appearances.

Padres fans had little to cheer about the rest of the season. The team finished in fifth place in the NL West Division, 21 games behind the division-leading Los Angeles Dodgers.

## SOURCES

In addition to the sources cited in the Notes, the author consulted the following:

baseball-reference.com/boxes/SDN/SDN200805250.shtml.

*San Diego Padres Media Guide* 2009.

Sullivan, Tim. "Yo, Adrian Should Get the Call as Team's Rep at All-Star Game," *San Diego Union-Tribune*, May 26, 2008: C1.

Wilson, Bernie. "Gonzalez's 3-Run Homer Wins It in 18th for Padres," foxnews.com, May 25, 2008. Accessed December 18, 2018. foxnews.com/printer_friendly_wires/2008May25/0,4675,BB-NRedsPadres,00.html.

## NOTES

1   John Fay, "Their Flight Home Won't Be That Long," *Cincinnati Enquirer*, May 26, 2008: C5.

2   Tom Krasovic, "Eighteen Is Enough for Gonzalez and the Padres," *San Diego Union-Tribune*, May 26, 2008: D4.

3   Fay.

# CINDERELLA CAME UP A GAME SHORT

## OCTOBER 3, 2010: SAN FRANCISCO GIANTS 3, SAN DIEGO PADRES 0, AT AT&T PARK, SAN FRANCISCO

### BY TOM LARWIN

"Cinderella came up a game short" was the lead sentence in the *San Diego Union-Tribune's* game recap of the Padres' season-ending game, played on October 3, 2010.[1]

At the start of the season both the San Francisco Giants and San Diego Padres were not considered to be 2010 National League pennant contenders. *Sports Illustrated's* annual baseball issue predicted the Padres would claim the National League's West Division cellar by a large margin.[2] *SI* had this to say: "The Padres, who will be closely watched only because the baseball world is waiting for them to trade slugging first baseman Adrian Gonzalez, have no such problems with imbalance. They're equally poor on the mound and at the plate." Largely because of their pitching staff, the Giants fared better in *SI's* analysis and were predicted to wind up in third place.

As the season entered October it was clear that the predictions were far off: The Giants and Padres were locked in a battle for the division championship. Most surprisingly, the Padres had been in first place for most of the season. However, a 10-game losing streak from late August into early September allowed the Giants to get close. From September 15 until September

26 the Padres and Giants traded the division lead back and forth, with neither team more than a half-game ahead. Then, from September 26 to 30, the Padres lost four of five while the Giants were hot, winning four of four, and opened a three-game lead on the Padres.

By October the races in the other two National League divisions had been decided. The Philadelphia Phillies had the best record in the National League and had sewed up the East Division title. Likewise, the Cincinnati Reds had won the Central Division title. Left to be decided for the two remaining National League playoff spots were the West Division champ and the wild-card team.

Entering the season's last weekend at the start of play on Friday, October 1, there were three teams competing for the two playoff spots:

| | |
|---|---|
| San Francisco Giants | 91-68 |
| Atlanta Braves | 90-69 |
| San Diego Padres | 88-71 |

Each team had a three-game series to finish the season: The Padres were in San Francisco to meet the Giants head-on, while the Braves, second in the NL East, were at home to play the Phillies.

The results of the October 1 games left the race tightened up as the Padres beat the Giants, 6-4, and the Braves lost to the Phillies, 11-5. Going into October 2 the Padres had gained a game on both the Giants and the Braves:

San Francisco Giants    91-69

Atlanta Braves    90-70

San Diego Padres    89-71

The Saturday games replicated Friday's results, as the Padres won, 4-2, and the Braves lost, 7-0. With the last game of the season on October 3, the three teams were one game apart:

San Francisco Giants    91-70

Atlanta Braves    90-71

San Diego Padres    90-71

The Saturday outcomes created four scenarios for deciding the final two National League playoff teams:

**Scenarios (showing the team's final record depending on a win or loss its final game on October 3, 2010)**

|  | 1 | 2 | 3 | 4 |
|---|---|---|---|---|
| If Atlanta: | Loses (90-72) | Wins (91-71) | Loses (90-72) | Wins (91-71) |
| If San Diego: | Wins (91-71) | Wins (91-71) | Loses (90-72) | Loses (90-72) |
| If San Francisco: | Loses (91-71) | Loses (91-71) | Wins (92-70) | Wins (92-70) |
| Then the National League West Division Champ would be: | San Diego* | San Francisco at San Diego | San Francisco | San Francisco |
| and the National League wild-card Team would be: | San Francisco | Decided by an October 4 playoff game, the loser of SF-SD at Atlanta | Decided by an October 4 playoff game, San Diego at Atlanta | Atlanta |

*In Scenario 1 San Diego would win the division on the basis of a 13-5 advantage in head-to-head games during the season.*

For the deciding October 3 game between the Padres and the Giants, the starting pitchers were Mat Latos and Jonathan Sanchez respectively. Latos at age 22 and in his first full season, was having a good year with a record of 14-9 and an ERA of 2.92. However, he was coming into this game with four straight losses and his ERA had shot up from 2.21 to 2.92. Sanchez, who a year earlier had pitched a no-hitter against the Padres, came in with a record of 12-9 and an ERA of 3.15.[3]

Played before an afternoon crowd of 42,822,[4] the game was scoreless going into the third inning. The Padres had left runners in scoring position in the first and second innings and the Giants did the same in its first inning. In the top of the third the Padres staged a rally with Chris Denorfia leading off with a single. Two groundouts left him at third base with two outs and cleanup hitter Adrian Gonzalez at bat. The Giants intentionally walked Gonzalez[5] to bring up right fielder Ryan Ludwick. Traded from the St. Louis Cardinals at the end of the trade deadline[6] to give some slugging support to the team, Ludwick struck out swinging, stranding the runners at first and third.

In the bottom of the third, with one out, Giants pitcher Sanchez stunned the Padres, hitting a triple to deep right-center field. Sanchez was a .125 hitter at the time and that was his eighth hit of the season. Latos struck out the next batter for a second out but Giants second baseman Freddy Sanchez singled, driving in pitcher Sanchez, and the Giants took the lead, 1-0. Aubrey Huff followed with a double that scored Freddy Sanchez from first base. Catcher Buster Posey grounded out to close out the inning with the Giants leading, 2-0.

In the top of the sixth inning, the Padres attempted another rally. Gonzalez singled to lead off and Ludwick walked. With runners on first and second, Giants manager Bruce Bochy brought in pitcher Santiago Casilla to face the next batter, Yorvit Torrealba. As a late-inning reliever for the Giants, this was appearance number 52 for Casilla in 2010 and he entered the game with a 2.01 ERA. After a first-pitch strike, Casilla got what he wanted when Torrealba grounded into a double play with runners forced out at third and second. The potential rally ended as the Padres' next batter, Scott Hairston, grounded into a force play and the Giants remained ahead, 2-0.

The Giants were stranding runners, too. In the bottom of the sixth, two-out singles by Pat Burrell and Juan Uribe placed runners at first and second, but Jose Guillen grounded into an inning-ending force out.

The Padres were at it again in the seventh when two batters reached base after two were out. Denorfia got his third hit of the game and David Eckstein reached on an error by pitcher Casilla. With the Padres' Miguel Tejada on deck to bat, Giants manager Bochy brought in Ramon Ramirez. With the Giants for slightly more than two months, Ramirez had proved to be an outstanding addition as he posted a 0.68 ERA for the Giants over his 24 relief appearances.[7] Tejada, a former American League MVP, was another late-July acquisition for the Padres in an attempt to bolster the team's offense.[8] In his 58 games with the Padres, he had done just that with eight home runs and 32 RBIs. However, Ramirez had the advantage this time as Tejada struck out swinging on a 3-and-2 pitch. Another opportunity lost by the Padres as they went into the bottom of the seventh still down 2-0.

The Giants threatened to score in the bottom of the seventh but left two runners on base without scoring. The Padres went three-up, three-down in the top of the eighth. Then, in the bottom of the eighth with Padres' reliever Luke Gregerson on the mound, the eventual National League Rookie of the Year, Posey, added to the Giants' score with a solo home run, his 18th.

The Padres went down quietly in the ninth, without a batter reaching base. The Giants' closer, Brian Wilson, handled the ninth inning, striking out Will Venable to end the game, pick up his save number 48,[9] and give the Giants the West Division championship.

In Atlanta the Braves defeated the Phillies 8-7 and won the wild-card race. The final records of the three teams after this last day of the season were:

| | |
|---|---|
| San Francisco Giants | 92-70 |
| Atlanta Braves | 91-71 |
| San Diego Padres | 90-72 |

The next day's headline in San Diego captured in words the Padres' season: "Padres Run Out of Surprises, San Diego Falls One Game Short of the Playoffs With Loss to the Giants, But the 'Little Team That Could' Surpasses All Expectations."[10]

Despite not reaching the playoffs, the 2010 team had achieved the franchise's fourth season with 90 or more wins.

## SOURCES

In addition to the sources cited in the Notes, the author consulted Baseball-Reference.com and Retrosheet.org.

## NOTES

1    Bill Center, *San Diego Union-Tribune*, November 4, 2010.

2    Pablo S. Torre, "Colorado's Turn, at Last," *Sports Illustrated*, April 5, 2010: 110.

3    Sanchez pitched a no-hitter against the Padres on July 10, 2009, allowing no walks and striking out 11 in an 8-0 win in San Francisco. In his 137 career starts it was his only complete game.

4    This was a standing-room crowd as seating capacity was 41,915.

5    This was Gonzalez's 35th intentional walk for the season, placing him second behind the major-league leader, Albert Pujols (St. Louis Cardinals), who finished with 38.

6    Ludwick was part of a three-team trade on July 31 with the Cardinals trading him to the Padres, the Padres sending pitcher Corey Kluber to the Cleveland Indians, the Indians sending Jake Westbrook to the Cardinals, and minor leaguer Nick Greenwood going from the Padres to the Cardinals.

7    Ramirez was acquired on July 31 from the Boston Red Sox for a minor leaguer, Daniel Turpen.

8    Tejada was acquired from the Baltimore Orioles on July 29 for minor leaguer Wynn Pelzer.

9    This save made Wilson the major-league leader in saves and placed him ahead of the Padres' Heath Bell, who had 47 saves.

10    Center.

# EDINSON VOLQUEZ ONE-HITS ASTROS

## JULY 19, 2012: SAN DIEGO PADRES 1, HOUSTON ASTROS 0, AT PETCO PARK

### BY PAUL HOFMANN

As of the start of the 2019 season, the San Diego Padres are the only existing major-league team that has not had a pitcher toss a no-hitter. While they have never had a no-no, the club has thrown 30 one-hitters.[1] One of these one-hitters took place on Thursday, July 19, 2012, when journeyman Edinson Volquez held the Houston Astros to a single hit at Petco Park.

The Padres entered the game with a 38-55 record, 14 games behind the front-running San Francisco Giants in the NL West but having won four of their last five games. The Astros entered the game with a 34-58 record, 17½ games out of first in the NL Central Division and having lost 15 of their last 17 games. Houston was in the midst of one of its worst offensive funks of the season and its anemic offense had been victimized by Giants right-hander Matt Cain's perfect game just over a month earlier.[2]

The right-handed-throwing Volquez had been acquired by the Padres in December of 2011 in a trade that sent Mat Latos to Cincinnati. Latos himself had come within a hit of throwing the Padres' first-ever no-hitter in 2010 and had another one-hitter preserved by the bullpen during his rookie season in 2009. Volquez was making his 20th start of the season for the Padres

and came into the game with a 5-7 record and a 3.61 ERA. He sported a career record of 5-0 against the visiting Astros. In his 109 career starts, he had never tossed a complete game; he had completed eight innings only three times.

The Astros sent rookie Lucas Harrell to the hill.[3] Harrell entered the game with a record of 7-6 and a 4.43 ERA. The right-hander had enjoyed some success against the Padres in 2012. On June 27, a little more than three weeks earlier, he held the Padres to six hits and pitched the only shutout of his career, a 1-0 victory at Houston's Minute Maid Park.

It was a perfect evening for baseball in San Diego for the 26,735 in attendance. The game-time temperature was 72 degrees and there was a gentle 7mph breeze toward right field. The third-base grandstand had begun to cast its shadow across the infield when Volquez delivered the game's first pitch at 7:06 P.M.

Volquez made short work of the Astros in the top of the first. Leadoff hitter Jose Altuve grounded out to second and Marwin Gonzalez was retired on a foul pop to third before Scott Moore grounded out to second to end the inning.

The Padres jumped on Harrell quickly in their half of the first. Center fielder Alexi Amarista sliced a ball into the left-field corner for a leadoff double and scored what turned out to be the winning run when Logan Forsythe singled to right field. Harrell settled down and retired the next three Padres in order.

The Astros threatened to tie the game in the top of the second. Volquez walked left fielder J.D. Martinez to lead off the inning. First baseman Matt Downs hit a weak groundball to third baseman Chase Headley, whose errant throw allowed Martinez to advance to second. Justin Maxwell hit a sharp liner toward right field, but it was caught by the leaping Forsythe. The second baseman threw to shortstop Everth Cabrera to double up Martinez and Cabrera fired the ball to first but Downs dived safely back to the bag to avoid an inning-ending triple play. The inning ended with Jordan Schafer grounding out to second base.

Volquez worked a one-two-three third inning and retired the first two hitters in the top of the fourth before walking Martinez again. That brought up Downs, who hit a checked-swing dribbler past the mound toward shortstop that Volquez briefly had his hand on but couldn't completely corral. The official scorer ruled it a base hit. Maxwell followed with a groundout to Yonder Alonso at first and the second and final Astros threat of the day was thwarted.

After the game, Volquez was asked how close he was to nabbing Downs's roller. He grinned sheepishly, as if to suggest that he should have had the ball, and said, "I don't want to talk about it. I'm going to have defensive drills tomorrow. I have to make that play."[4]

Volquez continued to set down the Astros and allowed only one more runner, walking Gonzalez with one out in the top of the sixth inning. Harrell was equally impressive as he kept the Padres in check. He pitched seven strong innings (four hits, one walk, and six strikeouts) before being relieved by left-hander Wesley Wright, who stuck out two in a perfect eighth inning.

In previous outings, Volquez had struggled with his pitch count, and left the game earlier than both he and Padres manager Buddy Black would have liked. Only four times did he manage to complete seven innings. But on this day, Volquez's pitch count was manageable, and he entered the ninth inning having thrown 103 pitches. Before the ninth, Black asked him what he had left. Volquez replied, "I got two strikeouts and a fly ball." So he went back out to the mound to finish what he had started. He got Altuve on a fly ball to deep right-center, struck out Gonzalez, and retired Moore on a fly ball to deep center, ending the game 2 hours and 2 minutes after he had thrown the first pitch. Smiling, Volquez told sportswriters after the game that Black had needled him: "He's like, 'Hey, you only got one strikeout and two fly balls.'"[5]

The one-hit shutout was Volquez's first complete game in the major leagues.[6] He gave his batterymate much of the credit for his excellent command. "I got to give some credit to Yasmani Grandal, he did a pretty good job. We were working on the same page tonight and that gave me more confidence," Volquez said.[7] Grandal returned the praise, saying, "That was a lot of fun. One hit on a jam shot. … That should have been a no-hitter. Volquez came up and in on Downs and he got enough of it to make it a hard play."[8]

Manager Black said he had considered bringing in closer Huston Street to pitch the ninth. Of Volquez's gem, he said, "It's an understatement to say it was a well-pitched game. Volquez was in command. He was in control of every pitch. Tonight was all Volquez. You could see the confidence in him from the first pitch to the last."[9]

Volquez's masterpiece was a rare pitching feat in the Padres' first 45 years. It was their 26th one-hitter, their fifth 1-0 one-hitter, and the first since Latos beat the Giants with a 1-0 one hitter on May 13, 2010, in San Francisco. It was just the third complete-game shutout by a Padres pitcher at Petco Park, the first since Jake Peavy shut out the Astros 2-0 on August 23, 2005. The one-hit shutout at home was the first since Kevin Brown tossed a 4-0 one-hitter against the Milwaukee Brewers on August 16, 1998, at San Diego's Qualcomm Stadium.

Five years after coming so close, Volquez attained the list of no-hit pitchers. On June 3, 2017, pitching for the Miami Marlins, he held the Arizona Diamondbacks hitless in a 3-0 win at Marlins Park.

## SOURCES

In addition to the sources cited in the Notes, the author also consulted Baseball-Reference.com and Retrosheet.org.

baseball-reference.com/boxes/SDN/SDN201207190.shtml.

retrosheet.org/boxesetc/2012/B07190SDN2012.htm.

## NOTES

1    "Padres One-Hitters." Retrieved from nonohitters.com/padresonehitters/.

2    "Volquez Tosses One-hitter." *Palm Springs* (California) *Desert Sun,* July 20, 2012: 25.

3    Lucas Harrell entered the 2012 season with a career record of 1-2 in limited action with the Chicago White Sox and Houston Astros in 2010 and 2011.

4    Bill Center, "Volquez Blanks Astros 1-0 on One Hit," *San Diego Union-Tribune,* July 19, 2012. Retrieved from sandiegouniontribune.com/sports/padres/sdut-volquez-blanks-astros-one-hit-2012jul19-story.html

5    David Dodd, "Volquez One-Hits Astros, Padres Win," *San Diego Reader,* July 20, 2012. Retrieved from sandiegoreader.com/weblogs/game-day/2012/jul/20/volquez-one-hits-astros-padres-win/#.

6    As of Opening Day 2019, Volquez had four complete games. He missed all of the 2018 season after having Tommy John surgery.

7    Ibid.

8    Bill Center.

9    Ibid.

# AFTER 7,444 GAMES, MATT KEMP BECOMES FIRST PADRE TO HIT FOR THE CYCLE

## AUGUST 14, 2015: SAN DIEGO PADRES 9, COLORADO ROCKIES 5, AT COORS FIELD

### BY MIKE HUBER

For the first 46 years of their history, from Opening Day in April 1969 until well into the 2015 season, the San Diego Padres were a team without two significant individual accomplishments: (1) having a pitcher throw a no-hitter, and (2) having a batter hit for the cycle. The second streak ended on August 14, 2015. Playing right field against the Colorado Rockies in his inaugural season with the Padres, Matt Kemp became the first Padre to deliver a single, double, triple, and home run in the same game.

One month after the 2015 All-Star break, the 55-61 Padres were sitting in fourth place in the National League West, 10 games behind the Los Angeles Dodgers. They had lost seven of their last nine games and, except for an 11-6 win against the Cincinnati Reds, San Diego was having trouble scoring runs (averaging 2.5 runs per game in those other eight contests). After nine seasons playing for the Los Angeles Dodgers, Matt

Kemp was traded to San Diego,[1] but for the first few months of the season, he was not making a difference offensively. The home-team Rockies were even worse, holding down the bottom of the West Division standings with a mark of 47-67. Colorado had lost eight of its last 11 games.

Before a Coors Field crowd of 33,697 fans, Yohan Flande (2-1, 3.86 ERA) started for the Rockies, opposed by San Diego's Tyson Ross (8-9, 3.39 ERA). In the top of the first, the Padres jumped on Flande. After Yangervis Solarte grounded out to open the game, Derek Norris singled to right. Kemp then drove a line drive deep beyond the center-field fence, giving the Padres a 2-0 lead. Melvin Upton singled and advanced to second on a wild pitch. Jedd Gyorko stroked a double down the left-field line, plating Upton. The Rockies answered in their half of the first, with Nolan Arenado hitting a two-out home run deep to left with Carlos Gonzalez aboard, cutting the Padres' advantage to 3-2.

In the third, Kemp led off with a line-drive single to center. Upton walked, but Gyorko grounded into a double play, erasing Upton at second. Clint Barmes flied out to left to end the inning. Colorado loaded the bases in its third on a single by Jose Reyes and back-to-back walks to Arenado and Ben Paulsen, but they could not score, either.

An inning later, the Rockies tied the game when Nick Hundley tripled into right field and jogged home on Brandon Barnes' sacrifice fly to right. San Diego regained the lead in the top of the fifth inning. Norris smashed a 2-and-0 pitch into the seats in left for a solo home run off Flande. The Colorado southpaw retired the next six batters before departing at the end of the sixth inning.

Ross was tagged for a first-pitch leadoff double in the bottom of the sixth by D.J. LeMahieu, and Padres skipper Pat Murphy brought Bud Norris on in relief. LeMahieu moved to third when Hundley grounded out to short, and then Barnes launched a triple into the gap in right-center, once again knotting the score.

Rockies manager Walt Weiss sent in lefty Kenny Roberts to start the seventh. Roberts allowed a single to Wil Venable (pinch-hitting for Bud Norris) but then flashed the leather by throwing Venable out at second when Solarte dropped a bunt in front of home plate. Weiss strode to the mound and called for Rafael Betancourt, who fanned Derek Norris for the second out. Kemp followed with an RBI double to deep center that "ignited a four-run rally."[2] Upton was intentionally walked. With two outs and two on, Gyorko hit his eighth homer of the season, breaking the game open and giving his club the 8-4 lead.

The Rockies added a run after the seventh-inning stretch on back-to-back singles by Gonzalez and Arenado. The latter was a slow roller to Padres third baseman Solarte, who threw the ball away, allowing Gonzalez to race around the bases and score. Arenado was credited with a single (with no RBI) but ended up at second base.

As the ninth inning began, San Diego still held its three-run lead. Justin Miller replaced Gonzalez Germen on the mound for Colorado and walked Solarte on four pitches but struck out Derek Norris. That brought Kemp to the plate. Kemp admitted, "Before I went up to bat, I heard [Melvin Upton Jr.] say, 'Hit a triple.' And I did."[3] Kemp took the first pitch from Miller for a ball. On the next offering, Miller threw a slider that hung out over home plate. Kemp connected, and at first, he admitted, "I was actually looking at the ball because I thought I hit a home run, but I didn't get as much as I thought I did. It just kicked off the wall. I like home runs, but it was my first cycle … so I

think the cycle would be better."[4] Hitting coach Mark Kotsay also predicted the feat, telling Padres manager Murphy, "He's going to hit a ball off the right-field fence and it's going to ricochet."[5] And sure enough, it did. Solarte scored the ninth and final tally for San Diego. Despite Arenado's single in the bottom of the ninth, the Rockies went quietly, ending the game. A Padres batter had finally hit for the cycle!

The milestone triple was Kemp's third and last of the season. According to mlb.com, Kemp said, "When I slid into third base, [third-base coach Glenn Hoffman] says, 'That's the first one.' I said, 'Yeah that is my first one.' He said, 'No … that's the first one for the Padres.'"[6] Later, Kemp was told that it had been 7,444 games without a Padres batter hitting for the cycle.[7] Kemp also remarked, "I've come close plenty of times. I've just never gotten that one hit I definitely needed. That triple is the hardest one to get."[8]

Murphy praised Kemp, saying, "That was special. I knew about it a few years ago, no one has ever thrown a no-hitter, no one has ever hit for the cycle. It's a matter of time before these records are broken. I think it's fitting it's Matt Kemp, he's part of a new beginning."[9]

Eleven pitchers were used in the game, and they faced 81 batters. Kemp was the hero for the Padres, while Arenado was 3-for-4 in a losing cause for the home team. The seventh-inning rally made a winner of Bud Norris (3-9), who had just joined the team,[10] and he pitched the sixth against the Rockies, although he did allow an inherited runner to score.

According to the San Diego Padres staff, "There have been 361 times when a player finished one hit shy of a cycle. Of these, 258 times a player was a triple short."[11] The great Tony Gwynn had never hit for the cycle. Hall of Famers Roberto Alomar, Willie McCovey, and Dave Winfield had never hit for the cycle while in a Padres uniform.[12] Beat writer Alec Nathan wrote, "Although the Padres are on the outskirts of the playoff picture, Kemp's late-season improvement has given them something to take solace in as the 2015 campaign begins to wind down."[13]

Kemp said, "Anytime you make history, it's special. Not everybody does that, I'm just glad I got the opportunity to do it."[14] Two seasons later (on April 10, 2017), the Padres' Wil Myers hit for the cycle against the same Colorado Rockies, becoming only the second Padre to accomplishment the rare feat. As of the end of the 2017 season, only the Florida/Miami Marlins do not have a player who has hit for the cycle. However, the Padres remain the sole major-league team without a no-hitter.

## SOURCES

In addition to the sources mentioned in the Notes, the author consulted Baseball-Reference.com, MLB.com, and Retrosheet.org.

## NOTES

1    On December 18, 2014, the Dodgers traded Kemp and Tim Federowicz (plus cash) to the Padres, in exchange for Yasmani Grandal, Joe Wieland, and Zach Eflin.

2    Pat Graham (Associated Press), "Kemp Hits for Cycle, First in Padres History," *Fort Collins Coloradoan*, August 15, 2015: C2.

3    Corey Brock and Dargan Southard, "Padres Down Rockies Behind Kemp's Cycle," mlb.com, August 15, 2015. Found online at mlb.com/news/padres-down-rockies-behind-matt-kemps-cycle/c-143147474.

4    Corey Brock, "Kemp Completes First Cycle in Padres History," mlb.com, August 15, 2015. Found online at mlb.com/news/matt-kemp-hits-first-padres-cycle/c-143243112.

5    Ibid.

6    Ibid.

7    Ibid.

8    Brock and Southard.

9    Ibid.

10    The Baltimore Orioles released Norris on August 8, and the Padres signed him on August 11.

11    Graham.

12    Dave Winfield hit for the cycle on June 24, 1991, while playing for the California Angels. As of the end of the 2017 season, 64 members of Baseball's Hall of Fame had hit for the cycle.

13    Alec Nathan, "Matt Kemp Hits for Cycle vs. Rockies: Stats, Highlights and Twitter Reaction," bleacherreport.com, August 15, 2015. Found online at bleacherreport.com/articles/2548202-matt-kemp-hits-for-cycle-vs-rockies-stats-highlights-and-twitter-reaction.

14    Brock.

# FACTS, FIGURES, TRIVIA

# A HALF-CENTURY OF PADRES FACTS, FIGURES...AND TRIVIA

### BY TOM LARWIN

PADRES IN THE NATIONAL BASEBALL HALL OF FAME

PADRES RETIRED UNIFORM NUMBERS

SUNNY SAN DIEGO: FEW RAINOUTS

SAN DIEGO PADRES HALL OF FAME

AWARDS RECEIVED BY PADRES PLAYERS AND MANAGERS

SAN DIEGO PADRES LIST OF MOSTS

SAN DIEGO PADRES LEAGUE LEADERS: BATTING

SAN DIEGO PADRES LEAGUE LEADERS: PITCHING

PLAYERS WHO HAD RELATIVES PLAY OR COACH FOR PADRES

BORN IN SAN DIEGO – AND ON THE PADRES

SAN DIEGO PADRES ALL-STAR PLAYERS

# PADRES IN THE NATIONAL BASEBALL HALL OF FAME

Over the team's first 50 years, 12 Padres players and one manager have been inducted into the National Baseball Hall of Fame. Willie McCovey was the first, inducted in 1986, and Trevor Hoffman is the most recent inductee (2018). Three of the players have the Padres logo on their Hall of Fame plaque cap: Dave Winfield, Tony Gwynn, and Trevor Hoffman. Inducted as a manager was Dick Williams in 2008. Six other Hall of Famers have been associated with the club as coaches or broadcasters.

| Induction Year | Name | Years with Padres | Inducted As |
|---|---|---|---|
| *Players, Manager Inducted* | | | |
| 2018 | Trevor Hoffman | 1993-2008 | Player |
| 2016 | Mike Piazza | 2006 | Player |
| 2014 | Greg Maddux | 2007-2008 | Player |
| 2011 | Roberto Alomar | 1988-1990 | Player |
| 2009 | Rickey Henderson | 1996-1997, 2001 | Player |
| 2008 | Rich Gossage | 1984-1987 | Player |
| 2008 | Dick Williams | 1982-1985 | Manager |
| 2007 | Tony Gwynn | 1982-2001 | Player |
| 2002 | Ozzie Smith | 1978-1981 | Player |
| 2001 | Dave Winfield | 1973-1980 | Player |
| 1992 | Rollie Fingers | 1977-1980 | Player |
| 1991 | Gaylord Perry | 1978-1979 | Player |
| 1986 | Willie McCovey | 1974-1976 | Player |
| *Others Inducted with Stints in San Diego* | | | |
| 2018 | Alan Trammell | Coach 2000-2002 | Player |
| 2015 | Dick Enberg | Broadcaster 2010-2016 | Broadcaster |
| 2005 | Jerry Coleman | Broadcaster 1972-1979, 1981-2014; manager 1980 | Broadcaster |
| 2000 | Sparky Anderson | Coach 1969 | Manager |
| 1980 | Duke Snider | Broadcaster 1969-1972; batting instructor 1973 | Player |
| 1975 | Billy Herman | Coach 1977-1978 | Player |

## PADRES RETIRED UNIFORM NUMBERS

Six uniform numbers have been retired by the Padres over the team's first 50 years. The retired numbers recognize five Padres players along with Jackie Robinson.

| Retired Uniform Numbers | | | | Last Padres Player to Wear Number (Other Than the Honored Player) | | Total of Padres Players who Wore the Number (1969-2018) |
|---|---|---|---|---|---|---|
| Number | Year Number Retired | In Honor Of: | Worn by Player These Years: | Player | Year(s) Number Was Worn by Player | |
| 6 | 1989 | Steve Garvey | 1983-1987 | Keith Moreland | 1988 | 11 |
| 19 | 2004 | Tony Gwynn | 1982-2001 | Gene Richards | 1978 | 2 |
| 31 | 2001 | Dave Winfield | 1973-1980 | Matt Clement | 1998-2000 | 15 |
| 35 | 1997 | Randy Jones | 1973-1980 | Al Osuna | 1996 | 9 |
| 42 | 1997 | Jackie Robinson[1] | 1947-1956 | Pedro Martinez | 1993-1994 | 14 |
| 51 | 2011 | Trevor Hoffman[2] | 1994-2008 | Mike Maddux | 1991-1992 | 6 |

Notes

[1] In April 1997 number 42 was retired for all major-league teams in honor of Robinson.

[2] Hoffman wore number 34 for the Padres in 1993.

# SUNNY SAN DIEGO:
# FEW RAINOUTS

In 37 of the 50 seasons there were no rainouts in San Diego. The 20 games rained out represent less than 0.5 percent of all games played in San Diego since 1969. Over the 50 years there has never been a rainout in August and only one in July. One game in Petco Park was delayed because of a swarm of bees on the field (July 2, 2009, vs. Houston).

| | |
|---|---|
| April 27, 1970 | Montreal |
| April 14, 1971 | Chicago Cubs |
| May 7, 1971 | Cincinnati |
| May 28, 1971 | New York Mets |
| June 5, 1972 | Pittsburgh |
| June 6, 1972 | Pittsburgh |
| April 8, 1975 | San Francisco |
| April 9, 1975 | San Francisco |
| Sept. 10, 1976 | Houston (2 games) |
| May 8, 1977 | Montreal (2 games) |
| April 15, 1978 | San Francisco |
| April 28, 1980 | Atlanta |
| April 29, 1980 | Atlanta |
| April 20, 1983 | Atlanta |
| May 12, 1998 | New York Mets |
| April 4, 2006 | San Francisco |
| July 19, 2015 | Colorado |
| May 7, 2017 | Los Angeles Dodgers |

## SAN DIEGO PADRES HALL OF FAME

Fifteen individuals have been inducted in the San Diego Padres Hall of Fame. The honored include eight players. The first player inducted was Nate Colbert, a member of the 1969 Padres. Six were on the executive/management/broadcasting side of the organization. Finally, one person honored was not directly involved with the major-league Padres: Ted Williams. Williams, a baseball legend and San Diego native, played for the Pacific Coast League San Diego Padres in 1936-37.

| Year Inducted | Individual | Tenure with Padres | Year Inducted | Individual | Tenure with Padres |
|---|---|---|---|---|---|
| 1999 | Nate Colbert | Player 1969-1974 | 2014 | Trevor Hoffman | Player 1994-2008 |
| 1999 | Randy Jones | Player 1973-1980 | 2015 | Benito Santiago | Player 1986-1992 |
| 1999 | Ray Kroc | Owner 1974-1984 | 2015 | Garry Templeton | Player 1982-1991 |
| 2000 | Dave Winfield | Player 1973-1980 | 2016 | Ken Caminiti | Player 1995-1998 |
| 2001 | Buzzie Bavasi | President 1969-1977 | 2016 | Ted Williams | Player, San Diego PCL Padres, 1936-1937 |
| 2001 | Jerry Coleman | Broadcaster 1972-1979, 1981-2014; Manager 1980 | 2017 | Jack McKeon | General Manager 1980-1990, Manager 1988-1990 |
| 2002 | Tony Gwynn | Player 1982-2001 | 2018 | Kevin Towers | General Manager 1995-2009 |
| 2009 | Dick Williams | Manager 1982-1985 | | | |

Notes for AWARDS RECEIVED BY PADRES PLAYERS AND MANAGERS on following page:

[1] For acronyms see below:

BA: Baseball America

BBWAA: Baseball Writers Association of America

BD: Baseball Digest

DRC: Denver Rotary Club

MLBPA: Major League Baseball Players Association

NL: National League

NLCS: National League Championship Series

TSN: *The Sporting News*

[2] Co-winner

[3] Combination of media members and major-league officials. 0.50

# AWARDS RECEIVED BY PADRES PLAYERS AND MANAGERS

San Diego players and managers have received a variety of annual awards over the years. Hall of Famers Rollie Fingers, Tony Gwynn, and Trevor Hoffman were prominent recipients for a relatively large number of the annual awards.

| Player/Manager | Source of Award[1] | Year |
|---|---|---|
| *Major League Player of the Year* | | |
| Gary Sheffield | TSN | 1992 |
| *NL Most Valuable Player* | | |
| Ken Caminiti | BBWAA | 1996 |
| *NL Outstanding Player of the Year* | | |
| Ken Caminiti | MLBPA | 1996 |
| *Major League Rookie of the Year* | | |
| Khalil Greene | BA | 2004 |
| *NL Rookie of the Year* | | |
| Benito Santiago | BBWAA | 1987 |
| Butch Metzger[2] | | 1976 |
| *NL Manager of the Year* | | |
| Bud Black | BBWAA | 2010 |
| Bud Black | | 2010 |
| Bruce Bochy | TSN | 1996, 1998 |
| Bruce Bochy | BBWAA | 1996 |
| *NLCS Most Valuable Player* | | |
| Sterling Hitchcock | Combination[3] | 1998 |
| Steve Garvey | | 1984 |
| *All-Star Game Most Valuable Player* | | |
| | Combination[3] | |
| LaMarr Hoyt | | 1985 |
| *Branch Rickey Community Service* | | |
| Trevor Hoffman | DRC | 2008 |
| Tony Gwynn | | 1995 |
| *Roberto Clemente Award* | | |
| Tony Gwynn | Major League Baseball | 1999 |

| Pitcher | Source of Award[1] | Year |
|---|---|---|
| *Major League Outstanding Pitcher* | | |
| Kevin Brown | | 1998 |
| Mark Davis | BD | 1989 |
| Gaylord Perry | | 1978 |
| Randy Jones | | 1976 |
| *NL Pitcher of the Year* | | |
| Jake Peavy | | 2007 |
| Kevin Brown | TSN | 1998 |
| Mark Davis | | 1989 |
| Randy Jones | | 1976 |
| *NL Outstanding Pitcher of the Year* | | |
| Jake Peavy | MLBPA | 2007 |
| *NL Relief Man (Rolaids)* | | |
| Heath Bell | | 2009, 2010 |
| Trevor Hoffman | Formula based on performance | 1998, 2006 |
| Mark Davis | | 1989 |
| Rollie Fingers | | 1977, 1978, 1980 |
| *NL Reliever of the Year* | | |
| Heath Bell | | 2010 |
| Trevor Hoffman | TSN | 1996, 1998, 2006 |
| Mark Davis | | 1989 |
| Rollie Fingers | | 1977, 1978, 1980 |
| *NL Rookie Pitcher of the Year* | | |
| Andy Benes | | 1989 |
| Bob Owchinko | TSN | 1977 |
| Butch Metzger | | 1976 |

## SAN DIEGO PADRES "LIST OF MOSTS"

Hall of Famers Tony Gwynn and Trevor Hoffman dominate the Padres' "List of Mosts." Other players whose names appear often are pitchers Randy Jones and Eric Show and infielder Garry Templeton.

| During their Career with the Padres Which Padres Player Had the Most: | Player | How Many? | Second Most? Player | How Many? |
|---|---|---|---|---|
| Seasons Played? | Tony Gwynn | 20 | Trevor Hoffman | 16 |
| All-Star Game Selections? | Tony Gwynn | 15 | Trevor Hoffman | 6 |
| Games Played? | Tony Gwynn | 2,440 | Garry Templeton | 1,286 |
| Plate Appearances? | Tony Gwynn | 10,232 | Garry Templeton | 4,860 |
| At-Bats? | Tony Gwynn | 9,288 | Garry Templeton | 4,512 |
| Runs Scored? | Tony Gwynn | 1,383 | Dave Winfield | 599 |
| Hits? | Tony Gwynn | 3,141 | Garry Templeton | 1,135 |
| Doubles? | Tony Gwynn | 543 | Garry Templeton | 195 |
| Triples? | Tony Gwynn | 85 | Gene Richards | 63 |
| Home Runs? | Nate Colbert | 163 | Adrian Gonzalez | 161 |
| Runs Batted In? | Tony Gwynn | 1,138 | Dave Winfield | 626 |
| Stolen Bases? | Tony Gwynn | 319 | Gene Richards | 242 |
| Walks (as batter)? | Tony Gwynn | 790 | Brian Giles | 509 |
| Strikeouts (as batter)? | Chase Headley | 864 | Nate Colbert | 773 |
| Wins? | Eric Show | 100 | Randy Jones | 92 |
| Losses? | Randy Jones | 105 | Eric Show | 87 |
| Games Pitched? | Trevor Hoffman | 902 | Craig Lefferts | 375 |
| Games Started (as pitcher)? | Randy Jones | 253 | Eric Show | 230 |
| Complete Games? | Randy Jones | 71 | Eric Show | 35 |
| Shutouts? | Randy Jones | 18 | Eric Show | 11 |
| | | | Steve Arlin | 11 |
| Saves? | Trevor Hoffman | 552 | Heath Bell | 134 |
| Innings Pitched? | Randy Jones | 1,766 | Eric Show | 1,603⅓ |
| Strikeouts (as pitcher)? | Jake Peavy | 1,348 | Andy Benes | 1,036 |
| Runs Allowed? | Randy Jones | 759 | Eric Show | 703 |
| Hits Allowed? | Randy Jones | 1,720 | Eric Show | 1,464 |
| Walks Allowed? | Eric Show | 593 | Clay Kirby | 505 |
| Batters Hit by Pitch? | Joey Hamilton | 46 | Brian Lawrence | 45 |
| | Eric Show | 46 | Jake Peavy | 45 |
| Balks? | Eric Show | 21 | Andy Hawkins | 17 |
| Wild Pitches? | Clay Kirby | 48 | Trevor Hoffman | 42 |

# SAN DIEGO PADRES LEAGUE LEADERS: BATTING

Most notable was Hall of Famer Tony Gwynn having the National League 's highest batting average in eight seasons and the most hits seven times. A Padres player led the league twice in runs batted in: Dave Winfield (1979) and Chase Headley (2012). A Padres player had one home run title: Fred McGriff (1992).

| Year | Category | Player | Statistic |
|------|----------|--------|-----------|
| 2012 | Runs Batted In | Chase Headley | 115 |
|      | Stolen Bases | Everth Cabrera | 44 |
| 2009 | Walks | Adrian Gonzalez | 119 |
| 2005 | Walks | Brian Giles | 119 |
| 1997 | Batting Average | Tony Gwynn | .372 |
|      | Hits | Tony Gwynn | 220 |
| 1996 | Batting Average | Tony Gwynn | .353 |
| 1995 | Batting Average | Tony Gwynn | .368 |
|      | Hits | Tony Gwynn | 197* |
| 1994 | Batting Average | Tony Gwynn | .394 |
|      | Hits | Tony Gwynn | 165 |
| 1992 | Batting Average | Gary Sheffield | .330 |
|      | Home Runs | Fred McGriff | 35 |
|      | Total Bases | Gary Sheffield | 323 |
| 1990 | Walks | Jack Clark | 104 |
| 1989 | Walks | Jack Clark | 132 |
|      | Batting Average | Tony Gwynn | .336 |
|      | Hits | Tony Gwynn | 203 |
| 1988 | Batting Average | Tony Gwynn | .313 |
| 1987 | Batting Average | Tony Gwynn | .370 |
|      | Hits | Tony Gwynn | 218 |
| 1986 | Hits | Tony Gwynn | 211 |
|      | Runs | Tony Gwynn | 107 |
| 1984 | Batting Average | Tony Gwynn | .351 |
|      | Hits | Tony Gwynn | 213 |
| 1981 | Triples | Gene Richards | 12* |
| 1979 | Runs Batted In | Dave Winfield | 118 |
|      | Total Bases | Dave Winfield | 333 |
| 1977 | Walks | Gene Tenace | 125 |

Note:

* Tied with others

## SAN DIEGO PADRES LEAGUE LEADERS:

## PITCHING

Four Padres pitchers led the league in saves: Rollie Fingers (1977-78), Mark Davis (1989), Trevor Hoffman (1998, 2006), and Heath Bell (2009). Three pitchers led the league in wins: Randy Jones (1976), Gaylord Perry (1978), and Jake Peavy (2007).

| Year | Category | Player | Statistic |
|------|----------|--------|-----------|
| 2017 | Complete Games | Clayton Richard | 2* |
| 2016 | Games Pitched | Brad Hand | 82 |
| 2009 | Saves | Heath Bell | 42 |
| 2007 | Earned-Run Average | Jake Peavy | 2.54 |
|      | Strikeouts | Jake Peavy | 240 |
|      | Wins | Jake Peavy | 19 |
| 2006 | Saves | Trevor Hoffman | 46 |
| 2005 | Strikeouts | Jake Peavy | 216 |
| 2004 | Earned-Run Average | Jake Peavy | 2.27 |
| 1999 | Shutouts | Andy Ashby | 3 |
| 1998 | Saves | Trevor Hoffman | 53 |
| 1994 | Strikeouts | Andy Benes | 189 |
| 1990 | Shutouts | Bruce Hurst | 4* |
| 1989 | Complete Games | Bruce Hurst | 10* |
|      | Saves | Mark Davis | 44 |
| 1986 | Games Pitched | Craig Lefferts | 83 |
| 1981 | Games Pitched | Gary Lucas | 57 |
| 1978 | Saves | Rollie Fingers | 37 |
|      | Win Percentage | Gaylord Perry | .778 |
|      | Wins | Gaylord Perry | 21 |
| 1977 | Games Pitched | Rollie Fingers | 78 |
|      | Saves | Rollie Fingers | 35 |
| 1976 | Complete Games | Randy Jones | 25 |
|      | Wins | Randy Jones | 22 |
| 1975 | Earned-Run Average | Randy Jones | 2.24 |

Notes:

* Tied with others

# PLAYERS WHO HAD RELATIVES PLAY OR COACH FOR PADRES

Over the 50 years 11 sets of relatives have played or coached for the Padres. Included are nine sets of brothers, three father/sons, one grandfather/grandson, and an uncle/nephew.

| Last Name | First Name | Years with Padres | Relationship | First Name | Years with Padres | Relation-ship | First Name | Years with Padres |
|---|---|---|---|---|---|---|---|---|
| Alomar | Sandy Sr. | 1986-90[1] | is *Father* of both | Roberto | 1988-90 | *and* | Sandy Jr. | 1988-89 |
| Clark | Phil | 1993-95 | is *Brother* of | Jerald | 1988-92 | | | |
| Garcia | Dave | 1970-73[1] | is *Grandfather* of | Greg | 2019[2] | | | |
| Giles | Brian | 2003-09 | is *Brother* of | Marcus | 2007 | | | |
| Gonzalez | Adrian | 2006-10 | is *Brother* of | Edgar | 2008-09 | | | |
| Gwynn | Tony Jr. | 2009-10 | is *Son* of | Tony | 1982-2001 | is *Brother* of | Chris | 1996 |
| Hairston | Scott | 2007-09, 2010 | is *Brother* of | Jerry Jr. | 2010 | | | |
| Hoffman | Trevor | 1993-2008 | is *Brother* of | Glenn | 2006-18[1] | | | |
| Lee | Leron | 1971-73 | is *Uncle* of | Derrek | 1997 | | | |
| Maddux | Mike | 1991-92 | is *Brother* of | Greg | 2007-08 | | | |
| Upton | Justin | 2015 | is *Brother* of | Melvin | 2015-16 | | | |

Notes:

[1] Was a coach for the Padres

[2] Acquired November 2018

## BORN IN SAN DIEGO – AND ON THE PADRES

A total of 31 native San Diegans have played or coached for the Padres since 1969 (and one even managed – albeit for only one game). The most games played by a San Diegan for the Padres was 833, by Brian Giles.

| Name | | With Padres | | City of Birth[1] | San Diego High School Attended |
| --- | --- | --- | --- | --- | --- |
| | | Years | No. of Games Played | | |
| Heath | Bell | 2007-11 | 354 | Oceanside | --[5] |
| Bret | Boone | 2000 | 127 | El Cajon | --[5] |
| Trevor | Cahill | 2017 | 11 | Oceanside | Vista |
| Brooks | Conrad | 2014 | 13 | San Diego | Monte Vista |
| Kevin | Correia | 2009-10 | 63 | San Diego | Grossmont |
| John | D'Acquisto | 1977-80 | 152 | San Diego | St. Augustine |
| Jerry | DaVanon | 1969 | 24 | Oceanside | Herbert Hoover |
| Alex | Dickerson | 2015-18 | 95 | Poway | Poway |
| Greg | Garcia | 2019 | --[2] | El Cajon | Valhalla |
| Bob | Geren | 1993 | 58 | San Diego | Clairemont |
| Brian | Giles | 2003-09 | 833 | El Cajon | Granite Hills |
| Marcus | Giles | 2007 | 116 | San Diego | Granite Hills |
| Adrian | Gonzalez | 2006-10 | 799 | San Diego | Eastlake |
| Edgar | Gonzalez | 2008-09 | 193 | San Diego | Eastlake |
| Aaron | Harang | 2011 | 28 | San Diego | Patrick Henry |
| Mark | Langston | 1998 | 22 | San Diego | --[5] |
| Ray | McDavid | 1994-95 | 20 | San Diego | Clairemont |
| Kevin | Mitchell | 1987 | 62 | San Diego | Clairemont |
| Chris | Nelson | 2014 | 27 | Escondido | --[5] |
| Graig | Nettles | 1984-86, 1995 | 387[3] | San Diego | San Diego |
| Nick | Noonan | 2016 | 7 | Poway | Francis Parker |
| Sean | O'Sullivan | 2013 | 7 | San Diego | Valhalla |
| Alex | Pelaez | 2002 | 3 | San Diego | Chula Vista |
| Kyle | Phillips | 2011 | 36 | San Diego | El Capitan |
| Royce | Ring | 2007 | 15 | La Mesa | Monte Vista |
| Bob | Skinner | 1970-73, 1977 | --[4] | San Diego | La Jolla |
| Brent | Strom | 1975-77 | 64 | San Diego | San Diego |
| Jason | Szuminski | 2004 | 7 | San Diego | --[5] |
| Jim | Tatum | 1996 | 5 | San Diego | Santana |
| Nick | Vincent | 2012-15 | 161 | Poway | Ramona |
| Mark | Wiley | 1978 | 4 | National City | Helix |

# SAN DIEGO PADRES ALL-STAR PLAYERS

In 1985 seven Padres were selected to play in the All-Star Game and five of the players were in the starting lineup for the National League All-Stars. In addition, Dick Williams managed the team. Catcher Chris Cannizzaro was the Padres' first All-Star selection, in 1969, and pitcher Brad Hand was the most recent, in 2018. Hall of Fame outfielder Tony Gwynn was selected to play in 15 All-Star Games.

## Number of Times Selected

15    Tony Gwynn

6    Trevor Hoffman

4    Benito Santiago, Dave Winfield

3    Heath Bell, Nate Colbert, Adrian Gonzalez, Terry Kennedy

2    Andy Ashby, Ken Caminiti, Mark Davis, Steve Garvey, Goose Gossage, Brad Hand, Randy Jones, Jake Peavy, Huston Street,

1    Roberto Alomar, Andy Benes, Kevin Brown, Everth Cabrera, Chris Cannizzaro, Dave Dravecky, Tony Fernandez, Rollie Fingers, Steve Finley, Cito Gaston, Johnny Grubb, LaMarr Hoyt, Ruppert Jones, Ryan Klesko, Mark Loretta, Fred McGriff, Wil Myers, Graig Nettles, Phil Nevin, Gaylord Perry, Drew Pomeranz, Tyson Ross, Gary Sheffield, Ozzie Smith, Garry Templeton, Justin Upton, Greg Vaughn, Rondell White, Chris Young

## Number of Times in Starting Lineup

12    Tony Gwynn*

3    Benito Santiago

2    Steve Garvey

1    Ken Caminiti, LaMarr Hoyt, Randy Jones, Terry Kennedy, Fred McGriff, Wil Myers, Graig Nettles, Jake Peavy, Dave Winfield

*Note:

In 1996 and 1999 Tony Gwynn was voted in as a starter but was injured and did not play.

Sources:

Baseball-Reference.com, *2018 San Diego Padres Media Guide*

Notes for BORN IN SAN DIEGO – AND ON THE PADRES
AND MANAGERS on previous page:

[1] In other words, a city within San Diego County.

[2] Garcia was acquired in November 2018.

[3] Nettles was a coach in 1995.

[4] Skinner was a coach in 1970-73 and 1977, and served as manager for one game in 1977 (which the Padres won).

[5] Did not attend a San Diego region high school.

# AFTERWORD

# AFTERWORD

## BY MAJOR GARRETT (SAN DIEGO NATIVE, LIFELONG PADRE FAN)

There are no Padre gods, but being a Padre fan feels something like a religion to me.

There is no scripture, sanctuary or ritual. There is faith.

When I was a child growing up in San Diego, the Padres marketing department asked me to keep it – the faith, that is.

I did. I have. Not for the marketing department.

For me.

Faith is easiest for a child because children have little sense of cruelty, heartache, and random tragedy. Adulthood brings this and more, testing faith and belief with every tear. When age advances and the end draws near, faith returns and innocence is a quiet indulgence and nostalgic daydream.

I have loved the Padres for 50 years and somehow kept my innocence and faith about them and little else. That is by turns mildly poetic and patently pathetic.

Owners have not inspired my faith but, as if conspiring across the decades, tried to kill it. Players inspired some of it; but the demi-gods were always out-numbered by the semi-blobs.

For every Tony Gwynn, Greg Maddux, Ozzie Smith, Dave Winfield, Ricky Henderson, Rollie Fingers, Willie McCovey, Craig Nettles, Steve Garvey, Greg Vaughn, Steve Finley, Roberto Alomar, Trevor Hoffman, Cito Gaston, Randy Jones, Ken

Caminiti Jake Peavy or Gaylord Perry there were dozens more like Broderick Perkins, Archi Cianfrocco, Bob Barton, Enzo Hernandez, Oscar Gamble, Rich Troedson, Dann Bilardello, Juan Eichelberger, Danny Frisella, Tito Fuentes, Doug Gwosdz, Adam Hyzdu, Fred Kuhaulua, Eddie Oropesa, Termel Sledge, Gene Locklear, Brian Tollberg, and Ed Wojna.

What is the source of this faith?

Certainly not wins and losses. In 50 years the Padres have won 3,661 games and lost 4,284 for a .461 winning percentage, dead last among all MLB franchises. Its expansion brother, the Montreal Expos (now the Washington Nationals), have won 3,884 games and lost 4,080 for a .488 winning percentage – good enough for 17th place. As a bit of solace, only 13 franchises have a career winning percentage at or above of .500 – two have exactly that, the Atlanta Braves and Los Angeles Angels of El Segundo (wait, it's Anaheim). The Padres have won two pennants and amassed a World Series record of 1-8. The last time the Padres were in the World Series Dennis Rodman and Carmen Electra were married (okay, for only nine days).

It's not the owners, it's not the players, it's not the record, it's not post-season glory. What then? What keeps the Padres faithful....faithful?

It starts with the Swinging Friar, the greatest logo in major-league baseball history. It epitomizes optimism and faith. See the Friar's eyes tilted upward, ever hopeful. See his sandal-covered feet, humble, coiled, balanced and vaguely balletic. Can you behold this and lose hope? You cannot. It does not matter that Padres logos have evolved (I say devolved!) from this original gem. It persists because long-time fans cherish it and new fans cannot avoid its irrepressible charms.

Faith is also about The Chicken. For those of us who remember his comedic stylings and playful fan interactions, it was a tonic for the times (the dawn of *disco*) and the dismal 1974 product on the field. In 1979 after a radio station firing and subsequent litigation, the Chicken was hatched anew (a drama far more compelling than the team in question) to the tune of Also Sprach Zarathrustra? What major-league franchise has carried out an unofficial, sold-out mascot reboot like that? Answer: None.

The point about loving the Padres is it has always been about the intangibles – or the additives. Baseball is at the center of it, of course, but not winning baseball. Being baseball. Being baseball in San Diego. Being in a place of sunshine, touched by a subtle sea breeze and feeling a sense of belonging both deeper and more trivial than craven competition. To love the Padres takes faith and innocence, endurance and good humor. It also comes with gratitude for the unexpected. Padre fans do not begin each season confident of success but hopeful the season to come, like life itself, will not turn out as badly as we fear. Being a Padre fan is, in essence, an under-appreciated existential challenge. How many franchises have produced that? Don't say the Chicago Cubs or Boston Red Sox. Decades between World Series glory and dog-eared myths about curses of the Bambino or Black Cat do not count. Why? Because glory, no matter how distant, sustains. What sustains in the absence of glory and the myths that arise from its wispy memory? Only Padres fans know.

Which brings us to the present. Can the Padres know a better, richer future in their next 50 years? How could they not? The law of averages strongly suggests no 50 years could be as futile as these first 50. Of course, that same law would have said the same about the first 25 years.

The farm system circa 2019 has never been better. There is a veritable horn of plenty. Management has patiently assembled the best collection of can't-miss stars in Padres history. For the first time in my memory, the Padres have too many qualified

outfielders, middle infielders *and* catchers (but still no reliable third baseman…in 50 years we've only had two: Nettles and Caminiti – Doug Rader, Ed Spezio, and Kevin Kouzmanoff do not count). This means the Padres have the talent to trade for front-line starting pitchers and relievers – and can therefore contemplate years of competitive, dare I say *winning* baseball

What's more, I have every confidence the current front office will not do what wasn't done in 1998 when the Padres did not trade for future Hall of Famer Randy Johnson. Johnson was about to be a free agent and the team willing to jettison him, the Seattle Mariners, asked for Ruben Rivera, a minor league phenom who for three years (1995 to 1997) was on Baseball America's top-10 prospect list. In '95 Rivera was No. 2 on that list, behind Alex Rodriguez and ahead of Derek Jeter (who we will come back to in a moment).

Instead of trading for Johnson and having him serve as the starter behind ace Kevin Brown, the Padres planned for the future, kept Rivera and saw the Houston Astros sign Johnson at the trade deadline. Johnson pitched two NL Division Series games against the Padres, gave up only three earned runs and, unbelievably, lost both games. The Padres went onto to the World Series and could have faced the Yankees with Brown and Johnson in Games One, Two, Five, and Six. No one knows how that would have turned out, but we can be fairly certain the Padres would not have been swept (Andy Ashby, the actual Game Two starter, was, charitably, no "Big Unit").

The Padres held fruitlessly onto Rivera until releasing him 2001. He landed with his first club, the Yankees, in 2002 whereupon he became the inglorious answer to this Happy Hour trivia question: Who stole Derek Jeter's bat and glove during spring training and sold them for $2,500? For that the Padres of 1998 could have had Randy Johnson and possibly a World Championship.

I am certain the front office contemplating the Padres 51st year and all the years immediately to follow will not make the same mistake. The Padres have assembled two clubhouses worth of top-notch minor league talent. The club, for the first time in franchise history, is in the skimming-the-cream-off-the-top business. After the skimming will come the trading.

And after 50 years of faith and innocence, will come our just desserts.

# CONTRIBUTORS

**Eric Aron** has contributed a number of bios for the SABR Bio-Project website and publications. Originally hailing from Rye, New York, he now lives in Boston. He holds a Master's degree in History & Museum Studies. Currently, he is a researcher and exhibit interpreter at The Edward M. Kennedy Institute for the United States Senate.

**Thomas J. Brown Jr.** is a lifelong Mets fan who became a Durham Bulls fan after moving to North Carolina in the early 1980s. He was a national board-certified high school science teacher for 34 years before retiring in 2016. Tom still volunteers with the ELL students at his former high school, serving as a mentor to those students and the teachers who are now working with them. He also provides support and guidance for his former ELL students when they embark on different career paths after graduation. Tom has been a member of SABR since 1995 when he learned about the organization during a visit to Cooperstown on his honeymoon. He has become active in the organization since his retirement and has written numerous biographies and game stories, mostly about the NY Mets. Tom also enjoys traveling as much as possible with his wife and has visited major-league and minor-league baseball parks across the country on his many trips. He also loves to cook and makes all the meals for at his house while writing about those meals on his blog, Cooking and My Family.

**Frederick C. (Rick) Bush** always thought that the Padres' 1970s mustard-and-brown uniforms were appropriate for a team owned by burger baron Ray Kroc, even if they did bring to mind a BK Mustard Whopper more than anything that Kroc's McDonald's chain offered. Rick and Bill Nowlin co-edited the 2017 SABR book *Bittersweet Goodbye: The Black Barons, the Grays, and the 1948 Negro League World Series* and are currently co-editing another Negro Leagues book about the 1946 Newark Eagles. Rick lives with his wife Michelle and their three sons Michael, Andrew, and Daniel in the greater Houston area, where he teaches English at Wharton County Junior College.

**Bob Chandler** has relied on SABR for baseball facts and historical information since becoming a member in 1978. A San Diego resident he has been active as a sports broadcaster for several radio and TV stations since 1961. Chandler's specialty is baseball; before 1969 he covered the PCL Padres and then was part of the National League Padres' broadcasting team for 31 years. An authority on Padres' history he authored a 2006 book entitled *Bob Chandler's Tales from the San Diego Padres.*

**Alan Cohen** serves as Vice President-Treasurer of the Connecticut Smoky Joe Wood Chapter, and is datacaster for the Hartford Yard Goats, the Double-A affiliate of the Rockies. He also works as a volunteer with Children's Reading Partners, working with at-risk elementary school students. He has written more than 40 biographies for SABR's BioProject, and has expanded his research into the Hearst Sandlot Classic (1946-1965), which launched the careers of 88 major-league players. He has four children and six grandchildren and resides in Connecticut with wife Frances and their cat, Morty.

**Rory Costello** has contributed to an array of SABR's book projects, and being a lifelong Mets fan is one of the running themes. He has yet to have the pleasure of visiting San Diego and seeing a game there. Rory lives in Brooklyn with his wife Noriko and son Kai.

Born and raised in Colorado, **Lauren Cronin** had the misfortune to be raised a Red Sox fan when it wasn't a pleasant thing to be. Currently residing in Wheat Ridge, Colorado, she roots for the Rockies and Rays and fits in studying art conservation around her busy baseball-watching schedule.

**Richard Cuicchi** joined SABR in 1983 and is an active member of the Schott-Pelican Chapter. Since his retirement as an information technology executive, Richard authored *Family Ties: A Comprehensive Collection of Facts and Trivia about Baseball's Relatives*. He has contributed to numerous SABR BioProject and Games publications. He does freelance writing and blogging about a variety of baseball topics on his website TheTenthInning.com. Richard lives in New Orleans with his wife, Mary.

**Dan D'Addona** is the author of *In Cobb's Shadow: The Hall of Fame Careers of Sam Crawford, Harry Heilmann and Heinie Manush*, published by McFarland & Co. He is an award-winning journalist as sports editor at *The Holland Sentinel* in Holland, Michigan, where he lives with his wife Corene and daughters Lena and Mara. He also writes for *Swimming World Magazine* and interned at the National Baseball Hall of Fame in Cooperstown. He is a member of SABR's Negro Leagues Committee and Deadball Era Committee.

**Paul E. Doutrich** is a retired professor of American History living in Brewster, Massachusetts. Among the courses he taught was a one entitled "Baseball History." He has written scholarly articles and contributed to several anthologies about the Revolutionary era, and has written a book about Jacksonian America. He has also curated several museum exhibits. His recent scholarship has focused on baseball history. He has contributed numerous manuscripts to various SABR publications and is the author of *The Cardinals and the Yankees, 1926: A Classical Season and St. Louis in Seven.*

**Amy Essington** is a lecturer in the history departments at California State University, Fullerton, and Cal Poly Pomona. She is the Executive Director of the Historical Society of Southern California. She completed a Ph.D. at Claremont Graduate University and is the author of *The Integration of the Pacific Coast League: Race, Baseball, and the West* (University of Nebraska Press, 2018). Amy was an intern at the National Baseball Hall of Fame Library and the Smithsonian's National American History Museum.

**Charles F. Faber** was a native of Iowa who lived in Lexington, Kentucky, until his passing in August 2016. He held degrees from Coe College, Columbia University, and the University of Chicago. A retired public school and university teacher and administrator, he contributed to numerous SABR projects, including editing *The 1934 St. Louis Cardinals: The World Champion Gas House Gang*. Among his publications are dozens of professional journal articles, encyclopedia entries, and research reports in fields such as school administration, education law, and country music. In addition to textbooks, he wrote 10 books (mostly on baseball) published by McFarland. His last book, co-authored with his grandson Zachariah Webb, was *The Hunt for a Reds October*, published by McFarland in 2015.

**Steve Ferenchick**, a SABR member since 1994, attorney and lifelong Phillies fan, lives with his wife, Rebecca, and children, Ellie, Kate and Sam, in Wynnewood, Pennsylvania. He contributed to this book as penance for the bad luck he has brought to the Padres throughout his life. By repeatedly leading Phillies fans in chanting "DER-EK, DER-EK" from behind home plate, Steve likes to think he caused Derek Bell's 0-for-4 performance in the Padres' July 2-3, 1993 loss at 4:41 A.M. in major-league baseball's latest-ever game. Then on July 26, 1998, he was in attendance in San Diego when Trevor Hoffman lost his then-MLB-record streak of 41 straight saves converted. Finally, Steve held tickets to Game Seven of the 1998 World Series, ensuring the Yankees-Padres series would go six games or fewer. For these and other forgotten sins against the Padres, Steve duly apologizes.

**Jeff Findley** is a native of Eastern Iowa where he did the logical thing growing up in the heart of the Cubs/Cardinals rivalry — he embraced the 1969 Baltimore Orioles and became a lifelong fan of the team. An information security professional for a large financial services company in central Illinois, he writes a daily sports "Pages Past" column for his local newspaper.

**Gregory Funk** joined SABR in 1981 and serves on the steering committee for the local Ted Williams Chapter. He prepares tax returns and plays the organ for his living, but his passion has been baseball and its statistics, strategy, and trivia. He is lifelong Padre fan who has never missed attending a home opener.

**Major Garrett** is the Chief Washington Correspondent for CBS News.

**Mark Hodermarsky**'s latest book, *Born to Lead: Americana Music Trailblazers* (New Haven Publishing), is his eighth. A retired English teacher, Hodermarsky's love of baseball and baseball writing remain passionate. He lives in Olmsted Falls, Ohio.

**Paul Hofmann**, a SABR member since 2002, is the Associate Vice President for International Affairs at Sacramento State University. Paul is a native of Detroit, Michigan and lifelong Detroit Tigers fan. He currently resides in Folsom, California.

**Mike Huber** is Professor of Mathematics at Muhlenberg College in Allentown, Pennsylvania. One of his research areas involves modeling and simulating rare baseball events, such as hitting for the cycle. He enjoys writing for SABR's Games Project.

**Jay Hurd** is a librarian, retired from Harvard University where he worked as the Preservation Review Librarian for Widener Library. He is also a museum educator and interpreter. Jay, a member of the Society for American Baseball Research (SABR), is a contributor to the SABR Baseball Biography Project, and presents on baseball related topics including the Negro Leagues, baseball literature for children and young adults, women in baseball, and baseball and the Blue Laws. Currently, he is studying baseball in Rhode Island, with a focus on baseball in Bristol. A longtime fan of the Boston Red Sox, Jay relocated from Medford, Massachusetts to Bristol in 2016.

**Jorge Iber** was born in Havana, Cuba and raised in the Little Havana neighborhood of Miami, Florida. He taught in the public schools of Miami before pursuing a PhD at the University of Utah. He currently serves as Associate Dean in the Student Division of the College of Arts and Sciences and Professor of History at Texas Tech University. He is the author/co-author/editor of 10 books and numerous scholarly and encyclopedic articles. His most recent project is a full-length biography of Mexican American pitcher Mike Torrez (he of the pitch to Bucky Dent in the 1978 playoff game between the Boston Red Sox and the New York Yankees). He is currently working on two other projects: an anthology on Latinos/as and sport, and a book on Latino participation in all levels of football.

**Chuck Johnson** has been a SABR member since 1991 and is a co-founding member of Arizona's Hemond-Delhi Chapter. Chuck has provided minor league content to SBNation, Bleacher Report, and MLB.com and is a frequent contributor to the Bio and Game Projects. A member of the Minor League Alumni Association through his work with the Eastern League, Chuck lives with his wife and daughter in Surprise, Arizona where he works for the Arizona Rookie League and MLBAM.

**Gerard Kwilecki** and his family reside near Mobile, Alabama. He is a native of Bainbridge, Georgia and graduated from Valdosta State University. He is employed by the University of South Alabama in Mobile and is a member of the Jaguar Baseball Dugout Club. He has been a member of SABR since 2015 and is a lifelong Atlanta Braves fan. This is his first contribution to a SABR publication.

**Tom Larwin** is a retired transportation engineer. He was born and raised on Chicago's south side as a die-hard Cubs fan, but after moving to San Diego in 1976 has admitted to becoming a die-hard Padres fan. Tom heads up SABR's San Diego Ted

Williams Chapter and has authored several biographies for SABR's BioProject. He has participated as an author on two books: *The Kid: Ted Williams in San Diego* (2005) and *San Diego's First Padres and "The Kid," The Story of the Remarkable 1936 San Diego Padres and Ted Williams' Professional Baseball Debut* (2019).

**Bob LeMoine** grew up in Maine and has been a Red Sox fan since the days when Carl Yastrzemski was taking his final swings. He works as a librarian and enjoys research and writing for any SABR project. He is a co-editor with Bill Nowlin on a forthcoming book on the Boston Beaneaters of the 1890s. Bob lives in New Hampshire.

**Len Levin** is a retired newspaper editor (*Providence Journal*). He works part-time editing the decisions of the Rhode Island Supreme Court, and also spends a lot of time copyediting SABR's books, including this one.

**Mike Madigan** is retired from a career in the development industry. He served as the City of San Diego's "Ballpark Czar" during the development of the PetCo Park project. A native San Diegan, he attended his first Padres game in 1948.

**Max Mannis** is a diehard Yankees fan who has been a SABR member since 2013, when he, as an 11-year old, began writing blogs as a special correspondent for *Sports Illustrated for Kids* covering the annual SABR conferences, conventions and other events. In 2016, he wrote a biography of Trevor Hoffman for SABR's bioproject. He currently covers SABR's many yearly events for SABR.org and also writes for unhingedyankees.com. He lives in New York City and attends the Abraham Joshua Heschel High School when he isn't at Yankee Stadium. He is an avid baseball card and memorabilia collector. You can follow him on Twitter at @maxmannissabr or @MannisCards.

**Seth Moland-Kovash** is a lifelong passionate baseball fan and amateur historian. He grew up in Minnesota and his love of the game and the Twins has carried through many years, many moves, and many Twins eras. During the day, Seth is a Lutheran pastor in suburban Chicago where he lives with his wife Jennifer and their son Carl. Carl has also inherited the love of baseball and plays whenever the fields are not covered by snow. Seth's favorite teams are the Twins and whatever team Carl is on.

**Dave Nielsen** grew up in Modesto, California where he attended professional baseball games at Del Webb Field, home of the Modesto Reds. He attended Wheaton College in Illinois and the Graduate School of Public Affairs at the University of Washington. He was living in Puerto Rico in 1971 when native son Roberto Clemente figured prominently in the Pittsburgh Pirates' World Series victory over the Baltimore Orioles, a cause for national celebration. He has resided and worked in San Diego since 1972. He was part of Larry Lucchino's planning team during the development of PetCo Park.

**Bill Nowlin** lives, writes, and edits from Cambridge, Massachusetts. A lifelong Red Sox fan, he respects partisan fandom in others (perhaps feeling more generous after waiting nearly 60 years and then experiencing four World Series wins.) He has edited a few dozen books for SABR during the current decade. A co-founder of Rounder Records, he's also written a few other books (and sets of liner notes) on music.

**Bill Parker** is co-host of the podcast *This Week in Baseball History,* and has written about baseball for espn.com, Baseball Prospectus, and many others. An employment lawyer by day, he grew up in Minnesota and lives in Minneapolis with his wife and three sons, and has thus far managed to continue to root for the Twins.

**Jim Patrick** is a librarian from Yuma, Arizona who grew up in the Midwest as a Minnesota Twins fan. Having moved to Yuma over 30 years ago when it was still a baseball town, he was able to experience firsthand several seasons of Padres spring training. This is his first SABR contribution.

**Carl Riechers** retired from United Parcel Service in 2012 after 35 years of service. With more free time, he became a SABR member that same year. Born and raised in the suburbs of St. Louis, he became a big fan of the Cardinals. He and his wife Janet have three children and is the proud grandpa of two.

**Joel Rippel**, a Minnesota native and graduate of the University of Minnesota, is the author or co-author of nine books on Minnesota sports history and has contributed as an editor or writer to several books published by SABR.

**Fred O. Rodgers** is retired and living in Houston, Texas. He is the former President of the San Diego Ted Williams SABR Chapter in its formative years in the early 1990's and head of SABR 23 in San Diego in 1994. He started *Baseball Gold*, the San Diego Padres newspaper, with Kurt Bevacqua in October of 1982 and was the editor until June 1986. He was researcher for *The Stan Musial Scrapbook* published by *The Sporting News* in 1993. Currently the owner of one of the largest *Sporting News* collections in the country.

**Paul Rogers** is co-author of several baseball books including *The Whiz Kids and the 1950 Pennant* with boyhood hero Robin Roberts and *Lucky Me: My 65 Years in Baseball* with Eddie Robinson. Most recently he co-edited *The Whiz Kids Take the Pennant – The 1950 Philadelphia Phillies* and *The Team That Time Won't Forget – the 1951 New York Giants*, SABR team projects. He is president of the Ernie Banks – Bobby Bragan DFW Chapter of SABR and a frequent contributor to the SABR

BioProject, but his real job is as a law professor at Southern Methodist University where he served as dean for nine years. He has also served as SMU's faculty athletic representative for over 30 years and counting. Since the age of 8, he has always looked at the box scores before reading any other part of the newspaper.

**Michael See** lives in Las Vegas, Nevada with his wife Kay along with their two children Taylor and Ben. Michael has a passion for baseball history and music from the 1960's and 1970's. When he is not listening to old records or reading a baseball book, he can often be found doing re-play simulations of old baseball seasons with his friends in their www.seasonspastbaseball.com historical baseball leagues. This is Michael's first SABR biography and he hopes to write many more in the coming years.

From an early age **David E. Skelton** developed a lifelong love of baseball when the lights from Philadelphia's Connie Mack Stadium shone through his bedroom window. Long removed from Philly, he resides with his family in central Texas where he is employed in the oil & gas industry. An avid collector, he joined SABR in 2012.

**Doug Skipper** first joined SABR in 1982. A member and former president of the Halsey Hall (Minnesota) Chapter, Doug has written a number of BioProject and Games Project articles for SABR publications and websites. He serves as chairperson for the Larry Ritter Award Committee and has been a member for several years. A native of Texas, who grew up in Colorado, lived in Wyoming and North Dakota, and now Minnesota, Doug has been an avid Red Sox fan since his maternal grandfather took him and his two brothers to see their first major league game, on Thursday, August 3, 1967 at Fenway Park (a 5-3 win). Doug and his wife Kathy have two daughters, MacKenzie and Shannon. He is a marketing research, customer satisfaction and public opinion consultant who reads and writes about baseball.

**Curt Smith's** 17th book was released in 2018, *The Presidents and the Pastime: The History of Baseball and the White House*, from the University of Nebraska Press, the first book to chronicle in-depth the relationship between two American institutions—baseball and the Presidency. It was praised by MLB TV, BBC TV, *Parade* Magazine, *The Wall Street Journal*, *SI Now*, *FOX Nightly News*, and the Franklin D. Roosevelt Presidential Library and Museum. Smith's prior books include *Voices of The Game, The Voice,* and *Pull Up a Chair.* From 1989-93, he wrote more speeches than anyone else for President George H.W. Bush. Smith is a GateHouse Media columnist, Associated Press award-winning commentator, and senior lecturer at the University of Rochester. He has hosted or keynoted the Great Fenway Writers Series, numerous Smithsonian Institution series, and the Cooperstown Symposium on Baseball and American

Culture. The former *The Saturday Evening Post* senior editor has written ESPN TV's *Voices of The Game* series, created the Franklin Roosevelt Award in Communication at the National Radio Hall of Fame, and been named to the Judson Welliver Society of former Presidential speechwriters.

**Mark Souder** is a retired Member of Congress. He and his wife Diane live in Fort Wayne, the area in which his ancestors arrived in the 1840s and which he represented in Congress for 16 years. Souder was one of the primary questioners at the Congressional Hearings on Steroids. His writings on baseball history have been published in *National Pastime* issues for the Chicago, New York and Pittsburgh SABR conventions. He has twice presented at the 19th Century Committee FRED conference at Cooperstown. His articles have appeared in SABR books including *Boston's First Nine* and *Puerto Rico and Baseball*.

When **John Stahl** and his wife are not busy chasing around their three small grandsons, he has been fortunate enough to contribute to over 20 SABR bios. He has been a baseball junkie since birth.

**Mark S. Sternman** rooted for the other National League team born in 1969, the Montreal Expos. Also a fan of the Yankees, Sternman well recalls the 1998 World Series, which ended happily for him with a New York sweep of San Diego.

**Wayne Strumpfer** is Of Counsel for the law firm Young, Minney & Corr in Sacramento, California. At his first baseball game in May of 1971, Gaylord Perry tossed him a baseball and he's been a Giants fan ever since. Wayne has written several SABR biographies and accounts for the SABR Games Project. He enjoys American and baseball history from the 1960's and 1970's.

**Alfonso Tusa** is a writer who was born in Cumaná, Venezuela and now writes a lot about baseball from Los Teques, Venezuela. He's the author *Una Temporada Mágica* (A magical season), *El Látigo del Beisbol. Una biografía de Isaías Látigo Chávez.* (The Whip of Baseball. An Isaías Látigo Chávez biography), *Pensando en ti Venezuela. Una biografía de Dámaso Blanco.* (Thinking about you Venezuela. A Dámaso Blanco biography) and *Voces de Beisbol y Ecología (*Voices of Baseball and Ecology). He contributes to some websites, books and newspapers. He shares many moments with his boy Miguelin.

**Nick Waddell** is an operational risk manager and life-long Detroit Tigers fan. He has been a SABR member since 2007, and once had a private dinner with Ernie Harwell thanks to an old-school letter. He has contributed to books on the 1968 Tigers, the 1986 Mets and Red Sox, and the Pirates.

**Bob Webster** grew up in NW Indiana and has been a Cubs fan since 1963. Now living in Portland, Oregon, Bob spends his time working on baseball research and has contributed to a few SABR books, as well working as a Stats Stringer for the Gameday app for the past three years. Also, a member of the Northwest Chapter of SABR and on the Board of Directors of the Old-Timers Baseball Association of Portland.

**Steve West** considers himself fortunate that he once got to see Tony Gwynn play. He recently co-edited the 2019 SABR book *The Team That Couldn't Hit: The 1972 Texas Rangers.*

**Gregory H. Wolf** was born in Pittsburgh, but now resides in the Chicagoland area with his wife, Margaret, and daughter, Gabriela. A professor of German studies and holder of the Dennis and Jean Bauman Endowed Chair in the Humanities at North Central College in Naperville, Illinois, he has edited nine books for SABR. He is currently working on projects about Comiskey Park in Chicago, Shibe Park in Philadelphia, and the 1982 Milwaukee Brewers. As of January 2017, he serves as co-director of SABR's BioProject, which you can follow on Facebook and Twitter.

**Brian Wright** is the author of *Mets in 10s: Best and Worst of an Amazin' History*, released by The History Press in April 2018. He was also the managing editor of *Met-rospectives*, a SABR publication released in September 2018 which chronicles the greatest games in franchise history. Prior, he wrote for Bleacher Report, the *Washington Examiner*, NESN.com, SB Nation, and *The Cauldro*n. For three years, he served as Lead MLB writer for *The Sports Daily* and from 2014 through 2017, Brian hosted his own interview-based sports history podcast, "Profiles in Sports." He has contributed to multiple SABR books, including the most memorable moments in the history of Wrigley Field and old Comiskey Park.

**Geoff Young** founded Ducksnorts, one of the world's first baseball blogs, writing there from 1997 to 2011 and publishing three books under that name. A SABR member since 2008, he penned regular columns at The Hardball Times from 2007 to 2011 and at Baseball Prospectus from 2011 to 2013. He is a co-author of Baseball Prospectus annuals 2012-2016, a co-editor of *Baseball Prospectus 2018*, and a contributor to several other baseball books. A recovering corporate desk jockey who now works in the craft beer industry, he lives in San Diego with his wife Sandra and their pug Charlie.

# PHOTO CREDITS

Photos/images courtesy of:

1 – San Diego Padres (Andy Hayt)

2 – San Diego Padres (Chris Hardy), both

3 – San Diego Padres Media Relations

4 – San Diego Padres (Andy Hayt), both

5 – National Baseball Hall of Fame (with bat);
San Diego Padres Media Relations

6 - San Diego Padres Media Relations, both

7 – National Baseball Hall of Fame

8 - San Diego Padres Media Relations

9 - San Diego Padres Media Relations

10 – National Baseball Hall of Fame (Giles);
Tom Larwin (scoreboard)

11 – San Diego Padres (Andy Hayt, Joel Zwink,
and Chris Hardy)

12 – San Diego Padres (Andy Hayt),
Scott Wachter (both at Hall of Fame)

13 – San Diego Padres (Andy Hayt);
with fans (Shana Siler)

14 - San Diego Padres Media Relations

15 - San Diego Padres Media Relations

16 – San Diego Padres (Andy Hayt), both

17 - San Diego Padres Media Relations

18 – In sequence: San Diego Padres (Andy Hayt), batting,
and Jackie Siragusa, fielding

19 – San Diego Padres (Andy Hayt), both

20 - San Diego Padres Media Relations

21 – Tom Larwin

22 – Andy Strasberg

23 - San Diego Padres Media Relations

24 – San Diego Padres (Chris Hardy), both

25 – National Baseball Hall of Fame, first,
and San Diego Padres Media Relations, second

26 – San Diego Padres (Scott Wachter), all

27 – San Diego Padres (Andy Hayt)

28 – Tom Larwin

29 – In sequence: San Diego Padres (Andy Hayt), in booth; San Diego Padres (Scott Wachter), with statue

30 – Andy Strasberg, both

31 - San Diego Padres Media Relations

32 – In sequence: San Diego Padres (Shana Siler), both

33 – Andy Strasberg, all

34 – San Diego Padres (Andy Hayt)

35 - San Diego Padres Media Relations

36 – Jim Patrick, all

37 – In sequence: San Diego Padres (Chris Hardy), San Diego Padres (Andy Hayt), National Baseball Hall of Fame, National Baseball Hall of Fame, and Tom Larwin (final three)

38 – San Diego Padres (Andy Hayt), and Tom Larwin (final three)

39 – Tom Larwin (first), Andy Strasberg (final two)

40 – Tom Larwin

41 – National Baseball Hall of Fame

42 - San Diego Padres Media Relations, both

43 – National Baseball Hall of Fame

45 – Tom Larwin, all four

46 – Fred O. Rodgers, all three

48 – Tom Larwin

49 – Tom Larwin

50 – Tom Larwin, both

57 – Tom Larwin

59 – San Diego Padres (Andy Hayt)

61 – San Diego Padres (Chris Hardy), first; Tom Larwin, other two

65 – Tom Larwin

Made in the USA
Las Vegas, NV
22 December 2020